READINGS

in the

LANGUAGE

ARTS

VERNA DIECKMAN ANDERSON

Formerly Associate Professor of Education
Wayne State University

PAUL S. ANDERSON

Professor of Education
San Diego State College

FRANCIS BALLANTINE

Professor of Education
San Diego State College

VIRGIL M. HOWES

Administrative Assistant
San Diego County Department of Education

THE MACMILLAN COMPANY, NEW YORK

FOURTH PRINTING, 1966

THE MACMILLAN COMPANY, NEW YORK
COLLIER-MACMILLAN CANADA, LTD., TORONTO, ONTARIO

Printed in the United States of America

Preface

THIS BOOK is designed to meet the needs created by three conditions of modern academic life. First, the large enrollment of today has placed a burden on existing library facilities. It is difficult for students to have readily available many of the references listed in bibliographies. Second, a great deal of valuable material appears in what librarians classify as ephemeral publications. Some of these are out of print a short time after their initial distribution. Third, curriculum bulletins are in very limited supply. Schools create these guides for their own use and are not in a position to make them available to the public. Frequently, students have no way of knowing of their existence.

The reading selections made will help elementary teachers understand contemporary trends of teaching the various aspects of the language arts and provide specific suggestions useful in classroom practice. Some of the material we felt should be known by teachers was not available. However, thanks to the willingness of many outstanding authorities and their publishers, no essential area of interest has been omitted.

In addition to the authors and publishers whose material appears in the book, we wish to thank others who graciously granted us permission to use articles that were not included because of space limitations. To Dean F. Schrupp of San Diego State College and Dr. Cecil D. Hardesty, County Superintendent of Schools of San Diego County, we wish to express a special word of appreciation. Without their cooperation this work could not have been completed.

Contents

Introduction

ENGLISH IS A VITAL SUBJECT *

J. N. Hook

English *is* a vital subject. It is vital for two reasons, which I shall attempt to explain in the few minutes at my disposal. [English is a tool subject, and English is a cultural subject.]

In almost every line of work, communication plays an essential part. I looked through the yellow pages of my telephone book and asked myself concerning each occupation or business, "Does communication enter into this kind of work?" I saw first "Abstracts of Title" and "Accountants." Obviously communication is important in both of those. "Acoustical Contractors" have work because the sounds of the human voice, and the thoughts that are transplanted to paper, must not be drowned out by machines. "Advertising"—another obvious one. "Air Conditioning"—I had trouble with that one until I thought of the communication necessary in manufacturing, selling, and installing the equipment. "Air Line Companies"—planes literally could not fly if there were no communication. And so on through the A's until I came to "Automobiles." There I stopped and pondered for a long time. I wrote some automobile manufacturers for information, and talked about the subject with friends. You may be interested in my conclusion and how I arrived at it, for I believe it demonstrates dramatically the contribution that the use of language makes as a tool in the modern economy.

I'll give you the conclusion first. Approximately fifty per cent of the price of a new automobile is expended for spoken and written words. When you drive a new $3000 car down the street, you are riding on $1500 worth of words.

* Address before the 44th annual convention of the Association of Secondary School Principals, 1960. Used with permission of the author and the Association.

Some of the words were spoken in meetings of boards of directors—as many as two or three hundred boards of directors of companies that supplied parts of your automobile—companies that mine iron ore or copper or zinc or molybdenum, companies that grow rubber trees or make artificial rubber, companies that manufacture cloth or glass or wire or spark plugs or generators, companies scattered throughout the Western Hemisphere or even beyond. Not only did the board members have to communicate in all these companies, but also the officers, the foremen, and the workmen themselves. It seems probable that several thousand persons exchanged written or spoken words pertaining in some way to the parts of your automobile. And all the companies involved had to write letters, make telephone calls, and send telegrams as they conducted their work. The average cost of a business letter today, the experts say, is between $1.50 and $2.00.

The parts of your automobile had to be brought together, some from hundreds or even thousands of miles away. Before there can be transportation, there must be communication. How many more messages were exchanged before all the parts for your car arrived at the place of assembly?

The maker of your automobile spends many millions of dollars a year for communication—within the plant, with stockholders, with dealers, and in advertising. A conservative guess is about $300 per car that rolls off the assembly line.

Several hundred dollars—up to a third—of the cost of your car are spent for direct or hidden taxes. If I had time, I could demonstrate that about half of our local, state, and Federal tax money is spent for communication. Most of the people in Washington are communicators; they make words, not something tangible. The same comment applies to most local and state employees. About half of our huge military expense is for communication. Approximately half of the taxes you pay on your car, then, is expended for words.

The salesman and the dealer get a sizable commission for persuading you to buy this make rather than another. You pay handsomely for their words—perhaps from $100 to $500.

Add together the costs of all these words, and you can see why I say that you are driving about $1500 worth of words when you step into your new car.

I have dwelt upon this example because it dramatizes the importance of this tool called language. Unclear or misunderstood letters, orders, or directions cost industry hundreds of millions of dollars each year. Clear communication, accompanied by the clear thinking that the schools **must** also teach, results in speed, accuracy, and efficiency.

But in addition to being a tool subject, English is also a cultural subject. This is harder to talk about in concrete terms, because culture is not concrete.) It is a way of looking at the world and at life, it is a state of mind, it reflects a set of values. It is not something long-haired and lisping and effeminate. The cultured person comes closer to seeing life whole than does the uncultured. Matthew Arnold said that culture is "a study of perfection." And the philosophical Novalis said that "The highest purpose of intellectual cultivation is to give a man a perfect knowledge and mastery of his own inner self."

Through literature our students become familiar with some of the noblest ideas that mankind has conceived. As the statement in your hands says, "Literature, at its finest, is one of the most effective vehicles for the study of values through teaching great themes which have pre-occupied men of all times, such as the struggle between good and evil, the search for identity, and the conflict between the real and the ideal."

All life is a search. Its object is not clearly defined for most of us, so that we are forced to use vague but rather evocative phrases such as "the pursuit of happiness." We all want something—generally something not completely attainable—for ourselves and our children and their children. Merely tangible things do not fully satisfy our craving; it is possible to be unhappy with a full belly. We want understanding, we want love, we want immortality—even though we never say those things. We want wider experiences than any of us can ever have; we want to taste all the world's wisdom, all the world's excitement, all the world's pleasure, but our years are too few.

Literature extends our experiences, carries us to distant lands, ac-quaints us with people we would never otherwise know. It makes us think, makes us wonder, makes us feel more deeply. It takes us into the minds and hearts of men and women who lived two thousand years ago, and makes us better understand the family next door. It will never make us perfect, but it may give us a glimpse of why imperfections exist and of what perfection can be.

Such are the cultural riches of English, well taught. Unfortunately, too few of us have sat at the feet of teachers who understood those riches. Too often a literature class is just a memory exercise in "What happened next?" or an excuse for vocabulary drill or outlining. That is one reason why we need the statement you are now going to consider: so that teachers and administrators alike will clearly realize that English is not just a tool subject, but also a study of what it means to be a human being.

CHAPTER 1

The Language We Use

The English language, it is said, has more than 750,000 accepted words. Multiply these by their contextual meanings. Compound the number whenever each word is accompanied by a smile or a snarl, by a grumble or a purr. Multiply again by the people who are never the same hour by hour, and the statistical potential for misunderstanding reaches astronomical figures. Then add the unspoken signals of lifting an eyebrow, clenching the fists, or shifting the feet; you will begin to see that effective communication is one of the most extraordinary achievements of human beings. From Mrs. Ethel R. Oyan, "Words: Their Power and Their Glory," in Tete-A-Tete (Evanston, Ill.: Harper & Row, 1961).

YOUR SPEECH IS CHANGING *

Bergen Evans

We're in the middle of a language explosion. New words are created in a chain reaction; grammar is being simplified, speech made more colorful. Dr. Evans, master of ceremonies of the TV show, "The Last Word," approves. His advice to all of us: "Don't be afraid to break a few rules of grammar."

If a contemporary Rip van Winkle had slept for 40 years and awakened today, he would have to go back to school before he could read a daily paper or a magazine. He would never have heard of atomic bombs or baby sitters, of coffee breaks, contact lenses or flying saucers—nor of eggheads, mambo or microfilm, of nylons, neptunium, parking meters or smog.

* Reprinted from *Think* (August 1959), by permission of the author.

And this is the briefest sampling of the innumerable new words added to our language in a mere 40 years. Only recently, a nuclear physicist reading a year-old glossary of electronic and atomic terms, found himself saying over and over, "That's what we used to call it."

The vocabulary of physics is, plainly, exploding with a violence commensurate with the new devices it has to describe. And physics is not alone in this. Almost every major industry now finds it necessary to issue a glossary of its own special terms to its workers. Yet they are unable to keep pace with the increase of their own knowledge, and the most striking feature of these word lists is not their newness—though the ink is scarcely dry on their pages—but their obsolescence.

Since Shakespeare's time, the number of words in the English language has quintupled, increasing from about 140,000 to somewhere between 700,000 and 800,000. And most of these have come, not from borrowing, but from the natural growth of the language, from the adaptation of the elements already in it.

The language has always changed, of course. But the rate of change, in some respects, has been uneven. Minor changes have slowly accumulated in every generation, but there have been periods of rapid change as well. The most important was the two and one-half centuries following the conquest of England by the Normans in 1066.

At the time of the conquest, the inhabitants of England spoke Anglo-Saxon, an inflected Germanic language. The Normans were Norsemen, who, after generations of raiding, had settled in North France (Normandy) in the tenth century. By 1066 they were speaking a form of French.

At the time they invaded England, Anglo-Saxon could hardly be considered one of the world's significant tongues. Certainly, there was nothing in it to suggest that it might become an important language, let alone the greatest ever known. The Normans, who were never much more than a garrison, established Norman French as the speech of the dominant group. It was the language of the upper classes, of law, of government and of such commerce as there was. Latin, of course, was the language of the learned.

For more than 200 years nobody who was anybody at all spoke Anglo-Saxon. It is doubtful if Richard the Lion-Hearted, for example, spoke one word of English in his entire life. Angle-ish was strictly for the churls, for the hinds and the hicks. As Wamba the Jester pointed out to Gurth the Swineherd in Scott's *Ivanhoe*, while animals were living and had to be cared for in muck and mire, they were Saxon—as cow, calf, sheep and pig. But when they were dressed for the table— when the rewards of labor were to be enjoyed—they were Norman French: beef, veal, mutton and pork.

But the masses went right on speaking Anglo-Saxon because they didn't know anything else. There was, however, no reading or writing of it to amount to anything. There was no teaching of it. It was simply used every day for generations by millions of common people, who just said things as effectively as they could, and got on with the business of living. And never—as any schoolteacher could have foretold—did a language become more "corrupted."

But after having been submerged as a "common" language for some 300 years, Anglo-Saxon was again being spoken by the upper classes—as English. And it had become the most flexible, exact, splendid and moving instrument of expression that mankind has ever known. Norman French had become something comic, spoken by the villains in the old mystery plays just for a laugh.

There have been other periods of vigorous change. Two generations after Chaucer's death in 1400, printing was invented, and this set into motion a chain of events whose full force upon the language is only now beginning to be felt.

The seventeenth- and eighteenth-centuries saw the stabilization of spelling. But, even more important, they saw the establishment of colonies in America, and, from the beginning, the language in the new world and the parent language in the old world began to draw apart in many particulars (though in the past 60 years or so this tendency has been reversed). American speech developed its own rhythms and vigor, found or adapted special words for its own special needs and (more west of the Alleghenies than east) rioted with a sort of defiant exuberance. The language was for a while of the people, somewhat as Anglo-Saxon had been during the rule of the Norman overlords.

In *The Adventures of Huckleberry Finn* (1884) the full power of the American idiom was first shown. It had been heard clearly in Franklin and Thoreau. But Mark Twain first showed the passion of its cadences and the subtlety and range of which it was capable. He used the idiom of the Great Valley with no apologies and scorn. It is true that he did it through the person of Huck, but it is equally true that in so doing he wrote not only his own greatest novel, but a novel which every American feels, somehow, speaks his language.

The liberating effect on American writing can hardly be overstated. With it we ceased to be a literary colony. The source of all modern American literature, Hemingway has said, is *Huckleberry Finn*. Of its effect on Hemingway himself there can be little doubt. One sample will suffice—a comparison of the description of Huck's diving under the paddle wheel of the riverboat, which had struck his raft, with Hemingway's description, in *A Farewell to Arms*, of Frederick Henry's plunge into the Po.

Huck says: "I dived—and I aimed to find the bottom, too, for a thirty-foot wheel had got to go over me, and I wanted it to have plenty of room. I could always stay under water a minute; this time I reckon I stayed under a minute and a half. Then I bounced for the top in a hurry, for I was nearly busting. I popped out to my armpits and blowed the water out of my nose, and puffed a bit. Of course there was a booming current; and of course that boat started her engines again ten seconds after she stopped them, for they never cared much for raftsmen. . . ."

Henry says: "I ducked down, pushed between two men, and ran for the river, my head down. I tripped at the edge and went in with a splash. The water was very cold and I stayed under as long as I could. I could feel the current swirl me and I stayed under until I thought I could never come up. The minute I came up I took a breath and went down again. It was easy to stay under with so much clothing and my boots. . . ."

COLLOQUIAL VS. FORMAL

Anyone can hear the authentic rhythms of American speech in both passages. And anyone who thinks he can get equal action, and the same shades of menace, tension, courage and excitement in the literary idiom that such writing displaced—well, let him show us! Though if he does, his triumph will be purely academic. For the use of the colloquial in effective writing is increasing rather than diminishing. It is one of the changes that definitely is accelerating. The purist angrily labels it "pandering to the masses" and accuses those who accept it of "debasing" the language. But the new way is better, more flexible, more expressive, communicates more directly.

Much of what is objected to in contemporary writing has been common for centuries. From all the uproar over "Winston tastes good *like* a cigarette should," for instance, one would have assumed that the R. J. Reynolds Tobacco Company had launched a subversive attack on established English and was determined to overthrow the Constitution and set up *like* as a conjunction. But if it was a conspiracy, it had been assisted in advance by Shakespeare, Dryden, Burns, Shelley, Masefield, Maugham and millions of Americans.

Similarly, *none* had been regarded as a plural when its idea was plural (according to the King James Version of the Bible) from the very First Commandment (Deut. 5:7). And double negatives have strengthened, not denied, negation as long as men have spoken English. Purists may insist that "two negatives make a positive," but no one in his right mind has any doubt what Chaucer meant when he said that his Knight "didn't never do no villainy to no man."

Prepositions are not supposed to come at the end of sentences; but from Shakespeare ("What great ones do, the less will prattle of."), through Milton ("Thee all living things gaze on."), to G. B. Shaw ("What are the police for?"), and Sir Winston Churchill's humorous rebuke ("This is pedantry, up with which I will not put."), all people who have the feel of the English sentence put them at the end to their heart's content. *That*, not *which*, has always been the common relative pronoun in English; the modern insistence that there is a clear distinction between them is pretentious nonsense.

Then there's *who* at the beginning of a question, even when in the accusative. "Who did you give it to?" would have seemed as natural and "To whom did you give it?" as strainedly elegant 100 or 500 years ago as they do today. At least that's the way Marlowe said it ("Who have ye there, my Lordes?"), and Addison ("Who should I see there but the most artful procures?"). Noah Webster was emphatic: "Whom did you speak to was never used in speaking, as I can find, and is hardly English at all."

The increased use of the colloquial in our writing is an interesting change that is bound to have far-reaching consequences. Our speech, of course, has always been colloquial. That's what the word means. The sensible man *speaks* colloquially most of the time. When he wants to be formal or unusually impressive he tries to speak as he thinks he writes. But on these occasions he often makes a pompous ass of himself and—worse—fails to convey his meaning.

Yet, whenever he stops to think, the common man feels guilty about his speech. He feels he *ought* to be more formal and that he ought not to use in writing (about which he retains a semiliterate awe) the expressions that just come naturally to his mind.

Hence, when he sees a form marked *colloq.* in the dictionary he thinks he ought not to use it at all, though actually the colloquial meaning of most words is to him the "real" meaning. For instance, *guy* in standard English means a rope, a stuffed effigy or a weirdly dressed person. Yet no one blanched or was bewildered when Nellie Forbush sang in *South Pacific* that she was in love with a wonderful *guy*, which means, of course, *man* colloquially. A *kit*, in standard definition, can be anything from a fox to a fiddle, but its colloquial meaning of a group of separate parts ready to be assembled is the one that would first come to mind.

Some modern linguists feel that the designation *colloq.* is so often misunderstood that it might be better, a safer guide to current usage, if the term were dropped and certain words marked as *formal*, so that the ordinary speaker or writer' will be warned that the word is not in everyday use.

Opposed to this increased use of the colloquial, it must be said, is a minor but increasingly vocal group that insists on "rules" and "correctness." They base their stand on a puritanical liking for absolutes, and they may be motivated in part by a sense of insecurity which the rapidly changing social status of millions is producing. At best, the demands of this group, if acceded to, will sacrifice vigor to "propriety."

And at worst it is producing a new kind of bad grammar—the uncertainty and pretentiousness which leads to the substitution of *myself* for *me* ("He gave it to John and myself."), to sticking *ly* on the end of abverbs that don't need them ("Our missile program is moving fastly." He's doing finely.") and such vulgar elegances as "Whom shall I say is calling?"

INTIMIDATED ENGLISH

This new bad English might be called Intimidated English. No nation in the world is as afraid of its schoolteachers as we are. We have no upper or lower classes to defy them, and the new semiliteracy which has replaced the old illiteracy timidly accepts their academic pronouncements as law. This would be all right if their "laws," like other scientific "laws," were based on observation. But they are more like moral laws; they are promulgated on the assumption that there is some sanction for them beyond speech itself—logic, or decorum or social prestige.

One of the effects of this, as it relates to our speech is a belief that pronunciations which don't correspond to spelling are debased. "Slurred" is the common term for it, and those who let what their eyes have seen once overrule what their ears have heard 10,000 times, have had a field day with this particular "corruption." Inspired by the humor of Orpheus C. Kerr, they have grown hilarious over such pronunciations as *mare* for *mayor*, *kloz* for *clothes*, *histri* for *history* and *ak choo uhli* for *actually*.

Unfortunately for the fun, however, these slurred forms happen to be accepted, standard pronunciations. Though they may not be for long. The dogmatic righteousness of the antislurvians is having an immense effect among the semiliterate and the insecure. Increasingly, words are being pronounced as they are spelled. The "l" in *almond*, *salmon* and *palm*, for example, is heard more and more. Only the most aristocratic and the most unaristocratic now dare say *Saint Looey*. One used to be able to go from *Kayroh, Illinoy* up to *Saint Looey*, but now one usually has to go from *Kyeroh, Illinoyz* to *Saint Loois*.

If this brings spelling closer to pronunciation, it will be good. But if—as seems more likely—it brings pronunciation closer to spelling, it will be bad, because spelling at the best is only an approximation of past speech and much of it is simply erroneous (like the "s" in *island*, the first "l" in *colonel* and the "c" in *acknowledge*).

The enormous enlargement of our vocabulary, the increasing use in our writing of our spoken idiom and changes in our pronunciation are not the only changes that are taking place, however. There have also been significant grammatical changes in our language. Such changes take place only by generations or decades, at the fastest, so they pass unnoticed by all but grammarians; but even the layman can perceive them when he is told that something which seems "quite all right" to him was regarded as erroneous only a few years ago.

Take, for example, the extraordinary increase in the use of the infinitive, one of the characteristics of modern American speech and writing. Ask any educated American to point out what is "wrong" with, "The government has a duty to protect the worker," or "We have a plan to keep the present tariff." The chances are that for the life of him he couldn't see anything wrong with either sentence. Yet in 1925 Fowler listed both of these sentences as ungrammatical. He felt they should read "of protecting" and "of keeping." Today, the old form has been completely superseded.

A further example of change in our grammar is the great increase in the use of what are called "empty" verbs. That is, where people used to say, "Let's drink," or, "Let's swim," there is now a strong tendency to say, "Let's have a drink," "Let's take a swim." Where people formerly said, "It snowed heavily," we are inclined to say, "There was a heavy snow." Our fathers *decided;* we, on the other hand, more often reach a *decision.*

Nobody knows *why* such changes are being made. Perhaps we are in the process of reducing our verbs to a few simple basic words of action—like those handy household tools where one handle serves for a blade, for a screwdriver, for a hammer, a corkscrew and a dozen other diverse implements that can be attached to it individually. That is, we may be reducing the language to an even more functional simplicity. If this is so, it may mark a change as significant as that which took place after the Norman Conquest, when the whole paraphernalia of declensions and conjugations was sloughed off.

THE BIG CHANGE

One of the most remarkable grammatical changes that has been taking place is the increased use of the passive—of verb forms, that is—that indicate something is being acted upon. Some think that our increased use of the passive may indicate a decay of will. The barbarians who overran the Roman Empire, these people say, had lost most of their passive; they seemed to think only in the active voice: "I do." Those they destroyed were enfeebled in endless consideration of the way things were done *to* them. The more pessimistic of this school point out that the Russians *shot* their first satellite into space while we debated the reasons why ours *was not launched.*

Others, however, take a brighter view. They see in this same increased use of the passive an increased awareness, and increased ability to express subtleties, greater sensitivity, not decadence but greater sophistication. To them this change in our speech shows us to be increasingly a people who are interested in what was done rather than in who did it. They see it as indication that we are more detached, more scientific, more mature.

Whatever the reasons for the changes that are taking place, the vocabulary will probably continue to expand because the expansion of our knowledge and experience requires the invention of new words or the adaptation of old ones. What few inflections remain will probably disappear. Meaning will depend more and more upon word order and context. Spelling will become simpler, with fewer common variants, and pronunciations, because of the great mobility of our population and the spread of radio and TV, will tend to become more uniform.

One thing by now seems certain—that the speech of the men who lost at Hastings, the sturdy, surly, freedom-loving thegns and churls who did not attempt to ingratiate themselves with their conquerors by learning their speech—will adapt and endure.

THUMBPRINTS AND THOUGHT PRINTS *

Harry W. Sartain

Last year an eighth-grade girl in our laboratory school wrote a paper in which she told how a composer had won a "pullet surprise!" The real "surprise" is the fact that she had an I.Q. higher than 160! Her achievement on standard tests, including spelling, was truly superior. Why would a bright girl make such an obvious error?

Frequently, we hear kindergarten and primary teachers tell anecdotes that reveal the faulty ideas of their pupils. One story is that of the child who drew a round, fat man to illustrate his favorite Christmas carol. He said that this was Round John Virgin from "Silent Night!" Another child cut out a large black kettle to illustrate part of a fairy tale that delighted him; he explained that it was "once-a-pot-a-time."

* Reprinted by permission of the author and publisher from *The Packet*, **17**, No. 1 (Boston: D. C. Heath, 1962).

What may be taking place in the minds of our pupils when we speak to them in terms that seem quite logical? What pictures are flashing in their brains in response to printed words and sentences which stand for concepts that seem simple to us? The possibilities are alarming!

Lest we think it can happen only to children, let us put ourselves in their places for a few minutes. Suppose that I asked you to draw a picture which would show your understanding of this statement: "In reality, the antirrhinum is acropetal, but not amygdaloid, acronycal, nor cleistogamous." Would the drawings by several teachers look alike? Perhaps I should ask you to be more imaginative by illustrating: "Susurrating, the hircine suzerain maundered about his diaphanous undine!" In these days of great concern for quality in education, would you rather be described as "a hippophagous fucus," "an amaurotic anchoret," or "a bit of propaedeutical tourbillion?" [1]

It is highly improbable that all of us would respond to these examples in the same way. Written or spoken symbols do not trigger the same thought pattern in every person, because we have not had the same experiences. The concepts which we have for each word or phrase differ because of our varied personal values and backgrounds. Despite our lack of full and equivalent understandings of the statements cited, we could memorize them in a few minutes. Then we could answer factual test questions such as "What was the suzerain doing?" Our teacher might believe that we had learned something, when really we were only mouthing sounds, or verbalizing.

A famous poet declared. "A rose is a rose is a rose." But is it? The poet assumed that everyone has had so many experiences with roses that no words can define "rose" in the way that the noun itself recalls our impressions of the scent, the form, and the beauty of the rose. This assumption certainly is more valid in the case of a rose than in other instances such as "battlefield," "authority," or "plantation life." Still, for some personal reason, the rose that *you* visualize may be quite different from the one which *I* call to mind.

RAW MATERIALS FOR THINKING

It becomes evident that *an essential aspect of language instruction is helping children use written and spoken symbols which convey precisely the thoughts that they want to convey.* Likewise, the listener and the reader must be prepared to absorb ideas with equal precision.

---

[1] These illustrations were used by the author in "Percepts and Concepts," *Reading and Thinking*, papers of the Reading Conference at the University of Pittsburgh, Donald L. Cleland, Editor, 1961.

Evidently teaching children to communicate and teaching them to think are fully interwoven.

In his book *Children's Thinking*, David Russell says that the raw materials of thought are percepts, images, memories, concepts, emotions, and attitudes.[2] A percept is an awareness of the external and internal environment at any moment; percepts result from sensations or observations. While a percept pertains to the present, an image refers to past sensory experience. An image is a percept recalled.

(Our concepts range from simple concrete meanings to abstractions of a high level.[3] The word "house" stands for a generalized understanding of all houses, without specific reference to a brick house, a white house, or a split-level house. "Friendship" is a more abstract concept, as are "justice," "perseverance," and "integration." Concepts are substantial ingredients of memory; Russell says that memory is the recalling of percepts and concepts, or related information from the past.[4])

As language teachers we want to help children attain percepts and concepts that are vivid, accurate, and complete. Otherwise their communication will be inept and faulty. Erroneous concepts may have effects that are far more harmful than merely the confusing of communication. As examples, we know of the injustices caused by some people's concepts of *caste* and *racial segregation*.[5]

BUILDING A FUND OF PERCEPTS

Percepts are the fabric from which concepts are fashioned. We perceive through all of our senses, and each percept seems to evolve through stages of vague awareness of a total situation, discovery of its separate elements, and combination of these elements into a clear pattern against a background of nonessentials. The whole process takes place in a moment, giving us a percept that may be highly accurate or grossly incorrect. Percepts involve form, space, time, movement, weight, number, social matters, aesthetics, and humor. Because of this complexity some inaccuracies are inevitable. The degree of accuracy of our percepts can be influenced by a number of factors.

1. We tend to perceive what we have learned to perceive. We hear some types of music as pleasant, while other types are strange and unpleasant. "Mother" is always beautiful. Roasted ants are seen as a delicacy by some people and as something repulsive by others.

---

2 David H. Russell, *Children's Thinking* (Boston: Ginn & Co., 1956), Ch. 3.

3 William H. Burton, Roland B. Kimball, and Richard L. Wing, *Education for Effective Thinking* (New York: Appleton-Century-Crofts, 1960), Ch. 9.

4 Russell, *op. cit.*, p. 157.

5 Burton, Kimball, and Wing, *op. cit.*, p. 157.

Evidently our past experiences have a great effect on how we sense things. An eighth-grade girl hears "pullet surprise" instead of "Pulitzer prize" because experience has taught her to hear "pullet" but not "Pulitzer." We teachers can plan experiences which affect the number and quality of children's percepts.

2. We tend to perceive what we want to perceive. The fond mother sees numerous fine qualities in the child, although the school staff may not be able to detect the same capabilities. A child trying on new shoes does not feel the pinch temporarily if they are the ones that strike his fancy. Thus it follows that the school situation can be motivated so that children will want to perceive as we wish; we can set the stage to produce desirable attitudes.

3. We tend to perceive accurately when our observations fit into a pattern that has meaning. You can prove this by showing a group of children a badly jumbled picture which includes a small dog perched in a tree. It will take them some time to locate the dog. Show them another picture in which an identical dog is following a boy down a path. Here they perceive the dog immediately, because it is in a familiar, meaningful context. Similarly, we fail to recognize an acquaintance when we meet him in a strange city, because he is not in a familiar context or "pattern." We must introduce new vocabulary and new ideas within a framework of the familiar, if we expect children to perceive them quickly and accurately.

4. We tend to perceive what others perceive. A hair arrangement which is classed as careless dishevelment at one time, suddenly becomes "beautiful" when certain movie stars adopt it. An adolescent girl sees a certain boy as "creepy" until an admired friend observes something very desirable about him. During the era of the open-toed slipper, a long, sharply pointed shoe was viewed as ugly and eccentric. A few years later it became so unbelievably "beautiful" that some women felt impelled to have toes sliced thin in order to follow the style. By regularly changing the fashions, the advertisers show their understanding that we perceive as others perceive.

Perhaps in school we can focus attention on the favorable enthusiasms of certain children in such a way as to develop good attitudes and language usage habits in others. Certainly we can avoid problems by anticipating situations where group attitudes can interfere with desired perception of poems and other literary works. By building solid standards of artistic good taste, we can free young people to read material that is of good quality regardless of what is currently sensational.

5. Errors in perception can be reduced, but not prevented entirely. Unfortunate personality problems are one cause of perceptual errors. Fearful people always see the remarks of others as being aimed at their vulnerable points. More commonly, perception errors are the result of inadequate experience "landmarks." In order to perceive "fifty yards" accurately, a child needs a percept of "one yard." In order to perceive quantity, time, or space on a large scale, it is necessary to have representative experiences on a small scale. This is one phase of readiness for any language activity.

In teaching the language arts the need for accurate perception is always evident. Listening skillfully, reading the printed page, telling story events in proper sequence, and all related language activities require a reservoir of percepts. Creative thinking and writing are especially dependent upon keen perception. The capable writer includes fascinating details which give integrity and beauty to his writing. These details are available only from his fund of percepts and images.

It seems reasonably certain that we can improve perception through teaching.[6] Some of the techniques are:

1. Provide daily opportunities for children to employ their senses —manipulating toys, feeling textiles, smelling liquids, tasting foods, sensing wind movements, hearing street sounds, assembling equipment, and similar activities.
2. Provide numerous first-hand experiences through field trips to farms and other locations.
3. Utilize contrived experiences with pictures, films, models, and mock-ups.
4. Capitalize on incidental experiences to direct observation of colors, forms, musical sounds, and sensations of weight, pressure, pain, and temperature.
5. Show sequence in charts, stories, and films.
6. Plan instructional materials which unify ideas—outlines, displays, and bulletin boards.

FROM PERCEPTS TO CONCEPTS THROUGH LANGUAGE

American Indian sign writing and Chinese symbol writing are known for their inefficiency. To communicate an idea through these forms, one must draw numerous small images to represent condensed percepts of the situations to be described. If this process is tedious, imagine how difficult it would be for us to think and to use language if we had to refer back in our minds to the realistic image of every item

[6] Eleanor J. Gibson, "Improvement in Perceptual Judgments as a Function of Controlled Practice or Training," Psychological Bulletin, 50 (1953), 401–31.

that we wished to consider. Instead, we have the capability of combining and classifying our myriads of percepts into concepts. Thus when we think or speak of "farm," it is not necessary to visualize and describe a specific farm. We have a general concept of "farm" which is an abstraction of all farms that we have experienced. Even more wonderful is our ability to develop concepts of things that are not concrete, such as "probability," "generosity," or "frugality."

It is only because of language that we are able to generalize related perceptual experiences into concepts. Words and phrases are the abbreviations which we use constantly to replace concrete experiences in making rapid thought and communication possible. Therefore it is apparent that concept development is the foundation of all learning.

A few facts about concept development may guide us in teaching language as a part of every school subject.

1. Concepts, being built on percepts, are the outcomes of experience. They grow from varied activities, including excursions, observations, projects, discussions, interviews, and every other first-hand or vicarious experience. The teacher who provides quantities of well-chosen experiences for children will be engendering in them the concepts which are the essential ingredients of intelligent thinking and communication. The classroom which is relatively barren and routine is one where the goals of concept development are extremely limited.

2. Verbalization of experience fosters the fixation of concepts. Raw experience creates concepts of certain types, but when the experience is carefully browned over the warm fire of conversation, it becomes more firmly fixed in the mind. The assimilation of concepts is dependent upon their being put into language symbols which the brain can classify and file for future reference. For that reason no field trip has served its best purpose until it has been discussed again in the classroom; no project is complete until a culminating experience requires a restatement of its purposes, principles, and revelations.

3. Concepts develop gradually over an extended period of time. Our concepts grow and change as long as we live. When a child has his first experience with a train, he will not be able to grasp all there is to perceive and understand about a train. He will need repeated experiences with many trains in various situations in order to develop an adequate concept of a train. Even an adult cannot absorb all of the percepts needed for complete concept development when he is in new surroundings or hears a complicated theory for the first time.

This is one reason why the curriculum in the modern school is organized in a spiral or developmental pattern. Such an arrangement provides new experiences every year to help the child build upon his earlier understandings. The new activities should not repeat the earlier learning experiences; rather, they should review and extend them.

Because of their travel and television viewing, today's children may be able to understand some things at earlier grade levels than we could. However, we must be cautious about moving content too low. Concept development is enhanced or limited not. only by experience but also by the child's *capacity* and by the *amount of time* he needs to absorb his experiences.

4. Concepts occur in various degrees of depth or richness for each individual. This is true because of the gradual growth factor. My favorite example is my own concept of "battlefield." From adolescent reading I gained a "battlefield" concept which consisted of a vague feeling of dread coupled with images of shell holes and darkness. This was a very superficial concept, lacking visual clarity and depth of sensory quality. Through experience my concept of "battlefield" became far more accurate, including sights of debris of buildings, bone-weary men, trees mowed off by artillery fire, and tanks approaching speedily down a hillside; sounds of dropping bombs, strafing and whistling artillery shells; odors of dead mules, dank dugouts, and mud; awareness that a friend had been cut in two by shell fire; and countless other sensations.

The accuracy and richness of each person's concept of anything depend upon the extent and the kinds of experiences he has had. In working with children we must strive to make their experiences as extensive and as authentic as possible. Even so, because no two people have identical internal and external experiences, their concepts probably will never be exactly identical. Mankind was made to be somewhat individualistic—from his thumbprints to his thoughts! If we want the child to appreciate good literature fully, we must help him build the concepts needed to relive experiences with authors.

5. Different people may associate different concepts with a given word or phrase. At a professional meeting last year a group of us had difficulty using the word "humility" in a written statement. Some felt that it implied a strength of character that recognizes worth in others; some understood it to mean a groveling attitude. Abstract concepts such as this are much more likely to cause problems than concepts of concrete object classifications. (One's personal background may cause slants or distortions in concept formation.) As an example, does "free enterprise" mean an economic system that stimulates production and a high standard of living for all, or does it connote an economic system that permits some people to profit from the efforts of others?

The necessity of developing undistorted concepts becomes readily apparent from these examples. Only study in depth can prevent half-baked concepts which cause confusion in communication. We teachers have a serious responsibility here.

6. Sometimes concepts are systematically related and overlapping. Like the cells of our bodies, concepts—the cells of thought— divide and multiply. They are differentiated and combined to form related concepts. As examples, the concepts of "plant," "tree," "conifer," and "Scotch pine" are specific ideas that have a patterned relationship. Children will be aided in concept development if we help them see these patterns when they have reached the proper maturation levels.

7. Concept development is nurtured by reflective thinking.[7] As verbalization of experiences helps to fix concepts, so the mental kneading of experiences helps to work the bubbles out of concepts as they are being formed. Careful thinking reveals flaws in understandings and clarifies relationships of significant elements. Thinking, of itself, is one kind of activity. We should encourage children to discuss, debate, and argue their ideas. The thinking this provokes will beat the dust of vagueness from their thoughts, leaving their concepts clear and precise.

8. Broad reading contributes to concept development. Obviously it is impossible for any human being to have enough direct experiences to build all of the concepts that he needs for efficient thinking and communication. Among the many valuable vicarious experiences, reading is particularly helpful because of the limitless number of topics which it can cover.

Of course, a person must begin with a supply of concepts in order to understand the meanings of the symbols which he sees on the printed page. Then he can use known concepts as clues for understanding and assimilating new and more complex meanings from his reading. A city child may combine his concepts of a steep hill and a tree in a park to develop a new concept of the timbered mountain slope about which he reads. Such a concept will not be as complete as that attained by the child who has visited the mountain. In turn, the concept of the second child would not be as detailed and emotionally toned as that of a third child who actually lived on such a mountain slope. However, extensive reading can supply in imperfect form a vast number of essential concepts. The more varied the sources of reading materials, the more accurately the reader's concepts will grow. Consequently we should demand a wide variety of books and materials to supplement the textbooks in every subject that we teach. Development of new concepts is the major goal in teaching every field of content.

EXPERIENCE, EXPERIENCE, AND MORE EXPERIENCE

Children gain both percepts and concepts through experiencing, observing, discussing, dramatizing, illustrating, reading, reflecting,

---

[7] Burton, Kimball, and Wing, *op. cit.*, p. 163.

modeling, acting, evaluating, questioning, and every other "ing" we could mention. Any limitation on experiences leads to lack of concepts, superficial concepts, or inaccurate concepts. Since our teaching hours are limited, it behooves us to select highly significant concepts for emphasis; then we should guide the children in discovering each major idea through as many *different* kinds of related experiences as possible. This will insure accuracy and precision in the child's thinking.

We cannot give the child ready-made concepts.[8] If we attempt this, he will learn only empty words. We must avoid *memoriter* teaching and guide youngsters in actively seeking and discovering ideas. Percepts and concepts are the products of many detailed activities, but this does not justify aimless activity. The child can be lost in a maze of separate facts and events unless we help him intellectualize, organize, and generalize these specifics into useful abstractions, understandings, and principles.[9]

The teacher who provides rich experiences will be rewarded. His pupils may not score appreciably higher on recall tests, but their eyes will gleam with pleasure or cloud with tears as they relive life in good literature. Their discussions in geography and science will reveal their ability to apply principles to new situations. They will thrill to an imaginative poem. And the keenness of their observations will be revealed by the color and truth of their creative writing.

LINGUISTICS: AN OVERVIEW *

George H. Owen

I

Today no one can claim to be a linguist without qualifying his terms carefully. John Carroll, whose book, *The Study of Language*, is an exposition of the various facets of language study, discusses descriptive linguistics, psycholinguistics, historical linguistics, comparative linguistics, and a host of other subdivisions of linguistics. Certainly all of these disciplines make interesting and valuable contributions to

---

[8] Burton, Kimball, and Wing, *op. cit.*, p. 165.

[9] *Ibid.*

* Reprinted from *Elementary English* (Champaign, Ill.: National Council of Teachers of English, May 1962), by permission of the publisher.

our understanding of language and its use, but the American teacher of English might find little that would help her in her classroom tomorrow morning from reading tonight a technical discussion of the differences between the morphemes of Tagalog and those of English. She might find the interspersed Greek and English dialogue of a movie like *Never on Sunday* more instructive, and the hours devoted to the instruction would certainly be more entertaining. Before anyone can talk about linguistics, therefore, and especially, talk *briefly* about linguistics, he has to limit his field.

II

First, then, let us consider the *attitudes* toward language which characterize linguistics. No discussion of linguistic theory will make much sense until we first understand the philosophy toward language out of which this theory grows. I am not going to try to arrange these attitudes in any order of importance, but certainly one of the most fundamental beliefs of linguists is that *language is speech;* that the spoken form of any language is more nearly *the language* than the written form. Speech, they point out, is older than writing. Speech satisfies the total communication needs of millions of human beings scattered all over the face of the globe who will never read or write a single word in their entire lives. Where once we used to say that writing is permanent and therefore enables us to communicate at a distance and at different periods of time, the development of telephones, radio, and tape recorders has extended these capabilities to speech. Speech is primary; writing develops from speech but can never be more than an approximation of speech. It never reproduces all of the factors of speech; gestures, stresses, speech tones, and intonation cannot be accurately recorded. Writing is slow and laborious and its difficulty of production hampers its value as a vehicle of communication. The permanency of writing limits its changes of form. Speech, on the other hand, changes constantly. Because of these differing characteristics, the degree to which writing approximates speech becomes smaller and smaller with every generation. For all of these reasons, linguists believe that language is speech and most of their efforts, therefore, are devoted to the study of speech. They do not ignore writing as they are sometimes accused of doing, but their interest in writing is in the ways in which, successfully or unsuccessfully, it reproduces speech.

A second fundamental attitude of linguistics toward language is that language is *systematic.* Specific principles govern its operation and these principles are all intertwined and interrelated. If this were not so, no one could ever learn by pure memorization the almost infinite number of combinations that are possible in every language. Actually, many of us know that language is systematic even though we rarely think about it. We know, for example, that to form the past tense of a verb in English, the *ed* suffix is usually added: *plan* becomes *planned, iron* becomes *ironed, flunk* becomes *flunked.* When a child learning to speak says *runned* ("We runned all the way home"), his parents smile and indulgently "correct" the little darling. But the child has caught one facet of the system of operation of the English language, and "correction" is not what he needs. He must now begin to learn the modifications of the inflectional system for the past tense in English. When he has really mastered the system, he will recognize that the change of *run* to *ran* is one of the fifty-two possible modifications of the inflectional system for the past tense in English. Most of these modifications he will learn to make accurately and fluently early in his life. A few of the modifications for the past tense, such as the distinctions between *sat* and *set, lay* and *laid,* he may not learn to make until he enters high school.

The system is a powerful force, however, in our use of our language. All of you listening to me today know that the verb *slay,* for example, has a past tense, *slew.* If I tested you on the sentence, "David slew the giant, Goliath," you would all get the verb form right. But a few years back when a popular comedian coined a new meaning for *slay* and made the expression, "You slay me" a household phrase, it was not long before thousands of persons, English teachers included, were saying "He slayed me with that answer" and "That slayed me." Youngsters who have heard the verb *slay* only in this context will find it doubly difficult to learn that the "correct" past tense is *slew.* And teachers who understand the systematic nature of the productive process in language change will find it easier to teach the verb form *slew* indulgently, rather than regarding their students' use of *slayed* as another indication of the complete stupidity of the younger generation.

Linguists think that language is speech and language is systematic. These concepts are clearly definable and therefore arguable even to those who insist they are not linguists. A third attitude of linguistics is harder to illustrate. It may be best to think of this attitude as a cluster of three related concepts. This cluster of three concepts may be stated briefly: language is *symbolic,* language symbols are *arbitrary,* and the symbolism of any language is *complete.* What does this mean?

Many words in English refer directly to objects that can be seen or touched. A *cat,* for example, is an object we all recognize. The recognition is so instantaneous for most of us that the word and the object blend together in our minds. When we see the animal, we think the word simultaneously; when we use the word, its referrant is recalled immediately. This stimulus-response pattern is so unconscious that we tend to forget that the word is not the object but is only a sound symbol or a written symbol for the object. This point may be a little clearer if we consider the morpheme *ed* for the past tense of the verb. Clearly this is a symbol. There is nothing about the sound of *ed* or its appearance in writing that intrinsically means anything related to the past. The words of a language, the inflectional changes, the prefixes and suffixes, all of these are symbols that speakers of English agree on and can manipulate in patterns of such great complexity that fluent language use is in reality a miracle.

Now, if language is symbolic, where did these symbols come from? In the very dim past, words may have evolved from pictures of objects or from attempts to reproduce the sounds that primitive man heard around him: the dog says "bow-wow" and the cat says "meow," for example. Historically, I believe this is uncertain, but it is perfectly obvious that no such relationship exists today between the words of a language and the objects which they symbolize. The word for *cat* might just as well be *geb* as *cat*. The symbols, in other words, are arbitrary. If they are arbitrary, then a person learning a language must learn it from some other person, either directly or from books or tapes or some other humanly developed vehicle. He cannot learn it by himself through observation or listening to the sounds of nature around him. If this is true, then language is the language that people use, the English that they speak in 1962 here in the city of Detroit. It is not the language of Shakespeare, of George Washington, of Franklin Roosevelt. Students learn the language of their parents, their friends, their community. If the language they learn is not the language their teachers speak, then they may have to learn a second language in school. But the language they bring with them is in every *linguistic* respect as good a language as the language of their teachers. Socially, it may not be as acceptable, but linguistically it is equally useful.

And, like all language, it is *complete*. It is capable of expressing every idea or feeling that its users wish to express. This does not mean that it is capable of expressing every idea that a poet, engineer, or a physician wishes to express, but then the ancient Greeks did not have a word for *TV* or *Sputniks* either. And we as teachers might as well admit that we ourselves cannot express every idea a nuclear scientist might wish to express. But the ancient Greeks could have invented a word for *TV* if they had needed it, we could learn to talk like a physicist, and our students can learn to express the new experiences they undergo in school. At each stage of their experience, however, their language is complete: capable of expressing any experience they encounter in symbols which are arbitrarily selected.

As part of their approach to language, linguists also accept two concepts which are shared with other intellectual disciplines. The first of these is that language use is *habitual*, not *logical*. All of us learn to use our language by slow steps, but we cannot be fluent in that language until we can manipulate it without conscious effort. By the time we are adults, this effortless, habitual use of our language is so deeply embedded in our subconscious mind that we never think about how we are using it. That is, we never think about it until we get in an English class and are told to "correct" our English by applying the rules that are listed in our textbooks. This implies that language use is logical: "Think, man, think!" "Here's the rule; now apply it next time you speak or write." Generations of teachers notwithstanding, students don't think when they speak. Neither do you nor I. Our attention is fixed on what we are saying, not the way we are saying it. And this is as it should be. If we need to change a student's use of language, the way to do it is the way we would change any habit: the habit of smoking, the habit of driving with a standard shift after we have been used to an automatic transmission, the habit of shifting our fork from our left hand to our right hand when we have cut up our meat and are now ready to eat it. Break down the old habits and build new ones, step by step, say the psychologists, and linguists agree with them.

Finally, linguists insist that any description of the way in which a language operates, that is, a grammar of the language, must be developed through the techniques of science. These, of course, are the techniques of inductive reasoning: careful observation and collection of data until a pattern begins to emerge, the formulation of a hypothesis to explain this pattern, the testing of the hypothesis against new data. The alternative is to start from premises and arrive at conclusions by deductive reasoning. This latter process has been the one by which most English grammars have been written. Linguists reject it.

III

The application of these five attitudes toward language, that language is *speech;* language is *systematic;* language is *symbolic, arbitrary* and *complete;* language use is *habitual*, not logical; and language descriptions must be *scientific*, has led linguists to some very precise analyses of English. While these analyses help us as teachers to understand how the language operates, they do not tell us how to teach English. They tell us a great deal about what is significant in our language, and therefore, what must be taught and what can be left out, but they do not tell us the best way to teach English phonology or syntax. In spite of ambiguities in popular use, we do not teach "linguistics" instead of grammar, "linguistics" instead of literature, "linguistics" instead of speech. Linguistics has given us much more precise descriptions of the way our language operates. Naturally these descriptions will change what we teach and how we teach it, but these changes are in the realm of pedagogy, not linguistics.

No brief paper on the theory of linguistics can possibly present completely the descriptions of English that linguistic scientists have been developing. But perhaps a brief outline of the major subdivisions of the work in structural linguistics will be helpful.

Linguistic analysis starts with the basic sounds of the language. Which sounds in the language are significant, it asks, and what is the system within which they operate? Obviously, all the sounds that we make as we speak do not contribute to conveying meaning. We could do without the "ahs" and "ohs" many of our friends insert in their speech, for example, or without the clicking of dentures. These sounds are not significant; they have no part in transmitting meaning. The sounds that do transmit meaning in English are the consonant and vowel sounds, the stresses and pitches, and the junctures, the ways in which we interrupt and break off the stream of speech. These significant sounds are the phonemes of the language.

The significant sounds are organized in a system of sound usage. Many linguists have worked out descriptions of this system. Today the most widely accepted phonology of English is the one published by George Trager and Henry Lee Smith in 1951. This phonology is logical, complete, and adequate to deal with the complexities of English speech. While many technical arguments have swirled around the Trager-Smith conclusions, their phonology will not be superseded until someone succeeds in putting together a better organization of all of the complexities of the sound system of English. American students who speak English as a native language know the language's sound system intuitively, and, therefore, do not have to be taught how to produce or understand its sounds, but there may be some advantage to them in understanding intellectually what they do when they speak. And, certainly, all English teachers should have this information as part of their technical background.

The phonemes of a language, its significant sounds, do not of themselves transmit meaning. The /k/, /t/, and /æ/ sounds, pronounced individually and in this order, are meaningless. Put together in the pattern, /kæt/, however, they do transmit meaning: *cat*, a furry animal that drinks milk, or *cat*, as in *that cool cat*, a thumb- and finger-snapping version of a human being, who, we are told, is unusually sensitive to the complexities of modern jazz. Combinations of phonemes which do transmit meaning are called morphemes, and the system of organization within which these morphemes operate is the morphology of a language. Many morphemes are words, but not all words are morphemes: *joy*, for example, is a morpheme which is a word but *enjoy* is two morphemes although still only one word. A morpheme does not have to be a combination of phonemes. The /s/ on the end of *cats*, for example, is a morpheme. It transmits the meaning that there are more than one of this animal. This same phoneme can be heard at the end of the noun *cat* in *my cat's bed, my two cats' feeding bowl,* and at the end of the verb *drink* in *my cat drinks milk.* The phoneme is the same, but in each of these examples the meaning transmitted is different. The single phoneme /s/ in these examples is four different morphemes.

The morphology of English is not complete when we have catalogued all the words, their possible prefixes and suffixes, and the various inflectional changes. Any native speaker of the language knows that it's not just what we say, but also how we say it, that counts. We know what the Western Badman means when he sneers, "Smile when you say that, pardner," and all of us can distinguish between "Really!" and "Really?" or "The rat," and "The rat! ! !" If the words are the same but the meaning is different, obviously something other than words is transmitting meaning. Careful analysis will show that it is the intonation patterns, the combination of stresses, pitches, and junctures, which are morphemic in these examples. A complete morphology of English would have to include a cataloguing of these patterns in addition to the words and word changings, and a description of the intonation system of English.

Finally, morphemes are put together in larger patterns which transmit ideas. These patterns linguists often call utterances. The study of the way utterances are created, the structures of which morphemes are the building blocks, is called syntax. Linguists working on a description of English syntax attempt to chart the various word order patterns in English, the functioning of the various parts of speech in English utterances, the uses English makes of function words, the connecting signals between parts of speech in English utterances, and the devices for compounding and modifying the patterns of English. In syntax, as in phonology and morphology, linguists are concerned not only with accurate observation of the phenomena of English speech, but with the discovery of the interrelations of the system within which the language operates.

COMMUNICATION: A GUIDE TO THE TEACHING
OF SPEAKING AND WRITING *

Minneapolis Public Schools

A TEACHING UNIT FOR A DIRECT STUDY OF
LANGUAGE ITSELF AS SUBJECT-MATTER

The following teaching unit is offered as a brief introduction to a point of view and a field of research not yet widely familiar to teachers of English. While there is now a growing body of authentic and readable material about the nature, development and power of language, it has only recently begun to appear in sourcebooks for teachers and only sporadically in textbooks. Yet both state and national curriculum committees endorse such material as needed content in our English courses of study.

Since the field is so new, any attempt to outline a teaching method for it must be regarded as strictly tentative. There is this advantage, however, to be found in a completely structured unit—tentative and suggestive, only, as it is designed to be: It will suggest a pattern for those teachers who wish to construct their own teaching units. While the structured unit as a whole, to be studied consecutively, is intended for the senior high school level, the ideas included will have implications for teachers at other levels and all teachers are invited to review it for stimulation of their own thinking about the language problem.

The Problem Defined

This unit is intended to suggest the broad outlines for an approach to language study which will recapture pupils' natural interest in language. The aim of the unit is to redirect attention away from an undue concern with their *difficulties with language* to a broader *interest in language*, through which they may find important clues for self-improvement.

Children just learning to talk, and later to read, reveal a spontaneous delight in language. They enjoy the mere sound of words. They ask freely about meaning. They try honestly to express themselves. As

---

* Reprinted by permission of Mr. Robert Fausch, Coordinator of Publications of the Minneapolis Public Schools, Minneapolis, Minn.

the need for social conformity arises in their use of language, however, they grow gradually more and more inhibited. By the time they reach senior high school, many of them "hate to write" and are shy about speaking before a group. English has become a dreaded subject: Do they *have* to take it? Why? They've been studying language all through the grades and through junior high school. It's old stuff.

To profit from further study, students need to become interested in language itself on a scale that is uplifting rather than merely irritating. They need to read about language and learn some of the thrilling discoveries made by the modern linguist. They need to think about language as an important social phenomenon influencing their own lives daily, as they listen to the radio, read the newspaper or watch television. In brief, for a time they need to be lifted out of their close preoccupation with correctness, and to gain a larger vision of the importance of language both to themselves and to the community.

Outcome Expected

In this unit language itself becomes the subject to be investigated, as well as the means of communication, and these specific outcomes should be sought: 1. Development of pupils' ability to observe language in action. 2. Understanding of linguistic concepts that will widen their interest in language and help them solve their own language problems. 3. Improvement of their sense of linguistic propriety, without blocking their desire and power to communicate their thoughts.

INITIATORY ACTIVITIES

To open the unit the teacher might relate any one or all of the three incidents recorded below, or any similar examples of his own choosing. These stories of actual uses of language are intended to awaken general interest in the problem of communication.

Story One

This sign appeared on a parking lot notice to patrons, as reported by a columnist in the local newspaper:

> Failure to pay Parking Fee when you
> enter will be considered trespassing.
> This lot is run on a strictly
> PAY AS YOU ENTER
> basis. Failure to have change will not
> be considered an excuse.

Next day the columnist had this to say about the sign:

"I'm asking you fellow parking-lot patrons who feel as I do to tear the bottom off this column and fasten it to the board where you pay your dime. (Or stuff it in the box with the little envelopes.) We try to be honest, most of us. If the lot doesn't trust us, they can keep a man there. A guard. Meanwhile:

NOTICE

Failure to have an attendant to make change when we enter this lot will be considered poor business practice and worthy of our earnest and gentlemanly complaint. This motorist runs on a strictly business-like basis. Failure to be able to make change will not be considered an excuse for tossing me or my car off your private property which you are permitted to run as a service to the public.

We appreciate your lot, but not that sign. Because we aren't crooks. Just . . . Joe Motorist.

There followed this reply to the columnist, published as a letter to the editor of the newspaper:

Poor Mr. G— who considers only his personal motives, not being able to see the other side of a matter, publishes a lot of stuff which should never appear in print. (But he must find something to try to write about!) His unjustifiable harangue against Parking Lots and their notices was unworthy of anyone's attention. If Mr. G— operated a parking lot business, his notices to his N. P. (No-Pay) customers would undoubtedly be of a sharper character than the one of which he so heatedly complained.

This smart scribe "knows" everything!—and yet knows nothing about the other fellow's business and business problems.

Parking Lot Operators

The columnist followed with this retort which closed the incident:

Well, Mr. B—, I know a gentleman when I see one. Even if he has problems. And I do understand some of the problems of those parking lot owners. One of them phoned me, gave me a fill-in, and reminded me that HIS lot wouldn't post a sign calling a self-parking motorist a potential trespasser. This gentleman has a pay-box lot. He says about one in three motorists fails to put the money in the box. On Saturdays, people are more honest (or may have more money) because only one in five is a dead-head. If there were an attendant on the lot, the parking fee would be higher.

It makes a difference *how* you say things. What angered the columnist was the manner in which the original sign was written. Notice the tone of his reply and how his *way of saying* things aroused the Parking Lot Operators. Which of the participants in the dispute seems the most reasonable? Did anyone cite facts without betraying feeling?

Story Two

Readers of London's *New Statesman and Nation* recently invited readers to play a game originated on a radio program by the well-known philosopher, Bertrand Russell, where he had humorously imitated the conjugation of a verb as follows:

> I am *firm*, you are *obstinate*, he is a *pig-headed fool*.

Among the winners picked by the *New Statesman* as illustrating most aptly how we tend to use different types of words to describe the same set of facts when talking about ourselves, the person in front of us, or the person beyond our hearing, are the following, quoted from the *Reader's Digest*, September, 1948:

I am sparkling; you are unusually talkative; he is drunk.

I am righteously indignant; you are annoyed; he is making a fuss about nothing.

I am beautiful; you have quite good features; she isn't bad looking if you like the type.

I have reconsidered it; you have changed your mind; he has gone back on his word.

I am an epicure; you are a gourmand; he has both feet in the trough.

I have the New Look; you have let down your hem; she has had that dress since 1934.

I am fastidious; you are fussy; he is an old woman.

I have about me something of the subtle, haunting, mysterious fragrance of the Orient; you rather over-do it; she stinks.

The condescension implied in each statement should be carefully observed, and perhaps the derivation of the word *condescension* itself noted.

Story Three

In an issue of *Time* (July 21, 1952) this news item appeared: †

In London, for *The New York Times,* a reporter asked the Labor Party's Aneurin Bevan how he really felt about Prime Minister Winston Churchill. The answer: "I've always looked upon him as more of an artist than an intellectual. This is to be seen most clearly in his speeches. He takes enormous care preparing them. Lloyd George once said to me, 'When Churchill has made a speech, he thinks he has won a battle.' Lloyd George made it clear he considered that Mr. Churchill's excessive preoccupation with words was

† Courtesy *Time* magazine, © Time, Inc., 1952.

a great weakness . . . It is Mr. Churchill's awareness that he is fundamentally a man of letters which compels him all the time to insist he is really
a man of motion. He is not a great orator, because careful preparation beforehand is not the way oratory is produced . . . His most endearing quality is
his mental generosity. He never spares himself in conversation . . . He gives
himself so generously that hardly anybody else is permitted to give anything
in his presence."

Students will need some introduction to the colorful figures of
Bevan and Churchill and the political situation in which the two are
involved. After that the questions might be put to them: Was Mr.
Bevan intending to compliment Mr. Churchill? Or to reduce his station
in the eyes of the world? How can you tell?

The three stories just offered are intended to help pupils appreciate
the fact that it makes a tremendous difference *how* we say things and
that many of our serious breakdowns in communication arise from
subtle psychological factors that creep into our use of language. The
purpose of this unit is to examine some of these factors, first by direct
observation.

LANGUAGE FACTS TO BE OBSERVED AND DISCUSSED—SET ONE

Language is a form of behavior which reveals our personality.
Note and record speech mannerisms—expressions that seem to express
or reveal the point of view or the character of the person who uses
them: habits of pronunciation or enunciation that set a person apart;
favorite words or expressions used constantly. Note especially the language personalities of radio and TV announcers or commentators:
What tricks of speech delight or irritate you? Can you tell why?

Collect examples of the highly individualized style of columnists
or feature writers from newspaper or magazine. How would you describe the style of Robert Ruark or Cedric Adams? What does their
manner of writing seem to reveal about their personalities?

Language habits as an indication of social status. Consider these
two ways of saying the same thing:

> I ain't gonna do it.
> I'm not going to do it.

Besides indicating what we mean, our sentences also reveal something about our social status. The speaker of the first sentence above
may never have had a chance to learn acceptable usage. Or, he might
prefer not to conform to standard usage for one reason or another.

Collect small bits of conversation which seem to you to indicate
differences in social station: Listen to people in various walks of life

talk about the weather, for example. *How* do they phrase their comments? What can you tell about a stranger just from hearing him talk?

Language inappropriate to the occasion. Collect examples of language that seem out of place: an undignified way of saying something when the situation called for dignity; an awkward way of saying something in a setting that called for an easy informality. How should the matter have been presented? Rewrite what was spoken in language which you regard as more appropriate.

Blocks to communication. Record for examination (as nearly as can be remembered) an account of an argument that didn't get anywhere, a conversation in which there was no meeting of minds, a complete misunderstanding of the other person's point of view. Try to analyze what caused the block in communication: To what extent, for example, was the way in which ideas were expressed responsible for the impasse? Wherein did strong feeling block thought? What particular words aroused hostility or caused confusion?

Inferences to be drawn from facts noted. Our manner of saying things, in either speech or writing, makes a difference:

> It reveals our personality.
> It indicates our social station.
> It affects our social relationships.

Related activities. Write a letter which attempts to meet a difficult situation. Try for clear communication of thought and appropriate expression of feeling. The letter should be to an actual person about a real situation, although names may be disguised and the letter withheld. Letters should be exchanged and discussed on the basis of what the language used seems to reveal about the writer and how successfully it meets the situation. Accompanying each letter submitted for discussion should be a brief digest of the situation itself that is being handled.

Write (to be read aloud) two versions of the same explanation written for two different people: an account of an actual mishap, for example; first, as you would tell it to a pal; second, as you would report it to the principal or someone else in a position of responsibility. On what basis do you justify your shift in style?

LANGUAGE FACTS TO BE OBSERVED AND DISCUSSED—SET TWO

The first set of observations is designed to open up the general problem of communication as it concerns us today; the second, to give students a brief introduction to the process of language development so that they may appreciate the tremendous importance of language in the evolution of man, and acquire a deeper respect for language itself.

How children learn to talk. If possible, observe and record how the baby in your family first learned to talk. Or ask your parents about yourself. What were the first words you learned? What part of speech is learned first? What, second? What was one of the first complete sentences uttered? Under what circumstances did it occur?

The sign language of animals. Collect examples of the kind of communication which can be carried on with your dog or cat. How do they signal to you what they want? With what words and gestures can you make them understand what you mean? What ideas is it impossible to make them understand? What does their name mean to them? It is a signal—of what?

Primitive modes of communication. Sign language, while a primitive mode of communication, is useful in civilized society. Collect examples of sign language commonly employed in sport, in surveying, by boy scouts, in the army. What facial expressions do you recognize as signs? What, for example, are raised eyebrows the sign of? A mouth drawn down at the corners? What bodily postures can you interpret as signs of self-confidence, discouragement, or resignation? What common gestures serve as signs? What are the advantages of sign language? What are its limitations?

The symbolic character of language. Read Chapter 14 of *The Story of My Life,* by Helen Keller, and report to the class on her first understanding of the symbolic character of language: that *w-a-t-e-r,* for example, as spelled into her hand, *stood for* the water from the pump that spilled over her hands. Explain how much this discovery meant to her. Up to this point, she, too, like animals, had been dependent on sign language. Now she possessed an important new tool. What did it enable her to do?

The importance of language to mankind. List the advantages which spoken language gives to mankind over animals. What advantages does written language give him? Without language, it would be impossible to build a civilization. Think of as many reasons as you can why. Suppose dogs were able to invent a language. What would a canine civilization consist of? Listen to your teacher read aloud and interpret the following poems about the permanency which writing gives to thoughts:

Shakespeare's Sonnets	Nos. 18, 60, 65
Michelangelo's Sonnet	No. 62
Keats'	*Ode to a Grecian Urn*

Keep a diary of thoughts during your study of this unit as a means of giving permanency to your experience or to help you hold onto fleeting thoughts.

The origin of language. Look up and report to the class the picturesque theories of the origin of language: the bow-wow theory and the pooh-pooh theory, etc. What myths reflect man's appreciation of the power of language long before he understood its origin?

Look up the story of the discovery of Sanskrit and comparative philology in 1784 and tell how it was discovered that all languages have a common origin.

Retell the Bible story about the Town of Babel, a story which is regarded by linguists as a figurative explanation that all languages have a common origin—not from an historically recorded source, but from a common form of early speech.

The development of written language. Look up and report to the class, by reproduction of examples on the blackboard, the various stages which written language went through in its development:

Pictographs—pictorial representation

Ideograms—representation of ideas

Phonetic alphabet—representation of sounds by symbols

Explain the advantages of the last-named over the others. (Consult unabridged dictionary or encyclopedia.)

Inferences to be drawn from facts noted. The ability of the human baby to learn our spoken language by imitation marks a tremendous advance in human development over the sign language of animals. Language learning begins unconsciously by ear and while other methods later supplement it, they do not supplant it. Adults, too, develop language power by unconscious absorption of language patterns which they hear and read.

The invention of language is a distinct cycle in man's evolution toward freedom and detachment from his physical environment. A bird, for example, is freer of its environment than a tree. The human mind is free to go beyond its own environment. Man can roam the universe, as he has done, by means of language. Animals live in a world of nature. They cannot escape from it. So early man once lived— until he invented language. Language set his spirit free. It gave him the tool to build his mental world—a world that transcends space and time. No longer need man be tied to his instincts. He can talk to himself and dispel his own fears. He can store impressions, weigh reasons, form judgments—all through language. He is no longer a helpless chip in a stream of happenings. He has a power for controlling and ordering his own destiny.

Man's development and control of language is his greatest single achievement. More than any other factor, language is responsible for his enormous superiority over animals in his control of his world. Language is the tool of reason. It is the means by which we think. We cannot think outside of language. Before he could think about what was happening to him, man needed a language. This urge to develop a language began with a noticing of objects separately, as things in themselves, and then naming them; of differentiating the factors in his environment: "This," for example, "is a stone; that a tree." Animals show no such mental recognition of stone, tree, flower or weed as such. They are aware of such objects only as they affect their physical needs. They have no mental interest in such things. Such interest would lead to language.

Language introduced permanence into man's otherwise vanishing world. Our mental world does not flow away from us as does experience. The flow of time is checked inside man's head. It is this aspect of language that has made possible the building of civilization. Language is man's most priceless possession: It is our best means of communication: to warn each other of danger; to share others' experiences and thus to extend and deepen our own; to learn from others' experience. It is our means of pooling information; of developing a reservoir of knowledge; of preserving our inheritance from the past.

Related activities. Compose a sentence in your mind and then try to communicate it to the class entirely by gesture and pantomime; a request, a command, a question or a comment about a situation. See whether the class can "read" what your actions say.

Bring to class for exchange and discussion, a reproduction of a statue or painting that communicates successfully by signs some thought or feeling. What are the signs? What, the facts or feelings communicated?

Write an imaginative story based on the idea that a particular species of bird or animal miraculously learns to talk our language or invents one of its own. What happened thereafter? Signifying what?

LANGUAGE FACTS TO BE OBSERVED AND DISCUSSED—SET THREE

The third set of facts to be observed relates to interesting facts about language change.

The saga of place names. Read Part One, Chapter VI, of *The Story of Language* by Mario Pei and recount to the class interesting examples of how places are named. Try to find out how the places in your community were named: the streets, parks, schools, and so forth. Look for the changes that have taken place in the spelling and pronunciation of odd names.

Origin of family names. Read Chapter VII, Part One, of *The Story of Language* and recount to the class interesting examples of the origin of family names. Find out, if you can, the origin and history of your own family names. What changes has time wrought in spelling and pronunciation?

Word borrowing from other languages. Look up and report to the class stories of word borrowing from other languages but especially by the English language. From what languages have we done the most borrowing? Read Chapter IX, Part II, entitled "The International Language Bank," from *The Story of Language* and cite interesting examples.

Word coinage. Collect popular words of recent coinage such as *know-how, hair-do, smog,* or picturesque phrases which are used metaphorically outside the setting where they originated. Try classifying the complete list compiled by the class, on the basis of the process involved: *smog,* for example, is built out of "smoke" and "fog"; *know-how* is a whole sentence reduced to a noun. Note the role of radio and TV in popularizing such new coinages. What examples can you cite? Check the words and phrases that have been popular a long time and seem destined to become eventually words in good standing.

Inferences to be drawn from facts noted. Pronunciation and spelling of place and family names undergo gradual modification over the years, and amusing bits of history are often to be unearthed in the study of originals. New words are constantly fed into language by popular coinage. Slang words become colloquial idiom; colloquial idiom may in time become acceptable, standard usage.

Related activities. Try your own hand at coining a new word by any of the processes identified by the class in its analysis.

Suggest an appropriate name for some school or community enterprise or commercial project. Or, set up a contest for securing a good name—where a good name or label is needed—which will stimulate thinking.

DEVELOPMENTAL ACTIVITIES

The activities suggested in the preceding section of the unit are intended largely to arouse pupils' interest in language itself as an important fact in life. If successfully carried out, these activities should also point to the need for further information about the nature of language. There follows a brief study outline touching upon the areas of grammar and usage, and semantics.

The usual approach to the study of grammar and usage is that of learning rules and forms in order to correct inaccuracies in speech and writing. In this unit the purpose is to discover reasons *why* a knowledge of grammar and usage is important, and *what* kind of help such knowledge offers. It is the building of a point of view toward language that the study seeks to accomplish.

Only a broad outline for study is offered here. It is assumed that teachers using the outline will amplify it as they see fit.

In the preceding section of the unit, pupils were set primarily to observing facts and to seeing how certain inferences, as listed, could be drawn from them. In this phase of their study, it will be necessary to introduce them to facts which they cannot discover for themselves. Such facts may be presented in outline form on the blackboard or on mimeographed sheets illustrated copiously and discussed thoroughly, followed by exercises in applying the ideas gained.

I. The Nature of Language

A. Language is built out of sounds (not letters) and speech (not writing) is the root of language development.

B. Writing is a way of representing speech. Letters were determined by sounds: sounds are not determined by letters. All languages have sound but not all languages have letters, or a system of writing.

C. Our printed alphabet does not represent all of the sounds in the English language; in other languages, moreover, there are many other sounds than those in our language.

D. To study language we must study the sounds themselves, and linguists have found a way of describing and analyzing the sounds of language in terms of the organs used to produce them. These sounds are of two types: Those we make by forming resonance chambers with the tongue in different positions (commonly called vowel sounds); and those produced by obstructing the breath and causing friction in one way or another (commonly called consonant sounds).

E. The letters of the alphabet do not adequately describe these two types of sounds and a series of phonetic symbols has been devised for vowels and consonants. All the different individual variations in sound that a speaker hears as a single sound constitute what linguists call a "phoneme." A phoneme is a class of sounds, any one of which is heard as the equivalent of any other. In the variety of American English used in the Middle West there are, for example, twenty-six consonant phonemes and thirteen vowel phonemes, or, loosely, twenty-six consonants and thirteen vowels. The study of individual speech sounds, or phonetics, and the study of the patterning of the sound-classes in a given language, or phonemics, provide the basis for linguistic analysis.

F. Language is a system of sounds for the purposes of signaling meanings.

G. Meaning is determined by usage, i.e., a certain sound or combination of sounds is invested with a definite, agreed-upon meaning and becomes a word. Different languages use different sounds for the same object: *dog* (English), *chien* (French), *hund* (German). Different languages also use the same sound, or combination of sounds, for different meanings: the English *do* (act); the French *doux* (sweet); the German *du* (you).

H. There are many different forms by which meaning may be signalled or communicated: *John! There! Look out! The deed is done.* Out of these forms (single words, phrases, clauses, sentences) language patterns are built.

I. These basic patterns of a language are generally referred to as the grammar of a language. Grammar includes a study of the sound-classes in a language (phonemics), of the different forms of words (inflection), and of the various relationships among words in structural patterns, such as a sentence (syntax).

J. In a very real sense, children learn their grammar when they first learn to talk and put words together to make sense. If they didn't know their grammar—i.e., know how to arrange words in accepted patterns—they wouldn't be able to communicate their wants or their ideas.

K. A knowledge of the basic elements of grammar is necessary to an intelligent discussion of language usage and to a profitable observation of language.

L. Terms which refer to the relationships of words or groups of words to each other—such as subject, predicate, modifier, agreement—are very useful in an analysis of sentence style or of a breakdown in sentence meaning.

II. English Usage

A. The actual language habits of the people in a community, speaking and writing for each other in varying circumstances, constitute *usage.* The term covers these six areas: (1) pronunciation, (2) vocabulary, (3) word forms to indicate time, possession, plurality, (4) construction, (5) idioms, (6) conventions of writing such as spelling, capitalization, punctuation, manuscript and letter forms.

B. "Correct" usage is *generally acceptable usage.* What is acceptable at one time and in one place, however, may be unacceptable in another. In those situations and with those speakers who accept *It is me,* it is not incorrect. In other words, a "mistake" which everyone makes is no longer a mistake.

C. People react unfavorably to language which varies from the customary and the generally accepted. "I ain't" has social connotations which sharply restrict its range of acceptableness. For this reason it is of practical importance to know and use accepted forms.

D. "Correctness," or acceptable usage, should not be confused with style. Good style transcends mere conformity and means clarity, appropriateness, orderly and pleasing arrangement of words. It signifies intellectual power.

E. Usage is not logical or consistent. It is constantly changing and varies at different times and in different places. It is the result of many forces playing upon language.

F. Usage determines grammar (that is, the description of word relationships): grammar does not determine usage. For example, *Many a man have tried* is logical agreement *(many have)* but usage has established *Many a man has tried* as preferable.

G. There is no single standard of "correct" usage but different levels of usage, each level carrying a social implication:

> *Standard English* is the language spoken by those who carry on public affairs. It is the language used in business, government, journalism, education, religion, literature.
>
> *Colloquial language* is the language of informal conversation used at certain times by all people. It is not inferior to standard English; it is merely different.
>
> *Ceremonial usage* is appropriate on formal occasions where dignity or reverence is in order.
>
> *Vulgar or illiterate usage* may indicate lack of formal schooling or limitation of social environment. Or, it may also indicate indifference or carelessness in the use of language.
>
> *Jargon* is the language of a particular sport or trade or profession. Sportswriters and pressmen use jargon.
>
> *Slang* is the experimental frontier of language development. It is the grass-roots source of new words and idioms added to our language. Most slang expressions are short-lived but a few withstand the test of time and are admitted first to colloquial usage and finally to standard usage.

H. Literature is the artistic use of language. It is not the root of language, but its flower. Therefore, it is not the basic element in language study.

III. Problems Created by Language

A. Language creates its own problems—problems which go far beyond the problem of grammatical structure and of acceptable usage, into the intricate problems of meaning. This field of language study is called semantics.

B. Language has a dual function: it can refer to a fact or to a situation, and it can at the same time express the speaker's or the writer's feelings about the fact. Both functions are legitimate but very often become confused in the minds of both speaker (or writer) and listener (or reader). We call these two uses of language *referential language* (because it *refers* to facts), and *emotive or affective language* (because if both expresses and *affects* feelings). We live in a dual world: the world of words and the world of fact. Confusion of the relation between these two worlds creates misunderstanding.

C. The growth of language is toward a close resemblance between the structure of language and the world which language mirrors. Originally, language sought to state what the eyes and ears and other senses perceived, or how the person felt. Nouns and verbs identified what was observed. "The car ran off the road." These words stated a fact which could be verified.

D. Words are always learned in context: physical, social or verbal context. No word has exactly the same meaning twice. It depends on the context in which it is used. This fact is a source of confusion: people disregard the context and misinterpret the meaning.

E. Meaning is of two basic kinds: denotative and connotative. Words name or identify or *denote:* they also suggest or *connote.* Denotative language is the language of accurate reporting: it is the language of science. Connotative language is the language of literature, whose purpose is to affect the emotions of readers or listeners.

F. Thus there are two basically different ways for words to be true: (1) they may be literally true, or scientifically true. Or, (2) they may be psychologically true; i.e., they may express a true feeling or a sincerely held idea.

G. The basic form of language expression is the report of what we have seen or heard or felt. A good report may be judged by the following: (1) The facts can be verified. The words fit the facts. (2) It will exclude judgments; i.e., what the reporter thinks or how he feels about the facts. Judgments stop thought on the part of the person listening to or reading the report. (3) It will avoid "loaded" words, i.e., words that arouse feelings (connotation) or "slanting" words, i.e., words that direct judgment. A good report, in other words, lets the facts speak for themselves. Good reporting is rare. People tend to disregard all three of the rules above and thus confuse others.

H. Words have other legitimate uses, however, than to report facts; they also communicate feeling by means of the tone of voice—its dramatic variations; rhythm, rhyme and repetition; the aura of association which words gather; by the pictorial devices of metaphor, simile and personification; and by the devices of irony and humor.

The aura of association of the word *home,* for example, has acquired a connotative meaning from the way it is commonly used and from the sentiments that are associated with it. Some words to many people are taboo because of association: they will not use the word *dead,* for example, but prefer *passed away* or *gone west.* The expression *gone west* above—a metaphor—is such a pictorial device.

I. All these devices are part of the *affective* use of words. They *affect* people. Sometimes they are referred to as *purr* words or *snarl* words: words that indicate and communicate a pleasant, happy feeling, or an angry and hostile feeling.

J. The central language problem is to recognize the difference between facts and judgment, between scientific and poetic truth, between denotative and connotative language. Misjudging the meaning intended, or confusing the two types of meaning, interferes seriously with communication.

K. Generalizing and abstracting are two language processes, absolutely necessary to thinking, but which often lead to empty talk, to what are sometimes called pure "verbalisms," that is, statements with no facts to support them. Generalizing from too few facts is a common error: "All the kids at school are wearing 'em."—when in reality, the speaker can name only three or four. High-powered abstractions like *democracy, faith, injustice* are often meaningless words. When we find ourselves talking mere words it is a good idea to go back to a specific *what,* in relation to a particular *who,* with a definite *where* and *when* and *how* in mind—an actual case of democracy or faith in operation: The women of Gary, Indiana, rose up en masse on such and such a date before the City Council to present a resolution demanding law enforcement.

L. Abstract words like *good* and *bad, right* and *wrong, black* and *white,* tend to lead us into a two-valued orientation toward the facts of life: It's either right or it's wrong. In truth, however, it may be right for a particular person in a particular situation and wrong for another under different circumstances.

M. The use of language may be viewed from four different angles: sense, feeling, tone and intention.

> *Sense* (or literal meaning) is the principal factor in referential language.
>
> *Feeling* is the attitude of the speaker or writer toward what he is saying.
>
> *Tone* is the attitude of the speaker toward his audience revealed through language.

Tone may be determined by his feelings. We speak of a sarcastic tone, a casual tone, a belligerent tone.

Intention is the purpose that lies behind an utterance. It, too, will determine the tone. It is the intention of some propagandists to arouse prejudice. The very word *propaganda* itself can be used to arouse prejudice.

N. Almost every utterance can be viewed from each of these four angles—

Feeling and *tone* are especially important in poetry.

Intention is the dominating motive in politics and advertising.

Sense is the principal factor in referential language—the language of work, business, science, education.

SUGGESTED ACTIVITIES

The Basic Structure of Language

Take a class inventory of the working knowledge which pupils already have of grammar. Devise a check list, perhaps, (not a test), and let the pupils indicate what they do know and can use: Can they name and recognize the eight parts of speech? Can they pick out subjects and predicates? Do they know the difference between phrases and clauses? What facts about the structure of sentences would they like to know more about?

It should be clear that the purpose of this assignment is quite different from the usual diagnostic test. Presumably pupils have at this point begun to take an interest in language and to see the need for a knowledge of grammar. Later on, after the whole unit has been completed, such an inventory should prove useful in suggesting needed content to be introduced at a time when a discussion of students' own writing is under way. It is important to note that the primary aim of this unit is knowledge *about* the significance of grammar rather than a knowledge *of* grammar for the purposes of sentence improvement. This last would presumably become one of the goals in another type of project; namely, the communication of an idea or the presentation of a point of view.

Levels of Usage

Students should be set to collecting examples of the various levels of usage and to noting what distinguishes colloquial usage from standard usage or ceremonial usage. They should listen carefully to the different ways in which people talk over the radio or TV and note such qualities as variations in the pronunication of words, idioms peculiar to different sections of the country, differences in dialect which are interesting (not incorrect), occupational jargon, and so forth.

A re-examination of the dictionary is also in order at this point: Students might look up the word *snob* in Webster's unabridged dictionary, for example, and note the history of the word: how it started out as a slang word and gradually acquired its present accepted meaning. Or, they might look up the word *run* and notice that while *ran* is given as the past tense, *run* is also given as a dialect form. They should note that the function of the dictionary is to record the history of words and their established usages and note the various abbreviations used: *obs.* for obsolete, and so forth. They might also read pp. 55–56 of *Language In Thought and Action* by S. I. Hayakawa and find out how dictionaries are made.

A question box might be set up for questionable usages, and a group appointed to run them down in something of the manner of the special page in the English journal given over to questions and answers. What purposes do conventions serve? This question might be explored in a panel discussion. Where else are conventions adhered to besides in writing? What are the values of uniformity in punctuation and spelling? What is a Style Book used by publishers and newspapers?

Problems Created by Language

Someone in the class might consider the significance of these famous words of Juliet from Shakespeare's play, *Romeo and Juliet:* "What's in a name? A rose by any other name would smell as sweet." Did the Capulets truly hate the Montagues? or only the name of Montague? How it is possible to hate a *name?* What examples of their own can pupils cite to show that people confuse names with facts?

It should prove profitable to list situations in which accurate reporting of facts is a first necessity and to recount cases where false reporting caused difficulties. Or to collect examples of biased reporting, pointing out "loaded" words; that is, words which show prejudice; or "fighting" words, words which immediately arouse antagonism because of their association.

Pupils might also be asked to bring to class samples of affective or emotive language—either in speaking or in writing—which had a high degree of influence—either good or bad. Or, to observe and analyze the language used in the famous speech by Mark Antony in Shakespeare's *Julius Caesar.* What were his methods of playing upon the emotions of the crowd? The class might discuss any political speech for bias, or analyze advertisements for their use of affective language.

Some student might read a favorite poem aloud to the class and point out the suggestive power of particular words, or bring to class an effective sales letter received at home and analyze its use of language to make a particular kind of appeal.

CULMINATING ACTIVITIES

Summary and evaluation of results. To conclude the unit, the following types of activity are suggested:

1. A review of the diaries kept during the course of the unit, referred to on page 32, by each pupil's rereading both his own diary and that of some of his classmates. High spots should be shared with all members of the class.
2. A test covering such topics as: how dictionaries are made and what kind of "authority" they represent; recognition of the various levels of usage; the usefulness of grammar; the denotation and connotation of words.
3. A vocabulary test on the meaning of such words as *usage, semantics, verbalism,* and so forth.
4. An analysis of a particular piece of writing or speech on the basis of its tone, the intention of the writer or speaker, the appropriateness of the language used, the emotional overtones of the language used, and so forth.
5. An original composition—either written or oral—in which a genuine purpose is clearly identified and the style is nicely adapted to it. An accurate reporting of an incident, for example, intended to give the student body a clear picture of what happened; or, an emotional appeal for support of some school project.
6. A carry-over plan for submitting language problems to the class periodically for discussion. These may be particular problems of usage. They may be interesting examples of advertising and propaganda devices discovered in newspaper, magazine or billboard or platform.

SPECIAL BIBLIOGRAPHY FOR UNIT

Estrich, Robert Mark and Sperber, Hans. *Three Keys to Language.* New York: Holt, Rinehart & Winston, 1952.
Fries, Charles. *Structure of English.* New York: Harcourt, Brace & World, 1952.
Hall, Robert A. *Leave Your Language Alone.* Linguistica, 1950.
Hayakawa, S. I. *Language in Thought and Action.* New York: Harcourt, Brace & World, 1949.
Johnson, Wendell. *People in Quandaries.* New York: Harper & Row, 1946.
Kenyon, John Samuel. *American Pronunciation.* Wahr, 1950.

Kennedy, Arthur G. *English Usage.* New York: Appleton-Century-Crofts, 1942.

Marckwardt, Albert H. *Introduction to English Language.* New York: Oxford U. P., 1942.

Mencken, Henry Louis. *American Language.* New York: Knopf, 1936.

Pei, Mario. *The Story of Language.* New York: W. W. Norton, 1949.

Pooley, Robert. *Teaching English Usage.* New York: Appleton-Century-Crofts, 1946.

CHAPTER 2

Listening and Speaking

Of all the sounds a man is capable of uttering, each culture selects a small number from which it builds a language. The oral language is the living language in which growth and change take place which are eventually reflected in its written form. The ability to use the spoken word to accurately communicate thought or express feeling is the most significant skill developed by individuals in the highly complex social organization of modern life.

LISTENING *

David H. Russell and Elizabeth Russell

"You can't believe your ears." Or can you?

As Wilson Mizner once said, "A good listener is not only popular everywhere, but after a while he knows something." This manual is concerned not only with "believing your ears" (or not), but also with Mizner's "popularity," in the sense of worth-while group skills, and with his "knowing something"—with learning through listening.

Children live in a world of sound. They are bombarded from morning to night not only with the sounds of the physical environment but with the words of peers and adults who want them to do something, or at least want to be heard. As Gerald Green puts it in *The Last Angry Man,* his novel of the television industry: "The most overwhelming fact of the twentieth century is the assault on

---

* Reprinted from *Listening Aids Through the Grades* (New York: Bureau of Publications, Teachers College, Columbia University, 1959), pp. 1–4; 6–10, by permission of the publisher.

the public ear and eye, the incessant, relentless avalanche of useless information."

Perhaps because there is so much of it, many children learn to ignore talk. Too many people are firing too many ideas at them, and so they take refuge in "nonlistening." They "listen with half an ear" when the radio is playing, but also transfer this habit to other situations such as the classroom when the teacher is giving directions. Some "noises" can be ignored—but not all.

Surely we all need to evade sound at times! But this book is not about escape. Rather it attempts to help teachers and children do something about what they hear. Sometimes this may be a negative rejecting. More often it means a positive selecting, listening to get an important idea, follow a sequence of events, carry out exact instructions, or do something else about what is heard. Most of us like to talk more than we like to listen, and so we need help in developing a liking for listening as well as skills in listening. Perhaps this collection of activities can help both the liking and the doing.

SCHOOL TASKS

When children first enter school there are wide differences among them in their sensitivity to sound signals. These differences occur in:

1. Auditory acuity, or the sensitivity of hearing as measured by the amount of *sound energy* necessary for a person to hear.
2. Auditory discrimination, or the ability to distinguish sounds which are somewhat alike, such as the sounds of the letters *p* and *b* or the words *seeing* and *ceiling*.
3. Auditory comprehension, or the ability to understand and remember the meanings back of the word signals.

The study and correction of difficulties in the first category may involve the school nurse, the use of such instruments as the audiometer, and, if necessary, the services of the school physician or a skilled otologist. The correction of difficulties and development of skills in the second area usually requires many language activities in the kindergarten and primary grades. These occur, for example, in the speech program, and in the development of phonetic skills in connection with reading. Some activities in this group are included as *listening* skills in Chapter Two of this manual. The development of abilities in the third category, concerned with meaning and use of words and passages, is the chief concern of this book. This group involves not only the general listening skills of the second division, but the understanding and interpretive abilities here developed as auding activities. The distinction between listening and auding is developed further below.

WHAT IS AUDING?

Today children have many purposes for listening. They listen to parent or teacher, they use the telephone, they engage in conversation and discussion, they enjoy stories and factual reports, follow directions or announcements, give some attention to radio programs, appreciate phonograph records, and hear (and see) movies and television programs. These varied activities suggest that words like *hearing* or even *listening* are not specific enough to describe accurately all of these modern activities. So we say that children hear generally, they listen to sounds, but they learn to *aud* or "to listen with comprehension and appreciation."

Donald Brown has explained his use of the term *auding* as follows:

I have adopted the term "auding" to avoid the ambiguities of such terms as "listening," "hearing," and "understanding" as well as to eliminate the awkwardness of such phrases as "getting the meaning from heard words," "listening with understanding to spoken language," or "interpreting vocal expression." Auding is to the ears what reading is to the eyes. If reading is the gross process of looking at, recognizing, and interpreting written symbols, auding may be defined as the gross process of listening to, recognizing, and interpreting spoken symbols.

The meaning of *auding* clears up when one compares it to reading. To put the relationship in quasi-mathematical terms:

Seeing : observing : reading = hearing : listening : auding.

Just as reading is more than seeing or observing because it involves accurate understanding and interpretation of written words, so is auding more than hearing or listening because it requires accurate understanding and interpretation of spoken words. Children hear the whistle of a train, the chirp of country frogs or the roar of city traffic. They listen, vaguely and passively or more accurately and actively, to a popular song or a news broadcast. But when they listen to teacher or parent to follow specific directions, to get the facts in a classmate's report on Norway, or to understand two sides of a panel discussion of teen-age driving they may be said to be auding, for they are listening with comprehension and interpretation of verbal symbols. Just as the child who reads must react to the words of the page with understanding and use, so the child who auds goes beyond mere listening to interpretation and use of what he hears.

THE IMPORTANCE OF AUDING

It is probably impossible to overestimate the importance of auding in the lives of children and youth. They listen in school and out of school. In an early and much quoted study, Thomas Rankin found that Americans spend 30 per cent of the time they devote to language use each day in speaking, 16 per cent in reading, 9 per cent in writing, and 45 per cent in listening. In another study consisting of observations of activities in elementary school classrooms, Miriam E. Wilt discovered that children spend about two and one-half hours of the five-hour school day in listening. This was nearly twice as much time as their teachers estimated the children spent on listening. In still another study, F. Corey found that the chances were about one to sixty of a particular pupil speaking compared to the possibility of the teacher speaking and, presumably, the pupil listening. One does not need to approve of all this listening, especially if learning is an active process, but the fact remains that pupils do listen a lot in school. Whether they are actively auding is another question.

Furthermore, in addition to all this listening in school, children hear parents and siblings at home, they may have a radio turned on part of the day, and they probably listen to television. Paul Witty has found that children in television areas spend, on an average, *over three hours per day* seeing and listening to television programs. Less frequently, but more or less regularly, they are expected to listen to public speakers, preachers, Scout leaders, peer members of groups, and to the characters in movies. From morning to night, the child or adolescent is buffeted with the stormy winds of words. He needs help in a deluge. His school is about the only place where he can get help in selecting or rejecting, in understanding and using, the torrent poured over him. . . .

If the third grade is asked by the teacher to follow carefully directions for making the Christmas box, a high level of listening for exact details will be in order. But if the television speech which the junior high class was asked to monitor turns out to be a boring affair, the students may listen only enough to get the main idea of the talk. Gertrude Strickland has suggested different amounts of involvement in listening. No one level is necessarily better than any other, but the following list of levels ranges from inexact to detailed, from aimless to purposeful, from passive to creative:

Hearing

1. Hearing sounds or words but not reacting beyond bare recognition (e.g., knowing that Joey is speaking).
2. Intermittent listening—turning the speaker on and off in aimless fashion, as the mind wanders (e.g., hearing one fact about sled-dogs but none of the rest of the social studies report on Eskimos).
3. Half-listening—following the train of discussion but only closely enough to seize the first opportunity to have one's own say (e.g., not really hearing what your classmate did over the week end but waiting to tell, during the conversation period, how *you* caught a fish).

Listening

4. Listening passively with little or no observable response. (The child who constantly "glues" his eyes on his teacher but offers no reactions in words or facial expression may or may not be responding.)
5. Narrow listening in which the main significance or emphasis is lost as the listener selects details which may be relatively unimportant but which are familiar or agreeable to him. (A junior high school pupil agrees heartily with two points made by a panel speaker but disregards other contributions on all sides of a question.)

Auding

6. Listening and forming associations with related items from one's own experience. (A second-grader notes the relationship between the words "hound" and "found"; a fifth-grader who has listened to the committee report on the gold rush of '49 tells of his visit to a ghost mining town in the West, relating his account to items in the report.)
7. Listening closely enough to the organization of a talk or report to get main ideas and supporting details, to follow directions, etc. (An eighth-grade pupil notes that the main topic of the report is the causes of the American Revolution and lists four such causes.)
8. Listening critically. (A sixth-grader gives evidence of critical listening when he asks for more data on the statement made by a classmate that most South American countries have democratic governments.)
9. Appreciative and creative listening, with genuine mental and emotional participation. (A pupil responds to the humor of the Benét poem *John James Audubon*, suggests several other poems that the group might read orally from *The Book of Americans* by the Benéts, and tells why these poems are exciting to him.)

These types of hearing, listening, and auding have been listed on successive levels, but obviously there is much overlapping among them. In general, pupils must have considerable experience and mental maturity before they can react as in levels seven, eight, and nine; but such responses are not limited to older children any more than aimless listening is typical of younger children. In every case the context of the material heard, and the concepts and purposes involved, rather than the mere age of the pupils, will determine whether the reaction is passive hearing or accurate, creative auding. The teacher and the other pupils have much to do with the level or quality of any one child's listening. With guidance a child's listening experience may become a genuine "meeting of minds." His auding may be selective, purposeful, accurate, critical, creative.

THE TEACHING OF LISTENING—AND WHY? *

Miriam E. Wilt

Prior to the invention of the printing press, knowledge and information were largely acquired through the ears. The printing press made books and other printed matter available to the masses. Four centuries have made people print-minded, and literacy has come to be measured in terms of reading and writing. In less than thirty years the invention of radio, sound recorders, and television has helped to swing the pendulum back. Perhaps there is something to be learned from the Hindus who, admittedly illiterate in terms of reading and writing, "have a literacy of the spoken word—thoughtfully spoken and thoughtfully listened to." [1]

WHY TEACH LISTENING?

Today, as never before, the ears of the peoples of the world are being bombarded by information and misinformation; by propaganda —good and bad; by drama, lectures, panel discussions, news reports of all types, and advertising campaigns. Sometimes what can be heard is worth while; sometimes it is actually harmful. The ability to listen intelligently and discriminatingly is important in these critical times. Recent scientific and technological developments have increased the amount of time that people spend in listening. In the opinion of many people, however, the ability to listen efficiently has not improved through increased use of the ears.

While "speech instruction is common, good listening is supposed

---

* Reprinted from *A Monograph on Language Arts*, No. 66 (Evanston, Ill.: Harper & Row, 1951), by permission of the author and publisher.

[1] Alice Sterner, *et al.*, *Skill in Listening*, N.C.T.E. Pamphlets on Communication (Chicago: National Council of Teachers of English, 1944), p. 5.

to be acquired naturally. Frequently it is never acquired, for ear specialists tell us that more than half of so-called deafness is nothing more than inattention." [2]

ARE WE TEACHING CHILDREN TO LISTEN?

A study [3] was made to determine whether teachers considered listening an important learning aid in elementary education. Five aspects of the problem were investigated: (1) the amount of time children are supposed to listen in 'the average classroom; (2) the amount of time teachers *think* that children learn by listening: (3) the relative importance teachers place upon listening as compared with other language skills; (4) teachers' opinions of the importance of listening skills in situations in which listening is the activity of the majority of the group; and (5) evidence of the teaching of listening in classrooms.

The data for this study were gathered from the answers to 1,452 questionnaires by teachers in forty-two states and by timing the listening activities of the children in nineteen classrooms.

In the opinion of the teachers answering the questionnaires, children spend the major part of the day reading. And also, in their opinion, learning to read is the most important skill to be learned. Contrary to what teachers believe, in the schools visited children were spending more time listening than in any other single activity. They were expected to listen 57.5 per cent of the classroom activity time.

In evaluating the relative importance of language activities common in modern schools, activities which are predominantly oral (such as group discussion, reports, and oral reading), only 29.5 per cent rated listening as the most important skill to the majority of the group. Paradoxical as it may seem in each situation, only one child spoke or read while the remainder of the group listened.

In the schools visited, seldom was there a real purpose for listening to what was being said. There was little reading of stories or poems that were new to the children listening. Rarely was oral reading used to prove a point, to give additional information, or to provide enjoyment. The most common uses of oral reading were in rereading stories, geography, history, or health lessons that had already been predigested by the class. This could scarcely be called purposeful listening. As

---

[2] Eda B. Frost and Rhoda Watkins, *Your Speech and Mine* (Chicago: Lyons and Carnahan, 1945).

[3] Miriam E. Wilt, *A Study of Teacher Awareness of Listening As A Factor in Elementary Education* (unpublished doctoral dissertation, The Pennsylvania State College, 1949).

for other oral-language activities, they were largely verbal ping pong with the teacher serving up a question to which some child parroted an answer from the book.

There was substantial evidence from the classrooms visited that the majority of elementary teachers do not consciously teach listening as a fundamental tool of communication. There was no evidence of its being taught. While children were expected to listen more than half the school day, purposes for listening, standards of achievement, and evaluation of the activity were conspicuous by their absence.

SOME BASIC PRINCIPLES

Teachers should realize the importance of skillful listening for effective living.

Present classroom listening practices should be evaluated to determine whether they are really learning experiences.

Purposeful critical listening should be a concomitant of many classroom learning experiences.

In the light of children's needs to learn by doing, children should do more talking and listening to one another and less listening to the teacher. The value of peer group learning through speaking and listening should be considered.

More use should be made of visual and auditory aids, experiments, excursions, and other experiences that require group discussion before, during, and after the activity.

Material read orally should be new, interesting, and meaningful so that the children are encouraged to develop critical and intelligent habits of listening.

Less time should be devoted to parroting questions and answers from the text and to making monosyllabic answers to teachers' questions. More time should be devoted to group discussion and problem solving.

A wide variety of listening experiences should be introduced into classrooms if children are to learn to adapt the kind of listening they do to that type which will best serve the purpose of the activity.

SUGGESTED ACTIVITIES FOR YOUNG CHILDREN

Classes primarily for the purpose of the teaching of listening are not the answer. They would be stilted and artificial. The listening inherent in so many regular classroom activities is a natural setting for the teaching of this skill. This presupposes a real purpose for listening and an evaluation of what has been heard. It must be functional if it is to be effective.

Teachers of the five- to eight-year-olds have an increasingly important role to play in helping children toward effective living and listening. The range of abilities is very wide. Some children are speaking in complex sentences and are able to comprehend long, detailed explanations and stories when they come to school. Others speak in monosyllables or not at all and are unable to follow simple directions or sequences of thought.

What are some of the incidental and more formal activities that can be used to capitalize on the keen sense of hearing many children have? How shall we keep alive this alert curiosity about things in their environment? The things children see, as well as those they hear, are a constant source of questions and new learnings.

Mike, scarcely able to talk, says "Whazzat?" And his puzzled aunt, looking around and seeing nothing, replies, "What's what, Mike? I don't see anything." Mike, impatiently, "Whazzat?" And she still sees nothing and says so. In a few seconds Mike says again, "Whazzat? Ooo-ooo-oo-oo." And suddenly, from far away, she hears the whistle of a locomotive scarcely discernible to her ears, which have become practically deaf to the sound symphony all around.

For Alertness and Discrimination (Indoors and Out):

1. Have the children close their eyes and see how many different sounds they can identify. They may hear dozens of things, as:
   Someone sweeping
   A baby crying
   A pencil being sharpened
2. Listen for sounds made just by people, as:
   Children singing
   A voice on the radio
   A mother calling
   A huckster calling his wares
3. Listen for nature sounds, as:
   The rain falling
   The murmur of a brook
   The roar of the surf
   The wind howling
4. Listen for mechanical sounds, as:
   A jet plane
   The subway roar
   A trolley car
   A train whistle
5. Have the children close their eyes. Either one of the children or the teacher may then make a variety of sounds for the rest to identify. See how many different sounds the children think of, as:

Clapping hands
Tapping with a hammer on metal
Tapping on wood with a hammer
Hitting the palm of the hand with the fist
Rapping on a window

6. With closed eyes, have one child say "Good morning" or some other short phrase and have the rest of the children try to identify the voice. Help children to refrain from guessing by listening for certain definite characteristics of individuals.

SOME LANGUAGE LISTENING ACTIVITIES

In all activities, it is important for children to learn to listen well to one another as well as to adults. In this learning to listen discriminately for information and pleasure, children should habitually give the same kind of attention to one another as they are supposed to give to the teacher. Too often the only things we expect children to hear and to remember are those things we say to them. One of the primary purposes of this program must be to see that children respect the contributions of their peers. A concomitant responsibility is that the speaker has something worth while to say. Courteous listening is important, but equally important is the realization on the part of the speaker of his responsibility to the group.

Teachers cannot and should not try to impose upon children standards for listening. Standards must be set by the people using them. As much of the talking as possible should be carried on by the children themselves. Even the youngest can decide what to listen for, why they should listen, and whether they have heard what they set out to hear. The teacher's function in this situation is to ask an occasional question or to make a comment that carries the thinking of the group beyond where they are.

For Sequences:

1. Today we are going to bake cookies. Nancy will read the recipe and the directions. Why is it important to hear what she has to say? What things must we listen for especially? (After the reading, the children discuss the steps to be followed and the necessary ingredients.)

2. Tomorrow we are going to the zoo. Let's see what we already know about the animals we are going to visit. What are the things we want to find out? If you have some information you want to share, be sure nobody else has said it (common with young children). You will also need to listen in order to know whether you disagree with what has been said.

3. Today Joan wants to tell us the story of "Cinderella." Most of us know this story. For what shall we listen, and why shall we listen to Joan tell it?

Is the sequence of events right?
Does she impersonate the characters well?
Are the facts correct?

Does she use good sentences and not string them together with "ands"?

Is her voice pleasant to listen to?

Can you see pictures as she tells the story?

4. Today I am going to play a record. You have asked for "Tubby and Tuba." For what shall we listen?

How many musical instruments do you hear?

Clap your hands when you hear Tubby speak.

Be ready to tell the story in your own words.

5. Today we're going to see a sound motion picture. The movie shows and tells about baby animals on a farm. Each of you choose one animal about which you will make a riddle. You will not only need to get all the information you can about the animal you choose, but you will have to watch and listen so that you can guess other children's animals.

6. (Give a child a series of directions to be carried out in the same order they are given. Increase the number and difficulty of the tasks as the child improves in the ability to carry the sequence in his mind.)

These ideas are merely suggestive. They can be varied to meet the needs of many ages and the content of the material. You will think of many additional ones. Unquestionably these suggestions are not designed for teaching listening. They are the activities of which the modern curriculum is made. Our plea is only that we capitalize on what is already the part and parcel of the things we are doing.

IN THE MIDDLE GRADES

In the middle grades the listening act becomes an even stronger force in influencing attitudes, as a source of information and in the forming of opinion. With panel discussions, guest speakers, news reports and analyses, political campaigns, advertising, and entertainment to be intelligently listened to and evaluated for pleasure or information, the variety of experiences is wide and the need is great.

1. As a group, have the children select some evening or week-end program, such as "Town Meeting of the Air," to which they will all listen. Ask them to take just the notes they will need to be able to discuss the major premises of the discussion and the manner of delivery and refuting.

2. Have the pupils listen to several different news reporters report on the same current event. Discuss the varied ways of saying the same thing and the many impressions listeners can get from the same words.

3. Compare the same current event discussed by a news reporter and a news analyst.

4. Choose some program or a recording which is definitely propaganda and discuss how public opinion is formed and influenced not only by what people say but the way they say it.

5. Have the pupils listen to advertisements of "name brands" of some common products and discuss what makes legitimate advertisement and how people are protected by law from false claims.

6. Documentary films and those produced with current social issues involved can be used as class projects for both Social Living classes and the valuable practice they give in listening.

7. Following silent reading around some topic of interest, either with everybody reading the same material or from a variety of sources, have the children discuss their findings and then have one member of the group summarize the main points. The remainder of the group will act as judges of both how well the reporter listened and how well he was able to summarize what he heard.

8. Listening to oral reading can be a valuable experience. It also can be a deadly one. If it's merely practice in word-calling for the reader, rereading of material already read, or reading stories with no surprise element, it has little value for listening or for anything else. If, on the other hand, it is new information, humor, story with a plot, beautiful prose or poetry, descriptions of persons or nature, or is a dramatic reading of conversation, it can challenge thinking and careful listening for some specific purposes.

9. Following oral directions of several steps is difficult for many adults. Use street and road directions for giving practice in carrying in the mind a series of directions that must be carried out in proper sequence.

Common shared listening experiences are the best activities for the teaching of listening skill. In common experiences the children and the teacher together have an opportunity to check each others' misconceptions and misunderstandings. There is also probably a better opportunity for helping children realize the critical need for accurate listening.

The teaching of listening is not something new to be added to an already overburdened school program. It is merely capitalizing upon those experiences which are already part of your day and using them to make living and learning more effective. If, as one writer has said, "The energy is there, also the time, and it is known that they listen," [4] then teachers need to assume responsibility for providing those experiences which will provide practice in this very important phase of the language arts.

---

[4] R. V. Burkhard, "Radio Listening Habits of Junior High-School Pupils," *Bulletin of the National Association of Secondary School Principals*, **XXV** (April 1941), 45–48.

WHAT CAN BE DONE ABOUT LISTENING? *

Ralph G. Nichols

*As adults most of us do not listen as well as we might. What can
we do to become better listeners? How can we, as teachers, help
children develop the skills that they need for efficient listening?*

Of the four language arts—reading, writing, speaking, and listening—listening is quantitatively the most important by far. Forty-
five per cent of the time we spend in verbal communication is spent
listening. Yet up to about ten years ago very little was known about
listening. Only a few research studies had been made, and almost
no schools were teaching listening. Since then, however, dramatic
developments have been taking place.

One landmark was the publication in 1952 of *The English Language Arts*, a report based on a five-year study by the Commission on
the English Curriculum of the National Council of Teachers of English.
This report stated clearly that good listening habits must be taught, not
left to chance; that, just as there is a need for continuous instruction
in reading throughout the school years, so there is a need for carefully
graded training in listening.

Today listening as a basic medium of learning is getting increasing
attention in elementary and high schools, and most of the notable universities in America are teaching courses in listening. Scores of industries have instituted their own listening-training programs.

What lies behind this tremendous surge of interest in effective
listening? It seems to me that it springs from an attempt to find answers
to two questions, both of great importance to teachers: Is inefficient
listening a problem, in and out of school? Can anything be done about
it?

IS INEFFICIENT LISTENING A PROBLEM?

If we turn to the schoolroom for evidence as to whether inefficient
listening is a real problem, the answer is a resounding "Yes."

---

* From *The Supervisor's Notebook*, Vol. 22, No. 1, Copyright © 1960 by
Scott, Foresman and Company, Chicago. Reprinted by permission of the publisher.

Much of the research on this question has been done at the universities. For example, a number of experiments have tested students' ability to answer questions about material presented to them in a ten-minute lecture. Almost without exception the students answered only about half the questions correctly. Retests from two weeks to two months later showed about 25 per cent of the answers correct.

This kind of evidence from the universities is shocking enough. But let us turn for a moment to industry. Is inefficient listening a problem there? Again the answer is an unequivocal "Yes." There are studies which indicate that because of poor communication often neither management nor workers understand very much of each other's hopes and aspirations.

I think it is accurate and conservative to say that without training in listening most of us operate at precisely a 25 per cent level of efficiency when we listen to a ten-minute talk. And we know from research that the longer the talk the less the comprehension of it.

WHAT CAN BE DONE ABOUT INEFFICIENT LISTENING?

Is there anything we can do about inefficient listening? The answer is fortunately "Yes." If we want to become good listeners, if we want our pupils to become good listeners, we can get results.

Currently every fall on the St. Paul Campus of the University of Minnesota we give training in listening to the 25 per cent of the incoming freshmen who are the poorest listeners. We have never trained a group that did not gain at least 25 per cent in listening efficiency.

Primarily the business of becoming a good listener consists of getting rid of bad listening habits and replacing them with their counterpart skills.

TEN BAD LISTENING HABITS

Several years ago I identified what seemed to me to be the ten worst listening habits in America today. Though my discussion of them here is in relation to the ways they may affect us in a formal listening situation, the effects of these habits can be just as devastating in less formal listening situations at home, at school, in business or social groups.

Teachers will perhaps get the most from this discussion if they think back to recent lectures they have listened to at educational meetings or public forums.

1. Calling the subject dull. The bad listener often finds a subject too dry and dusty to command his attention and he uses this as an excuse to wander off on a mental tangent. The good listener may have heard a dozen talks on the same subject before, but he quickly decides to see if the speaker to be heard has anything to say that can be of use to him. The key to good listening is that little three-letter word *use*. The good listener is a sifter, a screener, a winnower of the wheat from the chaff. He's always hunting for something practical or worth while to store in the back of his mind to put to work in the months and years ahead. G. K. Chesterton said many years ago that in all this world there is no such thing as an uninteresting subject, only uninterested people.

2. *Criticizing the speaker.* It's the indoor sport of most bad listeners to find fault with the way a speaker looks, acts, and talks. The good listener may make a few of the same criticisms but he quickly begins to pay attention to what is said, not how it is said. After a few minutes the good listener becomes oblivious to the speaker's mannerisms or his faults in delivery. He knows that the message is ten times as important as the clothing in which it comes garbed.

3. *Getting overstimulated.* Listening efficiency drops to zero when the listener reacts so strongly to one part of a presentation that he misses what follows. At the University of Minnesota we think this bad habit so critical that, in the classes where we teach listening, we put at the top of every blackboard the words: *Withhold evaluation until comprehension is complete—hear the man out.* It is important that we understand the speaker's point of view fully before we accept or reject it.

4. *Listening only for facts.* I used to think it was important to listen for facts. But I've found that almost without exception it is the poor listeners who say they listen for facts. They do get a few facts, but they garble a shocking number and completely lose most of them. Good listeners listen for the main ideas in a speech or lecture and use them as connecting threads to give sense and system to the whole. In the end they have more facts appended to those connecting threads than the catalogers who listen only for facts. It isn't necessary to worry too much about facts as such, for facts have meaning only when principles supply the context.

5. *Trying to outline everything.* There's nothing wrong with making an outline of a speech—provided the speaker is following an outline method of presentation. But probably not more than a half or perhaps a third of all the speeches given are built around a carefully prepared outline. A good listener is flexible. In his note taking he adapts to the organizational pattern of the speaker—he may make an outline, he may write a summary, he may list facts and principles—but whatever he does he is not rigid about it.

6. *Faking attention.* The pose of chin propped on hand with gaze fixed on speaker does not guarantee good listening. Having adopted

this pose, having paid the speaker the overt courtesy of appearing to listen to him, the bad listener feels conscience free to take off on any of a thousand tangents. Good listening is not relaxed and passive at all. It's dynamic; it's constructive; it's characterized by a slightly increased heart rate, quicker circulation of the blood, and a small rise in body temperature. It's energy consuming; it's plain hard work. The best definition I know of the word *attention* is "a collection of tensions inside the listener," tensions that can be resolved only by getting the facts or ideas that the speaker is trying to convey.

7. *Tolerating distraction.* The poor listener is easily distracted and may even create disturbances that interfere with his own listening efficiency and that of others. He squirms, talks with his neighbors, or noisily shuffles papers. He makes little or no effort to conceal his boredom. The good listener tries to adjust to whatever distractions there are and soon finds that he can ignore them. Certainly he does not distract others.

8. *Choosing only what's easy.* Often we find that poor listeners have shunned listening to serious presentations on radio or television. There is plenty of easy listening available, and this has been their choice. The habit of avoiding even moderately difficult expository presentations in one's leisure-time listening can handicap anyone who needs to use listening as a learning tool.

9. *Letting emotion-laden words get in the way.* It is a fact that some words carry such an emotional load that they cause some listeners to tune a speaker right out. I have pinned down a few: *mother-in-law, landlord, landlady, automation, clerk, big business, communist*—these are all fighting words to some people. I sometimes think that one of the most important studies that could be made would be the identification of the one hundred greatest trouble-making words in the English language. If we knew what these words were, we could bring them out into the open, discuss them, and get them behind us. It's so foolish to let a mere symbol for something stand between us and learning.

10. *Wasting the differential between speech and thought speed.* Americans speak at an average rate of 125 words per minute in ordinary conversation. A speaker before an audience slows down to about 100 words per minute. How fast do listeners listen? Or, to put the question in a better form, how many words a minute do people normally *think* as they listen? If all their thoughts were measurable in words per minute, the answer would seem to be that an audience of any size will average 400 to 500 words per minute as they listen. Here is a problem. The differential between the speaker at 100 words per minute and the easy thought speed of the listener at 400 or 500 words

a minute is a snare and a pitfall. It lures the listener into a false sense of security and breeds mental tangents.

However, with training in listening, the difference between thought speed and speech speed can be made a source of tremendous power to the listener. He can hear everything the speaker says and note what he omits saying; he can listen between the lines and do some evaluating as he goes along. To do this, to exploit this power, the good listener must automatically practice three skills in concentration:

1. Anticipating the next point. A good listener tries to anticipate the points a speaker will make in developing a subject. If he guesses right, the speaker's words reinforce his guess. If he guesses wrong, he'll have to do some thinking to discover why he and the speaker failed to agree. In either case, his chance of understanding and remembering what was said is nearly double what it would have been if he had simply listened passively.

2. Identifying supporting material. A good listener tries to identify a speaker's supporting material. After all, a person can't go on making points without giving his listeners some of the evidence on which he bases his conclusions, and the bricks and mortar that he has used to build up his argument should be examined for soundness.

3. Recapitulating. With the tremendous thought speed that everyone has, it is easy to summarize in about five seconds the highlights covered by a speaker in about five minutes. When the speaker stops to take a swallow of water or walks over to the blackboard to write something or even takes a deep breath, the experienced listener makes a mental summary. Half a dozen summaries of the highlights of a fifty-minute talk will easily double the listener's understanding and his ability to retain the important points in the talk.

LEARNING TO LISTEN IN THE PRIMARY GRADES [1]

This informal review of the bad listening habits that too often block the listening efficiency of adults leads us right to a question tremendously important to us as teachers. How can we keep children from developing the bad listening habits that plague too many of us? And conversely, how do we go about teaching the counterpart listening skills?

When we think about primary children, these questions are all the more important, because to them getting information from listening is

---

[1] Adapted from an article by Dr. Nichols in the Guidebook section of The Teacher's Edition of *Learn to Listen, Speak, and Write,* Book 1/1.

a necessary substitute to getting information from reading. Until they learn to read well, children must receive the bulk of their instruction, guidance, knowledge, and entertainment by ear. Ability to follow directions, to respond to signals—indeed, every school activity—is largely controlled by listening efficiency, and the thinking children do must be done in the language they have heard.

Certainly, then, we need to give early attention to teaching children how to listen. Fortunately, during the past years, we have made considerable progress in identifying the skills that underlie efficient listening and in working out techniques and materials that develop specific listening abilities—for example, listening to directions, organizing ideas while listening.

Interpreting Oral Reports

In addition to giving children formal listening exercises, we can also use their day-by-day experiences for the direct teaching of listening. Children spend hundreds of hours in primary classrooms just listening, and every one of these hours can help them improve in ability to listen if we will but bring the act of listening into conscious focus for them. Children need to be challenged to think as they listen and to organize and interpret what they hear.

In general our goal in teaching listening should be to develop the same levels of comprehension and interpretation in listening that we work for in reading. To this end, good use can be made of the accounts children give of things that happen on the playground or at home.

For example, suppose Nancy tells about going home to find that her mother had baked a cake. She wasn't allowed to eat any, because it was for her grandmother's birthday, but her mother let her decorate the cake, and after supper they took it to her grandmother's for a surprise.

To help children interpret Nancy's report, the teacher asks the same kinds of questions she would ask if she were helping the children interpret a story in their readers.

What did Nancy talk about? (Interpreting the main idea.)

What did she say first, next, and last? (Understanding sequence.)

How did Nancy feel when her mother wouldn't let her have a piece of cake? (Understanding emotional reactions.)

Recognizing Good Performance

In teaching listening as in teaching anything else, it pays to recognize a good performance. Children should be praised whenever they demonstrate that they have listened carefully and perceptively. If Jim's answers to questions about Nancy's story of the surprise party for her grandmother show that he caught the fun and the excitement of the event, this should be commented on. If Susan is asked to deliver a message to a teacher and does so successfully, this should be noted.

Demonstrating Good Listening

In developing good listening habits in children it is also important for a teacher to demonstrate these habits herself. If she is attentive to the words of her pupils, if she thoughtfully considers statements made by them, her influence for the good is tremendous. She should frequently ask pertinent questions and heed the answers given. And she should be highly sensitive to the great and truthful generalization that most teachers talk too much (about half of all classtime).

Eliminating Bad Practices

In addition to praising good performances and setting a good example herself, the primary teacher will undoubtedly have to work to overcome four bad practices that often interfere with children's learning to listen effectively. Two of these are things that children exhibit, two are things to which teachers are prone.

Inattention (or faked attention). Just as adults sometimes daydream when they seem to be paying attention, so do children. There are several ways a teacher can help them overcome this bad habit. She can alert the class ahead of time to specific things for which to listen. She can read or tell part of a story and ask each youngster to provide his own ending for it. She can use round-robin listening drills: One child says a word, a second child repeats it and adds another, the third repeats both and adds a word, and so on until some child misses a word, when the whole process starts again.

The important thing in meeting the problem of inattention is to keep listening an active process by specifying how the things learned are to be used. When a listener intends to put to use the things he hears, his listening efficiency at once increases.

Overstimulated response. Another bad habit that children, like adults, may exhibit is the overstimulated response. When Mary waves her hand throughout Frank's discussion or Dick breaks into a sentence to correct a "have did," the moment has arrived for some direct listening instruction.

Pupils need to learn to make their comments after, not before, a speaker finishes. A teacher must make it clear that an effective response to a speaker depends on an understanding of all that he has said—an understanding not likely to exist when the listener has been pre-occupied with his own thoughts or with his reaction to but a part of what was said. One condition of good listening is listening to the "WHOLE THING."

There are one or two bad habits of which teachers themselves may be guilty.

Needless repetition. In an earnest attempt to make sure that every-one understands, a teacher may repeat things several times. This kind of repetition breeds bad listening habits by creating boredom or a false sense of security. If repetition is necessary, a good listener in the class should be asked to do the repeating.

Demanding pupil attention. The second bad practice a teacher may be guilty of is demanding pupil attention. At the end of a hard day she may find herself sternly saying, "Pay attention, please." This is certainly understandable, but it is also regrettable. To be able to listen should consistently be regarded as a pleasant privilege.

To help children develop a positive attitude toward listening, several techniques may be used. Children might make an illustrated chart or booklet of what they think are good listening manners and practices. On an occasion when youngsters have listened especially well, their teacher might reward their good performance by reading another chapter in a story they enjoy.

Dividends for Teachers and Pupils

There is no denying that giving thought to listening practices throughout the school day will require an investment of time, effort, and ingenuity by the primary teacher. But the use of techniques like those described will help children develop responsive attitudes toward listening. And pupils can get practice in some of the specific skills that enter into efficient listening. The investment is sure to pay dividends in terms of teaching effectiveness for the teacher and learning efficiency for the children.

All of us, children and adults alike, will profit from utilizing to the fullest extent every means of learning at our disposal. And we need to develop competence in all four of the language arts if we are to achieve true efficiency in communication. The 45 per cent of com-munication time that we spend in one kind of listening or another should be time well spent. Twenty-five per cent listening efficiency is not enough for any of us. *We* can do better than that; children can, too. Let's take steps to make sure that they do.

TRAINING CHILDREN TO LISTEN *

Edward Pratt and Harry A. Greene

Listen carefully! What child has not heard these words time and again, in school and out? Haven't we often used these words, with the hope that the child will promptly "pay attention" to what is going on?

But just what do these words mean? What *should* they mean? Is a receptive attitude the only skill involved in listening? Or is listening like a jigsaw puzzle—many pieces that must be fitted together?

Research has provided us with definite *answers* to these questions. It points out that listening is *one of the most important areas of communication,* and as such, goes far beyond emphasis on attentiveness alone. If listening ability is to be an effective means of learning, attention must be given to the development of other associated skills as well.

We all know that every child enters school with some degree of listening ability. There may be a wide range of individual differences, but the general comprehension level is low. Yet, as proven in a recent investigation of the effect of a specific program of training in listening on a representative group of sixth-grade children, even a short training period of five weeks can be instrumental in raising the general level of listening ability.[1] This is possible only if emphasis is placed on all the skills associated with the process rather than on just the superficial aspects of listening.

What, then, are the skills needed for effective listening? We all know that listening is the act of receiving oral language. Such reception involves three things: (1) the recall or deduction of meanings for spoken word symbols, (2) the comprehension of ideas represented by different combinations of these word symbols, and (3) the ability to use the ideas presented to build understanding by adding to, modifying, or rejecting previous learning.

Recall of the meanings of spoken word symbols depends on the size of the *listening vocabulary,* while the deduction of *new meanings* depends on ability to make use of *context clues.* There is need for

* From *A Monograph for Elementary Teachers,* No. 80 (Evanston, Ill.: Harper & Row, 1958). Reprinted by permission of the authors and publisher.

[1] L. E. Pratt, "The Experimental Evaluation of a Program for the Improvement of Listening in the Elementary School" (unpublished Doctoral dissertation, State University of Iowa, 1953).

further research on the extent of the listening vocabularies of elementary-school children. The listening vocabulary consists of the words for which the child has made an association between the spoken symbol and the appropriate meaning. It is *larger than the child's reading, speaking, and writing vocabularies* and probably will remain so throughout his life.

Increasing the listening vocabulary can definitely improve other vocabulary needs. The wise teacher can help by using synonyms for the more common words and by stating definitions. For example, instead of saying, "How did Bill answer Jack's question?" she can say, "What was Bill's response to Jack's question? A response is an answer, or a reply." If word meanings so developed are to be retained, the teacher must repeat the words often in her oral expression.

In the listening process, only context clues can be used to aid in determining the meaning of strange spoken words. This skill must be developed to an automatic state. There is no opportunity to stop and analyze word meanings. The person who takes time to reflect on word meanings may find himself a few hundred words behind the speaker. *Children need training in deducing rapidly and accurately the meanings of unknown words from context.*

Comprehension of ideas presented orally requires a number of specific skills that are called into play according to the purpose for which one is listening. Children listening to the oral presentation of a story must know how to follow the sequence and to remember important details. When listening to the oral presentation of factual material, they must be able to organize the material into main and subordinate ideas. There also may be a listening activity to obtain a single piece of information. In such a situation, recognizing extraneous material is valuable. Directions are often given orally. They present a difficult problem that calls for ability to note detail and sequence explicitly. *Regardless of the purpose for which one listens, there is a real need for the ability to use clues that show how the speaker expects his thoughts to be interpreted.*

One skill needed in the use of ideas to build understandings or concepts is the ability to evaluate ideas presented orally and to supplement, modify, or replace previous learning. Although one may comprehend ideas without making use of them, it is the reflective process that makes listening a worth-while activity. A second skill needed for the use of ideas is making inferences that can be justified by the facts presented. Much of our learning comes from inference. Understandings arrived at through inferences can, and should, influence decisions and behavior if based on reliable evidence. *Briefly, these are the listening skills:*

I. *Word perception*

    A. Recall of word meanings
    B. Deduction of meanings of unknown words

II. *Comprehension of ideas*

    A. Noting details
    B. Following directions
    C. Organizing into main and subordinate ideas
    D. Selecting information pertinent to a specific topic
    E. Detecting clues that show the speaker's trend of thought

III. *Using ideas to build understandings*

    A. Evaluating an expressed point of view or fact in relation to previous learning
    B. Making justifiable inferences

A description and listing of skills is of little value without some suggestions as to the development of these skills. In the investigation by Pratt [2] "Lessons on Listening" were developed to give instruction in a number of the skills listed above. Discussions of these lessons, as well as lessons to develop the remaining skills listed, are presented in the rest of this monograph. They are given as samples of instruction in the development of listening ability. Special lessons need not be imposed, however, if the teacher takes advantage of the daily opportunities that present themselves. Furthermore, these lessons should not be considered complete in any sense. The material presented here simply indicates one approach in developing the various listening skills. The examples are designed for the sixth-grade level.

I. WORD PERCEPTION

The recall of known word meanings does not require instructional emphasis. Effectiveness will depend on the child's ability to respond correctly to the spoken symbols. If a word meaning cannot be recalled, the listener must automatically deduce meaning from the context or fail to understand what is associated with the word in question. If the word is a verb, the loss of understanding may be great, but for some adjectives the loss may be negligible. The

---

[2] *Op. cit.*

listener must be adept in using context clues. Words in parentheses are meant for the teacher.

Example 1

(Put these words on the board: *apostatized, leal, domicile, isolates, benignant.* Ask for and record meanings that the children supply for these words in isolation.)

> *To the pupils:* Listen to the article I am about to read. The words on the board will be used in that article. When I have finished reading, we will want to see whether you have any different ideas about the meanings of these words. Here is the article.

A neighbor of mine keeps a flock of perhaps a dozen hens. Four years ago one hen had a brood of ten chickens. A cozy little house and yard had been built for them, and for two days all went well. Then, for some unexplainable reason, the mother hen *apostatized* her offspring, and my friend noted to his great surprise that a beautiful dove had taken her place.

The dove remained *leal* to her task, feeding and watching over the chickens until they were big enough to care for themselves. Ever since then she has made her *domicile* with my neighbor's poultry. She associates with them by day, roosts with them at night, and *isolates* herself from other doves.

Every summer she lays three or four eggs and sits upon them with the greatest devotion, but they never hatch. The hens have never been *benignant* to the intruder and peck at her whenever she comes near them, but the roosters seem quite contented to have her in their company.

II. COMPREHENSION OF IDEAS

As indicated previously, purpose plays an important role in comprehension. It provides the reason for listening and a standard for sifting what is heard. Each purpose for listening calls for a specific ability.

A. Noting details

Sometimes a person listens for specific details. At other times it is important to note details without previous knowledge of the specific details for which he is listening. Example 2 is concerned with the first situation and Example 3 with the second.

Example 2

> *To the pupils:* I am going to read a short selection about a boy who had difficulty remembering the combination to his lock. *Listen for two pieces of information:* (1) the numbers of the combination and (2) the numbers given that are not in the combination. Here is the selection.

Jim felt grown up now that he was attending junior high school. He liked this school, and he especially liked the locker in which he kept his wraps and books. Just now he was trying to unlock the new combination lock that he had bought for his locker. 8—25— What was the next number? He always had trouble with it. Was it 15? No. Was it 20? No. Was it 17? Yes, that was it. Seventeen, and then to the last number, which was 4. Click! The lock opened. Jim decided to write down the numbers to make sure he could get the lock open the next time.

Example 3

To the pupils: I am going to read a short paragraph. (I want you to listen so that you can answer a question I will ask about the paragraph.) Here is the selection.

The big flying boat lifted slowly from the water and climbed into a cloudless sky. Her silver wings gleamed in the bright sunlight, and the four engines roared as they carried the plane aloft. Inside there was room for fifty passengers besides the crew. She carried enough gasoline to fly two thousand miles.

Question: What details describe the plane mentioned in the paragraph: (*1. flying boat, or seaplane.   2. silver in color   3. four engines   4. fifty passengers and crew   5. fuel for flying 2,000 miles*)?

B. *Following directions*

Many situations arise naturally during the school day that involve ability to follow oral directions. A very effective way to develop this skill is to use (oral arithmetic) to follow a series of computations. Both arithmetic and listening ability can be improved in this manner. Example 4 gives five problems in oral arithmetic.

Example 4

To the pupils: I have five arithmetic problems that I want you to compute for me. I will read the problem. You are to follow the steps I suggest without figuring on your paper. When I say, "Mark your answer," record your answer on your paper. Then be ready to listen for the next problem. Let's try one problem for practice. Here is the practice problem. Start with 8, multiply by 4, divide by 2, and subtract 10. Mark your answer. *(The answer is 6.)* Now get set for the first of the problems.

Problem 1: From the number that is four larger than 25 subtract 9, divide by 4, and add 2. Mark your answer.
Problem 2: Start with 15, divide by 3, multiply by 4, substract 5, and add 2. Mark your answer.
Problem 3: From the number that is two smaller than 7 substract 2, multiply by 10, add 5, and divide by 7. Mark your answer.
Problem 4: Add 4 to 13, subtract 7, multiply by 2, and divide by 4. Mark your answer.

Problem 5: Subtract 5 from 20, divide by 5, multiply by 3, and add 4. Mark your answer.

Answers to the problems: 1)7. 2)17. 3)5. 4)5. 5)13.

C. Organizing into main and subordinate ideas

Basic to comprehension of ideas presented orally is the ability to get to the heart of concepts discussed by the speaker. It is important that children develop this skill with material on their level. It is also important that they recognize statements made in support of principal ideas. Example 5 suggests the type of training to develop this skill.

Example 5

To the pupils: (Listen for the main idea in the paragraph I am about to read. You should also listen for statements that give important information about the main idea.) Here is the paragraph.

Speakers need to think very carefully about the words they are going to say. Even in conversation, people often talk about things they know little about. If we have ideas that we are going to try to get others to accept, these ideas should be based on facts. One of the most important jobs for the speechmaker is gathering the facts on which to base his speech. This usually means that he must read a great deal to make sure he has the important facts. In planning what he is going to say, the speaker must also think about the people to whom he is going to talk. If a college professor talks to a sixth-grade class, he cannot say the same things he would say to a group of college students. If we want our listeners to understand us when we talk, we must put our ideas into words that they should know. Correct use of language is another important matter for the speaker to consider. When we talk, we should feel a responsibility for using words correctly. If the speaker is careless in the use of language, his listeners may think that he is also careless about his facts. If the listeners have confidence in the speaker, they will be more willing to accept his ideas.

(*Main idea*—Speakers should select carefully the words they use. *Supporting ideas*—1) Ideas should be based on facts, 2) Words should be understandable to the listeners, 3) The speaker should use the language correctly.)

D. Selecting information pertinent to a specific topic

There are occasions when the listener's purpose is specific to the views expressed by the speaker on a single topic. Then the listener must be able to select pertinent facts, giving little attention to information irrelevant to the specific point of interest. Example 6 uses science information for practice in this skill.

Example 6

To the pupils: I am going to read a paragraph. Listen for information about *the other planets in our solar system.* See whether you can tell me what is said about this topic. Here is the paragraph.

Our sun is a star, but it is not the largest star in the universe. Astronomers tell us that our sun is only medium sized when compared to other stars. The sun is very large though when compared to the size of the earth. The diameter of the sun, or the distance through the middle, is 109 times the diameter of the earth. The planets in our solar system travel around the sun. As the earth and its eight sister planets travel around the sun, they are held in their orbits by the gravitational pull of the sun. Our seasons on the earth are a result of the yearly trip around the sun.

(*Information on other planets*—1) They travel around the sun, 2) There are eight planets besides the earth, 3) Planets are held in their orbits by the gravitational pull of the sun.)

E. Detecting clues that show the speaker's trend of thought

(The speaker usually gives clues to the importance of certain ideas and words. These clues may be either words that designate the important ideas or changes in volume and pitch of voice to designate emphasis and punctuation.)

1. Verbal clues

a) Designating important ideas by the use of number words.

Example 7

To the pupils: Sometimes the speaker uses number words to help you recognize the main ideas expressed about the topic. I am going to read a paragraph in which this has been done. When I finish, see whether you can tell me the main topic and the important ideas expressed about it. Here is the paragraph.

To speak well, we must have self-confidence. In simpler words, the speaker must believe that he knows the facts and that he can tell his listeners about them. There is no great mystery about learning to say things in a self-confident manner. First, the subject that you are going to talk about should be interesting to you. People can talk more easily and in more detail about subjects in which they are interested. A second thing that helps to build self-confidence is finding out everything you can about the subject. If you don't do this, you are always a little bit afraid that important points have been left out. Third, self-confidence in speaking becomes greater as you do more speaking. When you first learned to add, you probably made many mistakes, but with practice, the mistakes were corrected. It is the same way with making a talk. As you get more practice in speaking, you correct your mistakes. Fourth, speak to the listeners, not to the ceiling or the floor. When you speak to a friend, you look at him; and when you speak to a group, you should look at them. Good speakers make you feel that they are carrying on a conversation with you. Fifth, it helps to make you less nervous if you move your body while you talk. This does not mean that you should play with a handkerchief, a pencil, or some other object. Maybe there is a picture you can show to illustrate your ideas, maybe you can draw a simple picture or diagram on the blackboard, or maybe you can use your hands to emphasize a point. If you do not use your body in some way, you will probably be more nervous than you need to be. Don't forget, however, that it is normal to be a little nervous when you begin to speak. This nervousness will leave when you and your audience get interested in the subject.

(*Main topic*—How to achieve self-confidence in speaking. *Important ideas*—1) Interesting subject, 2) Know your subject, 3) Practice in speaking, 4) Speak to the audience, 5) Use your body, if possible.)

> b) Designating important ideas by the use of separating words or phrases.

(The paragraph in Example 7 above can be used by substituting for *first, second, third, fourth,* and *fifth* such words and phrases as *for one thing, in addition to, then, too, besides,* and *lastly.*)

2. Voice clues

> a) Use of inflection or voice modulation to show punctuation.

Example 8

To the pupils: The author of a book uses punctuation marks as signs to help the reader understand his thoughts. A speaker provides signs, too, but with his voice. In the paragraph that I am going to read, several sentences end with periods and two end with question marks. (Listen for the two questions and be able to tell how you knew they ended with question marks.) Here is the paragraph.

Most of us talk well enough to make people understand the words we are saying, but some of us do not make our ideas so clear to our listeners as others do. Do you ever wonder why some boys and girls are able to make the class understand them when they talk, while other boys and girls are not able to do this very well? People, for many reasons, want to make their ideas known to others or to find out what other people think about certain of their ideas. One way by which a person can make his ideas known is to write them for other people to read. Would you like to write everything that you wish to say? Another way of passing ideas from person to person is talking instead of writing and listening instead of reading. Exchanging ideas is called communication. Communication by talking and listening is called oral communication.

(The pitch of the voice is raised for a question mark and lowered for a period. The children may also point out that the structure of the sentence will indicate a question.)

> b) Showing emphasis by increasing the volume of the voice.

Example 9

To the pupils: To give a clue to the important words in the thoughts he is trying to express, a speaker will say *some* words louder than others. I am going to read two sentences. Listen to see whether you can discover which words are emphasized, or spoken louder than the others. Here are the sentences. (Italicized words are to be emphasized.)

Getting *prepared to listen* should become a *habit*. It is a habit that is important whether you are taking part in a *conversation* or are listening with a *group*.

III. USING IDEAS TO BUILD UNDERSTANDINGS

If we are to make use of ideas presented to us orally, we must relate them to learnings already acquired. In addition, we must make inferences that can be justified on the basis of the facts presented.

A. Evaluating an expressed point of view or fact in relation to previous learning

Example 10

To the pupils: (You have probably heard people say, "You can't believe everything you read." The same is true of listening. "You can't believe everything you hear.") (Besides trying to *understand* the ideas to which we listen, we must give some thought to their truth and value. One way to judge the truth and value of ideas is to consider the source of the statements.) If the speaker is very well informed on the subject or if he refers to the writings of someone who is an authority on the subject, we can be fairly certain of the accuracy of his statements. Another way to check the truth and value of ideas is to relate them to facts we already know about the subject. If we believe a certain statement to be false or misleading, we should ask questions at the proper time or find statements about it by authorities. You should also ask questions when you are not sure how the new ideas relate to ideas you have thought about before. I am going to read a paragraph. It contains a statement which you should consider as untrue because of facts you have already learned. Here is the paragraph. (The italicized statement is incorrect.)

The star nearest the earth is our sun. The sun is much larger than the earth or any of the other planets in our solar system. The gravitational pull of the sun holds the planets in their orbits as they travel around the sun. *Because the earth travels around the sun, we have day and night.* Although our nearest star is many millions of miles away from us, it provides heat and light, which are necessary to life on the earth.

B. Making justifiable inferences

Example 11

To the pupils: If we learn in geography that India, which is less than half the size of the United States, has more than twice as many people as the United States has, we can use that fact in our thinking. If the statement we have learned is true, we can be very sure that many people in India live under rather poor conditions. We can also make sure that farms are small. Inferences are not facts that have been stated. They are ideas judged to be true because certain conditions have been stated and, from experience or past learning, we know what the results are likely to be. (I am going to read a paragraph to you. When I have finished, I will suggest two inferences. I will ask you to tell me which inference is better on the basis of information in the paragraph. Here is the paragraph.)

Were you ever saved by a nail? I was, last summer. While I was at Grandfather's farm, I was playing in the haymow. All at once I slipped and started for the hole in the floor. The strap on my overalls caught on a nail as I went over the edge. There I hung! Grandfather pulled me back into the mow. That nail may have saved my life! [3]
Inferences: 1. Children should be careful when playing in the haymow. 2. Children should not be allowed to play in the haymow.

(The first inference is justified on the basis of the article. The second inference is not justified on the basis of the article inasmuch as this child may have been careless, and there is no evidence to show that this sort of accident happens to a large number of farm children.)

This Monograph has attempted to show that adequate listening ability depends on the development of a number of specific skills. It has also given examples of ways by which the teacher can help her pupils to develop these skills. There is evidence to support the belief that instruction and practice can raise the level of listening ability. It is hoped that the material presented here will serve to convince the teacher that she is asking for far more than mere attention when she asks children to "listen."

LISTENING COMPREHENSION: AN AREA FOR TEACHER EXPERIMENTATION [*]

Robert W. Kilbourn

Research has established a clear relationship between listening comprehension and reading ability of students in the elementary grades. There is some evidence that development of reading ability is facilitated

[3] H. A. Greene, *et. al.*, *Building Better English: Grade Six* (Evanston, Ill.: Harper & Row, 1952), p. 142.
[*] Reprinted from *Action* (November 1958), Metropolitan Detroit Bureau of School Studies, by permission of the author.

by experiences with the aural language. In fact, linguistic scholars suggest that a language can not be learned efficiently for purposes of reading and writing without the development of aural-oral language skills. This suggests increased emphasis in our schools on skills developed through listening and speaking.

When a child enters first grade, the focus of teacher and student attention is typically on the development of reading skill. The child has an understanding of aural-oral language far beyond any potentials he may have for skill in reading. Too often, the child is limited in his communication in school to the confines of his reading ability. He speaks when he reads from his reader. He listens and watches when others read from their readers.

The content of the child's communications in school often does not interest or challenge him. Television is only one of the factors that have made him a sophisticate in both content and aural-language skill. Boys and girls in first grade are not interested in the immature language of Dick and Jane. The language of Dick and Jane is not that of first graders unless they are coerced.

Some teachers spend a good deal of time reading stories and informational materials to students that are more challenging than anything children could read for themselves. These teachers, however, will feel that there is not enough time in the school day for this activity. Teachers feel direct pressures from the public and the profession to spend more and more time in efforts to develop reading ability. In some cases, teachers spend a major portion of their day working with reading groups.

What can harried teachers do to get more materials for students to hear and talk about? One technique that has been used in only a few classrooms is the listening center. In this center, a tape playback or disc record player is equipped with six or eight headphones so that children may listen without disturbing others in the class. The listening center becomes another of the small group techniques used by a teacher to diversify and individualize student activity in the class.

The listening center should be available in the classroom for full-time operation. Tape and disc playback equipment has been developed for ease of operation and in a reasonable price range. If tape equipment is used, it is economical for teachers to record stories and programs for use in the listening center. Tapes of many educational radio programs are available from local audio-visual centers, state film and tape libraries, or The National Tape Duplication Center at the University of Colorado, Boulder, Colorado.

We do not know the exact kinds of materials that will be most effective in listening center use at the various grade levels. Many of the stories that teachers read to students could be recorded on tape. Programs of science and social studies information could be recorded.

In some cases, social studies text information has been recorded for students who have difficulty in reading the textbook. In this way, these students have gained information that allows them to participate in class discussions of these subjects as never before. Success in this way may help students gain courage to overcome their deficiencies in reading.

The idea of the listening center is offered to teachers as a frontier for further exploration. It is a technique that may increase the effectiveness of student communication. It is a technique that may save teachers' time if recordings are kept for use in future years. The listening center facilitates the use of special materials keyed to the interests and abilities of the gifted and the not-so-gifted student. The listening center is another focal point for small group activity in the classroom. It can operate while the teacher works with reading groups or in other capacities in the class.

Imaginative teachers can take the idea of the listening center and develop it beyond anything that can be envisioned now. Some teachers will be interested to see what kinds of more-or-less routine functions can be taken over by the taped materials. Several teachers have recorded multiple listings of spelling words for use by various groups or individuals. Others have recorded listening exercises, number combinations and mathematical problems that can be used as self-teaching and self-testing activities by students.

SPEECH IN THE ELEMENTARY SCHOOL *

Los Angeles Public Schools

An outstanding course of study in speech is presented in Publication No. 479 of the Los Angeles City Schools. The excerpts following contain ideas for all teachers. A valuable feature of this publication, is a collection of stories and verse for each of the speech sounds.

ELEMENTS OF SPEECH

The voice mechanism is naturally a kind of musical instrument, and, like other musical instruments, must be played in the right way if the music is to give us pleasure.

---

* Excerpts from Publication No. 479 (1949), Los Angeles Public Schools, reprinted by permission of Los Angeles City School Districts.

A well-balanced speech program considers the key qualities—*voice, rate, rhythm,* and *articulation.* These four elements of speech will, when mastered, insure and accurately reflect an integrated, self-reliant, alert personality.

Speech may be improved by taking advantage of the usual opportunities of home, school, and community life. It grows and is refined through language in action wherever we find children living and learning together.

Speech is not a distinct entity that can be taken by itself, polished as a jewel or sharpened as a knife. The improvement of speech is the enrichment of the quality of a whole, living human being in the natural language setting of his environment.

Speech to be effective must be woven into the very life and thought of each child. The great thing is to build up that inner potential, or mental speech, and establish correct motor habits, so that its expression will be free, flowing, and communicative.

True education comes through the stimulation of the child's powers of communication by the demands of the social situation in which he finds himself.

The goal of speech education is the weaving of the speech strands through experience into the finished pattern of adequate speech so that each child may take his place in society as a happy, contributing citizen.

Key Qualities of Speech

VOICE	*Volume*	A voice is loud enough to be heard.
	Pitch	The voice is pitched in a natural key. It may be high, medium, or low. The pitch changes and varies with meaning.
	Inflection	The voice glides from one pitch to another.
	Quality	A voice is clear and distinct. It is free from huskiness and nasality. It is free from shrillness and harshness. It has fullness rather than breathiness.
RATE	*Tempo*	Timing. How fast or slow is the speech? Rate varies with the mood or emotions.
RHYTHM	*Flowing*	Normal speech is uninterrupted. It is free flowing.
	Smooth	It is rhythmic. It is free from repetition or prolongation.
ARTICULATION	*Formation of sounds*	The mechanics of speaking. Accurate production of speech sounds. How the organs of speech move and function in forming the speech sounds.

Speech is spoken easily—and joyfully. Simplicity, even in speech, is a mark of beauty.

Speech is not merely the movement of the organs of speech, but it is the functioning of the whole organism, the physical mechanism, the mental capacities, and the emotional patterns.

The adjusted, happy individual is usually one whose speech is well-modulated, clear, distinct, pleasant, and rhythmic.

One's speech is personal and revealing.

A teacher expressed an interesting thought when she said, "Now that I begin to recognize the pitch of voices, the rhythms of speech, the differences of speech sounds, and am on my way to improvement, I find that I get more enjoyment out of listening—even to myself."

THE NATURE OF SPEECH

No human behavior is so intricately and beautifully coordinated as speech.

To the majority of persons speech is as casual a function as breathing and walking. To many others, its difficulties are great.

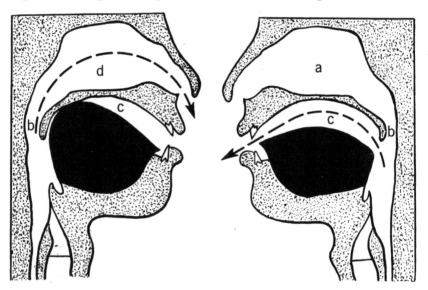

The breath stream passes through the throat and nasal passage for all nasal consonants.

It passes through the throat and mouth for all vowels and consonants other than nasals.

The VOCAL Instrument

The *source of energy* is the breath stream which, as it passes from the lungs, acts as the motor force that sets the vocal cords into vibration.

The *vibrator,* or the vocal cords, is located in the larynx and vibrates as the breath stream passes through.

The *resonator* is made up of three cavities: the throat, the mouth, and the nasal passages.

The size and shape of the resonator can be changed by the action of these four organs:

The *lips* which close and open, round and spread

The *tongue* which moves freely because of its mass of muscles

The *lower jaw* which moves downward and upward, and changes the size of the mouth opening by varying the distance between the teeth

The *soft palate* which moves and serves as a kind of curtain between the nasal passages and the mouth and throat passages

Muscles, fine, fine muscles, control these movable organs and by regulating the size and shape of the resonator quickly and accurately move to produce clear, distinct speech. The first function of these organs is the preservation of life; their second function is the production of speech.

HOW SPEECH SOUNDS DEVELOP

"A child's approach to speech should be a happy one." The newborn baby starts his speech development with the birth cry. Soon he has many different types of cries. Toward the end of the second month he begins his babbling and vocal play. From babbling the child passes into the lalling stage. Now he begins to repeat sounds or syllables he himself has produced. The imitative process of speech has started.

The infant learns to listen to sounds about him. Speech noises made by members of his family begin to have meaning when the words represent things in his personal experience. Soon his responses with appropriate bodily movements to words and phrases pronounced by others show that he is increasing in understanding. When this understanding goes hand-in-hand with his ability to discriminate between speech sounds we say—"he understands."

The child listens. He imitates the sounds of pets and noises in his environment. He imitates the speech about him. He is learning a language. He is now ready to understand and interpret what is said to him. He learns to manipulate the delicate muscles of the speech machine with the fine coordination required for speech. Vocabulary develops rapidly. In this process of listening and speaking the child develops the foundation for effective language.

The child's first sounds are vowels. Then appear combinations of vowels. Soon consonant sounds are formed as an accompaniment to the sucking and swallowing of vocal play. Then vowels and consonants are combined in words.

Chart of Development of Consonant Sounds [1]

  3½ years—b, p, m, w, h (lip sounds)
  4½ years—d, t, n, g, k, ng, y
  5½ years—f
  6½ years—v, th, zh, sh, l
  7½ years—z, s, r, th (as in there) wh

Factors Motivating Normal Development

Need for speech
Example of good speech
Conversation directed to the child
A comfortable environment
A happy parental attitude
Good muscular coordination
Normal hearing
Normal physical development

Factors Which Retard Normal Development

Being left alone
No speech stimulation
Examples of poor speech
Emotional problems such as negativism
Baby talk by family members
Bi-lingualism in the home
Dentitional development
Hearing impairment
Retarded muscular development

INDIVIDUAL DIFFERENCES IN SPEECH DEVELOPMENT

The speech age of the child is determined by the number of sounds he can use consistently in words and the number of substitutions he makes for those sound patterns not yet established. Variations in the speech age are due to physical, functional, and mental causes.

Physical: Maturation rates of the physical factors from which

---

[1] Irene Poole, "The Genetic Development of the Articulation of Consonant Sounds," unpublished doctoral dissertation (University of Michigan, 1934), p. 60.

speech sounds are developed influence the ability to articulate speech sounds.

Functional: Emotional attitudes rising from difficulties and conflicts with parents, siblings, teachers, and social groups influence the ability to articulate speech sounds.

Mental: Mental age is a determinant of the rate of learning and development of speech.

Teachers analyze the speech of children. The speech of each child should be analyzed to determine speech age; discover and remedy speech defects as early as possible; note individual differences in language responses; base speech improvement work upon the findings of speech needs; help individual children having speech problems.

Teachers observe key qualities of speech: voice, rate, rhythm, articulation.

Teachers observe the speech of children. The teacher listens to the speech of children at play; listens during oral reading; is alert to speech during participation in classroom activities; analyzes during conversation; evaluates by objective means.

Teachers observe speech and check progress in speech development. Listen to one-at-a-time speech sounds as the child names an object:

Listen to *s* in *s*un, bi*c*ycle, bu*s*.
Listen to *z* in *z*ipper, sci*ss*ors, no*se*.
Think of the correct enunciation of sounds which make the word.
Listen to the speech sounds as you say the same word.
Listen to the exact sounds the child makes.

Watch the mouth and lips and tongue to see how the child articulates the word:

Think of the correct way of saying it.
Feel your organs of speech as you say it.
Watch the child's speech machine as he says it.

Ask yourself:

1. Are all sounds articulated in an acceptable way?
2. Which sounds, if any, differ from the normal?
3. How rhythmic is his speech flow?
4. Does he repeat sounds, words, or phrases?
5. How fast or slowly does he speak? Why?
6. Is he excited, angry, fatigued?
7. Is he a slow-moving child or a hyper-active one?

8. How pleasant is his voice?
9. Is it low or high pitched, husky or hoarse, pleasing or unpleasant?

Have some *objective means* of discovering the specific speech diffi-culties of each child (see Speech Tests which follow).

Teachers give Simple Speech Tests

Let the child count from one to ten.
Let the older child count to twenty.
Most of the speech sounds likely to be incorrect appear in these numbers.
Ask the child being tested and wait for his answer:

Which would you rather have?

| s | spinach or soup |
| | sandwich or soda |

| sh | brown shoe or black shoe |
| | little fish or big fish |

| ch | cherry pie or cherry jello |
| | cherry juice or cherry jam |

| r | a rabbit or a row boat |
| | red kite or a red car |

| k | candy or cake |
| | cookies or crackers |

| g | gold watch or gold ring |
| | goat or goose |

| f | four balls or five balls |
| | forty tops or fifty tops |

| v | a vase or a valentine |
| | seven marbles or seven dolls |

What are the colors of our American flag

| r | red |

| wh | white |

| bl | blue |

What do you like?

| l | I like............ |
| | I like........... |

Let the child look through each of several thin colored plastic discs.

1   Teacher—Look through the red disc.
             How do I look?
   Child   —You look red.
   Teacher—Look through the blue disc.
             How do I look?
   Child   —You look blue.

Teachers give objective speech tests

SPEECH TEST I.   OBJECTS

This test has been designed to analyze the speech of the child and reveal the articulation of simple consonants and vowels through the naming of certain objects.

Place small objects or miniature toys in a box. A good collection makes it possible to test the thirty-eight consonant and vowel sounds in more than seventy situations.

Let the child name the objects as they are taken from the box.
Devise other interesting ways of using these toys.

SPEECH TEST II.   PICTURES

This test has been designed to analyze the speech of the child and to reveal the articulation of simple consonants and vowels through the naming of certain pictures. The child says the words suggested by the picture. As far as possible, the pictures have been selected to test consonants and vowels in these positions: initial (beginning of a word), medial (middle of a word), and final (ending of a word).

SPEECH CORRECTION

> The primary concern of speech correction is the person. It is not enough to know *what sort* of *speech defect* a person has. In addition, one should know what kind of *person* has a speech defect. The speech defect has no particular meaning apart from the person who presents the defect. We are not interested in speech defects alone, but in the person who has the defect.
>   —*Lee Edward Travis*

Need for Speech Education

We do not know how many school children in America are handicapped by speech so defective that they require special treatment. Estimates run all the way from one million, in 1931, to five million, in 1948, with a few estimates as high as ten million. To find all of the children whose speech is impaired there must be a greater awareness of the problem and increased vigilance on the part of parents and teachers.

From the many and varied reports it has been estimated that for every group of one hundred children in the United States there are, on the average, ten who have some form of speech defect. Of these 10 children:

5 or 6 have simple defects—sound substitutions as:
wun for *run, wike* for *like;* sound omissions as:
pay for *play.* Four or five have defects of a more serious nature:

1 or 2—hearing loss
    —malocclusion
    —spastic paralysis
    —cleft palate with or without harelip
1   —retarded speech
1   —stuttering

Impairments which call for special examination and care are:

Stuttering:
Audible or visible spasmodic action of the speech organs.
Rapid repetitions of the initial sounds in words.
Sometimes delay in answering questions or refusal to recite, or excessive self-consciousness may indicate a speech disability.

Articulatory Defects:
Lisping on consonants sounds—s, z, sh, zh, ch, j.
Other substitutions or omissions of consonant sounds or infantile speech; as w for l, b for v, etc.

Defects in Speech Organs:
Cleft palate
Tongue-tie
Malocclusion of teeth

Voice Defects:
Monotonous
Nasal
High-pitched

Delayed Speech:
Physical causes,
    poor muscular control, deafness.
Mental causes,
    lack of perception of speech sounds,
    mental deficiency.

For best results in any type of speech education, early recognition of the defect is imperative. Early treatment aids a program of prevention as well as correction.

The Teacher Can Do This:

The child needs guidance and direction in learning to make the correct movements of speech from the moment he begins to talk. Parents and teachers provide this assistance, direct the speech movements, show him how to produce the sounds in the correct sequence and with the proper patterns. The parent and teacher help the child *listen* to the word pronounced correctly and *see* it on the mouth of the speaker.

When Ricky says "shire-cracker," do not repeat his incorrect pronunciation; instead, take this as your cue that here is a perfect teaching-learning situation. He needs to hear the word pronounced correctly. He needs to see you as you say it. He needs to try to say it.

RICKY: "shire-cracker"
TEACHER: "fire-cracker"
        "See my lips and teeth."
        (Wait until he looks at you then repeat the word at least three times.)
        fire-cracker
        fire-cracker
        fire-cracker

If he repeats the word after you, well and good. If he does not repeat it, or if he doesn't say it correctly, be patient. Help him again the next time he uses it.

In every case of word-difficulty, refrain from repeating the child's incorrect pronunciation; instead, take it as your cue that he needs to hear the word and see you say it.

In each case, if you can get the child's attention focused as you have directed before you repeat the additional correct forms, you will be rewarded for your effort by an accelerated speech growth.

The child says:	You say:
fank you	thank you
	See my tongue peek
	between my teeth.
	thank you
	thank you
	thank you
	(Say no more at this
	time but repeat later
	if child again needs
	help.)

wed ball	red ball Listen how I say red ball red ball red ball
thee me	see me See my teeth together see me see me see me
I wike you	I like you See my tongue jump high I like you I like you I like you
muvver	mother See my tongue mother mother mother
seben	seven See my lips and teeth seven seven seven
sherry pie	cherry pie See my lips and hear me say cherry pie cherry pie cherry pie

The Stutterer Shows Improvement When

The School

1. The school sets the example of right attitudes toward these children.
2. In the classroom or out, the child feels that he is a normal individual.
3. Nothing is done to make the stuttering child feel that he is different.
4. Nothing is done to make stuttering acquire value, or become worth maintaining because of use in the avoidance of normal responsibilities.

Teachers (as members of school community)

1. The teacher sets an example for right attitudes.
2. She learns to control her reactions, and helps the children control their reactions to the speech of the child who stutters.

3. If necessary, she talks (in the absence of the child who stutters) to children of the class to help them see that the child who stutters will at times have difficulty with his speech but that they must behave toward him as they would toward any other child.

4. She confers with the speech teacher so that together they may plan for the speech growth of the child.

Children

1. They control their reactions to the child's stuttering.
2. They do not avoid looking at him when his speech blocks.
3. They wait, and listen until the child finishes what he has to say.
4. They do not supply words for him.
5. They behave toward the child who stutters as they do toward any other child in school.

The Boy or Girl Who Stutters

1. Feels that he is a normal person.
2. Believes that he is more like other children than different.
3. Accepts his problem with the right attitude.
4. Works in a positive way toward more normal speech.

Principal

1. Makes it possible for the child to have help from the speech teacher.
2. Makes it possible for the classroom teacher to have conferences with the speech teacher, the nurse, the counselor, and parents, concerning the problems of the child who stutters.
3. Talks with the child informally. Listens for clues in his conversation which might lead to the discovery of his problem.
4. Encourages a friendly relationship between the home and school. Listens to the parents. Lets them help solve the problem by telling their story.
5. Asks the parents to read the "Suggestions for Parents" in this publication.
6. Encourages the teacher and parents to learn more about stuttering, child training, and mental hygiene by reading books selected from the bibliography. Makes available to all parents *How Parents and Teachers Can Help Prevent Stuttering in Children,* by Leon Lassers; *Speech Correction in the Elementary School,* a Bulletin of the California State Department of Education, Vol. XVI, No. 1, March 1948; and "An Open Letter to the Mother of a Stuttering Child" from *Speech Handicapped School Children* by Wendell Johnson.

Remember that all of us on occasion do what the stutterer does more frequently.

AN OPEN LETTER TO THE MOTHER OF
A "STUTTERING" CHILD *

Wendell Johnson

Dear Mrs. Smith:

I deeply appreciate your concern about the speech of Fred, your four-year-old boy. You say that he is healthy, alert, and generally normal by any standards you know about. But you feel that, in spite of all this, he stutters.

It will interest you to know that the great majority of four-year-old children regarded as stutterers by their parents fit that general description. I want to say to you what I should say to the mothers of the many thousands of other "Freds."

Toward the end of this letter I am going to make a few suggestions which I believe might prove helpful. If you are like other intelligent and conscientious mothers, however, you would like to understand clearly what is back of these recommendations before you try them out on your own child. For that reason, I shall introduce the suggestions by giving you certain information.

This information has been obtained in the course of several years of research. Certain studies made of very young children regarded by their parents as stutterers have been particularly revealing. In summarizing the main findings of this research, I shall try to emphasize those points which will help you most to understand the problem that you feel you have with Fred's speech.

*   *   *

First of all, I want to try to put you at ease by stressing that our research findings indicate that children and adults who are thought of by themselves and others as stutterers are not generally abnormal or inferior. Concerning this point, I should like to make as clear a statement as possible—and I make it on the basis of several hundred scientific studies, including a series of investigations involving some 1,000 mothers and fathers and 500 of their young children. Half of these children had been classified by their parents as stutterers and half as nonstutterers.

The statement I have to make is this. About seven out of every 1,000 school children are classified as stutterers. I think any expert can be quite safely challenged to examine 1,000 children who have not yet begun to speak, and to pick out the seven among them who will be regarded as stutterers five to ten years later. In fact, I should be willing to let the expert examine the children after they had begun to speak but before any of them had come to be labeled as stutterers. I should not want him to talk with the parents, but he could examine the children as much as he liked in search of any physical abnormalities that he might suppose to be causes of stuttering. And if he were asked to pick out those who would later be thought of as stutterers, my best judgment is that he could do little better than make pure guesses.

Indeed, I doubt that any examiner could go into a room in which there are 1,000 adult men and women and pick out the seven stutterers whom we shall include in the group. He may use any physical or psychological tests he prefers on each person, except that he may not hear him speak or obtain information about how he speaks or feels about his speech. I should be surprised if the examiner could make clearly better selections with his tests than he could by means of eenie-meenie-minie-moe.

So far as I know persons classified as stutterers are not significantly different as a group from persons regarded as nonstutterers, aside from their speech behavior and the way they feel about their speaking experiences. In fact, even the speech of most young children who are taken by their parents to be stutterers is essentially and for the most part not unusual—but it does become more or less unusual in most cases after their parents begin to think of them as stutterers.

♦   ♦   ♦

This last point is particularly important. I mentioned above that we have made several studies involving some 500 young children regarded by their parents either as stutterers or normal speakers. As the first findings came in we were frankly puzzled. We soon discovered that it was difficult in most cases, often impossible, to see any difference between the speech of children *newly classified* as stutterers and the speech of other children.

We decided to make a series of precise studies of the speech fluency of normal youngsters. Since this had never been done, nobody knew just how smoothly young children do talk. We found that two-, and three-, and four-year-old children in a large nursery school spoke on the average with about 50 repetitions per 1,000 words. It was taken for granted by everyone that these children were normal speakers. They repeated *suh-suh* sounds like that, or-or-or words, or-two-or-two or more words. We found no child who never did this sort of thing and those who repeated the most did it more than 100 times per 1,000 words. These are norms—figures for fairly representative normal children.

Now, we were greatly puzzled by the fact that most of the youngsters whose parents believed they had begun to stutter appeared to be speaking as fluently as that—at the particular moment of the particular day *when their parents first thought of them as "stutterers,"* so far as this day or moment could be determined. After a great deal of research, we were forced to conclude that these children were in general like other children—and that even their speech itself was in most cases apparently like that of other children during the general period when they were first regarded as "stutterers."

This is not to say that they were talking perfectly. It is only to say that when we compared them with other youngsters of their age, and when we took account of the circumstances in which they were speaking, their speech behavior seemed "understandable or acceptable for their stage of development and under the circumstances." They were more disfluent—hesitant and repetitious—sometimes than other times, and this is true of children generally. To all appearances, most of the parents had applied the label "stuttering" to essentially the same types of speech behavior that other parents apparently take in stride and do not call "stuttering."

        ❋   ❋   ❋

We were faced with the question of whether the name used by a child's parents in referring to him or to his manner of speaking could make any difference. Doesn't a rose by any other name smell just as sweet?

Our research findings suggested that, Shakespeare notwithstanding, a rose by certain kinds of other names doesn't smell the same at all. If you regard your child as a "stutterer" you are likely to get one kind of speech development, and if you evaluate him as a "normal" or "good" or "acceptable" speaker you will probably get another kind of speech behavior.

I can illustrate what I mean by telling you briefly about two cases. The first is that of Jimmy, who as a pupil in the grades was regarded as a superior speaker. He won a number of speaking contests and often served as chairman of small groups. Upon entering the ninth grade he changed to another school. A "speech examiner" saw Jimmy twice during the one year he spent in that school. The first time she made a recording of his speech. The second time she played the record for him, and after listening to it, told him he was a "stutterer."

Now, if you can remember the first time you tried to speak into a speech-recording machine you can understand what seems to have happened. In the studies referred to previously all the children spoke with hesitations, repetitions, "uh-uh-uhs," etc. It is easy to see how the apparently inexperienced examiner misjudged Jimmy who was, after all, a superior speaker as ninth graders go.

He took the supposedly "expert" judgment to heart, however. The examiner told him to speak slowly, to watch himself, to try to control his speech. Jimmy's parents were quite upset. They looked upon Jimmy's speech as one of his chief talents, and they set about with a will to help him, reminding him of any little slip or hesitation. Jimmy became as self-conscious as the legendary centipede who had been told "how" to walk. He soon developed tense, jerky, hesitant, apprehensive speech—the kind that a speech pathologist would call stuttering in the clinical sense of the word.

The second instance involved Gene, a three-year-old boy. His father became concerned one evening because now and then Gene repeated a sound or a word. (He had been doing this all along, of course, but his father hadn't noticed it before.) The father reported that Gene didn't seem to know he was doing it and wasn't the least bit tense about it. The next day the father remarked to the family doctor that Gene "was beginning to stutter." Taking the father's word for it, and evidently taking for granted that the father meant the same thing he did by the word "stutter," he told the father to have Gene take a deep breath before trying to speak. Within forty-eight hours Gene was practically speechless. The deep breath had become a frantic gasping from which Gene looked out with wide-eyed bewilderment.

These are real cases, and in their essential features—though not, of course, in specific detail—they seem to be representative. We were mystified as our investigations went on and such results as I have sketched kept coming in. Not only were practically all of the so-called stuttering children, at the time when someone first began to think of them as stutterers, speaking like other children who were not thought to be stuttering, but also we could find no evidence that they had suffered more injuries and diseases. Moreover, contrary to the traditional theory that stuttering usually begins as the result of serious illness, severe fright or shock, and the like, we found that just as an amazing proportion of traffic accidents occur on dry, straight highways, in daylight, in the country, in good automobiles, so in most cases *the problem* called "stuttering" develops in ordinary homes, under conditions that are not dramatic, in children who are apparently not unusual and who speak as well as other youngsters of their age.

✿   ✿   ✿

The so-called stuttering youngsters were so puzzling just because they appeared to be so normal—until we decided to give up the assumption that they should necessarily be abnormal. Then the mystery began to lift. Slowly we saw more and more clearly what was staring us in the face. I suspect that it had been overlooked for so long—for centuries, in fact—just because it is so obvious.

What we had overlooked, and what we now noticed, was simply that in case after case stuttering, as a serious problem, developed *after it had been diagnosed.* The diagnosis of stuttering—that is, the decision made by someone that a child is beginning to stutter—is one of the causes of the stuttering problem, and apparently one of the most potent causes.

Having labeled the child's hesitations and repetitions as "stuttering," the listener—somewhat more often the mother than the father—reacts to them as if they were all that the label implies. She seems to do this—to react to *the label* that she herself has decided to use—without realizing that she is doing it at all. By her very facial expression and tone of voice, as well as by what she tells the child, she tends (without meaning to certainly!) to convince him that he is not speaking "well enough" and that she disapproves of the way he speaks. She disapproves of it because she disapproves of the label she herself has given it. In her zeal to "control" what she now calls his "stuttering," she might, with the very best of intentions, even influence her child to feel that she no longer loves him, or at least that she is disappointed in him.

Her label "stuttering," you see, implies to her that her child needs help, and she, of course, is eager to help him because, like you, she loves her child deeply. She may show the child how to inhale and how to exhale, how to speak more slowly, how to breathe "with the abdomen" or "with the chest," how to place the tongue for certain sounds. She may urge him—perhaps with considerable urgency—to "relax" and "take it easy," or to stop and start over, or to "think out" what he intends to say before he tries to say it. Occasionally a parent might, shall we say, scold her child if he does not speak smoothly after all these "helpful" instructions. The major and unfortunate result of all this is that the child "catches" her own attitude of anxiety and disapproval of his speech when he does not speak smoothly.

As soon as he has acquired this attitude he too begins to have feelings of uneasiness and disapproval. He begins to make ingenious attempts to speak according to the standard of fluency which his mother appears to favor. He tries hard. He does so want to do the thing properly—so his mother will smile again. Naturally, he exerts effort, he strains. Of course, he cannot strain without holding his lips together tightly, or holding the tongue against the roof of the mouth, or constricting the muscles of his throat. He cannot exert effort in certain ways without holding his breath.

By doing these things he interferes with his speech even more. He feels that he is "stuttering" worse, therefore, and so he makes greater efforts to "keep from stuttering," and these greater efforts, in turn, are felt by him—and are regarded by his mother and father and other listeners—as "more severe stuttering." His mother, understandably, tries harder to "help." She urges her husband to pay more attention to "the stuttering" and "do something about it." Maybe she talks to her close friends about it, and they also try to be "helpful." Any child reacts to all this, if only slightly, and some children become quite tense and unsettled. In some cases the child finally reaches the point where he is straining much of the time and so speaks with what appears to be great difficulty.

This, then, is a general account of how *the problem* called "stuttering" usually begins and develops. I believe this sketch might help you to understand better the problem which *you and Fred* are experiencing. If other factors also are operating in your situation they are to be given due consideration.

In giving you this information, I have by no means intended to say that you have done something for which you are to be criticized. On the contrary, it is to be taken for granted that you have acted from the finest of motives—the love you feel for Fred. Fred knows this and you know it. You have done the best that you have known how to do. My sole purpose in writing as I do is to help you see how best to help Fred, which is what you want so very much to do.

✿   ✿   ✿

If I have outlined then, in the main essentials at least, the problem with which you have to deal, I believe the following suggestions will prove helpful:

1. It is far from likely that Fred speaks the way he does because of any physical fault. You might, perhaps, have other reasons for taking Fred to see a physician. If he has any need for medical attention it should be provided for him. Nothing should be done, however, to suggest to him that he is frail if he is not, that he is sick if he is well, or that he should get more rest and sleep than he actually needs.

2. Do nothing at any time, by word or deed or posture or facial expression, that would serve to call Fred's attention to *the interruptions*

in his speech. Above all, do nothing that would make him regard them as abnormal or unacceptable. If he has begun to notice his own hesitatings help him to feel that they are understandable under the circumstances and so, of course, acceptable. In doing this, however, do not make the mistake of "protesting too much." You can make Fred self-conscious about his speech even by praising it—if you praise it to excess. Err, if you must, on the side of approving it a bit more than is justified.

I am not suggesting that you "pay no attention to Fred's stuttering." You may often be given advice in these exact words. The people who give it to you have good intentions. Meanwhile, the wording of the advice is not quite right, in my judgment. Here is what I mean: If Fred repeats and hesitates (speaks disfluently) in the ways that are more or less ordinary for his age and for the sorts of situations in which he is talking, he is simply not doing anything that might usefully be called by such a grave-sounding name as "stuttering" in the first place. He is just speaking normally, and normal speech is more or less disfluent. If he is more hesitant in speech than most children are, and especially if he hesitates with strain or tension, look about him, and at yourself, and try to find out the reasons. Then do what you can to remove them. Don't "pay no attention" to the *unusual* reactions Fred is making to the *unusual* things in his surroundings that need to be changed.

3. In order to see Fred and his speech in proper relation to the things and persons about him, and to develop a proper perspective in viewing Fred's hesitating and repeating, you should observe carefully:

a. the conditions under which he hesitates and repeats;

b. the times when he speaks smoothly and easily;

c. the ways in which he is, generally speaking, a "regular boy";

d. the times when other youngsters of his age also speak hesitantly and repetitiously more or less the way Fred does, especially when they are "excited," or "talking over their heads," or when frustrated and under other such conditions;

e. the times when Fred does not speak fluently but yet does not fail utterly or "go all to pieces"—rather, he repeats sounds or words or says "uh-uh-uh" more or less smoothly (or did before and at the time when you first began to wonder whether he might be a "stutterer").

4. Do not label or classify Fred as a "stutterer." If you do, you will have a very powerful tendency to treat him as if he were as abnormal and unfortunate as the label suggests, and this may affect badly the way he feels about himself and weaken his self-confidence.

This is a great and needless risk. Instead of saying vaguely and ominously that he "stutters," say more clearly and calmly what you mean, that under certain conditions *(and describe these specific conditions)* he repeats sounds or words, says "uh-uh-uh"—or whatever it is he does *(and describe specifically what he does).*

You are your own most affected listener, and when you tell yourself that Fred "is a stutterer" you do something to your feelings about him that you don't do when you tell yourself that he repeats words or says "uh-uh" in talking about a new family of squirrels he is excited about and doesn't know how to describe to you while you're busy trying to fix dinner—or to his father who is watching television or reading the newspaper and not paying much attention to what Fred is saying. It's pretty difficult for you, too, to talk smoothly about something you consider very important to someone who doesn't pay much attention to what you are saying. It's hard for you to do that without a certain amount of hemming and hawing and backing and filling even when you know very well what you want to say and when you know exactly the words you need to use. Much of the time Fred doesn't quite know what he's talking about and he needs words he has never used before.

What you tell yourself about Fred is a matter of such profoundly fundamental importance that I could not possibly emphasize it too much. The way you classify Fred—and the names you give to what he does—will determine very largely the way you feel about him and react to him. This is as true of his speaking as it is of everything else about him. If we label a boy a thief, no good will come of it because it will become harder and harder for him to do anything honest or honorable in our eyes. If we frequently call a youngster "stupid," it will be very unlikely that we will ever see the intelligent ways he behaves. Just so, if we think of a child as a "stutterer" we will worry about him, keep our ears tuned for the bobbles and imperfections in his speech, and literally not hear what he does well when he speaks.

5. You are already "tuned in" to the disfluencies in Fred's speech that you call "stuttering." Take a tip from the noted speech pathologist, Dr. Dean Williams, and "tune yourself in" to the disfluencies in Fred's speech that you would call "normal" or "normal under the circumstances for a child of Fred's age." The chances are that you will notice more and more "normal repetitions and hesitations" and fewer and fewer "stutterings" as times goes on—and Fred will sense the difference this will make in you and your feelings about him, and he will find it easier to talk to you with your new feelings.

6. There are certain conditions under which practically any child tends to speak smoothly and other conditions under which he tends to speak hesitantly. You will find it wise, therefore, to observe the following simple rules:

First of all, and above all, try to be the kind of listener your child likes to talk to. You know a great deal about how to be this kind of listener, but it may be that no one has ever helped you realize how tremendously important it is to Fred—and to you, and to the two of you together—that you be such a listener whenever he talks to you.

He should never have reason to doubt that you love him and that you enjoy hearing him talk.

Read to Fred whenever you can. In reading or speaking to him enunciate clearly, be interested in what you are reading, and avoid a tense, impatient, or loud voice. Enjoy this reading and make it fun and companionable. Do some of it every day, preferably just before bedtime, if possible.

Don't say, "No, you can't" or "Don't do that" when it really wouldn't matter if he did go ahead and do what he wanted to. Try to keep "Stop that" and "Don't do that" remarks down to a fourth or less of all the things you say to Fred—and see what you do say to him then, most of the time. You'll probably enjoy the time you spend with Fred much more if you do this.

Say, "That's fine!" to Fred much more often than, for example, "Don't be so careless and awkward!" Rewards are far better than punishments.

Avoid asking Fred to "speak pieces" for company or to "show off" in other ways.

Don't keep him in a state of excitement by too much teasing, nagging, bullying, or too much "running and jumping."

See that Fred's brothers and sisters are not always "bossing" him, or not always talking when he wants to talk.

In general, try to avoid situations that are needlessly or unduly frustrating, exciting, bewildering, tiring, humiliating, or frightening to Fred.

When you take Fred to strange places or ask him to do something that is new to him, prepare him for it by explaining ahead of time.

When he is "talking over his head" be patient, and now and then supply him with a new word which he has not yet learned but which he needs at the moment. To a reasonable extent and *in meaningful ways* help him to add to his vocabulary—preferably at those times when he needs words he hasn't yet learned in order to tell you things he has never tried to say before.

As for "discipline," so far as possible help Fred to discipline himself. Help him to understand how others feel and to be considerate of them. If Fred is to be loved he must be lovable. Help him learn how to be.

My last suggestion may sound quite drastic, but I believe you might find it worthwhile: Try at all times when it seems practical to be as friendly and considerate toward Fred as you would be toward a house guest.

*   *   *

Unless the speech problem that *you and Fred are in together* is in some way exceptional, or has developed into a truly serious form, these suggestions should prove helpful. You will not, I am sure, expect more from the printed page than would be reasonable—and you will remember that Fred is only human. His speech—or yours or mine—will never be as fluent as a faucet. All children hesitate and repeat and stumble more or less in speaking—and so do all adults. Even the most silver-tongued orator makes an occasional bobble. But if within six months or so you feel, for any reason, that Fred is not talking as smoothly and easily as he should, I hope you will consult a speech clinician—preferably, of course, one who is certified by the American Speech and Hearing Association.[1]

Yours very sincerely

WENDELL JOHNSON

CREATIVE DRAMATICS FOR CHILDREN *

Geraldine B. Siks

WHAT IS CREATIVE DRAMATICS?

It is many things at once. First, it is philosophy on a child's level. It is a child's way of playing out many different roles of man as he gradually becomes one. It is a way of stimulating children to become aware of the world of nature and the works of man. "Drama arose out of fundamental human needs in the dawn of civilization and has continued to express them for thousands of years. Drama represents humanity in moments of maximum tension, conflict, and crisis, and it tries to resolve them in broadly human terms. Drama brings the life of

[1] The American Speech and Hearing Association is the recognized professional organization of speech pathologists and audiologists in the United States. The address of the Association is 1001 Connecticut Avenue, N. W., Washington 6, D. C.

* Reprinted from *Contributions in Reading*, No. 26 (Boston: Ginn and Co.), by permission of the author and publisher.

man visibly before mankind." [1] It encourages children to wonder, to think, to discuss ideas and conflicts, and then to "play out" their wonderings with spirit and belief. To children, this experience becomes thought and feeling expressed in action and dialogue in the form of dramatic play.

Creative dramatics is simultaneously a creative art and a creative process. It aims for truth and beauty as it motivates children to express freely. Creative dramatics may be defined as a group experience in which every child is guided to express himself as he works and plays with others for the joy of creating improvised drama. This means that children are guided to create characters, dialogue, action, and interaction without the use of scripts or memorized dialogue. No costumes, scenery, or stage are required, only children, an understanding teacher, a space in which to play, and an idea from which to create. Ideas may be selected from children's experiences, such as a trip to a beach. Each child is guided to think, and to show in pantomime a happy feeling he experiences when he enjoys one special moment at a beach. Thus motivated, each child, in a group with five or six other children, expresses his idea in rhythmic action. Children express such ideas as "wading," "swimming," "splashing," "having a water fight," "listening to a shell I found," "dancing with the waves," "drawing a picture of Daddy in the sand," or "sitting on the warm sand and listening to what the waves are saying."

Children may also create characters and conversation. For example, a group of seven- and eight-year-olds who found great enjoyment in Rose Fyleman's fairy poetry skipped away to fairyland on a spring morning and became fairies and elves "doing one thing to make fairyland happy." When the Fairy Queen (the teacher) called to each one, active fairies and elves had these spontaneous answers to share:

"I'm a little elf swinging in a tree. I have a leaf for my swing-board."
"I have a wand with stars on it. See! I'm making flowers grow."
"My fairy has gray wings and a shiny wand. I'm touching leaves to make them sparkle."
"I'm a happy fairy, flying."
"I found a baby deer. See, she follows me."
"I found a ruby stone. It opens and has sugar inside."
"I am a silver fairy herding a herd of golden horses."

Once children have been introduced to the disciplines of expressing themselves through basic drama forms such as these, they will be ready to create scenes or an entire play from a verse or story.

---

[1] John Gassner, *Masters of the Drama* (3rd rev. ed., New York: Dover Publications, 1954).

Creative dramatics is also an art movement for children and youth which is now being shared in our country and in many other countries throughout the world. It has found its way into classrooms and community programs because of its appeal and unique contribution in a child's total educational program.

UNIQUE CONTRIBUTION TO CHILD DEVELOPMENT

Creative dramatics offers a natural, lively way for a child to exercise, synchronize, and manipulate his active body. A child is rhythmic from the first beat of his heart, which sends life into his being, to the rhythmic way he walks, talks, moves, eats, sleeps, shouts, lives. Rhythm is the basis for expression in all the arts. It starts with the individual. Each artist expresses through a medium unique to his art. A painter expresses rhythmically in space with line and color. A musician expresses rhythmically in space with sound. A child expresses rhythmically in space with movement. In creative dramatics a child releases vital energy in rhythmic movement as he becomes a variety of exciting things such as a chugging train, a zooming plane, a galloping horse, a hopping frog, a dancing fairy, a growing flower, or a blustery north wind.

Creative dramatics exercises a child's creative abilities. Among the many miraculous "built-ins" within every child are his senses and his imagination. These are his antennae, his ways of tuning in to receive impressions from his environment. A child is curious. He wonders, thinks, combines ideas, and expresses. He needs a steady intake followed by a steady output of expression if he is to develop his sensibilities and creative abilities. In the art of creative dramatics a child's awareness is stimulated. He is required to observe, to think, to concentrate, to discipline his mind as he strives to create convincing characters who speak and act with belief.

Creative dramatics also nourishes a child's uniqueness. Just as there are no two trees in all the world exactly alike, no two children are exactly the same. Each child has a personality of his own. He may long for beauty, understanding, friendship, confidence, idealism; for someone to admire, respect, worship, to be important to. In creative dramatics a child is introduced to many different aspects of life. As he discusses and explores characters and universal truths in many different situations, he satisfies his yearnings to know more of life. Whenever he becomes involved in his play, he is filled with belief and empathy. His playing often satisfies moments for which his spirit has longed; and feelings of satisfaction and dignity come from group experiences where each child is important to the whole.

THE CREATIVE PROCESS IN GUIDING

"The teacher's own feeling about creative dramatics is the biggest single factor in the extent to which she uses it in her teaching." [2] Once a teacher understands the creative process in guiding, she will recognize a wealth of material from which children may create in everyday happenings, in their reading, and in stories or verse which are read or told to them.

Guidance in creative dramatics requires, above all, a teacher who enjoys and understands children and drama. It flourishes with a teacher who is aware and appreciative of the unexpected and dynamic powers of children's hearts and minds. It calls for a teacher to set up an environment in which every child feels socially and emotionally free to experience and to express. The process of creative dramatics follows a basic pattern which evolves in a continuous five-way cycle. A teacher guides by: (1) Motivating children into a strong mood; (2) Presenting or clarifying a story, verse, or experience from which children are to create; (3) Guiding children to make a plan before each playing; (4) Guiding children to play with conviction and belief; and (5) Guiding children to evaluate playing in relation to the art of drama.

Motivating Children into a Mood

Because all art is created in the realm of mood, a teacher aims to get children into a "high rare mood." This is done largely by getting attention and asking motivating questions which cause children to think and which lead to a discussion that centers on the desired mood. Motivating questions are generally asked with *when, where, what, why,* and *how.* For example: *What* one thing did you do during summer vacation that made you feel happy deep down inside? *Why* was this such a happy time for you?

Presenting or Clarifying a Story, Verse, or Experience

This is done in a way which is appropriate for a group and situation. A teacher may tell a favorite story so that it "lives" for children. Or children may ask to "play" a story which they have read. In this instance, a teacher may guide children to read again specific parts of a story. Or she may guide them to read by asking questions to determine the comprehension and understanding of the dramatic content of a

2 Winifred Ward, *Playmaking with Children* (2nd ed., New York: Appleton-Century-Crofts, 1957).

story. Before children are ready to create, it is essential that they understand a character in relationship to his actions and his attitudes toward others in the story, why the character does what he does, and the way he feels toward other characters in the story.

Guiding Children in Making a Plan

If a child is to create with belief and enjoyment, he must be able to see, feel, and do whatever a scene or situation calls for in a way which is true for each child. For example, let us suppose a group has been motivated into a strong mood for the enjoyment of summer vacation experiences. A teacher then guides a group to plan through motivating statements or suggestions such as these:

Seeing. Close your eyes to get a picture in your mind of one special place where you had fun this summer. See yourself in this very place. Breathe deeply to smell the good smells. Listen to hear the special sounds of summer in this place.

Feeling. Remember the good feeling you had when you were there. Remember how happy and excited you felt inside your whole self. See if you can get this same good feeling deep inside yourself now.

Action. See yourself doing one thing that brought such a happy feeling to you. See yourself doing it in your own way. See yourself doing it clearly and vividly so that you may share this experience with others in the space we have in this part of the room. See how you may use your whole self to make others see and feel whatever you are doing in your own free way with spirit and fun. By reaching down inside for your own honest feelings and ideas, you will be able to make a moment of your summer fun come alive for others.

The responses and feelings aroused by these suggestions are discussed. When children understand a situation and are enthusiastic about "showing," they are then ready to pantomime for each other.

Guiding Children to Play and Create

For first and early playings a teacher designates a space within a room as a stage or playing area. She casts: (1) by inviting five or six volunteers to play for a first time, (2) by selecting confident children to play in first playings, or (3) by explaining that everyone will play, in turn, according to rows, tables, or whatever arrangement is best suited to the group. It is important to encourage every child to participate. Frequently a shy, sensitive child will not volunteer but will willingly and cheerfully participate when he is included in a group.

A teacher uses drama terms in explanations. She indicates that the children playing are "players" and the children watching are "audience." She suggests that there is an "imaginary curtain" between the audience and the stage which she will open (in pantomime) when it is time for the magic of the playing to begin. A teacher sustains mood by "setting the stage" with a clear and enthusiastic description. In this instance she may suggest somewhat as follows:

Setting a Stage. It is summer time. It is warm, beautiful, sunny. Each of our players, here on the stage, is in his own special place where he enjoys his summer vacation. For one player the stage may be a special indoor place. For another it may be a place in the outdoor world. Each player uses his imagination to see just where he is.

As soon as we are ready, each player will show with action and feeling just where he is and what he is doing. Each player will move freely in the space around him. He will be careful not to disturb other players. Above all, he will strive to make our audience believe. He will do this by seeing, feeling, believing, and enjoying whatever he is doing. In this way his playing will come alive for our audience and they will feel happy, too. This is an important secret of creative dramatics. A player never worries. He thinks, concentrates, and enjoys creating in his own way.

Getting Children Started. A teacher calls "curtain" and opens an imaginary curtain in pantomime. If she prefers, she may join with the players and pantomime to help get the children started. Or she may provide appropriate background music by a recording which suggests the desired mood, rhythm, and idea. In this instance, a recording of "Morning" from Grieg's *Peer Gynt* or "Sunrise" from Ferde Grofé's *Grand Canyon Suite* would heighten the enjoyment of summer vacation pantomimes.

Once children are creating, a teacher will encourage them to sustain their pantomimes for two or three minutes. If children "break the mood" before this time, she will make it clear that other "players" will continue to play and enjoy their playing until "curtain" is called.

Guiding Children to Evaluate Playing. Children who have served as audience are generally ready to share comments. The teacher guides by first asking for positive suggestions. This is done by asking questions which are focused on fundamentals of dramatic expression (seeing, feeling, believing, doing). For example, after a first playing of summer vacation experiences a teacher guides by asking evaluative questions similar to the following:

1. What summer fun experience came alive for you?
2. What moment in the playing did you enjoy most? Why?
3. Which player used his whole self to create his experience?

4. Describe a moment when a player made his actions so clear that you knew at once what he was doing?
5. Which player made good use of the playing space?
6. Which player enjoyed his playing so much that he caused you to enjoy it, too?
7. Who saw one way a player could make his playing clearer?
8. Who has a suggestion as to how a player might make an audience believe even more than our audience believed this time?
9. Who has a suggestion as to how a player may put more spirit and enjoyment into his playing?

Creating Plays from Stories

After a gradual foundation in the basic experiences of drama, involving rhythm and characterization, children should be ready to enjoy the experience of creating a play from an entire story. A close examination of the dramatic content of stories in basal reading series and in individual library books will reveal excellent stories for playing. Winifred Ward's *Stories to Dramatize* offers an outstanding collection of over one hundred stories from classic and modern literature which are particularly suitable for dramatization by children from five through fourteen years of age.

When children are motivated into strong moods for creative dramatics, they find enjoyment in writing or drawing about many of these experiences as well. Teachers have found that creative dramatics stimulates unusual expression in creative writing of poetry and stories.

Creative Dramatics in Intermediate Grades

Accurate characterization and the dramatizing of a whole story come within the province of older as well as of primary-grade children. However, the intermediate-grade teacher faces certain problems if her pupils have not experienced creative dramatics in the preceding grades. Older children will feel embarrassed, hold back, or "clown" unless they feel free to express with enjoyment and security. Consequently the chief problem is discovering how to begin, and a teacher needs to discover the way which is right for her and for the group.

Many classroom teachers in the fourth, fifth, and sixth grades have introduced creative dramatics through charades, action songs, or choral verse speaking. In each of these approaches children are motivated by the rhythm of the charade chant, the song, or the verse. Experiences are focused on pantomimes and a teacher strives to build a mood of enjoyment which breaks down emotional barriers. After several beginning experiences children generally start to request this kind of expression, and frequently suggest songs, verse, and charade ideas. After a gradual foundation in the basics of expression through rhythmic movement and characterization, older children will usually be ready to enjoy playing short scenes from stories and entire stories.

CONCLUSION

Once a teacher introduces creative dramatics in a classroom she will become aware of the strong appeal and benefits it brings to boys and girls. A teacher will also recognize the need for further study in the philosophy and techniques of this art if she is to guide children to creative heights and dramatic depths. Above all, a teacher will see for herself the vital way in which this art causes children to become aware of the world around them and to discover the creative power that is real and deep within each child. She will see, too, that this is a group art where children laugh and talk together, think and feel together, work and play together, and so learn to live happily together, with each respecting and admiring the unique individuality of the other.

STORYTELLING
THE UNIVERSAL URGE TO SHARE *

Mabel F. Rice

"Tell us a story!"

Down through the ages has come that request. The first fire with people sitting around it must have inspired the first story. Storytelling is the oldest of the arts. Not only was the storyteller man's first entertainer, but he was his first teacher. Storytelling was first used as a method for giving information. In the hands of the great teachers from Socrates and Jesus down to Abraham Lincoln, it became a vehicle for imparting truths.

The early storyteller told his story within the narrow limits of his

---

* Reprinted from *The Packet* (Boston: D. C. Heath Co.), by permission of the publisher.

own personal experience. He told of the hunt, the pursuit, the slaying of the wild beast. When the art of storytelling developed to a point where the story was related in the third person, then storytelling was elevated to the plane of entertainment.

In ancient tribes, as today, some individuals showed more talent than others. Gradually the responsibility for storytelling shifted to the talented individual. He was freed from some of the burdens of the day that he might prepare amusement to brighten the evenings for the tribe. Thus the professional storyteller became the chief priest and the medicine man. Thus originated the tradition that the leader of the group—the teacher—be the storyteller, a tradition that persisted. With the development and the application of the philosophy that one learns by doing, gradually the concept of storytelling has broadened until today not only the teacher but every child participates in the story-telling activities.

The roots of the desire to tell a story lie in a basic urge to share. Relating personal experience stories is a universal language activity. Children and adults alike enjoy telling unusual or exciting experiences and in the telling the need arises for vivid and dramatic use of words and phrases. In the nursery school, the kindergarten, and in the primary grades the sharing period presents an opportunity for the personal experience story as well as for the storybooks the child wants to share. The teacher tells the first stories, her narratives serving as a model and an inspiration to the child. She chooses her stories from a wide variety of types that will stimulate the listener to create his own mental pictures. Some days, as he listens, he will be moved to smiles or even to laughter. On other occasions he may sit in suspense as he follows the adventures of a story child or animal, and he will relax in happy satisfaction or enthusiastic acclaim at the end of the story. Sometimes he will travel in mental flight to distant places.

Again as he listens the child begins to sense certain standards of sportsmanship and behavior. He develops a feeling of sympathy and understanding for small creatures, for other girls and boys. He may even find a solution to his own problems. As the overlarge child listens to the story of *Amandus Who Was Much Too Big*, he arrives at the comforting thought that no one is too big or too small but that he is just the right size for him. As the timid child hears the repeated refrain "I-THINK-I-CAN, I-THINK-I-CAN" change to "I-KNEW-I-COULD, I-KNEW-I-COULD," along with *The Little Engine That Could*, he has a feeling of growing security.

Although a child grows and develops as he listens creatively to an excellent selection of stories, he grows even more through the telling of a story. A child's storytelling experience repeats the experience of the race. His first stories are the first person narratives emphasizing *I*, *me, my, mine.* The time is the present; the place is his immediate environment. The young child is interested in the activity and the story that goes along with getting dressed in the morning, with putting on new red birthday shoes. Another year and he tells of "My Puppy," and "My Kitten." Gradually his story horizons widen to include other members of his family and his friends. The time line expands to include yesterday and last week. With further maturity, he projects his story into the realm of the impersonal third person. When he can begin a story with "Once upon a time," the young storyteller has gone beyond the Here and Now and is creating a new story world in the Far Away and Long Ago.

Spontaneous and free expression is the keynote of the child's storytelling in the kindergarten and primary grades. His innate interest in animals and his love for them gives animal stories a coveted place among the story favorites. Unobtrusively, through her own contributions, the teacher can guide the grouping of the stories. A story about a pet stimulates the telling of stories about pets. The care of pets becomes a part of the discussion. From pets it is an easy step to inanimate animal toys. *Winnie-the-Pooh* makes delightful reading-aloud and forms the nucleus for a grouping of Milne stories and poems.

As children tell their own stories they may be led to develop an awareness of picture words, color words, action words, and sound words. There is careful attention to clear, distinct speech with emphasis on the pronunciation of syllables and word endings. By the time the child reaches the fourth grade, he may be made conscious of some of the simple but fundamental principles of storytelling:

1. He chooses a title that suggests the nature of his story.
2. He uses a beginning sentence that attracts the immediate attention of his listeners.
3. He keeps to the subject of his story and relates the events in the right order.
4. He uses a variety of interesting words to show definitely where the sentence begins and ends, thus eliminating unnecessary *ands.*

Analytical technique should never be permitted to interfere with the spontaneity of a story. No amount of technique or analysis can make a storyteller. However, in the upper grades pupils enjoy observing and studying the methods used by excellent storytellers. For instance they have learned that in the written story, through proper spacing, the title of a story is made to stand out and catch the eye of the reader. Now they learn that in the oral story the title is made to stand out and to catch the ear of the reader through a space in time, a brief pause before and after the title: The title of my story is . . . "The Elephant's Child" . . . Once upon a time. . . .

Although speaking names distinctly has been stressed in every grade, upper grade girls and boys are interested to learn that the name of a character will be clear to the listener if the storyteller pauses briefly before and after the name the first time it is mentioned in a story. In that way he tells *whom* the story is about. With equal clarity he must make sure that his listeners know *what* the story is about, *when* and *where* it takes place.

Older pupils glean much satisfaction in developing a procedure for the preparation of a story. Coupling a class discussion with the laboratory preparation of a story, they can evolve a method of work. No one plan is as important as the fact that pupils do have a plan. Thus the following plan is merely suggestive.

Choose a short story for the laboratory study, taking one that can be and should be cut somewhat. Read the story to the class or select a story from a reader and have all the pupils read the story for themselves. Since the pupils may be invited to tell their stories to a lower grade or to a mixed audience, there need be no limits to the age appeal of the story studied. In fact the class might develop one story for younger children and one for older, discovering that the steps in the preparation of the story are the same.

After the pupils have read the story, lead the group through discussion to discover for themselves that a story may be shortened through a pruning of the descriptive parts, through the elimination of one or more characters, or through omission of scenes. The story of Rip van Winkle, for instance, may be shortened by cutting descriptions. Edith Rickert's *Bojabi Tree*, a favorite with young children because of its delightful rhythm and repetition of the theme, may be successfully cut through omission of one or two of the animal characters and the scene with the king.

Edward Everett Hale's *The Man Without a Country* may be greatly improved for storytelling purposes by omitting the first four paragraphs and other descriptive passages, keeping the narrative to the main incidents. Armstrong Sperry's *Call It Courage*, an excellent reading-aloud story, with judicious cutting may be shortened for storytelling. Excerpts from junior novels can be edited and streamlined. An unusual Christmas story is found in the Newbery Medal winner *Dobry* by Monica Shannon. Choose the part which tells of Dobry's modeling the Holy Family from new-fallen snow. The young storyteller should read all of *Dobry* to obtain the background and the spirit of the story. Then in his introduction to the Christmas story he sketches the plot, thus giving his listeners the background and significance of Dobry's creation of the Christmas manger.

Through the class laboratory story let pupils discover for themselves the following desirable steps in the preparation of a story.

The storyteller chooses a story he likes and reads it carefully.

He reviews the story in his mind to see how much he remembers, then he rereads it to check on points he may have forgotten. He decides upon the parts that may be cut, and checks to see that the facts he has kept answer the questions *who, what, when,* and *where.* He plans a good opening sentence or two that will catch the attention of the listeners and thinks through the concluding sentence to bring the story to an effective climax. The rest of the story he plans to tell in his own words in free easy sentences.

Aside from having his first and last sentences well in mind, the results are more spontaneous if the storyteller avoids memorization. However, an occasional story such as "The Elephant's Child" or selected chapters from *Winnie-the-Pooh* lose much of their charm if retold in language other than that of the author. The experienced storyteller finds that successive oral readings of these and other stories fix them in his mind to such an extent that eventually he can lay aside the book and tell the story.

Even the best oral reading can never equal the personal appeal of the eye to eye contact of the storyteller. A teacher with a rich repertoire of stories is ready for those situations that arise when one needs a temporary "filler" and there is no story collection at hand. However, the reading-aloud story fills a very definite need, and the teacher with a wide knowledge of children's stories has an unfailing source of reference.

On the occasion of an impending landslide which occupied newspaper headlines for several days in a West Coast city (chamber of commerce tradition forbids mentioning the name), one teacher remembered Kipling's story of a landslide in the *Second Jungle Book* and brought "The Miracle of Purun Bhagat" to his seventh-grade classes.

In a vacant lot near the school a class of eighth-grade boys discovered an abundance of spiders, several of which they smuggled into the classroom for purposes not entirely scientific. The teacher had the spiders secured in bottles and read the group the story of Arachne. The pupils not only became interested in spiders and made a study of them, but they wrote their own dramatization of the story of the classic weaving contest between Arachne and Pallas Athene, presenting the play in the auditorium. Thus can a discipline situation be turned into a learning situation, both scientific and aesthetic.

The use of the feltogram story is an excellent method of inducting children gradually into storytelling experiences. Although for most children the telling of a story is as natural as eating, for the shy or backward child the feltogram story provides a means for motivating him to participate in the storytelling activities. A frame for the feltogram may be constructed from a piece of plywood or other light wood. The feltogram may rest on an easel, or a brace may be attached to the back of the feltogram forming a simple easel model which stands on a table. The frame is covered with felt or flannel in a pastel shade. Pale blue or green is preferable since it serves as the base for the sky and landscape backgrounds that can be used in most stories. Other materials to which felt or flannel figures will cling may be used for the easel covering. One teacher made an effective background from a red corduroy hunting jacket. Another used an old blue velvet skirt for the covering.

Story characters for the feltogram or flannelgram may be drawn freehand or traced and cut from felt or flannel which will adhere to the cover material. "Dime-store" books lend themselves well to feltogram stories. The gaily colored pictures can be cut out. A piece of flannel, felt, or sandpaper pasted to the back clings to the feltogram as it rests on the easel. Stories such as *Goldilocks and the Three Bears, The Three Little Kittens, The Three Little Pigs,* and many others are available in brightly colored, inexpensive editions. Numerous stories excellent for feltograms are in editions too expensive to mutilate, but the figures may be copied. Ideal for this purpose are stories such as Wanda Gág's *Nothing At All* and Carolyn Sherwin Bailey's *The Little Rabbit Who Wanted Red Wings.*

The teacher first tells the story herself, placing the figures on the feltogram as the story progresses. For the second telling of the story, usually on a subsequent day, the children place the figures on the feltogram as the teacher tells the story. Soon a child may relate the story while his classmates help with the building of the feltogram.

A stimulating reciprocal program on a schoolwide scale may be worked out between the upper and lower grades. Upper grade girls and boys enjoy the construction of a feltogram and the fun of telling the story. First the pupil tells the story to his own group, asking for suggestions for improvement. Primary children and their teachers are delighted to receive guest storytellers from other grades and to reciprocate with a return story. The result is an exchange program involving most or all of the school classrooms and many pupil storytellers, all of whom gain poise and confidence with each storytelling experience.

The feltogram technique suggests a wide variety of uses. It is ideal for creative storytelling. The teacher may procure ten-cent-store editions of paper-covered books on farm animals, pets, wild animals, city life, and other familiar subjects. The pictures are cut out, and adhesive material is pasted to the back. The assorted figures are placed on a table near the easel. The child selects those he needs to create and tell a story, perhaps about the mother cow and her calf, and the collie dog that prevented the calf from running away. The listening situation for the other children is equally creative as individuals see and suggest variations of the story. Young children develop amazing ingenuity and creative power in building stories about a set of figure characters. They can be encouraged to create new stories and make their own set of simple figures to use in telling the story.

In an upper grade as well, the feltogram proves a helpful stimulus to storytelling and to science. A unit of work on astronomy, for instance, has creative possibilities that challenge the ingenuity of girls and boys either in the classroom or in a science club. The study of the sky, the sun, moon, stars, planets, and constellations is made graphic through the use of a feltogram or a star box. A dozen stars cut in felt about the size of a quarter may be used for the construction of innumerable star groups, stimulating scientific explanations and storytelling.

The construction of a star box is an activity of absorbing interest to an upper grade group. An apple box or a box of similar shape is suitable for a star box. On a piece of cardboard the pupil draws the stars for a constellation; then he cuts them out. The cardboard is inserted in grooves prepared on the open side of the box. A hole is bored in the back of the box to permit the inserting of an electric light socket and bulb. As the bulb is lighted the constellation shines forth. The pupil describes his star group and tells the story from the classic myths, the American Indian myths, or from other mythology. A cardboard box with a flashlight used to light the constellation makes a simple and effective star box, one that is particularly adapted to summer camps or other places where electric lights are not available.

In all ages the night sky has moved people to storytelling. The story of Callisto and Arcas, symbolized by the Big Dipper and the Little Dipper, is a popular subject for a star box and for feltogram stories. Orion, the mighty hunter, shown with his dog and the frightened little Pleiades is another happy choice. The heroic adventures of Perseus are favorite subjects with storytellers and stargazers as is the beautiful story of Castor and Pollux.

An activity planned on a schoolwide basis that proves an incentive to storytelling is the painting of picture windows. In many cities and towns, artistic window painting on the part of school children has been initiated by the merchants in the community as a means for the release of the Halloween spirit! The merchants themselves provide the materials needed for the window painting. The work is done under the direction of the art department of the public schools. Pupils from grade schools through high schools are invited to contribute designs for plate-glass windows. Sometimes prizes are offered for the different age groups. During the week before Halloween, windows are lighted and steady throngs of people parade the business streets. Through a constructive plan the creative ability of youth is directed into channels that are productive.

Although the motivation is different, some communities have used window painting enterprises as a form of Christmas decoration. Within the schools the creation of designs based on favorite Halloween or Christmas stories is a motivation for wide reading and for storytelling. In one city an eighth-grade boy who designed a Halloween window based on the encounter of Ichabod Crane and the Headless Horseman was invited to tell the story of "The Legend of Sleepy Hollow" in several grade-school anditoriums. Listeners then were invited to see the story window. The "windows with stories" proved the most popular with both adults and children. In one situation the story windows led to creative writing, for pupils were invited to write synopses of the picture window stories for the local newspaper.

Storytelling is not an activity for one period in the school day nor for special occasions. Every phase of school work, be it history, science, music, art, or health, has its story possibilities. The alert teacher seizes every opportunity to use this universal method of sharing experience.

CHAPTER 3

Composition

The desire to communicate accurately is the learner's best motivation for the development of skills necessary for successful written expression. The teacher who is able to stimulate these desires will be successful in teaching composition. These articles discuss various approaches and techniques.

AS USEFUL AS A TOOTHBRUSH *

Mauree Applegate

WHAT IS CREATIVE WRITING?

What is creative writing, anyway? How is it different from work-type writing? Can *all* children write creatively? How can I get the children in my grade to write? These are a few of the questions I'd like to talk over with you teachers in this paper.

Creative writing might better be called *recreative* writing, since it *recreates* for the reader the experience of the writer.

A child in your schoolroom may write, "I have a dog." Because that sentence is lean in imagery, it may convey little to you. But a child may say on paper, as Nancy did, "Dad flopped his coat into a heap in the middle of the kitchen floor: Then out of the pocket waddled the cutest roly-poly pup! Her little white paws were so clumsy she seemed to always be stumbling over them." And Nancy's pup waddles right out of the page into your heart.

As we read such a re-creative description, we begin to experience this child's dog through her words.

* Reprinted from *A Monograph for Elementary Teachers*, No. 75 (Evanston, Ill.: Harper & Row, 1955), by permission of the author and publisher.

Creative writing does precisely that. It enables us to experience another's feelings through words.

CAN A DEFINITE LINE BE DRAWN BETWEEN CREATIVE AND WORK-TYPE WRITING?

In general, work-type writing tends to appeal more to the sense, and creative writing more to the senses. But bear in mind that the more senses writing appeals to, the more sense it makes to the reader, for our five senses are the antennae through which we learn. An article or book creatively written provides five doorways to the mind: sight, sound, smell, hearing, and touch. The right words can produce Keats's "unheard melodies" in the ears of the mind; they can cause the olfactory nerve to quiver with scents distilled from fragrant phrases; they can rebuild the writer's experience. To be fine, all work-type writing must take on some of the characteristics of creative writing.

IS CREATIVE WRITING A USEFUL ART TO TEACH CHILDREN?

I truly believe so for five reasons:

1. Creative writing is a necessary social tool. At least ninety per cent of all writing done by the average adult takes the form of notes and letters. What makes a letter interesting? It is the recreation of the little everyday happenings in the lives of our friends. If we are good letter writers, we paper-talk across the miles; and if we write well, our letter has been a real visit between two—a reliving through the medium of words.

How about business letters of application? Someday this school child will be applying for a job. Do you suppose he is ever going to get that job, unless his letter stands out from the others because it has taken on his personality? A letter is a word-photograph of the writer; it must be individual if it is to attract attention.

Suppose a young teen-ager is writing a letter of complaint to a department store about a blouse that was not up to specifications. Somehow or other she must make the adjustor at the receiving end feel just as she felt when she received the faulty merchandise. In the world of business, letters, to be effective, must be creative.

Then there is that report a child must write for the school club about his paper trip to Norway. How effective is a report which tells *where, when,* and *how* he traveled, but neglects to appeal to the five senses? Creative writing is as useful and necessary in a child's life equipment as manners and a toothbrush.

Since creative writing, then, seems to be one of the most useful of the arts, we teachers must start the habit early in a child's school living and refine the ability in each grade. And yet, in many schools, filling in blanks and answering true-false statements virtually take the place of any creative writing—and children enter adulthood unequipped with this major tool of gracious and effective living.

2. Creative writing helps the teacher understand the child. We must teach each child—not the class is the premise on which today's education is based. But since so many children have learned to roll up their secrets and put them behind shuttered windows when they come to school, how hard it is to get to know each child. How to get behind those shutters and find the real child is the aim of every true teacher. Although a single piece of creative writing seldom tells *all* about any youngster, each piece may add to the total picture in a teacher's cumulative file.

This excerpt from *Helping Children Write* [1] was just another indication of a condition of almost total frustration in a fifth-grade child's feelings about his home conditions:

We are always in trouble breaking windows with the baseball. When we paint, we paint our faces. Our mother does not know who we are. When we look at books, we rip the good pages. When we climb trees, the policeman comes after us. Then our mother makes us stay in the house. It is trouble, trouble, trouble!

A child, in an imaginative story, may hide behind a fictional character he has created; but the character is often made in his own image, yet daring to do what the child himself lacks courage even to attempt.

Yes, an astute teacher can learn much about her school children from their writing.

3. Creative writing is a safety valve. Each year on the program "Let's Write," on Wisconsin's School of the Air, the children are urged to write out their gripes and frustrations.

Can you imagine how much better this seventh-grade boy felt after he got this bit of writing out of his system?

I think practicing is worth while to a certain extent, but when it comes to slave labor that's the limit. Siberia is nothing compared to an hour and a half of working your fingers and your lips to the point where you think they are going to fall off. I come home for lunch, practicing . . . after dinner, practicing! I go to bed at night. What do I dream about? Practicing! Books are black and white. What do they remind me of? Practicing! I go to

---

[1] Mauree Applegate, *Helping Children Write* (Evanston, Illinois: Harper & Row, 1954).

orchestra. What do we get there? Practicing. There's a trumpet at the bottom of every glass of milk I drink. I could be playing football and get everything knocked off. But no, I'm practicing and getting my fingers knocked off.

In these days of child pressures—living in a yardless apartment, being a dangling part of a broken home, feeling oneself a member of a minority group—a child needs to use every possible chimney or valve to release his tensions. Creative writing is one easy means to this end.

4. Creative writing can give shy children something to be proud of.
Pride is the starch limp souls often need to buffet the brisk winds of living. The shy, retiring child is often the "writingest" child. Even though he may not be a universal favorite, if his poem or story or letter gains a place for him in the sun of approval, creative writing in the schoolroom has been worth while—for him.

5. Creative writing gives the teacher a chance to discover and encourage the talented child. Outstanding ability in any of the creative arts should not be lost, and the world be deprived of another contribution it needs. Although a teacher must be careful not to overpraise any child-masterpiece—since overpraise tends to stifle rather than develop—she still should encourage early signs of talent in a child.

Note the unusual insight in this third-grade child's perception. Her teacher writes:

Jean, in my third grade, is an exceptionally book-conscious girl. By the end of the year she found it difficult to find a book to read in our well-supplied library. One day she approached me saying, "I'm glad there weren't any books left to read because otherwise I would have never read any poetry. They aren't books, you know. Poems are the minds of my best friends."

I suggested she write a poem using this idea. This is the result:

We don't know what the birdies think
How they know what to eat
And how they know what to drink,
But poems know what they think.

We don't know what's in the mind of bees
Why they fly instead of walk
Why they make honey and never make cheese
They seem to know they can't do as they please.

This little poem even knows me
It tells you what I think
I never told him, don't you see
And I'm not even a birdie or a bee?

It is appalling to think how often, in the elementary grades, unusual talent starves from lack of encouragement.

Indeed, creative writing *is* an art useful to children—more useful than drawing and painting, useful to even more people than is music.

BUT CAN I TEACH THE CHILDREN IN MY ROOM TO WRITE CREATIVELY WHEN I CAN'T EVEN DO IT MYSELF

I believe I can answer you best by countering with another question: "You can teach children to paint and draw effectively without being an artist yourself, can't you?"

A teacher is an artist at releasing the arts and abilities in *others*, not in *herself*. Creative writing cannot be taught; it can only be released and guided. A teacher of creative writing needs to stimulate children to write, not to be a writer herself. Often the quietest teachers are the most stimulating. No, indeed! A teacher need not be talented in writing to lead children to write.

HOW TO GET CHILDREN TO WRITE

I promised you, didn't I, that in this article I'd not only answer your questions about writing, but I'd actually help you in the techniques of helping children? Of course, this is only a monograph, not a whole course in creative writing; but we can get a good start right here and now. Shall we be general first and then specific?

1. Create a writing climate in your schoolroom. Don't hurry as if the devil were after you all day (even if he is)! Have a spirit of largeness abroad in your room. Creativity grows most easily in mild climates. Take time in your schoolroom to enjoy things. Even plants do most of their growing at night when things are quiet.

2. Teach children to be see-ers. Stop to study real people the children know and talk about, and imaginary people they get acquainted with in books, and in pictures of faces, hands, and animals. With them, study the story that is there to see. Lead your children to read stories from chance encounters on the way to school, from animal tracks, and, easiest of all, from pictures. A writer must, first of all, *see*. Get a youngster to notice just how a hungry cat acts; just how his dog comes to meet him. First let him pantomime and then write what he has pantomimed. Writing is just a written fact of seeing.

3. From the short stories and books you read, interest the children in picturesque expressions. Picturesque speech is the beginning of creative writing. A little boy wrote of his cat, "fresh as a pillow in a case because she has washed her face." Later in the same poem he says, "off she goes like water spurting out of a hose." A first-grader told his teacher that the hole where his front tooth had recently been felt "like a pond with fish swimming in and out." This is picturesque speech because the sentences are images, and imagery is a short cut to understanding.

    4. Read fine poetry and prose to your children every day. Literary taste is developed gradually. One's taste comes from what he lives with. Children who hear poetry can more readily make poetry. Children who grow up with stories can more easily write stories. *Read to the children every day* if you would have them write.

    5. Let writing be a challenge in your room, not a chore. Daily give the invitation to write. When a story idea pops up, suggest that somebody develop it. Have a stimulating bulletin board which fairly calls out to the passerby, "What story do I suggest to you?" Make poems and stories together. Children who can never write well alone get a real feeling of having a part in a co-operative poem or story. Keep a story box where children can slip in their private writings unseen. Make writing a privilege, not a chore.

    Getting children to write, then, is like getting a garden to grow. First the climate and soil must be right. Later, at the proper time, we must plant some seeds and provide the proper care, keeping the soil loose and moist.

    Let's talk together a moment about this business of planting the seed. Do you know that some of you teachers would make mighty poor gardeners? *You never plant any seeds or get the seedbeds ready!* At least, you don't in your creative writing classes!

HOW TO PREPARE CHILDREN FOR WRITING

    For years we have hesitated to have much discussion before the writing begins, lest children copy someone else's idea. Shall we look at this matter of creativity squarely and with reality?

    Suppose that each woman in a group of ordinary club women decides to create a hat. Where will these women get their ideas?

    An exceedingly small group at the top will, from their own inventiveness, create true originals which will bring admiring "Oh's" and "Ah's" from their less creative sisters. An even smaller group at the other extreme will exclaim, "I just can't make one!" and fail the assignment. But the majority of those women will study *Vogue* or *Mademoiselle,* will try on hats in millinery shops, will take an idea from here and another from there, and will produce a fairly good creation and perhaps an original one. Some creative minds are just not self-starting.

    In creative writing the analogy holds. If ideas are suggested and talked over by all the children before writing begins, all those who need help will be helped; and the truly creative writers will not be hindered. The creative artists can help the less creative with ideas without in any way making copyists of themselves. To the truly inventive, thinking up a new idea is a challenge, but using the idea of another is anathema. If you do not agree with this statement, experiment with groups of children in any grade. The results may astonish you.

This "getting-ready" period will not be at all a teacher's getting her ideas into the heads of children.

But, wait—I'll explain just what I *do* mean—

WHAT ARE THE SPECIFIC STEPS IN GETTING CHILDREN READY FOR CREATIVE WORK?

I believe there are two essential steps which must precede classroom creativity of almost any sort: the first, *enriched experience;* the second, the *I-W-S formula.*

Let's start with the first step—enriched experience.

Natalie Cole in *Arts in the Classroom* (one of the most delightful books I have ever read) says, "Children cannot create out of a vacuum." Creation comes out of richness of some sort—experience either real or vicarious.

All children want to write if they have something to write about. Words bubble right out when a youngster has something to say. All this is what I mean by experience. If a teacher will help a child to grow rich in experience, that child will usually be more than willing to share his riches in writing. A *doing* schoolroom can easily become a *writing* schoolroom.

The best kind of experience is real, of course, not vicarious, but so facile are children's minds that vicarious experience is almost real to them. Via a *unit* or *experience learning,* children visit the whole world without leaving Forty-seventh Street. They read factual material about Mexico, study Mexican art, sing or listen to Mexican music (even create music of their own).

Vicariously, in storybooks, they wander hand in hand with Pedro or Manuel and learn to feel as he feels. These characters come alive in movies shown in the school theater. If the teacher is alert, she can locate a visitor who formerly lived in Mexico, who will talk to the children. If possible, the whole class can visit a Mexican home or a Mexican exhibit or, better still, interview Mexican children. Modern-day learning in the social studies is far from the anemic experience hinted at in popular magazines. The teaching of the social studies has left the flat page of the geography book and has gone three-dimensional; it is a present teaching, drawing on the past, and projecting itself into the future.

Such richness of experience cries out for expression. Think of the opportunities in such learning for creative writing: poems in which the child can pretend to be a Mexican donkey, a fighting cock, a flower seller, a market woman, or a sombrero talking to himself. Before the children realize it, they find themselves taking an adjective tour across Mexico, decribing every sight and sound with technicolor words. What a chance to write warm, friendly letters to pen pals in the Kingdom of Flowers to the south of us! What an opportunity to inform parents in a letter home about "that wonderful trip to Mexico!" What a stimulation for creating skits and dramatizing stories! To tell the truth, creative writing is a more natural end product of rich schoolroom experience than a grade on the report card.

Richness *just must have* an outlet. Experience must, therefore, precede creative expression.

And now what about that second step before creative writing—formula mixing?

This particular mix has to do with the *I-W-S* formula: *ideas, words,* and *stimulation.* Leave out any one of these three, and the result may be worse than the homemade cough syrup Grandpa used to make.

So that *all* the children will write, the noncreative must be stimulated by the creative. Let us take a real situation and think it through together.

In my fifth grade (one with which I often experiment) I have an average group of boys and girls—only three unusually gifted in the writing field. We have just finished a unit in the social studies on the opening up of the West, and every child has been able to experience, vicariously, many of the feelings and fears of the early pioneers.

Today I am getting the whole group ready for writing. I sell them on the idea that it would be fun on our sharing day with the parents to read or tell our own adventure stories as we sit around a "pretend" campfire. This must have been a proper sort of stimulation, since the whole bunch are wildly enthusiastic over the idea. (This is the S ingredient of the *I-W-S* formula: *Stimulation.*)

"What sort of adventures might pioneers want to talk over?" I question the class. Immediately ideas begin to flow. That Indian attack which they successfully routed, the time a scout got lost, that adventure with a grizzly, the day the horse broke its leg, the evening the covered wagon collapsed in midstream. The ideas run on until I laughingly stop them and say, "Yes, any of these and a dozen more you may think of later—the more different the idea, the better. Choose your own or think of a different one. (This is the *I* of the formula: *Ideas.*)

"And now, for such good ideas, we shall need technicolor words and phrases," I point out.

From pictures or from memory of moving pictures, we try to translate into words the landscape over which the pioneers traveled: rocky terrain, low hummocks, wind-swept mesas, barren wastes, fruitful valleys, prairies as level as a floor. Together we find words to express how the wagons jolted and lurched over the ruts and the boulders.

Whenever the children were low in suggestions for any area, I added a few picturesque phrases or apt words to the list. (The function of the teacher here is to guide and enrich—*not* to dominate.)

Together we tried to find words to express the wide reaches of the sky, the skyscraper aspects of canyon walls. We discussed how pioneers walked in their hard-soled boots; how their faces looked at night around the campfire. (This was the *W* of the *I-W-S* solution: *Words.*)

"Ah," but I can hear you say, almost in chorus. "But we haven't *time* to teach like this!"

May I say this to you? If we write less often in our schoolrooms and write better, we shall truly help our children to improve.

Yes, and not only can one improve the children's creative writing with the *I-W-S* formula, but think of the practice in social imagination the children will get. We are entering a new era in which we must feel as the other fellow feels: when the man who sits in the office running the business must get into his muscles the feel of the man who mines the coal; and the miner who does the actual work must learn the strain and the long hours of the man who runs the business. Our very life in the days to come depends on creative imagination. Truly the concomitants of the preparatory period are almost as important as the writing itself—perhaps more important.

Will this kind of preparation make all the children write alike? I have never found this to happen except in the cases of those who never could have any ideas of their own. And, pray, where are such people to get ideas if not by catching them from others? Catching is better, is it not, than copying from a book?

May I submit to you copies (complete with misspelling and mispunctuation) of four bits of children's writing? These youngsters had been studying clothing and had just had their last study-lesson about wool, following which their teacher had used the *I-W-S* formula. The results tell us a great deal, not only about the individual youngsters, but about what the same formula can do for different children.

Billy the Lamb

Hello! I'm Billy lamb, its spring on Uncle Johns farm. All the lambs are being born today. The ewes are as busy as bees, right this very hour I am two hours old, we're not the only baby's on the farm, their's colts, calf's, and even piglets, as we walk around on our shaky legs, and nibble at the grass that sticks up. We bleat a little bit, and then stop, theirs so many noise's their's baa's, duck's, quack's and even little squeeks from piglets. O hum I'm getting sleepy all ready. Oh! look at the sun in the west isn't it pretty mother, oh well here come's Uncle John Boy! He must be having some fun, do you know what he's doing, he's running us into the shed. Weeeew, that was the fastest run I ever had in 2 hour's O hum well good night.

by Mark Edward

The Story of Blackie a Little Lamb

I am a baby sheep. They call me a lamb. They call my mother a ewe and my father a ram. My name is Blackie. They call me that because I have black wool. My masters name is Patsy. I don't know why they call her that though. I asked my mother but she didn't know either. She told me to forget about it. One day when Patsy came out she told me I was to be sheared. I wondered what that was but I soon found out. They took me into a garage. They took some funny thing and cut all my wool off. It was summer so I didn't get cold. I wondered where it was going. I found out when I got older. Here is the story. First they put it into bags. Then it was sent to a factory. There they soded it into long and short threads. They put it into a big tank and men stirred it until it was clean, then they rinsed it. Then they dyed it. Some of it was woven and some was made into yarn. It was made into sweaters and other things. Could you guess how I found out? Patsy told me but she said maybe she wasn't exactly right but that was all she knew.

by Cele

Strawberry the Lamb

One day a little lamb was born and do you know who it was it was "me." They call me "Strawberry." One day some people took my mother away from me. I got so mad that I got my nose caught in with the piglets. The mother pig thought it was pig food and she took a bite of my "nose."

by Carolyn

The Spinning Wheel and the Mouse

Once there was a spining wheel. He was very tired of spining wool every day. When he wasn't so busy he would talk to a little mouse in the corner. His name was Sardine. I don't know where he got such a name, but he just got it. Every day they got together and talked and talked. One day the mouse said to the spining wheel, where does wool come from? From sheep said the spining wheel. How did you know said Sardine. Oh I heard some men talk about it. About what asked the mouse. Sheep silly said the spining wheel, and stop asking silly questions. Alright then I'll never speak to you again. So till this day mice and spining wheels never talk again.

by Mary Jean

Is creative writing a useful art for children? When I read what the most ordinary of them has written and know that I had an infinitesimal part in helping him to *see* and *feel* and *say* just a little better, what is in his heart, I feel as if I had just come into a great deal of money.

May I close with a fifth-grade boy's prayer, which his teacher sent me from Michigan?

> God, keep the trees growing beautiful
> God, keep the streams going beautiful
> God, keep the world going beautiful.
>   Amen.

CHILDREN COMMUNICATE THROUGH *WRITING* °

Helen E. Buckley

A CHILD'S REAL MIND

"Perhaps you've wondered how a child can see things you never dreamed about. Well, I happen to be one, so I shall tell you in my own words what I think about it.

"I think it is a wonderful thing when you have a good imagination. You can be out West, or in space, or in a plane. You can be anything you want to be and do anything you want to do there.

"Another mighty power of a very small child is that he is always the center of attraction, and likes it—ha, ha! A child is a very delicate thing. It can be hurt very easily on the inside as well as on the outside. It is a stronger thing than a hundred tanks or four forts, because in its own way it can capture your feelings, and your feelings are one of the most precious things to you and to the child.

"A child will always try to please you in his or her own way."

Thus did a nine-year-old boy write to his fourth-grade teacher, revealing not only his inmost thoughts but also his feelings toward his teacher. If he had not regarded her as an acceptant person who recognized that small boys have other thoughts along with baseball, snakes and television, he would not have been able or willing to express his feelings in such a fashion.

° Reprinted from *Childhood Education* (February 1960), Vol. 33, No. 4, by permission of the Association for Childhood Education International, 3615 Wisconsin Avenue, N. W., Washington 16, D.C.

Acceptance, respect for another's ideas, provision of time, opportunities, and materials are the ingredients which encourage a child to be creative in his writing.

LANGUAGE FIRST

Before writing, however, there must be many language experiences in which a child discovers his ability to put ideas together so that they convey meaning to others. If in the course of these experiences a teacher or parent records these ideas, the child begins to understand the nature and scope of writing. Written down, his story can be read not only today but tomorrow—next week— next month! Written down, his story can reach persons who are not even present for the original telling—his parents, an absent child, his brother in the room upstairs! Written down, his story is preserved forever!

BEGINNINGS OF STORIES

The 5 year olds who dictated stories to me, their kindergarten teacher, did not consciously *think* all these things about writing; but I am sure they *felt* them. They began by describing their drawings and paintings—first with single words, then with phrases, then with sentences, and finally with such lengthy stories that a typewriter and separate paper were needed.

As the year progressed, we discovered that pictures were not the only beginning place for a story. In fact, some of our favorite stories in books required that the listener make his own pictures—in his mind. An invitation was extended to all would-be storytellers that their "pencil person" would be available during activity time should they want something written down.

To this day I can see Butch—red-haired, lively—sitting across from me at the table, his chin supported with both hands, dictating slowly and thoughtfully. He was my first "customer," patient with my slowness in getting all the words down:

Today I was going out to hunt rabbits. But I decided not to. Do you know why? Because it would be horrid to hunt. You see a rabbit—and he runs away because he is afraid of you. I know where I saw *one* rabbit. Patty and I were going along and talking. We went past a clump of weeds. We heard something in the weeds. Out came a rabbit—hop, hop, hop. He had a brown back, a white cotton tail, and long ears. His ears didn't flop over, they stood up straight.

Today I said to myself: "Maybe I could go rabbit hunting, I'd get a couple of boys—I wouldn't get Freddy, he makes too much noise going through the woods! I would take two guns—one in my holster and one in my hand. We would go toward the water—One boy would go one way, and one would go the other. I would come up through the weeds, and there would be the bunny!"

How pleased he was with his story and with himself! How delighted when I read it to the group! Even Freddy beamed over his part in the story.

I learned early to be very quiet during these dictated stories— asking no questions, raising no eyebrows, but endeavoring to afford as much privacy to the author as he would have were he able to do his own writing. (It is difficult to organize one's thoughts if someone— even with the best intentions—keeps interrupting!) At the story's end, and during the reading of it to the group—if the child so desired or requested—interest, comments, even suggestions would be forthcoming.

PLAY WRITING

Greg wanted to write a play one morning. He asked if he could dictate "first thing" so that we would have time to "put it on." He promptly proceeded in a most businesslike manner: "Place: Hippety-Hop Town." Then followed an exciting tale involving three rabbits, some grapes, and a giant who might have been borrowed from *Jack and the Beanstalk*. In true five-year-old fashion, however, when the excitement became too much to bear, the three rabbits went home; and Mrs. Rabbit made a lovely grape pie! Fifteen minutes after the play had been written, the characters were chosen, the stage set, and the play presented—with Greg sliding into the role of author, stage director, manager and actor!

IMMEDIATE SHARING

It was not always necessary to "do something" with our stories. Like painting and block building, much of the joy was in the doing and in the immediate sharing. Occasionally, we would invite the children across the hall to hear some stories or to see a play.

When I taught six- and seven-year olds, however, this was not the case. These children wanted to take their stories home—they would illustrate them, make them into books, put them on the reading table, and add individual touches in their own handwriting. Their stories did not seem compelled to end on a "comfortable note"—people were always getting "eaten up," animals were being "shot dead," and humor was becoming more subtle. Robin's story, for instance, was dictated in a strictly serious voice and only the twinkle in the author's eye gave him away:

Once upon a time there was a beetle hopping on a hill.
He was gay and happy until a wolf came.
The beetle ate the wolf up!
Five hundred more wolves came.
The wolves got scared by the beetle!
They ran so fast they jumped into Snake River.
The beetle hopped into the river.
He saw his friends the tiger and the whale.
The beetle drank and drank—
But burped just in time!

CHILDREN'S STORIES READ

I remember the day well that we took our "Collection of Stories" to the children's library so that "Miss Rounds would have another book to read to the children who came there." How delighted they were on a future occasion when Miss Rounds, sitting down for the usual story, picked up *their* book and announced: "I have the most wonderful collection of stories here! Let me read some of them to you."

VALUES

"And where," you might ask, "does the teacher find time to be this 'secretary person'?" My answer is a simple one. I believe that we *find* time—no matter how busy we may be—to do that which we think is valuable. Creativeness does not flourish when one is in a hurry. For the following reasons I believe that creative writing is a valuable experience for children:

When we accept a child's story, we are accepting *him*, fulfilling in part one of the primary goals of education.

When we read his story to the group, we are giving him status, fostering good feelings among the listeners, and providing opportunities to learn respect for another's thoughts and ideas.

The writer himself builds confidence in himself as a worth-while person who can "do things." He experiences the satisfaction of seeing his thoughts and feelings transmitted into form.

The writer is given one more avenue of communication with the people of his world through the magic and the power of words. The whole world of literature opens before him, and he knows—because he *is* one—of the particular gift of self which the storyteller gives.

For these reasons I made time in my program for creative writing and gladly wielded my "silent pencil" and my "not-so-silent typewriter."

LIFELINES FOR TEACHERS OF COMPOSITION *

Sister M. Claude, S.C.C.

Two distress signals from the communications area on a single Saturday morning would force any teacher to the rescue. The first SOS sounded, "I love teaching grammar—but composition? I can't get the children to write a single straight sentence."

The second message wasn't coded at all. In a meeting of 600 upper-grade boys and girls, only two dared to offer an opinion on ideas previously outlined and conscientiously prepared. That frustrated teacher's admission was foolproofed. It is not the intention here to ask anyone to assume blame; I hope to offer some suggestions to upper elementary grade teachers that may clarify their position as teachers of English and assist them in meeting one challenge of their profession.

What is the usual procedure in teaching composition? Isn't it paging through one handbook after another in search of a list of suggested topics for paragraphs? Next day the confident teacher strides into her classroom sure of victory. Bewildered, uninterested pupils are offered a generous ten subjects about which they know nothing (and care less) and teacher fidgets for the moment when she can settle down to gloat over perfected themes ready for publication. To be sure, she will have helped. Outlines taught; picture words coaxed from Webster's thousands! Lo! The results do not meet her expectations; discouragement, even disgust, grips and causes her to ejaculate, "I can't make them write a straight sentence."

Let us here and now convince ourselves that "to write a straight sentence is not the prime objective in teaching language." In composition we compose; we put together. We put ideas into spoken or written symbols. First, then, teachers must aim to help the child discover his own ideas, things worth communication.

NO THOUGHTS, NO WRITING

The logical playback is, "What do you consider 'worth communicating?'" Any deed done, any project contemplated, any idea con-

---

* Reprinted by permission of the publisher from *Catholic School Journal* (Milwaukee: The Bruce Publishing Co., May 1962).

ceived, any person met is valuable. In general, anything worth saying is worth writing in one of the many types of written composition. Waiting for the extraordinary is wasting time. Life is not a succession of blue ribbons, expense-paid tours, or even of football games, yet people talk, and enjoy it. Their listeners, too, enjoy it; they do not turn a deaf ear because the topic would not make headlines.

Discovering these sources of ideas with the pupils may challenge our initiative, but it's worth the effort. We are teachers of language and language is the expression of thought. One workable attack is this: Pair off your class. Tell each couple to speak together for a few minutes. Afterward, have them write their message to the same neighbor in note form. Every child has a topic. Heads bend over papers. Pencils write; they are not being chewed. Given the topic, all concentration can be put on the manner of expression and on all the niceties of usage and punctuation we teachers love.

Or—begin the composition class with: "If you had time to talk now, to whom would you speak?" Write the name on line 2. "What would you say?" Write that on line 1. "What would you tell about the subject?" Jot down those ideas. Now say it on paper.

The best start in creative English is, I believe, the writing of social letters. Assure delivery by having the children write on stationery, address an envelope, lick on the stamp, but hand it in unsealed for the teacher's enjoyment. My class wrote in this way to the ladies at an old-folks home. No, the letters were not error free, yet all but two carried an interesting message.

Why stress the letter form? Solely, to have *someone* with whom to communicate. The only thing more uninteresting than talking to oneself is talking to no one. Yet isn't that what we expect of our pupils when we assign *that* paragraph from *that* list of suggestions. We had better admit that we're starting with two strikes against us. First, the youngster has no reason for writing since he is not communicating with anyone. Letter writing gives direction, dedication, to the written word. Someone is listening. He must make himself clear.

Sister M. Chrysanthe's "Secrets of Good Writing" published in the *Chicago Sunday Tribune Magazine* of October 16, 1960, emphasizes just that point as *the* essential of effective writing. Although "viewed from a college window" Sister's suggested technique of writing for a real live reader can be used with simplification in our upper elementary composition classes.

When once we move on to the noncorrespondence type of writing, we can and should retain the dedicatory note. The theme is humanized, the pen stimulated. As suggested by Sister M. Chrysanthe, have the student write, for example, about "Allowances" and then address his writing "To My Dad."

THINK IN THE PRESENT TENSE

Strike number two is our failure to realize how truly children live in the fast-moving present. It's what is tickling his tongue *right now* that he wants to drop from his pen. Someone may retort: "All children have seen a circus, so surely they can write about one"; or, "Every child likes money, so he'll have no difficulty telling what he'd do with a ten-dollar bill." But, dear teacher, the circus was in town last year, and the ten-dollar bill is nonexistent. I hold, that our first duty in teaching composition is to assist the child to dig up ideas from his own mine of experiences, reactions, likes, quirks. Our second responsibility is to help establish with him a flesh-and-blood reader.

To avoid the monotony of third-person writing, instruct the children in the delightful use of apostrophe. Now the subject of the theme becomes the main character in a "This is Your Life" production.

An excellent start in this kind of composition is the "Dear Diary" approach. But don't strike out without careful preparation. Read excerpts to the children from some literature of that type (*The Diary of Anne Frank* would well suit the purpose), so that they can begin to relish the flavor. Tuning the mind in this way whets the mental appetite and will prevent near collapse when you announce: "Today we shall write an entry in a make-believe diary. Think over your actions and reactions since you got up this morning. Tell your diary about them." With both topic and listener clearly established, the child is off to a good start.

USE THE CLASS PARAGRAPH

No, you need not discard the class paragraph. It's too essential to the teaching of good sentence patterns to be ousted. Your educational eyes and ears are keen. (Ask any of your pupils.) Tune in before class, on the playground, during intermission. When your radar detects a general-interest topic, attack: Joan's new skirt, Mary's third case of measles, Dick's latest hobby of raising turtles, Tom's brand-new, four-pound sister! No matter what your daily plan has scheduled, detour. Time is ripe for a free-for-all theme.

When sleuthing has brought no meaty ideas for class writing, try what Jacob W. Getzels and Philip W. Jackson of the University of Chicago call "stimulus" pictures. The October 31, 1960, issue of *Time* (p. 53) presents these two psychologists' stand on the invalidity of IQ's. Assuming creativity to be a mark of giftedness, they tested 500 teen-agers' IQ's by asking them to glance at a picture and to write an appropriate story.

So start your search for stimulus pictures, dear teacher. Let them assist you to arouse the dormant creative minds in your class. Executed first as an all-class activity, the pupils will get the feel.

STORE UP IDEAS

That we can, in an incidental way, feed ideas to children's minds for later communicative purposes is an opinion supported by successful experiment. Scrapbooks designed to include divisions such as likes, dislikes, daydreams, desires, etc. awaken the consciousness that such reactions exist for and in him. Squeezing a "time-out-to-think" five minutes between the square root of 144 and the altitude of Mt. Kilimanjaro is another suggestion for such vitaminizing. Connotative thinking about colors, numbers, grass, can be induced with simple questioning: "What comes to mind when I mention blue?" Answering on paper is the best way to assure high-percentage mental activity.

Some titles of young children's books are provocative. *What's a Shoe for* is one such teaser. Well, for what is a shoe, a thumb, or a roof, or an icy road?

Are you perhaps waiting for the next period to ask, "Do you expect these paragraphs to have unity, coherence, and emphasis? Do you suppose that an interesting readable style will come from this kind of procedure?" My answer: No, not immediately. But before you can shine the boots, there must be boots. Polishing a composition, presupposes the composition of an idea in some form—mental or written. The written form is certainly more tangible.

A successful device in learning better expression is the time-honored substitution of a related topic for the one treated in an existing well-executed paragraph. Take, for example, a splendid piece on a dog. Rewrite it in class, using a horse as the subject and making the necessary substitutions. A feeling of accomplishment is, more often than not, the result. Nothing encourages in the field of writing like the taste of success. It awakens not only the desire to articulate, but also the need to hear one's voice or to see it in print.

The suggestions here offered are lifelines tossed out in one direction to the rescue of struggling teachers of English. Listen to the other calls for help. How to correct compositions? How to score them? How to evoke responses in class writing from the mental "shut-ins?" How to get the class paragraph started? Won't someone respond?

TWO ROADS TO POETRY *

Dr. Patrick Groff

Bobby, filled with excitement, brings in a bird's nest he has discovered on his way to school, and his fourth-grade classmates respond with an eager interest. "Ah," many teachers would say, "this is a fine opportunity for a poem to heighten interest, to increase understanding and to affect esthetic sensibilities!" These teachers are generally agreed that the reading or study of poetry should result, whenever possible, from an incident such as this which captures the thoughts and emotions of a large portion of their classes.

A good poem to use in such an occasion, our hypothetical teachers might decide, would be *What Robin Told* by George Cooper. It relates in an understandable and straightforward way an actual, real-life phenomenon, and yet is movingly poetic in its use of figurative language, imagery, strong rhyme and rhythm, and through its colorful, descriptive words. At the same time, it is short enough to create a single over-all mood.

How do robins build their nests?
  Robin Redbreast told me—
First a wisp of yellow hay
In a pretty round they lay;

Then some shreds of downy floss,
Feathers, too, and bits of moss,
Woven with a sweet, sweet song,
This way, that way, and across;
  That's what Robin told me.

Where do robins hide their nests?
  Robin Redbreast told me—
Up among the leaves so deep,
Where the sunbeams rarely creep,
Long before the winds are cold,
Long before the leaves are gold,
Bright-eyed stars will peep and see
Baby robins—one, two, three;
  That's what Robin told me.

* Reprinted from *Grade Teacher* magazine by permission of the publishers. Copyright 1961 by Teachers Publishing Corp.

How then to proceed? At this point there seem to be decidedly different opinions.

With Bobby, the bird's nest and the class interest accomplished facts, let's see how two different hypothetical teachers reacted.

TEACHER NUMBER ONE

This teacher held the *hands-off* point of view. As soon as Bobby finished showing his bird's nest and noting the interest of the class, the teacher said, "Boys and girls, a poem has been written by Mr. George Cooper about robins and their nests. Would you like to hear it?" They agreed and she read the poem. When finished, she simply waited quietly for any reaction from the class. There was none, so the poem was dropped and the class moved on to its next activity. If there had been any statements by the class about the poem's meaning, language or effect, she would have accepted them attentively but without comment.

This point of view contends that the best way to develop understanding of, appreciation of, and sensitivity to poetry is not to study or analyze it. It views children as "naturally" poetic and therefore needful of little direct instruction in poetry. As a result, no poetry period as such is included in the language-arts curriculum.

A large portion of the material written about children's poetry, it must be said, supports this hands-off approach.

TEACHER NUMBER TWO

But there are those who take the *study-activity* point of view. They feel that poetry does not more "naturally" appeal to children than do other language forms—in fact it may be more confusing. Hence it must be studied in order for true understanding and appreciation to result. These teachers insist that the ability to distinguish the differences between poetry and prose are crucial and must be *taught, not caught*—quite the reverse of the thinking of the hands-off position.

Consequently one of these teachers treated the poem very differently from the one just described. After the class interest in birds' nests was evidenced, she selected and planned to use *What Robin Told* in a later poetry period. First, she had copies made of the poem, both in its original form, and in continuous discourse. Thus the class could easily notice the differing formats and realize that poetry need not always be written in lines and stanzas.

This teacher introduced her poetry period by displaying Bobby's bird's nest again. After reading a poem about birds' nests, she distributed the duplicated poem. Then she read it aloud as the children followed along in their copies. She was convinced that seeing as well as hearing a poem adds to its enjoyment.

The intent and mood of the poem then was discussed. Questions were asked: "What does the poem tell us about robins?" "What kind of man was Mr. Cooper—did he like birds?" "Is this a happy or sad poem?" "Why?" Each child was encouraged to read lines from the poem to make his answers more explicit. The central questions asked in the poem (such as *How do robins build their nests?*) were answered. Certain words were clarified: "What is a *pretty round?*" "What is *downy floss?*" "How much is a *wisp?*" Concepts were made distinct: "*Long before the winds are cold* means which part of the year?"

Following this, notice was taken of the meaning of the figurative language in the poem. "Was a *sweet, sweet song* really woven into the nest?" "Do sunbeams actually have feet on which to creep?" "Do stars truly have eyes with which to see?" "Can robins in fact talk to us?" The teacher and her class gave many further examples of figurative, therefore poetic, language in their everyday speech. The teacher, feeling that figurative language is one of the most distinct and distinguishing differences between poetry and prose, read to the class prose restatements of this figurative language to show that this prose did not sound as fitting as the original poetry.

The descriptions given in the poem were recalled. The teacher read the original lines and then the lines without the descriptive words to show how important they were. The class was encouraged to think of synonymous descriptive words that could have been used in the poem. Favorite descriptive lines, phrases or words were read by individual children.

The rhyme scheme of the poem was investigated. The pairs of rhyming words were written on the chalkboard with others added to them by the class. The teacher showed the class the vocabulary of rhymes in her dictionary and read some words that rhymed with ones used in the poem. As study of the metrical scheme of the poem was decided to be too advanced for elementary-school children, it was not attempted. The pupils were lead to discover the refrains of the poem, however, and they pointed out their significance.

The poem was used further by the class in many ways, most of which were creative.

Volunteers agreed to recite certain stanzas from memory during the following few days. Further instruction was given on how these lines should be recited, the rhythm to be used and the words to be stressed.

Some children were willing to find and bring to class other poems about birds to be read in poetry period.

Verse choirs were set up. Stanzas and/or lines of the poem were read by different groups with individuals reading certain dramatic lines, words or questions.

Additional stanzas of the poem were written by the whole class. These began *Why do robins build their nests?* and *Where do robins go when grown?* Following this, individual children wrote additional stanzas.

The poem was set to music. A simple melody was composed by the class which took notice of the refrains and the differing emphases within the poem.

Pictures were drawn of the various activities in the poem. The lines of the poem thus portrayed were remembered and recited as the drawings were shared.

Creative drama was played as the poem was read or recited aloud. Children took the parts of the birds building the nest and of the baby birds.

·Further, the poem was used as an impetus for scientific research. It was determined if robins' nests actually are built the way the poem described them and if the materials as listed were used. The other places robins build their nests were learned. The mating habits of birds and the number and behavior of the birds' offspring were reported on.

THE DIFFERENCES

These two teachers plainly had different opinions about the teaching of poetry. The former objected to what she called the overattention given to a single poem, remarking that many different poems could be read and enjoyed during this time. She alleged that the *study-activity* practice would turn children away from poetry.

The latter teacher denied this, believing that her classes grew to love poetry as their familiarity and understanding of its peculiar language forms and purposes deepened. She contended that at this point children are stimulated to read much poetry on their own. She maintained that the *hands-off* approach will not accomplish any of these purposes.

Here then are two conflicting roads to poetry. Which one will you take?

A GET-BETTER LETTER °

Mauree Applegate

ANNCR: This is *Let's Write* of the Wisconsin School of the Air. And here to help you write a get-better letter is Mauree Applegate.

NAR: Good Morning! Have you ever been flat on your back in bed at home or in the hospital when the mail came and changed a yallery-greenery morning into a flowing-glowing one?

If letters are that much fun for you to get, they must be just as much fun for other people to receive. That's why this morning we're going to learn to write a get-better letter.

This kind of letter is easy enough to write, after you learn how, but there are a few definite how-to's to learn before most of us can become truly good get-better letter writers.

How shall you begin a letter to a sick person? You know that very first line can be either a cheery hello or a cold, clammy handclasp. Which of these letters would you prefer to get? Notice the beginnings particularly. First please read the one from Gloria to Betty, Ray Stanley. Gloria has been having a tussle with rheumatic fever.

READER: Dear Gloria,

How awfully too bad that you will have to stay out of school for six months. We all feel so sorry for you.

You should especially be here now because at school we're having such fun at our Friday night parties. We square dance and have the most wonderful time. And the snacks! We'll tell you all about them when we have time to come to see you.

Love from us all

— Betty

NAR: Let's listen now to Richard's letter, Mr. Stanley—the one he wrote to his friend, Al, when he was out with that football injury.

° Reprinted by permission of the Wisconsin School of the Air, *Let's Write*, No. 22 (Milwaukee, Wis.: March 2, 1960).

READER:

Hi Pal!

Do we miss you! Hurry up and get back so our seventh grade won't be so dead. We haven't had a laugh in a week. The girls in the class are looking sad; they miss you, lad. So get those bones knitted or crocheted or whatever bones do and hurry back.

Even Miss Purvis looks sad, as if to say, "The I.Q. average of this class has gone down considerably since The Brain left us."

Are you lucky, Smarty Pants, to be out when we're learning new kinds of percentage problems. If it weren't for that smart girl with the brains, who sits across from me, I'd be a total loss in math since you left.

If you're smart, Bo, you'll make this absence from school last as long as possible. Or does penicillin make you willin' even to be educated? As for me, I may be down to join you if lessons get any rougher.

So be ready to move those broken bones over any time now.

Your pal, — Al

NAR:

Which one of those notes would you rather receive if you were flat on your back? I guess the answer to that one is obvious! There is a great deal of psychology needed in the beginning of a get-better letter.

Although Gloria meant well, she only made Betty feel sorry for herself by stressing how sorry everybody felt for her. She made Betty feel even worse by stressing the fun she was missing at school.

Richard, on the other hand, stressed how much the class missed Al, and kidded him about breaking his bones. He made Al feel good by telling him that even the teacher missed him. Richard had lots of fun teasing Al. A merry heart does as much good as medicine, the Bible says, and hope and laughter make everybody feel better. Remember, then, that your first rule in writing get-better letters is:

READER:

When writing letters to the sick, make this the gist
Put no accent on what the patient is missing
But on how much he is missed.

NAR:

I'm going to let you figure out the second rule from this gloomy one-sided conversation between Mrs. Brown and her old friend, Mrs. Watt.

READER:

Old Mrs. Watt called on old Mrs. Brown;
She wheezed a little as she sat down.
"Mattie," she said, "You look awful bad;
You're a sight to make a body feel real sad.
There's an awful lot of sickness all over town
Most every family, has at least one down!
The Simonses are sick and Jack and Dean's ailing

And old grandpa Snell is definitely failing.
I must go now, Mattie,
Hope you soon can sit
I just dropped by to cheer you up a bit.
If you're still living and I'm still here
I'll drop by soon with another word of cheer."

NAR:

Can't you just imagine how cheered Mrs. Brown felt after hearing all that talk about how bad she looks and how sick the whole town is! If she doesn't get worse immediately it won't be her friend, Mrs. Watt's fault.

I imagine this conversation tips you off immediately as to that second rule for the writing of get-better letters. Read it, will you please, Mr. Stanley?

READER:

Make your get-better letter a cheerful earful
Never write to sick folk what will make them tearful.
I'll never forget one lady who called on me one time when I was sick. The minute she found out what I had, she exclaimed, "My Aunt Mable died of that!" Then she proceeded to tell me how many of the people she knew had found that illness fatal.

By the time she left, I was so angry at all this "dreary-weary" talk that I decided to get well just to spite the woman. But I've been mighty careful since that day to remember that it's hope not gloom, a sick person needs. It's better not to dwell on the sickness end of a get-better letter, but on the better side of the situation. After all, this is a get-better, not a get-worse letter.

It's always a good idea in a letter to the sick-a-bed to chit-chat a little about some funny little thing that's happened to you since you last saw your friend.

Eighth-grade Carolyn Beth would make even a sick person grin with this description of a night at camp last summer.

READER:

Almost every night some girl had her bed shortsheeted. Thursday night was my night to be tricked. It happened that on that night there had been a banquet. After getting back to the cabin I was quite tired and glad to be getting to bed. I finally was ready and started to get in. All went well until I was half way in. Then I started to feel pop bottles, grass, combs, and even someone's hairbrush. That changed my mind about being tired and I started to laugh. All of a sudden the whole cabin was full of laughter. I found out later that every girl had donated something to the collection in my bed.

NAR:

Well now, we've learned to get off to a positive start and to avoid writing on dreary subjects. What comes next in this better-letter business? The next step is the easiest of all. Fill your letter with little newsy notes you know your sick friend will be interested in. He likes dogs?

Well then describe the new puppies born in your neighborhood. Babies—either animal or human—are always good for a quiet smile. Listen to this Let's Writer Judith's description of the puppy she got for Christmas a few years ago!

READER:

When my little pet gets up in the morning she is really funny. She looks so sleepy with her eyes half open and half closed. Her fur is so messy, but yet, she looks as if that is how it should. When she stretches, her paws spread apart, and her yawn is almost like a baby's. She almost seems like a little child when I come home from school. She jumps right over me and almost knocks me down. Her tail seems as though it might fall off; yet it still keeps on wagging. She certainly acts different when she is afraid. Her tail droops and she hides behind a chair. I will always love my Cindy.

NAR:

Why, a pup like that will wriggle his way into anybody's heart and make him feel better right away. So would this funny mistake Let's Writer, Sue S. told about when she was in grade five. Read that popcorn story, Mr. Stanley. It would make a sick person lose his stitches after an operation!

READER:

"I was mixing the batter for my 'cracked almond' cake when mother said, "Alice dear, don't forget the cracked almonds."

"O.K., Mother," I answered and put the cracked almonds in, mixed the batter and popped it into the oven!

One hour later, I opened the oven and to my surprise burnt popcorn hit me in the face. I opened my mouth to scream but that horrible tasting popcorn flew into my mouth. Just then mother came in to see what all the commotion was about. When she saw what was happening she nearly fainted.

"Alice!" she shouted in astonishment, "What <u>have</u> you done?"

"I didn't look at what I was putting in, and instead of cracked almonds, I put in popcorn," I said with a grin.

NAR:

You see it's just as important to get the right materials in a get-better letter as in a cake! Let's summarize those two get-better ingredients, Mr. Stanley:

READER:

Step 1. In writing letters to the sick, make this the gist;
Put no accent on what the patient is missing
But on how much he is missed.

Step 2. Make your get-better letter a cheerful earful
Never write to sick folk what makes them tearful.

NAR: And now step 3.

READER: Fill your letter with charming and gay
Little happenings of the day.

NAR: We could say all three of these rules in an eight-word slogan:
"For the sick, hope is the right dope."
There now! We're nearly ready to write and some of us are in the same predicament as the mountaineer who complained, "There's a sale on all the cold remedies at the drug store, but—worse luck—not a one of us is sick!"

What are you going to do today in writing time if nobody we know needs a get-better letter? Well the answer to that question is easy! In every hospital in the land are countless children, sick or crippled children, who never get a letter! What joy you could bring to one of these children with a get-better letter. What could one put into a letter to a sick child whom he doesn't know?

Well, of course, you'd just have to do a little introducing of your family—both the two and the four-footed members. I think it might help you to hear this letter from Let's Writer, Randy Figi, when he was in grade five. Randy's letter was written to a new pen pal, and the letter would make any stranger feel at home.

READER: Dear Friend,
Hi! My name's Randall Mig Figi; for short Randy. I'm ten, pretty good sized, and will be eleven August 14. I have blackish brown hair and dark brown eyes.

I have a pet—a small German shepherd. She is mostly black but with a couple of brown spots around the bottom of her legs. She can do many tricks such as roll over, lie down, sit up, play dead, bark, sneeze, sit up on her hind legs, get her tail, and many more tricks. Do you have a pet?

If you would like to know a little bit about my family I'll tell you. Well, I have a mother, a father, and a big sister who will be thirteen in March. Our family is partly Swiss and partly German. Our whole family was born in the United States. My mother's and father's grandparents were from the other lands.

I'm very interested in little miniature army men and everything to do with the army, navy, air force, and marines.

If you could please write to me, I would be very happy.

Your friend — Randy Figi

NAR: If you write to an unknown child in a hospital, write your letter with a light touch and your heart will glow

within you as will the heart of the child who receives it. Be sure to have the letters your school writes accompanied by an explanatory letter from your teacher and to have your name, age, and grade on the outside of your letter so a child your age will be sure to receive it.
Good-bye, now, Get-better Letter Writers!

ANNCR: This has been another program in the Let's Write series. Scripts and narration by Mauree Applegate, Wisconsin State College, La Crosse. Ray Stanley is the reader and producer. This is the Wisconsin School of the Air.

OUTLINING *

DEFINITION, PURPOSE, AND FORM

A written outline is an organized list of related statements of ideas pertaining to one subject. The preparing and writing of a formal outline is so difficult and technical that it is not usually introduced before the fifth grade. In this year a very simple form may be introduced. Pupils of this year are beginning to need the use of such a device with which to prepare reports, oral and written.

The purpose of an outline is to organize ideas in preparation for expressing them in a talk or speech; to organize ideas in preparation for writing them; to organize ideas as a helper to remembering them.

There seem to be two definite steps in the task of outlining: (1) to determine the relative importance and the relationship of ideas; (2) to state these ideas clearly in outline form.

The general form of an outline is always the same. Main topics are designated by the use of Roman numerals, with subtopics identified by the use of capital letters in alphabetical order.

I. Methods of approach, or introduction
   A. Show movie
   B. Using outline discuss author's ideas
   C. Find titles for paragraphs or short reading selections
   D. Plays
   E. Talks, reports
   F. Daily program
   G. Pictures (series)

---

* Reprinted from *The First R* by permission of the Supt. of Schools, Jamesville-DeWitt Central Schools, Board of Education Office, DeWitt, New York.

    H. Books
    I. Building of a house

II. Follow-up
    A. Find main ideas
    B. List subideas
    C. Re-organize subideas under main ideas
    D. Number main ideas with Roman numerals
    E. Letter subideas with alphabetical letters (A, B, C)
    F. Outline form always the same

III. Follow-up practice
    A. Selecting main ideas in games
    B. Arranging rules of games in proper order
    C. Writing an original play
    D. Make up own game
    E. Suggest use of outlining in studying other lessons
    F. Build outline with class
    G. Title of story or paragraph may express main idea

IV. Outline drill
    A. Research assignments
    B. Book reports, oral or written
    C. Study assignments in social studies, health, etc., arranged in outline form
    D. Read article and jumble ideas for the rest of the class to rearrange in outline form
    E. Continue using outline form of preparation in all written and oral reports
    F. From a given outline write as complete an article as pupil is able

V. Outlining highlights
    A. Stress organization of ideas in all oral and written work
    B. Help students see how authors or speakers have organized their material
    C. Discuss ways of introducing a subject clearly and interestingly
    D. Class examples of successful and unsuccessful introductions, contrast
    E. The importance of an adequate conclusion should be discussed
    F. By specific example show how ideas may be arranged in various ways for different purposes
    G. Show how one idea may be broken down or explained (division of a subject must not overlap)
    H. Have students organize their topic
    I. When they have completed this help them see that this organization is called an outline

        I.
          A.
          B.
          C.
        II.
          A.
          B.

III.
   A.
   B.
   C.
   D.

HOW TO TEACH OUTLINING

Subject:

Teaching a simple outline (Fifth grade)

Aim:

To improve reading comprehension by learning to outline

Specific Purpose:

The purpose of this lesson is to teach the building and form of a simple outline. Also to get the children to realize that the main ideas or thoughts in stories and paragraphs are brought into relationship through sub-thoughts or ideas.

Procedure:

Introduction and motivation of the lesson by the teacher: The story that I am about to read to you is about baby elephants. Listen carefully while I read it to you. I shall be wanting you to answer some questions. (Read the story without interruption.)

The Baby Elephant

A baby elephant is a funny looking thing. Its skin is wrinkled like its mother's, and at first, it is covered with soft down. It also has long eyelashes. The little elephant is dark brown in color.

The young elephant seems to be just like other kinds of babies in the way it acts. It loves to play tricks and is very mischievous. It teases other young animals just for the fun of it. Wrestling with other animals and sometimes with the elephant drivers is just part of its fun.

Of course, everyone knows that an elephant likes water and is a good swimmer. It uses its long trunk to spray water over its own back. It must be funny to see an elephant swimming below the surface of the water with only its trunk sticking out.

Discussion:

Questions	Anticipated Answers
1. What did the first part of the story talk about?	1. How the baby elephant looks. (write on board)
2. What did it tell next?	2. The way it behaves. (write on board)
3. What did the last part of the story tell about?	3. How it likes water. (write on board)

After these three things are on the board, letter the first with

    I. How the baby elephant looks
   II. How it acts
 III. How it likes water

Point out to the class that the little story talked about three different things concerning the baby elephant and get from them the answers as to how you numbered them on the board.

Read just the first paragraph again and ask:

Questions	*Anticipated Answers*
1. Who can give me one thing that the paragraph tells about how the baby elephant looks?	1. It looks like its mother with wrinkled skin. It's dark brown.
2. What else does it tell about its looks?	2. It has down on its skin.
3. Do you recall anything else about how it looks?	3. Its eyelashes are long.

(Write the above answers on the board as they are given.)

Follow the same procedure with the following two paragraphs. When finished have the children tell you under which of the three main thoughts to put the above answers. When completed it will look like this:

The Baby Elephant

    I. How the baby elephant looks

      A. Like its mother with wrinkled skin
      B. It has down on its skin
      C. Its eyelashes are long
      D. Dark brown in color

   II. How it acts

      A. Is very mischievous
      B. Teases other animals
      C. Likes to wrestle

 III. How it likes water

      A. Likes to swim
      B. Sprays water over its back
      C. Swims under water

Point out again that the main thoughts told in each paragraph are numbered with Roman Numerals I, II, III. Then that the little thoughts that describe the main thoughts are indented a little under the main thoughts and are lettered with *A, B, C*, etc.

Compare the outline to a skeleton or framework. Such things as the bones in the body, or the framework of a new house might be mentioned to bring a picture to the children's minds. Explain that an outline to a story is the same idea, and as we use an outline, we add to it to make a completed story, report or paragraph.

Assignment:

Have the children copy the outline from the board. Then read them the story again and have them put their pencil on each subtopic as it is read in the paragraph. Using the outline have several of the children retell the story as best they can with the help of the outline.

Suggestions:

1. For written work the next day, have the class rewrite the story from the outline that they copied from the board. Follow up the next day by having some of the written stories read. Ask the class to watch and see if they followed their outline in writing the story.

2. Continued practice may be done by giving the class a simple outline on some familiar subject and asking them to write an article on it with the outline as a guide. Have the class build an outline together from some short story that they have read. Write an uncapitalized and unpunctuated outline for the class to write correctly. Then from the correctly written outline have them write a complete article on the subject.

3. Assign a short topic for research and have the class bring any material they can find on the subject. Put all the different notes on the board. With the class rearrange the notes into main headings and subheadings. Build an outline. Have the children then write a report from that outline.

TEACHERS' CONCLUSION

Continued and long practice is necessary for complete understanding and ease in building and using an outline. It might be well to suggest that the class try studying their other lessons by building outlines for remembering the important facts in their lessons. It may help to make it easier for them.

CHAPTER 4

Handwriting

An examination of the written work of any college class will reveal that there are many individuals who cannot write with ease or legibility. Throughout our schools, writing presents many problems. The articles selected for this chapter are indicative of the efforts to find new solutions to problems familiar to most teachers.

WHY OUR KIDS CAN'T WRITE *

Theodore Irwin

It happened at the climax of evangelist Billy Graham's jampacked religious rally at Madison Square Garden last March. Mr. Graham had ended his fervent address by exhorting all who had made their "decision" to be saved to step forward. Silently, some 2000 men and women surged from their seats, clustered around the rostrum or stood in the arena aisles. Ushers passed out cards on which the converts were to write their names, addresses and church preference.

Suddenly, Mr. Graham raised his hand, and his voice rang over the loudspeaker. "Please, my friends, please print on your cards. It will save us hours and hours of work."

Thus, even in the realm of soul saving, the decline of handwriting in America has been recognized. That we've become a nation of scrawlers is officially attested to by Federal and state government forms, such as income-tax returns and driving licenses, which insist upon the printed word. Slogans like, "Don't Write—Telegraph!" and

---

* Reprinted by special permission of *The Saturday Evening Post.* © 1955 The Curtis Publishing Company.

the increasing reliance on the telephone, typewriter, dictating machines and electronic brains would seem to be making handwriting as obsolete as smoke signals.

When people do write, the results are too often as inscrutable as a waiter's check in a night club. From college, Junior scribbles something that looks like this: "Fgsikl trbumg iazyo dvqun emrekw rf $25. Juln." Memos to milkmen need decoding, and so do shopping lists for husbands. That word "cufflinks" is actually "cornflakes."

Business everywhere is having its handwriting woes. Recently, at the Philadelphia plant of the Minneapolis-Honeywell Regulator Company, accountants discovered an inventory underevaluation of $65,000. It took them over a week, working day and night, to trace the error—enigmatic figures jotted down by an inventory clerk had been read incorrectly. As a result of this and many other snafus, the company felt that "a return to old-style penmanship training was in order." A handwriting program was set up for employees, involving weekly forty-minute sessions for three months.

Telephone companies have long been victims of guess-what handwriting. Despite the automatic-dial system, operators still manually record millions of completed calls every day. In Chicago, the Illinois Bell Telephone Company realized that thousands of dollars were lost each month when illegible toll tickets had to be tossed out rather than chance an inaccurate charge. A scribbled exchange abbreviation could be read as either CO (for Columbus) or CA (for Canal); numerals could be interpreted as 4379 or 4819. Subscriber Herbert Smith, billed for a long-distance call to Pittsburgh, takes violent umbrage because neither he nor his wife and three daughters know anyone in Pittsburgh.

To cut down their losses and time-killing annoyances, Illinois Bell had to bring in Miss Ruth Kittle, former penmanship supervisor in the Topeka, Kansas, schools, to launch a "noble experiment." Using a streamlined method of writing she had originated, Miss Kittle organized special classes for the 4100 Chicago toll and long-lines operators.

In department stores, the Charga-Plate—ostensibly a means of charge-account identification—was introduced some years ago largely to combat hard-to-read names and addresses on sales checks. Still J. L. Hudson's, in Detroit, reveals that 20,000 sales slips representing about $165,000 in purchases are held up in Audit every year, often because of poor writing. The most common rhubarb arises when a scribbled sales check is sent to the warehouse to be filled out for delivery. A few weeks ago, for instance, a customer who had ordered "sleepers with grippers" for her baby received a pair of "slippers with zippers."

In its running battle against handwritingitis, J. L. Hudson resorts to a variety of tactics. One is to send a credit man armed with a fistful of incomprehensible sales checks to the guilty department. As the slips are passed around among the clerks, the credit man shoots his $165,000 question: "What do you think they mean?"

In the better-writing crusade which has become part of Hudson's sales training, employees are permitted to retain their own style, with stress on legibility.

At Bloomingdale's, in New York, salesclerks are being taught to print "because they never learned to write." At Gimbel's, diverse defensive measures are taken. Packages with labels that are not block-printed are stopped at the wrapping department and spot checks are made at the delivery belt. If a package slips through that can't be delivered because of "strangled" handwriting, it is brought back to the sales floor and the culprit confronted with the corpus delicti. At special staff meetings, prizes are offered for the first to decipher a particularly maddening sales check. Gimbel's even stages shows, starring careless Sybil Salesclerk, which dramatize handwritten whodunits.

The United Parcel Service, which delivers packages for stores in thirteen cities, finds poor handwriting an "expensive nuisance." Every day, in one city alone, about 1200 packages are undelivered, frequently because of illegible writing. To educate the stores, United Parcel sends out 6500 comic posters every month to its clients. Each month a new poster bears a different message—one shows a crystal-ball gazer trying to fathom a C.O.D. slip; another has a museum curator deciding that the hieroglyphics on a package are Sanskrit. Although such striking posters have been facing store employees for at least fifteen years, United Parcel sadly admits they have had "no discernible effect" upon handwriting. A black chiffon nightgown, size 12, still mysteriously finds it way to a seventy-two-year-old, 200-pound lady who had ordered a hot-water bottle.

Wherever one turns in the business world, the poor quality of handwriting is deplored. The drug industry, finding it more and more difficult to read orders for pharmaceuticals taken by salesmen—is it "Benzedrine" or "Benadryl"?—commissioned a handwriting publisher to prepare a 152-page text for drug salesmen that takes them through a twenty-seven-week "refresher course." When special checking accounts were introduced twelve years ago, many banks, whose bookkeepers were developing neuroses trying to identify signatures, considered it expedient to have the customer's name imprinted on his checks.

Through no handwriting deficiency of her own, one lady lost a cool $10,000 several years ago because of an illegible signature. After the death of Paul Perret, a New York chef, attorneys sought the two witnesses to his will. But the signature of one of the witnesses baffled the greatest experts of questioned documents. As the identity of this witness hadn't been established, the Surrogate's Court denied probate of the will. Under Perret's will, his $10,000 estate had been bequeathed to a lady friend. Instead, it dropped into the lap of his son.

Poor handwriting may mean the difference between landing a job or being passed over. More and more help-wanted ads ask the applicant to "reply in own handwriting." A survey several years ago, of 100 corporations employing more than 2,250,000 men and women, disclosed that most employers considered good handwriting a vital factor in appraising job seekers. It counted most where the applicant was a recent school graduate, without previous experience. One hospital personnel officer remarked, "I have noticed that employees filling out applications in a sloppy manner are the very ones to be inaccurate and lazy on the job."

Not only the lower echelons on the payroll are afflicted with atrocious penmanship. Last fall, a pencil manufacturer polled 850 secretaries, asking them what they thought of their boss' handwriting. More than forty per cent rated executives anywhere from "hard to read" to "downright impossible." One long-suffering Girl Friday observed, "My boss writes like an Egyptian." The handwriting of aviation executives was worst, with a grade of seventy-five per cent illegibility; architects, grocery, insurance and chemical-industry executives were rated at least fifty per cent incomprehensible. Most legible were educators and building executives.

Fortunately, nurses are required to print, to avoid having a patient treated for "hyperhidrosis" instead of "hypertension," but doctors have long been twitted for their preposterous scribbling. One morning last January a man walked into the pharmacy of William Astmann, in Yonkers, New York, and handed him a doctor's prescription for a narcotic. The druggist took one look at the prescription, asked the man to return in the afternoon, then phoned the doctor. It turned out that the man, a musician, had visited the doctor's office the day before; when his request for narcotics had been refused, the musician had stolen a pad of prescription blanks. After studying a book on prescriptions at the local library, he had forged the narcotics prescription.

What had aroused the druggist's suspicions? "That prescription," said Mr. Astmann, "was too clear to have been written by a doctor."

Perhaps the best-known tale about physicians' handwriting concerns the spider that fell into a doctor's inkwell. Somehow the spider managed to crawl out and walk aimlessly over the doctor's prescription pad, leaving intricate-looking track marks. A nurse, mistaking the sheet for a prescription, sent it to a pharmacist. After an hour of concentrated effort, the druggist, who prided himself on being the only person capable of deciphering the doctor's handwriting, called him up.

"Doc," he said, "I'm sorry, but this time I'm stumped. I just can't figure out the last word you wrote."

The average druggist, declares Prof. Joseph L. Kanig, of the College of Pharmacy at Columbia University, "must stand on his head at least once a day, trying to read what a doctor has written. Then, apologetically, he phones the doctor, perhaps using a subterfuge, saying that the patient spilled water on the prescription and made it illegible. Doctors are very touchy about their handwriting, even though some of their prescriptions look as if they were written with a post-office pen while traveling in the back seat of an ancient car on a bumpy road."

To prevent fatal errors of overdose or incompatible drugs, student pharmacists are taught always to phone the physician if his handwriting is dubious. Many times, however, when the pharmacist isn't sure of the dosage, he'll type on the prescription label: "Take as directed."

Pharmacists themselves are no great calligraphers. In an average class of 100 students, Professor Kanig has to warn at least a dozen students to print their essay-type examinations or their papers will not be graded. The situation is paralleled at other colleges.

Cacography has even crept into politics. A legend persists that an editor attending the Democratic convention of 1920 scribbled on his copy paper for the guidance of his staff: "This is not the time to support James M. Cox." His staff translated the message: "This is now the time —" Reluctant to call attention to its error, the newspaper supported Cox.

Assassins of the written word lurk in every community, as indicated by the 22,000,000 "dead letters" piling up in post offices every year; of these, over 1,000,000 are attributed to illegible handwriting. Every major postal station has special post-office clerks who work "hards"— hard-to-read letters. Most puzzling, the Post Office reports, are those from the South, where the tendency is to run words together like a written drawl and to scrawl a "tail" after a capital letter. "N—, M—," for example, is designed to read "Natchez, Miss."

Most poor writers fail to close o's, dot i's and cross t's. Illegibility, say the handwriting authorities, is also usually due to improper formation of the letters e, n, d, r, a, h and b, especially in making loops on letters that shouldn't have loops, such as t and i. Most frequently confused are the letters o and a, and u and v. Auditors find that most mistakes in digits occur with 1 and 7, as well as with 3, 5 and 8. An outstanding educator gives some simple rules for improving an ambiguous hand: Diagnose your own handwriting for its ailments, use more care in forming letters and numerals, avoid crowding, and always remember that, unless you're confiding to your diary, you're expecting someone else to read your prose.

What's at the root of our handwriting mess? The Railway Express Agency, whose claim-prevention department wages a continual crusade against poorly written labels, has made this comment: "Our general observation is that the quality of penmanship has declined, perhaps due to the fact that it is not sufficiently stressed in grade and other schools."

Many educators feel that the second "R" is not being adequately taught in our schools, and many a hot skirmish at P.T.A. meetings is being fought around it. One such hassle is still dividing the community at Briarcliff Manor, New York.

It started two years ago, when William F. Mattes, Jr., a General Electric executive, learned that his ten-year-old son, Bill, was interested in riflery. Mr. Mattes dug up his diary, notes and rifle scores dating back to his ROTC camp experiences. But Bill could not read his father's handwriting; the boy had never been taught cursive writing—ordinary longhand—at school. Mr. Mattes was shocked.

In a conference with the supervising principal of the Briarcliff schools, Mr. Mattes discovered that only manuscript writing—unjoined single letters, resembling printing—was being taught in all the grades. Mr. Mattes agreed that printscript was a worth-while skill to develop, but not to the exclusion of cursive. Corresponding with the education departments of forty-five states, he found that the general practice was to teach manuscript the first two or three years and then switch to cursive. Talking to Briarcliff graduates, Mr. Mattes heard about the acute embarrassment some had experienced. One young man couldn't open a checking account at a bank because his printed signature was unacceptable.

Backed by thirty other parents, Mr. Mattes protested again and again to the school board last year. But the board's president replied that "the public voice does not dictate school policies." The town was in a furor.

Said Mr. Mattes, "One of the three R's is missing in Briarcliff schools. I don't want cursive writing to be a foreign language to my son. I don't want him to be cut off from the outside world because he can't read letters from his grandparents or his friends in other cities."

The school board, in a lengthy report, retorted that "we're trying to get the students to learn a form of legible handwriting," and argued that the policy was predicated on three aims—legibility, speed and neatness. Unconvinced, Mr. Mattes decided to teach his son traditional script himself; other parents hired tutors for their children. Some concessions have been made by the Briarcliff schools; pupils are now taught to sign their names in lónghand and to read cursive from the fourth grade onward. The controversy still simmers.

While the teaching of printscript exclusively as a cure for illegibility remains a highly debatable issue, it's clear that a great many parents, businessmen and even educators believe that our schools are falling down in the mind-your-P's- and Q's department. The Commerce and Industry Association of New York, querying 288 business firms in fifteen different industries, found that two thirds of the companies maintained that high-school graduates had not been given enough basic training in writing. In a nationwide poll of 596 school systems, three out of four superintendents and principals agreed that in the past generation the penmanship of average students has either declined or remained the same.

One reason for this has been the virtual disappearance of handwriting supervisors and special teachers. In the 1920's there were over 500. During the depression and the emergence of the progressive movement in education most of these experts were dismissed or given other assignments. In the entire state of Texas today, only one town, Bryan, has a special handwriting supervisor. Wisconsin, too, has but a single handwriting expert. California has none at all.

Handwriting is being slighted in our schools, contends Dr. Frank N. Freeman, dean emeritus of the School of Education at the University of California, partly because classroom teachers are being inadequately prepared for it. "The emphasis in teachers' colleges," he says, "has been placed on general education and fundamental professional education instead of training in the technics of teaching. While this is a wholesome change, it was a great mistake to neglect the technics."

Few of our teachers' colleges have a course in the teaching of handwriting. A reverse trend, however, may be visible at Chicago Teachers College, where, after some urging by local business leaders, a specific handwriting course was introduced a couple of years ago. At Brooklyn College, a seventy-one-year-old retired penmanship expert, Max Rosenhaus, has been called in to give lessons to student teachers.

Most teachers' colleges today believe that, in the grade schools, handwriting should not be taught separately but as part of the language arts, which include reading, spelling, composition and grammar. A leading handwriting authority, Dr. Luella Cole, former professor of educational psychology at the University of Indiana, issued this stinging indictment of handwriting teaching: "Everywhere I have gone, I have found handwriting the worst-taught, the most-neglected and the least-understood subject in the elementary school. The progressive movement has done wonders in teaching children to manage themselves and to work together, but it has not been able to cope success-fully with handwriting."

What's wrong with the teaching of handwriting today, according to Prof. Alvina Burrows, of N.Y.U.'s School of Education, is that many children are asked to do too much writing before they've mastered manual dexterity. Writing requires fine muscular control—the co-ordination of about 500 different muscles is involved—and they get tired and tense.

Proper motivation is often lacking, and it's not uncommon for a child to refuse to learn to write. One youngster bothered by *a*'s and *o*'s dashed off a sentence which seemed to say, "This is a warm donut step on it," when he should have written, "This is a worm, do not step on it." Confronted with his hieroglyphics, he merely shrugged. "I'm going to be a barber—why should I have to write?" Another classic case concerns the high-school youth who ignored his handwriting because "I intend to have a secretary."

Greater incentives are necessary, asserts Raymond C. Goodfellow, director of business education in Newark, New Jersey. For years, New-ark has awarded certificates for writing competence, and at one time national contests were conducted which stirred up tremendous interest in penmanship.

Rapidly disappearing from our schools is the organized torture of "push-pull, push-pull . . . and now a nice round oval" drills, soon to be relegated to handwriting's history. The modern era of writing dates from about 1850, when attempts were made to improve the handwrit-ing originally brought over by the Pilgrims. Emphasis at first was placed on the fancy system devised by Platt Rogers Spencer, who announced his intention of presenting a method:

> Plain to the eye and gracefully combined
> To train the muscle and inform the mind.

Spencerian, mainly based on training of arm and hand muscles, "by appropriate movement exercises," went out of style in the early 1900's, and was replaced by a vertical system. The third phase involved the muscular movement, exemplified by Palmer, which has been modified to the present free movement of writing. In the early '20's, educators started to revive the legible, simplified "manuscript" writing used by monks during the fifteenth and sixteenth centuries. By 1929 more than 700 schools throughout the United States had added it to their curric-ula. The late 1930's and '40's, however, saw a swing back to cursive writing.

If we've failed to improve handwriting legibility over the years, the faults are sundry and complex. Educators point to the tensions of our age and talk of the declining need for handwriting in business. Most of them agree that school schedules are too crowded nowadays with other subjects, so that less attention is paid to handwriting in the curriculum and less time spent on practice.

Of course, there are educators who defend the present-day system of teaching handwriting. Several months ago, Frank W. Hubbard, director of the National Education Association Research Division, compared the handwriting of a group of students in 1846 with that of students today. He found that most of the students of a century ago wrote a "crabbed, laborious hand." Today's child, he says, doesn't do as well in the "copybook" writing so admired prior to 1910, but he develops a simple style suitable for almost every purpose.

Most schools today assume that handwriting can be taught, "incidentally" as it is integrated into the curriculum. Proponents of this idea say that utilitarian values are accented in contrast to attempts in the Gay Nineties to make handwriting an esthetic art, with sweeping flourishes and clever furbelows. Handwriting is now considered as a tool of communication, and a child should develop enough skill to meet the demands of school and life. In other words, like architecture and the world in general, handwriting has developed a "more practical style" that can stand up under the pressure of business.

Although the practical style being taught may eventually produce better penmen, businessmen meanwhile are stewing over what to do about the I-can't-read-your-writing trend. Latest declaration of war on illegibility was the formation, last fall, of the Handwriting Foundation, in Washington, D. C. Marshaling their forces behind the foundation are several hundred manufacturers of pens, pencils, greeting cards and handwriting textbooks, as well as educators, calligraphers and businessmen concerned with the problem.

Some crumbs of comfort remain for the adult whose handwriting defies comprehension. According to Herry O. Teltscher, a handwriting psychologist who is consulted by a dozen or more industrial firms, poor handwriting may indicate an attempt to think independently—to back away from school patterns.

"Generally, the more schooling a man has, the poorer his handwriting," says the psychographologist. "Education is supposed to develop independent thinking. And very quick thinkers are apt to write a script only they can read."

Geniuses like Beethoven, Napoleon and Einstein had abominable handwriting. So has Toscanini. One of the worst was Horace Greeley's; a compositor had to be specially assigned to dope out his editorials, tortuously written in what was described as "the tracks of a drunken hen."

Educators themselves are not immune to hen-track handwriting. Some years ago, Dr. George H. Denny, then president of the University of Alabama—and once voted "the most distinguished professional leader" in his state—wrote a letter to a man in Virginia who couldn't read the signature. In order to reply, the ingenious Virginian cut out the signature, pasted it on an envelope and addressed it to the university. Sure enough, the local postmaster solved the riddle.

MANUSCRIPT WRITING AFTER SIXTY YEARS *

Gertrude Hildreth

Sixty years have passed since Miss M. M. Bridges, an English educator, published her copybook, *A New Handwriting*, reviving the beautiful handwriting of the Elizabethan era derived from the 15th Century Italic style known as the "chancery" hand. For a period of nearly two hundred years this style of writing with unjoined, near-vertical letters was virtually lost, although William Blake, Lewis Carroll, Emily Dickinson and others used it for their literary work. Miss Bridges considered the conventional cursive longhand as a degenerated form. The gradual change from the old manuscript forms to cursive style longhand was attributed to the wide use of copper-plate engraving, the only known means of reproducing copybooks for school use. Joining the letters helped the copyist keep a straight alignment. Through the years the slant became more pronounced and fancy touches were added to the letters, producing a style of writing remote from the machine printed page. Not only in England and America, but in other countries where the written language employed the Roman alphabet or one somewhat similar, there was a noticeable trend away from the older unjoined letter forms.

The new movement received scant attention at first, but by 1913 the question of introducing manuscript writing into the schools was fully discussed at the London County Council Teachers' Conference. Toward the middle of 1914, Miss S. A. Golds worked out an alphabet for print script with the simplest possible style of lettering. Dr. C. W.

* Reprinted from *Elementary English* (January 1960), Champaign, Ill.: N.C.T.E. by permission of The National Council of Teachers of English and the author.

Kimmins, who was Chief Inspector of the London County Council, made the first extensive report of research findings concerning print script writing. By the early '20's English education authorities felt that the new movement had passed the experimental stage and that the new style of writing should become an established feature of the school curriculum. The new print style was expected to supplant cursive writing altogether instead of serving merely as a prelude to the use of cursive style writing.

Manuscript style writing, another name for print script, was brought to New York City by Marjorie Wise in 1921, and it was simultaneously introduced in private elementary schools in Boston. During the '20's the new style writing was confined largely to the smaller private and experimental or laboratory schools throughout the country, and suburban public school systems with experimental programs such as Winnetka, Illinois, and Bronxville, New York. During the '30's the trend steadily increased with more and more public school systems showing interest in the movement and introducing the new style of writing to beginners; from 1940 onward the trend was even more rapid so that by 1950 the teaching of script in the primary grades of public schools had become practically universal in American schools. Today in many countries around the world where the Roman alphabet is used, beginners are taught manuscript style writing.

The introduction of print script in the primary grades coincided with new views concerning the place of writing in the school curriculum and methods of teaching the skill. Possibly the wide adoption of print script was a significant factor in the activity movement. Formerly, handwriting was taught as a formal, isolated drill subject and treated as a mechanical skill. First came practice in separate strokes, then whole letters, and finally words. The children wrote laboriously in their copy books, slavishly copying line after line. A child who was asked what he had written would reply, "I don't know. I haven't learned to read it yet." Not until the children had reached third grade or beyond were they able to use handwriting for written expression.

In the early 1900's, Dr. Ovid Decroly, the Belgian educator, pointed out the fallacy in the older approach to handwriting for young children. He advocated teaching children to write by beginning with whole, meaningful words such as they used in speaking and were learning to read. He concluded: learning to write is not achieved best by motor imitation but by expression of ideas graphically. The visual images of whole, meaningful words are most easily retained because they express ideas.

Teachers of young children regarded manuscript writing as a functional tool from the beginning, not as preparation for composition work two or three years later. The children could learn to write while actually writing something to be read, instead of mechanically copying model samples written by adults. Teachers of primary pupils found that manuscript style was easier to teach; children could get good results with less effort than in the old style writing.

Beginners were saved the confusion of having to become familiar with two styles of graphic language, machine printed type-face and conventional longhand. It was now possible to teach reading and handwriting together and, in turn, to link these skills with the children's natural oral expression recorded in the chart text.

The use by the teacher of print style writing on the board in preparing experience charts furnished the incentive for children to do some writing themselves. As early as November of the first school year the children were writing by copying from the chart the text they had composed.

Manuscript style was advantageous for young bright children whose ideas and oral vocabulary ran ahead of their ability to record their thoughts in writing. Beginners could very quickly see improvement and be praised for achievement instead of feeling humiliated because the copy was far from the copybook model. Manuscript style seemed easier for boys to manage than cursive style writing. Non-English speaking children, slow learners, and physically handicapped children benefited immeasurably from instruction in print style writing.

With systematic daily practice the children's handwriting skill by the third grade was infinitely superior to results gained with cursive style writing. It was not only more legible and fluent, but more pleasing in appearance. With this style of writing children began composition work earlier, and became more independent in written expression.

In the '30's and '40's a new type of textbook for primary pupils began to appear: practice books that linked together lessons in reading, spelling, handwriting, and written expression requiring the use of print style writing.

Print script used by both teachers and students in foreign language instruction at all levels has values similar to those found in teaching primary pupils to write the mother tongue. An illiterate adult, an Arabian woman, quickly learned to read and write English through the use of manuscript written text prepared by her tutor, and through learning to write manuscript style; whereas her earlier attempts with cursive style writing had proved discouraging. An adult student of the Russian language noted at once the advantage in using unjoined vertical print script similar to book print instead of the conventional longhand with dissimilar letter forms.

PRINT SCRIPT VERSUS BLOCK PRINT

Various names have been given to this new-old style of hand writing—print script, print writing, and manuscript writing. The original term "print script" proved to be misleading because parents and the general public tended to confuse print script with "block printing," that is the use of all-capitals such as one sees in captions, maps, titles, advertisements, and so on; and the block printing the kindergartener does when he prints his name. This confusion has led to misunderstanding concerning the nature of manuscript writing. When done by hand, "printing" is associated with laborious, unaccustomed hand-lettering using all capital letters, wholly unlike long-practiced, fluent print style handwriting.

Manuscript-style writing uses letter styles similar to the typewriter or the simplified type face of the telephone directory, with only one or two exceptions, the letters *a* and *g*. The difference between manuscript writing, cursive style, and block printing can be observed by comparing such words as *plenty, surely, forget, scissors, draught,* written in longhand, written on the typewriter, and hand-lettered in capitals.

LEGIBILITY OF MANUSCRIPT AND CURSIVE WRITING

The superior quality and legibility of manuscript writing was evident when this style was well taught in the primary grades. Parents found it easier to read than conventional longhand, and realized themselves how frequently they were requested to "Print" in filling out important papers.

All perception studies show that the farther hand-written letter forms depart from the vertical the less legible they become. Joining the letters, increasing the slant, elongation of the letters, and added loops all decrease legibility, because legibility is directly proportionate to the degree of similarity between machine printed type-face and handwriting style. The reading of book print is the commoner, more accustomed type of reading; and personal handwritten context, notes, papers, records, etc., shows wide variation from person to person, unlike standard book print. Even one individual's writing varies with the occasions for writing.

Another factor in legibility is the impression or Gestalt of individual words in the sentences. To the extent that word forms in handwriting deviate from machine printed words, the words are less legible.

With increased speed, cursive writing tends to become a scribble, but according to George L. Thomson, manuscript writing deteriorates less under speed pressure than cursive style writing. This holds true even for wide variety in personal writing styles and rate of writing.

Today writing is less often done by American school children with steel pens. Modern children use cheap fountain pens, ball points, or pen-pencils. All these writing instruments are eminently suited to print style writing.

THE QUESTION OF "CHANGING OVER"

Both in England and in the early experiments with manuscript writing in America, teachers assumed that the children were being taught a lifetime hand, serviceable for all purposes. However, it has been reported that in England, although manuscript was the only style taught throughout the grades in some schools, in others only beginners were taught this style, or the children learned and used both manuscript and cursive styles. No sooner had manuscript writing been extensively adopted in this country than many questions and problems arose. The writing specialists who were committed to cursive style writing sought to confine the teaching of print writing to the primary grades. The enthusiasm for print style writing in the primary grades contrasted sharply with the rejection of manuscript writing in the intermediate and higher grades.

The standard arguments against continuing print script beyond the primary years were:

1. Print script is slower than cursive longhand in the upper grades and high school.
2. Manuscript is a babyish style of printing, remote from conventional styles of handwriting, not "real" writing at all.
3. The banks will not accept print script signatures because they could be forged more easily.
4. The children are unable to read conventional longhand.
5. Upper grade teachers are not familiar with instruction in manuscript style writing.

Parents became impatient with children who could not "write" their names by the end of the primary period. They inquired, "When are the children going to learn to *write?*" They were concerned about the style of handwriting the children would use as high school students and in adult life. *[Parental pressure]*

The children's attitudes also played a role in the changeover policy. Manuscript writing tended to become associated in the children's minds with the primary grades. A teacher commented, "The children are so eager to write like the grown-ups that they can hardly wait." "We're no longer doing baby writing," the children in one class reported to their parents. Older children who could have made faster progress in remedial reading if they had used print script would not even look at this type of "baby" writing, much less consent to learn it.

In the confusion some schools left the decision about continuing with manuscript style or changing over to the parents, or the children themselves decided how they would write.

Today in American schools manuscript writing is the form used almost without exception in the initial teaching of handwriting, with a change to cursive style before the beginning of the fourth grade. Schools that teach either cursive style or manuscript exclusively are in the decided minority. Dr. Freeman stated in his introduction to *Coordinated Handwriting*, a series of copy books for grades 1–8, "Manuscript writing is preferable for beginners, cursive writing is preferable for the upper grades."

Most teachers today assume that there is no alternative to changing over. As one supervisor expressed it, "Prejudice against continuation of manuscript in the upper grades is so deeply rooted that no change in attitude can possibly come about in our generation." After stating objections to the continuance of manuscript style beyond the primary grades, Luella Cole remarked, "Since, therefore, in the judgment of the present writer, manuscript writing cannot be continued with an expectation of satisfactory permanent results, it is best never to let it become established."

Upper-grade teachers approve the change-over because they themselves do not use manuscript as an all-purpose writing hand, are not familiar with instructional procedures in this style of penmanship, and have no copy books for the pupils.

By the time high school is reached objection to manuscript style writing has largely subsided because by this time both teachers and parents are chiefly concerned about legibility. Some children who do not write well in cursive style shift to the typewriter, others convert to shop printing.

RATE OF WRITING

The question about the rate of manuscript writing centers almost entirely in the upper grades. Speed of handwriting is a matter of practical concern as the child matures, because time for note-taking for school studies, even for personal correspondence, is always at a premium.

Miss S. A. Golds observed in 1916, "One objection raised to this style of writing by those who have not taught it is that children will never get speed with it. . . . As a matter of fact, we find that our children write just as quickly as they wrote in the old style." Dr. C. W. Kimmins was the first to report research findings relating to this moot question. His early studies showed that comparisons among groups having studied manuscript writing for only three years, ages 7 to 10, were always well ahead of cursive style writers of comparable experience. Results of a more comprehensive study on rate of writing were reported by Kimmins in 1916. The data for five-minute handwriting tests of 9,264 girls who had studied manuscript writing for two years or more are as follows:

Number Tested	Age	Letters Per Minute Manuscript	Letters Per Minute Cursive
373	7	21.6	18.8
1536	8	25.5	21.4
1609	9	34.9	29.3
1572	10	42.4	36.1
1449	11	48.7	44.5
1509	12	55.0	49.3
1216	13	60.9	61.0

Kimmins reported that in the boys' schools the results were slightly to the advantage of cursive writing at the 12 and 13 year levels. "This is due to the fixation of habits of cursive writing during a long period." Children who have been doing manuscript writing for three or four years had as great an advantage in speed at 12 and 13 years as those of the earlier ages. Handwriting tests of 15,000 English school children of elementary age showed no significant difference in speed when manuscript and cursive writing rates were compared.

Tests of children in the Winnetka schools proved that high school students wrote just about as rapidly using manuscript writing learned in the lower grades as those using cursive style writing, according to the report of C. V. Washburne and M. V. Morphett.

In a study by the writer of comparative handwriting rates of junior high school students, median scores for children using cursive style and manuscript writing from the first grade showed no important difference. The results of tests given to seventh and eighth graders were as follows:

Grade		Rate of Writing Letters a Minute	Ayres Norms	Number of Cases
7	Manuscript	70.5		25
	Cursive	70.0	73	25
8	Manuscript	80.2		28
	Cursive	85.5	77	42

Of the eighth-grade students writing at a rate of more than 100 letters a minute, six were manuscript writers and eight wrote cursive style, about the same proportion as the total number of students who wrote in each style. In both grades the manuscript writers varied more in speed, possibly because of greater differences in amount and type of drill through the grades. The legibility of the rapid manuscript writers was superior to that of the cursive style writers. On the question of handwriting rate, a Bronxville bulletin published in 1945 states: "We have accumulated data covering a period of three years recording the speed and legibility of natural handwriting of all pupils in the seventh and eighth grades. About twenty per cent of our seventh graders have never written anything but cursive script as they have come to us from schools where that form was taught. Our tests show that the average speed of manuscript and cursive writing is almost identical: for seventh grade, approximately 65 letters a minute; for eighth grade, 73 letters a minute. Both types of writing are represented among the slower writers and both types among the rapid writers." Tests of adults in Bronxville who write frequently showed that the average rate of speed for good legible handwriting of either type is in the neighborhood of 122 letters per minute.

In an extensive piece of research E. M. Foster studied the speed and legibility of children's writing in two public schools, grade 3–6, in which manuscript writing was taught in the early grades and a change-over was made in grade 3. Two handwriting specimens, one in each style, were collected from every child. Foster concluded that manuscript is only slightly more legible than cursive; that children who write one style legibly tend to write the other legibly also; in general, children who have been taught handwriting in the public schools write cursive style faster than they do manuscript; from grade 3 through grade 6 there is a consistent increase in the speed of writing both styles of handwriting; after it is introduced into the program, the speed of writing cursive style rapidly comes to equal and surpass that of manuscript style. These conclusions are not valid for comparative purposes because these are not matched groups of children with equivalent instruction and equal experience in one style exclusively, but "changed-over" cases. Frank N. Freeman, in reporting the results of Kimmin's study of 9,264 girls cited above stated, "He finds that the younger children write the manuscript style faster, whereas by thirteen years cursive writing becomes faster." Luella Cole observed that print writing is somewhat slower than cursive writing, but Virgil Herrick states the evidence concerning rate is inconclusive. Results indicate that manuscript and cursive styles are done with similar speed, but the legibility of cursive style seems to decrease more rapidly than manuscript under speed pressure.

In the studies conducted in English schools manuscript writing was not only systematically taught in the intermediate and upper grades, but the teachers themselves had learned the new style writing and used it in all class work.

Psychological illusions tend to distort impressions about speed of manuscript writing as compared with cursive style. The finished hand-written page of a good manuscript writer gives the impression of having been painstakingly hand-lettered. Authors of the Bronxville bulletin referred to above found it necessary to advise parents that the well-written manuscript writing examples in the bulletin appeared to have been laboriously hand-lettered by the children, though such was not the case. Actually, all the samples of writing were done at good speed with a free, easy, natural flow.

Some years ago a midwestern school superintendent asked the writer for proof that children attained good quality in upper grade manuscript writing. In acknowledging the receipt of a batch of seventh grade papers he commented, "How slowly the children must have written to produce such good results." Actually their speed was fully up to the level of seventh-grade standards for cursive style writing. Cursive longhand while being done looks "busier" than manuscript style; and it is, because the process is more elaborate. These illusions help to explain the impression that fluent, rapid writing is possible only in cursive longhand.

Two other lines of evidence throw light on the speed question. The writer conducted a test in which 70 eighth-grade boys and girls were asked to make joined and unjoined writing strokes on ruled paper. The tests were given individually and timed with a stop watch. The tests were preceded by warming-up exercises. To cancel out practice effect of joined and unjoined writing strokes, half the group were given the unjoined stroke test first, the other half, the joined stroke test first. Results in terms of the median number of strokes were as follows:

unjoined strokes	44.3
joined strokes	40.7

This is not a large difference, but it confirms the impression of common-sense observation that joining strokes in writing takes fully as long or longer than separate strokes.

The fact that the cursive writer must cover more mileage in the letter strokes of the words he writes can be easily verified by actually measuring the distance to be covered. Such comparisons show a proportion of 3 to 5, that is, for every 3 inches of strokes made in manuscript writing the cursive writer must write 5 inches on his paper.

Hebrew handwriting is both vertical and unjoined. College students familiar with Hebrew report that this style of writing is so rapid and economical of effort that they prefer it to their longhand English script for note-taking in class. Part of the economy is due, however, to the phonetic structure of the written language.

One argument against manuscript writing offered by handwriting experts is that it lacks rhythm and children cannot use arm movement. As early as 1916 Dr. Kimmins stated, "One reason why speed appears to come naturally to manuscript writers is probably that words with separate letters are more suitable for rhythmic purposes than words with joined letters." Miss Wise and other teachers subsequently reported that both rhythm and arm movement could be developed by the print-script writer. They found that taking the pen off the paper in contrast to joining the letters did not result in reduced rate. According to George L. Thomson, a rapid flowing hand can be cultivated equally well with manuscript style writing because the pen does not touch the paper so often.

The conclusion from all the evidence is that there is no significant difference in rate in the two styles of writing when experience and practice are comparable for upper-grade students. However, there still remain wide differences in individual rate of writing at all age levels, conforming to the general principle of trait variability in all motor skills and achievements, even with comparable instruction and learning effort. These facts suggest that rate of handwriting is more closely allied to quality of instruction, duration of practice, and traits of the writer, than to the particular style of hand writing.

The significance of speed of writing resides primarily in the indication it gives of increasing habituation of handwriting habits. Fluency in handwriting, just as in reading and other skills, is an indication of high level automatization of the skill in question, an index of degree of mastery.

There remains one essential difference between manuscript and cursive style writing as the child matures, and that is superior legibility with speeded up rate.

ARE MANUSCRIPT SIGNATURES ACCEPTABLE?

An early argument against manuscript writing was that the banks would not accept manuscript written signatures. This proved to be more a matter of the particular community, even of the particular bank or individual teller than a nationwide problem. Paradoxically, the Elizabethan script was the legal hand through the centuries of its popularity.

In 1935 the Bronxville school authorities reported that the signatures of adult manuscript writers were distinctive and characteristic enough to be entirely legal in all transactions. Virgil Herrick observed that most banks will accept a manuscript written signature if it is the writer's regular signature. Part of the confusion over this issue lies in the fact that officials may not distinguish between "printing" one's name, that is, the use of all capitals by a person unaccustomed to writing this way, and the long-practiced hand of the manuscript writer.

DIFFICULTY IN READING CONVENTIONAL LONGHAND

An argument offered by parents was that the children were unable to read conventional writing. Some years ago pupils in the fourth grade and above at the Lincoln School, New York, were tested in ability to read longhand done in a round bold hand. This presented no difficulty, but the children had more trouble interpreting sharply slanted, hastily written sentences. Individual longhand hastily written is difficult for anyone to decipher. The amount of such writing children will have to do in a lifetime in view of the popularity of typing is too slight to outweigh the advantages of print writing already mentioned.

PROBLEMS INVOLVED IN CHANGING OVER

Authorities agree that the earlier the change-over the easier it is to accomplish. The longer the change is delayed, the more likely the pupils are to retain vestiges of manuscript lettering. Primary teachers say they have not found "changing over" much of a problem provided they begin early enough, well before the end of grade 2. After that the problem becomes tougher in proportion to elapsed time. However, the advantages of primary children learning print script accrue more largely during the third grade, just the time when the change-over must be made.

One spring morning a school visitor in a third grade class admired the beautifully written spelling papers mounted on the wall board, all in manuscript style writing and all dated January. The teacher immediately apologized for this display, saying that she should long since have taken the papers down because the pupils were now practicing "changing over" with cursive style copy books. She admitted that she was proud of the manuscript written papers, but that changing over at this time was mandatory.

The continuation of manuscript style is a boon to slow learners who are not so far advanced as others by the third grade, who would be upset by the "change-over," who benefit from doing things the simplest way, and need this link between writing, reading, and spelling.

THE MECHANICS OF CHANGING OVER

Converting from print style writing to cursive longhand after three or even two years of systematic training in manuscript represents an abrupt change in a motor skill. This is not a simple matter of joining the letters but of learning new letter strokes and proportions, and slant. Some letters differ considerably from print style; the pen is not lifted from the paper in writing each letter of a word; and there are connecting strokes linking the letters within the words. In making the change-over teachers are asking the pupils to change their handwriting movements. Letters that begin at the baseline in cursive begin at the top in manuscript style. The strokes required in cursive style and manuscript writing are diametrically opposite for a number of the letters; compare *b* and *d*, *f* and *h*, *l*, *k*, *r*, *s*.

Cursive longhand is not a natural development from unjoined writing. No child joins the letters spontaneously; joining must always be taught and drilled. Unless instruction in the shifting process is persistent and thorough, children may show confusion in styles and never become fully efficient writers. The difficulties entailed in the change-over were vividly described by a young teacher in attempting to retrain her eight-year-old sister. This child, in third grade at the time, had been doing very well in print script. "She printed large and clear," says the teacher, "without too much effort." The first task she had to accomplish was to write her name in the new style in her notebook five times. Turmoil, frustration, and tears accompanied this task. Certain letters came out backwards no matter how many times the child tried. After many trials she refused to do it. By the end of the week, however, after many periods of practice she could write her name fairly well. She resented having to write out her spelling words instead of printing them, but after a few weeks writing became more natural for her, and she acquired skill with continual practice. Other children, it is true, experience little difficulty in making the shift provided they are well-taught and thoroughly drilled.

Although good copybook instructions are available for easing the task of making the shift, it still entails more hours of practice than would be needed to perfect print script. Changing over comes at a time when the children need to concentrate on the rudiments of written expression. In view of the fact that our national and world economy demand the most efficient instruction of elementary school children in all phases of literacy, this manifest source of waste in education should be eliminated at once.

1. Manuscript style writing is a practical, serviceable hand for all mature writing needs.
2. Changing over involves lost motion and in some cases actual distaste for writing.
3. The time and effort needed for mastering the new cursive style can be devoted to written expression and composition work.
4. Difficulties due to the fact that upper-grade teachers do not pay much attention to handwriting are avoided.

A growing proportion of older students and adults actually need manuscript style writing: all teachers of elementary school children, all high school boys doing shop work, all clerks in the larger stores, and all of us who are asked to "PRINT" at some time or other.

In summarizing the arguments against the continuance of manuscript writing in the upper grades, V. E. Herrick points out that cursive is the socially accepted form. Why force a child to learn something he will have to change later? Actually, in some "smart-set" communities adult manuscript style writing is a badge of having gone to private schools or high-class surburban schools.

Upper-grade teachers who teach manuscript writing like it very much. Instruction in manuscript writing through the years in the Bronxville schools has proved that this style of writing is serviceable and effective for lifetime use, resulting in attractive, legible script. Illustrations of upper-grade compositions and poetry in manuscript style will be found in the publications of Alvina Burrows, and others. These illustrations prove that print style writing has much the same values for advancing pupils in all phases of literacy as in the lower grades. The Bronxville schools encourage children who have developed a rapid, manuscript hand to retain it in high school. Occasionally the pupils have developed and retained both styles. Similarly, in Brookline, Massachusetts, manuscript writing has been retained throughout the upper grades.

Permitting the children to "keep it" is not the whole answer to upper-grade manuscript-writing instruction. Children above the third grade continue to need practice and drill until they show command of fluent handwriting. If individual children appear to be writing more slowly than need be, assist them in acquiring a slight slant, attaining a more comfortable writing posture, practicing for lighter pressure, more arm movement. To improve alignment, spacing, letter formation the pupils require drill books and worksheets. Among the Bronxville students, some had adopted a slight slant backward, or forward. George Thomson, a British handwriting authority, recommends the adoption of slight slant, more like the older Italic style, and he has prepared an interesting copy book for practice in this slight-slant, unjoined letter style.

At all stages, primary, intermediate, and in the higher grades teachers should avoid the use of the term "printing" when referring to handwriting because of possible confusion with block printing and tedious hand-lettering. Never refer to manuscript style as "printing" in contrast to "real writing," both because this is misleading and it prevents wider acceptance of print style handwriting. In one third-grade classroom a large sign announced, "Now We Write," giving parents and other visitors the impression that the children had not actually been writing up to this point.

An exhibit of upper-grade manuscript written papers is never seen at a local, state, or national teacher's convention; yet such an exhibit could be a genuine stimulus to teachers to experiment in handwriting.

Upper-grade teachers who wish to instruct children in manuscript writing should familiarize themselves with this style and learn to do it well. Teachers and others who attempt to instruct themselves sometimes unwittingly develop a peculiar combination of capitals and small letters in their print style writing as in this sample:

THANK you so much for the lovely gift.
(All letters except the first are of the same height.)

Only manuscript style should be used on the blackboard in preparing charts and for other classroom purposes.

EDUCATING THE PARENTS

The parents' prejudice against upper-grade print style writing springs largely from the impression that their children's writing is babyish, primitive. Parents attach higher values to a style of writing that looks more "educated," or "grown-up." No one looks over my shoulder while I am typing and comments, "How childish that looks. Why don't you "write"? The reason is that typing is associated with mature adult activities. Changing over to cursive style suggests to the parents that the children have now graduated to something more mature, that they have reached a higher level in school attainment, that learning to write in this style presents a more exacting learning task.

Parents of children in the junior high school in Bronxville were advised to support the school in continuing manuscript style writing in the upper grades and to show pride in their children's accomplishment. However, they were invited to request a change-over if they wished to do so.

The proper answer to the question, "When are the children going to learn to write," is, "They are learning to write, but it's new style, like your new model car or camera." Parents' attitudes might be changed if they realized how helpful they could be to their younger children by using print script themselves. A beautiful example of this is to be found in *Now We Are Six*, by Clara and Morey Appell,[1] in which the mother writes a letter to her three young children from the hospital where she is confined with a new baby. The letter, penned in clear manuscript style, was easily read aloud to the others by the seven-year-old. Fathers who rarely come to school need to have the reasons for modern instructional techniques fully explained to them.

NEEDED RESEARCH IN ELEMENTARY SCHOOL HANDWRITING

With the first introduction of manuscript writing in American schools on an experimental basis research proceeded vigorously, but the general impression today is that the issues raised in this paper were all settled long ago and no further attention need be paid to them. On the contrary, in this day of urgency in teaching literacy not only in America but around the world, the whole area of handwriting instruction needs to be thoroughly explored.

There is need of controlled studies in which comparable groups of pupils are taught different handwriting styles. American schools have never developed norms for rate and quality of manuscript writing throughout the elementary grades comparable to those reported by Kimmins or the cursive script norms established years ago by Ayres, Starch, Thorndike, and others.

An educational campaign among the parents and general public would be necessary to conduct new experiments with true impartiality. The full cooperation of the handwriting experts (penmanship specialists) and the copybook publishers would also be required.

YOU CAN TEACH MANUSCRIPT WRITING WITH 6 RULES *

Max Rosenhaus

Children may have difficulty in writing well because they feel hampered by too many rules. There seem to be so many things to

---

[1] Published by the Golden Press, New York, 1959.

remember when making a letter! Actually a few simple rules cover most of the manuscript writing problems. By following them, children will find it easier to form the letters, and greater legibility and speed will result.

Although it can be quite short, there should be a daily handwriting lesson. Most of this time should be spent in actual writing with only a few minutes devoted to discussion and checking. The teacher can discover children who need special help as she walks around the room during the lesson. As the boys and girls learn to evaluate good manuscript writing, they can check their own work and try to improve their handwriting.

1. ALIGNMENT

All letters must sit on the line.

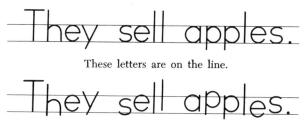

These letters are on the line.

These letters are not on the line.

2. PROPORTIONATE HEIGHT AND SIZE OF LETTERS

(a) Capital letters are all the same size. They are twice the size of short small letters.

These capital letters are not twice the size of short small letters.

These capital letters are twice the size of short small letters.

(b) Small letters are in the ratio of 2 to 1. Tall letters, *b, d, f, h, k,* and *l* are twice the size of short letters.

(c) Small *t* is one and one-half times the size of short letters. Extensions below the line—*g, j, p, q,* and *y*—are the length of a short letter.

(d) When children first write, they should make capitals about two spaces high and short small letters one space high. Later (by second grade), they will make capitals one space high with other letters proportionately smaller.

These letters are proportionate and of regular size.

These letters are irregular in proportion and size.

3. SPACING

(a) The space between two wide letters is narrow.

The spaces between these letters are narrow.

(b) The space between two thin letters is a little wider.

The spaces between these letters are wider.

(c) The space between two words is equal to the width of a pencil or a finger.

The spaces between these words are correct.

4. CIRCULAR LETTERS

Letters such as *a*, *b*, and *d* should be circular.

They sell large apples.

The spaces between these words are incorrect.

a b c d e g o p

These letters have circular shapes.

They sell large apples.

These letters are circular.

They sell large apples.

These letters are not circular.

5. PARALLEL STROKES

All down strokes are straight lines in a downward direction.

They sell large apples.

These down strokes are parallel.

They sell large apples.

These down strokes are not parallel.

6. VERTICAL DOWN STROKES

Except for the *k, v, w, x, y,* and *z,* all down strokes are vertical and straight.

They sell large apples.

These down strokes are vertical and straight.

They sell large apples.

These down strokes are not vertical and straight.

SELF-EVALUATION

An important element in any good lesson on handwriting is the practice of self-evaluation. Pupils should be encouraged to inspect their work critically at the end of each lesson to see if it adheres to the basic principles.

1. Are all the letters on the line?
2. Are all the letters of correct and proportional size?
3. Is spacing between letters and words correct?
4. Are all down strokes straight and parallel?
   CAUTION: Limit the checking process to one item per day per line; for example, on one day have the children check one line for alignment (writing on the line), on another day, check one line for straight down strokes, and so on.

SUGGESTIONS FOR THE "LEFTIES" *

Harold D. Drummond

Left-handed children often cause teachers real anguish. In spite of encouragement and exhortation, many left-handers gradually adopt the upside-down writing style. What can teachers do to help left-handed children with handwriting?

1. We need to understand why the lefty gradually brings his hand around to the upside-down position. There are at least two good reasons. First, the natural way to draw a horizontal line is from the middle of the body outward. A right-handed person draws a line naturally from left to right. A left-handed person draws a line naturally from right to left. Moreover, the natural way to draw a circle is counterclockwise for the right-handed child; clockwise for the lefty. Since English is written with the left-to-right progression, and since most ovals in cursive writing are made counterclockwise, we must recognize that we are trying to teach something which is unnatural. Second,

* Reprinted by permission of the author and publisher from *Elementary School Principal* (Washington, D.C.: Dept. of Elementary School Principals, N.E.A., February 1959).

the right-handed child can much more easily see what he has written than can a lefty who writes with his wrist in the natural position. Moreover, the hand of the lefty tends to smear what has been written unless he gets the hand out of the way. If he twists his wrist around and writes upside-down, so to speak, he can see what he is doing. Moreover, if he is using ink, the copy has a chance to dry before his hand rubs across the writing and smears it.

2. Specific suggestions can be made to help keep the lefty honest (straight wrist instead of crooked!):

a. Provide lots of writing on the chalkboard. It is practically impossible to use the upside-down style at the board.

b. Make sure the paper is properly placed on the desk. For manuscript, paper should be square with the desk. For cursive, the bottom right corner should be pointed at the body. It is hard to write in the upside-down position if paper is placed properly. Also, less hand-smearing occurs.

c. Permit lefties to continue manuscript writing indefinitely. Their writing is almost always more legible before they learn to write cursive than afterwards. As the left-handed children begin to change to cursive, though, watch the placement of the paper like a hawk.

d. Encourage children to hold pencils or pens so that the top of the writing instrument is pointing over the shoulder of the same arm.

e. Encourage lefties to develop a writing slant which feels natural and good. The slant will, undoubtedly, be a bit backhand compared to generally accepted handwriting styles because it's natural that way. A consistent slant makes writing legible, and a lefty is not likely to be consistent using a slant which is natural for right-handers.

f. Furnish lefties with pencils which have slightly harder lead than that used by right-handers. Harder lead will not smear as easily, thus providing less reason for twisting the wrist so that the hand is in the upside-down position.

g. When ink is used, be sure that all lefties have a good nonskip ballpoint pen which has a high-quality non-smear cartridge.

h. Encourage lefties to learn to type. Most classrooms should have typewriters to encourage children to write creatively. With lefties, the need for typewriters is even greater.

3. In spite of all our efforts, position for good writing feels wrong for most lefties—and it feels right when they get the wrist in the upside-down position. Many of them will write that way in spite of everything teachers can do—so don't make too big an issue of it. Consistently follow the above suggestions; but if it appears the war

has been lost, work to improve letter formation and writing style from the upside-down position. Good citizens write *legibly*—and it is better to have a cooperative, enthusiastic, eager lefty who writes legibly upside-down than to have a disgruntled, antagonistic, lethargic lefty, with a properly-placed wrist, who does not choose to write.

HANDWRITING "BLITZ" °

Nathan Naiman

PURPOSE, CONTENT, MATERIALS

The handwriting blitz is intended as a means of motivating children to improve their own handwriting. Definite goals are outlined in each lesson, and self-evaluation is the "motivating force" intended to lead to pupil improvement.

There are twenty lessons in the handwriting blitz. These lessons include the main elements that contribute to good handwriting. An introductory statement and a special "slant" sheet have been included.

Each child should have a folder that will contain (a) the "blitz" sheets as passed out by the teacher and (b) the handwriting samples done by the pupils. It is recommended that the pupils use 8½ x 11" foolscap paper with ⅜" ruling.

GRADES, USE, EXTENSIONS

The materials have been specifically geared to grades 5 and 6. They can be used in grade 4 if the teacher will take the time to interpret carefully. Vocabulary load may be too heavy for pupils in 3rd or 4th grade.

It is recommended that two lessons a week be used. This means that the "blitz" will normally run for a ten-week period. It can be used more frequently if the class interest indicates the desirability. In many cases it may be found that children need additional work on the skills introduced in any specific lesson.

° Reprinted by permission of the author.

TIMING, PROGRESS, REACTIONS

In general, a "blitz" lesson should be used in a twenty-minute handwriting period. Classroom usage will serve as a guide to the amount of time needed for each lesson.

It is especially important that attention be called to the progress made by pupils.

Recommendation: It is suggested that one sheet be passed out on the day the lesson is to be used. The surprise element can thus be maintained.

✿   ✿   ✿

Probably you have not heard of a *handwriting blitz*, for it is a new idea that is being tried. If it works well, then other people will hear more about it.

During war times, a "blitz" refers to an all-out push by an army to defeat its enemy. The army uses all means it can to win a victory quickly, in a short period of time, and with the greatest gains possible. The same kind of drive for victory is used in this handwriting blitz. You will be working to win a victory, but you will be striving to beat yourself—you will see if you can improve your handwriting in a short period of time. The enemy will be any handwriting habits that keep you from doing your best writing. The victory will be improvement of your own writing so it can be more easily read.

THE PLAN

You will receive a HANDWRITING FOLDER in which to keep all of the blitz materials. You will also receive LESSON SHEETS that give directions. The teacher will go over these directions with you, and then you will have your regular handwriting period to complete the assignment. By paying careful attention to the directions, you will know exactly how to improve your handwriting.

You will only take *one step a day*. By remembering the importance of that step in all of the writing you do, you will find that your handwriting improves daily.

There are 20 lessons in all. You will probably do only two a week— but at the end of ten weeks, the results should be such that you should see an improvement in your writing and you should have a better understanding of those things that make handwriting legible (easy to read).

MATERIALS

You will need your own handwriting folder which your teacher will give to you. You will also need to decide whether you are going to use pencil or pen for this work. You will also need some good writing paper that is lined. The lines will be ⅜ths of an inch apart.

You should plan to keep your printed lessons on the left-hand side of your folder. Your written samples should go on the right-hand side of the folder.

HEADING YOUR PAPERS

All writing looks better if the headings are the same for all papers. It is suggested that you head your papers as follows:

(Name)
(School)
(Date)
Lesson No.
(Start)

LESSON I

Handwriting Sample:

When you are ready to measure a board, you need a ruler or a yardstick. The same thing is true if you wish to measure improvement in handwriting— you need an instrument to use in doing the measuring. A ruler or yardstick will not do, however. In order to have a measuring tool, you will be asked to take some dictation today using the spelling words that were in your lesson last week. You will be asked to keep this paper and compare it to the sample of writing that you do on the last day of this blitz.

The teacher has taken the spelling words and used them in sentences. As you hear the sentences, write them exactly as given. Do your best spelling and also do your best writing.

Here are the steps to follow:

1. Head your paper correctly.
2. Listen to the sentence as your teacher reads it.
3. Write the complete sentence using your best spelling and handwriting.

The teacher will collect the dictation samples today, and will go over the paper carefully. The teacher will analyze the writing to note what you do well and to note where you need to improve. The paper will be returned to you—but not until after you have done Lesson II which asks you to analyze your own handwriting. It will then be interesting to see how you and the teacher agree or differ.

To the teacher: Short, easy sentences should be used. Each sentence should include two or three spelling words from the current or previous spelling lesson. The amount of time available will determine the number of sentences to be included in this lesson.

LESSON II

How Well Do I Do?

All of us have two kinds of handwriting. When we are in a hurry, we write for ourselves. When we write for someone else, we use our best writing. Today you will be asked to do an example of each kind of writing. Then take time to see how you analyze your own writing.

1. Here is how I write when I am in a hurry.
    Write: This is a sample of my writing.

    _____

    _____

2. Here is how I write when I try to do my best writing:
    Write: This is a sample of my best writing.

    _____

    _____

    _____

3. Here is how I grade my writing: Excellent   Good   Fair   Poor
    My fast writing (check only one
    grade)   _____ _____ _____ _____
    My best writing (check only one
    grade)   _____ _____ _____ _____

4. Here is how I analyze my *best* writing:
   a. *Slant*
      Do all of the letters slant in the same direction?   _____ ____ ____ ____
   b. *Spacing*
      Are the spaces between words even so each word can be read?   _____ ____ ____ ____
   c. *Size*
      Are the small letters ⅓ space tall? Are the capitals and tall letters almost a space high?   _____ ____ ____ ____
   d. *Alignment*
      Do all of the letters of each word rest on the line as they should?   _____ ____ ____ ____
   e. *Tall letters*
      Are all tall letters about a space tall and well formed? (*l, f, h, k, b*)   _____ ____ ____ ____
   f. *Closings*
      Are the following letters closed? *a, d, g, o, p, s*?   _____ ____ ____ ____
   g. *Roundness*
      Are *m, n, h, u, v, w, y* rounded on top?   _____ ____ ____ ____
   h. *Endings*
      Does each word have a good finishing stroke?   _____ ____ ____ ____

Adapted from *A Booklet To Help You Improve Your Writing* (Fort Madison, Iowa: W. A. Sheaffer and Co., 1958).

LESSON III

My Best Writing:

Today you are to write a paragraph using your best handwriting. Be sure that you try to do your very best.

When you have your paper, use the heading that was illustrated on the first sheet of the handwriting blitz. Then do what it tells you to do below:

1. Write the following paragraph. Use your best writing. Put in the correct numbers in the blank spaces.
     This is a sample of my best handwriting. I did it when
     I was in the _____ grade. I am _____ years old.
2. Skip one space. Then write all of the capital letters. Write them as carefully as you can:

   A B C D E F G H I J K L M N O P Q R S T U V W X Y Z

3. Now skip one more space. Then write all of the small letters. Write them as carefully as you can:

a b c d e f g h i j k l m n o p q r s t u v w x y z

4. And last, skip one more space. Then write all of the numbers from 1 to 10.

1 2 3 4 5 6 7 8 9 10

Your handwriting books often have materials that use every letter of the alphabet. If you have time, you may wish to try these. For example:

Paul said that the big, brown fox quickly and slyly jumped over the lazy dog.

LESSON IV

Finishing Strokes:

The finishing stroke on the end of a word can make your writing look much better if it is done correctly. Most finishing strokes at the end of a word end with an upward curve. This should be about the height of the letter *a*. The curve of the final stroke is downward on the letters *g, j, y, z*. Having a good finishing stroke on the end of all words can help improve the looks of your writing about 25%—check and see if this statement is correct.

1. Get the writing that you did for Lesson III from your folder. Look for the finishing stroke or "tail" on the end of each word. See how well you did. Does each word have a finishing stroke as tall as a small letter?

Word:	Yes	No	
This	____	____	
is	____	____	
a	____	____	
sample	____	____	
of	____	____	
best	____	____	
did	____	____	
it	____	____	
when	____	____	
was	____	____	
in	____	____	
the	____	____	
grade	____	____	
at	____	____	
am	____	____	Score of 15 to 20 yes—Good
years	____	____	Score of 10 to 14 yes—Fair
old	____	____	Score below 10 yes—needs much more work.

My score: _____

2. Did the following words have a final stroke that is downward on the letters?

writing	____	____
handwriting	____	____

3. Now head your new paper for the new work. Then do the following: Using *good finishing strokes,* write the following sentence *two* times. You will be interested to know that the sentence contains every letter of the alphabet.

> Paul said that the big, brown fox quickly and slyly jumped over the lazy dog.

Skip a line, and then write the following words using good endings on each:

> month   because   high   kite   west   held   fell   oak   broke

Skip a line, and then write the following using the right kind of end stroke:

> windy   string   away   try   hang   sly   easy   lazy

4. If you have time, write each word in the list in Part 1 of this lesson being sure that you have a good finishing stroke. You may even wish to try writing the whole paragraph from Lesson III to see what a difference good finishing strokes make.

LESSON V

Good Slant—Upper Loop Letters

Proper slant in handwriting is very important. It improves the appearance of your work. When all tall letters have backs that slant at the same angle, then the slant improves the appearance of your writing. Slant can be changed by moving the paper to the right position.

1. Get the writing that you did for Lesson IV from your folder. Take the "slant sheet" that your teacher gave you today. Put it under the material you wrote in Lesson IV. Then hold both sheets together up to the light. Check to see if the tall letters all slant the same way as the lines on the "slant sheet." Check these letters especially: *l, k, h, f, b.*
    How would you grade your slant?

    Excellent ___   Good ___   Fair ___   Poor ___

2. The lesson for today is to help improve your slant. Put the correct heading on your paper so you are ready.
    You know that all loop letters should have nice straight backs with a good slant. How do you do this? The answer is easy if you use this little skill—as you start your loop letter, you swing up until it is almost to the top line—now *pause* or *hesitate for just a second* before you start down making a straight line that is slanted until you reach the bottom line. Remember to make these letters almost a space tall: *l, h, k, b, f.*

Write one line of each of these letters. Then, check them with the "slant sheet." How well did you do?

3. Here are some simple words that have upper loop letters. Write each word two times. Remember to watch your slant, for it is important:

bib   fell   bell   hill   ball   back   hall

Write this sentence two times:
    "Up the hill went Jack and Jill."
Check this writing with your "slant sheet." How well did you do?
                                    Excellent ___ Good ___ Fair ___ Poor ___
4. Look back at all of the writing you did today to check for these things: slant; size of letters; finishing strokes.
    See if each loop letter reaches nearly to the top line. Circle the tall loop letters which are too tall or too short. Practice those which you circled. Look at all of the writing you did today. Check the words to see if you had a good finishing stroke. Put a check-mark by each word that you did nicely. If you did a good job, you should have a total of 28 check marks. How many did you have? _____
Your handwriting books have other practice material that will help.

LESSON VI

Good Slant—Lower Loop Letters

Lower loop letters must be made with correct slant, too. Be sure that the backs of these letters are straight and slanted at the correct angle, too: g, j, p, q, y, z.
1. The lesson for today is to help improve your slant with lower-loop letters. Put the correct heading on your paper so you are ready.
    Just as we paused briefly before making the back of the upper-loop letters, so do you pause briefly before making the back of the lower-loop letters. This makes it possible to have a nice straight back that is slanted just right. Remember, too, that these go a half space below the base line.
    Here are the lower loop letters. Write one line of each of these letters:

2. Here are some words that have lower loop letters. Write each word two times. Remember to watch your slant, for it is important:
        jig   pig   gag   pipe   gang   quick   yes   zig-zag
    Write this sentence two times:
        The big pig danced a jig.
3. Check today's writing with your "slant sheet." How well did you do?
                                    Excellent ___ Good ___ Fair ___ Poor ___
4. Look at all of the writing that you have done today. Check it for several things:
        Check to see if the lower loops reach half way below the line.
        Check to see if *all* loop letters have straight backs that are slanted?
        Check to see if the upper loop letters have an up-swinging finish stroke?
        Check to see if the lower loop letters have a down-swinging finish stroke?
        Circle those letters or words that need to be improved.

5.   Practice re-writing all letters or words that you have circled. Then see
     if you can think of a word for each of the lower loop letters. Write it:
     g, j, p, q, z, y.

Lesson VII

Good Slant—Intermediate Letters

There are three intermediate letters. They are called this because they
are taller than small letters. They are not as tall as loop letters. These three
letters are: *d, t, p.* They are ⅔rds of a space tall. They are sometimes
called "straight-back letters" because it is easy to see the straightness of their
backs.

1.   Take Lesson V from your folder. Put your "slant sheet" under it. Now
     check to see if the intermediate letters (*d, t, p*) have straight backs
     that slant at the correct angle. What did you find? How would you grade
     your work on these letters?

                          Excellent ___ Good ___ Fair ___ Poor ___

2.   The work for today is to practice writing the intermediate letters. Like
     the loop letters, it is easier to get nice straight backs if you pause at the
     top of the letter. Do be certain to see that the "d" and "t" come straight
     down the same line they went up. There is no loop in either letter.
     Here are the intermediate letters:

Carefully write a line of each of these letters: *t, d, p.*
Here are some words that use the intermediate letters. Write each word
two times. Check for good slant and for correct size of the letters:

            trip   dust   drop   party   tap   top   pot   stop

Write this sentence two times:
     Do not drop the top on the table.

3.   Look at all of the writing that you have done today. Check it for
     several things:
          Check to see if all of the intermediate letters in your words are a
          little more than ½ space tall. Check those that are not.
          Check to see if all of the intermediate letters have straight backs
          and good slants. Draw a circle around the words that do not.
          Check to see if all words have a good finish stroke.

4.   Practice re-writing all words or letters that you have circled.

5.   AND HERE IS SOMETHING ESPECIALLY IMPORTANT—FOR
     TWO OF THESE LETTERS ARE CALLED "HANDWRITING
     DEMONS" BECAUSE SO MANY PEOPLE MAKE THESE ERRORS.
     SEE IF YOU DID.

                                                          yes—no

     Did you close the circle part of the *d* or does it look like *cl?*   _____
     Did you retrace the stem of the *d* or does it look like *l?*   _____
     Did you cross the *t* on the stem or did you go above it?   _____
     Did you retrace the stem of the *t* or does it look like an *l?*   _____

Lesson VIII

Letter Size

To do good writing, you need to remember only four letter heights:
Loop letters and *capital letters* are almost one space tall.
Intermediate letters (*d, t, p*) are a little over ½ space (⅔rds) space tall.
Small letters are ⅓rd of a space tall (*a, c, e, i, m, n, o, r, s, u, v , w, x*).
Lower loop letters go ½ space below the line (*f, g, j, p, q, y, z*).

1. Take out the paper that you wrote for Lesson VII. Also take out your ruler. Look at the sentence that you wrote twice: "Do not drop the top on the table." Draw a line with your ruler from the top of the "D" in "do," to the top of the "l" in "table." Are they the same height, or does the line go up or down? Does it touch any other letters? If so, you will need to work on this.

   Draw a line from the *t* in *not* to the *t* in *table*. The following letters should just touch this line: t, d, p, t, t. How well did you do? Is this line about ⅔rds of the way from the base line?

   Draw a line from the *o* in *DO* to the *e* in *table*. Do all of the small letters just touch this line? Is the line about ⅓ of a space from the base line?

   How did you do on letter heights?

   Excellent ___ Good ___ Fair ___ Poor ___

2. Put the correct heading on your new paper. See how well you can do with the correct letter heights.

   Write each of these words two times. Then check with the ruler to see how well you did:

   little   baby   all   bill   kick   hall

   Remember the height of the intermediate letters. Write each of these words two times. Then check with the ruler to see how well you did.

   did   tied   pit   tipped   test   top

   The short letters sometimes cause trouble. Write each of these words two times. Then check with the ruler to see how well you did:

   am   or   seem   mice   saw   size   was

3. Write this sentence which uses all letters of the alphabet and all sizes of letters:

   "Everyone expected that the judges would quickly decide to award the beautiful prize for excellent work to Mary."

   Use the lines below to check the three different heights of the letters you wrote in this last sentence. Use it just as you used the "slant sheet."
   How did you do?   Excellent ___ Good ___ Fair ___ Poor ___

   _____
   _____
   _____

4. Look at all of the writing you did for today. What do you feel is the main thing you need to work on? Check that one.

   slant of writing   _____
   size of letters   _____
   finishing strokes   _____
   correct letter formation _____

Lesson IX

Spacing in Handwriting

After one word has been written, a space the width of a letter *o* is left before starting the next word. This space should never be smaller or larger than the letter *o*.

1. Look at the long sentence you wrote in Lesson VIII. See if the spacing between words is about as wide as the letter *o*. Are you leaving too much or too little space? How would you grade your spacing on the sentence you wrote in Lesson VIII?

    Excellent ___   Good ___   Fair ___   Poor ___

2. Put the correct heading on your paper for today.

    Write the following sentence, being careful to leave the space of a letter *o* between each word. Write each sentence two times:

    The quick brown fox jumps over the lazy dog.

    Whatever is worth doing at all is worth doing well.

    Well begun is half done.

3. It is harder to judge the spacing between letters in a word. Sometimes the letters are close together. This is especially true when you have two tall letters that come next to each other, as in: will, little, letter. Sometimes the spacing has to be wider so that each letter is separate and stands out clearly, as in: write, usual, summer.

    A good general suggestion is to use a little more space for the small hump letters and let the tall letters come fairly close together. You will have to be the best judge of this. You will be able to tell whether your writing is easy to read.

Lesson X

Alignment

Good writers try to have all of their letters rest on the base line. A few letters have lower loops that go half a space below the line. All of the other letters are written directly on the line. Because of a difficult connective stroke, some letters need to start out above the line, but some part of every single letter written always rests on the base line. This makes your writing neat and helps to improve handwriting.

1. Take the written work for Lesson IX. Look at the sentences you wrote. Check the alignment of each word. Are the letters and words just touching the line? Are any of these letters written above the line so they seem to float in the air? Are some of them below the line as if they were stuck in the mud? Even the lower-loop letters have a part which should be written on the line. See if these lower loop letters are properly aligned. Draw a circle around each word that needs better alignment. How would you grade your work?   Excellent ___   Good ___   Fair ___   Poor ___

2. Put the correct heading on your paper for today.

    Write the following proverbs twice, being careful to have all letters rest on the base line. See how many other correct items you can remember as you write.

Time lost is never found again.
Waste not, want not.
Pennies saved are pennies earned.
Always lend a helping hand.
Do a good deed daily.

3. Now check to see how good the alignment is. Draw a circle around any word that is either above or below the line. Put a check mark above each word that is just right. Now practice writing again any words that have been circled.

4. And do check all of your writing again:

	Excellent	Good	Fair	Poor
How good was your alignment?	————	———	———	———
How was the slant of your writing?	————	———	———	———
How was the spacing between words?	————	———	———	———
How were the finishing strokes?	————	———	———	———
How were the letter sizes?	————	———	———	———
What would be your total grade?	————	———	———	———

Lesson XI

Small Letters—the "Over-Curve" Family

There are a few letters that are difficult to make. They belong to the "over-curve" family, for they start with a curve or hump. These letters are *m, n, v, x, y, z*. They all start on the line. More important, they all need to have a good, rounded hump—especially the *m* and the *n*. The *m* and *n* also have another thing to watch—they need to have a retrace stroke after the first hump—just as the *d* and the *t* had retrace strokes coming down from the top.

1. Take the written work for Lesson X. Look at the first sentence you wrote. Check the letter *m* in the word *time*. Does it have three nice humps? Are they all the same height? Have you retraced on the second and third leg? Yes ___ No ___
Check all of the other humped letters in the same way. How did you do?

n	Excellent ___	Good ___	Fair ___	Poor ___
v	Excellent ___	Good ___	Fair ___	Poor ___
y	Excellent ___	Good ___	Fair ___	Poor ___

2. Now put the correct heading on your paper for today.
Write a line of each of the following letters:
      m, n, v, x, y, z—(if you have any doubts, look at the alphabet sample posted in your room or in your copy book).
Write each of these words three times, being especially careful of the letters with the "over-curve":
      man   many   nut   very   extra   yes   lazy

Check back over your work to see if each of the "over-curve" letters in these words started with a good stroke. Check to see if the letters are ⅓rd of a space tall. Put a check mark above any that could be done better.

3. Write these two sentences twice. Be careful of the hump letters.
   Many men ran to the hill.
   The lazy man took many extra steps.
4. Look back at today's writing. Grade it, thinking of all you know about good writing: Excellent ___ Good ___ Fair ___ Poor ___
5. See if you can improve your writing grade for today by writing this sentence, paying attention to all important points such as: height, slant, finishing stroke, alignment.
   I am improving my handwriting by doing careful work.

Lesson XII

Capital Letters—The "Cane" Family

There are 11 capital letters that start with a "loop-stem" or "cane." This is the family:

You will notice that each starts with a loop—made just like a letter *e* that might be written upside down. It is not difficult to learn to make this loop stem if you take time to practice.

1. Get out the paper that you wrote when you did Lesson III. Check the capital letters that you made then. See if they start with a good loop stem.

H	Yes ___	No ___	X	Yes ___	No ___
K	Yes ___	No ___	U	Yes ___	No ___
M	Yes ___	No ___	V	Yes ___	No ___
N	Yes ___	No ___	Y	Yes ___	No ___
W	Yes ___	No ___	Z	Yes ___	No ___
			Q	Yes ___	No ___

2. Put the correct heading on your paper.
   Try writing a line of each of these loop stem letters. Remember, start the "loop stem" just a little below the top line for your capital letters. Then swing around as if you were making a letter *e* upside down. Some of the letters then swing down with a straight line until they touch the bottom line that you are writing on. These are *H, K, M, N*. Other letters start the same way and then curve before they come to the bottom line. Use the examples in your handwriting book to be certain you are right.
3. Write each of these words two times. Start the words with capital letters:
   Help Keep Much No West Use Very Yes Question
4. When you are done, compare your capitals with the examples in your handwriting book. Put a check mark above any that need to be improved. Then write each letter ten times, trying to make it as near perfect as you can.
5. Put your slant sheet under today's paper. Check to see whether your capital letters have the correct slant. How did you do?
   Excellent ___ Good ___ Fair ___ Poor ___

If you had trouble, you may enjoy trying this exercise. Write it as often as you wish:

LESSON XIII

Capital Letters—The Compound Curve Group

There are seven capital letters that are sometimes a little difficult to write. This is because each of these letters uses a "compound curve." In other words, part of each letter has curves like those that are made when we write the number 8. This is what a compound curve looks like:

The letters are: *T, D, F, L, K, Q.* Notice in the example below how to make this curve. Can you find it in the capitals that are included in this lesson?

1. Look at these six letters as they are written in your Copy Book. Now get out your paper that you wrote when you did Lesson XII. See how well you did with the compound curve when you wrote *K* and *Q.* Did you make good compound curves? Yes ___ No ___

2. Put the correct heading on your papers.
   Make a row of the number 8, making the compound curve just as you see it in your copy book.
   Now make a row of the number 8, only have it lying on its side, resting on the base line. Be certain to keep the compound curve.
   Study these examples of the letters *T* and *F.* Note that they are the same except that *F* has the crossed line halfway up the stem. Notice that each letter has two compound-curves.
   Write a row of capital *T* and a row of capital *F.* See that the top stroke almost but not quite touches the downward stem.
   Study these examples of the letters *L* and *Q.* Notice that the compound curve rests on the line. The finish stroke ends below the line.
   Make a row of each letter—*L* and *Q.* Check to be certain that the compound curve rests on the line and the finish stroke is below the line.
   Look at the letter *D* in your Copy Book. See where its compound curve occurs. Look at the *K.* Can you find its two compound curves in the part that attaches to the "cane"? Work to make these like part of the number 8. Write a row of each.

3. Write each of these sentences twice. Be careful in making the compound curve. Be certain, too, to make your capitals as tall as your loop letters— almost a full space tall.

   Today is Friday.
   King David ruled the land.
   Lovely Queen Esther ruled, too.

4. How well did you do today? Make the number 8 on top of the word *Today*. Is the top part of your *T* a compound curve? Yes ___ No ___

Lesson XIV

Capital Letters—Boat Endings: *B, I, G, S, T, F.*

There are 6 capital letters that have "boat" endings. They are easy to make if you pause just before you start the back stroke that finishes the letter. The check mark ($\sqrt{}$) shows where to pause when making each.

1. Before starting to work on these, take out yesterday's paper. Two of the letters had "boat" endings—the *T* and *F*. Check to see if you made the ending correctly. Yes ___ No ___
While your paper is out, check your work on the sentences using the slant sheet. How well did you do?
        Excellent ___ Good ___ Fair ___ Poor ___
Check the finish strokes. How well did you do?
        Excellent ___ Good ___ Fair ___ Poor ___
Check for letter heights. In the first sentence, are the *t* and *d* about ⅔ rds of a space tall? In the second sentence, are the two *l*'s almost a space tall? Are they as tall as the capitals? In the third sentence, are all of the small letters in the word "Queen" the same height, about ⅓ rd of a space tall?
Grade your work: (thinking of height, slant, finish stroke)
        Excellent ___ Good ___ Fair ___ Poor ___

2. Put the correct heading on your paper.
Look at the six "boat-ending" letters. Now make a row of each letter, working on the following point as well as on the "boat" ending.
B—See that the back slants and then retrace to the top. Be certain that the "boat" point touches the slant part of the letter *B*.
F—Start with a good "cane" stroke. Then see that you have the two good compound curves. As you make the point of the "boat," be certain that it goes to the left beyond the "cane" that you started with.
G—Start on the line with a good upstroke. Make the point on the *G* before starting down. Then let the point of the "boat" go beyond the beginning stroke.
S—The *S* starts up just like the letter *G*. As you come down, cross the up-stroke in the middle of the space. Round the "S" nicely so it cannot be mistaken for a "G." Like the "G," let the point of the "boat" go beyond the beginning stroke.
T and F—Both letters are made much alike. Look back at the direc-

tions given for the letter *F* above. You will use the capital *T* more than most other capital letters. Work to make it look neat and legible.

    I—This is probably the hardest letter to make. It starts on the line just like capital *J* does, and swings up. *THE LETTER I SHOULD NOT HAVE A ROUND BACK.* Come down in a straight slant line. Curve up when you reach the base line, and then add the "boat" ending.

3. Write each of these words four times. Check for good "boat" endings, and also check for correct letter height.

      Boston   Fresno   Georgia   South   Idaho   Tennessee

4. Look carefully at the letters and words you have written today. Grade your writing as: Excellent, Good, Fair, Poor.

      Boat Strokes: _____   Slant: _____

      Finish Strokes: _____   Alignment: _____

Lesson XV

Handwriting Demons—*a, b, d, e, h.*

The dictionary says that a *demon* is an evil spirit. This is not true in handwriting. But the 15 handwriting *demons* are letters that cause much trouble for many writers. When these letters are written carelessly, it looks as if our words have been spelled incorrectly. Look at the examples of the demons when they are written incorrectly. Then practice the correct way to write these letters.

a instead of *o*   *a* instead of *a*   *a* instead of *a*   *b* instead of *l*

d instead of *d*   *e* instead of *e*   *h* instead of *h*   *i* instead of *i*

1. Get out your copy of the work you did for Lesson III. Look at the following letters that you wrote: *a, b, d, e, h.* Check with the correct form. Circle any letters that you did incorrectly. How many did you do just right? _____

2. Put the correct heading on today's paper.
   Write one line of each of today's letters. Be careful to make each letter perfectly. See if you can avoid the "demon" pitfalls.
   Write this sentence three times. You will note that it has all of the demons in it:
       A bad fog covered every hill.

3. Look carefully at the sentence that you have written four times above. Circle any letters that are poorly written. Copy them correctly on this line.

    _____

4. And now for an interesting spot-check on your handwriting. Grade your work by checking in the correct place:

                  Excellent   Good   Fair   Poor

    a. Use the slant sheet on the four
         sentences you just wrote.   _____   _____   _____   _____

    b. On the first sentence, draw a

line with your ruler from the top
of the *A* to the top of *l* in hill.
The following should touch it:
A, f, h, l.

_____ ____ ____ ____

c. On the second sentence, check
for finishing strokes. Circle any
word that does not have a good
stroke.

_____ ____ ____ ____

d. On the third sentence, check to
see if all letters rest on the base
line.

_____ ____ ____ ____

e. On the fourth sentence, check
to see if the space between
words is about the width of a
letter *o.*

_____ ____ ____ ____

WHAT GRADE WOULD YOU GIVE
YOUR WHOLE PAPER?

_____ ____ ____ ____

LESSON XVI

The Rest of The Demons—*m, n, o, r, t.*

There are only a few other handwriting demons. All of the demons
together make up about half of the problems that people have in writing.
Practicing to improve these letters will make your writing much better.
Study the correct way to make each of these letters. Avoid the common
fault that can make any of these a demon.

m instead of *M*   *n* instead of *N*   *o* instead of *o*   *r* instead of *r*

t instead of *t*   *t* instead of *t*   *t* instead of *t*

1. Put the correct heading on today's paper.
   Now write this complete sentence three times. Be careful, for all of the
   demon letters are in it.
         I can improve my handwriting greatly by practicing daily.
2. Write each of these words three times, being careful to make all letters
   correctly:
         many   not   nor   ton   rot   mother   north
3. And now for a spotcheck on certain letters. If you have made a letter
   that could be confused, then you have a problem to correct.

	Excellent	Good	Fair	Poor

a. Check the letter *a* in the first
sentence you wrote. It appears
five times. Draw a circle around
each. Now, how good was it?

_____ ____ ____ ____

b. Check the letter *b*. It appears
only once. Draw a circle around
it in each sentence. Grade it.

_____ ____ ____ ____

c. Check the letter *d*. It appears
twice. Draw a circle around it
in each sentence. Grade it.

_____ ____ ____ ____

    d. Do the same for each of the fol-
       lowing letters:
    e. The letter *e*.
    f. The letter *h*.
    g. The letter *i*.
    h. The letter *m*.
    i. The letter *n*.
    j. The letter *o*.
    k. The letter *r*.
    l. The letter *t*.

4. Which letters did you mark "Excellent" _____
5. Which did you mark "Good" _____
6. Which did you mark "Fair" or "Poor" _____
    Write a line of each of these to see if you can improve them greatly.

Lesson XVII

Writing Numbers

    Numbers are used quite often and must be written properly. Study the correct form of the samples carefully and be sure to avoid the incorrect forms. Correct any errors you have been making.

Correct Form	Common Problems
1	
2	2 2
3	3 3
4	4 4
5	5 5

Correct Form	Common Problems
6	6 6
7	7 7
8	
9	9 9
10	

REMEMBER, all numbers are made ⅔rds of a space high.
1. Take out your last arithmetic paper. Look at each of the different figures. Circle those that you need to improve. List those that you have circled on this line:

    _____

    How would you grade your numbers?
                     Excellent ___ Good ___ Fair ___ Poor ___

2. Put the correct heading on today's paper.
    Write one line of each figure. Be sure to make them correctly and the proper height.
    Write an extra line of any numbers that you circled on your arithmetic paper.

3. Copy and do these problems. Be neat and careful. Write the numbers carefully. Do what the sign tells you to do.

51	18	45	72	67	18	24	12
×3	+31	−23	+51	−34	−5	×2	+48

12	34	56	78	90	987	654	321
+91	+82	+73	−10	+64	−100	−123	+456

4. Look back at the figures you have just written. Check the last row of problems especially, for it contains all of the numbers several times.

 a. Are all of your numbers made correctly? Yes ___ No ___
 b. Do all of the numbers rest on the base line? Yes ___ No ___
 c. Are the numbers made with a good slant? Yes ___ No ___
 d. Are they all ⅔rds of a space 'tall? Yes ___ No ___

5. How would you grade your writing? Excellent   Good   Fair   Poor

_____   _____   _____   _____

Lesson XVIII

Page Arrangement, Margins

When we write any paper, it must be easy to read. If it is neat in appearance and well arranged on the paper, it can be most attractive. Besides knowing how to write correctly, we must know how to organize and arrange written work.

A good heading is important for nearly any kind of written work. You have been using a heading for these blitz papers that is often used in junior high and senior high school, too.

Margins help us to have a neat paper. For neatness, margins are left on all four sides of a paper. The left side margin is one inch wide so several papers may be fastened together along this side. The other three margins are about one-half inch wide. This means that one never writes on the top or bottom line. The left margin should always be straight. Sometimes the right margin will not be as straight because of the difference in length of some words. We do the best we can, though, to have the left and the right margin straight.

1. Take out the paper that you did yesterday. It was a number paper, but it should have been done neatly. How well did you do?

	Excellent	Good	Fair	Poor
a. Was the heading done correctly?	_____	_____	_____	_____
b. How neatly were the problems arranged on your paper?	_____	_____	_____	_____
c. How good were the margins on all four sides?	_____	_____	_____	_____

2. Now, knowing all that you do about good writing, margins, slant, finish strokes, and correct letter forms, see how well you can do in preparing a most attractive and correct paper. Copy the following story:

Handwriting Can Be Fun

There are some people who moan and groan when they have to write a letter. They hunt until they find a good writing tool. Then they search for the right kind of paper. Finally, when they sit down to write, they think they are tired before they start.

Handwriting can be fun, though. Think of being able to send

your own ideas thousands of miles away. Think of being able to "talk" to people you have never met. It can be done because "handwriting" is a tool of communication. When we use this tool well, we can make new friends. We can share our thoughts with others. We can open the door to world friendship.

3. Now check your writing to see how well you did:
   How would you grade it: Excellent ___   Good ___   Fair ___   Poor ___

Lesson XIX

Have I Improved?

When you first started the HANDWRITING BLITZ, your teacher dictated sentences using your spelling words. Today you will have some dictated sentences using the words you studied for spelling last week. Besides spelling the words correctly, you will want to check several things:

a. Heading—will it be neat and attractive?
b. Margins—have I planned in advance so I will have good margins on all four sides?
c. Writing tool—is my pencil sharp and long enough to use well?
d. Position—am I sitting correctly, and is my paper slanted properly?
e. Readiness—is my desk cleared of extra books and papers?
   Readiness—am I ready to give my best attention?
   Readiness—do I remember what I need to think about to do my best writing—letter form, height, slant, finish strokes?

1. Put the correct heading on your paper and wait for the dictation.
2. After you have written this dictation lesson, look over your writing very carefully. See how you would grade it:

	Excellent	Good	Fair	Poor
a. *Slant* Do all of the letters slant in the same direction?	___	___	___	___
b. *Spacing* Are the spaces between words even so each word can be read?	___	___	___	___
c. *Size* Are the small letters ⅓ space tall? Are the capitals and tall letters almost a space high?	___	___	___	___
d. *Alignment* Do all of the letters of each word rest on the line as they should?	___	___	___	___
e. *Tall letters* Are all tall letters about a space tall and well formed? (*l, f, h, k, b*)	___	___	___	___
f. *Closings* Are the following letters closed: *a, d, g, o, p, s?*	___	___	___	___
g. *Roundness* Are *m, n, h, u, v, w, y* rounded on the top?	___	___	___	___

h. *Endings*
    Does each word have a good fin-
    ishing stroke?   _____   _____   _____   _____

AND NOW FOR THE REAL TEST:

Take out the paper that you wrote for Lesson I. It was the same kind of test!

How do the two papers compare? Write your evaluation here:

I have improved my: _____

I need to work to improve my: _____

	Excellent	Good	Fair	Poor
The progress I have made is:	_____	_____	_____	_____

Lesson XX

A Sample of My Best Writing

You have now had nineteen of the Handwriting Lessons. Let us see how much you have improved.

1. Today you will again write some sentences and letters using your best handwriting. Be sure to use proper letter size, correct letter form, good slant, even alignment, and end each word with a good finishing stroke.

2. Put your heading on your paper.
   Write the following paragraph using your best writing. Put in the correct number in the blank space:

   This is a sample of my best handwriting. I did it when I was in the _____ grade. I am _____ years old.

3. Skip one space. Write all of the capital letters of the alphabet. Write them as carefully as you can.
   Now skip one more space and write all of the small letters of the alphabet.
   Now skip another space and write the numbers from 1 to 10: (1, 2, 3, 4, 5, 6, 7, 8, 9, 10).

4. Take out the paper that you did for Lesson III. Compare it with today's paper.
   Have you improved?   _____
   Is your paper neater today?   _____
   Does your writing slant more evenly?   _____
   Is your writing easier to read?   _____
   Are your letters more carefully made?   _____

IF THE ANSWERS TO ALL OF THE QUESTIONS ABOVE ARE "YES," then you know that you can improve your handwriting by giving careful attention to it and working to improve.

IF THE ANSWER TO ANY QUESTION ABOVE IS "NO," then you know that you will want to continue to work to improve your handwriting. Decide what you need to do to make your writing better. Then do the following:

1. Ask your teacher to help you decide what you need to work on most.
2. Practice improving writing *every time you write.*

ON ITALIC HANDWRITING [*]

Frank N. Freeman

Word has come to this country of a style of handwriting that is growing in popularity in Great Britain. The style is said to be superior to those commonly used there. Since the enthusiasm will probably spread to the United States, it is worthwhile to evaluate this style as best we can.

In the past we have adopted new systems on the basis of partial evidence and inadequate study, and later we had to backtrack. Certainly it behooves us to take a good look before we leap.

The style of writing in question is called Italic writing and is advocated by Reginald Piggott in his book, *Handwriting, A National Survey*. The style is not really new, but a slight modification of minuscule script, a style used for writing manuscripts before the age of printing. This style was revived by Sir Edward Johnston, the calligrapher, in about 1900. It was adopted for schools in what became known as manuscript writing and is now used in this country in 85 per cent of the schools as an introductory style of writing in the first two grades.

The Italic writing, advocated by Piggott is derived from Sir Edward Johnston's script. In the Italic style, Johnston's script is made over into a slanting style, and the letters are connected. The writing is still done with a broad-edged pen, so that the downstrokes are broad and the upstrokes narrow. This style is confused by Piggott with the early Italian *cancellaresca*, or chancery, hand, which is really the ancestor of our common script. According to Piggott, since 1950 some fifty textbooks, sets of copy books, and manuals have been published in the Italic style.

Piggott's book is profusely illustrated with examples of his own writing. Since he is an expert, his samples are attractive and legible. A great many examples by other writers are also included. Some of these specimens are admirable, others less so.

The author sketches the history of handwriting styles in England. He tells us that the copperplate style—with its long loops, extreme slant, and flourishes—is named for the copperplate engravings employed in copy books, which were used in teaching handwriting until the middle of the nineteenth century.

---

[*] Reprinted from *Elementary School Journal* (February 1960), by permission of the author and the University of Chicago Press.

The copperplate style was later modified and became the so-called civil service hand, typified in the Vere-Foster System. This system was plainer. It had less slant, shorter loops, "a comparatively high degree of legibility" and could be "written with reasonable speed," Piggott notes.

His opinion of this style seems a bit uncertain, for two pages later he writes, "Unfortunately the civil-service style is not compatible with speed, if it is to attain legibility. Written quickly the loops become

perche'aloechio mio la littera corsina onero (ancellarefcha) vuole hamere

you have one of dispose of please will call, and er

The chancery cursive hand of Italian writing masters of the sixteenth century.

Spencerian writing from the hand of Spencer.

enlarged and badly formed and the height of the small letters becomes inconsistent."

Piggott's ideas on legibility are quite confused. Italic style, he says "has the distinct advantage (in its model form) of being a hundred-per-cent legible due to the complete simplicity of the letters."

It is obvious that Piggott is using a dual standard for judging legibility. He is thinking, first, of the legibility of a style "in its model form" and, second, of its legibility as it is actually written. The latter is more to the point. All styles are completely legible in their model or ideal form, but handwriting has to be read as it is actually written, not as it appears in the copy book.

The only useful method of judging the legibility of various styles, therefore, is to measure their legibility as they are written by a large

half-uncial modern straight-pen writing round, upright, formal

horizon – as if the whole terre had been one jewel, one colossal single gem fashioned into a pl

The half-uncial letters of Edward Johnston, which were the basis of the movement toward manuscript writing in the United States in the 1920's.

Specimen of modern Italic writing based on Italian chancery.

number of randomly selected individuals, writing under comparable conditions. Piggott did not attempt such a test.

It is not clear from the author's account just what he included in his survey. He says that he has a comprehensive collection of all types and styles of handwriting that he has gathered over many years. According to his book, he has received many letters in response to articles that he has contributed to magazines from time to time.

Recently he made a request for samples that was carried in a large number of newspapers, journals, and trade periodicals. He asked that handwriting specimens be sent to him along with information on the writer's age, sex, occupation, handedness, and type of pen used. He reports that he received more than twenty-five thousand replies. We assume that the tables and charts in his book are based on this batch of twenty-five thousand letters.

When Piggott classified and tabulated the data from the letters, we assume that he included all of them, though he does not definitely say so. Nor does he give the data from which this fact may be established. His charts show only percentages, not actual numbers. This omission seriously limits the interpretation that can be placed on the findings.

Piggott classified the papers on the basis of the writer's occupation, style of writing, type of pen used, slope of writing, legibility, and use of right or left hand.

All occupations represented were grouped under twenty-six classes, but Piggott gives no table or chart telling the number or the per cent in each class, so that the significance of the comparisons between the occupations is doubtful.

He classified his specimens under five categories: copperplate, civil service, Italic, semi-joined, and others. Five categories for pens are given: fine, medium, broad, ball point, and others. Six degrees of slope are distinguished: backhand, upright, forward 1–10 degrees, forward 10–20 degrees, forward 20–30 degrees, and forward 30 degrees plus. Four gradations of legibility are noted: almost illegible, moderately legible, fairly highly legible, and completely legible. He classed all writers as right- or left-handed on the basis of their own statements.

The classifications for legibility are perhaps the most important. It would be highly desirable to have these judgments made objectively. The author evidently did the classifying himself and apparently did not try to get any check on his judgment. He gives no analysis of the criteria of judgment he used or any samples of the specimens he classified as almost illegible, moderately legible, fairly highly legible, or completely legible.

His remarks on legibility, some of which I have already quoted, give us reason to think that his standard of legibility may not be altogether objective. One could wish that this crucial step had been treated more satisfactorily.

More significant than the first-order classification are comparisons between the classes. The author draws comparisons only on the basis of occupation. For example, he gives the percentage of writers in the various occupations who use the various styles of writing. He reports that Italic style was used by 39.2 per cent of the artists and 2.1 per cent of the housewives. This information is interesting, but it would be more meaningful if we knew how many persons were in the two groups.

Piggott's findings tell us little or nothing about the value of the Italic style. He could have compared the legibility of this style with that of other styles. Even if we gave limited credence to the judgment of legibility, a comparison would give us some basis for evaluation. Since the author's main interest is to promote the Italic style, it is strange that he did not take this opportunity to test its merits. As it is, he gives no statistical evidence whatever about its advantages.

The other data he gives consist of 393 specimens of writing of different styles presented in random order. The author did separate the thirty-eight samples of children's writing from samples of adults' writing. Since he makes no statement as to how this series was selected, these specimens cannot be considered a representative sample of the twenty-five thousand he collected.

No estimate can be made of the legibility of the various styles. But some tentative conclusions seem to be justified from a casual examination. The legibility of a given style may vary from writing that is almost impossible to read to writing that can be read with no effort at all. Each style of writing may be so written that each letter is clear and distinct or so that each letter is poorly formed and hard to distinguish. The various letters in each style may be well spaced from their neighbors or crowded against one another. Words and lines may stand apart distinctly or be intermingled.

Hence, all styles are subject to variations that make the writing legible or illegible. The ideal shape of the individual letters does not determine legibility. Even the contour of a word as a whole has a definite influence, since for the most part we read by words, not by letters.

A recent doctoral dissertation by Elaine M. Templin brought out two important facts about handwriting: First, examples of a given style vary widely in legibility. Second, it is difficult to make a reliable comparison of the legibility of different styles.

The author gave examples to show the wide range of legibility within each of three styles. She used an objective method of measuring the legibility of the writing and an elaborate statistical technique for comparing the scores of the three groups.

Using these precautions, she was not able to establish a significant difference in the legibility of the three styles, one of which was manuscript writing. This style would seem to have at least as good a claim to legibility as the Italic style.

Since the claim to superior legibility of Italic writing rests on shaky evidence, we suspect that the preference for this style is due largely to admiration for its aesthetic qualities, not its practical advantages. In any case the supposed superiority in legibility is far from sufficient reason to warrant that a nation scrap the style of writing taught in its schools to adopt the style proposed.

In weighing the proposal, the history and the circumstances of the teaching of handwriting in the United States would have to be considered.

In the early part of the nineteenth century, the prevailing style in England was similar to that in the United States. This was derived from a slanting script that appeared in Italy in the sixteenth century and was called *cancellaresca,* or chancery, script. It was a slanting, connected script, written without the broad downstrokes of minuscule writing. It became widely adapted to commercial use because of the speed with which it could be written.

It was this script that was adapted for instruction in the schools and was reproduced by copperplate engraving in copy books. The use of these copy books disseminated and standardized the style. It is exemplified in the so-called copperplate writing in England and the Spencerian writing in this country. It was originally written with a quill pen, with long loops and heavily shaded downstrokes. Much of the writing was slow, painstakingly careful, and doubtless done chiefly with the fingers. Use was confined to a minority of highly trained individuals.

About the middle of the century a somewhat freer style was developed. In England it was called the civil service style, and it still persists. It has shorter loops and is somewhat more rounded but still uses shaded downstrokes made with a fine steel pen.

In this country the modification was more radical and took place in two stages, both in response to the commercial demand for an easier style and a wider diffusion of facility in writing.

The first stage was dominated by Platt R. Spencer, for whom the style was named. The letters in this style were simplified, the loops were shortened; and the writing was somewhat freer. But Spencerian writing did not differ much from the civil service style in England.

In the second stage elements were introduced that made the handwriting of both children and adults in the United States fundamentally different from the handwriting in England. These elements were first introduced into business schools and then into the public schools by such men as A. N. Palmer and C. P. Zaner, about 1890.

The element that was most emphasized, and for a time exaggerated, was the arm movement. What is essential is not arm movement only, but a free participation of the hand and arm in a swinging movement that carries the hand along from letter to letter across the page. The method calls for a fairly level position of the hand, which rests on the last two fingers, instead of the side. In this position the hand can slide easily across the page. The loops are shortened still more, the shading is eliminated, and the capitals are simplified.

The development of cursive writing in this country was interrupted in the nineties by the widespread adoption in the schools of the vertical style of writing, beginning about 1890. The style was advocated on two grounds: legibility and certain physiological considerations.

The legibility argument resembles that advanced for Italic writing and may be disposed of in much the same way. As for the physiological considerations, it has been argued that slanting writing causes the writer to bend his back and neck sideways. The position not only produces curvature of the spine, critics say, but causes eye strain by requiring a diagonal movement of the eyes.

The physiological objections to slanting writing were disposed of by showing that difficulties do not arise if two practices are followed. The paper should be placed directly in front of the writer at an angle with the vertical of about 30 degrees, and the forearms should be placed in symmetrical positions on the desk.

Vertical writing ran afoul of another difficulty which was not expected but became noticeable because of the American emphasis on movement as well as form. When the paper is placed with the sides perpendicular to the front edge of the desk, so that the downstrokes of the writing will be vertical, the forearm has to be drawn back as the hand progresses across the page to prevent the writing from running uphill. The position, of course, becomes awkward. The natural movement is to carry the hand across the page by a sideward sweep of the forearm across the page with the elbow as a pivot.

These difficulties led to the almost complete abandonment of vertical writing in the schools by 1910. Soon after the transition back from vertical writing to slanting writing, the method of psychological analysis and experimental study began to be applied extensively to the teaching of school subjects. This development made it possible to evaluate existing practices, to appraise proposed new practices, and to select their desirable features without including their disadvantages.

Our method of dealing with manuscript writing when it was brought over from Great Britain was mature. The style was studied carefully in the laboratory and the classroom. Its merits and limitations were considered, and it was finally incorporated into the lower grades as an introductory style. The method of handling this style was not left to the devices of the individual teacher but was carefully worked out in sets of textbooks and manuals.

In my judgment, Italic handwriting, like vertical writing, would not have the overwhelming superiority in legibility that is claimed for it. Italic handwriting, I believe, would fail to use the fluent, easy, and effective movement that has been developed and is used in the current American cursive style. My judgment is based on the history of the development of handwriting in this country and on various scientific experiments.

I am not opposed to all changes in style, but it seems desirable to make changes only after careful study. Once the decision to change has been made, the new style should be uniformly taught.

The situation would not then arise in which a great diversity of styles are taught with the result that a child frequently learns different styles as he moves from school to school or from grade to grade.

This confusion has existed in the past in our country. I myself was taught a modern version of the Spencerian system in the lower grades. I was converted to vertical writing in the upper grades and then subjected in high school to the mechanical drills of the arm movement system of an itinerant writing "professor."

It must be admitted that we have sadly neglected the technique of writing. The need is for a reform in teaching rather than a revolution in style.

I wish to again recommend emphatically that the style and the method of handwriting in the schools be reasonably uniform and that changes be introduced only after careful study and experimentation.

To bring about a sweeping and radical change throughout the country would require a revolution in the training of teachers, in the preparation of textbooks, and in the retraining of teachers already in service. The change would be even more drastic than the retooling of the automobile industry.

Even if our educational systems could stand the cost, we do not have the centralized authority to carry out such a retooling. Both the theoretical and the practical considerations inspire the hope that the school leaders of the United States will not be lured into a hasty and ill-considered adoption of the Italic hand now being advocated in Great Britain and discussed in this country.

REFLECTIONS ON THE TEACHING OF HANDWRITING *

Luella Cole

No subject in the curriculum is as neglected or as poorly taught, above the first three grades, as handwriting. And in no other subject are the results of instruction less impressive. The writer believes that much of the difficulty results from fundamental misconceptions about

* Reprinted from *Elementary School Journal* (November 1956), by permission of the University of Chicago Press.

the nature of handwriting, which differs from reading and arithmetic because it consists of muscular skills, not of ideas.

Handwriting is allied to athletic skills. One needs the same physical basis for producing a good script that one needs for hitting a ball, or rolling a hoop, or jumping a rope; namely, good muscular control, relaxed nerves, good eyesight, and excellent co-ordination between hand and eye. These nonintellectual traits develop largely as a result of mere age and growth, although training can accelerate the process. The main thing to grasp is that handwriting is purely a muscular tool, without content or end in itself, and without any fixed relation to intellectual development.

The average elementary-school teacher is not well equipped by nature, interests, or past experiences to be a good instructor of handwriting. To begin with the teacher is almost always a woman; and, because of her sex, she has not undergone a complete course of training in any skill or sport. She may have played this or that game in her younger days, but athletics have not been her main interest. Only an unusual girl spends endless hours "playing catch" or polishing any other rudimentary physical skill. With the coming of adolescence, most girls withdraw altogether from participation in sports. For one thing, they prefer to concentrate on social relations, and, for another, they soon learn that what boys want is admiration for athletic skill, not competition. As girls go through their teens, they run more slowly, jump to a lower height, and throw a ball less far with every passing year. Only a few ever show the passionate devotion to sports that characterizes boys of the same ages, and, by the time they are eighteen, the great majority of girls indulge only superficially and incidentally in any game. What athletic skill girls have is the result of natural co-ordination, plus casual advice from friends and some degree of spontaneous self-discipline and practice. It is rare for a girl to receive the meticulous muscle-training that is given boys who try out for school teams.

Women teachers, as a group, are therefore poorly prepared to teach muscular co-ordination. Moreover, a certain proportion of them are even less competent than the average in this respect, because they went into the "book learning" which subsequently led to their becoming teachers, precisely because they were not successful in the games and sports of childhood and early adolescence. Such women cannot give competent instruction in a purely muscular type of learning because they do not know from their own experience how muscular skills are acquired.

METHOD OF TRAINING A MUSCULAR SKILL

Perhaps the best way to explain the learning of a skill is to consider the course of training that a good tennis coach gives to a pupil. He begins by demonstrating, slowly and accurately, the precise series of movements that will lead to the establishment of a correct stroke— say, a forehand drive. He shows each movement separately, and he puts them together to demonstrate the final result. The pupil next tries to imitate what he has seen, while the coach watches and corrects each error as soon as it appears. Usually the pupil practices for some time without even having a ball to hit, and when he does begin to hit a ball, he is made to stroke is as easily as he can and is never allowed to hurry. The imitative learning continues until the pupil can execute the stroke perfectly and can diagnose and correct his own errors. He is then sent to the backstop for weeks of practice. He hits the ball gently, slowly, and correctly. If the coach sees him "pressing" or hurrying, he at once tells him to relax. During these weeks of training the pupil is not allowed to play with his friends, because the pressure of competition would lead him into trying to "slam" the ball and he would soon "unlearn" his new stroke. As time goes on, the series of movements becomes easier and easier, and the pupil presently is allowed to exert whatever strength he can, provided the smoothness of his co-ordination is retained. From this point on the pupil develops mainly because he grows older, bigger, and stronger. This improvement takes place even if he does not use his stroke, although it occurs faster if he does, provided he avoids strain and continues to diagnose his incorrect responses if and when they appear. If this system of training were to be reduced to precepts, these would run something as follows:

1. Base the teaching upon careful imitation of a good model, allowing only such minor variations as are necessary because of a pupil's age or size.
2. Continue the practice of simple skills under close supervision until the pupil can execute a series of movements perfectly.
3. Teach self-diagnosis and self-correction, until you feel sure that the pupil has the habit of self-appraisal.
4. Then introduce intensive practice, but without competition.
5. Permit no strain or pressure. If the pupil voluntarily tries to hurry, stop him.
6. Wait for nature to take its course in the development of speed.

CHAPTER 5

Spelling

The merits of the English Language are many but the way it is spelled is atrocious. Teachers have always been challenged to find ways to teach some of the illogical and irrational spelling variables. The fact that so many children spell the language reasonably well is a tribute to the dedicated efforts of countless teachers.

THOZE SPELING DEEMUNS *

Ralph Dornfeld Owen

A man named Mr. John Pough calls on you and hands you his card. To be polite you try to pronounce his name. What will you say?

Mr. Po	*o* as in dough or toe
Mr. Puf	*u* as in rough or cuff
Mr. Pawf	*aw* as in cough or off
Mr. Poo	*oo* as in through or too
Mr. Pou	*ou* as in bough or doubt

If you are wise you will say, "How do you pronounce your name, sir?"

This illustrates the fact that no one can know with certainty how to pronounce an English word which he has only seen written or how to spell a word which he has only heard but never seen written.

DIFFERENTIATION

English as a spoken language is easy to learn. Foreigners can pick up a speaking knowledge of English more easily than of any other

---

* Reprinted by permission of the author and publisher from *The Journal of Business Education* (May 1961), copyright by Robert C. Trethaway.

European language. But when they try to read English or try to write English, they have a rough time, because English is cursed with an outworn, illogical system of representing words.

Let us contrast English to German, Swedish, or Turkish. In Swedish *every letter* has one sound, and every sound is *invariably* represented by the same letter or combination of letters.

In other words, German, Swedish, or Turkish has an almost perfectly scientific method of representing its words. It is so simple that a child in the first grade learns to read and write and spell at the same time. In fact, *spelling is not taught as a separate subject.*

Why is German or Swedish or Turkish spelling so efficient? Because they are designed to perform only one function—namely to consistently represent the sounds of the words as pronounced today.

Why is English spelling so inefficient? Because it tries to do two things: (1) Show the history of the word; and (2) show the present pronunciation of the word at the same time as it shows its history.

The word *laugh* is spelled as it is, in order to show that it is a first cousin of the German word *lach* and that 500 years ago it was pronounced as the German word.

But today the word is pronounced *laf*. Here, then, the historical interest defeats the practical need.

CHAOS

English spelling is chaotic because of several variables:
1. *To illustrate single or double consonants:*

*Imm*une	*am*end	e*l*ude
*am*use	*comm*end	a*ll*ude

To gain control over this variable rationally, the average person would have to devote several years to the study of Greek, Latin, and French etymology. If he lacks the time for such study he must undergo the same kind of conditioning as a white rat in a maze or a monkey learning to ride a bicycle.
2. *Silent letters* and *duplicate consonants:*

Every silent letter is a mummy, a speech habit long dead but carefully embalmed and displayed, even though it has a musty smell. English spelling resembles an archaeological museum.

b in bomb, dumb, thumb, lamb, comb, tomb, debt, debtor
g in gnu, gnostic, gnat, gnome, gnaw
k in know, knowledge, knoll, knuckle, knot
l in calf, half, balm, calm, palm, psalm, stalk, talk, walk

p in psalm, psychology, pneumonia, pneumatic, pseudo-, receipt
w in write, written, wring, wrung, wrought, wrath, wroth

Then there are the *duplicate consonants:*

> *g* (soft as in gin) Duplicating *j* as in *jam*
> *gh* is useless wherever it occurs
> *c* (soft as in *cent*) Duplicating *s*
> *c* (hard as in *corn*) Duplicating *k*
> *ph* duplicates *f* everywhere

3. *Vowels:*

Even more serious is the confusion concerning the representation of vowel sounds.

In the pronunciation of present-day English we distinguish 17 vowel and diphthong sounds. Since we have only 5 vowel signs, we must use combinations of letters to represent most of the 17 sounds.

Here confusion reigns. More than 250 combinations of letters are used to represent the 17 vowel sounds, or an average of 18 different combinations for one vowel sound.

To illustrate: The long sound of *o* as in *open* is represented in our present system of spelling by 19 different letters or combinations of letters:

au	(chauffeur)	oo	(floor)
au - e	(mauve)	os	(appropos)
eau	(beau)	ot	(depot)
eo	(yeoman)	ou	(four)
ew	(sew)	o - ue	(rogue)
o	(no)	ou - e	(course)
oa	(coal)	ough	(though)
o - e	(more)	ow	(know)
oe	(toe)	owe	(owe)
oh	(oh)		

In the following sentence the long sound of *o* is represented in eleven different ways:

Our ch*au*ffeur, alth*ough* he stubbed his t*oe*, y*eo*manly t*owe*d f*ou*r m*o*re b*oa*rds through the *o*pen d*oo*r of the dep*o*t.

All of these useless, conflicting patterns are musty, smelling mummies for us adults, but they are nagging, taunting demons for the children who are learning to read.

Now let us turn to our bright-eyed, eager child entering the first grade. He can speak English, and he has a vocabulary of 1000 words or more. He wants to learn to read and to write. But in spite of the care exercised by the author of the reading book and by his teacher, he finds that learning to read is like a visit in the crazy house.

Here are some samples of his tormentors:

Mary, *watch* Tommy *catch* the ball.
Tommy, *put* your *cup* on the table.

The more intelligent the child is, the sooner he is annoyed by such inconsistencies as

watch	*catch*	*cow*	*low*
put	*cup*	*shoe*	*toe*

At the end of the first school year the German, Swedish, or Turkish child can help himself with phonics (because his language has a consistent, logical scheme of representing the sounds of words). But at the end of the first year of school, the English-speaking child, even if he has an I.Q. of 125, still is very much handicapped.

Is it any wonder that in English we have to compile such lists as W. Franklin Jones' "One Hundred Spelling Demons"? Is it any wonder that we have to organize remedial reading classes in secondary schools and even in colleges? Are we to "Point with Pride" at our having such classes? A visiting Turkish educator would think we should be ashamed of it. It is no accident that during World War II the Selective Service reported 1,750,000 draftees in need of reading instruction and made the statement that 12 per cent of our population is functionally illiterate.[1]

WHAT ABOUT IT?

Benjamin Franklin, scientist, and statesman, believed in extending scientific methods to language. In 1768 he composed and circulated "A Scheme for a New Alphabet and Reformed Mode of Spelling."
In a letter, defending his proposal, he wrote:

Whatever the difficulties of reforming our spelling now are, *they will be more easily surmounted now* than hereafter; and some time or other it must be done; *or else our writing will become the same with the Chinese as to the difficulty of learning and using it.*[2]

Dr. Frank Laubach, who has had amazing success in promoting literacy the world over has taught millions of people to read in 200

---

[1] "Literacy" in *American People's Encyclopedia* (Chicago: Sears Roebuck and Co.).
[2] *Complete Works of Benjamin Franklin*, ed. by Jared Sparks (Boston: Hilliard Gray and Co., 1840), vol. VI, p. 295.

languages. How has he done it? By using or inventing a consistent, phonetic system of spelling for each language. Thus, the pupil can concentrate on a single symbol for each sound. Dr. Laubach says:

. . . We could sweep the world with this system of phonetic key word teaching if it were not for one obstacle—the spelling of the English language! If we spelled English phonetically, American children could be taught to read in a week. We needed only a day with the Philippine dialects. I can see only one thing to do—start a strike against the way English is misspelled—become a spelling Bolshevist! I suppose that unless we revolt we shall be handing on this same accursed orthography to our children, and our children's children, to the crack of doom.[3]

ACTION

Let us recognize that language is a living, growing organism but its spelling is a hand-made garment which can and must be changed when it becomes a straight jacket.

Let us abandon our smugness ("what was good enough for me is good enough for my child") and our fatalism ("it can't be done" attitude). Let us catch up with the people of Germany, Sweden, Turkey, Russia, and most countries of Europe, by subscribing sincerely and without mental reservation to the principle that: *The only function of spelling is to represent consistently the sounds of the words as spoken (by the majority of speakers).*

HOPE

In 1930 the Simpler Spelling Society of Great Britain and the Simpler Spelling Association of America applied the principle of frequency count to the representation of English sounds. As a result they approved and recommended to all the people who speak English a system of spelling in which each sound is consistently and invariably represented by that letter or combination of letters which has represented it most frequently in our traditional spelling. Thus the sentence cited above.

Our chauffeur, although he stubbed his toe, yeomanly towed four more boards through the open door of the depot becomes

Our shoefur, auldhoe he stubd hiz toe, yeomanli toed foer moer boredz thruu dhe oepen doer ov dhe depoe.

---

[3] Frank Laubach: *The Silent Billion Speak* (New York: Friendship Press, 1943), p. 56.

PROGRESS

For twenty years this system has been used successfully in Scandinavia in teaching secondary school pupils to read and write English.

The Simpler Spelling Society, under the leadership of scholars like Dr. Daniel Jones, has begun publishing a series of beginning readers. The first one, *The Little Red Hen*, is a beautiful volume. It is being used successfully in beginning classes in a number of public and private schools in England and Wales.

In 1949 a bill to create a Commission on Spelling Reform was defeated in the House of Commons by only three votes. Many people in Great Britain believe that both the children and the millions of illiterate adults in the British Commonwealth of Nations would benefit by the adoption of this system of World English Spelling.

The use of World English Spelling in the schools of the English-speaking countries would release annually hundreds of millions of pupil-hours and hundreds of thousands of teacher-hours of effort, time which could be devoted to more useful learning.

Let us add another article to the children's Charter of 1930: "The right of every child to learn to read and write the English language through the medium of a consistent, phonetic system of spelling."

OPPORTUNITY

The members of the Educational Press Association of America can render a great service to education by:

1. Discussing spelling reform in their journals without prejudice or ridicule.

2. Encouraging the optional, alternative use of World English Spelling in beginning reading books.

3. Encouraging young people in schools and colleges to use World English Spelling in their written work.

4. Encouraging the optional, alternative use of World English Spelling in textbooks for adult illiterates and foreigners.

5. Encouraging the optional, alternative use of World English Spelling in books designed to be used for people who want to learn English as a second language, e.g., in Germany, Japan, Puerto Rico, and the Philippines.

6. Appointing a Standing Committee on Spelling Reform.

.   .   .

The limericks following are reprinted by permission of Bennett Cerf, author of *Out on a Limerick*, published by Harper & Row.

SPELLING 209

The fabulous Wizard of Oz
Retired from business becoz
 What with up-to-date science
 To most of his clients
He wasn't the wiz that he woz.

There was once a man not unique
In fancying himself quite a shique.
 But the girls didn't fall
 For this fellow at all,
For he only made thirty a wique.

A jolly old Southern colonel
Has a humorous sense most infolonel.
 He amuses his folks
 By laughing at jolks
That appear in the Ladies Home Jolonel.

There's a young man who lives in Belsize,
Who believes he is clever and wise.
 Why, what do you think,
 He saves gallons of ink,
By merely not dotting his "i's."

Langford Reed

SPELLING . . . DIAGNOSIS AND REMEDIATION *

James A. Fitzgerald

Research shows that many elementary school children are retarded in spelling. The causes for retardation are many and varied because of the differences in children, their needs, their interests, their backgrounds, and their learning powers and capacities.

Diagnosis and remedial instruction in spelling are highly important because nearly everyone has difficulty with the spelling of some words. Although there are the so-called "good spellers" and some others who require only occasional aid in checking the spelling of a word, there are those who need considerable help in appraising the correctness of words written in either social or business correspondence. Remedial instruction based on an adequate diagnosis should be of value to each individual, not only for spelling in the elementary school but also for writing activities in high school and later life.

* Reprinted by permission of author and publisher from *The National Elementary Principal*, 38, No. 7 (May 1959), Washington, D.C.

FOUR BASIC CONCEPTS

Four basic concepts are related to instruction of those who have difficulty in spelling. They are diagnosis, remediation, prevention, and motivation. These may be stated more precisely as principles to be followed in helping children who have difficulty.

Diagnosis concerns the identification of difficulties and the causes of the difficulties that a child encounters in spelling. It precedes remedial instruction and continues throughout the remedial program.

Remediation entails instruction based upon diagnosis, planned to assist children to overcome their difficulties.

Prevention of difficulties is an important concept and should be put into effect as soon as possible by every pupil who has trouble. Ideally, a preventive program would obviate diagnosis and remediation. However, once the child requires diagnosis and remedial instruction, the prevention of difficulties should not be neglected. As a child learns effective preventive techniques through remedial work, he should put them into practice and make them a permanent part of his spelling procedure.

Motivation and interest are vital to the success of a spelling program. The child must learn to spell correctly; but to do this, he must understand the value of spelling in writing and the need for correct spelling in written work.[1]

Diagnosis and remediation are the principal considerations of this presentation. Prevention and motivation are treated incidentally because of lack of space.

CAUSES OF SPELLING DIFFICULTY

In general, the causes for poor spelling may be summarized as follows: The child did not study the words he needed in writing; he did not study his spelling with an effective method of learning; he did not appraise his written work to determine his spelling errors; he did not correct his spelling and writing mistakes.

Davis listed the most frequent causes of spelling difficulty as follows: 1) lack of a systematic method in learning to spell, 2) poor writing, 3) faulty pronunciation, 4) poor attitude toward spelling, 5) failure to associate the sounds of letters with the spelling of words, 6) not enough time for study, 7) discouragement concerning poor

---

[1] James A. Fitzgerald, *The Teaching of Spelling* (Milwaukee: The Bruce Publishing Company, 1951), pp. 191–192.

records in tests, 8) speech defects, 9) faulty checking of papers, 10) transposition of letters, 11) copying words incorrectly when studying, 12) poor memory, 13) poor hearing, 14) excessive slowness in writing, 15) irregular attendance, and 16) poor vision.[2]

If the cause for poor work is determined, it can usually be eliminated. Sometimes there are several causes combined which give great difficulty. Each of these should be removed by careful remedial work.

DIAGNOSIS OF SPELLING DIFFICULTIES

The whole child should be considered in making an appraisal of spelling difficulties: physical qualities, mental abilities, educational progress, emotional stability, home background, school and neighborhood environment, and attitude toward school and life. It is obvious, for example, that in the area of physical qualities, the child's eyes, ears, nose, throat, breathing, nutrition, and health should be appraised and examined if necessary by a physician. It is equally obvious that in the emotional realm, for example, a child who dislikes spelling is not so favorably inclined toward instruction as one who enjoys it. Mental tests, achievement tests, and teacher-made tests have their place in diagnosis of difficulties.

A teacher should appraise the teaching-learning situation. To determine the causes of spelling difficulty, the teacher may check the answers to the following questions.

1. Are you enthusiastic about teaching spelling?
2. Have you evaluated the materials you use for spelling? Are they satisfactory?
3. Do the children understand the importance of learning to spell?
4. Do your procedures invite and motivate learning?
5. Can children see and hear the words they study?
6. Are the words pronounced correctly by teacher and children?
7. Do the children write legibly?
8. Do the children correctly associate sounds with symbols and symbols with sounds?
9. Is sufficient time allotted for the study of spelling?
10. Is the study time properly used? Does each child study the words he needs to learn?
11. Are tests properly administered? Are children attentive? Do they have time to write the words of the tests?
12. Are the pre-tests, final tests, and review tests properly corrected?

---

[2] Georgia Davis, "Remedial Work in Spelling," *Elementary School Journal,* 27:615–26 (April 1927).

13. Does each child understand that he should study the words misspelled in each test?
14. Does each child use an effective method of learning to spell words he missed in the tests?
15. Do children understand the meaning of the words they study?
16. Do children use in writing the words they learn to spell?
17. Do the children misspell words in written work that they spell correctly in the spelling tests?
18. Does each child correct the spelling mistakes in his own work?
19. Is each child improving in spelling and in writing?
20. Does each child keep a record of achievement and improvement, perhaps on a progress chart?
21. Does each child keep a list of hard words?
22. Does each child keep a record of new and interesting words.

Answers to these and to similar questions should help a teacher to find difficulties and some of the causes of trouble.

An analysis of each child's written work, pre-tests, final tests, and review tests will aid in determining the types of mistakes made. One child may persistently misspell words by transposing letters. Another may misspell non-phonetic words phonetically. A third may just spell words in a careless fashion. A fourth may misspell words in many ways. To determine the patterns of misspellings, the written work should be carefully appraised. To understand the types of misspellings is, of course, highly important in planning remedial work. Another technique is the observation of the child's behavior while he is taking the spelling tests or doing other writing. A child with a good attitude who makes mistakes in spite of that attitude has problems quite different from those of the child with a "don't care" attitude.

In pronounced cases of retardation, the interview, the case study, and the cumulative record folder are valuable techniques. For any retarded child, a simple cumulative record of assignments, work, success and failure, progress, achievement, change in attitude, and interests and changing interests is extremely useful in making advanced assignments and in guiding the child to improved achievement.

The results of diagnosis should show for each child, if possible, the following:

1. What are the difficulties of this child?
2. What are the causes of these difficulties?
3. What are the abilities and interests of this child?
4. How can these abilities and interests be used for instruction?
5. What remedial measures should be undertaken to help this child overcome his difficulties?

When a teacher understands the individual child—his difficulties, his interests, and his powers—he is in a position to guide him and reasonable improvement in his spelling can be expected.

THE REMEDIAL PROGRAM

Plans for remedial instruction must vary with the types of difficulty children have. No two children have exactly the same difficulties and no two children learn exactly in the same way. The important point is that remedial instruction must be carried on to help each individual with the difficulties he has. Important among the points to be emphasized are the following: the objectives to be achieved, the materials and the words to be taught, the adaptation of instruction to individual needs, teaching each child an effective method of learning to spell that meets his needs, the use of the corrected test in teaching, the right use of the words learned, the integration of spelling with handwriting and other language arts, the efficient use of the dictionary, and the recording of hard words, interesting new words, and progress.

Objectives for the child with difficulties. The principal objective of spelling for the child with difficulties, whether he is a slow-learner or one with other types of difficulties, is to learn how to spell correctly the words he needs when he needs them in expressing his thoughts in writing. Each child has his own problems and each must strive to solve them. In connection with the language arts program, each child must study the words which he needs and cannot spell. Each should learn to use correctly the words he needs, to understand various meanings of words, to build a strong desire to spell without error, and to achieve also a consciousness of the correctness or incorrectness of the spellings of words he has used. Finally, a child should develop a method for studying spelling under his own guidance and momentum.

Learning to spell the right words. Probably no list is adequate for any child. This does not mean that scientifically selected spelling vocabularies should be discarded. Every child will have some especially necessary words for his own work. Nevertheless, there is much to be said for well-selected lists of words. Hildreth has pointed out that "dull pupils will do well to master 500 words by the fifth- or sixth grade." [3] If this be true, and there is every evidence that it is correct, the words these children study should be the words they will use as children and as adults also. These words will be found principally in a well-selected spelling list. From most important spelling research,

---

[3] Gertrude Hildreth, "Spelling in the Modern School Program," *Language Arts in the Elementary School* (Washington, D.C.: Department of Elementary School Principals, National Education Association, 1941), p. 480.

Fitzgerald has selected *A Basic Life Spelling Vocabulary* of 2,650 different words, which comprises several important vocabularies. Among these are: 1) the 449 words of highest utility for writing; 2) a list of 970, including the 449 and others of high usefulness, which with their repetitions make up a high per cent of the writing that normal people do; 3) a list of highly useful derivatives—formed by base words plus either suffixes or prefixes or both. A child of limited learning capacity will be greatly helped by teachers who make use of such lists in the selection of words for spelling.[4]

The words which a child uses in his everyday spontaneous writing are words which he should study if he is misspelling them. It should be emphasized that a child should study the words that he needs and cannot spell. He should not waste time either on words he already knows how to spell or on words he cannot spell and will never use.

Adapting instruction to individual needs. Each individual's needs and difficulties, not some other child's, should be emphasized in teaching spelling to any individual. Group instruction is acceptable when it fits the needs of all the group, but attention to varying needs of individuals is mandatory if spelling aims are to be achieved for each member of the group. The practice of selecting for group study the five most difficult words of an assignment, for example, is excellent for those who misspelled them, but of little value for those who did not. Each child must study the words he cannot spell, not the words that some other child misspells.

Teaching each child how to learn to spell a word. Several authorities have indicated that one of the greatest weaknesses in learning to spell is the lack of an effective method. While it is true that children learn to spell in different ways, there are principles of learning to spell which should be followed by every child in his own way. These are:

1. Guide each child to approach the spelling of a word through use and understanding.
2. Guide the child to follow necessary active steps in learning to spell a word. Each should: a) develop a clear image of the word; b) recall the spelling of the word; c) write the word, if possible, from memory; d) check the correctness of each spelling; e) master the spelling of each word.
3. Each child should use the word in writing and check its correctness.

Some children master the spelling of a word in one writing. Others

---

[4] James A. Fitzgerald, *A Basic Life Spelling Vocabulary* (Milwaukee: The Bruce Publishing Company, 1951), pp. 50–127.

require two or more. Each writing should generally be from memory followed by a check of the correctness of the spelling.

Test correction in spelling. Efficiency in learning requires that valid testing must be a part of the spelling program. Pre-tests, final tests of the week's work, and review tests are highly valuable in a spelling program. The most valuable phase of such testing is the test correction for and by each individual followed by individual study of the words he misspelled.[5] Each child must concentrate upon learning his own difficult words. He must keep a list of his own demons; the spelling of these he must master.

Using words in writing. Some children write words correctly in spelling tests but misspell them in their written work. These children should be guided to proofread their work and to correct their spelling mistakes. The spelling of a word is mastered only when it has been used meaningfully and written correctly in various situations which call for its writing.

Using the dictionary. The dictionary truly becomes the spelling teacher of the individual after he leaves school. Because it is of such importance, children should be carefully taught dictionary techniques in school. They should learn how to find a word in the dictionary quickly, and how to find a word when only a few letters are known or when no letters are known. They should become able to appraise the meanings of synonyms, to determine the preferred spelling, to determine the correct pronunciation, and to differentiate among the various uses of words. Children who learn the many uses of the dictionary have an instrument that will make them independent in word study for life.

Integration of spelling in the language arts. Spelling is one of the language arts—closely associated with listening, speaking, reading, writing, and handwriting. In fact, in learning to spell a word, the child will listen to the pronunciation of the word; he will pronounce it; he will read it; he will use it in written work; he will use handwriting in forming the word on paper. All of these language arts are integrated in learning to spell in school. After school when an individual is writing, he uses several of these arts in learning to spell words he requires in his work. Accordingly, each develops techniques based upon the integration of the language arts.

IN SUMMARY

To conclude, each child's difficulties in spelling should be diagnosed. Causes of difficulties may be eliminated by well-planned re-

---

[5] Thomas D. Horn, "The Effect of the Corrected Test on Learning to Spell," *Elementary School Journal,* 47:285 (January 1947).

mediation techniques. In the remedial program, each individual should master practices which will help him to achieve spelling independence through his own efforts and which will prevent writing difficulties.

HOW TO CORRECT SPELLING ERRORS *

David H. Patton

Several studies have been made in recent years to determine major types of spelling errors.

A knowledge of the types of errors children are most likely to make when spelling a word is useful in helping to prevent such mistakes.

MAJOR TYPES OF ERRORS

Research has established that, at each level, spelling errors can be classified as to type. Daily diagnosis is essential in correcting these errors.

Errors at all levels. The rank order of the five major types of errors which occur at *all* levels is:

1. Substitution of letters
2. Omission of letters
3. Additional or insertion of letters
4. Transposition of letters in words
5. Spelling the wrong word

Other types of errors which contribute to the spelling problem include: doubling or non-doubling of letters, homonyms, lack of phonetic sensitivity, poor writing, and carelessness.

The majority of spelling errors occur in *vowels in mid-syllables of words*. Two-thirds of the errors are in *substitution or omission of letters.* Approximately 20% more of the errors are in *addition, insertion, or transposition of letters.*

Errors in primary grades. Studies show that types of errors vary in frequency at different levels. Most common errors to occur in beginning spelling at the primary levels are:

---

* Reprinted by permission of the publisher from *Education Today*, Bulletin No. 54 (Columbus, Ohio: Charles E. Merrill Books, Inc.).

1. Use of wrong letters for vowel sounds
2. Mispronunciations
3. Lack of knowledge of phonetic elements that make a particular sound
4. Confusion of words similar in sound
5. Inaccurate formation of derivatives
6. Omitting or inserting silent letters
7. Homonyms
8. Transposition of letters

CORRECTIVE PROCEDURES

There are certain corrective procedures which can be used successfully with each type of spelling error.

This bulletin contains a table which presents typical errors, causes, and suggested corrective measures. The table should prove a helpful guide to all teachers in overcoming persistent types of spelling errors.

*Causes of Spelling Errors, Typical Examples
and Suggested Corrective Procedures*

Causes	Typical Errors	Corrective Procedures
1. Incorrect Visual Image	*docter* for *doctor* *nitting* for *knitting* *familar* for *familiar*	1. Make pupils conscious of the need to see each letter in the word. 2. Break the words into syllables. Have pupils visualize the words. 3. Look at word for strong visual image.
2. Inaccurate Pronunciation and Inaccurate Auditory Memory	*ligting* for *lightning* *pospone* for *postpone* *erl* for *oil* *chimley* for *chimney* *choclet* for *chocolate*	1. Pronounce each word accurately on initial presentation. 2. Pronounce words in concert with class. Listen for inaccurate pronunciations. Check individual pupils for doubtful enunciation. 3. Repeat several times the part of the word which is difficult to enunciate.
3. Insertion and Omission of Silent Letters	*lite* for *light* *lineing* for *lining* *no* for *know* *ofen* for *often* *tabl* for *table* *gost* for *ghost* *stedy* for *steady* *lisen* for *listen*	1. Silent letters cause many difficulties in spelling. Since these letters do not appear for help in an auditory image, special stress must be placed on the visual image. 2. Observe each part of the word and have pupils practice writing the part likely to cause trouble. 3. Provide practice exercises to fix habits of dealing with silent letters.
4. Confusion of Consonant Sounds	*acke* for *ache* *parck* for *park* *gudge* for *judge* *visinity* for *vicinity* *sertain* for *certain*	1. Practice for correct image of the word. 2. Children need to know that some letters have more than one sound. S may sound like s or z. C may sound like s or k. G may sound like g or j.

Causes	Typical Errors.	Corrective Procedures
5. Confusion of Vowel Sounds	*holaday* for *holiday* *turm* for *term* *oder* for *odor* *salery* for *salary* *rejoyce* for *rejoice*	1. Have pupils break word into syllables, and look at its parts. 2. Practice for correct visual image of the word. 3. Practice writing the word for the kinesthetic feel of the letters.
6. Confusion of Double Vowels	*reel* for *real* *quear* for *queer*	1. Double vowels often take the sound of the single letter or another vowel combination.
7. Inaccurate Formation of Derivatives	*stoped* for *stopped* *haveing* for *having* *flys* for *flies* *sincerly* for *sincerely* *omited* for *omitted*	1. Work for more vivid visual image of word endings. 2. Emphasize auditory image of endings. 3. Break words into syllables. Have children observe the word in its parts. 4. Call attention to generalizations pertinent to regular ways of adding endings. 5. Stress closer understanding of adding suffixes. Provide practice exercises on word endings.
8. Reversals or transposition of Letters	*gose* for *goes* *form* for *from* *bread* for *beard*	1. Pronounce word distinctly. Have pupils listen for sequence of each sound in word. 2. Practice for correct visual image.
9. Incorrect Meaning— Homonyms	*dew* for *due* *our* for *hour* *hole* for *whole* *sum* for *some*	1. Illustrate use of the word with commonest meaning. 2. Use pairs of words in sentence to distinguish what each means. 3. Provide practices on homonyms and stress word meanings at all times.
10. Phonetic Spelling Applied to Non-Phonetic Words	*bin* for *been* *gon* for *gone* *sum* for *some*	1. While spelling embraces phonetics, the pupil must be taught to look for numerous exceptions in our unphonetic language. He cannot rely on sound alone. He must realize that his visual memory must be his guide in many words and word parts.
11. Confusion of Words That Are Similar in Sound	*an* for *and* *were* for *where* *merry* for *marry* *effect* for *affect* *cents* for *sense* *further* for *farther*	1. This error is often due to faulty auditory acuity. Care should be given to enunciation of these words. 2. Pronounce the words in pairs and give the meaning of each.
12. Lack of Acquaintance with Phonetic Elements	*ivlize* for *result* *haw* for *how* *inbean* for *imagine*	1. For pupils very deficient in phonetic sense or training, begin work with simple visual-auditory training (attaching beginning consonant sounds to appropriate letter symbol). 2. Use kinesthetic approach also. 3. Provide phonics readiness training.
13. Poor Handwriting	*stors* for *stars* *temt* for *tent*	1. Provide practice on letter forms which cause special difficulty. 2. Emphasize accurate formation of each letter. 3. Guide pupils in size, shape, slant, and spacing between letters and words.

Causes	Typical Errors	Corrective Procedures
14. Over-emphasis on Rules	Rules not helpful in learning to spell in lower grades and of limited value in upper grades.	1. Children should not be required to learn rules for their application as a means of learning to spell. Reference to certain rules in upper grades may prove helpful, but pupils need to know that numerous exceptions make rules an unsafe guide.
15. Nervousness	Inaccuracies due to lack of control for deliberate thinking.	1. Check child's health. Be sure vision and hearing are not defective. 2. Remove all possible tensions.
16. Carelessness	Errors due to poor concentration and careless habits of word study.	1. Stimulate pride in work well done. 2. Praise all improvement.

PHONETICS AND SPELLING *

Ernest Horn

English spelling is tough. Efforts to alleviate its difficulty have been the serious concern of many scholars for more than four hundred years. Any help, even though small, should therefore be welcomed by everyone. It is essential, however, that any proposed plan be soundly grounded in all essential related evidence if it is to be more than a passing fad.

Some of the claims recently made for the contribution of phonics to spelling, and the related proposal to spell by "word analysis, sounding, and logical reasoning by analogy," do not, unfortunately, appear to be so grounded. There is considerable evidence to suggest that well-planned instruction in sound-to-letter and letter-to-sound associations in appropriate relation to other learning procedures may be of benefit both in spelling and in reading. This is all the more reason for making sure that any plan for such instruction should be critically formulated on the basis of adequate evidence on all the important factors related to such instruction.

There are at least six types of evidence which should be considered in appraising the potential contributions of phonic instruction to spelling: (1) evidence on the uniformity or the lack of uniformity in pro-

* Reprinted from *The Elementary School Journal* (May 1957), pp. 424–432, by permission of The University of Chicago Press.

nunciation; (2) evidence on the ways in which the various sounds are spelled; (3) data from investigations of children's attempts to spell the sounds in common words; (4) evidence on the influence of word patterns and of the ways in which sounds are spelled in different word relationships; (5) evidence on the operation of the laws of association and of negative and positive transfer; (6) findings from the research on teaching generalizations, such as spelling rules. This article is chiefly concerned, however, with the first three types of evidence.

INFLUENCE OF PRONUNCIATION ON SPELLING

In a recent article the claim is made that the pupil who has been taught to relate sounds and written symbols can "arrive deductively at the spelling of most words that he can pronounce." This seems to imply that there is only one acceptable way to pronounce a word. The fact is that a very considerable portion of words have more than one accepted pronunciation and many have three or more. An inspection of several thousand words sampled systematically from Kenyon and Knott's *A Pronouncing Dictionary of American English*, indicates that at least a third of the words in that dictionary have more than one accepted pronunciation. Moreover the authors state in the Preface, "Almost certainly we have omitted many 'good' pronunciations." If the spelling of a word is phonetically regular in one pronunciation, it is not likely to be in another.

Regional differences in both formal and informal speech are readily recognized. The three chief speech regions in the United States are Eastern, Southern, and General American ("General American" refers to the rest of the country outside the East and South). Variations in pronunciations among these regions are recorded in *A Pronouncing Dictionary of American English*. Further differences are found in the speech of northern England, southern England, and Scotland. Yet, with few exceptions, words are spelled the same in all these regions in the United States and Great Britain.

There have been marked changes in the pronunciation of English words, especially in vowel sounds, but only to a small extent has the spelling been changed to conform to the changes in pronunciation. There are some words, although a small percentage of the total, that have had their pronunciations changed to conform to their spelling.

An important distinction in considering the relation of phonetics and spelling is that between platform speech or public reading and the speech that has been called "the familiar, cultivated colloquial." Phoneticians warn against the mistaken idea that "colloquial" is synonymous with "bad." On the contrary, this style, which has been termed "the speech of well-bred ease," is considered by Kenyon and others to be the most important of all styles. It is certainly the most important in its effect on spelling since it is the language that the pupil commonly hears and speaks.

CONSISTENCY WITH WHICH SOUNDS ARE SPELLED

Many modern spelling books recommend that, in learning to spell a word, the pupil should pronounce it carefully and should notice closely how each syllable or part is spelled. But observing how each sound in a word is spelled *as a method of learning a word* is a different thing from attempting to spell it by sounding, by analogy, or by spelling each sound in the way in which it is most commonly spelled, all of which involve the application of some sort of generalization.

The usefulness of teaching any generalization in spelling, whether phonetic or orthographic, is limited by the number of words covered by the generalization and the number of words which are exceptions to it. It is important, therefore, to have adequate information on these two points. In order to secure such information for the present study, it was necessary to select, first, the list of words to be analyzed and, second, the dictionary or dictionaries which were to be the source of authority on pronunciations. For the first, the ten thousand words in the writer's *A Basic Writing Vocabulary* were chosen because the analysis of this number of words, while laborious, was practicable and because these words, with their repetitions, make up more than 99 percent of the running words written by adults. Samplings made from Rinsland's *A Basic Vocabulary of Elementary School Children*, indicate that the results here reported would not vary greatly from those that would be obtained from an analysis of that vocabulary. They would probably not be very different from the results that would be obtained from an analysis of an equally extensive list of the words most frequently found in reading.

A succession of dictionaries were used as sources of pronunciation, according to their availability and suitability to the problem at hand. The pronunciations of the words containing the sounds given in Table 1 are from the *Thorndike Century Junior Dictionary* and the *Thorndike-Barnhart Junior Dictionary*, the latter being substituted upon its publication. In Table 2 the *Thorndike-Barnhart Dictionary* was used for the sound of *oi* as in *boil*, *ou* as in *out*, and long *u* as in *use*, but the other sounds were tabulated on the basis of the pronunciation given in *A Pronouncing Dictionary of American English*. In Table 3 the Thorndike dictionaries were used for all the consonant sounds except *ch*, *ng*, *sh*, and *y*. Kenyon and Knott's *A Pronouncing Dictionary of American*

English was the authority for the pronunciation of *ch, ng,* and *y.* The sound *sh* was originally tabulated from *Webster's Elementary School Dictionary,* but the recorded pronunciations were later checked against Kenyon and Knott. The data on the spelling of some of the sounds as here reported may vary from what would be found if one dictionary were used alone, but certainly not to an extent that would greatly change the practical significance of the evidence. The frequency of certain sounds would vary considerably if all accepted pronunciations were used.

In tabulating the various spellings of any sound, each occurrence of the sound was counted. Since some words contain the same sound two or more times, the number of words containing the sound is less— but, in most cases, not much less—than the number of occurrences.

Making such counts is not a purely objective, routine task. Many decisions must be made as matters of judgment, especially in the case of words containing silent letters. Some of these letters were earlier pronounced, as the *k* in *knife,* the *g* in *gnaw,* and the *gh* in *light;* others are capricious accidents in the history of spelling. In some instances, as when final silent *e* makes the preceding vowel long or *g* and *c* soft, the problem is relatively simple. In words in which the silent *e* is needed to show a long vowel and also a soft *g* or *c,* the silent *e* was counted as helping to spell both the vowel and the consonant sounds. In the word *range,* for instance, if silent *e* were omitted, the word would be *rang.* In many words, however, silent letters have no function, but, since all letters in a word must be written, each silent letter was assigned to some sound. In certain types of words the assignment of these letters was somewhat arbitrary. It could hardly be otherwise, since in many words the silent letters are not only phonetically superfluous but even, as in the case of silent *e* in the word *definite,* actually misleading. The policy in all cases was to consider the problems pupils face in spelling the sounds.

FINDINGS OF THE STUDY

Tables 1, 2, and 3 contain sounds for which (1) the commonest spelling makes up less than 90 per cent of the total spellings of the sound; or (2) even when the commonest spelling makes up more than 90 per cent of the total, other spellings are found in a large number of words.

Two vowel sounds of special spelling difficulty are not included in Table 1: the obscure vowel sound (*schwa*), as in the second syllable of *separate,* and the short *i* sound, as in *hit.* These are the two vowel sounds most frequently heard in the English language. They are

TABLE 1. *The Most Common Spellings of Certain Vowel Sounds*

Thorndike-Barnhart Symbol	Webster Symbol	Number of Occurrences of the Sound	Number of Different Spellings	Most Common Spellings	Examples	Number of Occurrences	Per Cent of Occurrences
ā	ā	1,237	14	a-e	date	636	51.40
				a	angel	249	20.13
				ai	aid	192	15.52
				ay	day	89	7.19
ē	ē	859	14	ea	each	263	30.62
				ee	feel	221	25.72
				e	evil	176	20.49
				e-e	these	56	6.52
				ea-e	breathe	34	3.96
e	ĕ	1,917	7	e	end	1,763	91.97
				ea	head	86	4.49
ō	ō	691	15	o	go	333	48.19
				o-e	note	179	25.90
				ow	own	95	13.75
				oa	load	54	7.81
ô	ô	497	11	o	office	281	56.54
				a	all	83	16.70
				au	author	60	12.07
				aw	saw	30	6.04
u̇	o͝o	108	4	oo	book	61	56.48
				u	put	36	33.33
				ou	could	7	6.48
				o	woman	4	3.70
ü	o͞o	371	16	u	cruel	93	25.07
				oo	noon	87	23.45
				u-e	rule	61	16.44
				o-e	lose	30	8.09
				ue	blue	27	7.28
				o	to	19	5.12
				ou	group	15	4.04
u	ŭ	721	6	u	ugly	548	76.01
				o	company	126	17.48
				ou	country	30	4.16

troublesome to tabulate because they are so frequently alternate pronunciations in unaccented syllables of the same letter or letter combinations. The pronunciations in *A Pronouncing Dictionary of American English* were used in investigating the spelling of these sounds.

The short *i* sound (ɪ) is spelled at least fifteen ways in common words and only in a little more than half the time with the letter *i* alone. Examples are (in one accepted pronunciation): *i (bit), e, y (pretty), ie (mischief), ui (build), ey (money), a (character), ay (Monday), u (busy), ee (been), ai (portrait), ei (foreign), ia (marriage), o (women),* and *ea (forehead).* There are. other spellings in less common words.

The short *i* is also pronounced in many words in which the vowel sounds, from their word patterns (vowel, consonant, and silent *e;* or two adjacent vowels), might be expected to be long. Examples are *furnace, mountain, favorite, minute* (time), and *coffee.*

TABLE 2. *The Most Common Spellings of the Stressed and Unstressed Syllabic r's* (ɜ, ə), *the Diphthongs* oi, ou, *and Long* u, *and the Syllabic Consonants* l *and* n *

Sound	Symbol in International Phonetic Alphabet	Number of Occurrences of the Sound	Number of Different Spellings	Most Common Spellings	Examples	Number of Occurrences	Per Cent of Occurrences
Stressed syllabic r ...	ɜ	430	12	er	her	160	37.21
				ur	church	93	21.63
				ir	first	63	14.65
				or	world	34	7.91
				ear	heard	26	6.05
				our	courage	24	5.58
Unstressed syllabic r ...	ə	1,044	11	er	better	720	68.97
				or	favor	165	15.80
				ure	picture	72	6.90
				ar	dollar	62	5.94
oi	ɔɪ	107	2	oi	oil	63	58.88
				oy	boy	44	41.12
ou	aʊ	225	2	ou	out	165	73.33
				ow	cow	60	26.67
u	ju	376	11	u	union	167	44.41
				u-e	use	130	34.57
				ue	value	29	7.71
				ew	few	17	4.52
Syllabic l	l	478	10	le	able	247	51.67
				al	animal	163	34.10
				el	cancel	34	7.11
				il	civil	16	3.35
Syllabic n	n	171	8	en	written	79	46.20
				on	lesson	33	19.30
				an	important	18	10.53
				in	cousin	17	9.94
				contractions	didn't	12	7.02
				ain	certain	10	5.85

* This table does not contain the sound of long *i* as in *ice*, although it is diphthongal. It is spelled in at least a dozen ways.

The *schwa* sound is found in at least one accepted pronunciation in more than half of the multisyllabic words in the ten thousand commonest words. It is a very frequent sound in the speech of people in the East and South who do not pronounce their *r*'s unless the *r* is followed immediately by a vowel sound. It is spelled with almost any vowel or vowel digraph, hence in many different ways. The multiplicity of possible choices makes it difficult to spell.

Unaccented syllables are a special problem. They are difficult to spell for two reasons: (1) they are less distinctly pronounced, the vowel sounds, especially, being weakened, and (2) in a great many

TABLE 3. *The Most Common Spellings of Thirteen Consonant Sounds*

Sound	Number of Occurrences of the Sound	Number of Different Spellings	Most Common Spellings	Examples	Number of Oc-currences	Per Cent of Oc-currences
ch	357	5	ch	church	212	59.38
			t(u)	picture	91	25.49
			tch	watch	42	11.76
			ti	question	11	3.08
f	1,117	7	f	feel	936	83.80
			ff	sheriff	91	8.15
			ph	photograph	57	5.10
j	484	10	ge	strange	161	33.26
			g	general	138	28.51
			j	job	118	24.38
			dge	bridge	26	5.37
k	2,613	11	c	call	1,681	64.33
			k	keep	290	11.10
			x	expect, luxury	164	6.28
			ck	black	159	6.08
			qu	quite, bouquet	113	4.33
l	2,590	5	l	last	2,205	85.14
			ll	allow	294	11.35
			le	automobile	84	3.24
m	1,712	7	m	man	1,500	87.62
			me	come	112	6.54
			mm	comment	66	3.86
n	4,007	8	n	no	3,724	92.94
			ne	done	170	4.24
ng ...	998	3	ng	thing	880	88.18
			n	bank, anger	116	11.62
s	3,846	9	s	sick	2,568	66.77
			ce	office	323	8.40
			c	city	315	8.19
			ss	class	299	7.77
			se	else	149	3.87
			x(ks)	box	140	3.64
sh	829	17	ti	attention	423	51.03
			sh	she	242	29.19
			ci	ancient	47	5.67
			ssi	admission	36	4.34
t	4,277	6	t	teacher	3,522	82.35
			te	definite	424	9.91
			ed	furnished	179	4.19
			tt	attend	145	3.39
y° ...	530	13	u	union	190	35.85
			u-e	use	155	29.25
			y	yes	55	10.38
			i	onion	44	8.30
			ue	value	42	7.92
			ew	few	17	3.21

Sound	Number of Occurrences of the Sound	Number of Different Spellings	Most Common Spellings	Examples	Number of Occurrences	Per Cent of Occurrences
z	1,792	8	s	present	1,473	82.20
			se	applause	183	10.21
			ze	gauze	64	3.57

° The *y* sound is the first element in the diphthongal sound long *u*. In many words where the long *u* sound follows a consonant—for example, *d* (*duty*) and *t* (*tune*)—the sound of *y* occurs in only one of two or more pronunciations.

words, as pointed out above, the obscure vowel sound, *schwa* (ə), or the short *i* is substituted for the vowel sounds which might be inferred from the printed letters.

Three other difficulties should be noted: silent letters, double letters, and the fact that syllabication in the pronunciations does not always conform to the conventional syllabication in the dictionary entries. If one includes letters not pronounced in digraphs, as in *please* or *boat*, and double letters where only one is pronounced, all but four letters of the alphabet (*j, q, v,* and *x*) are silent in some words. A systematic sampling of the words in the *Thorndike-Barnhart Junior Dictionary* indicates that probably at least half of the words in that dictionary contain silent letters. It is not likely that a pupil, by applying phonic "principles" or by "logical reasoning by analogy," can decide to insert a letter which neither spells nor helps to spell any sound.

More than a sixth of the ten thousand words most frequently written contain double letters. There is, of course, a rule for doubling or not doubling when adding suffixes, but the problem of double letters is not limited to adding suffixes. Double letters are far more frequent in the body of words.

The evidence here reported was compared with that furnished in an unpublished dissertation by J. T. Moore and summarized in an article by P. R. Hanna and J. T. Moore, which appeared in the February 1953 issue of *The Elementary School Journal*. The results agree rather closely as to the most frequent spelling of the sounds but differ considerably in some instances as to the percentage which each spelling of a sound makes up of the total and as to the number of different spellings. These differences may be due in part to differences in the nature and extensiveness of the list analyzed by the writer (ten thousand words as compared to three thousand) and especially to the fact that this longer list contained a greater number of multisyllabic words and hence more unaccented syllables. It is to be expected that more double letters and more *schwa* and short *i* sounds would be found in multisyllabic words.

There are marked differences, however, in the significance attached to the evidence by the writer and by Hanna and Moore. They state, "The letter or combination of letters most frequently used to represent a phoneme is called the regular spelling. This use of "regular" is at variance with the common meanings of the term, which imply a greater uniformity and fewer exceptions than are exhibited by the commonest spellings of the sounds reported above or the spellings of the same sounds in Moore's investigation. It is easy, in discussing the evidence, to slip over from this specialized definition of "regular" to the misleading use of the term to mean regular in the sense of dictionary definitions. The authors also state "that for almost every sound . . . there is what might be called a 'highly regular' spelling." The spelling of the thirty sounds cited above can scarcely be called "regular" and certainly not "highly regular." Neither the evidence here presented nor that given by Moore appears to warrant the statement that variants from the commonest spellings of these sounds are rare.

The data cited in Tables 1, 2, and 3 and in the paragraphs on the sounds of ə and ɪ show that these thirty sounds are spelled in many ways and that the commonest spelling accounts for too low a percentage of the total spellings to be called "regular" in the usual meaning of the term. Nine words out of ten contain one or more of these sounds. There are fifteen sounds in the tables that are spelled with the commonest spelling less than 60 per cent of the time. The frequency with which the sounds occur and the number of exceptions should be taken into account. The sound of long a (ā), for example, was found 1,237 times, with 601 exceptions to the commonest spelling; the sound of k was found 2,613 times, with 932 exceptions; and the sound of s in sick, 3,846 times, with 1,278 exceptions. One is hardly justified in calling spellings "regular" or in teaching the commonest spellings as principles or generalizations when the exceptions are numbered not merely by the score but by hundreds.

IMPLICATIONS FOR RESEARCH AND INSTRUCTION

With so many different spellings of these sounds from which to choose, it would be strange indeed if pupils did not spell unlearned words in a variety of ways. They do. In an early experiment by the writer, 195 pupils in Grades 1 and 2, all of whom had been taught phonics as one approach to reading, spelled circus in 148 ways. Tease was spelled in 44 ways. The "best" spellings were tes, teas, tease, tees, and teez. Subsequent investigations have shown a wide variety of misspellings even for more mature pupils who had had much greater experience in both wı. ing and reading. Harry V. Masters, for example, in an analysis of the attempts of 200 students in each of Grades 8, 12, and 16 to spell 268 difficult words selected from 5,000 words of high frequency, found miscellaneous to be spelled in 153 ways—113 ways in Grade 8, 40 in grade 12, and 22 by college students. An inspection of the attempts to spell these 268 words shows that the majority of the most common misspellings are analogically reasonable in the sense that the individual sounds were spelled in ways that represent the correct spelling of the sounds in other words. Examples are *adequate—adequit, amiable—aimiable, deny—denigh, scandal—scandle*. Additional examples, all reported as common misspellings by elementary-school children, are: *aid—ade, asleep—asleap, before—befour, boat—bote, busy —bizzy, crumb—crum, force—forse, honor—honer, mystery—mistory, tongue—tung*. Pupils need no encouragement to misspell by utilizing analogic spellings.

Attempts to account for a pupil's choice of a spelling of an unlearned word at a given time are largely conjectures. Why did one pupil, in attempting to spell *awful*, write *offul*, while others wrote *aufull, offel,* or *offle?* There must have been some influence or influences that, if known, would explain why these particular spellings of the sounds were written. Presumably any of the laws of association may operate in a given attempt to spell, and sometimes in combination. Both common sense and the evidence from research suggest that, when a number of reasonable choices are available, responses are uncertain.

The preceding discussions underestimate, rather than exaggerate, the complications which confront children in attempting to spell. How much more complicated the factors are can readily be seen by reading standard works on phonetics and philology, and treatments of transfer and the laws of association in the psychological literature. It is not the purpose of this article, however, to disparage the use of phonetics in teaching either reading or spelling. Its purpose is rather to call attention to types of evidence which should be considered in designing any plan for emphasizing sound-to-letter relationships, either for experimental purposes or for classroom use.

It seems important that children should learn the ways, not *the* way, in which each sound is spelled. This should at least eliminate many misspellings in which the sounds are spelled in ways in which they are never correctly spelled. Children should learn how to spell the principal prefixes and suffixes and should know how to add these to base words. They should also learn such orthographic aids as apply to large numbers of words with few exceptions.

The recognition of the importance of giving careful attention to the ways in which sounds are spelled is not new. For more than thirty years, authors of many series of spelling textbooks have recommended that, in learning a word, the word be carefully pronounced and that the pupils should note how each part or syllable is spelled. These procedures in themselves should promote an understanding of how sounds are spelled, but they are not the same as teaching principles or generalizations. As pointed out above, the criteria for deciding whether a phonetic generalization is possibly worth teaching are that it should apply to a large number of words and that it should have few exceptions, certainly not hundreds of exceptions.

What results should be expected from emphasizing as generalizations or principles the commonest spelling of sounds that have a large number of exceptions? Would pupils tend to spell these sounds in all words by the commonest spellings? If they should, as research has shown, they would misspell more words than they now do. Would it usefully sensitize children to deviant spellings? Would it give them a misplaced confidence in utilizing these commonest spellings, which would lead to disillusionment and therefore to a decrease in interest in spelling? These possibilities have not been adequately explored.

There are some characteristics of English spelling, however, that exhibit considerable consistency. Most of these pertain to word patterns, syllables, meanings, word positions, the adding of suffixes, and the influence of sounds or letters adjacent to the sound to be spelled. Most consonant sounds, whether single sounds, as the *b* in *bed,* or initial blends, as the *bl* in *black,* are regularly spelled at the beginning of words. The most important exceptions are the sounds of *f* as in *fun* or *physics, k* as in *cup* and *keep, s* as in *city* and *sad,* and *j* as in *jump* and *gem.*

Some consonant sounds, however, that are spelled regularly at the beginning of words are spelled in many other ways in other word positions. For example, the sound of *sh* is regularly spelled with *sh* at the beginning and end of words, but in other word positions it is spelled more often in other ways than with *sh.* The sound of *k* at the beginning of a word or a syllable is, with few exceptions, spelled with *c* before *a, o, u, r,* and *l,* but with *k* before *e, i,* and *y.* It is spelled in many other ways at the end of words and syllables. The letters *l* and *f* are, with very few exceptions, doubled at the end of monosyllables when preceded by a single short vowel. Other consistencies could be cited for the spelling of sounds in certain word relationships.

Some help, moreover, may be obtained from the knowledge of word patterns, at least in preventing obvious blunders. For example, it is not too much to expect that children should know not to spell *mad* m-a-d-e or *made* m-a-d, but note how the sound of *ade* is spelled in *aid, weighed, suède, stayed,* and *obeyed.* Actually, writing final silent *e* to indicate a long vowel sound is only one of four very common ways of showing vowel length, and long vowel sounds are more often spelled in other ways than this. Examples of other ways are: open syllables, *fatal;* double letters, *deep;* and digraphs, *boat.* There are many words, however, in which these four devices do not spell long vowel sounds. Examples are *definite, machine, been,* and *head.*

When the evidence, on both the consistency and the irregularities of English spelling, is critically and realistically assessed, little justification is found for the claim that pupils can arrive deductively at the spelling of most words they can pronounce. There seems no escape from the direct teaching of the large number of common words which do not conform in their spelling to any phonetic or orthographic rule. One must be exceedingly credulous to believe that authorities with the most complete knowledge of the English language (philologists, phoneticians, and lexicographers) have been in error in pointing out the serious lack of conformity between spoken words and their printed symbols, have been unaware of such orthographic and phonetic regularities as exist in the language, or would have so strongly urged that English spelling be simplified if its difficulties could be removed or largely alleviated by the teaching of phonetic and other orthographic aids.

SPELLING SIMPLIFICATION IN SCOTLAND *

The case for some simplification of English spelling is commonly put on educational grounds. The existing spelling with its confusions and inconsistencies imposes an obvious burden on pupils and teachers throughout the English-using world, and requires the expenditure of time and energy which could be better spent in meeting the increasing educational demands of a changing civilization. But the bad effects are not confined to childhood and youth; they are social as much as cultural. Spelling difficulties add substantially to the task of maintaining literacy in learning and communication in considerable sections of the adult population in all countries where English is spoken, and make English less effective than it might be as a second language. This again has an important bearing on the employment of English as an international medium. Two great wars have brought the nations of the world perilously close to each other, and one of the urgent needs of our times is a common speech to make mutual understanding easier.

---

* Reprinted by permission of the Scottish Council for Research in Education Studies from *Studies in Spelling* (London, 1961).

There are several candidates for this privileged position—national languages with great traditions already known over wide areas, and artificial languages avoiding nationalist prejudices—but taking one thing with another, English, by reason of its structural simplicity, no less than by the approval already accorded to it as a second language in the world's schools, has gradually established a certain priority in this competition of tongues. Its greatest defect is admittedly its rather perverse spelling. With a system of spelling freer from irrationalities and providing a better guide to pronunciation, its progress towards international acceptance would be surer and speedier.

While everybody is agreed that English spelling is far from ideal and many would welcome reform for one reason or another, most people are very doubtful whether the needed changes can now be made. The reception given to systematic schemes of simplification, like those propounded by Ellis, Sweet and Pitman in the last century and by the Simplified Spelling Society in this, has certainly not been encouraging. They have all made their converts, but they have not converted the public. Part of the difficulty lies in the conservatism which makes people dislike alterations of any kind in the familiar things of life. But difficulty in the case of spelling goes deeper. The seemingly insuperable obstacle is the fact that the changes proposed threaten a break in the continuity of written and printed English. With a logically reformed spelling in which every sound had its own symbol, print and script would look entirely different. School children might find it easier to learn the new forms once they were adopted, but for everybody else, both in the period of transition and after it, a considerable adjustment to new or old would be necessary. And the millions of pre-reformed books and papers would become almost as foreign to later readers as Chaucer is to us. No wonder people who are disturbed when they find 'honour' spelled *honor* shrink from the prospect!

The conclusion to which this leads is that there would be little hope for the adoption of any plan of simplified spelling, however modest, under ordinary conditions. But conditions, as it happens, are not ordinary. The world has been shaken to its depths by two great wars, and there have been so many revolutionary changes in the ways of life everywhere that the prospect of more change has ceased to disturb us overmuch. Any change like a simplification of currency or spelling which gives promise of definite social betterment can be sure to get at least serious consideration, and if the need for it be generally recognised, it may in time be accepted.

Even so, the chances of a particular change are always better if it can be kept within narrow limits. To be readily acceptable, the new ways must not be too different from the old. In the case of spelling, the revised form must not only satisfy the phonetician, but must approve itself to the ordinary reader. Previous schemes have sought phonetic consistency by introducing new letters and making extensive use of new combinations, and in doing so they have produced the impression of something foreign. To have any chance of adoption there must be comparatively few changes in the existing orthography and the printed page must in the main preserve its present appearance.

It is on these lines that the scheme now to be propounded proceeds. It has been developed in the course of an analysis of all the words in common use with a view to the intelligent teaching of spelling, and it only requires the changing of a comparatively small number of words. It has the added merit that even if it is not adopted, it may give help in the teaching and learning of the ordinary spelling.

There are two special features in the scheme. The first is that while a sound may be represented by one, two or more different letters or letter groups, each letter or letter group always indicates the same sound. Consider, for example, the words 'bow' and 'sow'. They have each two different pronunciations and two different meanings. To remove the ambiguity the -OW must be kept exclusively for one of the two sounds, either for the long O as in 'show', or the OU diphthong as in 'now'. As it happens, the two are almost equally common in monosyllabic words, but partly because the long O usage is more common in polysyllabic words, and partly because there is an extensive group of dissyllabic words like 'arrow' and 'fellow' with a distinctive appearance, it is recommended that the OW be reserved for the long O. OW thus becomes one of three symbols for long O (O-E as in 'more', OA as in 'boat', OW as in 'show'), all of them used for the one sound and only for that sound.

This principle applies to both consonants and vowels, but is of greater importance in the case of vowels and diphthongs than of consonants. There are comparatively few mixed uses of consonants. CH and GH are the worst offenders, and after them S and C. In contrast, there are confusions galore in the vowels, and it is to their removal that thought must specially be given.

To illustrate, take the EE sound. There are approximately 3025 words of one syllable in ordinary use, of which nearly a tenth have this sound. The 283 EE words are spelled in eight different ways:

EA (sea, dear)	110 words
EE (tree, weed)	98 words
E-E (here, scheme)	11 words
EA-E (please, leave)	15 words
EE-E (geese, sleeve)	9 words

E (he, me)	6 words
IE (chief, priest)	24 words
EI (weir, seize)	5 words
Other forms: league, key,	
suite, quay, pique	5 words

The obvious course here would seem to be to accept EE, EA and E–E to stand for the EE sound; and with them, to accept the subsidiary forms with the final E mute, as well as the 'he', 'me', 'we' group. There is no difficulty whatever with EE: it always stands for the same sound. EA is not so simple. There are 30 monosyllables like 'head' and 'heard', 8 like 'great' and 'break', and a solitary 'heart'. We have decided that EA is only to represent one sound. That being so, we spell 'head' and 'heard' *hed* and *herd*, which has the added advantage that with a single change it gives all the 265 words with the short E sound a uniform spelling. In the case of 'great', 'break', etc., a place has to be found among the accepted forms of the AI words. Most of these are spelled A–E (e.g., 'make') but a substantial number are spelled AI (e.g., 'paint'). Spell 'great' and 'break' and the half dozen words like them with AI (*grait, braik*) to distinguish them from the homonyms 'grate', 'brake', etc. Next comes the IE group, a troublesome lot, that are apt to be confused with the EI words, and in any case are misleading since the first letter of the digraph suggests the I sound. All the IE words can be spelled with EE: *cheef, preest*. For three of the five odd words EE may be used *kee, kee* and *peek*: spell the others *leag* and *swete*.

The second guiding principle of the scheme is that in the modification of words required to give every symbol a unique value, everything possible should be done to preserve the general appearance of words. In ordinary reading we do not distinguish the several letters in a word, but recognise the word as a block by its up and down letters, its length and peculiar combinations like OW and QU. We must endeavour to keep changes in these respects to a minimum. With this in view, we will continue to use alternative forms like F and PH, and S and Z. There is no objection to spelling 'stomach' and 'monarch' *stomack* and *monarck* to bring consistency into the use of the CH digraph, but we must hesitate to spell 'thought' *thot* or 'though' *tho*, and seek some alternative change. There are two ways in which this can be done. The one is to retain in the changes of the new spelling something of the effect of the old, as in the case of *stomack* and *monarck*. So again in words like 'half', 'calf' and 'often' with a consonant no longer sounded, we may minimise the difference in the changed form by spelling *haff*, *caff* and *offen*, of equal length with the present spelling. The second and more important course is to leave the anomalous forms unchanged, provided that there is no disturbing contravention of the principle of unique symbolisation, and that the particular form retained is in fairly common use.

This retention of forms which are commonly considered anomalous, but which are regular in their consistent employment, has many applications such as the following:

1. Redundant letters C, X, QU should be continued in their present use.

2. Initial combinations including an unsounded letter which are of frequent occurrence, like WR (as in 'wreck', 'wrong') and KN (as in 'kneel', 'knife'), should be retained. Words beginning with GN as in 'gnash' and PN as in 'pneumonia' being of lesser frequency should be spelled phonetically. So also should words like 'talk', 'half', 'debt', 'doubt' with a silent medial letter. Exception may be made in favour of words like 'thistle', 'fasten' (of which there are over a score) where the ST may be allowed to stand. It may also be worth keeping PS for the sake of 'psalm', 'psychology' (but spelled *psykology*) 'psychic' and 'pseudo-'.

3. The letter combinations, -ALL occurring in 'call', 'small' and WA occurring in 'watch', 'warn', 'want', 'dwarf', should be retained for the AU sound in this particular context.

The striking group of words that ring the changes on -IGH, -AUGH, -OUGH, -EIGH presents a special problem. What is to be done with a 'thought' that is pronounced to rhyme with 'caught', and an 'eight' that has the same sound as 'straight'? Above all, how can order be put into the use of -OUGH, when it represents OU in 'bough', OO in 'though', AU in 'bought' and 'cough', long O in 'though' and short U in 'thorough'? With an all-round phonetic simplification, the complications would disappear, but so would a most characterful set of forms. Plainly some of the -GH forms must be kept for appearance sake. We may begin by accepting the -IGH, the simplest and most numerous: 'high', 'sight', 'knight', 'fright' and the rest. 'Height' which is quite different from 'eight' can be rectified by spelling it *hight*. Next, there are the two sets like 'caught' and 'thought' pronounced alike but spelled differently. Since the sound is AU, we must spell them all -AUGHT: *aught* (instead of 'ought'), *thaught, braught,* ('daughter', 'naughty', 'caught'), -OUGH can now be used for the OU sound, in 'bough', 'plough', 'drought'. Then since the sound is AI, spell 'weigh', 'eight' like 'straight'; *waigh, aight.* That only leaves the words in which GH represents the F sound and odd words like 'though' and 'through'. These may be rendered phonetically as: *ruff, tuff, enuff, coff, troff, tho, throo;* or better perhaps, by giving the F sound the PH spelling (*ruph, enuph, troph*) and making 'though' *thow.*

CONSONANTAL CHANGES

To see the detailed application of the principles suggested, the consonants which are apt to cause confusion must first be considered. In actual fact it is possible to make do with a few changes.

Take the CH symbol. It is mainly used for the sound which appears at the beginning and end of 'church', but it has at least three other sounds: the guttural in the Scottish word 'loch'; the SH sound that occurs in words of French origin like 'champagne' and 'charade' as well as medially in 'machine' and terminally in 'bunch' etc; the K sound derived from the Greek *Chi* in words like 'character', 'chorus', 'school', 'scholar'. There is not a great number of words in the French group and it would not greatly matter whether the CH became SH or were allowed to remain. The same thing is true for 'bunch' and 'branch' in which the CH sound passes readily into the SH. Better spell them all with the SH. The words of Greek origin present a harder problem. If CH is to have a unique sound there must be a change here. The simplest course would be to represent the *Chi* sound by K, so that we would have *karacter, skool, Kristian*. A doubtful alternative would be to employ the combination which occurs already in 'bucket' and 'ticket' in order to retain the digraph form: thus *ckaracter, sckool, Ckristian, psyckology*. As for the Scottish guttural there is no simple symbol for it, and as only Scots are interested in it, it can be left to them to go on pronouncing 'loch' in their own way.

In the case of C and G, most of the difficulties experienced in spelling are connected with the facts that before E and I, C is always pronounced S (as in 'cent' and 'cinder') though the common association of C is with K, and that before the same two vowels G generally has a soft sound, though in some very common words like 'get' and 'give' it has its ordinary hard sound. As the usage with C at the beginning of a word or syllable is quite regular, nothing need be done about it beyond emphasising the regularity when teaching the CE and CI words. There is a complication, however, in the case of words beginning SC. Where SC is followed by E or I (as in 'scene' or 'science') the C becomes silent and there is a possible confusion with SC, pronounced SK as in 'sceptic'. The simplest method might be to accept SC as equivalent to S in 'scene', 'sceptre', 'scent' and the like, and spell works like 'sceptic' with a K (*skeptic*). In the case of GE and GI the only way of escape from the present confusion is to spell words like 'general', 'German', 'Geology', 'giant', 'gin', 'gipsy' with a J as has been done already with 'jet' and 'jig': there are 15 common words involved. Having done that the next thing to do is to remove the U from words like 'guard', 'guess' and 'guilt' into which the U has been inserted to indicate the hard sound which is no longer required.

There are also complications in the spelling of the sounds associated with C and G when these occur at the end of a word or syllable. Final C can have either the K sound or the unvoiced subilant. In the former case, it is generally accompanied by a K as in 'black' but there are one or two words like 'zinc' with the same sound. In the latter, E is added to make the digraph CE, and the vowel preceding may be either short, as in words like 'dance' and 'prince' ending in -NCE, or long as in words like 'face' and 'vice' where the terminal E has the double function of indicating a long vowel and denoting the unvoiced S. Much the same things happen with G. Final G has also a double reference. A few words like 'league' and 'vogue' have the original hard sound, but the majority with an added E as indicator have the soft J sound. Here again are two groups of words: on the one hand, words ending in -DGE (hedge), -NGE (hinge), -RGE (charge), -LGE (bulge), all except those in -ANGE (change) with a short vowel; on the other hand, words like 'page', 'oblige', 'seige' with terminal E indicating a preceding long vowel. There is little need for change. Words like 'scarce' and 'strange' might be spelled *scairce* and *strainge* with advantage to consistency, and *leag* and *voag* had better displace the curious -GUE spelling. So substitute *check* and *plack* for 'cheque' and 'plaque'.

A certain amount of confusion exists in the spelling of the voiced and unvoiced forms of the sibilant, but here also little change is needed. The initial single letter S is consistently unvoiced and Z consistently voiced, but there is considerable variety in the representation of the finals. The unvoiced sound in the latter case is expressed in three ways: SS (as in 'miss' and 'moss'); SE preceded by a short vowel as in the groups of words like -RSE (horse), -PSE (lapse), -LSE (pulse); CE as in 'grace' and 'dance'. The voiced sound also occurs in three forms: S as in 'his', 'was' and certain inflected forms like 'boys', 'waves', 'runs', 'robs'; SE preceded by a long vowel ('prose', 'phrase', 'rise', 'cause', 'grease'); and Z or ZE as in 'prize', 'gauze', 'freeze'. With the change of SE to CE in a few words like 'dense', 'chase', 'lease', 'mouse' and 'coarse' the scheme would be made reasonably consistent. Spell 'vase', *vas*.

Concerning the distinction between TH unvoiced as in 'thin' and TH voiced as in 'this' which is not shown in the present spelling, there is no great difficulty. The voiced TH as an initial sound is limited to a few monosyllables ('the', 'they', 'this', 'that', 'there', 'then', 'than', 'though', and related words). All nouns, verbs, etc., beginning with TH are unvoiced. Terminal TH again may be either voiced or unvoiced, but here also the two groups of words are fairly well marked. Almost all the unvoiced ones are monosyllabic noun words ('bath', 'breath', 'cloth', 'froth'); almost all the voiced are monosyllabic verbs distinguished by the addition of an E ('bathe', 'breathe', 'clothe', 'soothe'). The voiced sound also occurs in a few words like 'father', 'brother', 'weather'. Apart from writing 'smooth' as *smoothe,* no change is needed.

It is evident that there is no necessity for any drastic changes in the consonants in a scheme of spelling reform based on the two principles of consistent usage and continuity of form. Admittedly English would be much easier to learn and to use, both for children and adults, if it were possible to approximate to a phonetic representation of sounds, with but one symbol for one sound. But if that must be foregone in order to preserve the appearance of the existing print and script, the next best thing is a spelling in which every letter or letter group has one and only one sound. In the case of the consonants, as the survey of difficulties shows, that is not too hard to attain by a limited number of changes.

NEEDED CHANGES IN VOWELS AND DIPHTHONGS

The crux of the problem of a restricted scheme of simplification is in vowel and diphthong usage. The critics of English spelling have an easy case to make in the vagaries of the spelling of all the long sounds: the AI sound, for example, takes a very different form in the words: 'name', 'saint', 'pray', 'great', 'heir', 'prey', 'eight', 'there', 'plague', 'gauge', 'goal'. Contrariwise, they can point to the diverse sounds denoted by all the letters or letter combinations standing for the vowels: the EA digraph, for example, appears in 'spear', 'heart', 'head', 'bear', 'real', 'corporeal'. There is plain need to clear up this confusion.

Leaving over the question of what is to be done about it, we begin by noting that the source of the trouble is in the scheme of vowel notation which has been gradually evolved over the last five centuries by a long process of trial and error and with various efforts at reform. It is a simple scheme—too simple indeed for the complexity of the sounds to be denoted. There are twelve groups of vowel sounds (including vowel combinations) distinguished in English spelling: the five short sounds primarily denoted by the letters A,E,I,O,U, appearing in such words as 'ran', 'men', 'tin', 'don', 'fun'; the five long sounds corresponding with these, denoted by these same letters or some variant of them, as in the words 'make', 'cede', 'nice', 'bone', 'rule', and the two diphthong sounds OU as in 'foul', and OI as in 'boil'. All things considered, the notation has worked wonderfully well. In spite of all that is said about the irregularities of English spelling, most words as a matter of fact are spelled quite regularly. There are 265 monosyllables with the short E sound, for example, 229 of them are spelled with E (as in 'pet' and 'step'), and most of the rest represent the vowel by EA as in 'head'. To make the spelling quite consistent all that has to be done is to spell them all with the E. In the case of monosyllabic words with the long E, as we have seen before, 208 out of 283 are spelled either EE or EA in nearly equal number, with half of the rest so near akin to these that there is no need to change them. That leaves 33 words which may be described as anomalous (24 of them spelled with an IE as in 'chief'). It is not a big undertaking to bring the 33 into line with the others.

Working through all the vowel sounds in this way we get as the basic symbols: A,E,I (Y), O (AU), U; AI (AY), A–E; EA, EE, E–E; I–E (Y–E); OA, OW, O–E; OO, UE, U–E; EW; OU, OI. With these symbols, it is possible to construct a tolerably satisfactory system of consistent spelling in which about four-fifths of the common monosyllables would be spelled as at present.

But the percentage of change can be considerably reduced by the acceptance of subsidiary symbols of two sorts. The first are simple variants of the basic symbols—of two types: (a) words like 'me', 'we', 'so', 'go', 'by', 'cry'; (b) words with a final mute E like 'dance', 'praise', 'serve', 'leave', 'horse', 'curve', 'rouse', 'noise'. The second are certain letter groups like -ALL, -OLD, -OLT, -OLL, which consistently indicate a lengthening of the A and O sounds. With the addition of these extra symbols, about 10 per cent of the ordinary words of one syllable need to be changed to bring them into the scheme.

WORDS OF ONE SYLLABLE

The detailed application of this scheme of symbols begins as a matter of course with the words of one syllable, since the longer words are either made up of such words, or made up of syllables which with certain modifications behave like them. Apart from their length, these words have two special features that make for simplicity in spelling: (a) there is rarely if ever any difficulty in knowing whether the one-letter vowels have their short or long sound; (b) the complications introduced by differences of stress in the polysyllables are absent.

The following table shows in statistical form the spelling forms of all the ordinary words of one syllable, and suggests the changes necessary to make the spelling of the vowels reasonably regular.

*Needed Changes in the Vowels and
Diphthongs of Monosyllables*

The A Sound (376 words)

NO CHANGE:

Simple words like 'fat' and 'far'	338
Words like 'dance', 'charge', 'badge', 'valve'	25

CHANGE:

'are', 'axe', 'caste', 'have', 'vase'—*ar, ax, cast, hav, vas*	5
'aunt', 'laugh', 'draught'—*ant, laff, draft*	3
'heart', 'hearth', 'clerk', 'guard', 'plaque'—*hart, harth, clark, gard, plack*	5

The A-E Sound (302 words)

NO CHANGE:

A-E (make, face, blame)	161
AI (hair, paint)	68
AY (may, pray)	25
AI-E (raise)	4

CHANGE:

EA (great, bear—*grait, bair*)	8
EI (their, weigh—*thair, waigh*)	14
EY (they—*thay*)	4
-AGUE (plague—*plaig*) 2, -ANGE (change—*chainge*) 5, -ASTE (haste—*haist*) 6	13
'there'—*thare* 3, 'scarce'—*scairce*, 'gauge'—*gage*	5

The E Sound (265 words)

NO CHANGE:

Simple words like 'led' and 'step'	203
Words like 'hedge', 'fence', 'serve', 'delve'	26

CHANGE:

EA (head, breath—*hed, breth*)	30
'guess', 'guest'—*gess, gest*, 'cheque'—*check*, 'friend'—*frend*, 'were'—*wer*, 'said'—*sed*	6

The E-E Sound (283 words)

EA (sea, dear)	110
EA-E (please)	15
EE (tree, weed)	98
EE-E (sleeve)	9
E-E (here, scheme)	11
E (he, me)	6

CHANGE:

IE (chief, priest—*cheef, preest*)	24
EI (weir, seize—*weer, seeze*)	5
'league'—*leag*, 'key'—*kee*, 'quay'—*kee*, 'pique'—*peek*, 'suite'—*swete*	5

The *I* Sound (361 words)

NO CHANGE:	Simple words like 'bit' and 'sit'	327
	Y (myth)	9
	Words like 'since', 'bridge', 'hinge'	19
CHANGE:	'give', 'live'—*giv, liv;* 'sieve'—*siv*	3
	'build', 'guild', 'guilt'—*bild, gild, gilt*	3

The *I-E* Sound (228 words)

NO CHANGE:	I-E (bite, size)	140
	Y-E (type, tyre)	10
	IE (tie)	8
	Y (by, cry)	17
	-IGH (high, light)	21
	-IND (kind)	9
CHANGE:	-YE (dye, eye—*dy, y*)	7
	-ILD (mild—*mield*) 3, 'pint'—*pient;* 'ninth' —*nineth*	5
	'guide', 'guile', 'guise'—*gide, gile, gise*	3
	'height'—*hight;* 'buy', 'guy'—*by, gy;* 'climb' —*clime;* 'sign'—*sine;* 'isle', 'aisle'—*ile, iele;* 'choir'—*quire*	8

The *O* Sound (304 words)

NO CHANGE:	Simple words like 'dot' and 'for'	169
	Words like 'lodge', 'horse', 'solve'	10
	AW (raw, dawn, crawl)	36
	AU (haul, daunt)	18
	AU-E (cause)	6
	-AUGH (caught)	5
	-ALL (call)	11
	WA- (war, dwarf); WHA- (what); QUA- (quart)	25
CHANGE:	-ALK (talk); -ALT (salt); -ALD (bald)— *tauk, sault, bauld*	7
	-OUGH (thought); -OUGH (cough)— *thaught, coff*	10
	'broad,' *braud;* 'mosque'—*mosk;* 'gone'— *gon;* 'false', *faulse;* 'yacht', *yaught;* 'doll', *dall;* 'ball', *boll*	7

The *O-E* Sound (249 words)

NO CHANGE:	O-E (nose, stone)	101
	OE (toe)	9
	OW (grow, own)	21
	O (go)	5
	OA (boat, roast, coarse)	53
	-OLT, -OLD, OLL (bolt, gold, roll)	20

CHANGE:	OU (pour, soul, source—*poar, soal, soarce*)	11
	-ORT (port, fort—*poart, foart*); -ORD (ford, horde, sword—*foard, hoard, soard*);	
	-ORCH (porch—*poarch*)	8
	'post'—*poast* 4, 'both'—*boath* 2, 'folk'— *foak* 2, 'brooch'—*broach* 2, 'door'—*dore* 2, 'rogue'—*roag* 2, 'comb'—*coam*, 'owe' —*ow*, 'sew'—*sow*, 'beau'—*bow*, 'though' —*thow* 3	21

The U Sound (318 words)

NO CHANGE:	Simple words like 'hut', 'dull', 'fur'	260
	Words like 'judge', 'plunge', 'curve'	24
CHANGE:	O-E (come—*cum* 2, love—*luv* 4, done— *dun* 4, sponge—*spunge*)	11
	-ON (son—*sun* 3, front—*frunt*, month— *munth*)	5
	WOR- (word, worse—*wurd, wurse*)	8
	OU (rough, touch—*ruff, tuch*)	6
	'blood'—*blud* 2, 'tongue'—*tung*, 'brusque' —*brusk*	4

The OO and YOO Sounds (207 words)

NO CHANGE:	OO (book, poor)	76
	OO-E (goose)	10
	U-E (OO) (rule, flute, crude)	15
	UE (OO) (blue, true)	7
	EW (OO) (blew, crew)	14
	U-E (YOO) (sure, mule, duke)	21
	UE (YOO) (due)	4
	EW (YOO) (dew, stew)	12
CHANGE:	OU (group, could, you, route—*groop, cood, yoo, rute*)	15
	O-E (move, lose—*moov, loos*)	4
	O (do, to, who, two—*doo, too, hoo, too*)	4
	UI (fruit, juice—*frute, juce*)	6
	U (pull—*pool* 3, push—*poosh* 2, puss— *poos*, truth—*trooth*, put—*poot*)	8
	'feu', 'feud'—*fue, fued*, 'view'—*vew*, 'lieu' —*lue*, 'queue'—*cue*, 'shoe'—*shoo*, 'wolf' —*woolf*, 'tomb'—*toom* 2, 'whom'—*hoom*, 'through'—*throo*	11

The OU Sound (100 words)

NO CHANGE:	OU (loud)	52
	OU-E (rouse, ounce)	16
	OUGH (bough)	3

CHANGE: -OW (now, crown, browse—*nou, croun,*
                       brouse)   29

The OI Sound (32 words)

NO CHANGE: OI (join, hoist)   20
                     OI-E (voice)   4
                     OY (joy)   7

CHANGE: 'buoy'—*boy*   1

WORDS OF TWO SYLLABLES

From monosyllables we pass to dissyllables of which there are some 4000, to find that the coming together of two syllables has created some fresh problems in spelling. In general, the same principles of simplification apply to the spelling of the constituent syllables, but the scheme is complicated (a) by the effects of difference of stress, and (b) by the character of the medial consonant or consonants.

In most words of two syllables there is an inequality of accentuation. Usually when two words or syllables are put together in a single word the accent is put on the first of the two (as in 'eyebrow', 'kingdom', 'service', 'number'). Occasionally there is little difference of stress, or the accent falls on the second syllable (as in 'hillside', 'hotel'). Prefixes and suffixes as a rule are unaccented, so that in words like 'contain', 'above', 'decide' the accent is on the second syllable, while in words like 'judgment', 'famous', 'hateful' it is on the first. The common effect of diminished stress is a flattening of the vowel sounds and a loss of some of their distinctive quality. The endings of 'cottage', 'college' and 'certain', for example, are all pronounced in ordinary speech with much the same neutral sound. A word like 'granite' gets reduced to 'granit', and the IT sound is scarcely distinguishable from a dull ET. If it were considered necessary to make the letters follow pronunciation closely, many changes would have to be made in the spelling, especially in suffix endings. But seeing that in careful speech something of the original vowel sound makes itself felt in the reduced form, there can be no objection to retaining the original form in most cases. In a few words there is a marked difference in the current pronunciation which makes some modification desirable. -ITE and -INE are cases in point. 'Polite' must be spelled with an -ITE, but 'granite' should lose the final E. 'Canine' and 'divine' must remain as at present but 'marine' should be spelled *marene* and 'engine' be spelled *enjin*.

One letter with pronunciation peculiar to the unaccented second syllable is the final Y in words like 'happy' and 'merry' and in the suffix LY (as in 'softly' and 'happily'). An occasional variant is the digraph EY which occurs in 'donkey' and 'barley'. Since this final Y or

EY is readily distinguishable from initial Y with its consonantal value, and from the final Y in accented syllables such as occurs in 'rely' and 'supply', there is no need to make any change, unless perhaps it be to spell 'donkey' and 'barley' without the E.

The chief difficulty in the spelling of two-syllabled words arises when there is only a single mid-consonantal sound. When the first syllable ends in one consonant and another consonant begins the second, as happens in the majority of dissyllables, the two parts of the word are spelled just as if they were separate words: usually in this case the first syllable is simple with a short vowel preceding the consonant. If there is no consonant and the one syllable ends and the other begins with a vowel (as in 'lion', 'create', 'poem') the situation once more is simple: the first syllable has always a long vowel, and the second vowel is short or long as the case may be. But English spelling is confusing in the use of the single medial consonant. A clear distinction is made in some cases by doubling the mid-consonant to indicate the short vowel sound. Note for example 'tiger' and 'trigger', 'babel' and 'babble', 'bugle' and 'struggle', 'here' and 'herring'. But the rule suggested by these examples is not consistently followed. While the vowel before the double consonant is always short, the vowel before the single consonant is sometimes long (indeed very often long), sometimes short, generally uncertain for the ignorant child and the foreign learner. To take one set of words from many for illustration: Vary (long), very (short); tidy (long), pity (short); duty (long), study (short); pony (long), body (short).

There is one simple expedient which would clear away all dubieties at a stroke. Give every one-letter vowel that comes before a single mid-consonant its long value, and double the mid-consonant to indicate the ordinary short sound. The proposal has much to commend it and deserves serious consideration. Unfortunately it would entail a large number of changes, and some less drastic method of simplification is to be preferred.

The readiest solution of the problem is perhaps to be found in the fact that the character of the vowel sound before the single mid-consonant is largely determined by the following syllable. Certain suffixes or endings are usually preceded by the long vowel sounds, others usually by the short. As an example of the former we have the interesting group of two-syllabled words ending in O: halo, hero, negro, tyro, silo, solo, ludo: every one of them with the long sound. Almost but not quite so consistently short—to take an example of the other type—are the words ending in ISH: (a) banish, lavish, perish, relish, finish, British, polish, punish; (b) skittish, Scottish, rubbish; (c) slavish, stylish, mulish; (d) boorish, foolish. There is no reason why the present spelling of the first two sets of the ISH words should not be accepted, and for consistency 'Scottish' and 'rubbish' could be changed to *Scotish* and *rubish*. The third set are all derived from words with an E mute ending, and the E can be inserted to indicate the long vowel (*slaveish, styleish*), the more easily since EI has not been used as a digraph in the general scheme.

What is suggested is that the ISH group of words and the other groups with endings that are usually preceded by a short first syllable should be retained without change, as well defined exceptions to the general rule that a one-letter vowel before a single mid-consonant sound should have a long value. The following are typical examples of words in these special groups:

Words ending in:
IC: panic, cleric, critic, logic.
ID: rapid, tepid, timid, solid.
IT or ET: habit, facet, merit, visit, rivet, profit, comet.
ISH: as given above.
IN: Latin, famin(e), robin.
IST or EST: chemist, modest, forest.
ACE or ICE: palace, malice, menace, solace, novice (promise).
AGE: manage, image, homage.
URE or UTE: manure, salute, tenure, figure, tribute.
VEL, VIL, VEN, VER: travel, level, devil, seven, sever, swivel, civil,
        river, novel, hover, oven, shovel, cover.
(But note: uric, stupid, unit, future, all with the YOO sound.)

All other words with the short vowel in the first syllable will be symbolized by the doubled mid-consonant. Words ending in ON (for example, bacon, demon, bison, colon) have the long sound: *draggon, lemmon,* are the revised forms for the short. In words ending in ENT, like parent, silent, moment, where the first vowel is normally long, exceptions like 'talent' and 'lament' call for a doubling of the mid-consonant. Other changes to be made in common words are: *onnor, linnen, morral, verry, coppy, boddy, citty, mettal, meddal, widdow.*

Another difficulty of less consequence, affecting the mid-consonant is the existence of two sets of words beginning with A, the one with single, the other with double consonant following: words of Teutonic origin on the one hand—above, along, alive, asleep, ago, away, etc.; words of Latin origin derived from the preposition *ad,* on the other hand—afford, appeal, apply, arrive, assist, attract, etc. The logical course would be to bring the first set into line with the accepted practice by doubling the consonant. The alternative (to be preferred) would be to leave these very common words unchanged and depend for recognition of them on the fact that in most cases the second syllable is a word in its own right.

POLYSYLLABIC WORDS

The main difficulty in giving consistency to the spelling of words of three or more syllables is to distinguish the long and the short sounds of the vowels. The problem is much the same as with the dissyllables, many of which indeed are made into polysyllables by the addition of affixes. But there is one important difference in the fact that long vowels in the component parts of the polysyllabic words tend to shorten in their new context. 'Repeat' for example gives 'repetition'; 'prevail' gives 'prevalent', 'admire', 'admirable' and so on. It is not an invariable practice, however, as the word 'invariable' shows and it is therefore impossible to give any simple rule for the guidance of the spelling reformer. But as a matter of fact most of the vowels in the longer words are short, which suggests that the easiest way to remove ambiguities is to indicate by special spelling devices those long vowels which are not otherwise evident: for example, *doamestic, caipable, priemary, catheedral, arrieval.*

Polysyllabic words beginning with the prefixes *be-, de-, pre-, re-,* and *pro-* usually retain the long vowel sound they have in dissyllabic forms. Occasionally there is a shortening as in 'definite' or 'preposition' which may either be recognized by doubling the consonant (*deffinite, prepposition*) or be ignored as of minor consequence. Where one vowel follows immediately on another at the beginning or in the middle of a word, as in 'diagram', 'scientific', 'museum', 'violin', the first vowel is invariably long: and the same thing holds for U preceding a single consonant or another vowel. There is no need to make any change in these cases.

It is the suffixes which give most trouble in polysyllabic words. Those like *-ment* and *-ness* with a consonant in front are quite straightforward. So as a rule are the group ending in a silent E (-ate, -ite, -ute, -age, etc). But in some cases like 'engine', 'infinite', 'attractive', the final E is now misleading and must be dropped. Another case in which the present spelling is misleading is the digraph OU in words ending in *-ous* and *-our*: OU must be reserved for the sound that occurs in 'house' and 'hour'. In words ending in *-ous* such as 'enormous', the O is superfluous and should be dropped. In words like 'endeavour' and 'honourable', it is the U that is superfluous. Spell *enormus, endeavor, onorable.* One group of suffixes requiring special attention are those introduced by an I: *-ial* (burial), *-ian* (guardian), *-iar* (familiar), *-ion* (companion), *-iage* (marriage), *-ious* (glorious): all of them it is to be noted with a short I in contrast with the long I preceding another vowel at the beginning or middle of words. There are three different cases here: in 'marriage' and 'carriage' the I is not sounded and should be eliminated, in 'burial' and 'guardian', the ending is dissyllabic and should be left as it is; in 'familiar' and 'companion' the ending is monosyllabic and may be improved by changing I to Y, to indicate its consonantal character. Finally there is the rather confusing group of words already noted in which the suffixes prefaced with an I follow the consonants T or C or S (gracious, patient, ambition, permission— for example). There is something to be said for a phonetic spelling as a means of simplification. But so many words are involved, all very distinctive, and the spelling though not very obvious at first sight is consistent. So we are brought back to the conclusion that it may be better to accept 'shon' as the pronunciation of -TION and -SION, and 'shence' as the pronunciation of -TIENCE. Better that than disturb the ordinary printed page by the change. Following is an illustrative passage in the new spelling.

Robinson Crusoe

And nou our kace was verry dismal indeed; for we all saw plainly that the sea went so high that the boat cood not liv, and that we shood be inevitably dround. As to makeing sail we had nun, nor if we had cood we have dun ennything with it: so we wurked at the oar towards the land, tho with hevvy harts like men going to execution; for all we knew that when the boat came nearer the shore, she wood be dashd in a thousand peeces by the breach of the sea. Houever we committed our soals to God in the moast ernest manner and the wind driveing us towards the shore we haistend our destruction with our own hands, pooling as well as we cood towards land.

Friday was a cumly handsum fellow, perfectly well made, with straight strong lims, not too large, tall and well shaped, and as I reckon about twenty-six years of age. He had a very good countenance, not a feerce and surly aspect, but seemd to have sumthing verry manly in his face; and yet he had all the sweetness and softness of an Ewroapean in his countenance too, espeshially when he smiled. His hair was long and black, not curld like wool; his forehed very high and large; and a grait vivacity and sparkling sharpness in his ys. The cullor of his skin was not quite dark but verry tawny; and yet not of an ugly nauseus tawny, as the Brazilyans and Virginyans and uther natives of America ar, but of a bright kind of a dun oliv cullor, that had in it sumthing verry agreeable, tho not verry easy to describe.

Daniel Defoe

CHAPTER 6

Grammar and Usage

We'll begin with box, the plural is boxes,
But the plural of ox should be oxen, not oxes.
Yet the plural of mouse is never meese.
You may find a lone mouse or a whole nest of mice,
But the plural of house is houses, not hice.
If the plural of man is always men,
Why shouldn't the plural of pan be pen?
The cow in the plural may be called cows or Kine,
But a bow if repeated is never called bine;
And the plural of vow is vows, not vine.
If I speak of a foot and you show me two feet
And I give you a boot, would a pair be called beet?
If one is a tooth and whole set is teeth,
Why shouldn't the plural of booth be called beeth?
If the singular's this and the plural is these,
Should the plural of kiss be written kese?
We speak of a brother, and also of brethren,
But though we say mother, we never say mothren.
Then the masculine pronouns are he, his, and him,
But imagine the feminine: she, shis and shim!
So English, I think that you all will agree
Is the funniest language you ever did see.

—AUTHOR UNKNOWN

NEW FRONTIER IN GRAMMAR *

Sister M. Evelyn, R.S.M.

Anyone leafing through current periodical literature on education, at least on the elementary or secondary level, and observing the tenor

---

* From *The Catholic Educator* (New York: Joseph F. Wagner, Inc., May, 1962). Reprinted by permission of the publisher.

of so many of the articles might well conclude that this is the "Era of New Approaches," since there is scarcely an issue which does not carry an article on a new approach to one subject or another. Among the more controversial of these is the new structural approach to the teaching of English which has only recently begun to trickle down from the learned journals of the field of descriptive linguistics to the periodicals and textbooks of the field of pedagogy.

The attempt to apply the principles of descriptive linguistics to the teaching of English grammar is still in the pioneer stage, and there is not yet a definitive text. To my knowledge nothing has been done on the elementary level toward adopting this approach. Some high school texts have begun to incorporate a few of the new ideas in some areas, but their sections on formal grammar are still mainly traditional. The few authors who have fully adopted the approach on the high school and college levels differ among themselves in terminology and in the criteria which they set up for classifying parts of speech. However, all of them have this in common: they are trying to deal with the structure of the English language as it really is today rather than as it would have been if English had remained a highly inflected language. In other words, they are trying to make explicit those grammatical devices which native speakers of English subconsciously recognize and use from the time they first begin to speak in complete sentences.

Naturally, these devices differ, at least in degree, from those of other modern languages which still have personal endings and tense signs for verbs, endings to mark the number and gender of adjectives as well as of nouns, and similar grammatical signals derived from Latin which have long since disappeared from English.

NOT WISE TO ASSESS PREMATURELY

It would not be wise to assess prematurely the worth of any method before it has been well tried, since we know by experience that teaching methods which seemed in theory to possess great potential value did not always bring about the desired improvement when reduced to practice. However, teachers generally agree that the traditional approach to the teaching of grammar has never produced results commensurate with the time and energy devoted to it, nor have the students acquired a greater facility in their use of language either as a medium of communication or of art for having been exposed to it. It might, therefore, be worthwhile, despite our natural reluctance to turn aside from the familiar formulas and definitions, to consider seriously the reasons which prompted the linguists to abandon traditional grammar, and to take a look at just a few of the salient features of the system which they propose as a more accurate description of English structure.

FIRST ATTEMPTS

When they first attempted to systemize modern English grammar, the grammarians used Latin as their model and tried to force English into its mold despite the fact that English had lost most of its inflectional endings after the Norman invasion. As a matter of fact, some of the scholars of the time believed that the English language had no grammar of its own at all and the only way to analyze an English sentence was to translate it first into Latin and then to describe the Latin structure. They apparently failed to realize that unless it did have a grammar, English could not have been cast into an intelligible sentence in the first place.

In Latin the parts of speech have characteristic endings by which they can be recognized. For example, the case ending of a noun is a signpost telling us to interpret the word as a name of a person, place, or thing, as well as pointing out to us the relation of the word to the other words in the sentence. The structuralists' objection to the traditional definition of a noun is not that it isn't true but that it isn't helpful since we must first determine that a word is used as a name in a given context and then work backward to labeling the part of speech. To them this procedure is putting the cart before the horse, since one word form often has a number of meanings and the function of grammar is to act as a key unlocking the specific use of a word in a given context.

By the teaching of grammar, then, the structuralists mean more than merely helping the student distinguish those forms of language which are socially acceptable from those which are considered substandard, although, of course, they do not disparage this important aspect of language teaching as they are sometimes accused of doing. Grammar, as they conceive of it, means a set of signals or a kind of shorthand code which attaches certain meanings to words over and above their vocabulary meaning and which brings out their relationship to the other words surrounding them. These signals consist mainly of inflection, sentence position, and structure words.

WORD FORM

Elusive as it is in English, word form seems to be still the most tangible of the grammar devices and modern grammarians use it as a point of departure in constructing their system. They first make a distinction between vocabulary meaning and grammatical meaning. For example, the word *boy* has the vocabulary meaning, "male child," so the *s* by itself has no vocabulary meaning at all. However, the word *boys* means "more than one male child," so the *s* has the grammatical meaning of "more than one." Since nouns are the only part of speech to which we can add an *s* to make the word plural, this is one of the best signals by which they can be identified. Likewise, the fact that we can add the grammatical suffix *ed* to a word to signal "in the past" without essentially changing the meaning of a sentence, helps us to identify the word as a verb. Inflectional endings also provide economy in language, making it possible to express in a single word a combination of ideas for which we would otherwise have to use several words.

Despite the economy it provides, English has tended to drop the endings and to use instead certain little words called structure words to supply the grammatical meaning taken care of in some of the other languages by inflection. These words help to signal the part of speech of the words near them. For instance, if we change the sentence "Mary has driven to school," to "Mary has been driven to school," the insertion of the auxiliary *been* not only changes the relationship between Mary and the act of driving but also helps to signal that *driven* is the predicate verb in this context. If we say, "Her dress was as white as the driven snow," the article *the* preceding *driven* immediately excludes the possibility of its being a predicate verb in this sentence and helps to determine it as adjectival.

WORD ORDER

Another device, and perhaps the one on which we rely most heavily in everyday speech is word order or sentence position. Whether we say in Latin *Puer puellam videt*, or *Puellam puer videt*, makes no difference at all in communicating who saw whom since the subject-object relationship is expressed by the case forms of the nouns. However, in English "The boy sees the girl," and "The girl sees the boy," communicate quite different meanings because English nouns have long since lost distinctive nominative and objective case forms and the expression of the subject-object relationship depends on word order alone. The fact that pronouns have retained these case forms although the nouns have not accounts for the fact that we must always be correcting children for statements like, "Me and him saw it," and "Between you and me this is the way it is."

In the spoken language, intonation, or the variation of stress, pitch, and pauses, is an extremely important grammatical device and one which the writer must take into careful consideration if he hopes to avoid ambiguity. Many a comedy of errors has occurred because a reader has supplied a different intonation from the one intended by the writer. Intonation patterns differ from language to language and easily betray the difference between a native and a nonnative speaker of a tongue.

FORM CLASSES AND STRUCTURE CLASSES

On the basis of word form, the structuralists divide English words into two large classes which they call form classes and structure classes. In the form classes, some further distinguish lexical forms from grammatical forms. For example, the suffixes on the words *agreement, agreeable,* and *agreeably* are lexical suffixes because they change the part of speech and give us three different, though related, words. On the other hand, the forms *agree, agrees, agreeing,* and *agreed* are not four different words but four different grammatical forms of one and the same word. Some of the new grammarians would say, for instance, that a verb is a word that can be used in the same sentence position as the word *agree.* The only parts of speech which have distinctive lexical or grammatical forms are nouns, personal and relative pronouns, verbs, adjectives, and those adverbs which are formed by adding -ly to the positive form of the adjective. These, therefore, are generally considered the form classes.

The structure classes are made up of those words which generally occur only in one form but pass so freely from one function to another that they can be classified only by their position in a given context. Some of them are practically empty of vocabulary meaning and serve mainly as grammatical devices. Auxiliaries, for example, are the principal device for supplying tense, mood, voice, and aspect in the English verb-system. That is why we can get along with four or five verb forms in comparison to the great number employed in Latin or modern Romance languages. (The loss of personal endings with the exception of the *s* on the third person, singular, present is another factor which accounts for our few forms.) Some one-form words like *quite* or *somewhat* can stand only before adjectives or adverbs, while others like *that* can function as three or four parts of speech.

COMPLICATING FACT

English grammar is still further complicated by the fact that the form words also frequently shift into the position and function of one another. "Ring out the old, ring in the new," contains adjective forms used in noun positions as direct objects. "Close the kitchen door," contains a noun in adjective position. Some of the modern grammarians simply make the statement, unpleasing though it may be to the traditional ear, that nouns can be modified by nouns, verbs, and adverbs as well as by adjectives, and that the adjectives may be used as subjects or objects. Others follow a somewhat more conservative approach and distinguish four more classes of words based on the position that form words normally hold in a sentence—nominals, verbals, adjectivals, and adverbials. Thus, in the sentences given above, the words *old* and *new* would be classed as nominals and the word *kitchen* as an adjectival. In this way the break between form and function is bridged over.

Flexible as it appears to be, English structure follows a few basic sentence patterns and its variety is attained by interweaving modifiers around the basic nouns and verbs. However, even the modifiers follow a more rigid pattern than is apparent at first glance. Observe the modifiers in the following sentence: "The four very graceful prancing circus horses outside are thoroughbreds." If we tried to shift anyone of the six modifiers of *horses* to another position we would get a very un-English-sounding sequence or else sheer nonsense. The word *very* could pattern with no other word except *graceful* because it is the only word there with the lexical form of an adjective. *The* and *four* are structure words used as determiners which must begin the sequence; *outside* is an adjectival of place which normally patterns after the word it modifies. The participle *prancing* might follow *horses*, but if it did *outside* would become an adverbial; and *circus* could not be placed anywhere else in the sequence.

BECOME ALIVE TO SUBTLE SHADES OF MEANING

Thus we see that word form and sentence position are closely tied together, and even modifiers must accede priority to one another. As we play around with a sentence like this we become aware of what words can be substituted and where they must be put and we begin to realize that there is a reason for learning all the distinctions and classifications that make up grammar. Moreover, the more gifted students might become more alive to the subtle shades of meanings and shifts of emphasis that the careful placing of word patterns can effect.

This new approach to English grammar is not exactly simple, nor could it be since language itself is a very complex thing. No living language develops strictly by logic and no system can be expected to provide any neat and undisputable pigeon-hole for every conceivable combination of words. But it is intelligible, and it seems to me to offer through the triple approach of word order, word form, and the structure words, a more tangible set of clues than definitions based on meaning or function alone. I believe, too, that if students really grasped the basic structure of their language, they would not only improve in the art of speaking and writing but would also add to their knowledge a new and richer dimension—an insight into the beauty of order governing the forms and structures of sound which constitute man's most marvelous accomplishment in the field of communication, the development of human speech.

GRAMMAR IN THE LANGUAGE PROGRAM *

Harry A. Greene and Walter T. Petty

EVALUATION OF GRAMMAR AS LANGUAGE METHOD

Failure of formal grammar as discipline. Formal grammar as teaching method in English remained secure and almost unchallenged in the school curriculum until the new science of psychology began to develop in this country around the turn of the century. Along about that time the efficiency of learning and the validity of the assumptions of transfers in learning supposed to take place under the disciplinary theory then in vogue came under critical questioning. Actually the problem of transfer was not of special importance so long as the major function of school training was to transmit previously accumulated cultural elements. At the time the formal subjects, such as Latin, algebra, geometry, and natural history were studied for two reasons. First, the knowledge of these fields was the mark of an educated man. Second, mastery of these and other generally difficult subjects was believed to strengthen certain mental faculties and thus provide the desired mental discipline, the primary educational objective of the time. The accomplishment of this objective was dependent upon general learning, not upon the acquisition of specific skills. Gradually the belief developed in this country that a much more important function of education is the production of change in the behavior of the individual. Under this philosophy, learning became the acquisition of

---

* From *Developing Language Skills in the Elementary School*, pp. 337–342. Copyright 1959 by Allyn and Bacon, Inc., Boston. Reprinted by permission of the publisher.

specific skills, not broad general abilities. The individual learned to read, to comprehend, to compute, to solve problems, to write, to spell useful words; not merely to remember, to reason, to visualize in general situations.

In 1890, William James,[1] the father of experimental psychology, reported the results of experiments showing that transfer effects in memory, perception, reasoning and others of the so-called mental faculties were so slight as to discredit the claims of formal discipline and the functional theory of learning. Numerous other studies in special subject areas followed promptly. As early as 1906 Hoyt reported that pupils in the seventh and eighth grades with no training in formal grammar did as effective work in writing compositions or in interpreting literature as did those with two years of drill on formal grammar.[2] A few years later, Briggs conducted a carefully controlled classroom teaching experiment designed to reveal the extent of the transfer of grammatical skills to language abilities of seventh grade pupils. He concluded that "these particular children after the amount of formal grammar that they had, do not, as measured by the means employed, show in any of the abilities tested improvement that may be attributed to their training in formal grammar."[3] This study offered conclusive proof of the failure of formal grammar to transfer to such readily identifiable language skills as the statement of a definition, the application of a definition, or the ability to correct errors.

Formal grammar fails to function as English method. During the early decades of the present century, critical students of the problems of teaching English were quick to question the practical contributions of formal grammar as method in the teaching of English. Segel and Barr gave a formal grammar test and a test of applied grammar to a large group of pupils and after analyzing the data concluded that "formal grammar has no immediate transfer value so far as applied English grammar is concerned."[4] In the next two decades Rapeer,[5] Boraas,[6] and Asker[7] in three independent studies corroborated the

---

[1] William James, *Principles of Psychology* (New York: Holt, 1890).

[2] Franklin S. Hoyt, "Studies in English Grammar," *Teachers College Record*, 7:467–500 (November 1906).

[3] Thomas H. Briggs, "Formal English Grammar as a Discipline," *Teachers College Record*, 14:251–343 (September 1913).

[4] David Segel and Nora R. Barr, "Relation of Achievement in Formal Grammar to Achievement in Applied Grammar," *Journal of Educational Research*, 14:401–2 (December 1926).

[5] L. W. Rapeer, "The Problem of Formal Grammar in Elementary Education," *Journal of Educational Psychology*, 4:125–37 (March 1913).

[6] Julius Boraas, "Formal English Grammar and the Practical Mastery of English." Unpublished doctoral dissertation, Department of Education, University of Minnesota, 1917.

[7] William Asker, "Does Knowledge of Formal Grammar Function?" *School and Society*, 17:109–11 (January 27, 1923).

earlier findings of Hoyt and led to the general conclusion that "knowledge of formal grammar influences ability to judge grammatical correctness of a sentence and ability in English composition only to a negligible degree." [8]

Teachers of formal grammar have long defended the thesis that a knowledge of grammar is essential to the proper understanding of the sentence. The study by Benfer indicated a very discouraging lack of relationship between the ability to identify sentence fragments and sentences, and grammatical skill in identifying subjects and predicates.[9] A similar lack of correspondence between usage test scores and the knowledge of the grammatical reasons for the accepted usages found in a critical statistical study of a well-known grammar-usage test prompted two parallel studies.[10, 11] Both of these involved the determination of the relationship of scores on a difficult and comprehensive test of punctuation skills and the knowledge of the rules governing the usages. Pupils with little knowledge of the rules made high scores on the usages and, with almost equal frequency, individuals with extensive knowledge of the rules made low scores on the usages.

In a comprehensive and carefully controlled experimental study by Butterfield,[12] definitely superior results in the teaching of punctuation skills were obtained by direct teaching of the desired skills rather than by methods based upon the pupil's knowledge of the grammatical elements listed by English teachers as contributing directly to the punctuation skills.

Diagramming fails to produce mastery of the sentence. The use of graphic analysis or sentence diagramming has long been a favorite teaching device of upper-grade teachers of language. Two different studies in this series lead unquestionably to the conclusion that while diagramming responds nicely to training and is readily learned, it has very slight value in itself so far as production of sentence mastery is concerned. Many children enjoy the mechanical exactness of sentence diagramming. Teachers like it too, perhaps because it is a convenient form of busywork. The only defensible reason for teaching children to diagram sentences should be the improvement it brings in their ability to create effective sentences. Unfortunately, the evidence shows

---

[8] *Ibid.*

[9] Mabel Benfer, "Sentence Sense in Relation to Knowledge of Subjects and Predicates." Unpublished master's thesis, State University of Iowa, 1935.

[10] E. R. Butterworth, "Mastery of Punctuation Usages as Related to the Rules." Unpublished master's thesis, State University of Iowa, 1932.

[11] William A. Ortmeyer, "Relation of Punctuation Rules and Practices." Unpublished master's thesis, State University of Iowa, 1932.

[12] Claire J. Butterfield, "The Effect of Knowledge of Certain Grammatical Elements on the Acquisition and Retention of Punctuation Skills." Unpublished doctoral dissertation, State University of Iowa, 1945.

that this is insignificant. Barnett [13] demonstrated that children could be taught to diagram sentences rapidly and correctly, but that the skills thus acquired did not contribute in any significant degree to an improvement in pupils' language usage or in their abilities to read and comprehend sentences.

Stewart examined this problem further in a comprehensive investigation involving twenty different school systems with classes selected and balanced in all essential respects.[14] Again the children in the experimental group demonstrated that they could be taught to diagram, but those in the control group, by spending the same amount of time given to the diagramming group, showed slightly more improvement in sentence mastery than did those who learned diagramming. These results raised a number of questions. Why spend valuable class time in acquiring a useless skill when the same time and energy would attain a useful objective? Is time spent in learning to diagram justifiable or is it mainly busywork? Why not proceed directly to the real goal of expression by having the pupils develop their sentence writing skills by writing sentences arising out of their classroom activities?

Formal grammar fails to satisfy research and teaching groups. In addition to these and many other investigations of the contributions of formal grammar to the elementary language program, the attitudes of two influential professional groups on this problem should be given serious consideration. These organizations are the *National Council of Teachers of English* and the *National Conference on Research in Elementary English.* The second of these organizations in 1937 reported evidence substantiating earlier research showing the failure of formal grammar to function as a method of teaching language expression, and supporting the statement that "training in formal grammar does not result in a great gain in the writing of correct English or in the ability of the individual to recognize correct English in writing." [15] Hatfield, as chairman of the *Curriculum Commission of the National Council of Teachers of English* expressed the conviction of the commission that "all teaching of grammar separate from the manipulation of sentences be discontinued . . . since every scientific attempt to prove that knowledge of grammar is useful has failed." [16] Again, this same organization has recently taken the position that "labeling the

13 W. W. Barnett, "A Study of the Effects of Sentence Diagraming on English Correctness and Silent Reading Ability." Unpublished master's thesis, State University of Iowa, 1942.

14 J. Reece Stewart, "The Effect of Diagraming on Certain Skills in English Composition." Unpublished doctoral dissertation, State University of Iowa, 1941.

15 Harry A. Greene, "Principles of Method in Elementary English Composition," *Elementary English Review,* 31:485–493 (December 1954).

16 W. Wilbur Hatfield, "What Grammar? And How?" *Virginia Journal of Education,* 29:318 (May 1936).

parts of speech has proved in one research study after another . . . to be futile so far as its effect on speech and writing is concerned. Intermediate-grade pupils should have practice in the *use* of language, not in the classification of forms." [17]

VALUES OF FORMAL GRAMMAR

The discussion of the meaning, history, and place of formal grammar leads to the conclusion that many of the claims made for it are unsupported by either the experimental evidence or the results. Grammar failed to function as a discipline, just as formal discipline failed as a theory of learning. It failed as method of teaching because it lacked the elements of good classroom method. It failed to develop effective language expression because language is a skill field, not a subject-matter area. Language is active, creative, not formal and analytical. Grammar failed at the curriculum level because its methods slowed the growth and development of a live and growing language. The learning of rules, the study of the sentence elements, the diagramming of sentences, the study of the parts of speech, in addition to other formal methods, have not enabled language teachers to attain th' desired objective of enabling the individual to express himself effectively. However, even though the results of research in the past fifty years have demonstrated that formal and indirect methods do not assure good, or even acceptable language expression, no one, least of all the present writers, would deny that grammar does have a value as a structural framework of a language and as an editorial tool.

The structural framework of a living language. Despite idiomatic peculiarities and irregularities of usage, growing rules with as many exceptions as elements that conform, any living, growing language must have its framework of usage. An understanding of the function of this framework and the ability to work within it are of obvious value in learning to use the language effectively. Accordingly, the problem of the classroom teacher, supervisor, or curriculum worker in language is to determine the ways in which grammar may be employed most effectively to improve the language usage habits of elementary school pupils.

It is the conviction of the authors that the grammar of the elementary school language program must be functional rather than formal. That is, pupils meet and master the essential language habits in situations that are as life-like as possible in order that they may use them to communicate effectively in real life activities. The organization of the

---

[17] *Language Arts for Today's Children*, Curriculum Commission of the National Council of Teachers of English (New York: Appleton-Century-Crofts, 1954).

grammar program in this functional approach may be seen in the following principles:

1. Pupils develop language habits as they are needed in actual meaningful situations.
2. Only a limited number of skills of high social utility are presented for attack in the elementary school.
3. The pupil is led to discover his own deficiencies and is given practice only on those skills in which he individually has need of practice.
4. Clear, complete, effective expression is stressed at all times.
5. The pupils are led to a gradual awareness of the function of grammar in correct and effective expression.

An essential editorial tool. The failure of the memorization of rules and the isolated study of grammatical structure to produce the desired quality of oral and written expression strongly suggests that the place of usage will result, the pupil should look upon the rule as an editorial tool for the improvement of language. The apparent failure of the rules of grammar does not mean that they are useless; they have been misused. Instead of memorizing the rule in the belief that correct habits of usage will result, the pupil should look upon the rule as an editorial guide or authority for use in handling debatable issues. The child should learn to consider the grammar of his language as the authority on usage in the same sense that he recognizes his dictionary as the authority on spelling. Rules do not make the usages nor do they aid appreciably in the formation of correct language habits, but they do point the direction for the learner and tell him when he has arrived at a point of adequate mastery. They aid in establishing a desire to use language effectively and acceptably.

PUNCTUATION *

E. L. Thorndike

The history of punctuation goes back over two thousand years, but we shall start with the first printed books. The early printers (1475–1500) made types for such punctuation marks as they found frequently in the manuscripts they used and inserted these marks as they appeared

* From *Teachers College Record,* 49 (May 1948), 531–537, Teachers College, Columbia University, N. Y., reprinted by permission of the publisher and Robert L. Thorndike, executor for the E. L. Thorndike estate.

in the manuscripts, unless they thought it more useful to readers or more convenient to themselves to do otherwise. The earlier scribes used (1) a round or square point (punctum); (2) two such, one above the other; (3) three such, one above another; and (4) a diagonal line (/), but with little consistency or clarity of purpose, being more interested in abbreviations to save labor and paper than in devices to aid the reader.

Printers up to 1500 did slightly better by readers. Their commonest punctuation mark was the /, which is probably the ancestor of the comma but was not used as we use commas. Their next commonest mark was the punctum (round, square, or in the form of a tiny cross), which is the ancestor of our period, but was not used as we use periods. Two "points" one above the other is rarer. What the /, ., and : signified to the printers of 1475 to 1500, or to the readers of their books, was confused and variable. A printer could even for page after page use no /'s, or no :'s or no .'s. He could leave an entire page or more with no punctuation marks whatever. A pair of short diagonals was used unambiguously at the end of a line to show that the remainder of a word would be found on the following line. But if there was not room for it, it could be omitted. Capital letters were used, but not in accord with any clear rules or customs.[1]

```
We read of a hermit which much marveled of the
divers and obscure judgments of our lord jesus christ and
by temptation of the fiend he said in his heart that his judgmen
ts were not just. For god suffered the good men to have ma
ny tribulations. and the evil people many good things: and
god sent to him an angel in form of a man which said
to him in this manner/ Come and go with me for god hath     .
sent me to thee. For to lead thee in diverse places: to the end that
I should show to thee of his diverse and obscure judgments: he
led him first in to the house of a good man / the which recei
ved them benignly. and made to them right good cheer. and
held them wel at their ease On the morn early the angel robbed
his good host of a fair cup. which cup he loved mar"
velously. Then the hermit was much angry and thought he
was sent from god: the night after they were lodged with an
evil host which made to them right evil cheer. & supped evil
and had right evil bedding: & in the morning the angel gave to the
evil host the cup that he had stolen from the good host the ni"
ght before. & when the hermit saw that he had evil suspicion
upon the angel. the III night they were lodged with a good
```

The meanings of punctuation marks prior to 1500 were confused and variable, but the books were doubtless easier to read than they would have been without any marks or with only one mark of punctuation.

---

[1] In the sample shown (from the *Doctrinal of Sapience* printed by Caxton about 1489), I have modernized the spelling so that the punctuation and capitalization can be examined more easily.

Printers were abler men than scribes, and more concerned with pleasing readers.

Some of them were specially able men who tried deliberately to improve punctuation. A famous instance is the Italian, Aldus Manutius (1450–1515), who was an excellent scholar in Greek and Latin, and who became a printer primarily to promote learning. He introduced the round comma (,), question mark, "curves" around a parenthetical phrase or clause, quotation marks, and the semicolon. He and his son and grandson made, as printers of the Aldine books, innovations and systematizations in punctuation that had great influence on printing all over Europe. His grandson included in his book on spelling (*Orthographiae ratio*, 1566) a section of about 1000 words which stated rules for the use of the semicirculum or comma, semicirculo junctum, geminum punctum, and punctum. Orthodox doctrine followed these rules more or less for three hundred years.[2]

The variability, inconsistency, and confusion in punctuation were reduced, but by no means eliminated, by the improvements made by the Aldine and other thoughtful printers. Even by 1600 the best scholars and printers had no surety in their use of punctuation marks. Below are some familiar passages from the first folio edition of Shakespeare (1623) and the original (1611) King James version of the Bible.

> To be, or not to be, that is the Question:
> Whether 'tis Nobler in the minde to suffer
> The Slings and Arrowes of outrages Fortune,
> Or to take Armes against a Sea of troubles,
> And by opposing end them: to dye, to sleepe
> No more and by a sleepe to say we end
> The Heart-ake, and the thousand Naturall shockes
> That Flesh is heyre to? 'tis a consummation
> Devoutly to be wished. To dye to sleepe,
> To sleepe, perchance to Dreame; I, there's the rub,
> For in that sleepe of death, what dreames may come,
> When we have shuffl'd off this mortall coile
> Must give us pause.

> The quality of mercy is not strain'd,
> It droppeth as the gentle raine from heaven
> Upon the place beneath. It is twice blest,
> It blesseth him that gives, and him that takes,
> 'Tis mightiest in the mightiest, it becomes
> The throned Monarch better than his Crowne.
> His Scepter shewes the force of temporall power,
> The attribute to awe and Majestie,
> Wherein doth sit the dread and fear of kings:
> But mercy is above this sceptered sway,

---

[2] The names semicolon, colon, and period were not used by Manutius.

It is enthroned in the hearts of kings,
It is an attribute to God himselfe:
And earthly power doth then shew likest Gods
When mercie seasons Justice.

And they lift up their voyce, and wept againe: And Orpah kissed her mother in law, but Ruth clave unto her.

And shee said, Behold, thy sister in law is gone backe unto her people, and unto her gods: returne thou after thy sister in law.

And Ruth said, intreate me not to leave thee or to returne from following after thee: for whither thou goest, I will goe: and where thou lodgest, I will lodge: thy people shall be my people, and thy God my God.

Where thou diest, will I die, and there will I be buried: the Lord doe so to me, and more also, if ought but death part thee and me.

But when yee pray, use not vaine repetitions as the heathen doe. For they thinke that they shalbe heard for their much speaking.

Be not ye therefore like unto them: for your Father knoweth what things yee have need of, before ye aske him.

After this manner therefore pray ye: Our Father which art in heaven, hallowed be thy Name.

Thy kingdome come. Thy will be done in earth as it is heaven.

Give us this day our daily bread.

And forgive us our debts, as wee forgive our debters.

And lead us not into temptation, but deliver us from evil: For thine is the kingdome, and the power, and the glory, for ever. Amen.

It has been asserted by Percy Simpson (*Shakespearian Punctuation,* 1911) that the punctuation in the first folio was arranged to guide the speeches of the actors. And Harrison (*Introducing Shakespeare,* 1939) has asserted that the "authorized" Globe Edition's changes are not beneficial. But neither of these authors could rightly deny that the first folio's punctuation was variable, inconsistent, and confused.

It was only after printers and grammarians drew up elaborate sets of rules for using punctuation marks so as to give the maximum help to readers that consistency was even approximated. It was hard to frame and apply such rules. It still is. Consistent punctuation is a difficult art. If the reader will give to a dozen friends unpunctuated copies of any of the passages above and have them supply punctuation marks, he will find many disagreements. By the kindness of Dr. Irving Lorge I have records from 57 college graduates who supplied punctuation marks for all four of these passages.[3] No two identical treatments

---

[3] If the reader will punctuate all four passages, and do so again after some weeks, he will not agree with himself.

of any of the four passages resulted. These 57 persons punctuated the first line of Hamlet's soliloquy in 23 different ways as shown.

To be or not to be, that is the question.
" " ;
" " !
" ; " .
" ! " .
" : " .
" : " :
" : " ;
" — " .
To be, or not to be, that is the question.
" " !
" " ;
To be or not to be. That is the question.
" . " ;
" . " !
" ? " .
" ?— " .
'To be. or not to be,' that is the question!
" " ;" " .
To be or not to be that is the question.
" " :
" " ;
" " !

They punctuated the first twenty-four words of the Lord's prayer in 32 different ways as shown in the table below, in which A, B, C, D, E, F, and G refer to places in the text as shown here: Our Father (A) which art in heaven (B) hallowed be thy name (C) thy kingdom come (D) thy will be done (E) in earth (F) as it is in heaven (G).

	A	B	C	D	E	F	G
1			,	,	,	,	·
2			,	,	,		,
3		,	,	,			,
4		,	,	,			·
5			,	,			,
6			·	,			·
7			·	·			·
8			·	,	,		·
9		,	·	·		,	·
10			;	;		,	·
11		,	;	;			·
12		,	;	;	,		·
13		,	:	,	,		·
14		,	;	;	;		·
15		,	·	,		,	·
16		,	·			,	·
17		,	·	·			·
18		·	;	;	;		·

	A	B	C	D	E	F	G
19		—	.	,			.
20		:	,	,			.
21	,	,	.	,	,		.
22	,	,	.	,	,	,	.
23	,	,	.	.			.
24	,	,	.	;			.
25	,	,	.	,			.
26	,	,	,	,			;
27	,	,	.	.		,	.
28	,	,	.	.	,		.
29	,	,	;	;			;
30	,	,	;	;			.
31	,	,	!	!			.
32	,	,	,	,			.

From 1600 on, customs of punctuation changed greatly. Probably no book printed in the seventeenth century was correctly punctuated by the standards of 1850. Most novelists of the last fifty years would have been greatly annoyed if their books had been punctuated by the standards of 1850.

These changes are caused partly by changes in the ideas of publishers and printers about punctuation, and partly by changes in the ideas of authors. The influence of authors upon punctuation has increased greatly. It is possible that Shakespeare would have let printers alter his script as they felt inclined. But Ibsen and Shaw certainly did not. The printers of Ibsen's day would have deleted many of his dashes. It is possible that Richardson and Fielding left the punctuation of their books to the tender mercies of printers, but George Meredith certainly did not. No printer of his day would have willingly tolerated his use of . . . as a sign of an omitted thought of the speaker. Authors have become increasingly aware of punctuation as an element in style. Many of them now scorn the printer's love for a page of evenly spaced words, with few short lines, unmarred by dashes short and long, rows of dots, or unnecessary exclamation points, or sentences devoid of periods. Such a page now suggests uneventfulness, not to say dullness, to many authors. They prefer short paragraphs and many dashes, suggesting action and vivacity. Many of them disregard manuals and codes which use a dash to mean a break in thought, which limit single quotation marks to a quotation within a quotation, exclamation points to exclamations, and in general attempt to reduce ambiguities. If they use colons except as formal introductions to speeches, arguments, lists, and so on, it is not by rule but for some special purpose, such as to give a flavor of the upper classes to the characters in their books. For reasons of their own they use two length of dashes. Rows of dots (. . .) are so used that readers cannot tell what is meant. They may be used with the intention of giving a sense of mystery, or to suggest a very long pause or a less abrupt break in thought than a dash would.[4]

The influence of authors has made punctuation less pedantic and less subservient to grammar and more potent in expressing the movement of a conversation or action and the emotions of persons. Their influence has, however, caused new inconsistencies and confusions. In 1850 a writer, editor, printer, or teacher could find in the second edition of John Wilson's *Principles of Punctuation* a set of rules representing reputable and reasonable customs. But in 1950 there cannot be so simple and authoritative a guide. Summey[5] describes some of the new uses of the ordinary dash, long dash, and . . ., and the new freedoms in the use of the older marks. But writers of poetry, fiction, and probably of essays and histories also, have already gone beyond those he describes.

TEACHING STUDENTS HOW TO PUNCTUATE

The teaching of punctuation has been misled by a number of myths. One is that for any piece of writing there is one right or, at least, one best punctuation. Another is that the differences in merit between the one best punctuation and the inferior ones are great and important. Another is that the reasons for its superiority are logical consequences of principles of grammar or rhetoric. Another is that the unit of writing is a declarative, interrogative, or exclamatory sentence beginning with a capitalized word and ending in . or ? or! Still another is that the reasons for punctuation marks within such a sentence are to be found by examining it alone. These and other fictions may be useful to teaching on certain occasions just as legal fictions are useful to the law. But they are none the less dangerous fictions. In advanced courses in writing, in schools of journalism, and in publishers' code such "punctuational fictions" should be exposed: (1) by quoting instances where . and : are equally good, where : and ; are equally good, where ; and , are equally good, where . and — are equally good, and so on; (2) by quoting instances where the only reasons for the superiority of a usage are that it helps the reader more or that more and/or better writers use it; (3) by showing the impossibility of getting the units of a writer's flow of words by cutting up passages into pieces beginning with a capitalized word and ending

---

[4] The extreme case of authors' control of punctuation is furnished by the comics or picture stories. The adventures of Superman are related with exclamation points, dashes, or rows of dots (. . .) in place of periods. Half the marks in the samples I examined were exclamation points; a quarter were either — or . . . ; the last was used three times as frequently by the authors of Superman as by any other author for whom I have counts.

[5] George F. Summey, Jr., *Modern Punctuation, Its Utilities and Conventions* (New York: Oxford U. P., 1919).

with a . or ? or !; [6] and (4) by showing sentences whose internal punctuation is dictated by the context.[7]

(The older methods of teaching punctuation begin with the marks and try to show the proper uses of each. It is more reasonable to begin with the thought or feeling or act to be aroused in the reader, and try to show how punctuation marks help the words to cause it.) But this is harder to do. A dozen marks are a convenient basis for the organization of textbooks, explanations, exercises, examinations, and so forth. If we use the more reasonable way we must revise many instructive problems and emergencies. This can be done; and I venture to prophesy that someone with enough ability and ingenuity will do for punctuation marks what has already been done with the parts of speech, and make the facts about them secondary to effective writing.

We learn to punctuate partly by rules and examples, as in learning the salutations for friendly letters and formal letters, partly by imitation of the punctuations we see in our reading.

An almost perfect rule is, "If you ask a question in writing, put a ? at the end of it." Few rules can be framed that will rank with the rule for questions. A corresponding rule for ! after expressions of surprise, fear, approval, and other exclamatory sentences is not so clear, neat, or dependable. Corresponding rules for the terminal punctuation of a statement or command are: "If you make only one statement, put a period after it. If you make two statements, one right after the other, put a period after each, or put a colon or semciolon after the first and a period after the second. If you make two statements joined by such a word as *and, but, also,* or *however,* put a semicolon or a comma after the first and a period after the second. Punctuate commands as you punctuate statements." These rules are great improvements over, "A period is put at the end of each declarative sentence," which is not true. But they are somewhat ambiguous, and the extension to

---

[6] Any long passage from any edition of Shakespeare will do. If even the modernized punctuations of Shakespeare are considered "wrong," almost any long passage from any modern author will serve. Thus we have from Shaw's *Caesar and Cleopatra:*

Unit 1. In the little world yonder, Sphinx, my place is as high as yours in this great desert; only I wander, and you sit still; I conquer, and you endure; I work and wonder, you watch and wait; I look up and am dazzled, look down and am darkened, look round and am puzzled, whilst your eyes never turn from looking out—out of the world—to the lost region—the home from which we have strayed.

Unit 2. Sphinx, you and I, strangers to the race of men, are no strangers to one another: have I not been conscious of you and of this place since I was born?

Unit 3. Rome is a madman's dream: this is my Reality.

[7] For example, the last two lines of the following:

The girl.	Old gentleman.
Caesar.	Immortal gods!
The girl.	Old gentleman: don't run away.
Caesar.	"Old gentleman: don't run away!!!"
	This! to Julius Caesar!

sequences of more than two statements or commands is very clumsy.

Helpful rules can be stated for the use of commas in series of words or phrases, for example, "cats, dogs, horses, and cows," "they came early, stayed late, and went home happy," "red, white, yellow, and pink roses," and "she went to the station on the bus, from there to New York by train, from New York to Miami by airplane." The proper habits for clear cases of the principle can be established in children in grade 6 or earlier. Most of the rules in textbooks, however, are inadequate, ambiguous, or dependent on correct interpretation of such terms as sentence, clause, phrase, conjunction, coordinate, and subordinate.

Learning to punctuate by imitation is beset with serious difficulties. The book most revered by children, the Bible, is punctuated badly. Their most popular reading, the comics, are deplorable as models. Many authors from the worst to the best have forsaken the customs developed by three hundred years of experimentation with punctuation.[8] In spite of these difficulties, imitation is a great help in acquiring the preferred customs of punctuating. Fortunately most newspapers are reasonable and conservative in punctuating their items of news.

The facts reported in this article agree in opposing bigotry and pedantry as cardinal sins in the teaching of punctuation. From the elementary school to the graduate school the main aims should be (1) to induce the learner to try to punctuate what he writes so as to help the reader understand and enjoy it, and (2) to give practice in certain tried and true means of doing this.

PUNCTUATION ERRORS:
WHAT TO DO ABOUT THEM [*]

Hardy R. Finch

Do your students make many punctuation errors? Do they leave out commas and periods again and again? Here are several suggestions that may help:

---

[8] Suppose that a schoolboy wrote the following: "The trouble was, I didn't know what to do; he was all alone, he seemed to be sick, he was crying, and I wanted to help him: it isn't nice to see a boy break down before your eyes, and act like a loony. . . and . . . .I can't get over it. . . ." His teacher might penalize him for ten or more errors. Yet his punctuation follows exactly that of a comparable passage in Graves' *It's a Queer Time.*

[*] From *The Announcer,* The Prentice-Hall Newsletter for Language Arts Teachers, Vol. 4, No. 1. © 1960, Prentice-Hall, Inc., Englewood Cliffs, N. J., reprinted by permission of the author and publisher.

Find out just what errors the student is making. Don't rely too much on objective tests in punctuation. Instead, study the student's compositions and note the errors that are made there. Observe especially which errors are most frequent; which ones need immediate attention; and which ones he seems to have in common with the whole group. With this information available, you can plan your strategy.

Help the student to realize that punctuation is important. In every way possible, show the student how punctuation helps to make the meaning clear. Ask him to bring to class examples of the use of punctuation in magazines and newspapers. Present evidence such as the following to show how punctuation really makes a difference in meaning:

"The cannibals," said Mary, "ate the fat trader."
The cannibals said, "Mary ate the fat trader."
Don't shoot Mary!
Don't shoot, Mary!
Mrs. Smith, the bricklayer will be here tomorrow.
Mrs. Smith, the bricklayer, will be here tomorrow.
While George was eating Mary was playing the piano.
While George was eating, Mary was playing the piano.

Teach punctuation along with other English work. When teaching business and personal (friendly) letters, ask the students, "Why does one usually place a colon (:) after the salutation in a business letter and a comma (,) after the salutation in a personal (friendly) letter?" The distinction between the colon, which is formal, and the comma, which is informal, sometimes provides interesting discussion material in the classroom.

When presenting dependent or independent clauses in grammar, teach the punctuation of these clauses also.

Help students recognize the different punctuation marks. Students often confuse the colon (:) with the semicolon (;). This may be easily remedied by giving examples of their use in sentences and by explaining that the colon indicates that something will follow while a semicolon is thought of as a weak period.

Concentrate on one error at a time. If a student is making a number of errors, don't work on all of his mistakes at the same time. Have him concentrate his energies on one at a time. For example, after he has mastered his use of the period at the end of a sentence, then develop his skill in placing commas about appositives.

Make him an expert on his own special punctuation error. Appoint him to be the expert on his own special error. Whenever another student makes this error on the board, call on the expert to correct it and explain it.

Have him make his own guide to punctuation. This guide should contain examples and rules dealing with his own errors in punctuation. If he wishes, he may illustrate it by means of drawings or pictures.

Encourage the copyreading of papers. Train your students to reread carefully all of their written papers and to correct all errors before turning them in to you. Each time they are copyreading in class, show them one particular punctuation use to check especially. As you are observing the students at work, you can see whether or not they are finding this particular use.

Work with groups of students. When several students need help on the same error, work with them while the others are having a reading or study period. If all but one or two students need help on a type of error, let those who have mastered the skill work on other projects while you concentrate on those who need the drill and explanation.

CREATIVE LANGUAGE TEACHING *

John Maxwell

The literature of language arts teaching is full of admonitions to the teacher to use oral approaches in dealing with problems of usage and to use speech heavily in all work because it is closer to the natural mode of expression of elementary children.

The exercises that follow are based on the premise that we must first of all strive to work efficiently against the thousands of exposures to incorrect forms which have marred the student's language. The teacher's time and opportunities for dealing with usage problems are sharply limited; hence, time must be used with maximum efficiency. For speed and impact there is no medium which can match the oral-aural method. What is more, the method can be and is fun for the pupil.

Anyone can think of additional ideas in this framework. This monograph is presented as a springboard to effective, creative language teaching.

---

* Reprinted by permission of the author and publisher from *A Monograph for Elementary Teachers*, No. 100 (Evanston, Ill.: Harper and Row).

SOME SAMPLE TECHNIQUES BY GRADE LEVEL

Kindergarten

Problem: *saw* and *seen*

The object here is to increase perception of children to the correct form through thinking and hearing.

The children are seated in a circle with the teacher, who holds ten cards, each bearing the picture of a common object. One by one, the cards are displayed quickly to the class. Hands are raised; a child is called on. "What did you see, Tommy?" "I saw an apple." This continues until all cards are used.

Next, the teacher holds the cards, two at a time, in random order. (Example: orange, first; dog, second.) "Which did you see first and which did you see second?" (Hands are raised.) "Mary?" "I saw the orange first and then I saw the dog."

Problem: *did and done*

The teacher, with the children in a circle, asks each one to think of something he or she did the day before with brother or sister or playmate. Example—

TEACHER: What did you do, Jimmy?
JIMMY: I went to the store.
TEACHER: When did you do it?
JIMMY: I did it yesterday.

Problem: *bought* and *"buyed"*

The teacher requests each child, in turn, to think of something he or she bought recently. Example—

TEACHER: What did you buy, Jessie?
JESSIE: I bought some gum.
TEACHER: When did you buy it?
JESSIE: I bought it yesterday.

This process will yield seventy oral-aural exercises in a typical class during a brief period of time.

First Grade

Problem: "my brother, he . . ."

The teacher asks each child to think of something he or she could tell (that is nice) about a brother, sister, or some member of the class. She asks the class to think through what they are going to say, and to avoid using "he" or "she."

Each child then turns around to his neighbor to the rear and tells his bit of information, with the teacher judiciously correcting each child who uses an incorrect form. The end purpose is to have the correct form used twenty-five to thirty-five times. The problem is deepseated at this age, and although it will disappear naturally with maturity, the teacher can hasten its disappearance.

Problem: *brought* and *"brang"*

The teacher requests the class to think about something they received last Christmas. Digressing briefly into thoughts of Santa Claus and the story of his toy shop, the teacher then branches into round-the-class questioning. Example—

TEACHER: What did Santa bring you, Louise?
LOUISE: He brang me a big doll.
TEACHER: Oh, Santa *brought* (slight pause) you a doll. How nice. Jimmy, what did Santa bring you?
JIMMY: He bra-brought me *a* Erector set.
TEACHER: *An* Erector set. My you must have liked that!

Problem: "him and me," "her and I"

The teacher gives the class one minute to converse with a neighbor across the aisle to determine what they both like. Each tells the class one of the things he likes.

TEACHER: Donna, what did you and Sam decide?
DONNA: He and I like chocolate ice cream.
TEACHER: Sam, what else do you and Donna like?
SAM: She and I like Zorro.

The exercises (as with most oral-aural exercises) should be repeated from time to time, since the problem is deep-rooted and not easily corrected.

Second Grade

Problem: "if I were"

Although this seems to be a rather mature structure, there is little reason that smaller children cannot be attuned to it and accordingly not have to struggle with the problem later when "if I was" becomes solidly entrenched. Conceivably, imaginative work on this problem in the primary grades could eliminate completely the necessity to consider the subjunctive mood in the eleventh grade.

The teacher asks the children to imagine what they would like to be when they grow up. After they have done so, they should think what they would do in their adult roles to do something nice for others.
Example—

TEACHER: Mildred, what would you do if you were what you want to be?

MILDRED: If I was a nurse, I'd . . .

TEACHER: Oh, excuse me, Mildred. I forgot to tell you. Let's all start out by saying, "If I were. . . ."

MILDRED: If I were a nurse, I would help make people feel better.

TEACHER: Fine. Now would you ask the question of Michael?

MILDRED: Michael, what do you want to be?

MICHAEL: An aviator.

MILDRED: Well, what would you do if you were an aviator?

MICHAEL: If I were an aviator, I would give people rides in my plane.

Third Grade

Problem: "I couldn't hardly"

The teacher explains the exercise to the children. The first child turns and asks the one behind him, "Were you sleepy?" The next child responds, "I was so sleepy I could hardly keep my eyes open."

The teacher then places on the board seven words: *tired, nervous, happy, angry, pleased, surprised, excited.* Each child can then draw on any of the words in framing his question. Example—

FIRST CHILD: Billy, were you surprised?

SECOND CHILD: I was so surprised I could hardly tell what my name was.

THIRD CHILD: Alice, were you nervous?

FOURTH CHILD: I was so nervous I could hardly erase the board.

This may be too difficult for some classes. The teacher may prefer an alternate plan in which she asks everyone in the class a question and then gives him time to think. As each child's turn comes, the child would then respond to the question.

Problem: "that was real good"

In ten years, this may become an accepted form, but at present it is classed as a colloquialism, not suited to educated speech or writing.

Emphasizing the acceptability of *very* over the form *real*, the teacher calls upon the pupils to recall something they have seen, tasted, touched, smelled, or heard (note the use of the five senses) that they enjoyed very much. The pupils answer as shown in the following—

> TEACHER: What did you see? (Asked generally.) Raise your hands if you saw something you'd like to tell. Mary?
>
> MARY: I saw a real cute dress at the store.
>
> TEACHER: That's nice. Mary saw a *very* (slight pause) cute dress. Anyone else?
>
> HELEN: I saw a very funny squirrel on the tree outside a little while ago.
>
> TEACHER: Oh, did you? Boys and girls, did you notice that Helen said she saw a *very* funny squirrel. This is what I was talking about before. We should always use *very* when we tell how much we like something.

Problem: *is* and *are*

Usually the difficulty concerns the use of *is* with a plural subject. The teacher writes pairs of plural topics that often occur in children's conversation: *compact cars—standard cars, wide-screen movies—regular movies, clear days—rainy days, new shoes—old shoes, westerns—mysteries, movies in theaters—movies on TV.*

Each child in turn gives one sentence *comparing* the topics in whatever pair he chooses, using *is* or *are* in the comparison. Example—

> LYNN: Compact cars are cheaper than standard cars.
>
> AL: Compact cars are easier to park than standard cars.
>
> BOB: Compact cars are slower than standard cars.

Problem: period at the end of sentences

The teacher places six words on the board (all verbs): *stop, walk, run, jump, read, save.* Pupils then build their own sentences, starting with one of the words as a quiet command, and adding words in each subsequent sentence. The object is to build as long a series as possible without producing a run-on sentence or failing to place a period. Five points are given for each sentence, but there is a ten-point penalty for each run-on sentence or omission of a period at the end of a sentence. The teacher reviews all sentences over seven words long. Example—

Jump.—Jump high.—Jump very high.—She jumps very high.—She often jumps very high.—She jumps too high for me.—She often jumps too high for me.—Often she has jumped too high for me *(Minus 10 points for omitting period)*—Yesterday she jumped over the top of the sandbox.—The large brown and white cow jumped over the moon.—I can jump very high my sister can jump high too. *(Minus 10.)* *Total: 55 − 20 = 35.*

Fourth Grade

Problem: "hasn't got no"

The teacher retains for the purpose of the exercise the "got" form, which some authorities frown upon but which is necessary to attack the immediate problem.

The class is divided into two teams which follow down the rows in order. The first child says, "He (or she) hasn't got any _____." The first missing word should begin with the letter "a" ("She hasn't got any *a*pples."); the second with the letter "b" ("He hasn't got any *b*aseball bats."); and so on through the alphabet. As soon as one side misses or takes too long (ten seconds time limit) the turn passes to the other side. The first side to go around, completely, wins.

Fifth Grade

Problems: *leave* and *let*

This problem can be resolved as a game involving the alphabet, knowledge of the noun, use of *leave* and *let*. The class is divided in two and the game proceeds by rows until one side has finished. When a team errs, the turn goes to the other side. Example—

Side I	Side II
1. Let me see the apple.	Let me see the cherries.
2. I'll leave it in the aisle.	I'll leave them in the box.
3. Let me see the bun.	Let me see the doughnut.
4. I'll leave it in the bakery.	I'll leave it in the doghouse.
5. Leave me see the cauliflower.	
(*Error*)	

Some stress should be placed on the appropriateness of the response (i.e., *where* the item will be left).

Problem: avoiding overworked words

The teacher calls upon the class to produce a group essay on a familiar topic, in this case softball in the playground. She selects and underlines certain phrases in the essay to work on and asks individuals to think for a few minutes of a more exciting and descriptive way of saying the same thing. Example—

"We *like* to play softball. We play games each morning from eight o'clock until *the 8:25 bell rings*. Some of the players are *good*. *Some people like to watch*. Some fellows can *hit the ball a long way* and can *run fast*. We're sure of having a *nice time* when we play."

After discussion of the underlined words, a second version of the essay is placed on the board and comparisons are made.

This practice is followed by a few minutes of writing on "I Like Television." The papers are exchanged with neighbors who are instructed to find two places where some improvement in wording could be made. (This can also be done in groups if the class is capable of it.)

Problem: outlining (organizing)

The teacher brings a box of odds and ends to class (or collects them from the classroom). The items are studied by the class, who seek to organize the various items into groups.

Items		*Possible Outline*
comb	pencil	I. School materials
book	penny	A. Book
scarf	milk carton	B. Pencil
cup	map	C. Writing paper
writing paper	toothbrush	D. Map
sandwich	clothes hanger	II. Personal materials
button	spool	A. Scarf (etc.)

This activity serves as an introduction to outlining, to show its purpose and emphasize the thinking involved in outlining.

Problem: keeping to one idea in a paragraph

The class undertakes to write a class composition. Six committees are formed and the class is requested to contribute several ideas about a topic (in this case, ice cream). Results may be: "Most boys and girls like ice cream." "Ice cream can be purchased in many places." "Ice cream comes in many flavors." "You can buy ice cream in several forms." "Ice cream is a very healthful food." "Ice cream is popular in other countries, too."

The teacher then directs each committee to write three or four more sentences which will stay within the limits of the idea given to it. Each of the sentences above is then given to a committee for further development. The teacher judges what will make a good order and writes the sentence on the blackboard. As each group finishes its three or four sentences, the class as a whole discusses the group's work for its effectiveness in staying within the limits of its "topic sentence."

The daily work in social studies is a helpful source of information for selecting a topic.

Problem: "he don't," "he doesn't"

One child is sent out of the room while an object (pencil, eraser, glasses case, or the like) is given to another child in the room. The first child returns to search for the object. He may look at each person in turn, but must speak to the person behind his "suspect." Example—

"Does he have it?"
"No. He doesn't have it."
"Does she have it?"
"No, she doesn't have it."

Sides may be chosen if desirable and points given for each failure-to-find and a large number of points removed for each finding. The side receiving the smaller number of points wins the game. Use of "he don't" could be a penalty factor.

Sixth Grade

Problem: *lie* and *lay*
This problem can be handled first as a whole group and then in small groups of five or six.

The teacher or a student leader announces to the class that he has found a dollar bill. The purpose of the game is to find out by asking questions of him just where he found it. For each correct use of "lying," a player receives one point; each time he identifies the spot, he receives five points and becomes the new "finder." Example—

LEADER: I found a quarter in this room. Gerry, where did I find it?
GERRY: Was it lying on the window-sill?
LEADER: No. Ann?
ANN: Was it lying on the teacher's desk?

Problem: *"gimme"*
Played somewhat like the old game of "Geography," a game can be developed out of this problem stressing a form of "Give me" which must begin each request. The person making a request is told he can't be given the item, for it is in another place. The name of the place must begin with the last letter of the word requested.

The dialogue would proceed like this: "Give me a blotter." "I can't. It's in the round house." "Give me an elephant." "I can't. It's in the tool chest."

One point can be given for each correct use of "give me" and one point for following the rules of the game correctly.

Problem: "he could have taken (took)"
The teacher sets the scene: a bear has broken into a store and needs something heavy to break a window that stands between him and freedom. The class is asked to determine what he might have taken

to do so. The teacher has previously selected the item the bear eventually used.

Sample comments are: "He could have taken a can of pumpkin." "He didn't." "He could have taken a bag of flour."

If scoring is used, one point is given for using the correct form and five points for guessing the correct item. The game might be played in groups.

Problem: "he would have broken (broke)"

Problems of articulation (like "would'a") and usage are present in this problem.

The problem can be resolved as a "sides" game. The first side appoints a player who says, "If he (perhaps a dog) were in the china factory . . ." and leaves the sentence unfinished. The other team's defender must finish the statement, thus: ". . . he would have broken some crockery." He then begins, "If he were in the flower shop . . ." The other side's representative would say, ". . . he would have broken a flower pot." The game continues until one side fails to say "would have broken" correctly or fails to finish the sentence.

Problem: understanding inverted sentences

The teacher places four words on the board: *ball, window, desk, bird.* With the class divided into two sides, the first side creates a sentence in which something happens to one of the objects listed, as in "He pushed the desk close to the door." The opponent's task is to turn the sentence around, placing the thing acted on ("desk") at the beginning of the sentence (subject position) and change the verb to a "was" construction. Side 2 then creates a sentence, with Side 1 inverting the structure. Example—

> *Side 1:* The centerfielder hit the ball over the fence.
> *Side 2:* The ball was hit over the fence by the centerfielder.
> *Side 2:* The hunter standing in a deep field of wheat shot the rabbit.
> *Side 1:* The rabbit was shot by the hunter who was standing in a deep field of wheat.

In the first stages, it would be best to have three persons on a side.

As long as the four words are listed on the board and the students know that the "object" must appear at the beginning of the inverted sentence, this exercise can be worked. From success in this simplified form, we can hope to build a sensitivity of ear to reverse-order or "inverted sentences."

Problem: Understanding prepositional phrases

The subject has been broached and some blank-filling has been done, possibly. The teacher then gives the class this pattern:

The man _____ ran _____

She then lists twelve or fifteen prepositions: *with, under, in, after, over, to, beside, next to, without, through,* etc. The assignment (done orally twice) is to write four or five original sentences in which one of the words listed would be the first word to appear in the blank space. The words in the blank should *not* contain a verb; if a verb appears, then the form used would not be a prepositional phrase. (It would be a subordinate clause.)

Problem: "isn't there any," "aren't there any"

This problem can be made into a fast-moving game. One person asks, "Aren't there any elephants in the room?" A second person responds as rapidly as possible with "Yes" or "No," depending on the question, and forms a question to be thrown to the next person. If desired, the class may name the objects in alphabetical order: viz., artichokes, billy clubs, copper pennies, dandelions, etc.

CHAPTER 7

Reading Instruction Today

Research shows that it is fatal to "push" young children along in the initial stages of learning to read, particularly if there have not been activities to create a functional language background beforehand. Many children fail in reading because they are plunged into formal reading with an over-analytic method employing abstract symbols before they really understand what words and sentences mean in spoken, let alone printed, form. Young immature minds need opportunity and time to "sort things out," to understand what they are doing, and to see the purpose in the operations with which they are confronted. My strongest plea in the teaching of reading is, don't hurry the children, don't expect too much in the early stages—do all you can to provide a language background. This slower, wider approach will repay doubly later on.—Sir Fred J. Schonell, The Psychology and Teaching of Reading (New York: Philosophical Library, 1961).

READING INSTRUCTION—
A FORWARD LOOK °

Paul Witty

During the past decade we have had in the United States much adverse criticism of reading methods and materials of instruction. The strictures have emphasized the inadequacy of repetitious and uninteresting presentations in textbooks and associated materials. Critics have stressed too the school's failure to make extensive use of films,

° From *Elementary English* (March 1961), pp. 151–164. Reprinted with permission of the National Council of Teachers of English and Paul Witty.

filmstrips, and other aids. Some have cited the neglect of interest and motive, and have deplored an insufficient emphasis on phonics. Others have pointed to the unjustifiably high per cent of reading failures among children and to the lack of reading skill and interest on the part of many youth and adults today. Still others have cited the school's failure to treat reading as a thinking process. Undeniably there is ample reason for criticism, but the wholesale condemnation of our schools and the oversimplification of causes and cures are not only unjustifiable but deplorable.

A most insistent criticism has centered about the teaching of phonics, a topic which persists as a controversial issue. This criticism and a related one directed toward oral reading were in part justified by the neglect of phonics in some schools and by the abandonment of instruction in oral reading in others. Inconceivable as it may now appear, a group of educators at one time sponsored a nonoral reading program. Few schools adopted nonoral methods, and phonic instruction was usually offered, although the procedures and the extent of the emphasis varied widely. A few critics attributed all or almost all poor reading to lack of phonic training and appeared to believe that the inauguration of particular "approaches" would provide a cure-all for every kind of reading failure or problem. This unfortunately is not the case.

A critical study of the literature will demonstrate the significance of a number of factors which contribute to poor reading, including unfavorable home conditions, lack of readiness, emotional disturbances, few and unsuitable materials, and so forth. Of course, lack of phonic ability is sometimes associated with poor reading, but so too are other factors in various combinations. This fact has been well established by studies of the past. At the present time, several investigations are yielding additional valuable insights concerning causation as attention is being given in extreme cases to the significance of brain damage and other factors inadequately explored in earlier studies. The role played by attitude and emotion is receiving renewed attention, and interest and motivation are also being investigated. The future will bring, we hope, a greatly reduced tendency to over-emphasize single items in studying causation. Moreover, we hope that the prevention of reading difficulties will receive greater attention in the coming years.

PHONICS AS A CURE-ALL

Some writers, however, continue to oversimplify the problem of effective reading instruction and attack with vehemence current educational practices. Perhaps the most exaggerated position was represented by Rudolph Flesch,[1] who stated: "Teach the child what each letter stands for and he can read." Moreover, Mr. Flesch recognized no limitation in the phonic approach—in teaching children to read or in remedial reading. Thus he stated: "The reading 'experts' of course will say that such a program of remedial reading is much too simple. What about Johnny's emotional troubles, what about such nervous habits as reversals, what about correcting his eye movements? But my answer to all of that is phonics. Phonics is the key." [2]

Mr. Flesch's book reiterates the statement that children "never really learn to read" in our schools (p. 18). Parents therefore must take over since "the teaching of reading is too important to be left to the educators" (Preface, p. IX). Two other writers have examined current problems a little more realistically, but have arrived at a similar conclusion concerning the role of phonics. It is stated on the book-jacket of *Reading Chaos and Cure* that the authors, Sybil Terman and C. C. Walcutt, "advocate an application of the phonics method as opposed to the 'reading readiness' and 'word configuration' program now widely in use." [3] In the book the following statements are found: "It is absurdly easy to teach a child to read with the proper method. Most of the children in America could be taught in a few weeks or months at the age of five. We shall tell you about various schools, now functioning, where a problem reader is virtually unheard of . . ." (Preface, p. ix).

Some critics, like Mr. Flesch, are apparently interested chiefly or solely, it appears, in mere pronunciation of words. They have a very limited appreciation of reading as an intelligent, meaningful act by which thinking is promoted. Mr. Flesch makes this position abundantly clear in a story he tells: [4]

I once surprised a native of Prague by reading aloud from a Czech newspaper. "Oh, you know Czech?" he asked. "No, I don't understand a word of it," I answered. "I can only read it."

Later (p. 103), he describes a group of first grade children reading a newspaper and states: "But the fact is, and I testify to it, that those children read what was in the paper. They were perfectly able to pronounce words they had never seen before." In describing one child, he continues: "Needless to say, that six-year-old child hadn't

---

[1] Rudolph Flesch, *Why Johnny Can't Read* (New York: Harper and Row, 1955), p. 3.

[2] *Ibid.*, p. 116.

[3] Quotes are from the book jacket of *Reading Chaos and Cure* by Sybil Terman and Charles Child Walcutt (New York: McGraw-Hill, 1958).

[4] Rudolph Flesch, *op. cit.*, p. 23.

the slightest idea of what the word meant. How could he?" Certainly pronunciation without understanding is not the aim of modern reading instruction. Nor is meaningless pronunciation thought of as reading. Reading is considered by some as a thinking process through which meaning is obtained from printed symbols. It is recognized that we do not get the meaning of a word—invariably or generally—from its spelling or from its pronunciation. To some of us, failure to obtain meaning is the most significant and unfortunate outcome of faulty or inadequate reading instruction. The child who is not encouraged to find appropriate meanings in various ways, such as by examining the context, is not being taught to read effectively. Rather, he is engaging merely in a parrot-like, routine exercise. It is recognized, too, that reading is both oral and silent; and that it is a two-way thinking process involving the individual's reaction to the symbol or statement and his interpretation of it in terms of his experience.

Some critics ignore and ridicule much that experimentation has divulged in the past 20 or 30 years about child growth and development in relation to effective instruction in reading. For example, they categorically deny that there is such a thing as readiness for the various steps in the process of learning to read. They discount, too, the importance of the interest factor and of goals, purposes, and needs in the reading process.

PHONICS AND INTEREST

Criticisms assume various guises. A few advocates of simple procedures such as phonic instruction recognize the possibility that other factors also cause or contribute to poor reading. For example, Glenn McCracken has some reservations about the complete adequacy of phonic approaches. He states that interest should come first:

> I do not agree with Dr. Flesch, however, that phonics constitutes the only important teaching technique necessary for producing superior readers. The maintenance of interest must always come first. If interest is low, success will be lower. Particularly among slower learners better results will accompany accelerated interest.[5]

We should like to stress the fact that "accelerated interest" also will foster learning among average and rapid learners. To obtain interest, McCracken recommends heartily the presentation of materials in film-strip form:

---

[5] Glenn McCracken, *The Right to Learn* (Chicago: Henry Regnery, 1959), p. 156.

Another value associated with the textfilm approach is its facility for promoting class discussion. We have found this feature to be particularly pertinent to reading growth. Avid group conversation brings out many ideas. It stimulates interest and is helpful to pupils with good as well as weak mental abilities. When there is only one object of interest to look at in the room and when all children can see it equally well, conversation naturally ensues. It is common practice in these classes for the pupils guided by the teacher, to arrive at group decisions. This is learning in its finest form.[6]

This group approach is coordinated with the use of a basal text, and outstanding results are reported.

The filmstrip approach undoubtedly has merits. It was used with remarkable success in the Army's program for functionally illiterate men during World War II. Concerning the problem of illiteracy, Terman and Walcutt state:

> When the Army launched the great draft at the beginning of World War II, it discovered that between ten million (over twenty-five years old) and sixteen million (over twenty years old) Americans were unable to read up to fourth-grade level! By 1943 a million draftees had been rejected for illiteracy and three-quarters of a million had been accepted who read at or below a fourth-grade level. These millions could not all have come from Al Capp's mythical communities in the Southern mountains.[7]

But it should be pointed out that analyses of the origin of these men *did* disclose a meager background of educational experience. The majority of the men *did* come from educationally deprived areas. Moreover, the poor reading was not attributable primarily to inadequacies in their education but instead to lack of education. Terman and Walcutt also fail to indicate that we developed and used an unusually efficient program of instruction based upon research in child development and education.

ARMY PROGRAM FOR FUNCTIONALLY ILLITERATE MEN

In order to satisfy the need for manpower in the Armed Forces, it was necessary to induct large numbers of illiterate and non-English-speaking men. Special Training Units were organized to give the academic training these men needed to become useful soldiers. In these units they participated in an educational program characterized by (a) definite objectives, (b) high motive and interest, (c) careful study and proper grouping of individuals, (d) use of functional methods and materials in small classes, (e) wide application of visual aids, (f) hygienic conditions insuring a sense of security and general well-

---

[6] Glenn McCracken, *op. cit.*, p. 171.
[7] Sybil Terman and Charles C. Walcutt, *op. cit.*, p. 19.

being, (g) provision for success from the start and for steady progress, and (h) the use of thoroughly trained, enthusiastic instructors.[8]

Under the above conditions, it became possible for functionally illiterate and non-English-speaking men to acquire the reading skills needed in the Army in the short period of eight weeks.

THE ROLE OF INTEREST

Again and again the writer has referred to the value of ascertaining and utilizing children's interests.[9] In this emphasis, he has found support in research which provides convincing evidence that the curriculum should be developed in accord with the children's needs, interests, and problems if it is to have maximum significance and application. For years capable teachers have utilized children's interests as strong motives for learning. Committees engaged in curriculum development or reconstruction have also given recognition to the interests of boys and girls at different ages.

Specialists in reading too sometimes recommend that teachers utilize interests as a starting point in remedial endeavor. These workers are aware that some interests are transitory and that others are unworthy of extension. Therefore it has been suggested that teachers aim to modify old patterns, create new interests, and raise the level of pupils' tastes. In fact, the interests of boys and girls on coming to school may be thought of as constituting a unique opportunity for teachers. The interests of pupils at the time they leave a class or school may reflect the extent to which the teacher has accepted responsibility for directing pupil growth. Thus in a balanced reading program the study of children's interests becomes a primary consideration.

It is recognized also that learning to read with meaning increases the child's sense of power and opens the doors to new satisfactions and new sources of knowledge. Throughout all stages of the learning process, the child's satisfaction in real achievement and progress is a primary concern. This is the logical corollary to the foregoing emphasis on the interest factor. This dual approach guarantees the child the chance to follow worthwhile interests in a program characterized by systematic guidance and continuous evaluation. In such a program, successful achievement and disciplined growth are objectives.

In the Army program widespread use was made of films and filmstrips, as motivational and instructional devices. Following World War

---

[8] Paul Witty, *Reading in Modern Education* (Boston: D. C. Heath, 1949), p. 10.

[9] *Ibid.*, p. 11.

II, filmstrips were gradually introduced and employed successfully in certain phases of reading instruction. And films, too, were used with outstanding success in association with reading materials. For example, in an experiment conducted by James Fitzwater and the writer, films were employed to present simple narratives of strong appeal to second-grade children.[10] After the children had seen each film and had listened to the commentary, they read the story in a film-reader. Then they developed their own story which was reproduced and heard by them *via* the magnetic sound track. This experiment, combining reading with listening and discussion, was demonstrably successful. Under these conditions, the acquisition of concepts and of skill in interpreting presentations was greatly enhanced. The film played an important role in this program; however, it was recognized that the use of the film was one factor only in effecting success. Similarly, the use of filmstrips has been found to foster the development of reading skills.

It is the hope of the writer that the future will bring increased use of films and filmstrips soundly articulated in a developmental program with full recognition of their motivational and instructional worth. The value of visual and auditory devices is unquestionably great; their use should not be looked upon as a panacea but rather as a way of facilitating learning when they are employed in appropriate context or used as a part of a balanced program of instruction. These statements apply also to the use of tachistoscopes, reading accelerators, and "teaching machines." Similarly the use of "closed circuit TV" should not be looked upon as a cure-all device, nor regarded as a substitute for the teacher and as *the* way to solve the teacher shortage. The worth of each of these devices and approaches should be acknowledged and research should be undertaken to ascertain when and how they can be employed most advantageously.

THE ROLE OF INTEREST IN A DEVELOPMENTAL PROGRAM

Although many authorities in reading have recommended the use of interests in motivating instruction, relatively few studies of the interest factor have been made during the past fifteen or twenty years. During this period the emergence of TV has altered greatly the recreation of boys and girls and has deeply affected their interests. A recent comprehensive study reveals that the impact of TV and the mass media has altered children's interests greatly and has probably

---

[10] Paul Witty and James Fitzwater, "An Experiment with Films, Film Readers, and the Magnetic Sound Track Projector," *Elementary English* (April 1952).

increased the need for guidance.[11] We believe that in the future, knowledge concerning the interests of pupils will be regarded as essential in planning the reading curriculum and in guiding each pupil. We hope the principle of interest will receive greater recognition not only in the elementary school but also in the high school and in the college.

THE ROLE OF TEXTBOOKS

There are, of course, various ways to teach children to read. Some teachers have succeeded through the conventional textbook approach; others have utilized an "individualized method"; some have employed films and film-readers with success; and still others have combined effectively group and individual approaches. It has become clear that various means may be used to establish and improve reading skills. Although reading skills may be achieved by different approaches, we should observe that there are different outcomes and relationships associated with each. Increasingly, educators are recommending a comprehensive program of instruction which stresses meaningful reaction and reading as thinking. Accordingly, greater recognition is being given to the effects of reading experience upon the pupil.[12] In efforts to provide a more valid evaluation than that reflected only by the acquisition of skill, teachers are asking questions such as: Do pupils read more widely? Are they more interested in and better able to read the materials of the subject fields? Have they obtained competency in using the library to satisfy interests and meet recurring needs? Have they developed, as a result of instruction, a strong interest in reading and independence in the selection of materials?

Recently we have had our attention directed to certain inadequacies of the instructional program that follows the typical textbook pattern to achieve the objectives implied by the foregoing questions. Criticisms have centered in some cases on the content of elementary school textbooks. Indeed, the first-grade reading program has become a subject for ridicule or scorn on the part of some critics, and the textbook has served as the special object of attack. The assumption

---

[11] Paul Witty, *The Effects of the Mass Media,* Golden Anniversary White House Conference on Children and Youth, Washington, D. C., 1960. See also *A Study of the Interests of Children and Youth,* a cooperative research project between Northwestern University and the Office of Education, U. S. Department of Health, Education, and Welfare, directed by Paul A. Witty, Northwestern University, 1960.

[12] See Paul Witty (Chm.), *Development in and through Reading,* Sixtieth Yearbook, National Society for the Study of Education (Chicago: U. of Chicago Press, 1961).

that children may obtain maximum benefits from the presentation of words in highly repetitious contexts woven about trivial situations *is* highly questionable. Certainly more meaningful materials closely related to children's current experiences are essential in a sound program of reading instruction.

The design for textbooks of the future (and the instructional guides and practice materials) will, we hope, provide for greater flexibility and make more ingenious provision for individual differences through the inclusion of richer and more varied content. It is hoped that greater attention will be given to concept building rather than to repetition of words in routine patterns. Reading in the content fields, critical reading, and reading to satisfy personal and social needs, deserve, and should receive far greater attention. There will be too, we hope, a much needed enrichment for superior pupils, as well as provision for wide use of materials to afford opportunities for pupils to apply reading skills in the subject fields. The elementary school of the future will, we hope, have a central library and a school librarian. The school librarian, like the teacher, will be thoroughly trained in child study. The librarian will encourage teachers and pupils in the use of the library aids, reference books, catalogs, indexes, and bibliographies, and will also keep teachers informed as to new books and visual and auditory materials as well. Through the foregoing steps, we shall see the diffusion of developmental practices throughout our schools.

A developmental reading program will recognize the value of continuous, systematic instruction, utilization of interests, fulfillment of developmental needs, and the articulation of reading experience with other types of worthwhile activity. The chief aim of this program will be to help pupils *become* skillful, self-reliant, and independent readers, who will continue to enrich their understandings and satisfactions throughout their lives by reading. At all stages, reading as a thinking process will be cultivated.

INDIVIDUALIZED READING

The above objectives will be conceded to be desirable. But how they are to be achieved is a matter of controversy.

With some of these in mind, one group of educators and teachers is advocating what is called "Individualized Reading." This term means many things to different persons who advocate the practice. Leland Jacobs, in a practical manner, discusses the topic and states:

In the first place, "individualized reading" is not a single method with predetermined steps in procedure to be followed. It is not possible to say that every teacher who would individualize guidance in reading must do this or that. It is not feasible or desirable to present a simple, single methodological formulation of what is right in "individualized reading" which every teacher shall follow.[13]

Certain writers have attempted to define "individualized reading" as a unique program and have emphasized its value as a method of instruction. We would agree with the persons who recommend "individualized reading" if the following conditions were recognized. Individualized reading should be accepted as a *part* of (not a subordinate to, or an adjunct of) the basal program, but not as *the* program. We see little need for calling the program "individualized" and designating this approach as "the method" to be followed. May Lazar in a generally admirable discussion states: "Individualized Reading is not subordinate to or an adjunct of the basic reading program." However, she adds "*it is the basic program.*" [14] Why can't we recognize that neither group nor individual practices alone constitute the reading program? Why can't we grant the importance of both approaches and cease to think of them as mutually exclusive practices? Isn't it possible to find a way by which agreement can be reached so as to utilize the undeniably desirable features of both approaches in a program which encourages thinking, independent choice, and self-directed behavior? Admittedly, this will necessitate the abandonment of some practices associated with the typical textbook pattern of instruction; it will necessitate too the disavowal of belief in a single pattern to be followed by all children in a class. Adaptations, revisions, and extensions of current practices will be necessary.

CHARACTERISTICS OF INDIVIDUALIZED READING

Various persons have described the distinguishing features of "individualized reading." For example, Dorothy M. Dietrich emphasized some of the characteristics of individualized reading as follows:

Presently, numerous articles have been written concerning the individualized approach to the teaching of reading. Although these reports vary as to the organization and methods used, they do agree that the elements necessary for conducting an individualized reading program include: (1) a large classroom library made up of basal and supplementary readers, books brought from home by the children and/or materials borrowed from public

---

[13] Leland Jacobs, "Individualized Reading Is Not a Thing," in *Individualizing Reading Practices*, edited by Alice Miel (New York: Bureau of Publications, Teachers College, Columbia U., 1958).

[14] May Lazar, "Individualized Reading: A Program of Seeking, Self-selection, and Pacing." Jeannette Veatch, *Individualizing Your Reading Program* (New York: G. P. Putnam's Sons, 1959), Ch. 15, p. 196.

or school libraries; (2) a free choice by the children of the reading materials depending upon interest and/or readability; (3) a follow-up activity which may be a series of questions devised by the teacher pertaining to each book, a general report of the book read, a visual presentation of the highlights of the book to the class as a whole, or a discussion with other children concerning characters, plots, etc.; (4) a conference between each child and the classroom teacher, the number of conferences depending upon class size and individual need; (5) a reading skill program which may be taught to the class as a whole, or in some cases, on a flexible small group basis depending upon the emerging needs of the individual.[15]

May Lazar and two members of the Bureau staff, after visiting about 50 classes and making a survey of current practices in the schools where individualized reading had been started, found that "although no two teachers worked exactly in the same way even in the same school, there emerged a general picture of their procedures."

Teachers generally gave some directions to the class as a whole. A time was given when all children read independently from self-selected material. Teachers held sessions or "conferences" with individual children or with a small group. Teachers kept records of children's abilities, needs, and interests.
The children kept simple records and reports of their readings.
There was class or group discussion or sharing of books read.[16]

It will be found that most teachers who have tried the individualized approach are enthusiastic about its results.[17] Some schools have reported that a combination of the individualized approach with the traditional basic method has proved more satisfactory. Several writers have concluded that the most desirable procedure is to adapt the best features of individualized and of group instruction to the reading situation and the needs existing in different schools.

Both strengths and weaknesses in the individualized method have been noted. H. W. Sartain reports the results of an experiment "to determine whether second-grade groups would make greater progress in reading skills when taught for three months by the method of individualized self-selection or when taught for an equivalent period by the method of ability grouping using basic readers plus a variety of supplementary books."[18] He drew the following conclusions from his study:

In summary, because this study and others that have been carefully controlled show that the individualized method does not produce better reading

[15] Dorothy M. Dietrich, *International Reading Association Conference Proceedings*, 4 (New York: Scholastic Magazines, 1959), p. 233.

[16] May Lazar, *op. cit.*, p. 198.

[17] For the individual approach, see the essays in Jeannette Veatch's *Individualizing Your Reading Program*.

[18] Henry W. Sartain, "The Roseville Experiment with Individualized Reading," *The Reading Teacher*, 13 (April 1960), p. 277.

gains than a strong basal program, there is no reason to forfeit the advantages of a well-planned basic system. Instead the benefits of the individual conferences should be obtained by their addition to the basic reader plan.[19]

Sartain notes some strengths and weaknesses of the individualized method as listed by the teachers who participated in the study:

Strengths of the Method of Individualized Self-selection

1. Individual conferences provide a valuable personal relationship with pupils.
2. Children are motivated to read more extensively.
3. There is a keen interest in sharing.
4. There is a strong motivation for individual improvement.
5. Top readers are especially responsive.

Weaknesses of the Individual Method

1. All slow pupils and others who cannot work well independently become restless and tend to waste time.
2. There is no opportunity to teach new vocabulary and concepts needed before reading.
3. It is impossible to provide a systematic program of word attack skills.
4. It is exceedingly hard to identify pupils' difficulties in short infrequent conferences.
5. There is some doubt about the permanence of skills taught so briefly.
6. The method is inefficient because of the time required to teach skills to individuals instead of teaching groups who are progressing at a similar rate.
7. The conscientious teacher becomes frustrated in attempting to provide individual conferences for all pupils who need them each day.[20]

Eleanor Johnson, too, in evaluating the individualized reading approach, lists the following values and limitations:

Values. Individualized reading allows a pupil to read at his own level without being frustrated by those of differing reading ability. A child can follow his own reading interests. Tensions are reduced. Pupils enjoy the personal attention they receive in teacher-pupil conferences.

Limitations. The individualized approach to basic reading has at least four important limitations. (1) *Readiness.* For maximum achievement, every child on every level needs readiness for reading any story. Individualized reading appears to ignore the principle of readiness. (2) *Skills.* Reading skills are many and complex. A child does not learn them merely by reading. Leaving them to individual teaching can open a Pandora's Box of reading deficiencies. (3) *Purpose.* Reading is a thinking process. Skill in thinking needs more guidance than can be given in a brief conference. (4) *Efficiency.*

---

[19] Harry W. Sartain, *op. cit.*, p. 281.
[20] Harry W. Sartain, *op. cit.*, p. 279.

It is a waste of time to do individually what can be done more efficiently on a group basis.[21]

May Lazar also points to some values of and some items of concern about the individualized approach.

This approach: Really provides for individual differences; satisfies children's needs of seeking, self-selection, and pacing.

Better integration with other language arts—more creative thinking and critical reading; wide increase in vocabulary; motivation for listening, writing, and spelling; strong desire to communicate ideas.

Decided carry-over to homes; more self-initiated reading; extensive use of public library.

Social interaction—good relationships within the class; acceptance of one another's contributions; "caste system" is broken down.

The child has a better sense of his own worth—self-understanding; he is a participating member of the group;—he relies on his own self-management; he feels that he is a real part of the program and is learning from his own efforts and not always because of what the teacher wants him to learn.

Child actually reads; learns to cherish and handle books; respects authors and their ideas.[22]

May Lazar mentions some problems that were encountered.

The teachers and principals expressed concern about:

Materials—there are not enough books as yet to fit the needs of the classes; administration and organization of the books are serious factors.

Children's ability in selection—some children may need special guidance that the teacher does not foresee.

Teacher attitude—fear of something new.

Teacher effectiveness—would all teachers be able to handle this approach?

Supervision—flexibility makes procedures more difficult to assess. If the supervisor understands and has the same objectives, evaluation will not be too difficult. He may, however, have to employ evaluative measures somewhat different in nature from the existing ones.

Parents' reactions—skepticism about changing procedures.[23]

Although some of the writers on individualized reading do not recommend dropping basal textbooks, Sartain states that "most of the enthusiasts recommend dropping the basal reader program entirely, but several teachers have found that a combination of basal and individualized reading is more desirable.[24] We have noted some examples of effective combination of group and individual approaches. Thus, Maida Wood Sharpe describes an ingenious program in which

---

[21] Eleanor M. Johnson, "The Trend Toward Individualized Reading," *My Weekly Reader*, XXIX (May 2–6, 1960).

[22] May Lazar, *op. cit.*, pp. 200–201.

[23] May Lazar, *op. cit.*, pp. 199–200.

[24] Harry W. Sartain, "A Bibliography on Individualized Reading," *The Reading Teacher*, 13 (April 1960), p. 262.

the teacher worked "one or two days each week in the basal readers for systematic study and instruction in basic reader skills," and used on the other days an individualized reading program.[25] Also Louise G. Carson reports that in her school district the teachers were "not yet convinced that a completely individualized program" was "necessary or advisable," but that they were interested in the idea. She thought that were she to embark on such a program, she "would retain reading groups of basal reading" and "would individualize all supplementary reading." [26] This suggestion has been made by a number of writers including John J. DeBoer.[27]

Another distinct innovation is suggested by Margaret Kirby who described a program in which reading skills are presented and demonstrated to the children. For three days each week the children work independently and on the other two days they work together. An important feature of this program is in the arrangement for books. Six to eight books of like levels are placed on shelves covered with varying colors of shelf paper. Kirby thus describes the use of these books by the children:

Each child is told to choose the book he wants from a shelf of a particular color. No book may be put back on the shelf until checked by the teacher. A move to another shelf is determined by the child's own progress. When a new shelf is started, the basic book is required reading. In this way every child is getting the basic vocabulary.

If a child asks for a book from another shelf, I let him try. In most cases the child has come back and asked to go back to the shelf he had originally been assigned. This gives the child a chance to make an evaluation of his own ability. One child read a book much below his reading level. Together teacher and child evaluated this reading experience and decided that sometimes a book is worthwhile because of the enjoyment it gives or the information it presents. Another child wanted a book from a more advanced level and proved that she was capable of handling this level because she was willing to put forth the extra effort it required.

During the independent reading period I work with one child at a time at my desk. Theoretically each child has one ten-minute conference each week.[28]

Esther Dornhoefer,[29] after following for several weeks an individualized program with her children, has "some problems" to solve:

[25] Maida Wood Sharpe, "An Individualized Reading Program," *Elementary English,* **35** (December 1958), pp. 507–512.

[26] Louise G. Carson, "Moving Toward Individualization—A Second Grade Program," *Elementary English,* **34** (October 1957).

[27] John J. DeBoer, address given at Northwestern University, Summer Reading Conference, 1959.

[28] Margaret Kirby. "Tete-a-tete Lessons Develop Independent Readers," *Elementary English,* **34** (May 1957), pp. 302–3.

[29] Ruth Rowe and Esther Dornhoefer, "Individualized Reading," *Childhood Education,* **34** (November 1957), pp. 118–122.

. . . selective reading also involved some problems. Many of the children were in primers and first readers. The stories were longer and it took more time to read. It was now impossible to read with each child every day. I had tried taking half the group one day and the other half the next day but the children didn't like it. "I didn't get to read today" was the complaint. Again I thought, "Oh joy, they really do like to read. This is what I have been working for."

By this time, of course, I was almost sold on individualized reading except for one thing. There is a certain sense of pleasure in sharing a story with your classmates—in other words, group reading. But if I added group reading to our individual reading the day would be heavily overbalanced with language arts. And yet—the next teacher might prefer to use group reading and it seemed only fair that the children should have the experience. . . .

The longer I teach the more I feel that there isn't any *one* approach—rather a combination that ultimately shapes the results. This past year has been one of experiment, mistakes, and problems. But next year with some changes, I shall use a variety of approaches—group reading, the newspaper, the reading table with the freedom of choosing books to take home—but the backbone will be individualized reading.

We would most certainly concur with the conclusion of this excellent teacher in recognizing that there isn't any *one* approach to efficient instruction. Moreover, we believe that we should continue exploration to determine which combination of approaches is most effective. We admire greatly the courageous efforts of teachers to solve this problem and we agree too with the following statements of John Marcatante about possible reactions to the *Individualized Reading Program:*

. . . One teacher may attribute panacea-like powers to it, while another will maintain that it is a waste of time. Both these extremists may stand in error.[30]

This is precisely the point we attempted to make in an article published in *Elementary English,* October, 1959. In this article, we tried to give a rather representative summary of investigations and to evaluate the results. This summary was critized as incomplete (which it was intentionally). Since that time, additional summaries have been published, such as that by Harry W. Sartain who concludes that because his own study and others "that have been carefully controlled" show that the "individualized method does not produce better reading gains than a strong basal program, there is no reason to forfeit the advantages of a well-planned basic system." [31] However, he does recognize some of the strengths of the individualized approach.

---

[30] John Marcatante, "The Programmatic Fallacy and Individualized Reading," *High Points* (May 1960), pp. 47–50.
[31] Harry W. Sartain, *op. cit.,* p. 263.

Several other accounts demonstrate clearly some of the distinct values of individualized reading. One of these, by Helen F. Darrow and Virgil M. Howes, gives examples of effective reading instruction.[32] In the preface, the authors state that "The individualized method is no panacea, no quick trick to solve all reading problems," and that "At best it is a means to achieve the major goals of reading instruction." We were most impressed in this account with the care and success of the teachers in studying the interests of boys and girls and in associating interests with reading materials. Called by either name (individualized or developmental) this is an admirable practice. We were greatly pleased too with the consideration of skills and the various methods used to establish them. Perhaps the greatest strength of this admirable pamphlet lies in the ingenious provisions for recording development and evaluating growth through reading. The title of this booklet is *Approaches to Individualized Reading.* We believe that this monograph could just as appropriately be entitled *Approaches to Developmental Reading* as we have described the latter.

It seems to us that it is idle to debate whether individualized *or* group approaches are preferable. Common sense as well as some of the studies would support the use of both approaches in effective combinations and not with one subservient to the other. In doing this, we should, of course, recognize the need for the abandonment of the routine *basal* approach in using a single reading series; but this would not rule out systematic instruction in which reading textbooks in various combinations are used as needed.

Ruth Strang and Donald M. Lindquist also recognize this point of view in their interpretation of individualized reading. They state:

Individualized reading is an essential part of the developmental reading program. Children should be guided in selecting books of interest to them and at their reading level, and teachers should give them individualized help with their chosen reading.[33]

They point out that there are many ways of individualizing reading. "The most common method of individualization on all educational levels is subgrouping within a class." Other procedures are discussed and are followed by this conclusion; "These and other methods of individualization do not constitute the whole reading program. They are features of a classroom procedure that provide for both group and individual instruction and practice."

---

[32] Helen F. Darrow and Virgil M. Howes, *Approaches to Individualized Reading* (New York: Appleton-Century-Crofts, 1960).

[33] Ruth Strang and Donald M. Lindquist, *The Administrator and the Improvement of Reading* (New York: Appleton-Century-Crofts, 1960), p. 86.

It is difficult indeed to appraise scientifically a "method" which is interpreted in so many and such varied ways as is "individualized reading." And, we should hasten to add that developmental reading has many interpretations, one of which is found in this article. Similarly, instruction using the *basal* materials is difficult to evaluate since many plans are employed; in some, multiple texts and varied practice materials are used in different combinations; in others *a* basal reader and its accompanying materials are meticulously followed. Perhaps it would be well to admit these facts and abandon trying to ascertain the value of "individual" versus the textbook approach. Instead we might try to agree upon common objectives and seek to evaluate some aspects of both approaches, such as when and how pacing may be utilized successfully, when and how self-selection may be engendered and practiced most effectively, when and how skills under-emphasized in most textbooks can be most advantageously developed, and under what conditions films and filmstrips can be most efficiently utilized. The role of self-teaching devices should also be explored.

In summarizing the results and implications of studies and experiments to discover ways of improving reading achievement through the means of program organization, methods and materials, Lofthouse comments thus on some of the pitfalls to be avoided in making comparisons:

Individuals who undertake experimentation should try to control or at least take account of the numerous factors which might bias their findings. Pitfalls to avoid include comparing results achieved by teachers who are of unequal ability, experience, preparation, or motivation or who used classes of different socio-economic backgrounds. The amount of time spent and the emphasis placed on the subject being taught should be equivalent when plans of organization or procedures are being evaluated.[34]

And Clare B. Routley makes the following recommendations for reading practices and materials for the future:

Teachers in the future must pay more attention to individualized reading programs. Grouping must be planned to meet the needs of all pupils. Even gifted children may be retarded readers. Other gifted children may be reading below their potentialities. . . .

---

[34] Yvonne M. Lofthouse, *International Reading Association Conference Proceedings,* 4 (New York: Scholastic Magazines, 1959), p. 177.

To meet the unprecedented demands in reading which the changing characteristics of our age will demand, there must be more research, more experimentation, more testing and increased use of clinical procedures. The best of the New Castle Plan, the Joplin Plan, and all other plans must be made available for teachers in order that a sound developmental program may be followed.[35]

With the foregoing statements we are in full agreement. Moreover, we find in the following conclusions of John DeBoer and Martha Dallman an interesting commentary on needs in today's schools.

While it is true that some children learn to read well without any systematic instruction, acquiring all needed skills through abundant and highly motivated reading, the vast majority of children need instructional assistance if they are to learn to read at their best. The regularly scheduled reading period and the basal reader will continue to be indispensable for most teachers and with most children if essential skills are to be developed. Extensive reading may be sufficient for bright children under the guidance of skillful teachers, and it is likely to produce rapid readers, readers who readily grasp the total meaning of a passage. For most pupils, however, it should be supplemented with intensive instruction for the continuous development of increasingly difficult skills such as word recognition, comprehension of sentence meaning, and following directions.

DeBoer and Dallman make the following suggestions for modifying conventional textbook practice:

Certain general cautions should be observed in the planning of a basal reading program. These cautions grow out of facts and principles developed earlier in this book. For example, reliance should not be placed upon a single basal reader for the whole class; indeed it should not be placed upon an entire single series. In any given class, basal readers designed for many levels of reading ability and containing many different kinds of material should be provided. Basal readers should not be labeled according to grade level of difficulty, although the publisher's estimate of difficulty level may be indicated by some code device. All basal readers should be amply supplemented with general reading materials on many subjects and representing many levels of reading difficulty.[36]

A provocative point of view is also expressed by Russell G. Stauffer who states:

It is recommended, then, that a modified basic reader approach be used. To do this effectively one must, first, drop the notion that a basic reader program in and of itself is final and sacred. It is not. Second, one must drop the notion that time can be equated with equality. Not every group must

[35] Clare B. Routley, op. cit., pp. 144–145.
[36] John DeBoer and Martha Dallman, The Teaching of Reading (New York: Holt, Rinehart & Winston, 1960).

be met every day for the same length of time. Third, the idea that a basic book recommended for a grade level must be "finished" by all pupils in a grade before they can be promoted must be discarded. Fourth, teaching reading as a *memoriter* process by presenting new words in advance of the reading and then having pupils tell back the story must be stopped. If reading is taught as a thinking process, even short basic-reader stories will be read with enthusiasm. . . . Sixth, effective skills of word attack must be taught. Basic reading books do not provide for such skill training; neither do trade books.[37]

Following is an illustration, again from Darrow and Howes, of the way textbooks and group instruction have been combined effectively.

On certain days, instead of sharing individual reading, children worked on skills in small groups. For practicing certain skills, the children worked from a common reader; for others, they used workbooks, their individual reading books, and other aids. All kinds of skills were practiced: speed, word meanings, dictionary skills, word analyses, use of indexes and tables of content, and others. The teacher checked frequently with the county course of study in reading and in other books so as to keep in mind the range of reading skills.[38]

It will be granted that some widely followed basal programs are inflexible. Other programs and textbooks are more flexible. It is clear that we need new designs for texts and related materials. When these are developed, they will, we hope, stress reading as a thinking process to a greater extent. In the meantime, it is desirable to follow a flexible program using the best texts available and combining group with individualized reading, as DeBoer and Dallman have suggested. Stauffer, too, makes a distinctive recommendation:

. . . the reading program should be divided so as to allow about half of the time for each approach—a basic reader program and an individualized program. This might be done by using the group approach with basic readers for about a week or two, and then the individualized or self-selection approach for a similar period of time. When a pupil is free to select day after day for two or three weeks, he is almost forced to examine his interests and decide more carefully about what he wants to do.[39]

The suggestions given above seem plausible. It would be desirable for teachers to try out these approaches. What outcomes will they yield? Similarly we might through cooperative efforts seek answers to other questions, such as:

a. How can children be best prepared for self-selection and for successful

---

[37] Russell G. Stauffer, "Individualized and Group Directed Reading Instruction," *Elementary English* **XXXVII** (October 1960), p. 381.

[38] Helen F. Darrow and Virgil M. Howes, *op. cit.*, p. 16.

[39] Russell G. Stauffer, *op. cit.*, p. 381.

silent reading experiences? What is the role of readiness? How can phonic skills be best acquired?

b. What combination of individual and of group endeavor is most advantageous in various situations?

c. What provision should be made for "conferences" between pupil and teacher in classes of various sizes? How often should conferences be held in various situations?

d. How can we use films, filmstrips, and film readers more effectively to promote pleasure and success in reading?

e. What provision should be made for the acquisition of skill in oral reading? In story-telling? In creative endeavor of various kinds?

f. How can individual and group interests be best ascertained? And how can individual and group interests be best provided for?

g. What is a desirable combination of group and individual practices to follow in the subject areas? How can such practices be encouraged and evaluated?

h. What is the best combination of group and individual practice to follow in guiding exceptional children? In encouraging creativity?

i. In what ways can we encourage reading as a thinking process? How can we foster critical reading most effectively?

One of the values of individualized reading insufficiently stressed, is the opportunity it offers the creative child or the gifted pupil to explore his interests and to develop his background through reading. The principle of self-selection has special relevance here since its use may permit the expression or the development of gifts.

The above questions and others can be answered best through various types of classroom endeavor accompanied by research. They are not questions at present to be answered primarily by debate. Certainly we have few dependable answers at present to most of these questions. New and bold departures are necessary if we are to make the most of our present opportunities. During World War II, we demonstrated the value of films and filmstrips in teaching reading. And after World War II, the value of films associated with film readers was shown in the development of habits and skills in reading. Schools have been remiss by neglecting to incorporate such approaches in the teaching of reading. We should recognize, however, that some teachers are at present courageously making efforts to depart greatly from established practice and to test new approaches. With the unparalleled opportunities today for the use of new approaches and devices to foster enjoyment and success in reading, it is hoped that in the future we shall extend these efforts greatly and shall not be forced to acknowledge our neglect with its far-reaching consequences.

DEVELOPING BASIC READING SKILLS . . .
THROUGH EFFECTIVE CLASS ORGANIZATION °

Emmett Albert Betts

How can basic reading skills be more effectively developed through class organization? This question is an old one, beginning with the introduction of the concept of mass education. The history of education is, in fact, the story of the rise of regimentation and subsequent attempts to break the lock step created in our classrooms.

Of professional literature on this topic there is no shortage! Administrators have devised plans to *regiment* a whole school system into *differentiating* instruction. Other educationists have experimented with grouping and individualized instruction in the classroom. Today ardent protagonists of some plans cause many teachers to approach the problem with mixed emotions. And someone has defined mixed emotions as the feeling the young man has when he watches his mother-in-law drive over a cliff in his brand new Thunderbird convertible.

Sincere and dedicated teachers of America are raising these questions:

1. Should language readiness and reading readiness books be used for *all* beginners?
2. What is to be said for five-year-olds having a need for reading?
3. How do we know when a child is ready for reading?
4. How much reading should a child achieve before promotion?
5. What can we do for children who omit and substitute words, use lip movement, and finger point?
6. How can we group children to help slow readers? Average readers? Fast readers?
7. How many groups should I have in my class?
8. How can we take care of individual differences in reading abilities in a social studies class?
9. What is the best and most reliable reading test?
10. How do you find the reading level of a child with a serious reading difficulty? Of an average child? Of a gifted or talented child?
11. Where can we get materials of a low reading vocabulary with high interest level?

° Reprinted from the May, 1958 issue of *Education*, pp. 561–576, by permission of Bobbs-Merrill Co., Inc., Indianapolis, Indiana.

12. Is individualized reading the best way to take care of individual differences? Can individualized reading be substituted for group reading of a basic reader? If so, how can I organize the class? How can I be sure each pupil is learning phonic and thinking skills?

These questions and variations of them reflect concern about the improvement of reading instruction through class organization, appropriate materials, and effective methods. It is quite evident that the organization of the class is directed toward the goal of providing for individual differences in the maturity of pupil skills and interests. It is equally clear that the use made of instructional materials depends upon class organization as well as the teacher's concept of the goals of directed reading-studying activities. Then, too, procedures and methods are tailored to fit different types of situations. Class organization, therefore, is of necessity discussed in terms of (1) goals of instruction; (2) appropriate materials; and (3) effective methods.

LEVELS OF PROFESSIONAL COMPETENCE

The key to the problem of class organization is the professional competence of the teacher. At the lowest level are those teachers who operate at a zero level of competence—the regimenters who give all pupils in the class the same textbook and evaluate growth in terms of A-B-C-D or S-U report cards. At the top of the list are the "tenth-level" teachers who challenge all pupils in the class by means of teacher-pupil planned class, group, and individual activities. Between these two extremes are the teachers at different levels of competence—ranging from those who group primarily to help the *low achievers* to those who administer efficiently group and individualized reading programs for *all* pupils. How to help teachers at different levels of competence to improve their teaching requires differentiated supervision, in terms of individual levels of professional achievement.

REGIMENTATION

In early American elementary schools, instruction was largely individual. Following the Revolutionary War a great experiment in mass education was undertaken. As the American free-school system was taking its first faltering steps, graded schools were introduced followed by graded textbooks. While the avowed purpose of these schools was to equalize educational opportunity, they fell into a lock step and the narrow, calendar-dictated curriculum was organized on the basis of adult interests and needs. Regimentation, therefore, became—and still is—a serious peril in education.

ADMINISTRATIVE PLANS

About one hundred years ago, William T. Harris, Preston W. Search, John Kennedy, and other stalwarts in education began to wage a vigorous, ceaseless campaign against the lock step in education. Their plans, however, were administrative procedures for a whole school system, including (1) the frequent reclassification of children during the school year; (2) individualized activities preceding group recitations; and (3) coaching laggards by an assistant teacher in the classroom.

Later—in 1913—Frederic Burk introduced an individualized plan of instruction, which is now better known as the Winnetka Plan. By 1920, the Dalton, or contract, plan of providing for individualized instruction was favorably received.

Following the introduction of the intelligence scale by Binet and Simon in 1905, special classes were organized for the mentally handicapped. Over the years, special classes have been expanded to include the physically handicapped (including the brain injured) and the gifted. More recently, clinical services have been developed to help emotionally disturbed children and the educationally retarded.

With the exception of plans for special classes, administrative plans for providing for individual differences had serious weaknesses. They tended to regiment classroom administration and promotion policies. They perpetuated a one-ladder curriculum for all children to climb. In general, they fell into disfavor because differentiated instruction is, in reality, put into operation by different teachers in different classrooms in different communities.

CLASSROOM PLANS

During the 1920's, standardized test and informal inventories for evaluating reading achievement were developed and favorably received. While the standardized tests did not reveal the *wide* range of differences in the classroom, they did call attention to the *fact* that the same educational prescription could not be given to all children in the same grade.

In 1921, Fernald and Keller published their tracing technique for teaching word perception skills to certain types of non-readers. Their use of this technique heightened interest in both remedial and corrective reading. Equally important, it called attention to the *fact* that the same methods could not be used for all children in the same class.

In the early 1930's, many challenging data were reported on retarded readers and non-readers: (1) Eighty per cent had normal or superior intelligence; (2) Eighty per cent were boys. At this time, twenty-five to forty per cent were failed in the first grade because they had not achieved some adult standard set for them in reading. Furthermore, there was more retardation among the pupils in the upper fifty per cent of the class than in the lower fifty per cent.

The above and other events appear to have stimulated experimentation on how to develop basic reading skills through effective classroom organization. Between 1921 and 1938, three basic plans were reported: (1) grouping on the basis of achievement; (2) grouping on the basis of pupil interests; and (3) individualized reading. Most of these plans also provided for the occasional, informal grouping of children who need special help on blending in phonics, outlining, or some other specific skill. All of them emphasized the rôle of the teacher in providing for individual differences. Variations of these three basic plans have been reported recently in a spate of articles.

GROUPING: READING LEVELS

Since basic textbooks in reading are used in most schools, grouping children by reading levels is a generally accepted practice. In the beginning, this plan was used primarily to do something for low achievers, and slow readers. Gradually, however, the concept of helping *all* the children in the class has emerged.

There have been variations of the plan for grouping by reading levels. First, children in the primary grades and in the intermediate grades have been grouped by reading levels for departmentalized reading instruction one period a day. While this plan may be better than regimentation, it increases the chronological age range within a group, regiments the school schedule, introduces problems of the child's integrating his school experiences, and tends to divorce reading from the language arts and the rest of the curriculum, and often underemphasizes the rôle of interests and motivation in learning. In reality, this plan regiments differentiated instruction in the classroom, defeating accepted goals of reading instruction.

In most schools today, however, children are grouped for reading instruction within the classroom. Three or more groups are organized to provide for the slow, average, and fast readers. How many groups are organized depends upon the professional competence of the teacher, the range of pupil abilities, and other factors.

Effective grouping by reading levels embraces several important concepts: (1) independent reading level; (2) teaching, or instructional, level; (3) listening, or hearing, comprehension level; (4) interest level; (5) directed reading-studying activities; (6) etc. It is essential to the success of this plan, for example, that the teacher knows how to estimate reading levels and how to guide the group from their teaching to their independent reading levels in each directed reading activity. While the sequential skill program is built into the teaching plans for *different* basic textbooks, this plan is effective to the degree that the teacher understands these concepts.

Most teachers who group by reading levels also plan for (1) class projects; (2) free, or independent, reading; (3) small informal groups to help individuals with specific skill needs; and (4) grouping in science, social studies, and other learning areas on the basis of interest.

Some teachers have experimented with pupil leaders—monitors or helpers—of groups. Others have depended more on self-aids for groups working on study-book and other independent activities. Teacher-pupil planning is one of the keys to the successful working of other groups and individuals while the teacher is directing the reading activity of a group.

Grouping by reading levels, like all other plans, has its limitations. In the first place, there is a wide range of reading abilities and interests within a reading group. The twelve-year range in a typical sixth grade, for example, poses some very real problems regarding the number of groups and the availability of appropriate materials. Some teachers report they can manage no more than three groups, which, of course, does not meet the needs of all pupils in the class; other teachers can administer several groups. In addition, teachers are always searching for books, magazines, and other materials of interest to different individuals in the class. A basic reader, for example, is written for a given age level, but some retarded readers may have mature interests and a very low level of reading ability.

GROUPING: INTERESTS

It is a fairly common practice to organize groups of children to pursue different interests. This is done in preparing a play, a dramatization, or a puppet show; in performing science experiments and preparing reports; in pursuing a unit of the social studies; and so on. This type of group activity extends reading into the heart of the curriculum, promotes the dynamic relationships between pupils, develops the ability to select and evaluate relevant materials and to draw conclusions, and motivates learning. Effective grouping in terms of interests usually requires considerable *class* planning and evaluation as well as *group* and *individual* activities.

When interest groups are organized, materials are made available in terms of the independent reading levels of the pupils. This requirement makes it necessary for the teacher to know the reading level of each pupil and the readability of a generous supply of books and other materials.

Pupil selection of relevant topics of interests and readable materials —of books they want to read and can read—is basic to interest grouping. For self-selection of reading materials to operate effectively, the pupil needs to have a firm grasp on the reality of his own reading abilities and to have clearly in mind the purposes of his contribution to the group undertaking. In other words, the group needs guidance; self-selection does not mean a laissez-faire, or "hands-off," policy is followed by the teacher.

Interest grouping, too, has its limitations:

1. Teachers need to achieve a high level of competence to administer effectively the diverse activities of groups.

2. More time is required for the teacher to plan when and how reading skills are developed and there is the ever-present possibility that skill development is haphazard rather than sequential.

INDIVIDUALIZED READING

The major goals of reading instruction are to help the child (1) mature in his interests; (2) make automatic his use of phonic and other word-learning skills; and (3) develop thinking and related abilities required for *independence in* reading and study activities. The acceptance of these goals—and they appear to be reasonable!—requires systematic planning for the sequential development of interests and skills, and for self-selection when the child has achieved to the point where readable materials are available to him.

In the 1930's a number of plans for individualizing reading were reported in grades one to six. These plans made use of "single copies of a large number of books" on the assumption that "learning to read is an individual job." These plans provided for (1) informal estimation of reading levels; (2) records of daily or weekly progress; (3) "simple check ups" with emphasis on audience-type reading; (4) a wide range of references, fiction, and other materials; and (5) individual guidance, combined with group and class instruction.

These early plans were reported as "individualized reading," "individual guidance," "reading for enjoyment," "informal reading," and so on. The authors of these plans were not deluded into thinking that the goals of reading instruction could be achieved by a *plan* or *the* plan of individualized reading. Instead, they were deeply and justifiably concerned that individualized reading should be encouraged by definite planning. At the same time, they organized for class and group instruction to insure interest and skill development. That is, they recognized the values and limitations of individualized reading in an effective reading program.

Individualized reading is receiving increasingly popular approval. In fact, a relatively large amount of literature is now available, although the great bulk of it is an expression of opinion rather than validated facts. Probably no scholars in the psychology of pedagogy of reading, however, would recommend individualized reading as the sole basis for reading instruction. For that matter, very few teachers would go that far.

Self-Selection. One of the outstanding merits of individualized reading is the emphasis on self-selection of independent reading. This emphasis can place a high value on pupil and peer motivation when appropriate group and class activities are planned around independent reading. The value is defaulted, however, when the child has to merely read to the teacher for five to fifteen minutes each week.

Recently, a cartoonist showed a frustrated master sergeant drilling recruits and yelling: "How are you going to learn to think for yourselves, if you don't do what I tell you to do!" Unlike the frustrated sergeant, master teachers do give children opportunities "to think for themselves" in setting up their purposes for reading, in selecting appropriate materials, and in evaluating what they read in terms of their purposes. But these master teachers do not confuse self-selection with aimless, unguided, and unfruitful activities of their pupils. They know that self-selection operates effectively when they give competent guidance.

Individual Development. Another significant merit of individualized reading is the opportunity for the child to proceed at his own pace. This opportunity, too, is of high value when he is maturing in interests and acquiring the skills needed to meet those interests. But this opportunity is denied pupils when they fail to get systematic guidance in the myriad of interests and skills they need for growth in reading. The extent to which individualized reading is developmental depends upon how expert the teacher is in providing for specific learnings, either through the use of a well-planned basic reader or some other equally well-planned sequence.

Individual Attention. A third merit of individualized reading is the attention given to each child in the class. Of course, the value here depends upon the professional competence of the teacher. However, there are very real limits to the amount of time a teacher has for twenty-five to forty pupils in a class. There is also a limit to the amount of time a teacher can give to reading instruction. There is always a need to help individuals in all curriculum areas, but can reading instruction be effective when the child receives only seven to fifteen minutes of help a week?

A highly individualized plan of reading instruction requires special administrative skills on the part of the teacher. If administering three or more groups in reading has taxed her skills, she may find the record keeping and other administrative details of a highly individualized plan overwhelming. Since small group activities are necessary to most individualized plans, this type of teacher might well perfect her skills in handling small groups before organizing her class into one-member "groups."

Leaders in education long ago emphasized the fact that *learning is an individual matter.* They also realized that teaching is concerned with a social *group,* ranging in size from the total class to one member of the group. The goal of differentiated instruction, therefore, is to help each individual realize his potential, without penalizing any other pupil in the group.

Learner Needs. A fourth merit of individualized reading is the attention given to the specific needs of each pupil. In most plans these needs in word learning, thinking, and interests are indentified in individual conferences and small group activities. Help is given to the child, who is motivated by an awareness of his needs, in both individual conferences and small groups of pupils having common needs. For this purpose, basic readers and study books, special workbooks, and informal activities are used.

How effectively individual needs are identified and provided for depends upon the professional insight of the teacher, the adequacy and systematic use of informal inventories, the sequential introduction of new learnings in the instructional material, and many other factors. Since *individualized* instruction is the goal of all plans for classroom organization, this problem of meeting individual needs is not peculiar to any one plan.

Library Facilities. A fifth merit of individualized reading is the attention given to the need for a wide range of reference books, fiction, magazines, and newspapers. This wide range covers both interests and reading abilities. Since children, like adults, can read only that material which is available to them, the teacher uses all of her initiative in keeping a flow of books through the classroom from the school library, community library, homes, and other sources.

Here again, library facilities are essential for individualized reading regardless of which basic plan of organization is used. Basic readers used in grouping by reading levels, for example, serve as springboards to worthwhile independent reading.

INDIVIDUAL AND GROUP ACTIVITIES

Fortunately, there are few teachers willing to depend upon individualized instruction alone. All master teachers provide for individualized reading. But they also use class activities to plan and evaluate projects. They plan for grouping by reading levels and interest areas. They know that having a child read to them only every fourth or fifth day would not make sense to an educational psychologist, a competent business man, or a parent.

OPINIONS AND FACTS

For developing basic skills in reading, class organization goes hand in hand with the use of effective methods and of appropriate materials. One of the major problems in class management is the study of and provision for individual needs in motivation, achievement, interests, word-learning skills, and thinking abilities. How this problem is handled depends upon teacher competence, size and composition of the class, library and textbook facilities, and other factors.

In recent publications on the teaching of reading a wide variety of *opinions* are expressed. There are those who sincerely believe, for example, that individualized reading, or grouping by reading levels, or grouping by interest areas or some other single plan of differentiating instruction is the *one* way for *all* teachers to teach *all* pupils in *all* classrooms. Then, too, there are those who believe that a two-book plan for the intermediate grades is an adequate solution. Though the road of progress in reading is strewn with ill-conceived, one-shot plans of improving reading instruction through classroom organization, each generation seems to breed its own variety of cultism.

Experimentation by classroom teachers needs to be encouraged, but generalizations cannot be based on one teacher's experience in one classroom in one school system. It is a well-known fact that teachers vary widely in their levels of professional competence. For this reason, supervision is differentiated to help individual teachers mature in their professional competence. For this reason, too, plans evolved in classrooms must be tested and evaluated over a period of years by scholars in the psychology and pedagogy of reading with the help of experts in statistics and experimental design.

DIFFERENCES

In a typical fourth-grade class, the children range in reading abilities from those who can barely struggle along in a pre-primer to those who enjoy the *Reader's Digest*, encyclopedias, and other materials which would challenge the best efforts of the average eighth- or ninth-grader. There are those, too, with anxieties and other emotional problems which interfere with their learning. Then occasionally there is a child with a subtle brain injury which blocks his attempts at learning. Overlaying these differences are wide variations in maturity of interests, word-learning skills, and thinking abilities.

Since education increases differences, this range of achievement in attitudes, skills, and abilities is increased as the children progress (or regress!) through the fifth and sixth grades. In a typical sixth-grade, for example, there are the Johnnies who have never read a book on their own—even a pre-primer—to those who read avidly high school and even college books on meteorology, satellites, radio communication, and other areas of interest.

Yes, educating all the children of all the people has been attempted in few places on this planet. But we are committed to this task because we are firm in our belief that all citizens are born free and equal—that we must, therefore, provide equal learning opportunities for all individuals. It is to this end that a century of progress has been made. The history of this century is the story of many leaders' attempts to break the lock step in education created by the post Revolutionary War plan for mass education.

READING LEVELS

Basic to any plan for differentiating instruction is the achievement of each individual in the class. In the fifth-grade class, for example, Johnny is unable to remember *her, the, my,* and other common words in a pre-primer. For him, self-selection of reading materials exists only in fantasy rather than in reality; he needs special help. If he has normal or superior intelligence, he may require the help of a clinical psychologist who understands language disturbances.

In the same fifth-grade class, Tommy can read a second reader on his own—without lip movement, finger pointing, substituting words, and other signs of difficulty. In a third reader, Tommy shows no signs of difficulty but he occasionally comes to a word he cannot identify or an idea he doesn't understand. He needs help from his teacher who knows how to teach him the necessary skills so that the next time he can recognize the word and can apply that skill to similar words. He also needs help from his teacher who knows how to identify and to help him with specific comprehension needs. His independent reading level, therefore, is second-reader; his teaching, or instructional, level, is third-reader.

But Tommy is not interested in reading second readers written for seven-year-olds. His fairly high intelligence, his curiosity about science and history, and his opportunities to listen in on reports and conversations have helped him to mature in his interests. He, therefore, needs books with a high interest level but a low readability level.

Mary, another fifth-grader, can read a fourth reader on her own and a fifth reader under teacher supervision. When seeking books and magazines for independent reading, she selects those at or below fourth-reader level. She has an adequate concept of her own skills in a reading situation.

Mary, along with eleven other pupils, is having an enjoyable experience in a fifth-reader story book and the accompanying study book. In each selection of the story book, Mary finds the need for new word-learning and thinking skills. At the beginning of a directed reading-study activity, the selection is at her teaching, or instructional, level. After the teacher has prepared the group for reading the selection, guided the silent reading, and given specific help on word perception and comprehension, Mary can read the selection—silently or orally—on her own. Also, on her own, she can complete the study book activities which improves her use of reading skills. In each directed reading-study activity, therefore, Mary and the rest of her group are taken from their teaching level to their independent reading level.

GOALS OF INSTRUCTION

Over the years a substantial amount of respectable research has been accumulated on three major goals of reading instruction:

1. The development of worthwhile *interests* which take the child to reading and which are satisfied through his increasingly effective reading-study skills.

2. The acquisition of *phonic* and other word-learning skills to the point where they are used automatically.

3. The maturing of *thinking* and related comprehension abilities needed to solve problems and to get genuine satisfaction from reading-study activities.

A comprehensive plan for the teaching of basic skills through class organization is effective to the degree that it embraces the above three goals. When any one of these goals is underemphasized or overemphasized, pupil progress is impeded.

Highly competent teachers know the interests of their pupils, understand how interests change and develop, and are alert to the need for helping children mature in them. For these reasons, they systematically use informal inventories of interests to estimate levels of maturity and to evaluate growth. They confirm these estimates by systematic observation of pupil interests in different types of situations and by encouraging the self-selection of books and other materials for independent reading and study.

Master teachers, too, are keenly aware of the phonic and other word-learning skills of the different pupils in their classes. They systematically use informal inventories of phonic skills, for example, to estimate achievement and specific need. They know that when a word, or telling, method is used, their pupils resort to saying the letters of words and to using other inappropriate skills.

To offer positive guidance, a master teacher takes these necessary steps:

1. *Readability of material.* Provides appropriate materials which each child can read without signs of difficulty.

2. *Need.* Gives the child—in an individual or group situation—help on word learning when he has a need for it. The kind of help given depends upon the part of the word causing the difficulty, previously learned skills, and the need for learning a new skill.

3. *Meaning.* Insures pupil understanding of the use of the word in its context.

4. *Listening.* Helps the child to hear the undistorted sounds of letters and syllables in the word.

His help on listening gives the child a learning set to see the letter and syllable phonograms in the word.

5. *Seeing phonograms.* Guides the pupil in relating the sounds heard in the spoken word to the phonograms representing those sounds in the written word.

This guidance requires the sytematic teaching of phonic skills, beginning with the first words the child learns. It includes the sequential development of skills to deal with initial consonants, final consonants, and vowels of one-syllable words. It also includes the application of these skills to the syllables of words—without setting up for the child an artificial dichotomy between phonics and syllabication. It includes, too, the extension of phonic skills to the interpretation of pronunciation symbols in the dictionary. For the best interests of the learner there need be no trichotomy of phonics, syllabication, and pronunciation symbols; instead, his learning is facilitated by well-planned sequences of learning.

6. Blending. Takes the pupils a step further by blending the parts of two whole words to make a new one.

This includes, for example, blending the *b* of *bill* and the *l* of *left* to make the *bl* of *black*. It also includes blending the first part of one word with the rhyming part of another; for example, the blending of the *sk* of *sky* with the *ate* of *late* to make *skate*.

7. Checking meaning. Helping the child to form the habit of making sure the word he identified by means of phonic skills fits the context in which it is used.

8. Making rules. Helping the pupils to make generalizations about consonants, vowels, and syllables.

9. Applying skills. Giving the pupil opportunity to apply his newly learned phonic skills to unknown words.

In addition to being keenly aware of each child's interests and phonic needs, master teachers are very much concerned with teaching children how to think. With pupil interest to motivate the reading and with the pupil's automatic use of phonic skills, the teacher is prepared to deal with the major concern of reading instruction: *thinking*.

Here again the teacher is as much concerned with specifics of comprehension as she is with specific interests and specific word-learning skills. These needs in learning how to think embrace six major concerns:

1. Purposes—felt needs—which motivate the child to read.

2. Personal experiences out of which the child makes his concepts.

3. Attitudes which influence the child's inclination to read on a topic, accuracy of interpretation, recall of ideas, and tendency to rationalize.

4. Use of language to deal effectively with ideas (language ability includes interpretation of definite and indefinite terms, classifying, indexing, awareness of shifts of meaning, use of context clues, differentiating between language used to report facts and to influence attitudes, etc.).

5. Ability to discriminate between fact and opinion, to evaluate relevance of ideas, and to draw conclusions.

6. Versatility in adjusting rate and depth of comprehension to purpose.

These three goals of reading instruction—interests, word-learning skills, and thinking abilities—are inseparable essentials. These goals are ever kept clearly in mind by master teachers and conscientious authors of textbooks. To understand these goals requires a reasonable degree of scholarship in phonetics, phonics, perception, semantics,

language structure, psychology of thinking, child development, differential psychology, and children's literature as well as in the pedagogy
of reading. How a typical class of children with a possible twelve-
year range of reading abilities is to be organized to achieve these goals
has been a formidable challenge to thinking educators for more than
a century.

SUMMARY

To find one plan of class organization to be executed effectively by
all teachers with all children is as difficult as finding a word to rhyme
with *orange*. The purpose of class organization is to provide *equal
learning opportunities for all children* in the classroom—to promote
better learning conditions in all curriculum areas. This *is* a worthy goal
of reading instruction, but the fact remains that a few children need
special services; for example, the mentally limited, the brain injured,
the emotionally disabled.

Challenging differences. In the first place, there is no such thing
as a homogeneous group. When children are grouped by reading levels, for example, the best readers need to meet at least one new idea
or word in about eighty running words in order to be challenged by
new learnings. The less able children in the group may meet as many
as one new word in twenty-five or thirty without showing signs of difficulty. Furthermore, differences in mental ability, verbal aptitudes,
motivation, experience, etc. make occasional regrouping necessary.

Nor is there such a thing as a homogeneous group so far as interests are concerned. While master teachers can help a class or a group
to develop a community of interests, nevertheless, individuals vary
in the strength of their interests in a given topic.

Moreover, grouping in reading does not dictate the membership
in an arithmetic or science group. Differences in the educational pro-
file of each individual explain this fact. A given pupil, for example,
may be a poor speller but a whiz in arithmetic and even in reading.
This fact is both a blessing and a challenging problem in education.
It is a blessing for a child to excel in art or arithmetic computation
when he is a poor reader. It is an interesting challenge in a classroom
to deal with the *different* needs of children and to depend upon the
special contributions of different children.

Emotional climate. Some teachers complain that poor readers have
weak defenses for their egos because they stand out in contrast to their
age mates. They may go to absurd extremes to conceal the reading
levels of books. This is done on the false belief that children cannot
and do not evaluate themselves and others.

Yet, some of these same teachers will appoint group leaders to *tell* other children words they want to know. This practice is bad for at least two reasons: (1) a word, or telling-method is notoriously ineffective for developing phonic and other word-learning skills; (2) many poor readers are not aware of their perceptual inaccuracies. Furthermore, very bad human relationships can be developed unless both leader and pupils are prepared, in attitudes, for the undertaking.

How a child feels about his low status in reading does not depend upon the class organization but upon the emotional climate in the classroom. Awareness of real achievement, the attitude of the teacher toward the pupils, and the attitude of the pupils toward each other—all these attitudes contribute to the child's self-concept. These attitudes can be developed in classroom situations where instruction is differentiated by some practical means. Of course, frustration is compounded in a regimented classroom.

High achievers. Most teachers know that a child who either can't read or is a very poor reader is like a soldier without a gun or a baseball player without a bat. Probably for this reason the history of differentiated instruction highlights concern with mentally, physically, emotionally, and educationally handicapped children. For the same reason, low achievers tend to have higher achievement quotients than high achievers. One of the chief dangers in group or in completely individualized instruction is the tendency of the teacher to give the lion's share of her time to the low achievers.

A lay person can identify a non-reader or crippled reader, especially one who cannot remember words. But it takes a highly competent teacher to identify the child who has not learned to organize information, to draw conclusions from related facts, and do other types of thinking.

Many teachers, for example, are lulled into neglecting high achievers by the cliche: "If children enjoy books, the more they read the better they read." While there may be a grain of truth in this platitude, there is real evidence that high achievers need as much, or more, guidance in reading as the low achievers. Nevertheless, these high achievers too often are turned loose in their classrooms or the library, without benefit of competent guidance.

Differentiated instruction. Discussions of interests, phonics, thinking, group dynamics, and other crucial elements in education are so much prattle when the child is frustrated in a regimented classroom. Therefore, the purpose of any plan for differentiating instruction is to reach the individual in the group, where he is in attitudes and skills.

How to provide for individual differences is a problem of mutual concern to children, parents, and teachers. In no successful plan, for example, can the active participation of parents be sidestepped. The dreams of educators must face the test of reality because, in a democracy, the citizens will have the kinds of schools they want.

When the last word is written on the topic, it will be seen that differentiated instruction reflects an attitude toward the individual. In our democracy, individuals have equal opportunities to participate in government. It has long been the responsibility of teachers—dedicated to the concept of democracy—to provide equal learning opportunities for all children in the classroom.

A DESCRIPTION OF THREE APPROACHES
TO THE TEACHING OF READING *

Department of Education, San Diego County

Much improvement has been made over the years as the schools have struggled with the task of improving the teaching of reading. Hundreds of studies conducted in the field of reading instruction have modified the methods and materials employed in the teaching of reading. But the complexity of the nature of the reading task indicates the need for even more research studies. We now realize, as a result of much information concerning human growth and development, that because of the diversity of our school population, no single approach to the teaching of reading is apt to be the best or only solution. Improved practices and deeper insights will be forthcoming as a result of a broad front of investigations probing into method, materials, and the learning process.

As a contribution to the investigation of improved methods of teaching reading, a Reading Study Project was undertaken by twelve elementary school districts in San Diego County during the 1959–1960 school year. Sixty-seven teachers, grades one through six, were selected to participate in an analysis of and experimentation with three selected approaches to the teaching of reading. The San Diego County. Department of Education was asked to develop the design for the study and to provide the necessary leadership for its conduct. The broad

* Reprinted from *Improving Reading Instruction, Description of Three Approaches to the Teaching of Reading*, Monograph No. 2 (May 1961), by permission of the San Diego County Department of Education, San Diego, California. Reading Study Project Committee: Warren C. Vogt, K. Boyd Lane, Chairmen; Ralph E. Kellogg, and William W. Norin.

assumption underlying the study was that any improvement in teaching approach must be related to a basic philosophy which states general aims of education, principles of reading instruction, and a broad definition of reading. For this study the following philosophy was formulated:

1. *The aims of education* are to help children develop a democratic faith, to mature in the ability to think creatively, and to become self-directing and cooperative members of all human groups in which they operate. The reading program should serve to provide experiences which will contribute to the development of these traits and ways of working.

2. *Principles of reading instruction* which should be included in any approach to the teaching of reading should draw from the following areas of educational theory: growth and development; readiness; individual differences; experience; and evaluation.

3. *The definition of reading* established for the study was as follows: Reading is a process. In its broadest sense it is the development of meanings in response to stimuli for the purpose of guiding behavior. The categories of stimuli are: (a) objects or things; (b) persons and social processes and relationships; (c) symbols of varying degrees of abstractness.

The general aims of education, principles of reading instruction, and the broad definition of reading were stated as basic assumptions. From these basic assumptions criteria and rationale statements were developed to describe the main ideas of three approaches to the teaching of reading. These selected approaches were in current usage by teachers in San Diego County at the time of the study.

This monograph explains the organization and use of "A Description of Three Approaches to the Teaching of Reading," the basic document used in the study. The monograph (1) explains the organization of the criteria and rationale of the Basic, the Individualized, and the Language Experience Approaches to the teaching of reading, (2) describes how the monograph might be used in classroom reading experimentation and in in-service education, and (3) lists the criteria and rationale of each of the three approaches.

CRITERIA AND RATIONALE ORGANIZATION

In the document, "A Description of Three Approaches to the Teaching of Reading," the criteria and rationale statements of each approach are preceded by a concise description of the approach. The criteria column describes the selection and organization of activities and experiences in each reading approach. The rationale relating to each criterion indicates the reasoning, logic, psychology, or philosophy which supports that particular criterion. By this organization one can quickly grasp the essential concepts of an approach and their justification. The criteria and rationale statements do not include detailed information regarding specific techniques of reading instruction.

BASIC APPROACH

The Basic Approach, in its most definitive sense, is concerned with providing children with experiences which will help them learn *how* to read printed symbols. This may be contrasted with programs providing broader experiences in reading different types of printed materials and engaging in other independent activities for the purpose of greater generalized learning. Personal growth and recreational appreciation through reading are not primary objectives of the basic program. (Remedial or corrective instruction is not considered a part of the basic reading program.)

In this approach skill development is central, the skills being those of analyzing, locating, interpreting, and comprehending written or printed symbols from the page. The development of reading skills which are common to all reading situations involving printed or written words is the primary objective of such a program. The method of fulfilling this objective involves direct, systematic instruction, usually on a daily basis, through the use of a basic "reader" text or series of basic "reader" texts. These readers present a sequential organization for development of reading skills. A controlled vocabulary is utilized in presenting and providing for this sequential organization. To provide for the differences in abilities of pupils, three or more flexible groups in the class are utilized. Pupils may advance at different speeds through this sequential program but all must follow the predetermined sequence.

CRITERIA	RATIONALE
1. The teacher attempts to assess the reading ability of each student for the purpose of establishing reading groups. He uses results of standardized reading tests, observation of pupils, intelligence tests, information from other teachers, previous books read, and consideration of class size and make-up.	1. Information concerning the child's reading ability, intelligence, interest, attitudes, previous learning experiences, need to be analyzed if he is to be placed in the best possible reading instructional situation. Children with similar reading abilities can be taught more effectively in groups than can groups of children with wide differences in reading ability.

CRITERIA

2. On the basis of available student information the teacher assigns each child to a reading group. Groups are formed on the basis of reading ability with some flexibility for placing children in groups on other bases. Children may be moved from one group to another when they have need for a new group experience. In the typical class of 25 to 30 children three groups are considered adequate.

3. At reading instruction time the teacher works with each group separately (usually in a reading circle situation). The teacher follows the suggestions for sequence, content, etc., set forth in the manual which accompanies the basic and supplementary series. While the teacher works with one group, the other children work at seatwork assignments or in self-selection activities such as art, word games, etc.

4. Generally, the plan of instruction for individual groups entails a definite procedure which includes these steps (procedure varies in different series and at different grade levels):

a. Setting purpose (motivation, background information, etc.).

b. Introducing new vocabulary and teaching necessary skills.

c. Silent reading by pupils.

RATIONALE

2. Children of similar abilities placed in small groups can be more easily instructed in reading skills. Materials of instruction can be prepared in terms of group needs on the basis of group ability. Children progress at different rates, which necessitates flexibility in assigning a child to different groups when his reading development indicates need for change.

3. Since the needs of the group differ and since there are more opportunities for individual help in a small group, the teacher works most effectively through direct instruction activities geared to the ability of each group. In the small groups it is possible for each child to read orally, take part in discussion, tell a story, participate in skill building activities, etc. Children learn to work independently as they have opportunity for independent work (seatwork) while the teacher is working directly with one of the groups in a reading circle. (The teachers' manuals offer directions for carrying out a systematic reading program which accommodates several levels of ability.) Seat-work assignments which are correlated to the basic reader stories are included in the manual. Assignments for creative activities are also included.

4. Certain logical procedures have proven successful in the teaching of reading printed symbols. Children learn best when they are motivated. To enhance accurate reading and provide for success, skills related to the lesson and new words taken from the lesson may become part of the daily reading activity. Silent reading provides for the fortification of skills. Oral reading provides the child with an opportunity to communicate with others. The teacher is able to evalu-

CRITERIA

d. Oral reading by pupils.

e. Discussing story read.

f. Independent activities (workbooks, seatwork, teacher-guided skill development, supplementary silent reading).

5. The teacher attempts to establish the purposes of reading in a given lesson. He generally follows the suggestions of the manual. Interests of the group on a particular topic may be used when related to the lesson story to be read.

6. New words are introduced to the children before they encounter them in a story context. These new words are part of a carefully controlled vocabulary around which the entire series is built. Word attack skills which are needed in solving these new words are taught. Other skills to be emphasized are suggested in the manual. (In primary grades much emphasis is given to developing a basic sight vocabulary.) Instruction is aimed at developing meanings for new words being introduced for a given lesson. New words follow a sequence which is based upon criteria of relative difficulty, interest as to age level, etc.

7. After discussion of new words and points developed in the story, children are generally required to read the story silently, keeping in mind the purposes that the teacher established with the group. (This procedure varies with grade level and may range from short sentences to complete stories.)

8. Children in each group are given many opportunities to read orally. Oral reading is generally done in the group itself by individuals while the others serve as a small audience.

RATIONALE

ate the child's reading progress during oral reading. Follow-up activities provide for additional opportunities to use skills and vocabulary previously introduced as well as to pursue interests related to the content of stories read. Follow-up activities can be used to evaluate student progress.

5. Children's interest in and understanding the purpose of a task improves the learning situation. The suggestions offered in the teacher's manual take into account what is known about children's interests and ways in which children may be stimulated.

6. Children have more success with printed symbols when they are prepared to cope with specific problems they will encounter when reading the new story in the basic text. When the vocabulary is controlled in this manner only a few new words are introduced in each lesson. In addition, words which have been previously introduced are repeated in succeeding stories. This technique enables the child to handle a small number of new words and to maintain a growing number of previously learned words from a basic vocabulary list.

7. Questions are used to focus on the main points of the story and to guide reading for certain purposes. By then reading the story silently, children are better able to understand the content of the story.

8. When children read orally, the teacher gains an opportunity to evaluate such reading abilities as pronunciation, phrasing, word attack skills, expression, speed, and fluency.

CRITERIA

Children in the group discuss and react to elements of the study and the presentation of the individual reader. The teacher may provide individual instruction in specific skills as he reacts to the oral reading.

9. Prior to and following directed reading lessons, pupils are expected to engage in a variety of planned independent activities. Many of these activities are related to the lesson, such as workbook exercises which accompany the basic text, use of teacher prepared worksheets, and related recreational reading. Activities not directly related to the lesson itself are provided for by the teacher. These include reading in various content fields, recreational reading, expressive activities (group dramatization, creative writing), practice activities.

RATIONALE

The teacher is enabled to appraise listening skills of group members. Oral group reading also serves as a means of sharing.

9. It is necessary that children not under the direct supervision of the teacher be provided with a variety of well-planned independent activities to reinforce and extend reading skills.

INDIVIDUALIZED APPROACH

The major objective of the Individualized Approach is to provide opportunities for each pupil, progressing at his own rate of growth, to gain experience in a variety of reading situations. This approach is based upon the child's own desire to discover, explore, and react to stimuli in his environment. Guided by his own motivation to learn, his reaction to those stimuli which he selects enables him to develop meanings which are essential to behavioral change. Basic to this approach is the principle of learning theory which recognizes that each individual learner is most genuinely motivated in terms of his own needs, and that when provided with the appropriate environment, guidance, and materials he will tend to choose materials most suitable to his maturity, ability, and interests.

Among the major functions of the teacher using this approach are these: to provide a balance of reading materials, to evaluate growth, to teach reading skills, and to develop pupil interests and attitudes. These functions are fulfilled primarily by the teacher helping pupils in their selection of printed materials, offering guidance during individual conferences, keeping records of pupil progress, and offering individual and group encouragement during silent reading periods.

CRITERIA

1. The teacher with the help of the children selects a wide variety of reading materials (books, magazines, pamphlets, etc.) from all possible sources. These materials, representing varying degrees of reading difficulty, interest, content, style, format, etc., become the media for reading instruction.

2. The teacher encourages the children to become familiar with the material available by providing opportunities for them to browse, to discuss the materials, to hear passages or stories, to use book lists, etc.

3. To prepare children for initial selection of materials for reading, the teacher guides children in the development of effective techniques for appraising printed materials quickly. Examination of preface, introduction, table of contents, index, topic sentences, pictures, etc., is encouraged. Skimming and other surveying techniques are developed through explanation, demonstration, and try-out.

4. During the initial stages of using varied printed material in the classroom, the children are encouraged to "try out" different materials in terms of their own interest, purpose, and ability to read. They are allowed complete freedom within the range of material available in arriving at their choice of material which they will make more concentrated use of during the time scheduled for reading.

5. Children are encouraged to proceed in their selected material at their own rate. Vocabulary growth, skill development, interest, and time available are the major factors regulating this growth.

RATIONALE

1. Children differ in native ability, interests, and emotional needs. As a result, their purposes for reading will vary from one child to another. In order to better accommodate these differences there is no limit to the amount and kind of reading material needed.

2. Familiarity with material promotes more intelligent use. When children discover reading materials in the areas of their particular interests, they are naturally motivated to read and to appreciate the rich variety of reading material available. New interests are thus continuously aroused.

3. Because of the great amount of printed material available today, it becomes a primary task of the teacher to provide each pupil with the necessary techniques for selecting materials appropriate to his individual needs and purposes. The pupil needs more than knowledge of the techniques, he needs also to be able to apply them in meaningful situations.

4. Since interest and purposes are individually unique, the children themselves are more likely to choose materials which are appropriate to their individual needs. Children are also more highly motivated when they are able to pursue tasks of their own choosing. A more valid assessment of their true ability to read print is possible under such conditions.

5. A child will advance more rapidly if he is encouraged to proceed at his own rate of progress, which is not limited by the rate of progress of a group.

CRITERIA	RATIONALE

6. Guidance in developing reading skills, vocabulary growth, interest, and attitude is provided by the teacher through scheduled individual conferences with each pupil as the need arises. These conferences help the pupil develop an understanding of the skills necessary to his reading growth. The teacher points out the areas of the child's success in reading and helps him to plan additional reading experiences in areas where he needs further development.

6. Because no two students have identical specific reading characteristics at any given time, instruction can best be performed on an individual basis. The close working relationship between teacher and pupil inherent in individual conferences helps the child see that someone is concerned about his interest and progress and is willing to give *,iim* needed assistance. In pointing out the child's successes in reading, the teacher is encouraging the pupil to achieve future success.

7. Group situations may be employed when:

a. Two or more children have similar needs in skill development.
b. There is an expressed desire to share reading interests.
c. There is need to share ideas of different students gleaned from their individual or common reading.

Structure of groups changes as needs change.

7. Children will at times exhibit common specific needs which can best be taught in group situations. They occasionally have need to identify with a group situation wherein they feel they have peers in reading skills, interests, and attitudes and where they can see that different people bring different meanings to a reading selection.

8. An individual reading record for each pupil is kept by the teacher. *In diagnosing the child's progress,* the teacher keeps frequent anecdotal notations of the child's growth based upon daily observation. In this observation the teacher looks for evidence of the pupil's interests, attitudes, reading level, rate of progress, and difficulties with reading skills. The number of conferences and amount of time spent with each child is also noted. *Over-all reading growth* is recorded periodically to survey the pupil's variety of reading experiences and physical characteristics in reading situations. Results of informal and formal testing are also included.

8. An individual reading record facilitates the teacher's diagnosis of each child's reading strengths and weaknesses. This enables the teacher to work in individual conferences so that each child gains an understanding of his own progress.

9. Children engage in many types of creative independent activities during the time when they are not

9. As children acquire new skills, interests, and attitudes from their reading activities, many opportunities are

CRITERIA	RATIONALE
involved in group or individual conferences.	needed for them to fortify these new learnings and apply them in different situations.
These activities are related to many areas of the curriculum but reading is given top priority.	Because reading is the core from which these activities are extracted, it should receive the most attention.
A balance is maintained in that children participate in individual silent reading, oral reading in small groups, art, communication, and construction type endeavors.	However, children need to realize the interrelatedness of all the curriculum areas.
	The creative nature of these activities promotes self-direction which is a major goal of all instruction.
10. Opportunity is provided for individuals or groups of children to share what they have read with others.	10. It is important that children be enabled to evaluate their own growth through self-testing situations. Of lesser importance, and yet a factor, sharing allows for teacher evaluation of pupil growth in all areas of the language arts.
These sharing activities may be carried on in small groups, total class situations, or during the pupil-teacher conferences.	Even though each child at any given time is reading self-chosen materials, he must receive encouragement and opportunity to develop new interests and understanding of the range of reading materials available.
A wide variety of means of sharing are possible, among them being dramatization, use of audio-visual aids, oral reading, pantomimes, etc.	

LANGUAGE EXPERIENCE APPROACH

The Language Experience Approach to teaching reading recognizes in daily practice that learning is based upon the experience of the learner. The development of the language experience approach is founded upon fundamental understandings which are cultivated in the thinking of each child as he lives and learns with other children and adults. The teacher recognizes that each child brings to school a unique language personality. He strives to preserve the individual's personal language at the same time that certain common understandings and skills are being habituated.

The Language Experience Approach to teaching reading requires that each child be given opportunities to work individually with the teacher, in small groups, and in the total class group. In each situation the child is expected to express and record his own thoughts, ideas, aspirations, and ideals as well as to read and understand the thinking of others. His own expression is encouraged through the use of a variety of media such as painting, speaking, and writing.

Student-prepared materials are used as *basic* sources of reading, along with printed materials which are developed for general reading and the expressed purpose of teaching reading skills. The use of all kinds of books is necessary for the child to get a balanced program of reading and to increase his skills of word recognition and interpretation of reading. The child *makes progress* in reading and writing through self-expression. He *evaluates his progress* as he uses materials prepared for teaching reading skills.

CRITERIA

1. The teacher creates situations in which each child feels encouraged to produce something of his own thinking and interest using familiar media such as crayon, pencil, and paint.

2. The teacher gives each child an opportunity to express his thinking through oral language. The child responds as an individual, as a member of a small group, or in the total class group.

3. In the primary grades, the teacher extracts from the oral expression of the individual a sentence or two which summarizes his story. The teacher records the child's story in summary form for the child and in his presence, using as much of the child's language (his particular mode of expression) as possible.

4. When using small groups, the teacher records the story in the presence of the children, having them arranged so that they can observe the writing.

5. As the teacher writes he takes opportunity to call attention to letter formation, relationship of beginning sounds to the symbols used, repeti-

RATIONALE

1. All learning must be based upon the previous experience of the learner. In expressing what he knows the child should use familiar media of expression. Those which are normally used in the home and the kindergarten should be continued into the first grade and beyond.

2. Oral language is a base from which written language emerges. Until the child is able to express his ideas through speech, he is less able to communicate effectively with others and has a limited basis upon which to build a writing-reading vocabulary.

3. A fundamental concept which the child must hold about "what reading is" is that it is speech written down. As the child sees his own speech taking the form of writing he is developing readiness for both writing and reading. By using the child's expressed thoughts, meaningful content related to his background of experience is provided. He is thus able to identify more closely with the written material.

4. The informal grouping around the teacher as he writes the dictation of one child after another gives all children a feeling of participation in the total experience of the group.

5. The natural way for a child to understand "what reading really is" is to observe the recording of his own speech with the letters of the alpha-

CRITERIA	RATIONALE

tion of sound and symbol in many situations, capitalization and punctuation, and sentence sense.

bet. Teaching language skills with reference to an actual meaningful task is an effective procedure.

6. The teacher and children carry on informal discussions which relate to the problem of helping them understand that what they say is being symbolized with the letters of the alphabet.

6. When the child has insight into and understanding of the reasons and procedures underlying a written language system, his ability to make use of the system is enhanced.

He understands that what he has represented in painting and drawing and said orally can be symbolized in conventional written form and read.

7. The teacher binds the productions of small groups into books that can be used in follow-up activities in the classroom. The teacher may have the same group involved in such activities as recalling what was recorded on a previous day, recognizing letters and words, matching words that are alike, suggesting a new story, etc. One group of children might read pupil-produced books developed by other groups.

7. Interest in learning to write and read is stimulated by the use of materials produced within the classroom. Reading books authored by pupils in a class motivates the child to try to achieve competence in reading beyond normal expectations. As the teacher and children work with reading material which has been produced in the classroom, there is increased interest in analyzing the skills involved in producing a book. The appreciation and skills derived from these activities help children to move with enthusiasm into the reading of commercially prepared reading materials.

8. As soon as the teacher is aware that a few children can copy simple words, he helps them to write what they call their own stories. These are usually such stories as might accompany a self-portrait, recording a recent experience, planning individual or group activities.

8. Children who are helped to move into writing on their own at an early age are developing a balance in communication skills which is desirable for better understanding of our language and its use in daily life. Simple beginnings in writing in the early part of the first grade are challenging and interesting to children. A basic objective of language instruction is to help the child recognize and capitalize upon the natural interrelatedness of writing, reading, speaking, and listening.

9. A variety of independent activities (using crayon, pencil, paint, etc.) is open to the child during the

9. Most children seek activities such as painting, crayon sketching, dramatizing, etc., because they have ex-

CRITERIA

time in which he is not directly involved in individual or small group sessions with the teacher. These pupil products may serve as the bases for total class experiences in language. The child's interpretation of his independent work is recorded by the teacher or the child himself for the whole class to see. In this way, provision is made for an additional experience from which the class is able to see how thoughts are recorded in writing. Instruction in skills appropriate to the task at hand, plus further discussion of the purposes of writing can be carried on in this type of situation.

10. The teacher and children develop a simple routine for guiding and utilizing children's independent activity productions. This routine might include (a) procedures for selecting and distributing materials, (b) procedures for displaying or storing products, (c) procedures for presenting the material and sharing experiences.

11. The teacher utilizes the activities and procedures which provide the background and motivation that enable the individual child to make a self-commitment to write on his own. The teacher is constantly alert to the emergence of such a development in each child.

12. After the child makes the self-commitment, the emphasis in the teacher's role changes from one of motivating the child to one of facilitating his development in the communication skills. The teacher encourages the child to express his experience in appropriate forms of communication. Assistance is given the child in planning his independent effort and in the specific skills required for it.

RATIONALE

perienced some previous success in using these media. Young children are able to express their ideas more freely through such activities as these than through writing alone since these activities place fewer restrictions on ideas and vocabulary. The individual child sees a clearer purpose for his independent work when his own product is used for instructional purposes. Children who have mastered the basic skills of writing in conjunction with reading will continue to find it helpful to use a variety of media in communicating.

10. The establishment of simple routine procedures allows the teacher and children to plan activities over an extended period of time. Thus language activities that are held on different days are more clearly seen as interrelated; e.g., writing to reading, speaking to writing, etc. The routines necessary for this type of organization give the children the security that comes from knowing what comes next.

11. There is a period of maturation when the child is physically, socially, and mentally ready to write. This stage of development is unique to each child. One of the best evidences of readiness for writing is the child's own indication of his desire to write.

12. One of the major goals of language instruction is to help all children to become more and more independent in their ability to communicate. This independence develops over a period of time, necessitating varying degrees of teacher guidance depending upon the child's level of development.

CRITERIA	RATIONALE

13. The teacher may invite other children to react to a child's independent production (a painting, a model, an idea for a play) and to indicate what they would write about it.

13. Children learn from other children and develop a feeling of cooperation as they interact through sharing their own communication efforts. The children begin to sense the great variety of ideas possible in interpreting a production, and gain some experience in making discriminative responses. The elements of creative thinking as well as critical thinking are utilized.

14. Children learn how to utilize a wider selection of communication materials as the environment of the classroom is enriched with their own productions and with other resources which they and the teacher bring. The teacher is working toward a goal of independence in each child, thinking through what is to be done, the difficulties to be anticipated, and the resources available to help the child solve his problems.

14. Children learn to evaluate and select appropriate materials when a wide choice is available. Abundant resources help motivate the child to pursue an interest further or to develop a new interest; they also help him develop proficiency in using communication skills.

15. As children continue to write independently, the teacher meets with them in small groups and works with them on vocabulary development. Children are provided with word lists which contain basic vocabulary words for their level as well as lists of general interest. The teacher encourages children to use these additional words in many ways. This enables children to increase their vocabulary with a minimum of direct teaching.

15. As children gain some confidence in reading and writing their own ideas, they need systematic help in expanding their vocabulary in reading by including in it those words they are most frequently using in their own language experiences.

16. As the child develops a firm grasp of a reasonably large sight vocabulary, including a good number of the basic words for his level, the teacher provides new printed materials for him to read. Opportunity is provided for the child to read orally when it is appropriate for him to do so. The teacher records the words with which the child has difficulty and provides experiences which enable the child to add them to his vocabulary.

16. Meaning of, facility in using, and recognition of printed words is enhanced when unfamiliar words are learned in contexts which are meaningful to the child. Success in first endeavors tends to sustain the child's interest in the task and inspires him to further effort.

CRITERIA

17. As children have successful reading experiences they are provided more and more "book reading" opportunities. The child's interest, needs, and abilities are the prime factors considered as the teacher assists the child to move to higher levels of independence in reading. The child is encouraged to read for a variety of purposes.

RATIONALE

17. The child needs the sense of achievement which comes as a result of increased independence in reading. He can recognize the pattern of his progress and realistically adjust his aspiration level at any given point. As the child branches out into many types and kinds of reading experiences, he begins to recognize his potential for greater independence in reading and the communication arts in general.

THROUGH SELF-SELECTION TO INDIVIDUALIZING READING PROCEDURES [*]

Marie Dickinson, and Others [1]

A long step toward individualizing reading procedures in classroom groups was taken when grouping within the class was introduced and the teacher thereby brought closer to each child. However, the potential for individualizing instruction in the groups was rarely realized, for certain weaknesses were inherent in the procedures used in forming the groups.

A nearly rigid patterning for the selection of groups developed. Three groups formed on the basis of a single index of ability became the rule in most classrooms, regardless of the changing academic and other needs of the children concerned. A kind of ritual took possession of the reading time during which both the teacher and the children often lost interest in what might have otherwise been an exciting experience. Every child listened to the reading problems of every other

[*] Reprinted from *California Journal of Elementary Education* (February 1959), pp. 150–177, by permission of the *Journal* and the author.

[1] The following teachers in Los Angeles County Schools contributed many of the specific examples cited in this chapter: Sara Brant, Nellie Brantley, Irma Coulter, Virginia Craghead, Keren Elgin, Lucille Gingras, Bernice Hensley, Beulah Larison, Evelyn Marshall, Marcia McVey, Lucile Neiter, Norman Peters, Claire Reichardt, Robert Rhoads, Dean Seeley, Anne Smith, Agnes Tuttle, John Van Sant, Rhea Wenger, Arlene Young.

child in the group. He practiced on the next skill as logically determined by the graded materials rather than on the skill he needed as determined by his own development. He adjusted his reading pace many times during the reading time to that of the child who was reading orally. He not only lost time from his own reading but was unable to develop the habit of concentrating. He was likely to depart from the reading period without a clear perception of his own problems or of how he might use what he had learned in the other reading he would do during the day.

The eagerness with which teachers are exploring more satisfactory ways of meeting individual needs in reading attests to the failure of ability grouping and controlled reading materials to provide in themselves an adequate means of guiding growing skills.

Wide-spread interest has developed in a promising practice which has come to be known as *self-selection in reading.* As implied in this label, one of the features of the plan makes available to the children reading materials of many types on many subjects and of varying degrees of difficulty. Each child chooses the material he reads during the regular period of reading instruction. This provision frees the children to explore and enjoy reading as they grow in ability to read.

The child's selection of his own materials for reading instruction makes it possible and necessary for the teacher to develop a plan for individualizing his practices so that each child works on his own problems at the time he needs to work on them and makes progress with a feeling of real achievement without reference to such labels as "slow," "average," or "fast."

THE CONCEPTS OF SELF-SELECTION AND PACING
APPLIED TO READING INSTRUCTION

The concept of "self-selection" as a means of growth was formulated during the early extensive studies in child growth and development.[2] Investigators noted the way in which children exhibit *seeking* behavior according to their needs. They observed the *selective awareness* children have, the tendency to get from a given environment those things for which they are ready. They found that by properly *pacing* instruction or learning tasks to a child's capacity that the child enjoyed success. The meaning of these concepts of *seeking, self-selection,* and *pacing* for guiding children's growing skills in reading might be made apparent in the following ways.

---

[2] See Willard C. Olson, *Child Development* (Boston: D. C. Heath, 1949), pp. 157; 340–43; and his article in *The Packet* (Boston: D. C. Heath, 1952), pp. 1–10.

Seeking. The urge to grow and learn comes naturally from within children. They can generally be relied upon to take the initiative and responsibility in the learning process. The more that children have opportunity to grow, the more change takes place within them. It follows that the reading environment needs to provide materials of varied content and difficulty if individuals are to find the materials which meet their needs.

Self-selection. When the environment provides alternatives, children generally select the specific means that best promotes their growth. In relation to books this means that when many books are available children choose the reading which both satisfies and promotes growth.

Pacing. The teacher's role in providing appropriate pacing for children is one of providing the materials on which children can grow. Since each child continues to strive when his responses are successful and to avoid experiences that are beyond his attainments, the teacher provides an environment in which each child can find materials suited to his needs. Increasing maturity gradually emerges with much self-initiated practice on self-selected materials. A child shows by his reaction to reading materials when he is ready for the next step. The teacher's observations and notes on a child's progress help him to make decisions about the reading materials that need to be provided to promote that child's growth.

Teachers have been exploring in many different ways the meaning of these clearly defined concepts of growth and development in the teaching of reading. Teachers are convinced of t⊦ soundness of the self-selection procedures they are developing. On⌄ ⌄eacher explained self-selection as follows:

Self-selection in reading is just what the words imply. It is an individual program of reading. Each child selects a book which appeals to him from a collection of well-chosen books. He reads at his own pace, without pressure, and reports in his own individual way. The self-selection reading program holds promise of meeting individual differences, because it combines the best elements of recreational reading and skill teaching.

PREPARING TO INITIATE SELF-SELECTION IN READING

A single teacher, an interested group within a staff, or an entire staff may discuss, read, and visit, and then begin to modify the pattern of children's reading experiences. Teachers indicate that the process of studying children and of providing the materials for reading, which are necessary for a successful beginning, continue through self-selection procedures.

A planned environment. Every available source of books, magazines, and other reading materials needs to be explored to secure the
materials needed to make the classroom environment offer an attractive fare covering many subjects and of varying degrees of difficulty.
The importance of the environment being appropriately planned is
pointed out in the statement that follows:

> Self-selection of reading material requires a carefully planned environ-
> ment. The first requirement of the teacher is to set up the room in such a
> way that there is provision for every child's ability and interest. The selec-
> tion will include all varieties—science, history, nature, readers, poetry, pic-
> ture books, encyclopedias, and magazines—every category of reading avail-
> able within the levels of ability of a particular class.

Arrangements can be made by the teacher to obtain several dozens
of books at a time from the different libraries. The school district library, the public library, the county branch library, and the county
school library are ready sources. Children's contributions from home
libraries, with the approval of the children's parents, may be encouraged. In one district the parent-teacher association subscribed a fund
for books for each class. Children helped select the books that were
purchased with this fund.

Materials prepared by the teacher have a place in the reading environment of every classroom. These may be provided for individual
children, small interest groups, or the total group. A fifth grade teacher
described the usefulness of materials she prepared as follows:

> To make this reading program a success more reading material at each
> child's ability and interest levels must be provided. At times I have found it
> necessary to write material dictated by some of the slower readers in my
> fifth grade to meet these requirements. John, with his limited reading vocab-
> ulary and great interest in his ranch and horses, was definitely not interested
> in pre-primers. The stories about his own ranch experiences served as a
> bridge until he was able to read the *Cowboy Sam* books.

Other teachers in the middle grades also find the use of the experience story a creative and effective way of helping inexperienced readers discover meaning and satisfaction in reading. A teacher of a combination third and fourth grade made the following statement regarding
how she handled stories the different children wrote:

> In his free time, or at home, a child draws a picture, or brings in a pic-
> ture or object. The teacher and the child talk about it. Whatever the child
> says, the teacher writes down as the child's experience, explanation, or fairy
> story. Then the child reads his story. Most of the children make books with
> their stories. Gradually as the child's confidence grows, it is very simple to
> move into book reading.

An uncommunicative child of any age may be led into reading and
eventually to responsiveness to other children through this use of the experi-

ence story. Barry, a nine-year-old who refused to communicate with anyone at any time except by painting, after four months found his way into the life going on about him in the classroom by dictating to the teacher and reading his story back to her.

Becoming acquainted with children's books is one of the many creative activities of the teacher who guides children's reading growth through self-selection.

The need to "sell books" which teachers have felt necessary in some classes may diminish more quickly than anticipated. One teacher noted with interest and amusement the written comment of a child who said, "The teacher shouldn't talk so long at the beginning of the period. It takes too much time from reading."

Learning more about the children. The teachers' first observations, acquaintance with permanent records, and simple, quick diagnostic procedures are followed by more extensive study. If a teacher is preparing for self-selection in reading, his initial observations tell him something about each child's attitudes toward reading—whether eager, reluctant, defensive, or bored—and about his interests and friends. Other information such as that from test data, interest inventories, parent conferences, personal writing, reaction stories, and sociograms helps the teacher provide more adequately for children's reading needs as self-selection procedures develop.

A card file or other simple system needs to be devised for collecting the information pertinent to the guiding of each child's growth. The usefulness of cards or a notebook is suggested by the following sample of a teacher's easy-reference record of an individual child:

Audrey K.
   Test Data: I.Q.: 142.   Reading Achievement
                                       9th grade
   Interests: Wants to be a nurse.
       Reads toward that end avidly.
   Observations:
       She chooses some quite difficult books.
       Looks at pictures and reads captions to help
           get meaning.
       Curiosity leads to a variety of activities.
       Works well with all the children.
       Disagrees courteously: "May I correct you?"
	Language
	problems
	
	Needs
	help with
	pronunci-
	ation of
	technical
	words.
	Seems to
	dislike
	writing.

STARTING THE CHILDREN IN SELF-SELECTION

Self-selection in reading is concerned with creating new ways of working with children. No set pattern, therefore, appears in reports teachers make of ways they begin. Many ways of initiating change in procedures are possible. Teachers reported the following ways:

The first year I divided my class into the regular three groups according to ability. Then I began introducing the children in the top group to individual silent and oral reading. Gradually I involved children from the other two groups until every individual was selecting his own reading material and there were no more static groups.

With the help of the principal I started with high groups, but the rest of the class seemed unhappy and restless. Before long we were all in it.

Since questions arise about the ways children may move into self-selected books in the first grade, a more detailed report of one teacher's experience follows:

In the fall my first grade class was still in ability groups and many of the children still not quite ready to read in books. The fast group had written many short stories, used readiness materials, the big book (state series), and had read several pre-primers: *Three of Us, Bill and Susan, Under the Tree, We Come and Go, We Look and See, Play With Us,* and *Busy Days.*

Our library corner contained many other pre-primers. I noticed a few of the children looking through these books. One day a boy who was reading very well brought one of the books up to me and said, "Mrs. Young, some of the books over there are easy to read! May we read them?" Before long others were doing the same and gradually the faster readers began to choose books to read.

The children who could not read independently seemed to shun the extra books. They sometimes browsed through the books but never asked to read them. One little fellow asked to read one of the pre-primers and I felt that he wasn't ready. After watching him in his group, I was certain that he could not read independently. He was persistent and I felt that I should not stop him, but just wait to see what might happen. We began to read! After the first two or three pages he very honestly said, "Gosh, this is too hard for me." I explained to him that it wouldn't be long before he would be able to read this book. He did not seem disappointed.

ORGANIZING MATERIALS AND TIME

Open shelves and table space for displaying reading materials and making them easily accessible are desirable. Adjustments and changes in shelving can be made to facilitate the finding of books by children and to highlight subjects or books that children are overlooking. In making the arrangement, questions like the following present themselves:

Which books should be shelved by subject? Should certain authors' books be shelved together? What interest centers should be arranged? What labels are needed to help children find books for which they are looking? How should "readers" be shelved?

A system of checking books out and in needs to be worked out with the children. In the middle and upper grades, where children may take turns helping with the returning and issuing of books, adequate table space and boxes or drawers for filing cards make the system orderly and quickly managed. Primary children can assist with some parts of a system of issuing, receiving, and shelving books.

The management of time needs to be flexible so that each child may think about and make a selection, read independently, work with the teacher, and share with others his ideas and feelings about what he is reading.

A plan for third grade. The teacher decided upon a block of 75 minutes in which she could hear nearly every child read or observe him at close range as he read. The children came in small groups to the reading circle each with his own book. Groups were formed without reference to ability in reading but on the basis of a sociogram. The membership of the groups changed every three or four weeks as new friendships and working relationships developed.

The schedule was changed from day to day, on a three-day cycle, somewhat as shown in the chart on the next page.

This plan was kept flexible. Sometimes children presented a dramatization of a story read. They planned and prepared the dramatization during activity periods and were free to borrow someone from another group occasionally. Some time was devoted to *Weekly Readers*. Children did much sharing in small groups, informally.

A fifth-grade schedule. One teacher varied the procedures during a period of 60 minutes so that the children could gain skills and other satisfactions from their reading experiences. In the time devoted to building skills, the teacher worked with an individual, a small group, or the whole class, depending upon the need that had emerged. During the silent reading period, each child read a book of his choice, and the teacher passed among the tables to help as needed. In the conference time some children read aloud so the teacher could appraise their progress and identify their needs for further skills. At this time, too, a child might read orally to the class a passage he had prepared of a beautiful, interesting, or amusing incident.

A first-grade plan. A first-grade teacher, who provides for success in reading as reading comes about naturally in the various activities, also has regular periods of instruction for those who have chosen charts, booklets, or books to read. This teacher described the arrangements for the reading period as follows:

The children are grouped for reading instruction for convenience. The reading group is gathered around on three sides of a table. The teacher sits on the other side. Next to her is a chair where each child takes his turn

Grade Three, Schedule for Reading

Group	Mon.	Tues.	Wed.	Thurs.	Fri.
1	Reading silently	Teacher-pupil conference	Activity		
				Same as Monday	Same as Tuesday
	Teacher-pupil conference °	Activity	Reading silently		
2	Teacher-pupil conference	Activity	Reading silently		
				Same as Monday	Same as Tuesday
	Activity	Reading silently	Teacher-pupil conference		
3	Activity	Reading silently	Teacher-pupil conference		
				Same as Monday	Same as Tuesday
	Reading silently	Teacher-pupil conference	Activity		

° Teacher-pupil conference time is used in different ways: conversing, reading orally, working on difficulties, noting progress.

reading to the teacher. The group usually includes six or seven pupils. Each pupil reads his book silently until his turn comes to work with the teacher. The teacher helps each child when he needs the help.

When teachers comment on their experiences in individualizing reading instruction through self-selected materials, they have much to say about the effect on children of involving them in determining what they read. Something happens to children's concepts of themselves when they are trusted to make decisions in choosing their own books, stories, and factual materials. Feelings of dignity and responsibility enhance a child's attitude toward himself and his achievement. For the first time, some children feel the incomparable pleasure that waits for them on the printed page. All these desirable feelings about their own powers and about the satisfactions in reading motivate further learning.

TEACHER-CHILD RELATIONS DURING THE READING CONFERENCES

During the teacher-pupil conference the teacher brings about a new kind of relationship between himself and the child. Each child becomes involved in making decisions, in assuming responsibility for doing his part, and in evaluating his progress. When the teacher changes his role to that of helper and partner each child is able to explore his abilities with safety. The security of knowing that the teacher understands and accepts his problems as well as his achievements increases a child's willingness to communicate. Progress in learning to read becomes steady.

A first-grade teacher describes her relationships with the children as follows:

> Each child has a turn reading to or talking with the teacher. This is important in the first grade. The child gains confidence sitting near the teacher. He is more relaxed because it is a personal contact and his ideas are more easily and more freely expressed. The shy child benefits much more this way. He will honestly and openly make comments about his own reading. The teacher gains insight into the child's limitations and learns much about his vocabulary and his methods of attacking words. Here, too, the teacher can catch concepts which are confused or inadequate and can help the pupil to clarify his understandings and to grasp meanings which the other children in the class have had explained or clarified earlier in their experiences.

The procedures used by a second-grade teacher indicate that she has the same view of her role. She reported as follows:

> If the slow children are not all in the same group the teacher has more time for each of them since the faster readers require less attention and can occasionally help the slow ones. However, other reasons are valid for eliminating ability groups. One purpose is to remove the stigma attached to a child for being in the "slow group." Another is that home pressure is often placed upon children who are not in the "top" group. Relieving this pressure is frequently a big step toward better reading.

Similarly, in a third grade, the teacher's relations with individual children during the time of reading instruction encouraged and made possible desirable attitudes toward reading. She reported as follows:

> I sat at the reading table with eight or nine children who chose to read during their "free" time. I felt that a little longer with each child, listening to him read, discussing the story with him, sharing his pleasure, helping him develop better word attack and occasionally analyzing usage and punctuation was more valuable than everyday checks.

In the upper grades, too, effective child-teacher relationships are furthered through self-selection in reading. The teacher's role is much the same as it is in providing for individual progress. An eighth grade teacher describes his procedures in the following way:

> We schedule time to read self-selected material two or three times a week and offer encouragement to "have your book available in case you finish other work early and have a desire to read."

Generally, reading is silent reading. Eighth graders like to get 'lost' in their books. However, it is necessary to do oral reading and I handle this in two ways. Sometimes I have a friendly, informal chat with the person at the library table. During the discussion of the book the pupil is reading I have him find a favorite passage or paragraph to read orally, softly so as not to disturb some of the 'lost' ones. At other times I bring together six or seven who have finished or almost finished their books. The children in this group share their ideas, reactions, and parts of stories. The boys and girls make recommendations as to who else in the class might enjoy the book. Individuals then read orally a part they found interesting, funny, beautiful, or that most clearly shows the 'sound' of the author's style.

BUILDING SKILLS IS PART OF THE PROCESS

Something about the word "self-selection" may suggest relaxing of the teacher's responsibility and concern for the systematic development of reading skills. Actually this idea is far from the truth. The same methods are used in teaching word recognition, word attack, and comprehension. The difference is that the development of these skills is guided with greater discrimination and success. Teachers who have previously followed someone else's plan for exposing children to the various reading techniques find themselves in new and stimulating situations. They make their own judgment of individual problems. They help children recognize their progress in reading skills, some of which is made through the process of reading itself if the practice is done with enjoyable and significant content that has special appeal to the child.

FURTHER DETAILS ABOUT TEACHING READING SKILLS

A purpose of reading instruction is to help children build a variety of reading skills. It is wasteful of a child's time for the teacher to teach the child specific approaches to reading problems which he has encountered and solved or which he is not yet ready to learn. The methods for teaching specific skills in word attack and comprehension are the same, whether all the children read from the same book or whether each child reads from a book he selected.

A second-grade teacher made the following comment regarding how she helps children with their reading problems:

As the child sits by me at the reading table I glance at his reading card. I can note where he is in his book and what difficulty he is meeting. If he is ready for more work with word endings, word attack, or phonics, help is given. Words that sound alike but have different beginning consonants may be the next approach for this child, or perhaps the child is showing readiness for silent reading. As I work and talk with a child, I make notes of his progress on his individual card.

A third-grade teacher emphasized that word attack skills may best be isolated for special attention when words are already out of context as in working on spelling lists. She reported her work as follows:

I did much with word attack skills in connection with spelling and saw a carry-over into reading. We made class booklets of long vowels, short vowels, compound words, phrases, and consonant blends. These were found in the book the child was reading.

Many teachers found that they increased their own understanding of a child's mental processes when he met a difficulty in reading. Their comments underscore the teacher's need to perceive the process of reading more in relation to a child's psychological processes than in relation to the logical steps into which reading skills may be analyzed and arranged. The teacher, of course, needs understanding of both the psychological and logical aspects of the reading process. Sometimes the teacher encourages a child to tell how he solved a problem, as in word recognition. This helps the teacher to see more clearly what went on in the child's mind. An example of this procedure follows:

A teacher looked over the page a child was reading for what she thought to be the most difficult word. She selected "command" and asked the child if he knew the word. The child knew. The teacher asked the child if he had read the word before and he said that he hadn't. The teacher then asked the child how he knew the word was "command." The child said that he knew "commandment" and that helped him to know "command." The child was then asked what the word meant. He gave this explanation, "Well, it would be like the king ordered you to do something."

Solving problems or making decisions like this by the children often go on so quickly and smoothly in the process of reading that the teacher need not, and indeed could not, follow all of them. To be aware of something of the nature of the intellectual process and to develop ways of tuning in on it when children have difficulties is the role of the teacher.

Introducing reading experiences through individually dictated stories in the first grade makes it possible to compile a list of the words used by the children and to note the frequency with which the words are used. This list reassures the teacher that the words commonly encountered in reading occur frequently in the children's own stories. The teacher may use the words in the list when he writes stories for the children. A partial list of the words, other than nouns, that one first grade teacher developed from work done during the first six weeks of school follows:

a	—23 times		love	—12 times
am	—18 times		like	— 7 times
are	—18 times		my	—19 times
at	— 7 times		on	—11 times
go	— 7 times		the	—58 times
going	—21 times		their	— 5 times
I	—39 times		to	—28 times
is	—51 times		this	—16 times
it	— 7 times		we	—17 times

The total list contained 192 words, 67 of which were nouns. These children, who moved into reading through experience charts and individually dictated stories, were introduced to pre-primers from a supply of 30 to 50 from which they might choose. The teacher added more books as the children gained in ability to read.

Primary teachers who individualized reading through self-selection of books reported satisfactory progress in skills as follows:

In this type of program good silent reading habits are learned early. The whole process makes a child much more of an independent reader. He discovers that all printed words can be read and that reading isn't just doing an assignment in a book read by all the children and that they must all stop at a definite time and place regardless of interest until the next reading period. These children have discovered that they can read and that learning to read is fun. It is a real thrill to the teacher when some child picks up a new book and exclaims, "I can read it!"

I have found it a valuable aid to write on small slips of heavy paper the words from his reading a child needs to learn and add to his sight vocabulary. I give these to the child in an envelope with his name on it and encourage him to study them in his spare moments. Most children enjoy doing this and take pride in learning as many words as they are able. Of course the child must help in selecting the words for study and understand their usefulness in his current reading or the drill has little meaning.

A very good reader may wish to read "Peanuts the Pony." The story may very well be too easy for him. But every child needs to read some material that he can read with ease.

In the middle grades, also, the teacher-pupil conference provides opportunity for the child and teacher to understand and appreciate one another's contribution to the development of facility and pleasure in reading. The child has the teacher's personal attention for a few minutes. This makes him feel worth while and that he has an important place in the group. The teacher, with her record at hand, is able to follow up previous conferences and explore new ideas with the child.

During part of the reading time the teacher has no conferences. As the children read their chosen books, the teacher moves about the room to help each child with his problems regardless of whether they involve word attack drills, meaning, pronunciation, or some other phase of reading.

In the upper grades, the same kind of planning for reading development suggested for primary and middle grades helps pupils build favorable attitudes and grow in good taste and appreciation, and encourages initiative in attacking problems in reading. An eighth grade teacher made the following report:

> Children who have problems learn that "reading" does not mean criticism and correction all the time. To be able to sit down and read a book of one's own choice is a satisfying experience. In individual conference time, the reading experience is extended as problems are discussed and made manageable.

Some children need the teacher's help to see a book through to completion. Once a child gets a taste of following a story all the way to the end, his sense of accomplishment may be the key to greater concentration and more interest in reading.

In discussing books with individuals or with the group, discrimination and appreciation are gradually built. Children learn from (1) discovering the difference between well and poorly written materials; (2) comparing the styles of authors; (3) comparing the ease of reading of one book with the difficulty of another; (4) learning to interpret paragraph, sentence, or poetry structure; (5) talking about the use of metaphors and similes; and (6) inferring character of an individual from his reactions discussing problem-situations.

The skills involved in using references in connection with seeking particular kinds of information become matters of everyday use as children learn the arrangement of a library, use the card file, and become acquainted with the different ways of finding information on a subject.

KEEPING RECORDS

Record keeping evolves as a necessary part of the individualizing process. Each teacher develops procedures for recording that best suit his ways of working. Many teachers who reported their experiences in record keeping emphasized that the notes made or referred to during teacher-pupil conference should be open to the children.

When a child knows what the teacher writes about him and is made a full partner in evaluating his progress and problems in reading, he is enabled to work with purpose and to assume his share of responsibility. Even primary children may be involved to a limited extent in participating in the record keeping. Children's questions concerning the records should always be answered so that the children will understand why they are kept and how they are used to help them.

Most teachers reported the use of 5x8 file cards as being desirable for use in keeping records. Several kinds of information may be kept on one card or several cards may be clipped together to provide the space required. Some teachers prefer a bound notebook. These offer a double-page spread which the teacher may divide into sections to systematize his observations and individual planning with each child.

Whatever the form of the record, the information needs to be systematically and regularly entered. The date of each entry is recorded. The titles of stories and books read are recorded. Specific problems that the child is endeavoring to solve are noted. Evidences are recorded of the child's growing powers in comprehension and critical thinking and of his growth in appreciation of good writing and artistic illustrations.

The teacher keeps records at hand for easy reference at times other than teacher-pupil conference time to recall data, to use in planning changes in reading materials, and to use in parent-child-teacher conferences.

One first-grade teacher who worked with every child for a few minutes every day kept a record of the books read and of the pages that she heard each child read orally. She asked questions about the other material the child read to check on his comprehension. The following notes from Candy's record show how the teacher did this part of her work:

Candy   *Age 6-6*

Under the Roof: Started 1/29, pp. 7–12. 1/30, pp. 24–28. 1/31, pp. 40–41. 2/3, pp. 51–55. 2/4, pp. 65–68. No problems. 2/7, Took the book home. Enjoyed this very much. Tells everyone the stories.

The Very Little Girl: 2/7, started and finished. Read aloud to group. Smooth.

Stories about Linda and Lee: started 2/10, pp. 48–53. 2/11, pp. 54–57. 2/13, has temperature. 2/14, pp. 79–81—Finished. Needs something harder.

Fun for Dick and Jane: started 2/17, finished 2/18. She made no comment.

The Cat in the Hat: 2/19 finished. Begs to read.

A teacher of a combination third and fourth grade used the following method in keeping records of the children's reading program. Each child helped complete the record and was free to look at it any time.

Name: *Jane*

Date	*Title*	*What We Did*	*Check the Skills*
9/30	*Lucky Pierre*	On p. 46, read aloud, finished chapter, discussed Pierre's punishment.	Discussed pronunciation. Reviewed *prefix* and *suffix*.

Comprehension:
    Story sequence.
    Projected possible outcomes.
    Summarized the chapter.

The teacher used the back of the card to note extra help needed and to record ways the child reported his reading to the class.

Children in the middle and upper grades usually become partners in the record-keeping. The teacher's notes are then directed to the child instead of recorded as observations about him. This is one of the ways in which children come to understand the teacher's role as guide. A page from the booklet of Don, a fifth grader, follows:

Title	Author	Date begun	Date ended	Class report
The Wright Brothers	Quentin Reynolds	January 15	January 19	Dramatized a portion
Our Trip into Space	Acceleration vehicle	January 19	January 24	Painting
Robinson Crusoe	Daniel Defoe	January 24	January 28	Read parts to class

Teacher's Comment

You are reading smoothly now. You summarized clearly, telling just the main points about the book.

Answered well some questions on content. Read aloud from p. 31. Quite good word attack on difficult words.

You told the story well. The class was interested. Words to review: *provisions, clefts, extremely.*

Teachers also used forms similar to the ones appearing on the next page for keeping records of children's reading. The first, "Self-selection Reading Record," was mimeographed on 8½ x 11" pages for use in a loose-leaf notebook. A separate page was provided for each child. A page of the type appearing on the form in the middle of the next page was attached to each child's record and the information was recorded to make sure the pupil's reading was varied.

Some teachers in the upper grades prefer a record on an individual file card for each book read by a child. Such a record is shown on the form appearing on the bottom of the next page. These cards may be placed in a central file to which the girls and boys have free access or they may be kept in a separate file.

SELF-SELECTION READING RECORD
(for teacher use)

Student's name _____

Grade	Reading vocabulary	Reading comprehension	INTERESTS		

TITLES OF BOOKS READ	Date checked	Page number	Progress in reading (anecdotal data)
1.			
2.			

Boys, girls, and grown-ups as well need to read different kinds of books so that their information will be well-balanced.

Animal Stories	*Classics*
_____	_____
_____	_____
Biographical	*Legends and Myths*
_____	_____
_____	_____
Fiction	*Fairy Tales*
_____	_____
_____	_____

Name of Student _____

Date started book _____

Date finished book _____

Where obtained _____

Bibliographical data:

Brief résumé, comments, or reactions:

When and where do you read besides during actual school time?

Discussion of the variety of topics in books helps children to become acquainted with subject matter that is new to them. It also helps children vary their reading and thus get a balanced fare. Except for children whose special needs for a time take them repeatedly to a certain kind of book, most children broaden their range of reading when many books are available for self-selection.

Teachers use different ways to help children get pictures of their reading. A sixth grade devised the following form [3] which was mimeographed and provided for each child to keep a record of the books he had read and to develop a picture of the comprehensiveness of his reading.

Directions
Give each book you read a number. Write the number of the book under each of the categories of the chart it might be placed in. No number should be placed in more than three different categories. Try to read books of different kinds so that you will have numbers in all the categories.

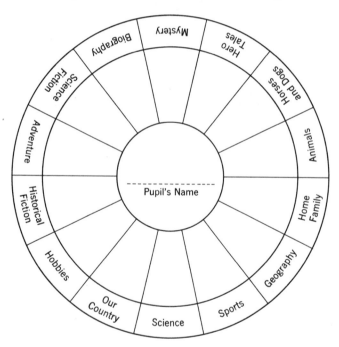

Use of the following forms does not diminish children's creative ways of expressing their ideas nor encourage them to write beyond

---

[3] Adapted from G. O. Simpson, "My Reading Design," *Reading Circle*, 1946 (North Manchester, Indiana).

what they really have to say. The information reported makes this fact apparent.

---

1. Harry E.   2. Jan. 13, 1958
                                                Jan. 15, 1958
                                                School Library

3. Freeman, Ira M. *All About the Atom.* New York: Random House, Inc., 1955 (140 pages).

4. If you could magnify a single grain of table salt until it became as big as the Empire State Building, each atom in it would look only as big as the grain that you started with!
    These and many more examples and facts about the atom are in this book.

---

1. Ervin N.   2. Jan. 5, 1958
                                                Jan. 8, 1958

3. Campbell, J. W. *Black Star Passes.* Fantasy Press (278 pages).

4. Gee Whiz! Invaders from space. This old theme is too corny. The book should be in Circular File.

---

1. Sherri G.   2. Feb. 14, 1958
                                                Feb. 17, 1958

3. Chandler, Ruth Forbes. *Two Many Promises.* New York: Abelard-Schuman, 1956 (216 pages).

4. It was either the farm or reform school so Niki took the farm. Anyway he liked animals so it wouldn't be bad at all.

5. Most of the book was read at home.

ACCEPTING MANY WAYS OF REPORTING READING

During pupil-teacher conferences children are free to express their reactions to what they have read. They also have opportunity to make comments about the books on the records they keep. Occasionally a child's enjoyment of something he has read needs to be extended through sharing his experience with other children. This experience gives him a feeling of elation and also opportunity to develop language and social skills. He learns effective ways of interesting others in his book, in deciding what to say, in practicing for reading aloud, in speaking before a small group or the whole class, in discussing ideas and answering questions, and in taking part in dramatization. If his report is written, he learns to express himself rather than to repeat in detail the action in the story.

Books may be shared in many ways. Boys and girls are ingenious and, if given the opportunity, will use their imaginations in developing their own ways of reporting. One fifth-grade group used the following ways to share with each other what they had read:

Painting a picture or a series of pictures to illustrate a book
Making booklets: may vary from two pages to four or five to contain illustrations and comments
Writing a comparable story of a personal experience
Depicting a scene in a diorama or "peep box"
Dramatizing
Giving a puppet show: paper bag, stick, string, and others
Making the figures and telling the story using a flannelboard
Painting a mural or picture roll
Making a poster for display case or library
Modeling with clay
Creating a mobile
Giving a radio or television program
Reading favorite poems or passages from stories
Telling part of the story
Writing a book review for the class bulletin board or school paper
Giving personal reactions to one of the characters
Writing a different ending to the story
Holding round table discussions or panels
Creating a book jacket for the story
Acting the role of the author in discussing the book
Fingerpainting
Making maps of areas told about in the story
Performing a scientific experiment
Drawing a diagram and explaining to a group

The teacher who worked with this group made the statement that follows:

Every two weeks we have an "audience day" in which the entire 50 minutes is given over to some form of oral reporting. The children seem to enjoy this and look forward to it. This may seem like a very simple process, but, I assure you, it is one that really motivates children to read.

A seventh-grade teacher also found children responsive to the appeal of books presented in an interesting way. He made the following statement regarding this discovery!

Our seventh-grade class endeavored to make books come alive in several ways to create more interest in reading. One was by means of dioramas. One group that had enjoyed reading about Stanley and Livingstone got a large piece of styrofoam and fastened it to a piece of plywood the same size. They painted the styrofoam for their earth; then they assembled on it trees, huts, animals, Stanley and Livingstone shaking hands, natives at various activities, and even birds in the trees. They made people and animals of pipe cleaners with bits of cloth for clothing. Many materials were used to make articles such as drums, rocks, fruits, and vegetables. The group showed much ingenuity in developing the diorama. Other dioramas, some in open-front boxes, some on boards or cardboard, were made to show incidents in *Tom Sawyer, Huckleberry Finn, Indian Paint,* and *Little Women.*

Reading has truly been enjoyed by this class. Never have I seen such interest as they have shown in the "Real People" books. Pictures and skits about some of these books led the class to reading and more reading. We can talk quite fluently about Queen Elizabeth, Peter the Great, Florence Nightingale, Julius Caesar, and Leonardo da Vinci. This has vitalized our social studies as we meet these friends in the lands about which we are studying.

In the first grade a child's enthusiasm for a good book is spontaneous. When he is reading something that is funny to him, a first grader simply laughs aloud and shares what he has read with the class. The child does not need to feel that he must report formally. Many shy children would not want to read if they had to stand up before the class and tell what they had read.

EVALUATING OUTCOMES OF SELF-SELECTION PROCEDURES

All the teachers who provided materials for this report had voluntarily adopted the self-selection procedures for use in their classrooms. They reported that they had done so in order to secure values in addition to merely acquiring reading skills. Their means of evaluating, therefore, were of several kinds. They used standardized instruments to measure growth in vocabulary, comprehension, word-study skills, and oral reading facility.

An example of test data from a fourth grade class shows how carefully the teacher tried to discover whether children gained in reading power in the freer procedures of self-selection. (See Table 1.) This class engaged in self-selection from the first day of school and at no time had ability groupings. The language scores for the class also soared. The class rose from the 15th percentile to 45th percentile in spelling.

Teachers expressed the opinion that many other measurable skills which developed in the individualized reading processes were not measured. From their observations they noted that children were growing in the following ways: [4]

---

[4] See also May Lazar and Wayne Wrightstone, "Effective Classroom Practices in Individualized Reading" (New York: Bureau of Educational Research, Board of Education of the City of New York, May 1958) mimeographed.

TABLE 1. *Test Data From Fourth Grade Class Showing Comparison of October Comprehension and Vocabulary by Grade Level With May Comprehension and Vocabulary*

	October Comprehension	Vocabulary	May Comprehension	Vocabulary
Boys				
A	6.0	4.0	moved	
B	1.7	2.1	6.4	5.5
C	6.0	6.0	8.0	9.1
D	3.6	3.1	3.0	3.9
E	4.8	5.7	8.7	7.7
F	3.6	3.0	4.2	5.2
G	1.9	2.1	Placed in Pt. I program	
H	2.7	4.0	4.3	3.6
I	3.1	2.7	7.2	5.6
J	3.3	4.2	6.6	6.8
K	2.5	2.3	3.9	4.6
L	5.1	5.1	moved	
M	5.1	6.0	3.9	3.8
N	3.9	4.5	3.9	4.5
O	6.0	6.0	9.3	8.4
P	4.8	5.1	9.6	9.1
Girls				
A	5.1	5.4	8.5	6.6
B	4.5	4.2	6.4	4.6
C	4.8	5.7	5.3	7.0
D	3.1	2.9	4.8	4.4
E	2.7	3.4	4.5	5.3
F	4.2	3.3	5.3	4.3
G	3.4	4.5	4.8	6.6
H	4.2	3.5	5.6	4.4
I	4.2	6.0	5.3	6.0
J	2.8	3.2	3.9	3.5
K	2.3	2.1	3.1	2.7
L	6.0	4.0	6.4	6.6
M	3.6	5.1	8.7	7.0
N	4.2	3.1	4.3	3.5
O	5.1	6.0	7.0	7.5
P	3.6	3.7	6.4	5.3

The ability to sustain interest over a long period of time on one piece of material

The ability to organize one's thinking in order to recapitulate the ideas in the material read

The ability to apply knowledge of word attack and other skills in the actual reading situation

The ability to seek out the relevant reference in relation to problem solving

The teacher also noted growth in some less tangible aspects of reading behavior, such as the following:

Improved attitude toward reading and increased interest in reading—broadening horizon of interests

Ability to use reading as a base for integrating all areas of the curriculum

Development of taste, discrimination, and judgment
Ability to verbalize about reading
Greater development of independent critical thinking
Increased stature in group situations
Development as a person through reading for personal purposes

Some of the indications of the less tangible kinds of growth were noted as children did the following:

Made choices of books over a period of time
Wrote creatively as a result of reading
Gave oral and written reports and reviews
Worked creatively in painting, drawing, construction, puppetry, dramatization, resulting from reading
Reacted orally to stories and poetry read by the teacher and other children
Appreciated and reacted to humor, both broad and subtle
Used the dictionary and other suitable aids—how, why, when

Most of the teachers asked children to tell how self-selection procedures helped them. Certain of their comments follow:

I read more with selective reading, and I try harder. I think I spell better, too, don't you? (Fifth grade)
I have learned a lot of new words I've never seen before. (Seventh grade)
A while ago I could read only fourth and fifth grade books. I like to go to the library and check out my own books. (Eighth grade)
I like reading books of my own choice. I can read thick books or thin books. Now I read stories I wanted to read before and couldn't. (Seventh grade)
I hope we can have self-selection reading next year. I think it has helped me read better, write better, and do better in school. (Eighth grade)
I like self-selection because you can stick to one story until you have finished it for yourself. (Seventh grade)
Instead of reading only when you called on me, I can now read the whole book myself. (Sixth grade)
I started to read when I was six years old. I read the names of cars and license plates on the way to California from Canada. I like self-selection because I can read different books, especially about science. (Seventh grade)
When I read in a group I didn't read much. Now I like to read. (Sixth grade)
I like it because you don't have to read a certain book. You can go to the library and look until you find a book you really like. (Eighth grade)
You have been like a mother to me and I have liked being in your room, especially reading. (Second grade)
I won't be in your room next year but if you get any more interesting books, be sure to let me know. Your books are keen! (Third grade)
I didn't like to sit in a group and stay on the same page while someone was reading out loud. (Fourth grade)

The following comments written by the teachers during their conferences with pupils indicate that children evaluate books and social situations fairly accurately:

There are lots of new words in here. It's a little hard. Maybe I'll save it awhile. (First grade)

I didn't think I'd be able to read this much when I couldn't read any last year. (Second grade)

This is a little hard right now. I'll just remember it and read it when I know a few more words. (First grade)

Sometimes I get tired of reading fat books. Then I read some thin ones. (Fourth grade)

I'll bet that house cost a lot of money. This is like *The Little House*. It became a home when a family moved in. (Third grade)

Parents' reactions were generally favorable. Many expressed amazement at the interest and progress of their children.

A mother who was concerned over having to move came to see what books we used. I explained to her that we used many books and that we would be able to get the book the child had been reading if it were not here. The child made a very quick adjustment, though shy. At the end of the week he said, "Boy, do I like this way to read! I can read all I want to." The mother assured me she felt John's easy adjustment was due to the kind of reading program. (First grade)

The teachers noted that certain kinds of difficulties were diminished when children were not regularly grouped for reading. Typical statements made by the teachers regarding this development follow:

We had an extremely high illness record this year. With self-selection in reading there seemed to be less pressure felt by both the children and the teacher when a child returned after an absence. After an illness, a child has one strike against him physically and, when his group has moved off and left him, his return is doubly difficult. With individualizing reading, he picks up where he stopped, gets special help without being made conspicuous in a group, and in most cases quickly moves forward. (First grade)

In a first grade room, 10 out of 28 pupils were well into second grade material. Many were writing creative stories, with the teacher giving them the words asked for. They had a reading and spelling vocabulary far beyond any "grouped reading" in my experience. (First grade)

Little boys who often are not interested during "groups," frequently read through two reading periods completely unaware of what is going on around them. (Second grade)

I never hear a complaint that it is reading period. (Eighth grade)

I have opportunities all day long to develop reading skills through science, social studies materials, arithmetic, and the *Weekly Reader*.

The children seem to understand and remember they have help when they need it.

I hope to be able to continue this way of working as I have seen what a difference it can make in a child's growth in reading.

These comments by teachers who have been working "at the grass roots" in planning and developing procedures in guiding children into reading show the professional attitudes and understandings of the teachers. Teachers know they do not have the answers for all problems that arise in the classroom. They are constantly asking questions in their quest for correct answers. They want to know more about the children, more about children's reading materials, more about the nature of reading skills, and more about how children can be helped to become proficient in using reading skills.

FURTHER RESEARCH AND EXPERIMENTATION NEEDED

Individualizing reading procedures when carried out systematically seem to hold much promise. The reports of children, teachers, supervisors, principals, and parents regarding these procedures are generally enthusiastic and contain evidence of growing insight on the part of all of them regarding the problems involved in guiding children's growing powers to attach meaning to and to gain satisfaction from reading materials.

Teachers discover some answers for themselves. Problems, questions, and cautions mentioned by teachers who have worked with self-selection in reading suggest that continual evaluation and adjustment of their teaching procedures are necessary. Because teachers have a class of children for the whole year, they emphasize working out systematic procedures that fit the children in the group and help the children to make progress in reading. The problems raised by teachers clustered about (1) reading materials; (2) time; (3) evaluation; and (4) finding opportunities to discuss procedures and questions with other teachers and supervisors.

The teachers' cautions were largely concerned with trying to change procedures in teaching reading before the teacher understands how the changes cause the teacher's role to change. Obviously, some of the very techniques which seem to stifle growth in reading group organizations may be carried over to individualizing reading if a teacher does not really understand.

It was apparent from the teachers' reports that they sensed their own needs for information, study, and change in their way of working. Certain of the statements they made follow:

We are merely scratching the surface of possibilities as yet in this program.

1. Not working enough on critical thinking is a weakness in my program.
2. I need help in giving a child or a small group the kind of help needed for a particular deficiency.

3. I need to develop better ways to discuss a book with a child.

The following are some questions raised by the teachers on one staff that held regular meetings on problems and procedures in self-selection that point up this concern:

1. Will interest in reading developed in the first grade stay with them?
2. Would it be possible to follow some of these children through from year to year?
3. How can we develop new standardized ways to evaluate results?
4. How can we be sure children are gaining vocabulary?
5. Is individualizing children's instruction the real reason teachers are having greater success in teaching slow learners to read?

Enough is now known about the way children grow and learn to lead to significant changes in classroom organization and teaching procedures.[5] Changes in the right direction are those which grow out of what we already know about the uniqueness of the individual, the individual differences among children, the importance of purpose and motivation, and the need for those conditions of living that foster good mental health.

READING ABILITIES INVOLVED IN THE CONTENT SUBJECTS [*]

Arthur I. Gates

When we realize that the content subject activities radiate into all phases of life and include newspapers, magazines, catalogues, bulletin boards, advertisements, technical materials, and many other items, we observe that a great many techniques are employed. The first general question is whether there are dozens or even hundreds of different specific techniques, each of which must be acquired by specific practice, or a smaller number which, when used in different combinations

---

[5] See Earl C. Kelley and Marie I. Rasey, *Education and the Nature of Man* (New York: Harper & Row, 1952); and Association for Supervision and Curriculum Development, *Growing Up in an Anxious Age* (Washington, D. C.: National Education Association), 1952.

[*] Paper presented before the New England Reading Association (October 2, 1952).

and permutations, make up the total array. I now think that a relatively small number of basal techniques or groups of techniques form the backbone of the reading process; that in one form or another they may be adapted to innumerable different purposes; that they comprise the most important equipment for economical and effective learning in the content subjects; and that the teacher of each content subject should know them and show the pupil how to use them in his subject.

SOME ILLUSTRATIONS OF BASAL TECHNIQUES

Let me begin by illustrating a basal type of technique. One was revealed by a girl, who from the first grade onward had been regarded not only as a first class student but a very fine reader. At the time of the examination she was the best student in a group of about one hundred twenty-five in the junior class of a high school. As far as I am aware, no question about her reading ability had been raised in school. Her parents, however, noticed that she spent so much time in study that she had very little left for other activities. They raised the question whether her slowness was due to slow learning, or learning wisely but too well, or, possibly, to poor reading.

An examination showed that this young lady read everything at the rate of about 130 words per minute. She read with very full understanding and in no other way. She thought it was improper—in fact, unethical—to skim or to jump over the material. She said, "How can I say I have read a selection when really I haven't?" In fact, she regarded as one of her special virtues her habit of never faking her reading.

Whenever she read, she really read. Her reading was in fact confined almost exclusively to her school books. She lacked some of the basal techniques or combinations of them required to skim over material, hit the high points, get the gist of the matter, survey the thing as a whole. She lacked some other reading skills which I shall mention later. Although, as this case illustrates, these techniques were not absolutely indispensable for achieving high scholarship in the various subjects, the art of rapid reading is essential for many activities, including the enjoyment of literature, and a great miscellany of light reading, and a lack of it is a serious handicap in school. This girl's high scholarship was due to a combination of exceptional intelligence and hard work. She was a very inefficient learner. I could report many other cases in which pupils with less scholastic aptitude and diligence than this girl possessed failed or were seriously retarded in their school work.

PROOFREADING A SPECIALIZED GROUP OF TECHNIQUES

Let me give another illustration of a specialized technique. There are, as you know, experts in proofreading, persons who can read material with more or less comprehension, and with almost unfailing ability to detect misspellings, improper punctuation, wrong type, wrong spacing, wrong symbols. Many of us who read primarily for the thought rarely notice the defects in composition and find it very difficult to do a good proofreading. The art of proofreading, I think, represents a very special combination of techniques—techniques which are involved in many other combinations in other forms of reading. Such specialized complexes of techniques would be difficult or impossible to acquire readily and effectively, were not certain basal techniques in hand in good form.

Let me now describe the basal techniques as I see them.

BASAL TECHNIQUES IN WORD ANALYSIS

A first technique is that involved in working out the recognition and pronunciation of words. I shall use this to illustrate my general thesis. Skill in word analysis is, of course, taught in the reading course from the first grade onward.

When a child reaches the intermediate grades he should have mastered a general method of attack which he employs in reading English words in all his school subjects and elsewhere. Typically, the pupil first views the word as a whole and tries to recognize it at a glance. If he is unsuccessful he then glances over the word, always from left to right, in an effort to spot familiar, especially large, components of the word, which will suggest the whole to him. If he makes one kind of guess, based on one kind of division, and fails to get the word, he tries again, attempting another division. He will vary the translation of the visual components into sounds, first giving, for example, the short sound to the vowel, and then a long sound. He may make two or three tries, using larger parts. This process failing, he will make a more detailed analysis of the word and try to find syllables or phonetic elements, or in some cases single letters, as the basis of getting a grasp on the word as a whole. He has several varieties of ways of attacking a word and he shifts readily from one to another.

This is a general type of attack which can be transferred to and employed upon almost any kind of item, whether the characters be Chinese, the symbols and formulae in mathematics, or the diagrams in statistics. There will always need to be a certain modification, certain differences in what the pupil looks for and exactly how he looks, but the general procedure of first trying to get the item as a whole, then moving in the direction of detailed analysis, varying the interpretation, varying the viewpoint, until telltale clues are found, is one which applies in many of these areas.

In most of the content subjects and in most areas of activity as well, the instructor should help the child acquire some of the special devices proved to be most helpful for achieving recognition of the item as a whole. There are different orders of procedure, different items to look for, different telltale features. In each subject, then, specific instructions and help are needed to modify and adapt the general technique which the good reader learns in his basal reading program.

TECHNIQUES IN DERIVING WORD MEANINGS

A second skill is that of deriving the meanings of words in context, and sometimes in isolation, combined with the ability to recognize cases of uncertain meaning, and the habit of stopping and looking in a dictionary, or otherwise finding the meaning when necessary. These are skills which we now attempt to teach in a good modern program in reading and exercise in all the content areas in the elementary school. I think that the general pattern can be transferred to material other than words. The child who is a "word-jumper," who is satisfied with very vague meanings, and who is disinclined to stop and review the context to try to figure out the more exact meaning of a word in his reading, or who is unlikely to look up the meaning of a word in a dictionary, is the child who is likely to work over the formula in algebra carelessly, content to get it in a vague way, and disinclined to take the trouble to make sure of all its details. In mathematics and physics vagueness probably leads to even more trouble than in most instances in reading. Here the instructor will have to encourage the child to be even more thorough, more exacting, more careful, than he has habitually been in reading.

RANGE OF SPEED

A basal skill of great importance in the content subjects is the ability to read with the mind directed to the thought at speeds ranging from slow rates, as, for example, the count of the number of words per minute, ranges from one hundred through various rates to the level of very rapid skimming, a procedure so rapid it becomes essentially meaningless. It is possible for children in the intermediate grades to learn to skim more than twelve hundred words per minute with a degree of comprehension adequate for certain purposes.

Investigations of the reading of children in the various grades have revealed the fact that many of them tend to fix a habit of reading at a particular speed in the third or fourth grade and thereafter to read at substantially that speed whatever the purpose and whatever the character of the content may be. The high school girl I mentioned earlier illustrated habitually slow, thorough reading. Many older adults who learned to read when exact pronunciation, careful and effective oral reading were required, when the subject matter was compact and difficult, and when the school and the home library contained relatively little light reading, habituated a slow speed. There are others who adopt an intermediate speed, in the neighborhood of two hundred or two hundred fifty words per minute. Still others consistently read at a more rapid speed, at four or five hundred words a minute or even faster.

The rapid readers tend to be pupils who in early years did a large amount of independent reading of light literary material. In general, they excell in the literary field. Their difficulty emerges when they are asked to read the heavier concentrated material, as in science, mathematics, handbooks, manuals, and the like. Here they are unable properly to slow down and adapt a more analytical procedure. The result is that their understanding tends to be superficial. The slow readers, on the other hand, other things being equal, tend to show relatively high accomplishment in the work of mathematics, science, and the heavier sorts of historical and other informative materials. They are typically pupils who do relatively little free reading of literature. The pupil who reads at average speed tends to be fair in both extreme types of work, but unless he is unusually bright, not outstandingly successful in either. The reading of literature is so slow and labored that it lacks the full flavor enjoyed by the fast reader. Inability to skim large amounts of material is a serious handicap in subjects in which extensive reading is required, and inability to slow the pace down for thorough analytical work is a handicap in the sciences, mathematics, and other heavy matter.

No one speed of reading serves all the purposes of the world at large or the content subjects in school. A most important basal skill is the ability to modify the pace from very slow careful reading up to an exceedingly rapid skipping and skimming. These skills we now attempt to teach in the basal reading program. Adaptability in speed is most important for work in the content subjects, and it should not be assumed that the basal reading course will teach the child all the tricks of making a nice adaptation to the needs of every type of material and purpose found in them. In mathematics and science or the social studies, in the reading of poetry, and in other areas the teacher should be alert to demonstrate the optimum skill, the variety of attacks that may be employed, where skimming is advisable, and where slow or moderate speed is optimum.

ACCURACY AND FULLNESS OF COMPREHENSION

In commenting on the rate of reading, I have unavoidably been referring to another basal technique, namely, learning to read with different degrees of thoroughness or accuracy or fullness of comprehension. This may properly vary from merely getting the high points or getting a sense of what a selection is all about, at the one extreme, to the very thorough reading with a full appreciation of every detail, as in the reading of a definition or the directions to operate a gadget, or the description of a diagram. Here again, ability to vary the fullness and accuracy of comprehension is something that must be learned. Pupils must acquire the skill and habit of trying to suit the thoroughness of comprehension to the demands of the situation.

A good basal program in the present-day schools provides much experience in varying the degree of thoroughness of comprehension. Work with modern preparatory books or workbooks, reading in special material, such as catalogues, newspapers, brochures, advertisements, diagrams, directions, and the like, provides realistic materials for a great range of thoroughness. The simple self-testing and self-diagnostic devices included in many of the basic reading materials are of great value for this purpose. One of the reasons many children comprehend at a fixed level, either very superficially, or intermediately, or very thoroughly, is that they are unable to appraise how thoroughly they have comprehended or they are not clear just how complete an understanding of the content is required for different purposes. By offering carefully devised exercises, questions, or discussions to pupils to test their comprehension after their reading, and then to compare the thoroughness and accuracy of their understanding with those of other children or with standards of some sort, we can help them appraise their habits and acquire new ones.

Much in the way of a basal technique in varying the fullness and accuracy of comprehension may, therefore, be taught and usually is taught in the basal reading program. Much of this, sometimes a very generalized approach and technique, will be carried over to the content subjects, but this is not sufficient. Mathematics sometimes requires a more thorough and somewhat different type of comprehension from that which children are accustomed to exercising in the materials found in their other school work and out of school activities. The content subjects present a great range of types and degrees of expectation in the way of thoroughness of understanding and accuracy of detail. The teacher of the content subjects is the best person to set up standards, to give the pupils hints, to help them appraise the character of their understanding, and to direct practice to achieve a more optimum level of comprehension. The content subjects, in fact, are ideal for developing proper types of comprehension.

REREADING AND RECALLING

The next important basal skill is that of recalling or trying to remember while reading. There is an important distinction between reading and rereading, on the one hand, and reading and recalling or adopting a policy in which one rereads when necessary and recalls when possible, on the other. The importance of this distinction was brought out in an experimental study conducted more than thirty years ago. It was found that there are many children in the intermediate grades and above who, while studying material, read it through from beginning to end, then proceed to read it through again in substantially the same way. There are other children, however, who glance over the material, selectively picking out phrases of sentences which suggest the content of paragraphs or several paragraphs, and then try to remember the substance, and if necessary some of the details of what is read. If they are unable to do so they proceed to read, but only as much as necessary. If they are uncertain of their recall, they may skim the material to check their memory. After a few perusals of this type the pupil's review consists chiefly in recall, reading only a few words or sentences here and there. The ability of these pupils to reproduce the material later was far superior to that of the pupils who were unable to break away from a slavish rereading, however rapidly or otherwise efficiently it may have been conducted.

The point is that one is able to recall ideas from a selection only to a limited extent without having actually practiced the activity of recall. Those who do so are the students who, other things being equal, can recall and reproduce at the time of the test or formal examination or informal discussion. Furthermore, they are on the whole persons who can think while they are reading, who can compare the ideas recalled with other ideas, or make a selection of the pertinent things, deciding which is important and which is relatively unimportant, and the like. Skill in recalling during reading is essential for learning to think while reading. The girl I mentioned earlier lacked this skill. She read, then recalled, then read again—never the two together.

This ability to combine reading and selective recall is one of the most important of all reading skills in the content subjects. It needs more attention than it usually gets. While much can be done in the basal reading course to develop it, it is important that the instructors in the content subjects give the children guidance in applying the art to their particular field. The content subjects are ideal for developing this type of ability. The exact nature of the procedure differs from one situation to another. Sometimes very rigid reading and rereading with attempt at full recall, with a long period of study of particularly important condensed portions, is necessary in mathematics, whereas a quite different procedure is often required in the reading of literature or history or geography. Moreover, in every subject, indeed in different parts of the same subject, variations in these techniques may be desirable.

THINKING WHILE READING

The next skill involves ability to think while reading. Here one may distinguish between reading or recall of the substance as it actually appears—mere reproduction—on the one hand, and on the other the kind of reading in which appraisal or evaluation or selection or judgment or comparison of the ideas takes place during the process. This is a subtle but important distinction. There are pupils of all ages whose reading is largely literal. It may be selective in the sense that they may not try to note and remember everything, but they are always engaged in direct recognition and faithful recall of what is offered. Some of these children acquire considerable skill in reproducing not merely all the details but also a summary or outline of the substance, but they still do little thinking beyond the accumulation of the ideas as they understood them. To think while reading, to evaluate, to judge what is important or unimportant, what is relevant or irrelevant, what is in harmony with an idea read in another book, is a technique that is somewhat difficult to acquire. It is difficult to teach it directly, but there are many things the teacher can do to help the student acquire it. Ability to skip and skim at various rates, and to recall what is not actually read, are prerequisite. These abilities free one's mind for thinking. Thinking may be encouraged by raising issues or explaining objectives before the reading is begun, and then by giving the pupils time to express themselves and to check up on their thinking after they have completed the reading.

Success in the content subjects depends greatly upon ability to read selectively and to think critically during the process of reading itself. How one thinks and for what purpose, to what end, of course, varies from one subject to another. Much can be done, and in good schools today a great deal *is* done, to help pupils acquire a general technique of reading beyond the page, comparing what they read with other things, selecting what is related to some issue. But the ideal procedures are somewhat specialized in different areas. The best technique for reading a problem in physics is somewhat different from that of reading critically a treatise on the Revolutionary War.

STRATEGY FOR ATTACKING AN ASSIGNMENT

The final basal technique is one which involves the development of strategies of attack on assignments as a whole. I have touched on this technique in discussing previous matters. For example, the ideal method of attack in history would depend somewhat on the length of the assignment. The best procedure of studying a highly compact, short chapter might be different from the best strategy for reading several chapters in each of several books for comparative purposes. In both these cases, the ideal attack would be different from that to adopt if one were reading theorems in geometry, definitions in grammar, compactly stated technical propositions in physics, or directions for operating a complicated machine. Still another approach might be taken if one were to survey several books for the purpose of picking up the information bearing on a particular topic.

By "strategy" I mean the method of attack at the first step, the second, the third, and so on. For example, in reading a long chapter in history, a good procedure in one case might be to skim the whole chapter as a first step, noting particularly the center and paragraph headings, the summaries interspersed through the context, the final summaries, illustrations, figures, and the like. In other cases a person might find it advisable to read the whole selection through very thoroughly and then proceed with the skim, skip, and recall process at different rates, or one child might prefer one, and another the other. In all the content fields the teacher should make a study of the different techniques which good learners use in studying different kinds of material or the same kind for different purposes.

Too often pupils have no variety in their approach. They have a simple, repetitive procedure, such as the read and reread activity. The teacher of the content subjects should demonstrate different strategies and induce the pupils to try them out in practice. Pupils can compare their techniques. If the teacher provides a good array of check-ups, tests, or discussion or other devices, a child can help himself decide which procedures are best for him. Obviously, the choice of the procedure depends somewhat on the time available, the pupil's familiarity with the material, the purpose of the reading, and other factors. In this area as in others, what the pupil needs is an array of strategies within his control, thus enabling him to find out which work most effectively and which work in one case better than in another. Pupils should understand that it takes practice to learn to use good strategy in the content subjects as it does in baseball or tennis.

SUMMARY CONCERNING BASAL TECHNIQUES

This completes my list of basal techniques. These are abilities which can be taught to a considerable degree in the program in reading in the elementary and high school. Give the pupil a good mastery of the skills of word analysis, the skill of deriving meanings from words in context, and the habit of looking up these meanings in dictionaries or other sources; give him the ability to read at different rates from one hundred words a minute to the skimming of materials covering say, at least twelve hundred words per minute; give him the ability to vary the fullness and accuracy of comprehension from practically complete absorption of all detail, at the one extreme, to a superficial grasp of the high points at the other; give him the ability to skip and skim sagaciously; give him especially the ability to combine reading and rereading with recall and recitation; give him skill to think selectively during the process of reading; give him knowledge of a few good general strategies of attack on various kinds of assignments, and you will equip the pupil to learn to do good work in all the content subjects. All these skills are basal. They are best developed by means of guidance in the basic reading course and in the content subjects as well. To meet the needs of all the content subjects they must be highly adaptable and flexible.

Learnings in the content subjects beyond those taught in reading. I do not mean, however, to give the impression that there is nothing more to learn. Beyond these basal skills there are many other things to learn, but primarily they are not new reading skills. Let me illustrate. I can read English and, to some extent, French and German but I cannot read Greek, Russian, or Chinese, or shorthand, or certain forms of mathematical materials. If I should undertake to read and learn effectively in these areas what would be left for me to master?

Learning the basal symbols. First of all, I must learn the basal symbols—the alphabet in Greek and Russian, and the symbols in shorthand and mathematics. Learning these symbols is more or less similar to first grade work with the alphabet, punctuation marks, and the like, but some instructions should be given at all levels in how to come to grips with the basal symbols of the subject. The number of such symbols in all the content subjects is great, however, and there has been a disposition, no doubt, to underestimate the amount of sheer work that is required to master them.

Learning the arrangement of symbols in wholes. Secondly, one who attempts to master a new field must learn to understand the arrangement of symbols into meaningful wholes and the typical orientation procedure required to deal with the wholes. For example, English, Hebrew, and Chinese words differ from one another in their structure and arrangement. A child who has learned the left-to-right orientation of English will be puzzled by Hebrew and Chinese. In mathematics the form of equations and the way one proceeds through them are new and the children must achieve familiarity with them. The inverted order in poetry is puzzling until children become accustomed to it. Here again, although six-year-old children do learn to read English, Hebrew, Chinese, and to handle other complex symbolic materials, the amount of learning required is considerable. A common error in teaching in the content subjects is to underestimate the amount of help and guidance that a pupil needs to get the hang of the different ways in which symbols are combined into more meaningful wholes in different subjects. While basal instruction in reading will help to some extent and give pupils some familiarity in the rigid requirements of such organizations, the major part of learning is specific to the particular subject.

Acquiring technical terms. When one goes into a new subject, one must also become familiar with the technical terms or expressions, the precise meanings which words and other symbols are given. Sometimes these are in conflict with everyday uses of the same words or symbols. Content subjects are very heavily loaded with technical words and expressions, which are often insufficiently explained, reviewed, and reintegrated, to enable the pupil to learn them fully by study of the text alone. Often difficulties in learning the subject are not really due to faulty basal reading habits as much as to the fact that the pupil is insufficiently acquainted with the technical meanings of the crucial terms.

Mastering general concepts and processes. A person taking up a new subject must acquire an understanding of many broader technical concepts: the notion of infinity, of Gestalten, of gravity, and the like. The tests of mastery in the content subjects often show superficiality and inadequacy in the pupil's understanding of the important concepts. Studies of disabilities in mathematics and physics have shown that often the trouble goes back to an inadequate or misleading idea of some of the basal concepts or processes, which block or misdirect future learning. Here again the teacher of the special subjects must realize that the basal concepts and processes are many, subtle, and difficult, and that a great deal is required that goes beyond mere reading techniques. The trouble often is not due to a faulty way of reading, but to inadequacies in what is given to be read. Additional help by means of diagrams, demonstrations, visual aids, discussions, experiments, as well as by better reading texts, is needed in the teaching of these subjects.

Clarifying the objectives of study. To do well in most of the content subjects, furthermore, it is necessary for the pupil to understand the nature of the assignment, the meaning of the problem, what he is to get out of his reading, how well and what he is to learn. To illustrate, if you merely give a pupil a selection and ask him to read it he will have no idea whether you want him merely to get a general temporary impression of it or to learn the main ideas, or all the details thoroughly for later recall, or whether you want him to proofread it for spelling or for punctuation, or to see what imagery it suggests, or merely to form a judgment as to whether it agrees or disagrees with the view you have previously presented. He cannot set up a good pattern of reading and learning unless he knows what the objective is. In all the content subjects the pupil needs help in understanding the objectives of the work. If he is reading poetry possibly you want him to try to sense the imagery of the selection, rather than the philosophic thought or the literary structure. If you assign him a piece of music you should tell him whether you want him merely to scan it to get some impression of the main theme or to look for certain details. The tremendous variety of purposes and problems in the content subjects, the indefiniteness of the child's understanding of the assignment, his uncertainty of what to do, are responsible for much inadequate learning, even in the case of pupils who have good technique both in reading and thinking.

General strategy of attack. Finally, a child must learn in each subject, indeed in different parts of many subjects, the various useful strategies of attack upon the material. I have already given a few illustrations of different approaches in reading. In every subject there are distinctive ones. It is too much to assume that, however good a reader a person may be in the field of literature, for example, he can without help hit on the best strategy for studying a particular subject assigned in all the content subjects. The teacher of each subject must know the various strategies, know how to demonstrate them, how to help the pupil understand them, how to help him appraise his own competence in using them, and how to encourage him to vary the attack in order to find out which one works well for him in each of many content areas. The strategy of attack must mainly be taught in each content subject. I believe this is a very important function of the teacher of each subject.

I realize that my emphasis on the importance of general strategy of attack may strike you as an approval of the "methods of study" approach, which achieved popularity a quarter of a century ago, but which proved to be less than fully satisfactory. The older "methods of study" approach has two faults. First, it was too largely a group of formal steps, a few tricks for all the trades. Secondly, and more important, the program failed to recognize that the general procedures were useless unless the pupil had the basal reading skills to make them work. Strategy in doubles in tennis is very important but it is of little value for a player who lacks the variety of basal strokes essential to hit and place the ball well. Likewise, it is of little value to show a pupil a good strategy to use in a history assignment unless he has command of such basal reading skills as I have outlined—skipping and skimming, combining re-reading and recall, and interspersed with thinking, and so on.

In summary, learning in the content subjects involves certain basal reading skills arranged in various combinations, adjusted to a particular purpose and operating under a general strategy of attack. The better a child has mastered the basal techniques and achieved flexibility in using them, the more easily he will learn to read and otherwise study well in the content subjects. There are, however, many adaptations to be made and these readjustments as well as effective patterns of grand strategy of attack are best cultivated in the content subjects themselves.

Now, finally, let me shift to certain principles in the teaching of reading which will, I think, apply not only to the teaching of reading but to the teaching of the techniques of reading and other forms of study in the content fields.

SOME GENERAL PRINCIPLES OF TEACHING

In the teaching of reading we find a principle of first importance is this: To get really competent reading it is necessary that pupils learn to love to read. Unless children learn to love to read they are unlikely ever to become good readers and good students in other subjects. Satisfaction, enjoyment in reading, is indispensable to learning to read well. This is more true today than it was a generation or two ago for the reason that reading now finds itself in the midst of so many strong competitors—radio, television, movies, comics, picture magazines, and an endless variety of toys and gadgets that the modern world supplies, and I judge the content subjects feel the same competition.

Secondly, teaching children to love to read and read well must be done in an atmosphere in which they feel they are reasonably successful and they must, in fact, *be* reasonably successful. They must be well equipped to learn and confident that they can learn. Embarrassments, misundersandings, errors in techniques must be detected and corrected at once. Serious disabilities may grow from minor faults, anxieties, oversights, and inappropriate procedures, which can easily be corrected if spotted, at once. This is notably true of most content subjects, especially those which, as in the case of mathematics and the sciences, are closely knit and developmental in character, in which each stage emerges from and depends upon the preceding stages.

Thirdly, children learn to read best in a full, rich, varied, enjoyable program, in which training in the technical skills is made an intrinsic component of a genuine, full-fledged reading, rather than in an isolated, formal drill. One principle of modern psychology is that the best way to help a child to learn a difficult task, such as reading, is to start him reading and then guide him as he learns to analyze words, to sense meanings from the context, to move along the line, and to do the other things in the course of reading itself. This principle can be applied to teaching the other content subjects. The way to do it is to launch the pupil on a realistic project and then show him how to maneuver. Give him some suggestions concerning techniques, tell him how to proceed, illustrate modes of attack, and then let him proceed on his own. There will be occasions when special attention must be given to one component or phase of the process, but even this is best done in the course of a genuine, full-fledged activity rather than in the form of an isolated, artificial drill.

A fourth principle or maxim is that success in learning depends greatly on the degree to which the pupil is taught to help himself. He should be encouraged to try out various techniques, to be an experimentalist, to go at it as best he can. In the teaching of most of the subjects, much more attention should be given, in my opinion, to the techniques and procedures of learning. If the child is to learn effectively in the future, what helps him most are not the particular facts in this book or lecture but the general techniques of attacking problems, of learning in typical situations, and of learning in different ways. Children, we are now discovering, are much more interested and competent in trying to steer their own course, trying to discover and correct their own difficulties, than we formerly assumed. Such ability does not grow best, however, in a *laissez faire* program. It develops best when the teacher is expert in helping pupils to become their own teachers, in helping them to try out their own devices and achieve competence under their own management. If a pupil should appear more interested in the strategy of studying reading or mathematics than in the substance of reading or mathematics, one should not worry. One should be more concerned about the pupil's ability to learn to spell words than about the number of particular words he can spell.

Finally, it seems very important that learning in reading or any other subject be carried on in a relaxed, friendly, cooperative situation. Much depends upon the skill of the teacher in dealing with the pupils as persons. One can get a clue to the importance of the relaxed, friendly, even somewhat carefree attitude by observing youngsters in their play and learning on the playground in baseball or basketball. Here, where they are not being subject to inquisition, not being held up to ridicule, not especially afraid of failure, where they are engaged in a cooperative enterprise, they are very alert and eager, active in searching for clues, likely to take pointers and most capable of self-appraisal and prolonged practice.

In order to achieve the properly relaxed, friendly, cooperative atmosphere which is so essential to good learning the teacher herself must be confident, relaxed, and, in a certain sense, carefree. This is especially true in reading and subjects dependent on reading. Many teachers, realizing the great importance of reading, tend to become anxious about it. The pupils, sensing the teacher's anxiety, become tense and worried themselves. The schoolroom atmosphere then becomes fraught with the sensitivities that lead pupils, according to their nature, to labor with fatiguing effort or to retreat from the contest (by means of many mental adjustments) or covertly or openly to rebel. All these adjustments are unfavorable to learning. They tend to make life in school less enjoyable and fruitful for the teacher as well as the pupil.

For some years a frequently stated slogan has been: Every teacher a teacher of reading. I have tried to show that this is a sound but an insufficient principle. Every subject-matter teacher should also be a teacher of the best strategy of attack in his subject. Finally, every teacher needs to know not only the strategy of teaching reading but also the strategy of managing pupils as persons.

HOW WOULD YOU LIKE TO BE
IN FIRST GRADE AGAIN? *

Paul McKee

Now put yourself in the place of the beginning first grade child by trying to read lines of print which are representative of the text given on the first ten pages of a hypothetical and quite mediocre but somewhat typical preprimer. The word given in parenthesis following each strange symbol the first time that symbol is used gives you the familiar pronunciation and consequently the familiar meaning for the symbol, just as the teacher's saying the name of a strange word makes the pupil recall the familiar pronunciation and the familiar meaning of that word. Do whatever you wish to do to try to become acquainted with each strange symbol so that the next time you see it you will think the pronunciation and the meaning without help. When you meet the same symbol the second and each subsequent time, try to think the pronunciation and the meaning without going back to the first use of the symbol. Whenever the fake text introduces different variants, these should not be too difficult if by the time you meet them you have the base forms fairly well in mind and are using the context.

Now try to read another page in the hypothetical preprimer. The question of the suitability of the content is not important in this instance. Notice, rather that the page contains two symbols which you have not had. If you have been observing enough to notice the forms that stand for *t* and *k* and if you use the context, you should have little trouble with those two strange symbols. If you can't read the page without getting much help by going back to the lines you have already read, you are not doing as well as first grade children are expected to do.

When you first met each strange symbol in the hypothetical preprimer, what did you do to try to become acquainted with that symbol? Did your mere association of the form with the pronunciation and the meaning which you were given at that time provide sufficient help? Did the mere repeating of that association through the first ten pages give enough help so that you could read the eleventh page readily? That is about all of the help that millions of first grade children receive as long as the teaching is limited to the use of the so-called sight method.

---

* Reprinted from *The Teaching Of Reading* by Paul McKee (Boston: Houghton Mifflin, 1948), pp. 25–36, by permission of the author and publisher.

⊥＋ የ (Sam)

⊔＋⊔⊔⊇ (Daddy)

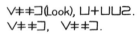

V‡‡⊐(Look), ⊔＋⊔⊔⊇.
V‡‡⊐, V‡‡⊐.

V‡‡⊐　⊔＋⊔⊔⊇.
V‡‡⊐ ＋∧(at) የ⊗(me).

⚬+∧X⊏(Watch) ℉⊗, ⊔+⊔⊔⊇.

⚬+∧X⊏ ℉⊗ ⊥⊏⧺⧺∧(shoot).

⚬+∧X⊏ ℉⊗ ⊥⊏⧺⧺∧ +∧ ∧⊏⊗ ⊔⚬X⊐

∨⧺⧺⊐, ⊔+⊔⊔⊇.

∨⧺⧺⊐ +∧ ∧⊏⊗(the) ⊔⚬X⊐(duck).

⊔+⊔⊔⊇ ⚬+∧X⊏⊗⊔ ⊥+℉ ⊥⊏⧺⧺∧.

⊏⊗(He) ∨⧺⧺⊐⊗⊔ +∧ ∧⊏⊗ ⊔⚬X⊐.

∧⊏⊗ ⊔⚬X⊐ ⊔⊔⊔(did) δ⧺∧(not) Δ+∨∨.

⊥⊏⧺⧺∧ +∧ ∧⊏⊗ ⊔⚬X⊐, ⊥+℉.

⊥⊏⧺⧺∧ ⊏⊔℉(him), ⊥⊏⧺⧺∧ ⊏⊔℉.

⊇⧺⚬(You) ⚬+∧X⊏ ⊏⊔℉ Δ+∨∨(fall).

⊔+⊔⊔ᒫ ∨+⌐⊓ᒪ⊗⊔ +∧ ⊥+የ.
ᒪ⊗ ⌐+∧Xᒪ⊗⊔ ᒪ∪የ Δ+∨∨.
⊔+⊔⊔ᒫ ∨+⌐⊓ᒪ⊗⊔(laughed) +∧ ⊥+የ.

⊔+⊔⊔ᒫ ∨+⌐⊓ᒪ⊗⊔ +∧ ⊥+የ.
ᒫ‡⌐ ⌐‡⌐∨⊔(would) ᒪ+⌐⊗(have)
∨+⌐⊓ᒪ⊗⊔.
ᒫ‡⌐ ⌐‡⌐∨⊔ ᒪ+⌐⊗ ∨+⌐⊓ᒪ⊗⊔
+∧ ᒪ∪የ.

"∨‡‡⊐,⊥+የ. ∨‡‡⊐ +∧ ∧ᒪ⊗ ⊔⌐X⊐
ᒫ‡⌐ ⌐+∧Xᒪ የ⊗ ⊐ᒪ‡‡∧ ᒪ∪የ."
⊥+የ ⌐+∧Xᒪ⊗⊔ ⊔+⊔⊔ᒫ ⊐ᒪ‡‡∧
∧ᒪ⊗ ⊔⌐X⊐. ᒪ⊗ ⌐+∧Xᒪ⊗⊔ ∧ᒪ⊗
⊔⌐X⊐ Δ+∨∨.
"ᒫ‡⌐ ⊔⊔⊔ ∫‡∧ ᒪ+⌐⊗ ∧‡ ⊐ᒪ‡‡∧,"
∨+⌐⊓ᒪ⊗⊔ ⊥+የ. "∧ᒪ⊗ Δ+∨∨
⌐‡⌐∨⊔ ᒪ+⌐⊗ ⊐∪∨∨⊗⊔ ᒪ∪የ."

PHONICS IS EASY? *

Lily Cable

Dough and Dough were twins. They looked so much alike that their mother decided to name them the same, with but one slight difference. Brother Dough's name rhymed with *bough*, while Brother Dough's name rhymed with *tough*.

Dough and Dough lived in a little town in the county of Hough (rhymes with *through*). At the age of six, not one day later, they entered Hough elementary school.

Their first day was rough; mainly because the teacher Miss Sew, (rhymes with *few*), couldn't tell Dough from Dough. Consequently, communication between her and the twins was somewhat less than adequate.

"Dough," she would say, looking at Dough (the other one). "Please come here."

Then Miss Sew would find her eyes swinging from Dough to Dough, wondering. Unfortunately for her sense of security, most of the time the wrong Dough would hear and come here please. It was very confusing.

Matters didn't improve when the principal came in for her visitation. Mrs. Lomen (rhymes with *women*), knew about Dough and Dough. She had learned about them when Mrs. Snead (rhymes with *bread*), came to enroll the twins.

"This is Dough Snead. And this one is Dough Snead." It had been quite an experience—that enrollment day.

Now Mrs. Lomen found Dough and Dough at the clay table. Observing them with a practiced eye, she noted they seemed well adjusted.

"What are you making, Dough?" she asked, bending over the little fellow.

"I'm not Dough, I'm Dough," said Dough.

"I'm sorry, Dough, I meant to say Dough. What are you making? It looks mighty interesting." Mrs. Lomen sized up the mass of clay that Dough was manipulating, willing to accept any answer.

"Can't you tell?" Dough sounded aggrieved. "It's a ewe. That's what it is."

---

* Reprinted from *CTA Journal* (March 1959), p. 22. Permission granted to reproduce by copyright owner, California Teachers Association.

At this, Brother Dough left his chair at the table to come over and see for himself.

He nodded his head. "Like he said. It's ewe, all right." Confirmation made, he returned to his chair.

Mrs. Lomen watched as Dough poked the ewe's left eye clear through the ewe's right ear. Then leaving the room, Mrs. Lomen whispered to Miss Sew. "These two will be a challenge to you, my dear."

Recess brought no respite. A wire fence separated the schoolyard from a farmer's pasture. In no time at all Dough had discovered the watering trough. It was a hot day, and Dough couldn't resist the nice cool water. In fact, when Dough saw Dough splashing in the trough he decided to join him. And there they sat, happy as babes in a bathinette.

When Miss Sew saw that the twins were not of a mind to leave their trough she hastily summoned the custodian, Mr. Frough, (rhymes with *cough*). Mr. Frough extricated Dough and Dough from the trough. By the time the two dripping twins reached the schoolyard the entire class was in a frenzy of excitement.

Most opportunely, the postman drove by. Mr. Maugh, (rhymes with *laugh*), liked children. He stopped his car to watch the activity.

"Looks like you could use a helping hand," he observed. "How about my taking them home? I'm going that way to deliver a package."

"Oh, could you? Would you?" A relieved Miss Sew turned to Mrs. Lomen, who had just come out of the building to see about the commotion. "They could go home with Mr. Maugh, couldn't they?" She tried to repress the rising note of hope in her voice.

Permission granted, Mr. Maugh took the drenched boys by their hands and led them to his car.

"Good bye, Miss Sew," called out Dough, remembering his company manners. "Thanks for everything!"

"Good bye, Dough," answered Miss Sew.

"I'm not Dough. I'm Dough," he wearily corrected her. "Good bye, anyway." He forgave her.

Mr. Frough and Mrs. Lomen took the shattered Miss Sew by her elbows and led her off to the Teachers' Room.

"It's time for a coffee brache," they gently told her.

PHONICS CLINIC *

Selma E. Herr

Phonics is being increasingly recognized as an effective tool in developing the ability to pronounce new words. This does not mean, however, that phonics alone will make a child a successful reader. There are many methods and techniques used in helping a child become a good reader and no one technique alone can do the job.

In analyzing the effectiveness of phonics, teachers have found:

1. Phonics can provide the child with a tool that will help him attack unfamiliar words which he encounters in his reading; but phonics will not provide the meaning of the word. (He may get the meaning from hearing the word pronounced or from the context of the sentence.)

2. Phonics can teach the child to associate the visual symbols with sounds known to him in oral-aural form.

3. Phonics should be an effective part of word analysis, so that the child will have some independence in working out new words.

4. Phonics is a means to an end, not an end in itself.

PHONICS TRAINING

1. Children should be helped to use several methods of attack in word analysis. These include: Looking at the word beginning to see if it starts the same as a word already known. Looking at the ending to see if it ends the same as a word already known. Looking at the ending to see if it has a rhyming element already known. Looking to see if the base word is recognizable, as in *looking*.

2. During reading class, if a child does not know a word, tell him the word quickly, but show him how to analyze it later.

3. In all phonics work, use meaningful words. Nonsense syllables have proved to be of little value.

4. Call the letters by their alphabetical names, not by sound. For example, "This is *a* and it has the *ah* sound." With the long vowel sound, "This is *a* and it says its name."

* Reprinted from *The Instructor* (May 1957), pp. 35–38, by permission of the author and publisher.

5. While some children can learn to read without phonics, show all of them the working processes of phonics. Then, those children who need phonetic help can be directed further and the others may develop their word analysis without extra work in phonics.

6. Never drill merely for the sake of drilling.

7. Avoid distorted sounds, such as pronouncing the consonants with an *uh* sound after them, as *puh-ah-tuh* for pat. The word is spoken as a unit.

8. Only the elements that are to be used at that time should be taught.

9. There is a tendency to use rhyming ends but when children begin to spell words, be sure that they know that all rhyming words are not spelled the same, as weigh and say.

10. Phonics can produce natural articulation and assist enunciation and pronunciation if taught correctly.

11. Phonics must be taught in close relationship with context.

12. Remember that phonetic analysis is only one of a number of techniques which help the child in attacking new words.

A PHONICS VOCABULARY

Phonetics   Science of speech sounds.

Phonics   Study of sounds as related to reading and enunciation.

Phonetic word   One in which every letter represents a particular sound as in run, sit, and did.

Phonogram   Ending on which a word family can be built as *at* (mat, cat, rat).

Digraph   Two consonants or two vowels that represent a single speech sound as *oa, ie, ph.*

Diphthong   A slurring together of two letters. The most common diphthongs are *oi, oy, ou* and *ow.* Occasionally some consonant combinations that give the slurring effect are called diphthongs.

Blend   Two or three letters show sounds are both pronounced as *bl, st, gr.*

Initial consonant   Single first consonant of the word as *s* in sit.

Initial consonant blend   Two or three consonants at the beginning of a word such as *bl* in blend.

Final consonant   Consonant at the end of the word.

Medial sound   Those vowel or consonant sounds in the middle of the word.

Level I

Goals

1. To grow in ability to differentiate many sounds around us—at home, at school, on the playground, in the country, and so on.

2. To develop ability to listen to records and stories and to be able to retell or explain parts that were heard.

3. To notice initial consonants (pick out words that begin the same way).

4. To notice final consonants and word rhymes (recognize words which end the same or have the same rhyming end).

5. To be able to match pictures according to initial consonants, final consonants, or rhymes.

Activities

1. Play records that include rhythms, stories, poems, and songs. Encourage the child to retell parts of the story, listen for certain parts, keep time to the music, and sing the songs.

2. Use a cardboard screen (about 2′ × 3′ cut from a large cardboard box) so children cannot see what you are doing. Show them the items and then put them behind the screen and have them tell what you are using. Suggested sounds might be:

Crumple a piece of paper toweling and a piece of typing paper.

Tap with a pencil and a fork on the table.

Shuffle cards and shake some buttons in a box.

Tear cloth and then paper.

Tap on a piece of wood—then a tin can.

Tap on soft-toned bells. Let the children guess which has been rung. Show the children buttons and pennies. Drop one or two of them on a hard surface. The children tell what has been dropped and if there is more than one.

Use kitchen equipment such as an egg beater, a can opener, and a wooden spoon.

Tap on an empty, a half-full, and a full glass or bottle.

3. Use a fork or some other object to tap a rhythmic pattern on the table. This should be very, very simple at first. A designated child repeats the pattern. The others listen to see if it is the same.

4. The children close their eyes, one child hops, skips, jumps, or does some other activity. The children guess what he did.

5. Bounce a ball and let some child reproduce the number of bounces.

6. Echo Game—A child hides behind the desk. Another child calls out in any intonation he chooses. The first child tries to imitate the sound and guess who made the first sound.

7. Supply the missing rhyming word. The teacher makes up rhymes and children add the word. "My little fuzzy bunny looks so very ———."

8. Have many large pictures. Each child takes a picture and tells all the things he sees that begin with a sound designated by the teacher, or he may tell all the things he sees that end like *cat*.

9. Familiarize the children with nursery rhymes. They listen while you say part of the rhyme. Then someone gives the word you left out.

10. I Am Thinking of a Word. Make up any story you wish. Develop word concepts but do not accept nonsense syllables. "I am thinking of a word that rhymes with *bake*. It is something good to eat. (Child says *cake*.) Can you think of some other words that rhyme with *cake* and *bake*?"

Level II

Goals

1. To further develop the ability to hear and distinguish various word sounds.

2. To learn the consonant sounds of *b, c, d, f, g, h, j, k, l, m, n, p, r, s, t, w;* and the blends of *ch, sh, th, wh.*

3. To match words with initial blends (first with picture and word, then with two words).

4. To match final consonants in words.

5. To match rhymes (first with picture and word, then with two words). (Note: Drill in achieving these goals should only be attempted after children have about 150 sight words, or when they begin to notice beginning letters.)

Activities

1. The teacher says, "Listen while I say some words and tell me which one does not begin like the other two; as *hat, house, cat.*"

2. The first child in the group says, "I am going to the farm (or China or Detroit)." The next child says, "I am going to the farm and I will take a fox." Each child gives a word with the same beginning sound of the place where the first child is going.

3. Place small objects in a box—button, ruler, pencil, shell, marble, bead, spool, scissors, and so on. In turn each child picks an object, names it, and gives another word beginning with the same sound.

4. "I will whisper the name of something. Watch my lips carefully and see if you can guess what I said." Children in turn whisper a word.

5. For the first lesson on specific phonic sounds, the teacher prints familiar words beginning with the same consonant on the blackboard. "Listen while I say these words. Did you notice anything that was the same in these words? Now let's look at them. Did you see anything that is the same? Can you tell me some other words that begin with this sound? Look in your books and see if you can find some other words." Each sound is presented in this way.

6. Match pictures with some beginning sounds. Next match pictures with letters, then pictures and words, then words that begin alike.

7. When drilling on initial consonants, give each child a duplicated story containing many words with the sound being learned. The children first read the story and then circle all the words that begin with the designated consonant sound. As the children increase in ability, they can underline all the words that begin like *house* and circle all the words that begin like *mother*. Endings and consonant blends may be used in the same way.

8. Find rhyming words. "Look at these pairs of words. Put a line under the parts of the words that are the same." Use words that have appeared in their reading; as *house, mouse, swing, thing.*

9. To pick out rhyming words, draw a red circle around the pairs of words that rhyme; as *take, bake; far, farm; make, walk; fish, dish.*

10. Draw or paste pictures of objects on 3″ × 5″ cards. The child sorts these according to initial consonants, blends, or rhyming words. He then says the sorted words.

11. The teacher passes out cards with half of the cards bearing word endings and the other half initial consonants or initial blends. The children find partners and say, "Our cards make —————."

12. Mark off squares on a piece of wrapping paper. In each square write an initial consonant or blend. The child throws his beanbag into a square and gives as many words as he can that begin with that sound. He gets a point for each word. The children keep score.

Level III

Goals

1. To learn the remainder of the consonant sounds as well as the blends *dr, fr, tr, bl, cl, sl, st, sm, sn, sw.*

2. To become proficient in the recognition of vowels and vowel combinations.

3. To know and pronounce the long and short sounds of vowels.

4. To become familiar with diphthongs.

5. To gain facility in blending all consonants and speech sounds.

Activities

1. When introducing the long and short sounds of vowels, write the word *dim* on the blackboard, and ask the children to tell you the word. Then add an e and ask the children to tell you the word. Do this with several words until the children notice that a final e, although silent, makes the long *i* sound. Divide the class into two groups. One group looks in books for words with short sounds. The other group finds words where the final e makes the other vowel long.

2. For a long-and-short-vowel game, collect pictures of objects with long and short vowel sounds as *bell, shoe, cat, cone,* and *glass.* Paste these on 3″ × 5″ cards and place in a box. Paste a picture of a short sound vowel word in the lid and one of a long sound vowel word in the bottom. The children sort the cards and put them in the right places. Later use words instead of pictures. Provide a key for self-checking.

3. Play a detective game to find the silent letters. Prepare a list of words from reading or spelling lessons. The children circle the letters that are silent; *before, coat, high, blue, leaves.*

4. List several words on the blackboard. The children rewrite them, substituting another vowel for the one given; *went, want; wish, wash; dish, dash;* and so on.

5. Give the group a duplicated list of words. They add another vowel to make a new word; *mad, made, maid; led, lead; din, dine.*

6. Everyone numbers his paper. The teacher says, "I am going to say

some words that have either a long or a short sound of *a* in them. When I say the word, write S on your paper beside the number of the word if the *a* has a short sound. Write an L if the word has a long *a* sound in it." Be sure the words are short and familiar.

LEVEL IV

Goals

1. To become familiar with the blends of *br, cr, gr, pr, pl, sp, spr, str, thr, qu.*
2. To notice that *oo, ow, ou* have two or more different sounds.
3. To know about the hard and soft sounds of *c* and *g.*
4. To have an understanding of what happens to the sounds of the vowels when they are followed by *r.*
5. To notice what happens to *a* when followed by *l* and *w.*
6. To be aware of the many phonic irregularities.

Activities

1. *oo* Teams—divide the class into teams to find words that have similar endings. Have six teams each working on an ending such as *ook, oom, oon, oop, oose,* and *oot.* Words with the proper sound but different spelling such as *prune, group, juice,* and *brute* should either not count at all or be worth only ½ point.

2. Eight words (*bow, brow, cow, how, now, plow, sow,* and *allow*) are the only words primary children need with the *ow* sound. They meet these words in which *ow* has the sound of long *o*—*blow, crow, flow, glow, grow, know, low, mow, row, show, slow, snow, throw, tow, sow,* and *below.* Once their meaning is clearly understood, have several activities to provide further study. Put them on flash cards and show. Have the children stand up if they have an *ow* sound, sit down if they have an *o* sound. (Notice that *bow* and *sow* are in both groups.)

3. Make separate flash cards for practice on phonic irregularities. Have a bulletin board with pictures and words that have unexpected sounds. Let children pair off and show the cards to each other. For variation show them in the opaque projector.

4. Duplicate a list of common words involving the hard and soft *c.* Read over the list with the group, then have the children write the words in two separate columns. Do the same with *g.*

5. Present *ar, er, ir,* and *ur* separately rather than treating the vowels alone. Use groups of words such as *sir, were,* and *blur* to show that *ir, ur,* and *er* have the same sound. Point out that with *ar,* the *r* usually says its own name.

6. *Aw, al* are also separate sounds. Play a game with such *aw* words as *draw, jaw, saw,* and *straw* in which one child pantomimes a meaning and the others guess it.

7. Make a triple-consonant list on your bulletin board. Any child that can think of a word with a blend of 3 consonant sounds may add it to the list and put his initials after it.

SEQUENCE FOR PHONICS ACTIVITIES

Auditory

1. Listening to sounds around us, stories, rhythms, music.
2. Listening to words that begin alike.
3. Listening to words having the same ending sound.
4. Listening to words that rhyme.

Visual

1. Matching pictures with initial sounds or blends.
2. Matching pictures with final consonants or rhymes.
3. Matching a picture with a word for initial sounds and blends.
4. Matching a picture with a word for endings.
5. Matching pictures and letters for beginning and ending sounds.
6. Matching words.
7. Recognizing the long and short vowel sounds.
8. Recognizing diphthongs.
9. Recognizing irregularities.

PARENTS AND READING *

Emmett Albert Betts

Last week a parent came to us upset by a book attacking ALL schools. He was confused by the statements of an irresponsible alarmist and the fact that his own nine-year-old Danny was having trouble with reading. He said that he wanted to know the facts so he could do something sensible about the situation.

There are many other level-headed parents like Danny's father, asking for the facts about how reading is taught in our schools today. They know that when an alarmist indicts all schools, all teachers, all methods, and all textbooks, he is like the soldier who claims that everyone is out of step except himself. Thinking parents know that schools are not ALL good or ALL bad; that teachers are not ALL stupid or ALL geniuses.

Danny's father wanted some facts so that he could draw a reasonable conclusion and take sensible action.

From Danny's mother we learned that he had been late in learning

---

* Reprinted from the November 1957 issue of *Education* by permission of The Bobbs-Merrill Co., Inc., Indianapolis, Ind.

to use words and sentences. Our tests showed that Danny's visual skills were not up to par for reading. We agreed that Danny had been forced into reading before he was ready.

Both the parents and the school had failed because Danny had normal intelligence but could read only a primer. In a first-reader he began to flounder; a second-reader was beyond his poor powers.

Danny's parents were in a mood for a serious discussion of what parents could do. Here are some points which made some sense to them:

1.   Expect boys to be slower than girls in getting on to the knack of reading.

Boys generally are slower in learning to talk. They are more likely to have speech difficulties. And they are more likely to be color blind. Moreover, the odds are better than four to one that a child having difficulty with reading is a boy. Therefore, don't force your boy into the first grade until he is at least six years of age—and be sensible about your little girl.

2.   Keep a record of your child's development, including facts about his birth.

Age of crawling, standing, walking, teething, talking, establishing bladder and bowel control, buttoning clothes, tying shoe laces—all these facts help teachers and child psychologists to understand educational needs. For example, day-time and night-time bladder control may indicate a need for a medical examination or a study of the child's emotional health. Lateness in learning to talk and to use sentences may have a direct bearing on when your child is ready to learn to read.

3.   Make sure your child is visually ready for school.

You are responsible for taking your child to a vision specialist once a year—and especially before he starts school. You should make sure that his eyes are O.K. and, equally important, that his visual skills are up to par. Remember that screening tests used in schools to detect visual handicaps are no substitute for diagnostic tests by a competent vision specialist.

4.   Expect big differences in the ages at which children learn to read.

Recently charlatans have been telling parents that ALL children can be taught to read at age five. This cannot be done in the United States and is not being done anywhere else in the world. Such statements are contrary to fact.

For many reasons, children learn to talk at different ages. For more reasons, they learn to read at different ages. We have seen a few three-year-olds who could read third readers and a few nine-year-olds who were not ready to learn to read.

5.   Find out why your child is having difficulty with reading.

Every week we see at least one mother who has cried herself to sleep every school night for years because her child has not learned to read. Sometimes the facts have been covered up by so-called social promotions in the schools. Nevertheless, neither the mother nor the schools can keep the facts from the child who must live in a world of reading.

The best solution to any problem is to get the facts from which to draw conclusions: Is my child mentally retarded? Is his brain injured? Is he tied to my apron strings? Is he trying to read material entirely too difficult? Can he learn to read by techniques which go beyond traditional phonic and look-say methods? Get the facts on your child and see that he gets the right help.

Above all, get on the job if your child has not gotten the hang of reading by age 7! The longer you wait the more confused your child may be. And the more difficult it will be to untie his emotional knots.

6.   Think many times before having your child repeat a grade.

No good and much harm may be done by having a child repeat third or eighth grade when he cannot read a first reader. It is equally absurd to drill a high school student on algebra when he doesn't know the facts of simple arithmetic. Likewise, it may be silly to have a child repeat a regular first grade when he cannot learn by the methods which his teacher uses.

Danny's parents were beginning to see that they needed to understand as well as to love him. That they could not afford to sit on the sidelines when he needed help on reading. In fact, they have asked for more time to go deeper into the problem.

CHAPTER 8

Children's Literature

> *Children read for many purposes: to experiment with a new reading skill, to satisfy curiosity, to seek information or direction, to share in the joys of the life of a person whose achievements are admired, or to be entertained. In the process a wide range and great number of books are read. A child's reading is not a substitute for experience, it is an experience that makes an impression that influences the structure of his personality.*

GIVE CHILDREN LITERATURE *

Leland Jacobs

From the beginnings of the movement for free public education in this country, literature has held a place as a curriculum experience for boys and girls. It is true that, in the beginning, it was a rather sad and sorry kind of literature. One of the first bits of verse which colonial children were expected to learn reminded them dolefully that "In Adam's fall, we sinned all."

It's probably characteristic of so much of the literature that was given to those poor little Puritans that, as Dorothy Baruch has said, "One would think from the kinds of reading experiences which were given to the young in those days that the adults of the community were in momentary fear of an infant revolt, and so they dangled them over hell-fire and brimstone to keep them in line."

As our country first looked to the Old World for its traditions and culture, so, similarly, we looked to the Old World for our first children's

* Reprinted from *Education Today* series, Bulletin No. 22 (Columbus, Ohio: Charles E. Merrill Books, Inc.), by permission of the author and publisher.

380

literature. Later, we developed a literature for adults that represented our declaration of intellectual freedom from other parts of the world. In the absence of a truly children's literature, we gave to children some of the masterpieces of this adult literature.

ADULT LITERATURE NOT
APPROPRIATE FOR CHILDREN

It is tragic that to this day, in some schools in the United States, the childen's literary heritage is confined pretty much to the old classical adult material. In some third grades one still finds children reading:

> Between the dark and the daylight,
> When the night is beginning to lower,
> Comes a pause in the day's occupations
> That is known as the Children's Hour.

As one looks at that poem inside out, he discovers that it is the reminiscences of an old man looking back upon the joys of having children in his household. If, in your school systems, you have any such individuals in the third grade, I recommend that you look at your promotional practices rather critically!

Or, along in the fourth grade—because, I presume, the title is "Little Boy Blue"—one still finds nine-year-olds trying to get into the experiences expressed by "The little toy dog is covered with dust, but sturdy and staunch he stands." Now if you analyze those lines sympathetically, you discover that this is the emotion of an adult who has lost a child. It is *about* a child—but not *for* a child.

As we moved on toward the Twentieth Century there began to develop a movement for a literature that was distinctively *for* children. It was promoted by men and women who believed firmly that the boys and girls of America deserve as significant a literature for *them* as do the adult readers in our culture. Our present age has seen the full flowering of this movement. The literature is here. This is truly the Golden Age of children's literature.

If we follow in the tradition of literature as an experience for boys and girls in the elementary schools, then, our job is so to provide it that, increasingly with their maturity, they grow in taste in reading. Without literature as a vital experience for children, I have the suspicion we have spent so much time on other aspects of reading, that we are in part to blame for the low level of adult reading habits in American life today.

There are six good reasons why children need literature in their lives.

1. Literature is entertainment. The first reason why children need literature is that literature is entertainment. I have no fear of entertainment as a noble end to education. The shortening of the working hours—for everybody but members of our profession, it seems—gives more time for leisure. Certainly, along with radio, picture magazines, movies, and television, some time ought to be reserved for reading. Unless children at school learn to love to read and enjoy reading for its own sake as entertainment, we are missing one of our wonderful citizenship opportunities. I would never apologize to anybody coming into my classroom and finding me enjoying literature with children. Literature as entertainment is a perfectly valid reason for it as a curriculum experience.

2. Literature refreshes the spirit. Literature sometimes helps to take us away from the urgencies of life that have become too urgent. Through the experience of reading fine prose and fine poetry, for the moment one learns to escape from the immediate cares and comes back to them recreated and refreshed. Unless children have many opportunities for this experience at school, they may never learn this wonderful value of literature in the refreshment of spirit.

Nor is that all of literature's contribution to the spirit. In all of our lives there are some books which—long after we have forgotten their titles, the incidents and the names of the characters—if one comes in contact with them again, they recall what I term a "residue of meaning," an overtone of spiritual values. Because such books have such vital meanings to us, the spiritual quality of their entertainment comes to the fore. We cannot expect that of every story or of every poem, but it is only as children have experiences with literature that this great potential is at least a possibility.

3. Literature helps explore life and living. Children need literature in order to explore life and living. There is no other medium—television, radio, or any of the rest—that quite compares with that wonderful experience of getting into the life situations of another person in the ways that one can do it with literature. A fine author is so cautious, in the sense of being careful with life—the realities of life—that somehow or other he reaches out to the young reader, and together, they go exploring into the life and the living, the customs, the mores, the habits of thinking of another character. Sometimes, first-hand experiences are best, but there are certain kinds of experiences that can come only vicariously through this kind of experience with literature. So, children need literature as an exploration of life.

4. Literature is a guidance resource. Literature can serve as a guidance resource for letting a person get insights into himself so that he can possibly change behavior. Not all literature can do it, nor can it always be done prescriptively. But everyone of us has in his life probably at least one book that helped to give him insight about him-self at a time when he needed it.

5. Literature stimulates creative activities. Children need litera-ture as a springboard to creative activities in other areas. Creative reading of literature, coupled with a rich program in the other arts, gets one art to feed another art. Reading stimulates drawing and rhythmic interpretation in dramatics. The richer the children's ex-periences in reading and dramatics, the richer they all become in the creative aspects of living.

6. Literature is beautiful language. Children need literature in order to enrich their own language. Literature is beautiful language, and who among us would not want children to get the beauty of their mother tongue at its best?

BUT WHAT LITERATURE?

But what kind of literature will provide the kind of values children need? I have three great parallels, which, if followed consistently, will provide the kind of literature program the children of today need.

Parallel 1: The new and the old. Today's literature program needs a balance of new literature and old literature, for one's literary heritage has its source in the combination of the two. A child needs a great deal of the modern literature—the things that have been written for children in his own generation—because it is written in the idiom and in the style, mood, and tempo that he understands because he's living it. The great modern writers for children know what the inside of a child's mind is like, and they write with a tempo, style, and spirit that is Twentieth Century modern.

The child needs a wealth of this material, but if his heritage is to be rich, he needs to know that before his time there came to us great stories, too—stories like "The Elephant's Child," who went down by the "great gray-green, greasy Limpopo River, all set about with fever-trees, to find out what the Crocodile has for dinner." Kipling is gone, but "The Elephant's Child" is with us yet. The child needs the old, old tales of Grimm, Asbjornsen, Joseph Jacobs, and all the rest of the wonderful crew of folklorists who collected the old stories of the world. Children love this old literature. They particularly love it if they can share it with an adult who had it, too, as a child. This is the kind of literature that May Lamberton Becker said is like the measles going through an orphanage. Generation after generation, the continuity of the literary experience going from the old to the young, and from the young to the younger is a great experience and a great combination of new and old reading experience.

Parallel 2: Realistic and fanciful literature. My second parallel is the balance between realistic and fanciful literature. Now, the child loves the kinds of stories that acquaint him with his own world, whether he is close to it in time and space, or far from it. He loves animal stories. He wants stories that take him out to the various parts of the United States, where people live like him as an American and yet different from him because they belong to an area that is different. This balance of realistic literature, which we call regional literature, he needs and wants tremendously.

But he also wants at this age to go out in time and space beyond our own country to the Orient, to Europe, up into the hills of Switzerland with Heidi, over into Japan with the little farmer boy who was saved from the tidal wave.

He wants to go back into time—to the time of Abraham Lincoln, when a little girl wrote and recommended that Lincoln would look much better on a platform if he had whiskers. So he raised whiskers, and she saw that he had them and met him in those days, as Hertha Pauli has written.

But along with these kinds of experiences in time and space with realistic literature, he also wants the kind of literature which takes him out of this world into the world of the impossible, the improbable, and the fanciful. So there is "Mary Poppins"; there are the "Three Wishes"; there are the fairy tales that transcend time and space. I think these are terribly urgent. Look what the child can do with such literature. He can get out of the plausible and the possible and look back on the real to get a greater perspective on both.

Parallel 3: Prose and poetry. I am sad that in so many schools today there is so little time for poetry. There are some good reasons for this. For, in the past, you know some of the things we did. "Mass memorization," for example—forty times around the room, "I wandered lonely as a cloud that floats on high o'er vales and hills," until you hope you never see a daffodil again. Or, "verse vivisection," where you tear it to pieces to see how it ticks. Or, "poetic preachment," where you give children poetry to improve their spirits, their souls, and their characters.

That isn't our idea of poetry for children. Today, we give them their wonderful heritage of poetry where they can read it and see it beautifully on a page, or hear it joyously.

THE PLACE OF LITERATURE
IN THE CURRICULUM

Children need literature, then, for entertainment, for refreshment of spirit, for the exploration of life and living, for guidance, for creative activities, and for the enrichment of language. We deprive them of these values at our peril.

There are some people who like to say that the social studies are the backbone of the curriculum. That's all right with me. Then there are some who think that mathematics give muscle to the curriculum. That's all right with me, too. Because, deep down inside, I am quite sure that literature is mighty close to the *heart* of the curriculum; and, as Edna St. Vincent Millay has said so well:

> The world stands out on either side,
> No wider than the heart is wide.

Give children literature!

EVALUATING AND SELECTING BOOKS FOR CHILDREN'S INTERESTS *

May Hill Arbuthnot

There is no field in which grownups should proceed with more caution than in the evaluation of books for children. It is fairly easy to set up hard and fast criteria of literary merit by which to judge a book, but there still remains the unpredictable child. One child reads avidly, another with reluctance. One demands factual books, another fairy tales. Children's needs and interests at any age level are as varied as their physical growth patterns. And these needs and interests must be taken into account in evaluating their books if we expect to make readers of them.

A book may meet every literary standard; but if a child can't read it or if by way of it he is bored or discouraged, it is not a good book for him. And if a child discovers and treasures that odd book the critics scorned, adults had best conceal their scorn and be thankful that at long last some book has given him a taste of the possible joys of reading.

Of course a good book can do more for a child than a poor one, so a critical sense is essential, but omniscience is dangerous. We can select and promote books, but we cannot force delight. Obviously

---

* Reprinted from *Reading in Action,* Vol. 2 (New York: Scholastic Magazines, 1957), by permission of the author.

then, we must ask of a book: Can the child read it? Does its content come within the level of his understanding? Has the book child appeal? And how does it meet the child's basic needs?

These needs, and specific types of books that satisfy them, are already listed in print in considerable detail.[1] Here there is only time to summarize them under a few general heads. We may well ask of a book, (1) Will it help the child to a clearer insight into the cause and effect of behavior? (2) Does it satisfy his varied curiosities? (3) Will it minister to his zest for living? and (4) Will it deepen his reverence for all life worthy of development?

INSIGHT

To get along in this complex world of people the child must grow in understanding of the cause and effect of human behavior, his own and other people's. The problems change with age, from the penalties of running away at four years of age to the uncertainties of a first date at fourteen. But because at every age level the child looks for pieces of himself in book characters and situations, his reading can and should influence his sense of right and wrong, of moral and ethical standards and resultant behavior patterns.

This should not mean a return to didacticism, although it must be admitted there is a trend in that direction. In the course of a perfectly good story, manners and morals can and should be made clear without moralizing. For instance, in two amusing tales, *Eddie's Pay Dirt* [2] and *Henry Huggins*, [3] both boys are confronted with painful ethical problems which they can't squirm out of but must solve for themselves. These problems in social relationships are not the focus of the story, but arise suddenly as they do in real life.

At adolescence, the pangs of having to face adult responsibilities can be grievous indeed, as the climax of both *The Yearling* [4] and *Good-bye, My Lady* [5] makes dramatically clear. And there are, of course, innumerable other problems of personal behavior which books illumine. They can also broaden the child's understanding of other times and peoples where the patterns of living differ from his own but problems may be similar. The fight for liberty that *Johnny Tremain* [6] knew in our American Revolution is still going on in other lands today. Stories of regional life in the United States and of everyday life in foreign lands can minister to the child's sympathetic approach to people who are somewhat different from his immediate neighborhood friends.

In short, many kinds of books may, without didacticism, help the child to grow from his egocentric concern with his own desires into an

increasing sensitivity to other people's needs and a sense of the kin-
ship of all peoples.

CURIOSITIES

The normal child comes into the world with the most diverse
curiosities. He asks about worms and weather, stars and stones, trains
and planes, animals and atoms or, as the walrus would say, "Of
shoes and ships and sealing wax." Fortunately, factual books are
better and more numerous today than ever. From dictionaries and
encylopedias to books about India or the Arctic, dinosaurs or the bees,
there are books for most age levels, in most fields, that will satisfy and
develop further the child's interests in the universe. Let's see that those
we choose are (1) scrupulously accurate, (2) conveniently organized
and indexed, and (3) understandably and interestingly written. Not
only does the child need and enjoy such books, but some children are
won over to reading by informational books rather than by fiction.

ZEST FOR LIVING

The healthy child comes into the world with a God-given zest for
living that experience seems bent upon quelling. Hence the value of
books that build a child's faith in the fact that life is good and may
be glorious, books that foster the frisky enjoyment in being alive that
most children possess. For instance, tales of adventure, from the
doughty deeds of folk-tale heroes to records of real people who have
struggled, failed, and risen again to carry the task through to heroic
conclusion, these lift the child's spirits and give him faith that he too
will achieve mightily.

Sea Pup [7] and Banner in the Sky [8] give city boys a vicarious
taste of outdoor adventures that lift their spirits and their imaginations
as well. Books are precious that show children the innocent absurdities
of life, and sheer nonsense that provokes laughter can relax tensions
and be as cheering as a burst of sunlight after a dark day. Sometimes
poetry can give children a sudden sense of wonder and beauty. Any
kind of literature that gives the child a keener awareness of the good-
ness and fun of life, the desire to "fight the good fight," to get on with
the task, and to welcome each new day with courage, is good reading.

REVERENCE FOR LIFE

Finally, because we are living in an age of conflict and violence,
children need to grow in that feeling of "reverence for life" as Albert

Schweitzer calls it, "all life worthy of development." Substantial stories of animals, written with integrity to the species, can make children keenly aware of a creature's virtues and limitations as it fights its enemies, men or other animals. *The Tough Winter*,[9] *Bambi*,[10] *Brighty of the Grand Canyon*,[11] *Big Red* [12] or the remarkable books by John and Jean George [13] will increase the child's knowledge of a particular species of animal and his compassion for its gallantry and vulnerability. Stories about everyday people, past or present, their hardships, self-sacrifice and persistence in the face of obstacles have special values. No child can read such books as the historical *Little House* [14] series or those remarkable books, *The Ark* [15] and *Rowan Farm*,[16] about a modern German family in a bombed-out city beginning all over and making a good life for themselves and others, without a quickened feeling of "reverence for life—all life worthy of development."

Turning now to literary yardsticks with which to evaluate children's books, these too must be general. There are specific criteria for judging stories about animal life, regional, religious or minority groups, life in other lands, historical fiction, biography and poetry. These detailed standards must be left to the textbook. But there are four broad criteria by which to evaluate the child's first literary love— the story.

FICTION

Characters. Someone once said of the novel that it never achieves greatness unless the characters are convincing. This is not always true of stories for children who are satisfied at first with the stereotypes of the folk tales—*Boots the Brave, Cinderella the Beautiful and Good!*

But children soon outgrow these symbols and demand real flesh-and-blood people in their books. The stereotyped "Beauty and the Beast" are replaced by the unique personalities of Pod, Homily and Arrietty in *The Borrowers*,[17] and the foolish and wise "Three Little Pigs" give place to absurd Wilbur, "the radiant pig," in *Charlotte's Web*.[18] Moreover, these well-drawn characters of fantasy are as real to young readers and as memorable as the realistic, equally well-drawn characters of Tom Sawyer [19] or Jo in *Little Women*.[20] Historical fiction is an area of writing for children in which an over-concern with theme or conflict is apt to reduce the characters to mere types. Not so with *Johnny Tremain* [6] or the characters in any of William Steele's [21] excellent historical tales. His people are sharply and cantankerously individual. Strong characterization is also one of the many elements of greatness in that Newbery winner *and now, Miguel*,[22] in which every member of the Chavez family is alive and memorable.

Theme. Look next at the theme of the book—what is it all about? Is there a substantial idea back of the story? In *Wheel on the School*,[23] for instance, two important questions launched the whole story: Why are there no storks in Shora, and how can we bring them back? These ideas started a chain of action that finally involved every person in the village. Sometimes the theme is stated or suggested by the title of a book. This year's Newbery Medal winner, *Miracles on Maple Hill*,[24] is concerned first with the lovely everyday miracles of the changing seasons and then, the miracles of healing which the outdoor world can bring to a sick spirit. And *The Ark* [15] revolves around a family's search for shelter and security from the storms of war. These are strong themes, and without one it is impossible to build a full-bodied story.

Just at present we are suffering from a rash of thin and themeless narratives for the youngest children. There are books about night sounds and daytime sights, smells, tastes, coldness, wetness and what not. These are designed to increase the pre-school child's awareness of this or that. They may be good language experiences occasionally, but their lack of humor and substance send the average child searching for something meatier—an honest-to-goodness story, not another so-what book. Nor is it necessary for the youngest to have this attenuated fare. *Circus Ruckus*,[25] *Little Angela and Her Puppy*,[26] *The Happy Lion*,[27] *The Bears on Hemlock Mountain*,[28] *John Billington, Friend of Squanto*,[29] and dozens of others, have substantial themes that support hilarious or serious action and guarantee a rousing story that will keep the small fry sitting up and demanding more.

Plot. Grownups may accept a stream-of-consciousness story, but children like plots. Plot is merely the action of a tale, what happens to or because of the theme. Plot involves obstacles, suspense, climax and a satisfying conclusion. Something must have been accomplished in the process of the action, for children and young people cannot accept the idea of defeat. Even in that fine story about Alpine guides and their stern code of ethics, *Banner in the Sky*,[8] brash young Rudi did not reach the top of The Citadel himself, but he accomplished the more difficult task of sacrificing himself for a moral principle, thereby proving himself a guide indeed. In adult fiction it is possible to have a strong theme with little action or plot, but in children's books that have lasted over the years—*The Tale of Peter Rabbit* [30] and *Tom Sawyer*,[19] for instance—the two generally go hand in hand.

Style. Finally, there is the matter of style, an unknown quantity to children and difficult to define for adults. In part it is the auditory effect of words, how they trip on the tongue and fall upon the ear. Try reading a story aloud and you can tell quite a bit about its style,

good or commonplace. The words must also suit the mood, or movement or matter of the story. When you read aloud *The Duchess Bakes
a Cake*,[31] the children are soon chanting with you, "A lovely, light,
luscious, delectable cake," but when you read from *Little House in the
Woods*,[14] they relax and are quietly absorbed. So style must vary
with the content of the tale. There are lovely descriptions of the outdoor world in *Miracles on Maple Hill*,[24] derisive chants in *What Can
You Do with a Shoe?* [32] *The Courage of Sarah Noble* [33] is soberly
and beautifully written with deceptive simplicity. The adventure tale
of *Little Tim and the Brave Sea Captain* [34] has a forthright style
that is oddly convincing. Style may and must differ with the content,
but it can be the essence of simplicity without being commonplace.
It can have great beauty without being artificial, and there is certainly
no excuse in a child's book for slovenly writing, slang or pretentiousness.

BIOGRAPHY

All of these criteria with the exception of plot may be applied to
the evaluation of biography which has come to play such a major
part in the modern child's reading. Obviously, the writer of biography
needs as acceptable a prose *style* as a writer of fiction, and the character of the man must emerge as vividly and uniquely as in fiction.
When the biographer has assembled all the facts about his hero, he
begins to see a unity in the life and chooses a *theme* accordingly.
Jeannette Eaton's old biography of George Washington, *Leader by
Destiny*,[35] is a good example. She saw her hero called away, over
and over again, from a life he loved, to assume a leadership he dreaded
but could not refuse.

Interestingly enough, the heroes of biography make their own *plots*.
Their obstacles, mistakes, action and suspense are not as neatly patterned as in fiction but carry them forward to some tragic or triumphant climax just as inevitably. When we read biography, we say
tritely, "Life is stranger than fiction." Of course, it is. Perhaps this is
why in writing biography for children it seems natural to fictionize it
here and there, to introduce dialogue where no dialogue is recorded
by the historian. And here biography and fiction part company.

Authenticity. Biography has one characteristic in common with all
informational books, it must be true to the facts. In a book for children, some of the facts may be omitted; but those that are used should
not only be scrupulously documented but should reveal the man.
Sources are generally omitted in juvenile biographies and more's the
pity. It permits altogether too much latitude in a field where authen-

ticity is of major importance. Children may ignore a footnote or an appendix, but they could be trained to look at them and to respect an author's regard for truth. Two fairly recent children's biographies of John Paul Jones give such different accounts of his childhood that the reader would never suspect the books were about the same man. Which was reliable? There was no documentation to say. Nevertheless, in spite of this one anxiety about juvenile biography, we hasten to add that most of the recent books are absorbingly written. The heroes emerge as fully drawn, convincingly alive human beings, and the great drama of human struggle has never been more movingly presented to children and youth than it is in modern biography.

POETRY

Poetry is another field of literature that requires special criteria for its appraisal. And here examples are needed but generalizations must suffice.

Melody and Movement. It is the melody and movement of poetry that most sharply differentiate it from prose, and these are the qualities that first attract children to the enjoyment of verse. So listen first for the melodic ear-appeal of verses for children and shun those so-called poems with halting lines and forced rhymes. If children begin happily with the tumpety-tumpety tunes and rhythms of Mother Goose and light verse of similar caliber, they can be carried from these to the subtler melodies of true lyric poetry. So listen first to the music of the verses you are appraising. Melody and movement are clues to the child's enjoyment and to the lyric quality of poetry itself.

Words of poetry. Examine also the words of the poems you are considering. They may be the ear-tickling words of nonsense verse or they may introduce the child to new words, startling and bright, or the poems may use quiet, familiar words in a fresh new way. But the words of authentic poetry will never be commonplace or pedestrian or forced. Poor verse is invariably marked by awkward lines and an unnatural use of words for the sake of rhyme. The result is something forced and dull that sets the teeth on edge like a harsh noise. True poetry has lightness, freshness and a lovely sense of surprise and joy. It sings with meaning.

Meaning. And of course, the child must understand it. Grownups may put up with obscurities, but not the child. He wants to know what it is all about. Examine it for meaning. Does it come within the child's easy comprehension; his comprehension with a few explanatory lifts? If it takes elaborate amplification it is not for him. Ask also of the poet what does it do for life and the child? Does it tickle his funny bone and provoke laughter as the verses of Laura Richardson or A. A. Milne [37] invariably do? Or does it suddenly set fire to the imagination the mystery and magic of life caught and held in a line? That is poetry! That is worth building toward. That is worth carrying children through the tumpety tumps of nursery rhymes, to simple lyrical dramatic ballads and on to authentic poetry until all by themselves they stumble on that magic verse or poem that speaks strangely and movingly to them. Then, and then only, poetry possesses them and your task is done.

In conclusion, you are you and I am me. Like children we bring to our reading different backgrounds of judgment. So let's be charitable with each other and devoutly thankful for all the gifted artists, writers, editors and publishers who continue to pay no attention to our pronouncements but go on producing surprising and wonderful books for children.

BOOKS IN THE ORDER MENTIONED

1. May Hill Arbuthnot, *Children and Books* (revised). Chicago: Scott, Foresman, 1957.
2. Carolyn Haywood, *Eddie's Pay Dirt*. New York: Morrow, 1953.
3. Beverly Cleary, *Henry Huggins*. New York: Morrow, 1950.
4. Marjorie Rawlings, *The Yearling*. New York: Scribner's, 1948.
5. James Street, *Good-bye, My Lady*. New York: Lippincott, 1954.
6. Esther Forbes, *Johnny Tremain*. Boston: Houghton Mifflin, 1943 (Newbery Medal 1944).
7. Archie Binns, *Sea Pup*. Boston: Little, Brown, 1954.
8. James Ramsey Ullman, *Banner in the Sky*. Philadelphia: Lippincott, 1954.
9. Robert Lawson, *The Tough Winter*. New York: Viking, 1954.
10. Felix Salten, *Bambi*. New York: Simon and Schuster, 1928.
11. Marguerite Henry, *Brighty of the Grand Canyon*. Chicago: Rand McNally, 1953.
12. Jim Kjelgaard. *Big Red*. New York: Holiday House, 1954.
13. John and Jean George, *The Masked Prowler*. New York: Dutton, 1950.
14. Laura Ingalls Wilder, *Little House in the Big Woods*. New York: Harper & Row, 1932.
15. Margot Benary-Isbert, *The Ark*. New York: Harcourt, Brace & World, 1953.
16. Margot Benary-Isbert, *Rowan Farm*. New York: Harcourt, Brace & World, 1954.
17. Mary Norton, *The Borrowers*. New York: Harcourt, Brace & World, 1953.
18. E. B. White, *Charlotte's Web*. New York: Harper & Row, 1954.
19. Mark Twain (pseud. Samuel Clemens), *The Adventures of Tom Sawyer*. New York: Harper & Row, 1923.
20. Louisa May Alcott, *Little Women*. Boston: Little, Brown, 1929.
21. William O. Steele, *Tomahawks and Trouble*. New York: Harcourt, Brace & World, 1955.
22. Joseph Krumgold, *and now, Miguel*. New York: Thomas Y. Crowell, 1953 (Newbery Medal, 1954).
23. Meindert de Jong, *Wheel on the School*. New York: Harper & Row, 1954 (Newbery Medal, 1955).
24. Virginia Sorensen, *Miracles on Maple Hill*. New York: Harcourt, Brace & World, 1956 (Newbery Medal, 1957).

25. William Lipkind and Nicolas Mordvinoff (Will and Nicolas), *Circus Ruckus*. New York: Harcourt, Bruce & World, 1954.
26. Dorothy Marino, *Little Angela and Her Puppy*. New York: Lippincott, 1954.
27. Louise Fatio, *The Happy Lion*. New York: Whittlesey, 1954.
28. Alice Dalgliesh, *The Bears on Hemlock Mountain*. New York: Scribner's, 1952.
29. Clyde Bulla, *John Billington, Friend of Squanto*. New York: Thomas Y. Crowell, 1956.
30. Beatrice Potter, *The Tale of Peter Rabbit*. London: Warne, 1903.
31. Virginia Kahl, *The Duchess Bakes a Cake*, Scribner's, 1955.
32. Beatrice Schenk de Regniers, *What Can You Do with a Shoe?* New York: Harper & Row, 1955.
33. Alice Dalgliesh, *The Courage of Sarah Noble*. New York: Scribner's, 1954.
34. Edward Ardizzone, *Little Tim and the Brave Sea Captain*. New York: Oxford, 1955.
35. Jeannette Eaton, *Leader by Destiny: George Washington, Man and Patriot*. New York: Harcourt, Brace & World, 1938.
36. Laura Richards, *Tirra Lirra*. New York: Little, Brown, 1955.
37. A. A. Milne, *When We Were Very Young*. New York: Dutton, 1924.

PRELUDE TO LITERATURE *

Katherine Reeves

It is through his senses and his feelings that the very young child takes the measure of his world, determines its character, and decides how he will relate himself to it. Long before he has any understanding of books as objects in his personal landscape, he has had countless experiences which will influence his feeling about literature and his interest in learning to read and to use the written word.

The sensing-feeling life is the vital content of preliterature. Every mother and father knows that the very young child is the pure pragmatist. All living is a doing-with the environment. To touch, to taste, to smell, to see and hear are organic hunger and thirst. And yet how often do we expect him to do all his learning through his ears—to listen and understand and be able to act appropriately. This is like asking a pianist to practice with his thumb only and to let the rest of his hand stay quiet.

Listening, hearing, important as they are, are not enough. "I must get closer to the source," say the urgent, restless body, the exploring intelligence of a young child. And he runs and climbs and pulls and pushes and carries. He squeezes and strokes and pounds. He toils up

* Reprinted from *The Horn Book* (October 1958), by permission of The Horn Book, Inc., Boston.

and down the stairs, not to go anywhere but to conquer the obstacle presented by the stairs. He opens all doors, drawers, and cupboards within his reach. He piles the kitchen pots and pans around him on the floor. He chews his rubber ball, his bath soap, the snow on his mitten, a dandelion he picks on the lawn, a neglected cigarette stub in the ash tray. "Why does water splash when I stamp hard in the puddle?" "Why doesn't the sand splash?" "Why does the robin fly away when I try to touch him?" "Why does the stone lie still?" "How do mashed potatoes feel when I squeeze them?" "Why does this other creature like me cry when I push him?" "Why doesn't my doll cry when I let her fall on the ground?"

Through his searching hands, his keen observing eyes, his delicate nose and tongue, his acutely hearing ears, he finds out the gross and the fine meanings of his world. All the infinite variety, the nuances of sound, texture, space, time, temperature become clear to him as he travels through his own sphere, using his senses for divining rods. These are meanings which must be discovered at first hand, these cannot be truly known except as they are experienced. The need to know, through perceiving and feeling, is not superficial, and the search for satisfaction is not random. There is a beautiful order in the young child's involvement of himself with the world about him. And through this involvement he finds out whether his world is warm, permissive and kind; whether it is hostile and cold; whether it can be easily manipulated or is rigid; just what constellation of qualities distinguishes the various parts of it.

The lines which Walt Whitman wrote about this kind of primary experience are so well known they have become almost a cliche in our efforts to find the perfect statement of the merging of child and environment. "There was a child went forth every day," Whitman wrote, "and the first object he looked upon, that object he became . . ." These lines, familiar to all of us, say so warmly what must be understood if we would discover how feeling and sensing become the young child's foundation for concepts of the natural world, the prelude to thought and imagination, the foreshadowing of attitude and perception. The child, the poet says, is made out of what he brings to the world and what he has a chance to absorb through blood and nerve and bone.

In the growth of our "preschool literature"—a literature which has a brief history in years but a thrilling and beautiful achievement through those years—the acceptance of the primary significance of the child's sensory-motor-feeling life has steadily enlarged. This acceptance has its own history, to be seen in a chronological look at the books which have been made for the very young in the past three decades. The artist, whether with words or brush, has made it his imperative concern to know a great deal about the actual facts of human development, the course of early language, the feeling-life within the child, the growth of imagination and perception, and to use this knowledge with sympathy and strength in creating books and pictures.

Before the nineteen-twenties there was little formal literature for young children. The very period of life was an unexplored country. The four-year-old was looked upon as a downward extension of the older child, and the two-year-old was perceived as an upward extension of infancy. Children between the ages of two and five or six had been given as their special literary property the nursery rhymes and simpler traditional tales, fables of Aesop, and certain gleanings from the didactic harvest of the nineteenth century.

Of course there has always been a mother-father-child literature. This is as old as mother-father-child in man's history. And many a parent must have discovered with joy that his child liked to hear the simple stories of his own doings, about himself and his intimate world of people, things, and creatures; and that the child's imagination and perception were enriched and stimulated by the hearing. This experience, too, is preliterature, and serves the little child today as richly as it has served other children through the decades and the centuries.

We might argue the point as to whether the picture book is literature or pre-literature; either yes or no will do us for an answer. But there is no argument as to the aesthetic usefulness of the good picture book to the child who finds in it some ordering of his own feeling, some reflection of his own desires, some extension of his own imagination.

The good picture book aids and advances the young child's search for answers; it confirms his faith; it stretches his understanding; it may give him something to struggle with, now and then; sometimes it gives him the springboard he needs for getting his feeling into words.

Although this is probably never its initial intent, the good book— at any level—may provide therapy for mind and heart. Adults go to books, often, with this need, and have it met. Why should children not be served in the same way? As we watch children with books we know that they are so served. This help rises out of the integrity and moral substance of the book itself—and this integrity and moral essence flow from the attitude of artist and writer toward the child. Conscience, important at all levels, must be most deeply and surely exercised by those who make books for the very young.

Writer and artist must enter as fully as possible the world of the young child, and taste and touch and see as nearly as possible in his way, if they would truly give to him, and not use him for their own purposes. It is when this real giving, in the child's own terms, occurs that the enduring book and the living illustration come into being. To our great good fortune, this kind of giving is abundant in the young child world.

And an interesting thing happens—as the writers and the artists create books which help the young child find his answers and learn what his world is, they help us—the naive and inexperienced—understand what a child is.

THERAPEUTIC READING *

Matilda Bailey

Reading for information is undoubtedly the kind used most widely in the public schools. However, English teachers talk of another type. It goes by a number of different names—"leisure reading," "free reading," and even the spirit-killing "extra-credit reading." Obviously, there is much overlapping in the two kinds of reading: reading for information often yields tremendous enjoyment, and reading for enjoyment frequently results in added information. As a consequence, it is difficult to pigeonhole kinds of reading according to any ironclad classification.

Therapeutic reading is not a third kind of reading, and it is certainly not a new type. Therapeutic reading is merely a new name for an old idea. The term *therapeutic* indicates that it is "of or related to the healing art." Surely boys and girls, as well as adults, are beset with all kinds of problems which bore into their hearts and minds. Often we can only vaguely guess at the things which are giving hurt. With such hazy appreciation of their problems, we naturally have difficulty in finding the right remedies. Fortunately, there is another way. Through the medium of books, children can find duplications of their problems and can see the ways by which other children have met their difficulties. Thus, therapy in reading occurs.

Illustrations of the value of therapeutic reading are endless. One adolescent girl suffered agonies because of her bright red hair and her bountiful and unbeautiful crop of freckles. All her friends were of the peaches and cream variety. Then one day she discovered L. M. Mont-

* Reprinted from *ABC Language Arts Bulletin*, Vol. 1, No. 6 (New York: American Book Co., 1955), by permission of the publisher.

gomery's *Anne of Green Gables;* and by identifying herself with Anne, who also had red hair and freckles, her problems were solved. A well-known fiction editor tells of having lost her father when she was very young. For a time the world seemed entirely black, and then one day she found a story about a little girl her own age who had lost both her father and mother. Through a story-book character, who exemplified courage, she found solace.

Physical handicaps are frequently crushing blows to youngsters. An example of what a make-believe story can do is seen in the experience of a boy named Jim. Jim was born with one leg shorter than the other; and he was always forced to wear a built-up shoe, which he hated because it clumped-clumped when he walked. That built-up shoe seemed to be a nemesis; and because of it, an otherwise normal boy was becoming moody and anti-social. Then one day his father found a story about a boy, like Jim, who had a built-up shoe. That boy played football, and he was a star because with his heavy shoe he could kick harder than any of the other players on the team. Because of that story, the real boy, Jim, took hope. Last spring he was graduated from high school. For his prowess in football as the best kicker in the district, Jim was awarded a special distinction. A book and a father's guidance had done the trick.

In an Anglo-Saxon community, the influx of "foreigners" often presents a problem in the schools. One teacher wisely anticipated difficulty by reading aloud to her class Eleanor Estes's *The Hundred Dresses.* The pupils quickly recognized that the little girl in the story, with her strange and almost unpronounceable name, was a very nice little girl made extremely unhappy by the Browns and Smiths and Joneses in her class.

One girl said after the reading of the story, "I wish she were in our class. We'd be nice to her."

Thus far the matter rested entirely in theory. However, one morning a few weeks later, three new little faces appeared in the classroom; their names were not easy to spell or to pronounce. There was a moment of silence—this was the acid test. Then suddenly smiles of welcome appeared on the pupils' faces, and the three new and rather frightened children smiled back. *The Hundred Dresses* had saved the day.

Many schools have the problem of the children of migrant workers. The children are here today and gone tomorrow. Certainly something can be done to make the today that they are here a happy one. If they are treated like outcasts, as they are very frequently, all their todays will be a dreary and lonely procession. Many teachers have found that Doris Gates's *Blue Willow* can do much to ease the way.

Parents are often more conscious of the value of books in character building than teachers seem to be. After all, we may argue, we are so busy taking care of facts and "figgers" that we haven't the time to "Build thee more stately mansions, O my soul." Let the parents take care of that problem! Recently in a public library two mothers were heard to ask the librarian, "My little boy tells lies. Do you have a book that would be good for him to read?" and "I want a book for my son. He can't play with the other boys on our street without fighting with them." Certainly we shall agree that parents and teachers both need to be concerned with fundamental qualities of character and personality.

METHODS OF USING BOOKS IN THERAPEUTIC READING

The first step, obviously, is to determine whether there are any serious personality problems in a class. If there are—and there usually are—the next step involves an analysis of them. Some may be aggravated cases, and others may be simply incipient. Some may be individual problems, and some may be class-wide. Not one can be solved with the mind alone. A little bit of love and understanding can go farther than all the statistics in an educational notebook. Hence, in speaking of the method to be used in therapeutic reading, one must agree with Parks that the teacher is always the best method.

Many of the problems in an average class are highly personal. Marie's family has had to go on relief, John's father and mother are getting a divorce, Ellen is an adopted child, Kathie lives on the wrong side of the tracks, Bob's father has died and he must help with the support of the family, Ted is fat and awkward, Carol's clothes look "funny," Bob has a new baby sister and no one at home is paying any attention to him. Little things, like a pair of squeaky shoes, can grind into the soul. Even such a little thing as "lining up" leaves one or two hurts: the first in line is always the "smallest," and the last in line is always the "biggest." Extremes can be painful.

As a consequence, personal hurts and problems should be dealt with individually. Often a sympathetic word or two and an understanding pat can do wonders. However, sometimes pride enters in; and the method has to be indirect. In the latter situation, it is usually best for the child himself *incidentally* to "discover" the book. Then there is no danger of his feeling that the privacy of his individual hurt has been invaded.

When a problem is a class problem, the matter can be brought into the open and discussed with all the pros and cons. Prejudices and fears and hates can be aired as common property. A story is told of a prominent contemporary painter, who in his early paintings had a lion phobia. In each of the pictures, a part of a lion could be seen; it would be crouching back of a column or tree or bush. The whole lion was never seen. Then one day the artist painted a picture and put a whole lion in the very center of it. That was the end of the lion phobia; he had brought the lion out in front, and that was the end of the complex.

When we bring our "lions" of hate and prejudice out in front, we usually are able to conquer them. Children pick up stereotyped adjectives to describe persons of minority groups. These adjectives set character appraisals: all persons belonging to those minority groups are what the adjectives say they are; there are no exceptions. Stories which give realistic pictures of persons of other races and of other creeds can do much to dispel wrong stereotyped thinking. Stories of this sort plus healthful class discussion are means by which the lion is brought out in front.

Often such discussions can begin with a single story read aloud by the teacher or read by the pupils themselves. If interests are aroused and thinking is challenged, the search for other stories dealing with the problem is certain to begin. Every possible source should be tapped. As the reading continues, interesting discoveries will be made. Thus, ideas can be pooled and evaluations made. The opportunities are endless.

POSSIBLE BOOKS TO BE USED IN
ALLEVIATING PERSONAL PROBLEMS

The bibliography given here includes books dealing with some of the most serious of the personal problems. It is merely a scratching of the surface, but it suggests possible remedies for the varied personal problems in each classroom.

The grade placement of the books, covering grades 1 through 12, is only approximate. Each teacher will know best the problems, the interests, and the reading abilities of her pupils and will use the books accordingly.

The numbers immediately after the name of the book give the approximate grade level, the numbers in parentheses give the key to the name and address of the publisher.

APPEARANCE

FAT: Engelbretson, Betty, *What Happened to George,* 1–2 (33)
Evers, Helen and Alf, *Plump Pig,* 1 (33)
Felsen, Henry G., *Bertie Comes Through,* 8–10 (9)
SIZE: Beim, Jerrold, *The Smallest Boy in the Class,* 1–2 (26)

Felt, Sue, *Rosa-Too-Little*, k–1 (8)
Field, Rachel, *Hepatica Hawks*, 7–9 (21)
Harris, Leonore, *Big Lonely Dog*, 2–3 (15)
Krasilovsky, Phyllis, *The Very Little Girl*, k–1 (8)
Lipkind, William, *Even Steven*, k–3 (13)
Seuss, Dr., *Horton Hears a Who*, k–3 (34)
Ward, Lynd, *The Biggest Bear*, k–3 (15)
PLAIN: Gates, Doris, *Sensible Kate*, 6–7 (41)
McGinley, Phyllis L., *The Plain Princess*, 3 (17)
Palmer, Nena, *That Stewart Girl*, 8–10 (26)
Reyher, Rebecca, *My Mother is the Most Beautiful Woman in the World*, 2–3 (12)

PHYSICAL HANDICAPS

VARIOUS: Herman, William, *Hearts Courageous*, 8–10 (9)
BLIND: Aldis, Dorothy, *Dark Summer*, 10–12 (32)
Bretz, Alice, *I Begin Again*, 10–12 (23)
Dickson, Marguerite S., *Bramble Bush*, 9–11 (27)
Knight, Ruth Adams, *Brave Companions*, 8–11 (8)
Putnam, Peter, *"Keep Your Head Up, Mr. Putnam!"* 10–12 (14)
Sherriff, Robert C., *Chedworth*, 11–12 (21)
Spellman, Francis J., Cardinal, *The Foundling*, 10–12 (37)
DEAF: Ehrlich, Bettina, *A Horse for the Island*, 10–12 (14)
Field, Rachel, *And Now Tomorrow*, 11–12 (21)
Murphy, Grace E. Barstow, *Your Deafness Is Not You*, 10–12 (14)
Warfield, Frances, *Cotton in My Ears*, 11–12 (41)
CRIPPLED: Angelo, Valenti, *Hill of Little Miracles*, 6–8 (41)
Baker, Louise, *Out on a Limb*, 9–12 (45)
Burnett, Frances Hodgson, *The Secret Garden*, 6–8 (11)
Menotti, Gian Carlo, *Amahl and the Night Visitors*, 9–12 (23)
PARALYZED: Barton, Betsey, *And Now to Live Again*, 10–12 (3)
Beim, Lorraine, *Triumph Clear*, 7–8 (13)
Berry, Erick, *Green Door to the Sea*, 8–10 (41)
Walker, Turnley, *Rise Up and Walk*, 10–12 (9)
Walters, Anne B. and Marugg, James K., *Beyond Endurance*, 10–12 (14)
HARELIP: Webb, Mary, *Precious Bane*, 11–12 (9)
SCAR: Leao, Sylvia, *White Shore of Olinda*, 11–12 (40)
Macken, Walter, *Rain on the Wind*, 11–12 (21)

TRAITS OF CHARACTER AND PERSONALITY

TIMIDITY: Cavanna, Betty, *Lasso Your Heart*, 8–10 (43)
Dalgliesh, Alice, *The Bears on Hemlock Mountain*, 3–4 (37)
Treffinger, Carolyn, *Li Lun, Lad of Courage*, 6–7 (1)
Williams, Gweneira, *Timid Timothy*, 1–2 (36)
CONCEIT: Boyle, Kay, *The Youngest Camel*, 5–6 (18)
Pope, Edith, *The Biggety Chameleon*, 1–3 (37)
Silliman, Leland, *The Daredevil*, 8–10 (47)
Tunis, John R., *Highpockets*, 8–12 (26)
Walden, Amelia E., *Marsha-on-Stage*, 8–10 (26)
LONELINESS: Bishop, Claire, *All Alone*, 4–6 (41)
Garner, Elvira, *Little Cat Lost*, 2–3 (25)

Glenn, Elsie and Morris, *Dumblebum,* 2–3 (22)
Smith, Dorothy E., *O, the Brave Music,* 10–12 (9)
Woolley, Catherine, *Ginnie and the New Girl,* 3–5 (26)
GREEDINESS: Cutler, Lin, *Peg-a-leg,* 2–3 (16)
Lipkind, William, *Finders Keepers,* k–3 (13)
SELFISHNESS: Bradbury, Bianca, *One Kitten Too Many,* 3–4 (15)
Cadell, Elizabeth, *The Cuckoo in Spring,* 9–12 (26)
Cavanna, Betty, *6 on Easy Street,* 8–10 (43)
Harkins, Philip, *Southpaw from San Francisco,* 8–10 (26)
Henry, Marguerite, *Geraldine Belinda,* 2 (31)
Latham, Frank B., *The Law or the Gun,* 5–8 (2)
Sigsgaard, Jens, *Nils All Alone,* 2 (29)
ACCEPTING RESPONSIBILITY: Beskow, Elsa, *Pelle's New Suit,* 1–2 (14)
Buck, Pearl, *The Big Wave,* 3–6 (6)
Du Soe, Robert C., *Three Without Fear,* 5–7 (19)
Farley, Walter, *The Black Stallion's Sulky Colt,* 8–10 (34)
Fisher, Aileen, *Homestead of the Free,* 5–8 (2)
Gray, Elizabeth J., *Adam of the Road,* 7–9 (41)
Hader, Berta and Elmer, *Cock-a-Doodle-Doo,* 2–3 (21)
Hazeltine, Alice I., comp., *Selected Stories for Teen-Agers,* 8–10 (1)
McFarland, Wilma, comp., *Then It Happened—,* 8–12 (42)
Rankin, Louise, *Daughter of the Mountains,* 7–8 (41)
Sperry, Armstrong, *Call It Courage,* 4–6 (47)
Stuart, Jesse, *A Penny's Worth of Character,* 4–5 (45)
Thompson, Mary W., *Pattern for Penelope,* 8–11 (19)

POVERTY

Crone, Anne, *This Pleasant Lea,* 10–12 (37)
Gates, Doris, *Blue Willow,* 5–7 (41)
Giles, Janice, *Miss Willie,* 10–12 (43)
Sawyer, Ruth, *Maggie Rose; Her Birthday Christmas,* 4–7 (14)
Seredy, Kate, *Tree for Peter,* 4–6 (41)

FAMILY RELATIONSHIPS

EVERYDAY LIFE: Alcott, Louisa May, *Little Women,* 7–9 (11)
Beim, Jerrold, *Kid Brother,* 2–3 (26)
Brink, Carol, *Family Grandstand,* 4–6 (41)
Carroll, Gladys H., *Christmas without Johnny,* 10–12 (21)
Cleary, Beverly, *Henry and Ribsy,* 4–5 (26)
Enright, Elizabeth, *Spiderweb for Two,* 5–7 (35)
Estes, Eleanor, *The Moffats,* 4–7 (13)
Estes, Eleanor, *The Middle Moffat,* 4–7 (13)
Estes, Eleanor, *Ginger Pye,* 4–7 (13)
Gilbreth, Frank B., Jr. and Carey, Ernestine G., *Cheaper by the Dozen,* 9–12 (5)
Holberg, Ruth, *Tomboy Row,* 4–6 (8)
Lenski, Lois, *Papa Small,* k–2 (29)
Millar, Margaret, *It's All in the Family,* 10–12 (33)
Partridge, Basil, *The Penningtons,* 10–12 (43)
Rawlings, Marjorie K., *The Yearling,* 9–12 (37)

Reynolds, Barbara L., *Pepper,* 4–6 (37)
Smith, Madeline B., *The Lemon Jelly Cake,* 10–12 (18)
Turnbull, Agnes S., *Gown of Glory,* 10–12 (15)
West, Jessamyn, *Cress Delehanty,* 9–12 (13)
Wilson, Hazel, *More Fun with Herbert,* 4–6 (16)
Woolley, Catherine, *Holiday on Wheels,* 3–5 (26)
NEW BABY: Flack, Marjorie, *The New Pet,* 1 (8)
Hawkins, Quail, *The Best Birthday,* k–2 (8)
TWINS: Du Jardin, Rosamond, *Double Date,* 8–10 (17)
Haywood, Carolyn, *The Mixed-up Twins,* 2–4 (26)
BROKEN HOME: Beim, Jerrold, *With Dad Alone,* 2–4 (13)
Cronin, A. J., *Green Years,* 11–12 (18)
L'Engle, Madeleine, *Camilla Dickinson,* 10–12 (38)
Lewiton, Mina, *The Divided Heart,* 8–10 (24)
Moody, Ralph, *Man of the Family,* 9–12 (28)
Smith, Dorothy E., *He Went for a Walk,* 10–12 (9)
Stone, Amy, *P-Penny and His Little Red Cart,* 3–5 (20)
ADOPTED CHILD: Daringer, Helen F., *Adopted Jane,* 4–5 (13)
De Leeuw, Adele and Cateau, *The Expandable Browns,* 3–6 (18)
Doss, Helen, *The Family Nobody Wanted,* 9–12 (18)
Goudge, Elizabeth, *City of Bells,* 11–12 (4)
Montgomery, L. M., *Anne of Green Gables,* 8–10 (30)
Rose, Anna P., *Room for One More,* 9–12 (15)
Runbeck, Margaret Lee, *Our Miss Boo,* 8–12 (3)
ORPHAN: Eustis, Helen, *The Fool Killer,* 10–12 (8)
Gallico, Paul, *The Small Miracle,* 10–12 (8)
Horgan, Paul, *One Red Rose for Christmas,* 9–12 (19)
Stuart, Jesse, *The Beatinest Boy,* 4–6 (45)

BOY-GIRL RELATIONSHIPS

Bro, Margueritte, *Stub, a College Romance,* 10–12 (8)
Cleary, Beverly, *Henry and Beezus,* 4–5 (26)
Craig, Margaret, *Julie,* 10–12 (5)
Daly, Maureen, *Seventeenth Summer,* 9–12 (7)
Du Jardin, Rosamond, *Boy Trouble,* 8–10 (17)
Gray, Elizabeth J., *Sandy,* 9–12 (41)
Horner, Joyce, *The Wind and the Rain,* 9–12 (8)
Stolz, Mary S., *To Tell Your Love,* 8–11 (14)
Summers, James L., *Girl Trouble,* 8–10 (43)

RELATIONSHIPS WITH PERSONS FROM OTHER COUNTRIES

Bannon, Laura, *Hat for a Hero* (Mexican), 1–3 (44)
Bard, Mary, *Best Friends* (French), 5–7 (17)
Beim, Lorraine, *Two Is a Team* (Negro), 1–2 (13)
Bemelmans, Ludwig, *Madeline's Rescue* (French), 1–3 (41)
Benary-Isbert, Margot, *The Ark* (German), 7–9 (13)
Blanton, Catherine, *Hold Fast to Your Dreams* (Negro), 9–10 (25)
Bontemps, Arna, *Lonesome Boy* (Negro), 1–3 (15)

Church, Richard, *Five Boys in a Cave* (English), 6–7 (6)

Clark, Ann N., *Secret of the Andes* (Inca Indian), 4–7 (41)

Davis, Norman, *Picken's Treasure Hunt* (African), 2–4 (29)

De Angeli, Marguerite, *Bright April* (Negro), 4–6 (8)

De Angeli, Marguerite, *Elin's Amerika* (Swedish), 4–6 (8)

De Angeli, Marguerite, *Up the Hill* (Polish), 4–6 (8)

Decker, Duane, *Hit and Run* (Negro), 8–9 (26)

Estes, Eleanor, *A Hundred Dresses* (Polish), 4–6 (13)

Flack, Marjorie, *Story about Ping* (Chinese), 1–3 (41)

Goetz, Delia, *Other Young Americans* (Latin Americans), 8–9 (26)

Guareschi, Giovanni, *Don Camillo's Dilemma* (Italian), 10–12 (10)

Lewis, Elizabeth F., *Young Fu of the Upper Yangtze* (Chinese), 7–9 (47)

Liang, Yen, *Dee Dee's Birthday* (Chinese), k–1 (29)

Lipkind, William, *Boy with a Harpoon* (Eskimo), 4–6 (13)

Long, Eula, *Faraway Holiday* (Mexican), 1–2 (26)

McSwigan, Marie, *All Aboard for Freedom* (Czech), 6–7 (9)

Mirsky, Reba P., *Thirty-one Brothers and Sisters* (African), 4–6 (46)

Papashvily, George and Helen, *Anything Can Happen* (Russian), 10–12 (14)

Politi, Leo, *Little Leo* (Italian), k–3 (37)

Prishvin, Mikhail M., *The Treasure Trove of the Sun* (Russian), 5–7 (41)

Ritter, Elizabeth, *Parasols Is for Ladies* (Negro), 4–6 (47)

Rugh, Belle D., *Crystal Mountain* (Lebanese), 4–7 (15)

Schartum-Hansen, Ingvild, *Ingvild's Diary* (Norwegian), 5–8 (20)

Seredy, Kate, *Good Master* (Hungarian), 5–7 (40)

Shannon, Monica, *Dobry* (Bulgarian), 5–8 (41)

Tunis, John R., *All-American* (Negro and Jewish), 8–11 (13)

Unnerstad, Edith, *The Saucepan Journey* (Swedish), 4–7 (21)

Walden, Amelia E., *Daystar* (Italian), 8–10 (43)

Woody, Regina J., *Starlight* (Negro), 6–8 (26)

PREVENTION OR CURE: BOTH ARE POSSIBLE IN WELL-CHOSEN BOOKS

The kind of reading described in this *A B C Language Arts Bulletin* may result in something that may be even more valuable than therapy. If we can anticipate difficulties, there is no need for remedy. For example, if we can help boys and girls to understand appreciatively the people of other races and from other countries, prejudices may be forestalled. If we can recognize in a child personality traits which may later grow into personality problems and if through books we can give him insight, we have been good teaching "doctors." If we can throw light upon all the dark crannies of the mind and heart before fear and hate and bias creep in, then we have gone a long way in educating healthy-minded boys and girls.

Therapeutic reading may be a kind of "laying up treasures." Today is good, but tomorrow may bring heartaches. When heartaches and failures and rejections come, what is the bulwark? It may be knowing someone who has had the same experience. It may also be a book, read years before, in which a character met and solved a similar problem. Thus, "remembrance of things past" may be the therapy for tomorrow.

KEY: PUBLISHER'S NAME AND ADDRESS

1. Abingdon Press, 201 Eighth Avenue S., Nashville 3, Tennessee
2. American Book Company, 55 Fifth Avenue, New York 3, N. Y.
3. Appleton-Century-Crofts, Inc., 34 West 33rd Street, New York 1. N. Y.
4. Coward-McCann, Inc., 200 Madison Avenue, New York 16, N. Y.
5. Thomas Y. Crowell Co., 201 Park Avenue S., New York 3, N. Y.
6. The John Day Co., 62 West 45th Street, New York 36, N. Y.
7. Dodd, Mead & Co., 432 Park Avenue S., New York 16, N. Y.
8. Doubleday & Company, Inc., Garden City, N. Y.
9. E. P. Dutton & Co., Inc., 201 Park Avenue S., New York 3, N. Y.
10. Farrar, Straus & Co., Inc., 19 Union Square W., New York 3, N. Y.
11. Grosset & Dunlap, 1107 Broadway, New York 10, N. Y.
12. E. M. Hale and Company, 1201 S. Hastings Way, Eau Claire, Wisconsin
13. Harcourt, Brace & World, Inc., 757 Third Avenue, New York 17, N. Y.
14. Harper & Row, Publishers, Inc., 49 East 33rd Street, New York 16, N. Y.
15. Houghton Mifflin Co., 2 Park Street, Boston 7, Massachusetts
16. Alfred A. Knopf, Inc., 501 Madison Avenue, New York 22, N. Y.
17. J. B. Lippincott Co., East Washington Square, Philadelphia 5, Pennsylvania
18. Little, Brown & Co., 34 Beacon Street, Boston 6, Massachusetts
19. Longmans, Green & Co., Inc., 119 West 40th Street, New York 18, N. Y.
20. Lothrop, Lee & Shepard Co., Inc., 419 Park Avenue S., New York 16, N. Y.
21. The Macmillan Co., 60 Fifth Avenue, New York 11, N. Y.
22. Macrae Smith Co., 225 South 15th Street, Philadelphia 2, Pennsylvania
23. McGraw-Hill Book Co., 330 West 42nd Street, New York 36, N. Y.
24. David McKay Co., Inc., 119 West 40th Street, New York 18, N. Y.
25. Julian Messner, Inc., 8 West 40th Street, New York 18, N. Y.
26. William Morrow & Co., Inc., 425 Park Avenue S., New York 16, N. Y.
27. Thomas Nelson & Sons, 18 East 41st Street, New York 17, N. Y.
28. W. W. Norton & Company, Inc., 55 Fifth Avenue, New York 3, N. Y.
29. Oxford University Press, Inc., 417 Fifth Avenue, New York 16, N. Y.
30. L. C. Page & Co., 53 Beacon Street, Boston 8, Massachusetts
31. Platt & Munk, Inc., 200 Fifth Avenue, New York 10, N. Y.
32. G. P. Putnam's Sons, 200 Madison Avenue, New York 16, N. Y.
33. Rand McNally & Co., 8255 Central Park Avenue, Skokie, Illinois
34. Random House, 457 Madison Avenue, New York 22, N. Y.
35. Holt, Rinehart & Winston, Inc., 383 Madison Avenue, New York 17, N. Y.
36. William R. Scott, Inc., 8 West 13th Street, New York 11, N. Y.
37. Charles Scribner's Sons, 597 Fifth Avenue, New York 17, N. Y.
38. Simon and Schuster, Inc., 630 Fifth Avenue, New York 20, N. Y.
39. William Sloane Associates, Inc., 425 Park Avenue S., New York 16, N. Y.
40. Vanguard Press, 424 Madison Avenue, New York 17, N. Y.
41. The Viking Press, Inc., 625 Madison Avenue, New York 22, N. Y.
42. Franklin Watts, Inc., 575 Lexington Avenue, New York 22, N. Y.
43. The Westminster Press, Witherspoon Building, Philadelphia 7, Pennsylvania
44. Albert Whitman & Co., 560 West Lake Street, Chicago 6, Illinois
45. Whittlesey House, 330 West 42nd Street, New York 36, N. Y.
46. Wilcox & Follett Co., 1255 South Wabash Avenue, Chicago 5, Illinois
47. The John C. Winston Co., 1010 Arch Street, Philadelphia 7, Pennsylvania

CHAPTER 9

Foreign Language in the Elementary School

Foreign language instruction on the elementary level is one of the most rapidly expanding trends in American education today. Current estimates indicate that there are between a million and a million and a half students studying a foreign language. Experimental programs are only beginning to test and develop the how and why of teaching it most effectively. Questions such as why teach a foreign language, what language, when to begin instruction, for whom and how long, are only a few which demand thoughtful consideration as foreign language programs are explored and initiated.

FOREIGN LANGUAGE ELEMENTARY SCHOOL *

Stanley Levenson

More than 200 natives teach more than 50,000 American elementary school children a foreign language in grades 1–8 in the dependents' schools of the U.S. Army in Europe. Of this total approximately 41,000 children are studying German, 7,500 children are studying French, and 1,500 are studying Italian.

This unique program is the largest of its kind in existence, and embodies the sum of over a decade of experience in foreign language study in the elementary school, while also giving thoughtful consideration to the results of research being done in higher institutions.

---

* Reprinted from *CTA Journal* (October 1961), pp. 46, 47, 48, 51. Permission granted to reproduce by copyright owner, California Teachers Association.

Many California school districts are presently teaching foreign language in the elementary school. These programs have been encouraged by the state department of education and the financial incentives of the National Defense Education Act. They vary from pilot courses given to selected children in one grade or one room, to city-wide programs articulated from kindergarten through high school. The fact that these programs have been almost universally successful wherever they have been undertaken with competent instruction is an indication that there are factors inherent in the experience appropriate to the child's development and geared to the time and world in which he lives.

I have spent more than one year in research toward a higher degree in studying the outstanding foreign language program in the U.S. Army Dependents' Schools in Europe, as well as other FLES programs throughout the United States. The implications contained herein should help in providing an incentive for educators throughout California to begin teaching foreign language in the elementary school, or to help in revising or enriching programs presently in the experimental stage. Many of the problems that school districts encounter when venturing into a so-called "virgin" field have been ironed out or alleviated by the dependents' schools. Teaching aids have constantly been improved and increased, as well as teaching techniques.

Objectives of the foreign language program: (a) To provide instruction in language of the host nation for all pupils in grades 1–8 in Germany, France, and Italy; (b) To develop a fluent speaking knowledge for ordinary conversation; (c) To familiarize with cultural topics insofar as they come within the intellectual grasp and interest of the elementary school child; (d) To enrich the basic curriculum by integrating as much as possible with all subject areas.

Experience has shown that certain children become proficient in a foreign language sooner than others, as is the situation in most subject areas, and it is believed that classes need to be divided into beginners and advanced groups. To alleviate the difficulty of teaching both groups in the same room, the beginners of two adjoining rooms of the same grade are combined in one room, and the same is done with the advanced group. Thus, two foreign language teachers teach simultaneously. This is the idéal situation, and is organized in most of the larger schools. Smaller schools with just one foreign language teacher find that they can only approximate the ideal. All arrangements, whatever they are, provide for continuity of instruction, which implies special provisions for beginners and advanced groups.

Foreign language teaching natives employed by the dependents' schools are specialists who teach from eight to ten sections daily, moving from classroom to classroom. They must possess a pleasing personality and a friendly spirit of cooperation with regular classroom teachers and with parents. They must be tactful, considerate, and patient with children in all grade levels, be able to meet both American and foreign school visitors, and be well informed in indigenous customs and conditions. They must be able to speak the English language correctly and fluently and be able to make proper translation and interpretation of printed matters in both English and the foreign language. Lastly, they are required to be free from pronounced dialects and colloquialisms, and use only the pure high foreign language in speaking and teaching American children.

The educational requirements for foreign language teachers are flexible enough to enable recruitment of the most qualified personnel for teaching positions. Salaries are commensurate with teaching experience and educational preparation.

The dependents' schools subscribe to the modified direct method or basically aural-oral approach to foreign language study in the elementary school. In the aural-oral approach to the teaching of foreign languages, "aural" means by ear and "oral" means by speech. Consequently, the aural-oral method means that the student has to hear the modern foreign language and then practice speaking it. The term audio-lingual which is sometimes used, refers to this same approach. Beyond this method, the foreign language teaching specialist is left to his own devices. However, several tools are provided to render the teacher's task easier and his effort more effective. Chief among these are the dependents' school teaching manuals, textbooks, audio-visual aids, and the periodic references to methodology and research published in the "Foreign Language Letters Series," by the Office of the Foreign Language Specialist, Department of the Army.

Whereas the philosophy of beginning the teaching of a foreign language in the first grade is controversial in the minds of some educators in the United States, it is perfectly evident in the U.S. Army schools where children have the opportunity to "live the language being learned" that this is the most advantageous time to begin foreign language study with greater ease and efficiency. First graders had their eyes glued to the foreign language teaching native, watching his mouth, his face, his gestures, his entire behavior. Their responses were sharp and clear, and their mimicking exacting. They seemed to arrange the foreign sounds almost intuitively into sense patterns, and within a few weeks were beginning to speak the foreign language.

In the primary grades as well as all other elementary grades, the teacher speaks nothing but his native tongue, thus creating a new climate of sound for the youngsters. It should be noted, however, that English is sometimes used when all explanations in the foreign language do not answer a specific question or convey a desired meaning. Action is used to illustrate by means of dramatization, presentations, and greetings. These are exploited in various ways. Games, songs, and dances of the native land are also utilized to their fullest extent.

While the foreign language work in the primary grades is confined to aural and oral experience, aided by the visual, tangible, and dramatic, and is therefore meant to initiate the child's articulateness in the foreign tongue, the function of the middle grades in the dependents' schools is to increase the oral articulateness of the child, and also to begin the process of making him literate in a second language.

By the time a child reaches the fourth grade the sound patterns of the second language are usually firmly established, and the written or printed symbol is logically introduced. Whereas the speaking objective is primary, practice in reading and writing is also given. This philosophy is based upon the theory that the fourth grade child will have learned to read and write his own language well enough so that there will be no interference between his first and second languages. It should also be brought out that some of the more advanced third graders are introduced to the written or printed symbol before they encounter this in fourth grade, and are meeting with much success.

In observing upper grade classes in the dependents' schools, it is felt that continuity in the over-all foreign language program is being provided. The minds of the average and superior students are being developed to the point where they crave greater intellectual exercise. The upper grades are where a great deal of grouping takes place. The slower groups or beginners stress conversation, and read about the foreign people and their culture, while the advanced groups are presented with grammar or structure of the second language.

Comparisons between the grammatical pattern of English, which the students are studying at this time, and the foreign language are continually made. Notebooks are often kept in the upper grade classes. Records of reading and other experiences, letters to pen pals in foreign schools, and contributions in creative writing as well as tape exchanges, are some of the activities in which upper grade classes participate. Although certain areas are stressed more than others, hearing, speaking, reading, and writing continue throughout the upper grade foreign language program.

The FLES program in the U.S. Army dependents' schools in Europe is one example of the outstanding results which can be obtained when beginning the teaching of a foreign language in the elementary school.

Americans need to become increasingly aware of the importance of languages in the communication between nations in a rapidly shrinking world. With millions of our soldiers distributed all over the face of the earth and in contact with other peoples, with thousands of representatives of our government distributed even more widely, with the sudden emergence of an American Peace Corps, and with more than a million American tourists visiting foreign lands each year, it is clear that we need to become more linguistically adept than we have been in the past. This result can be obtained if we begin a second language in the elementary school, proceed logically, and improve the quality of our teaching as we progress along intelligent lines.

AFTER FLES—WHAT? *

Theodore Andersson

The easy assumption, hitherto held by many, that foreign language instruction in our elementary schools would cure most of our language-learning ills is gradually yielding to a more balanced view. Excessive optimism inevitably resulted as teachers and parents, accustomed to the resistance and ineptitude of adolescent learners, observed with what skill and eagerness young children learned the elements of foreign speech. This feeling of optimism was increased by the realization that in many FLES [1] classes the children practiced listening and speaking in direct imitation of a native model. Here was little problem-solving, none of the time-consuming grammatical talk *about* language for which our high school and college teachers of modern languages have been so severely reproached. But events have proved that lessons learned from our experience with FLES are not automatically applied to FL teaching in the secondary school or college. And indeed many FLES programs that *appear* to be successful are threatened with failure because they are conducted under unfavorable conditions. However, FLES still holds much hope, and new and developing programs far outnumber the many less well publicized failures. FLES therefore is the focal point of the brief survey I should like to make of recent trends and future prospects in modern foreign language teaching. Such a survey falls naturally into five parts, each corresponding to a well defined program.

---

* From *The Educational Forum* (November 1961), pp. 81–86. Copyright Kappa Delta Pi, reprinted by permission.

[1] Widely used abbreviation for "foreign languages in the Elementary School."

STAGE ONE: THE TRADITIONAL TWO-YEAR COURSE

The first is the traditional two-year course of language study, in grades nine and ten or ten and eleven. If I were named Voltaire, I would say that this arrangement had been carefully planned to guarantee the *non*-learning of language. By age fourteen a person whose experience has been confined to one language has formed deep muscular and psychological habits which are in most cases an effective block to the learning of a second language and to the development of an understanding of another people. Add to this handicap our traditional teaching of modern languages as though they were Latin and the usual limitation of the learning period to two years and you can readily agree that it would be good to have a Voltaire around to help Bestor and Rickover in their useful work. Because guidance counselors still advise high school students not to continue their language study through the eleventh and twelfth grades, a large percentage of college freshmen who have had two or three years of a language are unable to demonstrate on a placement test enough proficiency even to get into a second-semester course. To all intents the high school language instruction for these students has been largely wasted, as professional educators have long contended.

STAGE TWO: THE FOUR TO SIX YEAR SEQUENCE

Stage two has been achieved in a few places. This program consists of four solid years of language learning in grades nine through twelve or six years in grades seven through twelve. The six-year sequence may consist either of five periods a week for six years or of, say, three periods in grades seven and eight, five in grades nine, ten, and eleven, and two in grade twelve. This program is often characterized by a slightly greater sophisticaton in method and may even consist of anywhere from a month to a year of bookless instruction at the outset. There is usually a greater emphasis on understanding and speaking than in traditional classes, and hence greater concern for providing learners with authentic models in the form of native speakers.

STAGE THREE: THE TEN-YEAR COURSE

Stage three I shall describe as the ten-year sequence, which, beginning in grade three, builds in each grade solidly on what has gone before and continues through grade twelve. Since most teachers understand that the traditional grammar method of instruction cannot be successful in grades three and four, they almost universally use an audio-lingual approach in the early years of the ten-year sequence. And since almost all learners are more interested in learning to understand to speak than they are in learning *only* how to read and write, this program is likely to be more successful than were the older ones.

We are of course speaking of a single ten-year program with a smooth articulation between the elementary and secondary grades, not of one in which children who have been learning a second language in grades three through six are put in the same class as beginners in grade seven.

Graduates of the ten-year program can be expected to have acquired greater skill in understanding, speaking, reading, and writing a second language than graduates of a four- or six-year sequence, but we don't yet know how much more. The administrators of one well planned program recognize an advantage of one year's achievement; but since tests show that the former hold an additional ten-per-cent advantage over the latter, it is possible that the actual differential is nearer two years than one.

STAGE FOUR: THE TWELVE-YEAR SEQUENCE

Stage four, almost non-existent at our present stage of development, I shall call the twelve-year sequence, beginning either in kindergarten or in grade one and continuing in one uninterrupted and cumulative program through the twelfth grade. At first sight it would appear that there is not much difference between stages three and four. From a quantitative point of view this is true. Graduates of the twelve-year course are not going to learn many more structures or much more vocabulary than graduates of the ten-year course. But there *is* an important difference.

This difference derives from the observation that in general children under ten are better able than children over ten to hear and reproduce linguistic signals. Hence, real mastery, acquiring the "feel" of a language, the ability to use it automatically, the freedom to think about *what* to say rather than how to say it, the easy acceptance and understanding of those who speak the second language, these intangible values of language learning are more easily acquired the younger the learner is. Hence the great superiority of the twelve-year sequence —if properly conducted—over the ten-year course.

BILINGUAL LITERATES OR ILLITERATES?

It is appropriate at this point to mention what might be called a variant program of stage four. This is a program which is possible in bilingual areas, of which we have many. For example, we could utilize our French resources in northern New England and New York State and in Louisana and our Spanish resources in and around New York City and throughout our Southwest.

In the early grades our teaching of children whose mother tongue is not English often violates the basic principles of developmental psychology in two ways: (1) We try to teach them to read and write English before they are "ready" and we fail to teach them to read and write their mother tongue, for which they are or soon can be made ready. In the Southwest, for example, it happens regularly that Spanish-speaking children receive no opportunity for formal instruction in Spanish until grade seven or grade nine, by which time motivation for learning has disappeared. The same children are often forced to learn reading and writing in English at the same time as English-speaking children, thus creating in them a sense of insufficiency which often ends by producing bilingual illiterates.

By the simple expedient of teaching them first the elements of reading and writing in Spanish while they are learning to understand and speak English and while their English-speaking classmates are learning reading and writing in English and the elements of spoken Spanish, most of these young Americans could become literate bilinguals. These are precisely the kind of people whose need was so sorely felt during and after World War II. It is partly because we have failed to cultivate these vast linguistic resources within our borders that we now have to spend millions under the National Defense Education Act on programs which are essentially remedial in nature.

LOOKING AHEAD TO STAGE FIVE

If stage four is largely beyond our reach, stage five lies still farther in the future. Such a program will, we hope, rest on a thorough understanding and a wide recognition of the principles of developmental psychology and of conditioned learning. Although François Gouin recorded vividly as early as the 1870's the results of his observation, we are still far from having learned or applied the simple lessons to be derived from watching any child learn a language between birth and age five and a half. The marvelous perceptive and imitative powers which enable him to do this remain with him for some years though they decline in proportion as his powers of conceptual learning increase. It appears that conceptual learning becomes dominant over conditioned learning at about age ten. So it is that by age fourteen or fifteen, the age we have chosen in the past to begin language instruction, the faculty which is most useful in learning a language is no longer of much use to the learner. If ten is still a favorable age to begin learning a second language, eight is better, six is better still, four is even better, and so on down to zero. Thus, while from an adult— or adultistic—point of view a program which begins in kindergarten or grade one seems ideal if not downright fanciful, it actually comes much too late. Stage five will have to be concerned with pre-school and out-of-school learning if it is to take full advantage of the child's powers of learning.

CONDITIONED LEARNING OR ENCULTURATION

FLES in stage three is still a somewhat formal kind of instruction though obviously much less formal than FL instruction in high school or college. In the early years of stage four FLES is more informal though still organized within the regular school day. In stage five the words "instruction" and "formal" are out of place. Indeed the word "learning" might well be replaced by the word "enculturation." A child learns the language or languages of his environment as a part of the total process known as enculturation. In this setting a language expresses and reflects the values of its culture, and both the language and the cultural values are learned together by a process of conditioning. Here language and culture are inseparable, whereas in our traditional language classes language and culture are almost never joined.

In this fifth stage all is speculation. Experience provides much evidence but there has been little experimentation. In an effort to point to possible ways in which we might take advantage of the psychological principles mentioned, let me suggest two lines of thought.

THE INTERNATIONAL NURSERY SCHOOL IDEA

One possibility for exploiting the young child's language-learning powers would be to experiment with the international nursery school idea. The exact procedures would have to be worked out carefully in collaboration with nursery school experts and child psychologists, but the general features of such a program might be somewhat as follows.

Since there is no known limit to the number of languages a small child can learn in a natural cultural setting, one might start with as many languages as there are days in the week. For practical purposes I should select Chinese, French, German, Russian, and Spanish. Necessary to the success of such an undertaking would be the selection of highly trained nursery school teachers who are native speakers of these languages and who can also speak English. On Monday the Spanish-speaking teacher would be in charge and would conduct her work in Spanish. On Tuesday the Russian teacher would direct the activities in Russian. On Wednesday the German teacher would take over, as would the Chinese teacher on Thursday and the French teacher on Friday. While observing basic principles governing the conduct of an American nursery school and thus maintaining a uniform policy under the direction of an English-speaking American nursery-school expert, each teacher would represent, as naturally as is possible in this artificial setting, her own culture. She would behave with the children—two, three, and four-year-olds—as one does in her country and she would urge them to behave as children do in her country. She would speak only her own language—except in an emergency—and would use gesture to convey meaning. The children would be instructed initially by the directress to respond in English or in any way that seemed natural or not at all until they feel ready. It is my guess, subject to verification in an actual experiment, that the children would understand everything that is said in this limited setting in all five languages by the end of the school year. The experiment should if possible be continued into a second and third year, for children who learn fantastically fast at this age forget just as rapidly unless habits are reinforced by long and continued exposure.

OUT-OF-SCHOOL LEARNING

There is room for much experimentation in this area: the establishment of more bilingual or multilingual summer camps, extended foreign travel for children, the placing of children in foreign families under carefully controlled conditions, movie and TV programs which would bring a foreign environment into one's own home. These and other ideas could be used to extend to our children opportunities for learning other languages and cultures. Through such initiatives we could implement our knowledge that language is behavior and that the intimate understanding of another people's behavior is the necessary foundation for better international understanding and cooperation.

The preceding five-stage survey of trends in FL teaching is intended to provide needed perspective. From it will appear how inadequate have been conditions under which in the past languages have been taught. And proper understanding of the facts that language is essentially a form of behavior and that the acquisition of anything approaching authentic linguistic behavior requires conditioned learning of an intensive kind is by no means universal. FL teachers have not until recently provided leadership in propagating this understanding, for they have themselves not understood the nature of language and of the language-learning process much better than other educators or the general public. Educational administrators and school boards cannot well be expected to provide long language-learning sequences, insist on qualified teachers, and assure modern materials and facilities until they understand these basic principles. Slipshod procedures will inevitably result in mediocre instruction and inadequate learning, in FLES as in high school and college teaching, leading to ultimate failure. Ironically, the more advantage we can take of out-of-school or pre-school learning, the better is our chance of establishing a satisfactory course of FL instruction in school. The cure for our language ills is therefore not to be found in FLES as such, nor in language laboratories, nor in new and better materials—though all of these are needed—but rather in a much higher quality of workmanship than has in the past marked our FL instruction and indeed our total educational effort.

FOREIGN LANGUAGE IN THE
ELEMENTARY SCHOOL *

Anne S. Hoppock

Pressures on the elementary school to teach a second language are mounting. Led by the Modern Language Association of America, using the cryptic battle cry FLES, teachers of foreign languages have sent out the fleet to invade the shores of the elementary school curriculum. The *FL Newsletter* of the Association reports each new beachhead with triumphant headlines.

But many people in elementary education take a distinctly dim view of the campaign. They do not quarrel with the belief that it is desirable for Americans to become bi-lingual. They do doubt that organized instruction in elementary schools is appropriate, even in terms of this particular goal alone. They observe the 50% decrease in enrollments in the high school language classes in the nation over the past three decades and reflect that unless more impressive results can

---

* Reprinted from *NJEA Review* (November 1956), by permission of the author.

be demonstrated at the elementary school level, the time and money are hardly justified.

RE-EVALUATE THE H. S. PROGRAM

This movement to produce Americans who speak other languages ought to start, it seems reasonable to believe, with a thorough re-evaluation of the language program in the high schools. The purpose should be to determine why high school pupils are not participating and what can be done to make the program more attractive.

Certainly high school teachers are not promoting "FLES" because the high school is unable to use procedures which interest adolescents in language study. And yet, what are the implications of this report of a northeastern conference on the teaching of foreign language in the elementary school, from the *FL Newsletter* of September, 1954?

"We have finally realized that the central language experience is *some-one speaking and someone listening;* that grammar is not the language itself. . . . We have learned that children can acquire most readily a second language when it is taught to them as a living experience. They enjoy learning it that way. We have come to understand that the modern elementary school, because of its basic philosophy and program pattern, can be the place for the acquisition of a second language as a *living* experience."

Here seems to be the assumption that a second language cannot be a living experience anywhere but in the setting of the "basic philosophy" of the elementary school. Are high school teachers willing to let it be implied that the basic philosophy of the high school requires it to teach as if grammar is a language in itself?

RESEARCH PROVES WHAT?

The children in the elementary school are a captive audience; they have no choice of courses. This creates the temptation to look outward (or downward) rather than inward and jump to the conclusion that the solution is to catch the children younger. Carried to its logical conclusions, this idea might lead us to include football, driver education, or Shakespeare in the elementary school curriculum. But, proponents of FLES argue, this does not follow for, in the case of foreign language, research proves that the elementary school is the best place to begin.

"Research proves" has a weighty ring and to hold out against an innovation which "research proves" to be "best" is to run the danger of being called either ignorant or reactionary. However, the skeptic must ask, "What research proves what?" and to insist that values and principles as well as statistics enter into decisions.

Research may prove that many elementary school children have learned some elements of a foreign language easily. The children can count to 20 or say "good morning" in Spanish; they can sing a song in French and speak and respond to simple directions. But this is not to say they can use the language to think with, or that they can communicate in the language with a non-English speaking person. The young child may acquire many words in a second language but it is a mistake to think that he learns it as a mode of communication in the sense he does his native tongue. A child learns to speak his own language in order to supply basic needs, to get food when he is hungry, to find refuge when he is afraid, to seek companionship when he is lonely. Unless he lives in another culture where he really needs a second language to communicate, it is doubtful if he learns it in any permanent or functional sense.

Other sweeping assertions are frequently made as supporting evidence. However, if assumptions such as these are supported by research, the findings have not come to our attention:

. . . that children who are given organized instruction in a language will thereby learn to admire and respect the peoples of the world who speak that language.

. . . that world peace will be furthered (Note that our most crucial need is for peaceful relations with people who speak Arabic, Chinese, and Russian).

. . . that, if they start early, appreciably more children will continue to study languages throughout the high school and college years.

. . . that at the conclusion of high school, and college, students who start early will be much further along (In one school system, pupils who had 6 years of instruction in French before entering high school are placed in second year French classes. In other words, 6 years of instruction set the children ahead only 1 year). Assumptions such as these should be tested before extravagant claims are made.

It is easy to confuse opinion with research-validated facts. Here is an example of a decision to continue and expand a program in the elementary school, reported by the *FL Newsletter* in an article headed "Success with FLES":

In 1952, Dr. . . . ., Professor of Foreign Language at . . . ., began teaching French to 4th and 6th graders of the Elementary Laboratory School. When the twenty-nine original 6th-graders finished 8th grade (and 3 years of French) they were asked for their personal evaluations of their French study. Of the twenty-five who felt they understood the French people and France much better than they could have done without the 3 years of language, 18 felt they probably had a better understanding of *all* foreign-speaking peoples because of their contact with French; 27 vowed that they'd be less apt now to laugh at foreigners who speak English with an accent; 25 expressed personal satisfaction in the fact that they had 'accomplished something'; 25 believed that there had been too little time for class periods in French (four 25-minute periods per week); 24 expected to go on with French in high school (only 2 expected to do no more work in a foreign language). Lamented one pupil: 'I might have done better if I had not had my braces. It is very hard for me to imitate anyone!'

Writes Professor ....:

By now there is no question about scheduling foreign language, and I am set for the program this fall in the 4th, 5th, 6th and 7th grades. The 7th grade will be entering their fourth year of French. Our fourth-grade critic read these evaluations and her comment was most encouraging to me. She said they showed her that our 8th grade (about whom everyone had been worrying the past two years) was NOT doomed to intellectual mediocrity. She thinks that the language work has been able to hold them to a high standard which they have felt and have appreciated. I do expect the children to do a high-level piece of work with French, and they have never disappointed me yet. I fear that too many elementary teachers do not expect enough from the children.

"By now there was no question," the Professor said, basing this flat and final conclusion on the opinions of 25 children and the reaction of a teacher who apparently assumed that the children's experience with French had rescued them from a lifetime of intellectual mediocrity and protected them from elementary school teachers who do not "expect enough."

People who know elementary school children know that they will become enthusiastic about anything which is taught attractively by an enthusiastic teacher. But it takes study over time to determine what the real outcomes are. It is small wonder that people responsible for the education of young children are alarmed when data such as these are offered as the basis for drawing upon the elementary schools' slender reserves of time and money.

"RESEARCH SAYS"

It is fascinating to find that research often seems available to "prove" that the same practice is both good and bad.[1] For example, study of the literature gives some indication that:

---

[1] See the *Encyclopedia of Educational Research* (Macmillan, revised edition). See also FLES Bulletin No. 1 (Modern Lanugage Association of America, 1953), which cites conflicting views of leading neurologists and psychiatrists.

1. Bilingualism in young children tends to retard their learning of the mother tongue.

2. Some children with language disabilities are further hampered academically and emotionally by instruction in a second language.

3. Older pupils learn a foreign language more rapidly than do younger children. The childhood years may have the advantage in linguistic flexibility but the late high school and college years are the period of greatest learning ability in general and are closer to the time of possible use.

4. Probably the truth is that dependable research is insufficient to indicate conclusively the "best" age to introduce a second language.

The "best" age to begin may be later than we think. The experience of the armed services gives strong support to the idea that young adults with strong motivation learn languages much more efficiently than any other age group. For example, service men currently in training for duty which requires facility in foreign languages can begin conversing in an Asiatic language after from 4 to 6 weeks of instruction. Granted that the men are selected, the training intensive, and the groups small, one can safely hypothesize that strong motivation and good methods of teaching are our best hope rather than adding years of instruction to those which already have proved ineffective.

STUDY THE STATISTICS

Sometimes administrators are pressured to institute a program because "everybody" is starting one. Actually, the statistics showing the growth of the program will bear some critical analysis.

In the February, 1956, joint report of the United States Office of Education and the Modern Language Association, "Status of Foreign Language Study in American Elementary Schools," programs were reported in 357 cities and towns throughout 44 states. When the figures are analyzed, it becomes clear that there are fewer well established programs in public elementary school districts than appears on the surface.

For example:

94 were conducted at college, in campus or demonstration schools, or in connection with summer workshops.

26 were summer programs only.

85 were voluntary, sometimes conducted in out of school hours, some on a fee basis.

39 were for "gifted" children. (For example, in the city of Cleveland, only about 1100 children were in the program.)

In a considerable number of districts, the program is available to relatively few children because the program is experimental, or because only a few elementary classroom teachers are working "on their own" with their children.

The report further specifies that 33 programs were being discontinued in 1955 and that 58 were introduced in 1955.

Only 39 programs have been operating prior to 1950. Of these, 13 are in demonstration or campus schools. A number are on a voluntary basis, or for "gifted" children. Highly significant is the fact that a number of the old programs are in border states, where some of the children have need for a second language.

Programs which have started since 1950 might reasonably be considered as still experimental. It is surely difficult to draw final conclusions about the worth of a program until the elementary school children involved have moved through the high school, perhaps through early adulthood.

QUALITY, NOT QUANTITY

Practical as well as philosophical considerations are involved. The elementary school curriculum is already overcrowded. Classes are often too large. Well trained teachers are in short supply. Elementary school classroom teachers who speak a second language well enough for children to imitate are practically non-existent, requiring that a special language teacher be scheduled for one or more short periods a week. This arrangement makes the assumption that children "live the language" and the culture of the people who speak it hardly credible. One specialist met 100 classes per week on a 15–20 minute schedule, and so worked with about 3500 children in a week's time!

The ill effects of a program which does not have competent teachers are discussed by William-R. Parker, Executive Secretary of the Modern Language Association, in the June, 1956 issue of "The National Parent Teacher." In the words of the writer:

When programs are improvised faddishly, when the teachers themselves have only a slight knowledge of a foreign language, what happens? Johnny imitates, with pathetic accuracy, his teacher's fractured French. Mary merely commits to memory a few isolated Spanish words that she'll forget over the summer. (And a good thing too!)

For the surest way of discrediting language instruction, causing the public to doubt its value and relevance, is to have it done by teachers who are not qualified. There are those who say we've been making this mistake in some of our high schools for years, but that's another problem. Let's not repeat it in the grades, at a level where children's more faithfully imitated accents would eventually advertise our folly to the world! . . .

Our plea—and we think it a reasonable one—is that it come from persons who not only understand elementary school children but who also speak and understand the foreign language. It must be solved by recruiting elementary school teachers who already have the language proficiency.

. . . a qualified teacher of a foreign language in the grades had better know the important differences between our culture and that of the people who speak that native tongue . . . This does not mean teaching the children the foreign words for American things; it does not mean teaching isolated words at all . . . Rather, in a measure he experiences that culture.

Hence my plea that we slow down this great rush to get a second language in the grades—much as we realize its importance . . . Why hurry to put it there before we are ready to offer the kind of language instruction that parents expect and that America needs? Let's not cheat our children.

THE BASIC QUESTION

Does research in human development and learning strongly indicate that a second language should be taught in the elementary school? In our opinion, it does not.

Children in a spirit of play respond to the learning of the vocabulary of a foreign language just as they enjoy the lingo of "pig latin." But the program serves no genuine need of children. Real motivation —that is, the need to communicate, is lacking. If "learning" is defined as "learning to use," it is doubtful if the children can be said to learn.

"Use or lose" applies here. Relatively few adults who have studied a foreign language in high school or college, even those who became fairly fluent, are able to communicate in the language after a few years have elapsed. They lose the skill because they do not use it. How ridiculous to assume that young children who are years further away from us will be better off.

This principle of "use or lose" throws light on the belief that our young children should be given instruction because European children become bi-lingual. Elizabeth Thompson, in a report worth careful study,[2] writes, "I had spoken German fluently as a child and had studied six years of foreign languages in high school and college, but I had so little occasion to communicate in the languages that I had forgotten them." She describes her inability to speak the languages of the nations she visited during her study and then says, "As I visited

---

[2] Elizabeth Engle Thompson, "Foreign Language Teaching in Elementary Schools," Great Neck Public Schools, New York, December, 1954.

foreign elementary schools where English and other languages were taught, I could well understand why the majority of educated Europeans are bilingual and multi-lingual. The school learning is meaningful, for the children live in an environment in which many languages are spoken. The need to communicate in more than one tongue has been and is a part of the experiences of living for many European children so that the languages they learn in school . . . are also part of their home and community life experiences. They learn the languages by using them." And, later, "Young children of army personnel quickly and adequately assimilated the languages of the foreign countries not only because of their youthful age, but primarily because of the foreign linguistic environment and need to communicate."

RELATIVE VALUES

In the final analysis, values must weigh heavily in reaching conclusions regarding the desirability of an organized program. Even if the claims made for the efficiency of early teaching were shown to be valid, school people and parents must assess the total needs and resources of the school and community, and ask, "Does this program have priority?"

Let's not fool ourselves that the program does not require time and money. If an itinerant teacher is responsible, as would be the case in most New Jersey schools, how else can the program operate except in regularly scheduled periods which, we are told, should be daily, or several times a week? In some districts as much as 175 minutes per week are devoted to instruction and it is obvious that much less time would be inadequate. Where is the time to come from? From the "3 R's?" From the arts? From creative experiences with the children's own language? From science, the social studies? From outdoor play?

As for money, one suburban district figured that it would cost nearly $42,000.00 to provide instruction from grades one through six. (Several "authorities" recommend beginning with kindergarten or grade one.) This estimate is modest since it is based on minimum salary figures. Train classroom teachers to do it, or use records? Can we assume that the speech of a teacher trained in a summer workshop will be a fit model for children to copy, or that records are good for anything but an interesting experience in hearing how people of other nations speak?

When time and money are spent for one thing, it automatically rules out something else. Forty-two thousand dollars and two hours a week are no small expenditures. Do the children need 30 minutes a day of French or Spanish more than other things the equivalent time and money would buy? Again, on a basis of our acquaintance with schools throughout the State, we are strongly convinced that the answer is no.

CONTRIBUTION OF THE ELEMENTARY SCHOOL

In our opinion, children in the elementary school are better off for having informal, meaningful experiences with several languages in the setting of the cultures involved than to be given formal instruction in one language. Rather than to develop facility with one language, the purpose is to develop interest in several languages, to realize that people everywhere communicate common feelings and experiences although the words they use have different sounds. Many resources are available for this purpose. The creative planning of elementary school people and language specialists might well be directed toward discovering and using these resources effectively.

In seeking resources, we do not have to start from scratch. We already know that there are many children in our classrooms today whose first language is a foreign language. We know that usually there are citizens in the community, and visitors to the community, who speak one or more foreign languages. Records, radio, and television programs are available. Books such as "See and Say," a picture book with captions in four languages by Antonio Frasconi, published by Harcourt, Brace, say to children that people use different languages to communicate the same things. Picture-story books from Asiatic as well as European countries are available. The language arts, social studies, and music all offer opportunities for meaningful experiences with languages. Informal study of our own language shows children how widely it draws from other languages.[3]

It is in face-to-face contacts, however, that language becomes a "living experience." It lives when it is used to communicate. If, in the process, those communicating learn to like and respect one another, then we can feel reasonably sure we are on the right track. In seeking the "living experience," contrast with the twenty minute lesson in Spanish by the teacher who comes and goes, the story of this group of nine year olds and their new friend Carmen:

Carmen, a shy nine year old Puerto Rican girl came unheralded with her brother to enroll in the school. The principal discovered she could speak no English and assigned her to the fourth grade teacher knowing she would be wanted and accepted there.

---

[3] "Passwords to People" (by Carol Denison, Dodd-Mead Co., 1956) is a fascinating story for children about words, their origins, uses, and importance.

The teacher and children planned how they would help Carmen quickly learn English to "get along" during the first weeks. Various youngsters assumed responsibility for needed learnings. For example, one took her to the corridor to learn "fountain," "water," "drink." To the delight of the children, Carmen said the Spanish equivalents. Gradually the idea developed that Carmen might teach the children some Spanish. So the learning of Spanish and English proceeded happily side by side. Then Carmen and the children began writing Spanish words and their English equivalents on the chalkboard. Carmen sang a song in Spanish. The music teacher took down the melody and the children learned to sing it. As Carmen learned the ways of working and playing in the United States, the children were becoming acquainted with the culture from which Carmen came. The children were not mastering Spanish but they were using it to learn to know Carmen. They were getting its "feel," finding it interesting, not funny or strange. They were learning that, although languages are different, human beings of other races and national origins are much the same in the basic needs and ideas they have to communicate.

This experience in getting acquainted was so fruitful that the children decided to share it with the rest of the school in an assembly program. They arranged a miniature classroom on the stage. One child was "teacher." They played out the ways they had worked, exhibited their facility with the new language, sang the song Carmen taught them, shared their valued new friend, Carmen, with the whole school.

Later, Carmen's mother came for a parent-teacher conference with a Puerto Rican child who spoke English as interpreter. At the end of a pleasant talk, Carmen's mother put her arm around the teacher and in a flood of Spanish told her, "Now, I know why Carmen loves to come to this school. This school is a loving place."

IN SUMMARY

Policy disagreements on the question of where to begin foreign language study has seemed in some instances to put us in a position of competing for the children's time and their parent's support. None of us want this. It behooves us, then, to work out together the broad outline of a program for all levels of the school based upon the best thinking we can do with the data we now have. Within the program is a place for carefully planned and objectively evaluated experimental study to seek new knowledge and insight and "action researchers" involved should lead in resisting the bandwagon approach to innovations.

Each district has the right and responsibility to do its own thinking regarding placement and program at various levels of the school. Our purpose, in this statement, is to share our thinking on the basis of our study. It leads us to believe that:

1. In the elementary school, children should have many vital ex-

periences with several cultures including the language of these cultures. Thus the elementary school curriculum becomes a broad based readiness program resulting in interest and readiness for more intensive study.

2. Leaders in our high schools should intensify their efforts to spread widely the leaven of creative teaching which makes language study in some of our New Jersey high schools truly a "living experience."

SEQUENCES OF GROWTH AND INSTRUCTION IN FOREIGN LANGUAGES IN THE ELEMENTARY SCHOOLS *

Edward Diller

The reasons for teaching foreign languages in elementary schools are (1) society now has greater need than it has ever had for linguistic ability; and (2) foreign languages are generally learned with greatest ease early in life. Society's need for linguistic ability makes it necessary for full consideration to be given to ways the need may be met most readily. The fact that foreign languages may be learned with the greatest ease during the early years of life directs attention to the feasibility of teaching foreign languages in the elementary school.

It was with the foregoing idea in mind that foreign language was introduced in the elementary schools of the Beverly Hills Unified School District in the fall of 1960. . . .

✲   ✲   ✲

SEQUENCE IN INSTRUCTION IN FOREIGN LANGUAGE IN THE ELEMENTARY SCHOOL

In planning the year's work for the foreign language program in the elementary schools of Beverly Hills the members of the plan-

* Reprinted from *California Journal of Elementary Education* (November 1961), pp. 115–120, by permission of the author.

ning committee were immediately confronted by three possibilities:
(1) They could lay out a series of subject units, such as home, school,
community, and the like and move with regularity from one to the
other; (2) they could construct a chart of sequential grammar,
progressing from the simplest and most functional concepts, to the
rarer and more abstract while searching out pragmatically any approaches or drills that would put the concept across; or (3) they could
attempt some composite of the two.

The guiding, but remote, linguistic objective was to bring the
children to the point of spontaneously communicating in the foreign
language within a reasonable period of time. Yet, the basis of the
program was to teach pattern sentences; that is, standard basic con-
versational patterns which might easily be used in their entirety. Such
units or sentences could be memorized in the form of a story, a song,
or a pattern conversation about home, school, or any other subject.
Arbitrary acceptance of the way that foreign sentences are formed
seemed the basis of the approach to foreign language learning, so it
was decided to begin with a story to be memorized.

"The Three Bears" (in the French Classes) and "Chicken Little"
(in the Spanish classes) were told and retold with pictures, flannel
boards, masks, or chalk drawings in order to make the story seem
constantly different, interesting, and exciting. The basic vocabulary
and syntax were relayed in the same pattern each time in order to
ensure an unadulterated assimilation of the native sounds and structures. Games were played, songs sung, and the story acted out. At
first, the children were enthusiastic, amused, and soon skilled in re-
telling the story, but then the interest began to wane. The children,
especially at the higher elementary level (i.e., fifth grades), wanted to
know the purpose of the story. Most first and third grade pupils were
willing to accept the story *per se* for its intrinsic amusement. The story
had captured the imagination of the older children at the outset, but
it did not offer adequate content to sustain interest for a long period
of time. The children soon desired to say common and meaningful
things to each other in the foreign language. They were anxious to
get on with fluency and a more practical vocabulary. At this point
instruction, therefore, moved on to another unit consisting of colors,
numbers, and self-description. Because these seemed to be of concrete interest, the children learned quickly and once again the planning group was confronted with the problem: "Shall we go on to
another subject matter unit or is there a basic grammatical structure
that we must follow?"

The question led to an investigation of three areas: (1) theories of learning, (2) the sequence of grammar, and (3) the interests of children.

1. The theory of language learning. Language skill begins with a basic stock knowledge. Forms and phrases must be learned through repetition in a rote manner. Words are the basic building blocks of a sentence, and grammar consists of the basic relationships between these words. What we often call "original speech" is actually the rearrangement or juxtaposing of words or phrases in a basically acceptable syntactical structure. This is the manner in which the mother tongue is learned. The child finds himself under a deluge of sounds and with time is allowed to sift and select them for his own use. But, is this process practical for children exposed to a foreign language for only 20 minutes daily?

2. The sequence of grammar. Frequency lists for vocabulary are readily available and the order of basic grammatical concepts used to build language skills is accessible in any traditional grammar text. Articles, basic verb forms, declarative and interrogative word order, personal pronouns, negatives, and adjectives are fundamental concepts. The fundamental concepts should be imparted to children explicitly in the foreign language as they are in the native language. When "j'ai un livre" has been thoroughly learned, then the concepts, in part, of subject pronouns, conjugation of "avoir," indefinite articles, direct objects, and transitive verbs have also been learned.

Upon further consideration, the variable and inflexible parts to the sentence are evident. The inflexible noun remains as it is, and the children will have little or no difficulty with it, whereas the verb is highly flexible and is at the same time the bulwark of the sentence. The subject pronoun may be considered equally variable, but yet with some drill the children consider the pronouns almost an integral part of the verb which they in turn begin to inflect mechanically and with facility. Measuring basic grammatical concepts against the ease or difficulty with which the children learn them, the plan for further development of instruction in foreign language began to be formulated. A concept was identified as necessary to be learned. This concept was then checked against a vocabulary frequency list. The teachers realized that "to be" and "to have" must be effectively taught and that thereafter teachers must embark upon the teaching of regular common verbs. Such logic was appealing, but to try to teach such abstractions as conjugations to elementary school children would be to court disaster.

3. The interests of children. The present program extends from the first to the fifth grades and naturally the interests vary widely.

Pupils in first grade, third grade, and fifth grade live in three different worlds and to capture interest and imagination the language instruction program must offer that which their minds are capable of absorbing. Primarily, it seems, that children incisively reject monotony. Teaching foreign languages effectively to elementary school children is to teach the same thing in many different yet carefully planned ways. Language learning demands endless repetition and yet young minds constantly require new, stimulating, and exciting learning procedures.

On the basis of the above considerations and of experiences in the classrooms, the teachers arrived at the formula "Realism and Romance," or "Content and Amusement," that is, alternate entertaining stock experiences such as stories, games and songs, with pattern rearrangement and drill. For example, drill can concentrate on certain verbs which have been introduced with stories, games, and songs.

The steps in the program are *Step 1, Romance:* "The Three Bears"— basic vocabulary, pattern sentences, and amusement; *Step 2, Realism:* verb (e.g., "to have")—to be drilled on in relationship to the story—"I (you) (he) *have (has)* the baby bear's bowl" ("chair," "bed," and the like)—varied but basic drill; *Step 3, Romance:* new story or content unit that emphasizes and depends on use of the verb previously taught.

Step 1, Romance. The stories, songs, games, and dialogues are designed to spark the imagination of the children; but insofar as the over-all foreign language program is concerned, this approach has the manifold purposes of introducing new work in an interesting fashion and of expanding the amount of material already known. It is through the story that basic vocabulary and sentence structure are taught in context; it is through the song that phonology is emphasized; and it is through games and poems that enthusiasm is stimulated. Of course, enthusiasm should be apparent throughout and phonology should always be a concern of the teachers, but the emphasis shifts according to the nature of the work being taught. Activities are varied frequently and are frequently repeated. During the "romance" cycle an attempt is made to add language quantity to the child's knowledge, and enthusiasm is kept at a high pitch; personal involvement should be complete, for what completely interests the child will be learned quickly and efficiently.

Step 2, Realism. Realism implies the "realistic" or practical application of what has been learned. Here flexibility and adaptability are emphasized. The children like the suspense and anxieties of a quiz-type drill. During this period of time the use of one, or at the most two, verbs is emphasized.

The teacher gives the child a blue pencil and asks, "¿Tiene el lapiz azul?" The answer is "Si, tengo el lapiz azul." There upon the teacher quickly asks another pupil while pointing to the first, "¿Tiene el lapiz azul?" The process is repeated often with different objects and in different relationships; for example, between pupils, between groups of pupils, or a pupil may ask a question of the teacher. Introducing different objects, pictures, and names add variation to a drill which could otherwise become monotonous. The drills are conducted for about five-minute periods and then a short game is played, or a song is sung for added variation, then back to the basic drill.

What is learned? The verb is practiced over and over again in varied contexts but the basic relationships remain the same. The various combinations of the verb (first, second, and third person) have been taught to the children. They are now aware of the vast possibilities of the sentence patterns they have already learned and they are now willing to experiment for themselves. Subject pronouns, or in the case of Spanish, personal inflections on verbs, have been inadvertently identified so that when the next verb is introduced, a subconscious pattern will already be at work to facilitate the acquisition of the new structures.

Step 3, Romance. New and interesting material is introduced on a broad scope. The children may visit a market or go to the zoo. The teacher may tell a new story or bring in new material about the home or community. The games and songs that fit in with these experiences add to their suitability and amusement.

In essence, the alternation of romance, realism, and romance as described here allows the teachers to view their efforts through a diametric structure and assures them that they will not limit themselves to a one-sided approach.

In conclusion one must state that the children's reaction to a varied program is rewarding. Basic content and teaching methods are changed periodically and yet the over-all course maintains a substantial structure which the children and teachers are aware of and rely on.

Instruction in foreign language must follow three rules which guide instruction in all fields. First, the activity must be suited to the needs and interests of the learner; second, it must be carefully planned; and third, the learning must be highly motivated. Effective learning takes place when the pupil is involved and interested in the material, and when he understands and accepts the reasons for learning.

FOREIGN LANGUAGES IN ELEMENTARY SCHOOLS:
SOME QUESTIONS AND ANSWERS *

At a work conference sponsored by the Modern Language Association and held at its headquarters (6 Washington Square North, New York 3, N. Y.) 11–13 December 1953, a group of authorities on the teaching of foreign languages in the elementary schools met to provide informed answers to the questions most frequently asked about this rapidly growing movement. At a second conference, 11–12 June 1954, specialists in elementary education met to criticize these answers and to discuss the problems involved in the introduction of foreign-language instruction in grades I–VI.

The majority of the participants in the second conference felt that the document formulated by the first conference, "Foreign Languages in Elementary Schools: Some Questions and Answers," was subjective, too sweeping in its claims, and lacking in documentation. The child-centered, integrated curriculum, in their view, makes it difficult to speak of allotment of specific amounts of time to foreign language study, and the current trend away from departmentalization is opposed to the use of foreign language specialists. Two of the participants felt that the principle of curriculum development should determine the answers to almost all the questions. A basic principle of curriculum development, in their view, is "that children must be dealt with as individuals. Study appropriate for one child may not be appropriate or suitable or needed for another. The learning experiences, activities, and opportunities in any grade should be developed on the basis of the needs of the children and of the community situation."

The Modern Language Association, a learned society, in reprinting the original Questions and Answers, is glad to include these friendly reservations about a movement which thus far has elicited almost no unfavorable comment in print. These criticisms may serve, not only as an antidote to the uncritical enthusiasm of some parents and some language instructors, but also as a suggestion of objective research needed in a field where conclusions have rested largely on the accumulated experience of foreign language teachers themselves.

---

*Mimeographed reports of two work conferences (December 11–13, 1953) (June 11–12, 1954). Reprinted by permission of Foreign Language Program Research Center, Modern Language Association of America.

THE QUESTIONS AND ANSWERS

What values does foreign language study have for elementary-school pupils?

We take for granted what is really a miraculous acquisition, by a kind of absorption from his environment, of the child's skill in understanding and speaking his mother tongue. We are impressed when we observe how easily young children learn a foreign language in an environment where it is spoken. We know moreover that the introduction of a second language at the beginning of the elementary-school program exercises the language-learning capacity of children when the capacity to understand and speak a foreign language is at its highest. Learning a language at this age is therefore not a chore but a joy, increasing the children's appetite for learning more. By releasing greater powers of self-expression than have formerly been tapped, the learning of a second language contributes to the general learning process of the child, whose pride and pleasure are fortified by his new sense of accomplishment. In fact, it has been noted with surprising frequency that even children who learn very slowly are stimulated by contact with a second language. The confidence gained through success in a foreign language often produces better performance in other areas as well.

By starting early and continuing his study as long as the experience is rewarding for him, the pupil can learn to understand, speak, and eventually read and write a second language much better than if he begins at a later age. His ear becomes more perceptive and his tongue more articulate. Later on, when the mind begins to make comparisons, the materials available for comparing his own language with a second language will make him more keenly aware of the resources of his mother tongue.

A language is not only a *means of communication;* it is the *vehicle of culture.* Young children are by nature eager to know how other people live, to learn their songs, their dances, their legends and stories, and their art. Moreover, the child who learns by heart jingles, songs, and verse in a foreign language is cultivating a taste for and a love for literature.

The values of foreign language study in the fields of art, music, the dance, drama, and the language arts are apparent. The opportunity to learn numbers and to review in the foreign language the simplest operations learned in arithmetic is just as obvious. The second language can be an element of enrichment and support for many parts of the curriculum.

Foreign language study serves to cultivate the child not only as an individual, but also as a member of society. It is possible to instill in the young child an early interest in and acceptance of children of other national backgrounds, both abroad and in his own community. It has been noted, particularly in bilingual areas, that the introduction into the school of the second language of the area tends not only to develop, in the child in whose family this language is spoken, a respect for the culture of his parents, but also to raise the social status of both child and parents in the community.

Teachers and students of foreign languages, social studies, and international affairs are more and more realizing the importance of international understanding in the shrinking world of the twentieth century, but many of them have not yet fully understood to what extent foreign languages are the key to understanding foreign peoples. The total education of the child will be strengthened when foreign languages and social studies combine forces to emphasize world understanding.

At what age in a child's development is it most desirable
to begin foreign language instruction?

The evidence of numerous experimental programs (Brooklyn, Carlsbad, Cleveland, El Paso) shows that a child, having mastered at the age of five the basic aural and oral skills of his native language,[1] is ideally equipped to begin learning these same skills in a second language. The younger the child the easier his acquisition of a new language: his ear is attuned to intonations, accents, and pronunciations, and his tongue imitates foreign language sounds with effortless flexibility and with none of the self-consciousness that is such a handicap at a later age. Foreign language instruction for the child at this period should present the language, insofar as possible, in the same natural manner as that in which he has learned his native tongue. At this early stage in the child's mental development, he does not think of analyzing the foreign language or comparing it with his own. He accepts it without question, learning sounds and accents through imitation, and ideas through his senses. Words and phrases acquire meaning through sensory aids and pantomime. Both common sense

---

[1] Children in grade 1 have an "understanding" vocabulary of 24,000 words and a "writing" vocabulary of over 5,000 words, according to studies by Mary Katherine Smith and Henry D. Rinsland cited in Ruth G. Strickland's *The Language Arts in the Elementary School* (Boston: D. C. Heath & Co., 1951), pp. 190–191.

and the observations of neurologists,[2] psychiatrists, and language researchers indicate that the years from five to ten are the best years for children to learn to understand and to speak a foreign language.

Should all children of a given grade be allowed to study foreign languages? If not, should such study be restricted, and on what basis?

All children of a given grade *should* have the opportunity to learn a foreign language. The elementary-school curriculum is properly considered as a sum of learnings acquired by individual children as they progress through the years at their own speed, in keeping with their individual talents. Language learning, then, should not be restricted to children of superior intelligence; but it should not be imposed *indiscriminately* on slow-learning children. However, any children who show a *desire* and *ability* to learn a foreign language should be allowed to participate in the program if their consequent feeling of success gives them greater confidence in their ability to learn.

In *border areas* and where there are frequent contacts with non-English speaking groups (and where the percentage of bilingual teachers is relatively high) there are obvious advantages in extending foreign language instruction to *all* children in a grade.

In other communities foreign language instruction may *at first* have to be limited simply because in these areas there may not be enough teachers qualified to give such instruction to all elementary-school pupils. It may be necessary, at the outset, to use these teachers with selected groups of pupils in order to insure the needed continuity of instruction.

What should be the content of the foreign language class?

The content will be determined by a number of basic considerations: the abilities and interests of the children involved; the scope and sequence of related areas of the curriculum as outlined for each age group; the time available for foreign language instruction. Basically, the content planned must have meaning for the children con-

---

[2] " 'To everything there is a season and a time to every purpose under heaven.' Educators, before all others, must realize that this is particularly true of the 'organ of the mind.' Physiological evolution causes it to specialize in the learning of language before the ages of 10 to 14. After that gradually, inevitably, it seems to become rigid, slow, less receptive. In regard to this function, it is soon senescent. But it is ready for life's fulfillment in other directions, ready for reasoning, self-discipline, understanding, even wisdom."—Wilder Penfield, "A Consideration of the Neurophysiological Mechanisms of Speech and Some Educational Consequences," *Proceedings of the American Academy of Arts and Sciences,* **LXXXII** (1953), 201–214.

cerned, and it must be of sufficient interest to stimulate active participation by all the pupils.

If the sequence established for language arts, social studies, and other related areas is to be used as a guide for determining children's interests at each age level, the choice of content for foreign language instruction becomes quite obvious. In the primary grades, phrases and units of vocabulary will center around exchange of greetings, expressions of courtesy, the family, pets, the home, the school, and the immediate community. Parallels in foreign communities may be indicated. The extent of the vocabulary included in each unit will, of course, depend upon the abilities and interests of the children in the group. Much can be done with a limited number of words and phrases if these are used in meaningful situations, in simple dialogues and dramatizations. Songs, games, and folk dancing will enrich the modest beginnings at these levels.

As the children progress through the grades, the units of vocabulary begun in the earlier years will be expanded. Children will still want to talk about their school, their friends, their activities at home and in the community. Much of the foreign language content will continue to be motivated both by the activities and interests developed in the other areas of the school curriculum and by the expanding experiences of growing children. Songs, games, dramatizations will continue to be highlighted. Folk stories and stories about children in the foreign country can be told and acted out.

All new words and phrases will be introduced orally with the use of pictures, objects, action, and dramatizations. Much oral practice in chorus and by individual children will be essential.

Since foreign language instruction may begin at any level from grade one through grade six, it is difficult to decide when reading and writing of the second language should begin.[3] There are two principal factors to be considered: Reading and writing of the second language, even of the informal sort, should not be introduced until: 1) the aural and oral skills of the second language are well established, and 2) the child's progress in reading and writing his own language has been developed to the point where he is secure in his ability to use these skills.

What teaching materials and techniques should be used?

The integration of the foreign language with the other areas of study in the particular grade is very important. Foreign languages

---

[3] In El Paso, where Spanish is introduced in grade one, reading and writing of an informal sort are begun in the third grade. French in Cleveland is begun in grade one, but reading and writing are not formally introduced until the seventh grade.

should *not* be taught in isolation. In the first grade, the child's family, home, pets, and toys are the persons and objects around which his life centers, and around which all language instruction should center. Since learning a language should be above all an experience, the child in the first grade must *live* the language; and because his experiences are limited, foreign language instruction must be brought to his level of understanding.

All materials discussed in the foreign language class period should be presented visually and orally at the same time, so that sound and concept are identified. One effective way of presenting visual aids in any grade, but specifically in the lower grades, is by mounting pictures on chart paper and presenting them as new words are introduced. The picture of a man is shown to the children as they hear the word "papá." They recognize the picture and hear the word associated with it. As the teacher points to the picture, he says: "*Este es el papá.*" Note that the word is immediately used in a *sentence,* not learned *in isolation.* The children repeat with the teacher: "*Este es el papá.*" When there is no doubt in the teacher's mind that the children have a clear concept of the word "papá," he asks: "*Niñas, ¿quién es este señor?*" (Children, who is this gentleman?) He encourages an answer by saying with the children: "*Este señor es el papá.*" Nothing is left to chance. Each new word is presented in this manner, *in a sentence,* to assure comprehension. Retention is maintained by repetition, and "thinking in the foreign language" is sustained by the direct use of the language, without translation.

Once the child has a clear concept of the meaning of a word, he must, if possible, actually "feel" the object. In units on furniture, foods, fruits, and vegetables, miniature or wax models may be passed around so that the child sees and feels the object designated by the word he has just heard.

In the first and second grades, correlated practice materials can be very effective. Their purpose is to teach the child to follow directions in the foreign language, to learn the names of the colors he is to use, the parts of the object that he is coloring, and finally the name of the whole object. Such work is fun, and the child is learning the foreign language without effort. For example, in the unit on the outside of the house, mounted pictures of houses are presented and each part of the house and the surroundings is identified in the foreign language: the *roof, chimney, bricks, windows, door, stairs, sidewalk, trees, street.* The child makes freehand sketches of houses, following instructions given in the foreign language. In order to test retention, a stenciled house with all the outside characteristics learned in the foreign language is handed to each child. Instructions are given in the foreign language. "Paint the roof black." "Now paint the chimney red," and so on, until the whole house is colored.

In the third grade, interest is created by presenting in the foreign language songs and folk tales appropriate for this age level, keeping the foreign language within the children's vocabulary and comprehension. Story-book characters are mounted on flannel board as the story progresses in very simple terms.

Other materials that have been found effective are doll houses with removable walls and roof, colored paper and crayons (for teaching the names of the colors), plastic table settings, dolls (or the actual clothes of the children), and photographs of children and adults in the foreign setting, especially those of middle-class groups (avoiding those of "quaint" but barefoot or sabot-shod children). When the children are old enough to tell time, a clock with movable hands is invaluable, and flags, maps, and globes will add variety to a geography lesson. At all levels of instruction, a browsing table stimulates interest and conversation. On it can be placed pictures and picture books printed in the foreign country, primers, arithmetic books, and song books.

Dramatizations and dramatic play are another effective device. In the unit on the living room, a natural situation can be created, since the members of the family meet guests in the living room. At first, a picture of a lady in a living room is presented: *"Niños, ésta es mi mamá."* (Children, this is my mother.) The children have learned to identify the members of the family in an earlier unit. Now all they have to learn is: *"Tengo mucho gusto en conocerla."* (I am very pleased to know you.) The mother, father, or other members of the family being introduced answer: *"El gusto es mío."* (The pleasure is mine.) Groups of children introduce each other, taking the part of the various members of the family, or introduce the foreign language instructor as a visitor in their home. In learning the words for dishes and silverware, children participate by dramatizing a mother setting the table: as she places each object, the class says: *"La mamá pone la mesa. Pone el mantel. Pone cuatro platos."* (The mother sets the table. She puts the cloth on. She puts four dishes on.) and so on until the table is set. The appeal in foreign language instruction to the first- and second-graders is the emphasis on natural situations in which they can participate.

How can records, tape recordings, radio, and television be used?

Records can furnish a model for songs and, if the diction is clear and the vocabulary limited, for speech as well. Participation records, with pauses for choral repetition by the class, are a still more effective teaching device.

Tape recordings can be similarly used, and they are adaptable to the needs and foreign-language ability of the class. In the upper grades, the voice of the teacher or another person fluent in the language can be recorded in supplementary stories within the vocabulary range of the pupils. If a reader is used, passages can be recorded and the children can read aloud with the narrator. Questions on the reading can be recorded, with pauses for the children to repeat the question and give (or repeat) the answer, to get practice in correct intonation. At any grade level, children can record their voices as an aid to correct pronunciation and intonation. The tape recorder can also be used to direct group work for part of a class while the teacher works with the rest of the children in another part of the classroom.

In some communities classes receive regular radio or television lessons, especially helpful in larger school systems that may lack sufficient teachers fluent in the foreign language. In Miami, daily 10-minute broadcasts of Spanish lessons to fifth-grade pupils in 35 schools are followed by related classroom activities in Spanish. In El Paso, a Spanish program is broadcast three times a week to the fourth- to eighth-grade classes of 17 schools. These programs maintain interest and aural practice in these pupils, who have had classroom instruction in Spanish in grades 1–3. In Cleveland, weekly 20-minute lessons in French and Spanish are broadcast to classes under the guidance of voluntary teachers. In these cities, the radio material is recorded on tape beforehand.

In Washington, D.C., foreign language classes receive weekly 15-minute TV lessons in French or Spanish. After-school classes receive TV Spanish lessons in Buffalo, N. Y., and French lessons in Schenectady.

What should be the length and frequency of the foreign language teaching period in each grade?

Experience has shown that the minimum desirable, in the kindergarten and 1st and 2nd grades, is 15 minutes from three to five times a week. In grades 3 to 6, 20 to 30 minutes have proved desirable, although an able class can continue for a longer time without tiring if the teacher is skillful in varying the activities.

Foreign language learning need not be confined to the period formally allotted to it. The teacher can create opportunities for children to use and hear the foreign language in everyday classroom situations, in simple arithmetic problems, in directions, in counting out for games or other activities, encouraging children to greet her and to say "please," "thank you," "pardon me," "good bye." The effectiveness of language learning will be in direct ratio to the amount of time given to its *use* in school and out.

What factors should determine which foreign languages are to be offered?

The chief factor determining the choice of the foreign language to be offered in school should be the known or inferred *preference of the majority of the parents.* Parents should, however, be urged to select (1) a language of international importance and (2) one for which continuity can be provided in high school. Whether one or more languages are offered in the same school or school system depends upon local conditions. In Public School 208 in Brooklyn, N. Y., for example, French *and* Spanish are offered from grades one through eight and there are enough children studying each language to keep one teacher busy all the time. If an approximately equal number of parents express a desire for two different languages, both should be offered. Some communities or schools might, however, not be able to provide this choice, for financial reasons or because of a lack of teachers.

What is the place of "general" or "exploratory" language in the elementary or junior high school?

In schools where a foreign language has been introduced in the grades there is little place for either general or exploratory language courses. Children making satisfactory progress in their foreign language will want to and should be encouraged to continue. For those who lack either the interest or the aptitude to continue profitably, a general-language course can broaden a language consciousness, emphasizing the place of language in our society and stimulating an interest in other peoples.

In schools where a foreign language has not been introduced before Grade 7, children of at least average aptitude could (except for comparative historical-cultural purposes) with greater profit begin a foreign language at this point than either a general or an exploratory type of course.

Can foreign language instruction be integrated into the curriculum without displacing other essential areas of instruction?

It can. It happens, as the administrators and foreign language teachers have agreed, whenever and wherever those responsible for the total curriculum accept the demonstrable fact that foreign language instruction is an enriching activity which contributes to the learnings in other areas.

In schools where all children are given the privilege of participating in foreign language study, two distinct patterns have emerged. In one, where the foreign language specialist comes into the classroom from the outside, careful joint planning by the language teacher, the classroom teacher, and the supervisor concerned is necessary to make sure that the vocabulary and content of the language units are directly related to the regular curriculum offering for the grade concerned. In the other pattern, where the foreign language instruction is given by the classroom teacher, it is planned primarily as an enrichment activity to be correlated with the other areas in the over-all curriculum. Activities in such fields as social studies, language arts, music, art, physical education, and arithmetic will give motivation and meaning to the experience in foreign language learning (simple dialogues, dramatizations, dramatic play, vocabulary games, songs, folk dancing, and pageantry), through many of which the child acquires understanding and appreciation of a foreign culture and people.

Wherever foreign language instruction is planned as enrichment for children of superior intelligence, there is no problem of displacing other essential areas of instruction, since such children can master essentials in less time than average children and need additional challenges. Foreign language instruction provides such a challenge. With continuity in such instruction provided through the school years, the outcomes in cultural appreciation and in fluency in the foreign language bring rich rewards to these young people and to American society.

How can continuity and progression be achieved in foreign language instruction up through the grades?

A course of study designed for continuous progression in a given language from grade 1 through 12 might have the following phases:

Grades 1–3: Development of aural-oral skills through conversation, songs, and activities related to home, community, and school experiences. The fostering of an understanding of and interest in children who speak the foreign language.

Grades 4–6: Further development of aural-oral skills and attitudes established as goals in grades 1–3. Content of the course related to other study areas and creative activities, with parallels in foreign communities indicated. Reading and writing may be introduced, but only after the firm establishment of the pupil's command of these skills in English and of oral-aural skills in the foreign language.

Grades 7–9: Continued emphasis on oral expression and the cultivation of attitudes. Reading begun or continued, with stories and other materials that give insight into the customs and culture of the foreign country. Language structure learned inductively. Planned sequence of functional drill projects on verbs, vocabulary building, and speech patterns.

Grades 10–12: Further stress on conversation and oral discussion; practice in writing original compositions. Extensive and intensive reading of works in the foreign language, with consideration of their place and value in the foreign literature. Systematic study of the essentials of grammar.

There is considerable variation in the organizational patterns of our public schools. The main types are: (a) the 8-year elementary and 4-year secondary plan; (b) the 6-year elementary and 6-year secondary plan; (c) the 6-year elementary, 3-year junior H.S., 3-year senior H.S. plan; (d) the 6-year elementary, 2-year junior H.S., 4-year senior H.S. plan.

In the majority of public schools, up to the present, foreign language study has begun in the 9th or 10th grade. Some elementary schools which have introduced foreign languages leave an unfortunate gap in grades 7 and 8, particularly in systems which do not operate on the 8-4 or 6-6 plan.

The following suggestions are offered as possible solutions of the articulation problem:

A. *Articulation under the 8-4 or 6-6 plans.* If one or more of the foreign languages currently in the high-school curriculum are also offered in the elementary grades of that system, and if present high-school foreign language offerings can be extended to cover all 4 or 6 high-school years, articulation can be attained in one of these ways:

1. The high school might offer two types of foreign language courses, one for pupils with previous training in the grades and another for pupils beginning a new language in high school. We might call the first type "continuing courses" (Continuing French I, II, III, IV), and the second type "beginning courses" (Beginning French I, II, III, IV). The two programs could be carried on concurrently. Yearly or semestral placement tests would show differences in individual progress.

2. The high school might gear its language offerings to the needs of pupils who had previous foreign language experience in the grades and offer intensive "conversation courses" for 1 to 4 semesters for pupils without such previous preparation.

3. Pupils who have had a language in the grades might be admitted to the second, third, or fourth semester of a high-school foreign language course either on the basis of a placement test or of a blanket transfer of credit at the rate of 1 high-school semester to 3 years in the primary grades or to 1 year in the upper elementary grades. Sec-

ondary-school foreign language teachers will have to adjust and to make adjustments for pupils with varying backgrounds of foreign language study.

B. *Articulation under the 6-3-3 and 6-2-4 plans.* The junior high school, as the link between elementary and secondary education, can also be the place for passing from the predominantly aural-oral training of the elementary-school to the more systematic study of the foreign language and culture in the senior high school. "Continuing" courses and "beginning" courses (or alternate plans as presented under "A") may be designed for both junior and senior high-school programs.

Who should teach foreign languages at this level?

In some schools the foreign language is taught by classroom teachers with varying degrees of foreign language preparation or by fully qualified classroom teachers; in other schools the classes are taught by foreign language specialists. The question of who should teach the foreign language depends upon the personnel and financial resources within the school or school system, and also upon the individual teacher's enthusiasm, preparation, and willingness to qualify. Any plan requires adequate supervision. There must be available an adviser or coordinator to raise and maintain the quality of instruction, to provide in-service training where needed, and to provide liaison among departments of the elementary school, and between the school and the community.

A. *The regular classroom teacher.* The teacher should have an acceptable pronunciation and be able to use the language in correct speech patterns, or at the very least, be developing this ability through in-service training. Prominent among the objectives of such a teacher will be the enrichment of the total elementary school curriculum through the foreign language experience, an understanding of other peoples, and the creation of an interest in and a readiness for serious language study.

B. *The fully qualified classroom teacher.* Qualified elementary classroom teachers who have majored in or are fluent in a foreign language teach foreign languages at different grade levels in a school. Such a teacher serves either as a "resource person" to assist others who are carrying on the foreign language instruction or provides continuity for the established program by teaching foreign languages on a class-exchange basis.

C. *The staff member with a part-time job.* A regular member of the elementary-school staff competent in a foreign language may combine teaching this language with part-time work in another field (e.g., the library).

D. *The foreign language specialist.* If he is thoroughly prepared in the foreign language, in elementary school methods, and in child growth and development, the specialist, who enters a classroom only to teach the foreign language, has an excellent opportunity for effective teaching. His planning and preparation are confined to a single subject, and since all his contacts with the children are in the foreign language, he can create for the children an atmosphere in which hearing and speaking the language seems natural and exciting. The specialist may be a secondary-school teacher qualified for elementary-school teaching or a qualified elementary-school teacher who is fluent in the foreign language.

How can elementary-school teachers without foreign language facility be trained to teach foreign languages?

An in-service workshop sponsored by the local school system is probably the best solution. Through such workshops or through courses at a nearby college, available throughout the year and offering functional training in foreign languages and in methods of teaching them, teachers can get the needed training. Their own study should be of the aural-oral type that they will use in their training. They may also be able to get advice and help from directors of foreign languages, supervisors, or consultants in the local school system, or from foreign language teachers in nearby colleges.

The community itself may furnish help. Parents, other townspeople, and high-school or college teachers who know the foreign language may be invited into the classroom to work with the teacher on the unit being studied.

Elementary-school teachers seeking training in foreign languages can clearly profit from summer workshops, summer-school foreign language courses, and foreign travel.

How can future elementary-school teachers receive foreign-language training?

The training can be obtained in teachers colleges or in schools of education working in conjunction with university foreign language departments. Addition of foreign language courses to the course of study for elementary-school teachers presents to administrators in teacher-training institutions a problem that they must consider in relation to other areas of study, since some courses have by legislative act become an established part of the program and are required for teacher certification. Members of the foreign language staff of an institution and those in charge of the preparation of elementary-school teachers should work together on this problem. One obvious place for the introduction of foreign language training is the materials-and-methods laboratory in the language arts.

In some universities a major in foreign languages is available as an elective course to prospective elementary-school teachers. Such majors will be more widely offered and elected when there is assurance of the local need for an elementary-school foreign language program, an assurance that can best come from local school systems.

Such foreign language programs may be stimulated by workshops in teacher-training institutions or in nearby colleges. Future elementary-school teachers can be interested in foreign languages, and in preparing themselves to teach them, through a variety of approaches, such as displays of children's books written in other languages, through demonstrations of music and dancing, and through foreign films, recordings, and transcriptions.

How can such a program get started?

Initiative by the school administration or by the elementary-school teacher is the most obvious and natural way of starting such a program. A college or secondary-school teacher may have difficulty in initiating a program of foreign language teaching in the elementary school if there is any "pressure" involved. Parents or interested laymen, too, will need to proceed in an objective way and without the use of "pressure tactics."

A. A *school superintendent* is in a position to bring together teachers, principals, and parents interested in foreign language teaching. He can set up a committee to study the problem, and a favorable report by the committee can lead to an experimental program. The programs in Atlantic City, El Paso, and Los Angeles were established in this way.[4]

B. An *elementary-school teacher with foreign language ability* can create an opportunity if he has initiative. To succeed, he will need the permission of his principal and superintendent and the cooperation of his supervisor in the experiment, and he should secure the interest and cooperation of the parents of the children with regard to the proposed class or classes. Such a procedure by a fifth-grade teacher in one school in Lawrence, Kansas, led to the introduction of Spanish into all the Lawrence elementary schools.

C. A *college or secondary-school foreign language teacher* may make known to the school superintendent, through the appropriate

---

[4] The establishment of the Atlantic City program is described in the *NEA Journal*, **XLII** (November 1953), 479–480.

channels, that he is available as a consultant to any elementary-school teacher who would like his help. Before making official contact with the administration in an elementary school, he should make sure that there are elementary-school teachers with an interest in foreign languages and that there is a community interest in having a foreign language taught at this level. A cooperative effort will bring the best results.

D. *Parents or interested laymen,* as individuals or organized groups (the PTA, Home and School Associations), should make a survey of the attitude of all parents in the school community and discuss the results of this survey with the principal, then with the principal and staff, and if the situation seems favorable, with the Superintendent of Schools. Such a procedure, advisable in initiating *any* new school project, will have a much better chance to succeed than if a campaign is started in a newspaper article or in a board of education meeting.

Once an experiment is started, every effort should be made, through talks and press notices, to bring it to the attention of the public and all the school officials in the area. But individuals or groups that hope to get cordial consideration of this or any other new idea should collect the facts, interpret them judiciously, and then proceed through the administrative channels appropriate to the situation.

How can a program at this level win the cooperation of classroom teachers, administrators, and the community?

To win and maintain their support, one must: (1) show that the program is practicable and desirable, (2) consult with everyone concerned with the program, and (3) evaluate continually what is being achieved to make sure that results are commensurate with effort.

In one large city school system, for example, official authorization to experiment with the teaching of French in a second-grade and a fifth-grade class was given in 1944 as the result of many consultations with the Associate Superintendent in Charge of Elementary Schools, the Director of Elementary Education, the principal of the school concerned, the parents of all the children in the two groups to be taught, the teachers of these classes, the senior-high-school teacher who was to conduct the experiment, her principal, and the latter's superior officer, the First Assistant Superintendent of Schools. The experiment was watched with interest not only by those immediately concerned but also by others in the community. Results permitted continuance of the experiment in two elementary schools until the Spring of 1951, when all agreed that it was no longer feasible to continue the program if it was necessary to depend upon secondary-school foreign language teachers loaned for the purpose when they could find free time.

After preparing instructional materials and securing the authorization of the Board of Education for a city-wide program insofar as teacher resources were available, the community was approached for its verdict. A questionnaire sent to all parents of elementary-school children in the city's public schools brought 22,860 replies in favor of the foreign language teaching, and only 110 opposed. A questionnaire sent to all elementary-school teachers through their principals brought approximately 200 volunteers to teach French, 150 for Spanish, and 75 each for German and Latin.

Such a program succeeds only if it is undertaken voluntarily, even enthusiastically, by teachers who recognize its possibilities in enriching the regular learnings of children and in broadening their own cultural equipment. It is doomed to failure if imposed from above upon the elementary-school teachers. As a result of the meticulous planning in setting it up, this program now enjoys the warm support of administrators (including principals), teachers, parents, and children.

Weekly TV lessons in French and Spanish serve as a unifying element in the city-wide program and give both pupils and teachers models of pronunciation and method. They also arouse the interest and enlist the support of people not directly concerned with the schools. Teacher morale is raised by eight workshops in area schools, where secondary-school foreign language teachers help elementary teachers with pronunciation and methods of teaching languages.

How can foreign language teaching at this level be financed?

In many places where foreign language teaching has been started in the grades, it is carried on without additional cost to the school system, the language being taught mainly by the regular elementary-classroom teachers, by foreign language teachers from the secondary schools, or by volunteers from other sources. Where language teachers from secondary schools do the teaching, it is done either as a voluntary service during free periods or before or after school, or on assignment by the school administration, sometimes as a traveling position, sometimes to fill out an incomplete language schedule in their schools, instead of giving the teacher assignments in a different subject-matter field.

In other communities (Lawrence, Kansas, El Paso, Fairfield, Conn., Somerville, N. J., and notably Cleveland) one or more foreign language specialists have been added to the elementary-school staff.

Sponsorship of the foreign language program by agencies outside the school system:

1. A nearby college, which lends the services of teacher or assigns a foreign language major to teach in the school as part of his practice teaching or in connection with a research project (e.g., University of Kansas, New Mexico Western College, Central Michigan College of Education).

2. A community agency (the PTA, Home and School Association, a foreign language group), which pays a qualified person to do the teaching (e.g., Staten Island, N. Y.).

3. Parents of the children receiving the lessons, who pay, through a yearly fee, the salary of the foreign language teacher (e.g., P.S. 208, Brooklyn, N. Y., where the optional yearly fee is $10.00).

Foreign language teaching should properly, however, be financed through regular budget appropriations. This will not occur on a general basis until the trained personnel are available to make possible a continuity of articulated courses from grade to grade and into the junior and senior high schools.

Meanwhile present enthusiasm and resources must be fully used to keep programs going, so that they may prove their worth and justify their inclusion in the regular budget.

CHAPTER 10

The Children We Teach

Children who have special needs because of mental, emotional, social, physical or cultural deviation from what is recognized as normal require specialized educational effort. However, the needs of the so-called normal child are often equally challenging to the classroom teacher.

DIMENSIONS OF ENRICHMENT *

William K. Durr

Children most capable of thoughtful learning are entitled to thoughtfully selected learning activities. What guides can a teacher use in choosing the enrichment which gifted children must have to achieve their full potential?

MEANING OF ENRICHMENT

The lack of definite terminology in some educational areas is illustrated in the literature on the gifted. The inconsistencies begin with the definitions of giftedness and extend to enrichment and beyond.

Those who have studied the literature find it difficult to agree on just what enrichment means.[1] Barbe,[2] Dunlap,[3] and McNamee[4]

---

* Reprinted from *Exceptional Children* (December 1959), pp. 202–206, by permission of the author and publisher.

[1] Philadelphia Suburban School Study Council, *Guiding Your Gifted: A Handbook for Teachers, Administrators, and Parents* (Phil.: Educational Ser. Bur., U. of Penna., 1954, p. 23.

[2] Walter B. Barbe, "Evaluation of Special Classes for Gifted Children," *Exceptional Children*, **22** (November 1955), pp. 60–62.

[3] James M. Dunlap, "Gifted Children in an Enriched Program," *Exceptional Children*, **21** (January 1955), pp. 135–137.

[4] L. V. McNamee, "Enriching Education of Rapid Learners," *Nations Schools*, **56** (December 1955), pp. 70–72.

reporting on three different special class programs, all refer to the kinds of experiences the children have in these special classes as enrichment. They do not, however, define the term nor indicate that they would apply it only to special classes.

Others use the term in connection with various administrative practices or organizational methods for improving the education of the gifted.[5,6,7,8] Some of these suggestions include enrichment in special classes and schools, enrichment in regular classes, enrichment by additional courses, enrichment through additional extra-class activities, enrichment through the library, and enrichment through community resources.

There have been efforts to tie the term to programs in regular, heterogeneous classes. "Enrichment alone, not accompanied by acceleration or special grouping, keeps the talented child in his own age group and with children of various levels of ability."[9] If this meaning was commonly accepted, one would know, when he sees the term used alone, that it refers to programs for gifted children who have not been accelerated or placed in special classes. Others, sometimes agreeing that the term is usually associated with a regular classroom setting, point out that it may be a part of special classes and many of the other organizational methods for dealing with the gifted.[10,11]

Sometimes the term is so inclusive that it is synonymous with good teaching and may refer to children of all intellectual levels. "Enrichment consists of the selection and organization of learning experiences appropriate to youths' adequate development. It is not, therefore, 'special education' . . . but rather the essence of all good education."[12]

While the writer hesitates to add still another definition to this already overlong list, it seems desirable that the term be clarified for

[5] W. F. Anderson, and L. R. Davis, "Guiding the Gifted," *School Executive*, **76** (February 1957), pp. 82–83.

[6] Earl M. McWilliams, "Enrichment Practices for Gifted Junior High School Pupils," *National Association of Secondary School Principals Bulletin*, **40** (September 1956), pp. 72–84.

[7] A. Harry Passow, *et al.*, *Planning for Talented Youth* (New York: Bureau of Publications, Teachers College, Columbia U., 1955), pp. 50–64.

[8] Paul Witty, and Samuel Bloom, "Education of the Gifted," *School and Society*, **78** (October 17, 1953), pp. 113–18.

[9] Robert J. Havighurst, *et al.*, *A Survey of the Education of Gifted Children*. Supplementary Educational Monograph No. 83 (Chicago: U. of Chicago Press, 1955), p. 20.

[10] Willard Abraham, *Common Sense About Gifted Children* (New York: Harper and Row, 1958), p. 82.

[11] Marian Scheifele, *The Gifted Child in the Regular Classroom* (New York: Bureau of Publications, Teachers College, Columbia U., 1953), p. 41.

[12] National Society for the Study of Education. *Education for the Gifted.* 57th yearbook, Nelson B. Henry (ed.) (Chicago: U. of Chicago Press, 1958), p. 193.

purposes of this paper. Although the following suggestions could apply to special classes, here enrichment means the special provisions made for the rapid learner in a regular, heterogeneous classroom. The child who has been accelerated may be placed in such a classroom; hence, the special provisions made for him once he is there would be enrichment. If our terminology is to have preciseness, other words should be used to describe programs in special classes for the gifted or good teaching for all children.

DIMENSIONS OF ENRICHMENT

Enrichment falls into one or more of three basic dimensions—horizontal, vertical, or supplementary. Effective teachers use these dimensions as guides. They know the strengths and limitations of each and how these dimensions are exemplified by the enrichment in their rooms.

Horizontal enrichment broadens the regular program for any one grade. Learnings do not cut across grade levels. Vertical enrichment provides content which will be learned by average children at a later time. Learning deliberately cuts upward through the grades. Supplementary enrichment stresses activities outside the normal curriculum. The regular program is neither broadened nor extended upward since these activities relate only indirectly to it.

HORIZONTAL ENRICHMENT

Horizontal enrichment involves a broader understanding of regular studies for more capable students. It may be visualized like this.

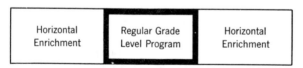

It emphasizes learnings directly related to the regular program; however, children would not proceed to advanced material if they learned at a more rapid rate. A first-grade child who had achieved mastery of the addition facts with sums through 8 would not be taught his "9's" if these sums were normally taught in the second grade. He would use the sums he did know in a greater variety of situations. A third-grade child who had completed the 3^2 book in the regular reading series might begin the 3^2 book in another series. Or, he might be encouraged to read widely for pleasure and information. He would not, however, be taught the skills which were developed in the 4^1 book.

VERTICAL ENRICHMENT

Vertical enrichment in its pure form stresses the mastery of increasingly more mature ideas for the child who learns at an above average rate. It may be pictured in this way:

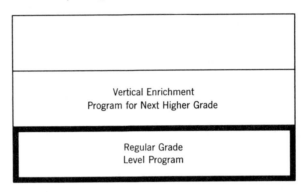

It deals with learnings in the regular school program which "average" children will be expected to attain at a later time and at a more leisurely pace. A first-grade child who had achieved mastery of the addition facts with sums through 8 would be helped to learn his "9's" even though these sums were normally taught in the second grade. A third-grade child who had completed the 3^2 book in the regular reading series would begin immediately on the 4^1 book. He would be helped to master more advanced reading skills in the sequentially arranged series instead of simply reading widely or reading the same level book in another series.

SUPPLEMENTARY ENRICHMENT

Supplementary enrichment places emphasis on activities which are least related to the regular school program. It might look as shown in the diagram on the opposite page.

In its pure form activities are deliberately chosen because they do not directly broaden the regular grade level program and because "average" children will not be required to have such activities at a later grade. In other words, it involves activities which are neither horizontal or vertical. It takes the child into fields normally unexplored in school at any level. A first-grade child who has achieved mastery of the addition facts with sums through 8 might plan appropriate displays for a school display case. A third-grade child who has completed the 3^2 book in the regular reading series might take full responsibility for the primary grades in a school fund drive.

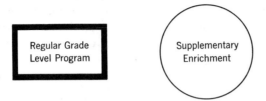

The above examples of supplementary enrichment are not totally unrelated to 'the learnings which children are expected to acquire. Enrichment which could not be related in some way, however diverse, to the program for all children, would be difficult to imagine. While the theoretical difference between supplementary enrichment and those which depend more on the school program may be a difference of degree, it results in a difference in kind when translated into classroom practice.

Although these three dimensions are not sharply divided and frequently do not appear in pure form, the teacher's tendency to adopt one of them as a guide in selecting enrichment activities is a powerful factor in determining what a child will be taught. The teacher looks for activities directly related to grade level learnings, activities leading to understandings at a higher grade level, or activities only indirectly related to the school program.

EVALUATING ENRICHMENT PATTERNS

Merely classifying an enrichment activity into one of these three dimensions will not, in itself, make that activity desirable. This truth, obvious as it may seem, does not always receive recognition from those whose vision is narrowed to one dimension. No pattern contains all of the advantages and none of the hazards of good enrichment practices. There are desirable attributes in each which, when carried to extremes, become hindrances to effective teaching.

Writings in this area indicate a general preference for horizontal enrichment. Understanding more about arithmetic facts at any given grade level, greater depth in social studies units while confining exploration to the unit topic—these kinds of recommendations receive major emphasis in suggested enrichment.

Helping a student broaden his understandings in this way has obvious merit, but it can lead to a violation of learning principles. "Children's interests should be considered when selecting learning activities," and "Children should be given opportunities to learn materials for which they are ready," are two principles of good teaching. The teacher who says, "No, you can't study about airplanes; you'll learn about them next year when you have a unit on transportation," ignores these principles.

When horizontal enrichment is followed and vertical enrichment is avoided, it is sometimes difficult to make a distinction between cause and effect. A teacher who follows horizontal enrichment does not tread on the subject-matter toes of those at higher grade levels. Is it this avoidance of another teacher's territory which results in the adoption of horizontal enrichment or does the conscious adoption of such enrichment merely result in not teaching "above grade level?" Deliberately choosing horizontal enrichment because of its merits may be defensible. Backing into it to keep from walking into another teacher's subject matter area is not. Grade level distinctions are merely lines draws for convenience; they are not fences abounding with threatening "Keep Off" signs.

Proponents of vertical enrichment show unconcern with grade level distinctions. Children are challenged to learn at their own best pace. This pattern of enrichment follows the readiness principle which may be ignored in horizontal enrichment and it also enables a child to follow his interests without fear of running into grade level fences.

Certain dangers in this pattern temper its obvious advantages. Insisting on vertical enrichment may also result in ignoring children's interests. The teacher who says, "You can't take that book home to read; it's too easy for you," substitutes an overly rigid concept of vertical enrichment for the interests of her students.

One criticism leveled by the opponents of vertical enrichment is unjustified. It is sometimes said that vertical enrichment results in the child being pushed too rapidly through a narrow and sterile curriculum. This unfortunate circumstance could occur, but vertical enrichment, even in its pure form, does not have to be narrow and sterile. All of the essential experiences for meaningful learning can be provided and no "pushing," with its unpleasant educational connotations, is necessary. Learning activities which allow the child to progress upward through a planned sequence are provided at a pace which is appropriate for him.

Supplementary enrichment puts no "regular curriculum" limitations on the child's interests. It is, in fact, designed to encourage explorations unrelated to the regular program. Not only does it re-move curriculum barriers, it encourages the teacher and the child to creatively explore for new ideas.

Although it is not limited by the necessary curriculum connections which characterize horizontal and vertical enrichment, it is limited, in its pure form, by its direct avoidance of such connections. The teacher who says, "No, you can't study ahead in arithmetic; it's time for you to clean the school display case," is carrying the values of supplementary enrichment to an absurd extreme. The advocate of pure supplementary enrichment would tend to reject activities directly related to the regular school curriculum even though these were in line with the interests and readiness of the child.

Since each of these three dimensions of enrichment has both ad-vantages and disadvantages, what pattern should be adopted? A good pattern of enrichment is a composite of the best features of each of the three basic patterns adapted to fit the individual learning situa-tions.

Enrichment should include the horizontal aspects which give de-sirable, added meaning to the regular school program. It should not, however, provide endless connections which soon lose meaning, nor be limited by grade lines. There can be no justification for closing doors to children whose readiness and interests might lead them to explore the sacred ground assigned to later grades. The advantages of supplementary enrichment should also become an integral part of any composite pattern. Children and creative teachers not infrequently conceive worthwhile activities which were undreamed by textbook authors or curriculum organizers. These activities should not be shunned because of the relative lack of creativeness by those who are responsible for programs of study.

EVALUATING SPECIFIC ENRICHMENT ACTIVITIES

Each teacher should adopt a pattern encompassing the strengths of the three basic enrichment dimensions. This pattern will provide guidelines and a theoretical framework for evaluating specific ideas. It will lead to the rejection of some suggestions which do not fit into a worthwhile pattern. It will not, however, prevent the adoption of useless or harmful activities which may be classified in that pattern.

For example, the practice of having fast-learning children repeat unneeded drill exercises in arithmetic may be rejected because it does not fit into a pattern containing the strengths of vertical enrichment.

In its place the children may spend a major portion of their time tutoring their slower learning peers. This may be classified as either basically supplementary (since tutoring is not a normal part of the school program at any level) or horizontal (since it is an extension of teaching children to work together). Although tutoring may be adequately classified within a desirable composite pattern, such a classification does not insure the desirability of the specific activity.

When a guiding theoretical pattern has been adopted, the next basic problem is *not* that we lack the answer concerning the activities to use—it is that we do not ask the right questions.

The question normally is, "What enrichment activity can I use with this child?" The answer to this is usually in the singular. It may be, "He can answer the telephone for the principal." Even if this activity can be classified in a defensible pattern, its merits have not been established. However, it answers the question and, since it does, it is sometimes adopted as an enrichment experience. The issue is settled, perhaps inappropriately, but it is settled; the child will answer the telephone.

The question should be, "What enrichment activity would be *best* for this child?" If honestly asked, it leads to a completely different orientation in selecting experiences. The answer requires comparison and an appropriate selection from a group of suggested activities, not a quick adoption of the first one which fits a pattern.

When this question is posed, the search for an appropriate learning must extend. What suggestion comes to mind? Perhaps the first one is that the child can answer the telephone for the principal. This, however, does not answer the question since a single suggestion does not allow for comparison. Now additional suggestions must be derived. He might work on a room newspaper, do additional research in a social studies unit, or many other interesting and worthwhile things. The list is limited only by the insight and imagination of both the child and the teacher. The question can now be answered because there are a number of ideas from which to choose.

It is unlikely that there will be universal agreement as each of us searches for the best activity for a particular child at any given time. The worth of certain enrichment activities will be evaluated differently, the needs of our children will change, and the opportunities in different learning situations will vary.

Universal agreement is not essential. There are two essentials for effective enrichment, a carefully chosen pattern using the best features of each dimension and a comparative judgment in selecting the best specific activity which fits that pattern.

FLYING MONKEYS AND SILENT LIONS *

E. Paul Torrance

CURRICULUM FRONTIERS FOR THE ELEMENTARY GIFTED PUPIL

Traditionally, it seems to me, our treatment of gifted elementary pupils has been designed "to make flying monkeys abandon such antics" and "to make silent lions roar." Today, we find the curriculum frontiers for the elementary gifted pupil leading to a reversal of this goal. I want to propose that we explore curriculum frontiers which will permit flying monkeys to fly at even greater heights and which will allow silent lions to remain silent, developing other important talents.

First, I shall try to describe some of the dynamics by which we are making flying monkeys swing by their tails and coax silent lions into roaring or be destroyed. Next, I shall identify some of the curriculum frontiers by which this process can be reversed. Finally, I shall outline some of the things which we must do in order to open up these frontiers.

Although I can support most of my ideas with research evidence from our studies of creative thinking in the early school years, the ideas which I shall present actually came from the wisdom of approximately 4000 gifted elementary pupils in Minnesota, Illinois, Oklahoma, Georgia and Massachusetts. Children express these ideas so much more eloquently and simply than research men.

The data to which I refer came from imaginative stories written by these elementary pupils. In a 20-minute period, they were asked to write imaginative stories about animals or persons with some divergent characteristics. In some cases, they were given a choice of 10 topics, such as The Duck That Won't Quack, The Cat That Won't Scratch, The Woman Who Won't Talk, and The Boy Who Wants to Be a Nurse. In others, they were given a choice of only two titles, The Flying Monkey and The Lion That Won't Roar.

SANCTIONS AGAINST DIVERGENCY

It is my hypothesis that curricular practices which seek to prevent flying monkeys from flying and make silent lions roar result pri-

---

* Reprinted from *Exceptional Children* (November 1961), pp. 119–127, by permission of the author and publisher.

marily from society's sanctions against any kind of divergency. People have a tendency to become suspicious, anxious, even fearful of anyone who is different from most other people. The sanctions are strongest, of course, against those who are so indiscreet as to permit their differences to show.

My proposal that we seek our curriculum frontiers in a reversal of this traditional approach and free ourselves from fears is based on the belief shared by an increasing number of behavioral scientists that the ways in which a person is different from all others are his most priceless possession and that it is these differences which have made our country what it is and are essential to a democratic society.

Many of the coercive influences against divergency are illustrated in this story about Pepper, a Flying Monkey by a Twin Cities girl:

> Far into the jungle of Africa lived a flying monkey named Pepper. Pepper was a well-educated monkey and very cute. . . . Pepper was unusual too. He was not like all of the other flying monkeys. You see, Pepper didn't eat bananas like everybody else. He wanted to be different. He ate peppers!
>
> No one ever went out of the jungle so Pepper, being different, decided to go to America! . . . When the people saw him, they began to laugh and then others began to scream. Then out of nowhere a man from a zoo came and took Pepper by surprise. . . .
>
> Now Pepper was sad. He didn't like the cage they put him in. He made a vow that if he ever got out he would never be different again and then minutes later he saw some bent bars big enough to fly through. All of a sudden he flew out and in two days was back in the jungle. He kept his promise too. He was never different again. He was a good little flying monkey.

I suppose *he ate his bananas!*

About two-thirds of the stories about flying monkeys, thus far analyzed, tell similar tales of conformity or of destruction. Some cultures, however, are more indulgent of divergency than others. Stories written by gifted children in special classes are far more hopeful than those of gifted children in regular classes. In about 70 percent of the stories of pupils in classes for high achieving pupils, the flying monkey is in some way able to persist in his flying. The stories written by children in a small Oklahoma town composed of Indians, whites, and a few Negroes also reflect this tolerance of divergency. In 74 percent of their stories, the flying monkey succeeds.

Pressures upon gifted children who lack or are weak in some characteristic or skill regarded as highly important by society are especially severe. Since verbal skills are highly valued in our society, the stories of ducks that won't quack, lions that won't roar, dogs that won't bark, and roosters that won't crow seem to give us valuable insights into this problem as viewed by children. The relentlessness of this kind of pressure is reflected in the following story by a sixth-grade girl:

Quack! Quack! They were after him again—the Ladies Duck Aid Society, with their hair up in pin curls and their screaming, fat ducklings swimming and holding on to their skirts. They never failed. Alas! It was getting too much for little Glob-Blob. Every day there would be quacking and screaming of ducklings while poor Glob-Blob would run as fast as he could to get away from the vicious ducks.

The reason for this was because poor Glob-Blob could not quack. So every day the Ladies Duck Aid Society would chase Glob-Blob, for they said it was for the good of the ducks, and it was not only right but they were doing a good turn.

It was luck for Glob-Blob that the ducks were fat and flabby, for if they were limber, I will not mention what would happen. But one day, these lazy ducks did reduce, and when chasing Glob-Blob dealt him a good many hard blows. And the next day, poor Glob-Blob was at last doomed. The vicious quackers came and the chase was on. Glob-Blob was failing. It is a shame that so noble a duck should be doomed, but "That is life," said Glob-Blob to himself as, slowly but surely, failing, he dropped to the ground. The quackers, very pleased with themselves, sat down for a chat.

But I shall always remember Glob-Blob and his death. So I shall let him finish his journey, where there will be no more quackers and chasers, and where at last, he may have passionless peace forever.

Many children see us as "quackers and chasers" when we work so hard to make them "better rounded personalities." They might contribute far more to society and be far happier and more successful by capitalizing upon their unique strengths rather than spending fruitless energy trying hopelessly to compensate for some divergent characteristic or behavior. I would, of course, emphasize the fact that it is necessary for some of our highly creative youngsters to achieve basic skills necessary for success in their chosen areas of specialization.

SOME OF THE FRONTIERS

With this introduction to the process by which flying monkeys are forced to desist and silent lions, to roar, I would like to identify some of the frontiers we discover when we reverse our goals.

Self-Initiated Learning

In my estimation, one of the most promising frontiers is to be discovered in efforts to provide for, and give credit for, self-initiated learning. In many of our stories, the monkey learns to fly or the lion learns to roar through self-initiated learning. One of the most fre-

quent devices is to secure the assistance of someone who is an expert.
The wise old owl and the eagle are some of the favorite teachers. Some
of the gifted children in our longitudinal studies of creativity are
experts at self-initiated learning. One third-grade girl wanted to learn
how to knit. Her mother did not know how to knit, so she started
going from door to door in her neighborhood until she found someone
who could knit and was willing to teach her. She mastered this skill
quite readily. One fourth-grade boy, who as a second grader gave me
the clearest and most accurate explanation of the principle of the
magnifying glass, became interested in high speed computers. He
went to the experts and is now something of an expert himself on
computers.

Learning On One's Own

Another curriculum frontier is to be found in provisions which
permit children to do things on their own and to learn on their own.
Last year, we conducted an exciting study in which we found that
children would do a great deal of writing on their own. In another
it was found that gifted children in a split-shift school showed more
growth in language development, science and social studies than under
a full-day schedule. Only in spelling was there significantly less growth
among the split-shift children (seventh graders). In still another we
found that children in a split-shift school engage in a large number of
creative learning activities on their own.

New frontiers are bound to open up whenever we open the tops
on the cages in which we imprison our flying monkeys or chase
the silent lions out on their own. The following story by an Oklahoma
sixth grader, illustrates some important points:

Once there were some monkeys sitting in a group. They were all alike
except three monkeys. They were very different because they could fly.

One day some men from a park zoo were looking for some monkeys
because theirs had died. They came upon the three that flew. So they took
them in a cage. The cage didn't have a top to it. They were in the sun one
day and one monkey said to the other, "I wish we could get out of here."

"Then why don't we fly out of here?" said the other.

They started to fly out. When they got about half a mile, some men
came to feed them. When they couldn't find the three monkeys, they saw
them flying away. One of them said, "If we would have put them in a cage
with a top, we would have had a real good thing here in the zoo."

I am particularly interested in the remarks of the keepers as they
saw the monkeys flying away. For their own gain or their own glory,
they would like to enslave the flying monkeys. It is perhaps rather
brutal to suggest this, but we should perhaps examine more honestly
our motives for making pupils so dependent upon us.

The Responsive Environment

Another important curriculum frontier is being opened up rapidly with experiments in creating responsive environments through which children are propelled by their curiosity. This concept of the responsive environment is illustrated in the experimental work of O. K. Moore at Yale University. Through the natural curiosity of children about electric typewriters, Moore has demonstrated that pre-school children can learn to read, write, type, and take dictation. Here we have skills being learned creatively which we have always assumed could be taught most economically by authority. In much of our own research at the University of Minnesota, I believe we have demonstrated that children can learn creatively many of the traditional educational skills.

One of the most common themes in the stories of gifted children is a failure to find a responsive environment. I am convinced that our failure to provide a responsive environment kills at a very early age much of the excitement of learning. The process by which this occurs in the kindergarten is described in a number of the letters I receive from parents. From these heart-rending accounts, we can understand why researchers such as E. G. Andrews find drops in the creative thinking of five-year olds.

Revising Concepts of Readiness

Everywhere educators of gifted children are revising their concepts about "readiness" and what can be taught at various levels of education. This is a frontier which terrifies many however. The following recent headlines reflect this fear:

"Caution Urged in Changing Primary into High Schools"

"Don't Turn Grade Schools into High Schools, Educators Warn at Parley"

"Reading for Kindergarten, Languages Too Soon Attacked"

J. S. Bruner's exciting book, *The Process of Education*, should help us chart our way through this frontier. Along with revisions about readiness, he develops the concept of structure of knowledge and interesting ideas about intuition and motivation. About readiness, he says, "Experience over the past decade points to the fact that our schools may be wasting precious years by postponing the teaching of many subjects on the grounds that they are too difficult . . . The essential point often overlooked in the planning of curricula . . . (is that) the basic ideas that lie at the heart of all science and mathematics and the basic schemes that give form to life and literature are powerful." For this purpose, Bruner suggests "the spiral curriculum," one that turns back on itself at higher and higher levels of complexity.

A very frequent theme in our imaginative stories is related to this problem. The young animal or fowl asks, "When can I roar? When can I crow? When can I quack? When can I fly?" Almost always, the answer is, "When you are a little older." We are too afraid that the young one might not be ready to learn and that he would be forever scarred by even the most temporary failure.

A common experience in the lives of almost all highly outstanding individuals has been their ability to cope with failure and frustration. Certainly, almost all highly creative scientists, inventors, artists, and writers attempt tasks which are too difficult for them. Had they not attempted such tasks, it is quite unlikely that their great ideas would have been born.

Search for Self

Generally, people feel that the elementary period is too early for children to start developing their self-concepts, to start searching for their selves. The trouble is that the process is well under way even before the child enters school. I think children have a natural concern about this and that our failure to help them blocks access to important and exciting curriculum frontiers, especially for gifted children.

I am reminded of these things by the following story by a sixth-grade boy:

There once was a South American monkey that didn't know what he was, who he was, or why he was even alive. He decided that he didn't know even a way to figure it out, so he thought he would make up a reason.

He had seen many airplanes fly overhead. He had seen many ferocious animals, many nice animals, and many machines. He had always thought that it would be nice to fly, so he pretended he was an airplane.

He had also heard that buzzing sound of the engines, so he called himself "Buzz." He also decided that he was a real fast flyer so that this was the reason he was alive.

Now we all know that monkeys can't fly, but he didn't know this. Why he didn't even know now that he was a monkey, so he kept trying and trying—and you know what? He flew!

Perhaps this has some implications not only concerning the need for helping children discover their potentialities but for helping them achieve their self-concepts creatively rather than by authority.

We also need to help children accept themselves, remembering that children may even despise an outstanding "gift," if their giftedness makes them different from others. This makes far too many gifted children willing to emasculate themselves and consciously and unconsciously hide or destroy their talents. They prefer to be like others.

Search for One's Uniqueness

An important curriculum frontier in the education of gifted elementary pupils is to be found in helping them search for and develop their uniqueness. Such a frontier has been under exploration during the past three years in the Riverside School at Bloomington, Minnesota, through what they call their "strengths and weaknesses program." Every other week, each afternoon is devoted entirely to this program. Opportunity is given for developing further their special enthusiasms or what might otherwise be hobbies. Guidance is also given in strengthening neglected educational skills which might cause them to bog down later in the pursuit of their enthusiasms, both vocational and avocational.

OPENING UP THE FRONTIERS

I have suggested six curriculum frontiers whereby we may aid flying monkeys and silent lions realize their potentialities more fully. Now, I would like to suggest some provisions which I believe will be effective in breaking through these frontiers.

Rewarding Varied Talents

Research for years has repeatedly shown that people will develop along whatever lines they find rewarding. Thus, the need for rewarding various kinds of talents and kinds of learning should be obvious. My staff and I have conducted over a dozen experiments concerned with rewarding creative thinking. We know now what some of the difficulties are, what some of the most effective principles and procedures are. The essence of what we know, however, is simply to be respectful of a diversity of talent.

Help Children Recognize the Value of Their Talents

We cannot open up curriculum frontiers for many children until we can help them recognize the value of their talents. Otherwise, they continue to despise their most valuable assets. Itchy, the flying monkey in the following story by a sixth-grade girl, made this discovery for himself:

Itchy was a monkey who lived in a deep, dark jungle in Africa. He came from a very fine family, but Itchy was ashamed of himself because he didn't have a long tail like his father or curly hair like his mother. He didn't even look good at all because he had a short, wide tail and smooth hair. But what made him look real bad were two wide wings just below his shoulders.

One day while Itchy was lying in the grass, looking up at the sky, he saw a flock of birds. . . . Then he started thinking (for he was a very smart monkey). "If the birds can fly, why can't I?" So he climbed to the tallest tree in the jungle and jumped. Right away the wings below his shoulders started working and Itchy was flying.

"Why," said Itchy, "I shouldn't be ashamed of myself because how many monkeys can fly?"

And off he flew to show his family that he was as good as they were.

Developing Creative Acceptance of Limitations

Inevitably there are limitations both within the environment and the individual. Both must be accepted, not cynically, but creatively. In an early study of the psychology of inventors, J. Rossman found that this characteristic differentiates inventors from non-inventors. Non-inventors only cuss the defects of their environment and of themselves. Inventors, however, take a more constructive approach, saying, "This is the way to do it." I like this story in which a fifth grade boy in Massachusetts shows how the lion can accent creatively his inability to roar:

Once there was a lion named Roary. He was the king of the beasts. But he didn't roar. Mostly every creature laughed at him and didn't listen to him. Everyone thought they should vote for another animal. They were trying to decide. Then the monkey said, "Can't I be the king? I'm very strong."

The animals said, "You'll have to prove it." So the monkey did, but the animals weren't satisfied. . . .

. . . Then one day the animals were frightened by the hunters. They told Roary, "Please save us!"

But Roary said, "I can't save you because I can't roar."

The animals said, "It's not time to be joking."

The hunters saw Roary. They started laughing because he couldn't roar. But Roary had a record player and the record was called "How to Learn to Roar." So he played it. Then he opened his mouth and the roars came from the record player. And it seemed as if he was roaring. Roary scared the wits out of the hunters. They ran like lightning. The animals were saved, thanks to Roary. So they asked, "Roary, did you really roar?"

Roary said, "That's my secret." So now they wanted Roary for king even if he can't roar.

Stop Equating Divergency with Mental Illness and Delinquency

One of the big barriers to opening up the curriculum frontiers I have suggested is our practice of equating any kind of divergent characteristic or behavior with mental illness and/or delinquency. Flying monkeys in our stories are frequently thought to be crazy or to be devils or under the spell of witches. Lions that won't roar and cats that won't scratch are thought to be mentally ill. Some of the stories make us more aware of the ways by which parents intensify this problem. Others painfully show how both parents and professionals fail in understanding divergency, as is exemplified by the following story:

> Once there was a cat that could not scratch. A lady came and the cat followed her so she took the cat home with her. The cat meowed and meowed, so the lady gave him some milk and he spilt the milk all over himself. So the lady put the cat in the bath tub and gave him a bath, but the cat did not scratch her. The lady did not understand so she took the cat to the cat hospital. The veterinarian did not understand so she let the cat go and that is the end of the cat that would not scratch and the lady and the doctor that did not understand that cat.

In our studies of highly creative children, we find many evidences that they feel that their parents and teachers do not understand them. Their teachers themselves admit that they do not know these children as well as they know highly intelligent (IQ) pupils.

Changed Emphasis on Sex Roles

Our overemphasis or misplaced emphasis on sex roles is a serious block to the development of many talents, especially creative talents. It has been pointed out frequently that rarely do women become scientific discoverers, inventors, or composers. Overemphasis or misplaced emphasis on sex roles, however, exacts its toll on the creativity of both sexes and creates serious problems of adjustment to highly creative individuals of both sexes.

Creativity, by its very nature, requires both sensitivity and independence. In our culture, sensitivity is definitely a feminine virtue while independence is a masculine value. Thus, we may expect the highly creative boy to appear to be more effeminate than his peers and the highly creative girl to appear more masculine. Anne Roe, F. Barron, and E. P. Torrance have all cited evidence in support of this phenomenon. In our longitudinal studies we are finding interesting examples of children who sacrifice their creativity in order to maintain their "masculinity" or their "femininity," as the case may be.

This cultural block to creativity comes out in many places. We first observed it in our Product Improvement Test in which children are asked to think of all the ideas they can for improving common toys so that they will be more fun to play with. In the first grade, boys excelled girls on the fire truck but girls excelled boys on the nurse's kit. Many of the boys refused to think of anything to make the nurse's kit more fun, protesting, "I'm a boy! I don't play with things like that!" Some of the more creative boys, however, first transposed it into a doctor's kit and as such were quite free to think of improvements. By the third grade, however, boys excelled girls even on the nurse's kit, probably because by this time girls have been conditioned to accept toys as they are and not to manipulate and change them.

The inhibiting effects of sex-role conditioning also showed up in our experiments involving small groups working with science toys. Girls are quite reluctant to work with these science toys and frequently protest, "I'm a girl; I'm not supposed to know anything about things like that!" Boys demonstrate and explain about twice as many ideas as girls in experiments involving these materials. We know already, however, that this situation can be modified significantly. In 1959, we found these phenomena operating quite strongly in this school. Later I had the opportunity to report these and other results to both the teachers and parents in this school. In 1960, we conducted some experiments in this same school in which we used a different but similar set of science toys. This time, we found none of this reluctance on the part of girls, there was no difference in the expressed enjoyment of the activity of boys and girls, and the mean performance of girls and boys was almost identical. In one way, however, the situation remained unchanged. The contributions of boys were more highly valued by peers than those of girls. Apparently, the school climate has helped to make it more acceptable for girls to play around with science things, but boys' ideas about science things are still supposed to be better than those of girls.

Help the Divergent Child to Become Less Obnoxious

In our studies of highly creative children, it is evident that many of them bring upon themselves many of their own woes. To open to them the curriculum frontiers I have suggested, we must help them to become less obnoxious without sacrificing their creativity.

Both our experimental and longitudinal studies and studies of outstanding creative persons reveal that highly creative individuals do, in fact, possess characteristics generally considered somewhat obnoxious. They do, in fact, create problems for their parents, siblings, peers, teachers and supervisors. Many of our young elementary school authors recognize this problem, but most, like the sixth grader who wrote the following story, feel that considerable sacrifice of creativity is necessary:

My brother was born a day before I was. But there was something wrong with him. He had wings! Can you imagine that? A monkey with wings!
He could fly where other monkeys couldn't get to, so they teased him. Well, he got tired of being teased and I got tired of being his brother (because of course I was teased too).
We decided to fly to some other place. So I climbed up his back and away we went.
The other monkeys were sorry then because my brother had always

gotten the best bananas for them. Everyone was sad, even my brother and I. We couldn't find anywhere to go and he was getting tired. Finally, we turned around and started walking back.

When we got back, everyone was happy again! But sometimes, for spite, the 'flying monkey' wouldn't get the best bananas for them and then the teasing would start again.

Finally, he learned how to keep his 'wings' out of sight. After that he hardly ever used them and was never teased again.

We also need to help children recognize that outstanding talents may threaten others and make them uncomfortable and afraid. Our young authors recognize this and offer some interesting philosophies. The performance of important services and courageous deeds on behalf of the larger social group is seen by our juvenile authors as one way of reducing the social pressures on divergent individuals.

In conserving creative talent, the problem resolves itself into one of helping the child maintain those characteristics which are essential to his creativity and at the same time helping him acquire skills for avoiding or reducing to a tolerable level the social sanctions against him. M. I. Stein, on the basis of his study of research chemists, has offered a set of helpful principles whereby creative research chemists can become less obnoxious without sacrificing their creativity. I have tried to paraphrase this advice to make it apply to gifted elementary pupils, as follows:

Help the gifted child maintain his assertiveness without being hostile and aggressive. He must be aware of his superiors, peers and subordinates as persons. He may work alone but be must not be isolated, withdrawn or uncommunicative. In the classroom he must be congenial but not sociable; outside the classroom he must be sociable but not intimate. He must "know his place" without being timid, submissive, or acquiescent and must speak "his mind" without being domineering. As he tries to gain a point, he can be subtle but not cunning or manipulative. In all relationships, he must be sincere, honest, purposeful, and diplomatic. In the intellectual area, he must learn to be broad without spreading himself too thin, deep without being "bookish" or "too scientific," and "sharp" without being overcritical.

This model probably asks too much of the gifted child, but it at least provides a model which might guide us in making possible the exploration of the frontiers outlined.

Develop Pride in the Achievement of Gifted Pupils

It seems to me that we miss many good opportunities for developing pride in the achievement of gifted pupils. We have long done a good job of developing pride in athletic teams, bands, and the like. Much is being done now to develop pride in a school's scientific talent, especially at the high school level. Some schools are organizing elementary school art shows. Much more could be done, however, to give favorable recognition to schools for their development of intellectual and creative talents.

You may dislike the blunt exhibitionism involved in the following story by a gifted sixth-grade boy. You must admit, nevertheless, that he has the rudiments of a potentially useful idea.

Once there was a monkey named Business. Because this was his name and he was a monkey, all of the other animals in the jungle called him Monkey Business. Of course, Business didn't like this. Why he was the laughing stock of the whole jungle! That is, until his friend Jacko the Bird taught him to fly! Now Monkey Business was the pride of the jungle. . . . Very soon nobody made any jokes about his name. As a matter of fact, whenever they had any visitors from other jungles, the first thing they showed them was Monkey Business, the fabulous flying monkey.

Reduce the Isolation of the Gifted Child

Much attention has already been given to the problems involved in reducing the isolation of the gifted child (Kaluger and Martin, 1960). Isolation has been a favorite technique for coping with individuals having almost any kind of divergent characteristic. In the imaginative stories, the following reaction is fairly common:

. . . His mother was so surprised to see him flying. She said that she didn't want any flying monkey in her family so she sent him away to some other part of the jungle.

One of the most successful techniques in the stories of our young authors is the discovery by one divergent individual of someone with a similar divergency. This happens to both the flying monkeys and the silent lions. Several current streams of research suggest that various kinds of groupings, both within classes and into classes, may open up some exciting frontiers, especially for children with divergent characteristics.

Provide Sponsors or Patrons for Gifted Pupils

Someone has observed that almost always wherever independence and creativity occur and persist, there is some other individual or agent who plays the role of "sponsor" or "patron." The patron or sponsor is someone who is not a member of the peer group, but possesses prestige or power in the same social system. He does several things. Regardless of his own views, the sponsor encourages and supports the talented individual in expressing and testing his ideas, in thinking through things for himself. He protects the individual from the counter reactions of his peers long enough to permit him to try out some of his ideas. He can keep the structure of the situation open enough so that originality can occur. In some cases, this sponsor for the gifted elementary pupil may be a teacher, principal, an older child, an adult leader, a school social worker or counselor.

Exploit the Opportunities of the Moment

Frequently questions are asked concerning the role of chance in scientific discovery. Certainly many great discoveries have resulted because someone exploited a chance occurrence, an unexpected incident, or the like. As teachers learn to exploit such moments and train their pupils to do so, there is no question but that unpredicted curriculum frontiers for gifted elementary pupils will emerge. Many of the stories of flying monkeys and silent lions tell stories of such exploitation of the moment.

Develop Values and Purpose

Studies of outstanding individuals in various fields almost always reveal that such purposes seem to be impelled by some feeling of mission or purpose. They believe that what they are doing is tremendously worthwhile and are thereby aroused to "all-out" effort. When learning and thinking is made to be "tremendously important and worthwhile," schools will become exciting places and curriculum frontiers will unfold. Even gifted children will achieve more than we thought possible. Such is the experience of a number of the monkeys in the imaginative stories of elementary pupils.

Help Gifted Pupils Cope with Anxieties and Fears

Neither gifted children nor creative scientists are free of handicapping anxieties and fears. Many gifted children will be unable to explore the curriculum frontiers already discussed unless they have help in coping with their anxieties and irrational fears. Not only will they fail to be fully functioning mentally; they will be afraid to break away from the safest, most frequently traveled paths.

An unusually frequent theme in the stories of animals and persons with divergent characteristics is the fear of one's own talent or the fear that its use will bring injury or destruction. The following pathetic story by a gifted Illinois girl represents an extreme fear of one's own talent:

. . . I will tell you about a lion named Elmer who was afraid of anything. Elmer had no friends at all. In the day he laid around all the time. At night he hunted for food. He saw his shadow, he started to cry. All the animals came running. The tiger, Mr. Peabody, said, "Why are you crying?"

Elmer just sat there. Then an elephant, Mrs. Atlas, said, "Why are you crying?"

Elmer said nothing. Then the lizard, mouse, horse, cat, cow and hen tried but could not get him to answer. Then a little boy said, "Why are you crying?"

Elmer looked up and said, "I saw my shadow and I'm scared of it."

"I don't see it," said the boy. The lion looked down. It was not there. He started to roar, then started to cry. The boy said, "Why are you crying?"

"Im afraid of my roar," Elmer said. All the animals and the boy laughed.

In one story, a lion would not roar because he was afraid that his roar might not sound like a lion's. Another would not roar because he was afraid that a banana might fall down his throat when he opened his mouth to roar. Thus, on and on, the animals created by gifted children are shackled by some of the same kinds of fears which shackle gifted children. Quite interestingly, almost all of these handicapped animals are able to rise to the occasion and transcend their fears when some necessity arises. I feel convinced that gifted children will leap many barriers to curriculum frontiers, if we educators will learn better how to create necessities for learning and thinking.

MY FRIEND PAULA *

Walter B. Barbe

Once in every teacher's life there comes a child who stands out from all the others. For some this child comes early in their teaching career; for others, the child does not come for many years. But as certainly as every good teacher loves to teach, some one child will stand out.

And when my friends ask me why I teach, I can only tell them about the child whom I can never forget. There are many children I will never forget, but above all these stands one child. I shall call this child Paula because that is her name. It would somehow take away part of her personality if I were to call her anything else.

I work in a reading center, where we see many children who are having difficulty with reading. Some of them want to learn, others

* Reprinted from (January 1958) issue of *Education*, pp. 263–268, by permission of the Bobbs-Merrill Co., Indianapolis, Indiana.

don't. Some of them come with the greatest of enthusiasm, for this is their opportunity to learn; others come because they must, expecting nothing but more of the same type of thing which has failed them in the past. The day Paula came to the Reading Center marked the beginning of a new period. She arrived, not to learn from us but to teach us. And oh the things we learned that day, when Paula came our way.

With clenched fists and bowed legs, Paula stomped into the Center. Never one to be taken back by a new situation, even at the age of eight, Paula had learned a technique for disarming people. "I wanna see the man who owns this place!" she demanded. Being the one who is nominally in charge of the Reading Center, I stepped forward. Being unaccustomed to such a bold approach I was, to say the least, taken back. At this point, I noticed for the first time a lady and another child about Paula's age standing in the hall. Before anyone could say anything more the lady began explaining that the little boy was her child and that she took neither any blame or responsibility for this outspoken little girl who stood with her hands on her hips and her feet wide apart waiting for an answer to her question. The mother of the boy, being somewhat more in awe of a "reading specialist" than Paula, was obviously quite distressed. Undoubtedly realizing the need for someone to say something, Paula, who had caused this dumbfounded silence, said, "Before I go any further, I want to get one thing straight. I'm not going to read and so don't try to make me." Since I knew that Paula was in the third grade, and obviously would not have been sent to the Reading Center unless she had some reading problem, the light began to dawn. She did not know how to read and was afraid that she would be exposed. With some degree of complacency, for I had confronted this problem before, I began assuring her that she did not have to read unless she wanted to. This was the last complacency that I was ever to feel around Paula for what should have worked never did and what worked with other children was certain to fail with Paula.

The approach that "you don't have to read unless you want to," usually works after the child feels secure in the Reading Center. He is usually quite willing to attempt some short reading paragraph. Paula, being somewhat skeptical of an adult's promise, reminded me many times that morning that I had told her that she did not have to read. She seemed almost to delight in the fact that she had control over me because obviously everything I was doing was attempting to lead her into the desire for reading. It became almost a game, and one in which I was a complete loser. Paula did not make any attempt to read for me for three visits, but on the fourth visit she admitted that she could not read and so there was no reason to try.

In getting acquainted with Paula, I asked her if she liked to read and she replied, "I would if I knew how." And the only answer which I could think of was, "who wouldn't."

In Paula's first visit she was administered an individual intelligence test. Test results at school in the first grade had indicated that Paula was about average in ability, but retesting later seemed to indicate low average mental ability. Paula had lots of fun with the individual intelligence test. She defined the word "conquer" as "hit her on the head" and said that if she were to find a child who was lost from its parents that she would take it home and raise it. She was aware that these answers were not correct, but she seemed to enjoy being different. She said that she had been told enough times how different she was and she didn't really care because she didn't want to be like the others. But even in spite of all of Paula's fooling around, she still scored in the superior range of intelligence. When confronted with the tests results, she replied, "Don't waste your time telling me, I never thought I was dumb. You had better tell some of those other teachers." Something seemed to click about this time and I knew that Paula and I were going to get along all right. I did not know what could be done next, but I knew that something could be done. I knew that the referral which said that Paula was a "non-reader" was wrong, for to be a non-reader means that the child will never be able to read. Then and there I said, "This is the child I am going to help."

Getting to know Paula was a form of self-therapy. She asked far more questions about me than I did about her. I wondered sometimes just who was interviewing whom. But I decided that this was all right, for here was a child who was getting what she apparently needed most—the complete attention of someone who was interested in her. Paula was not a pretty little girl, but with her straight hair and bangs which seemed to frame her plump little face like a picture window, there was something about her that was very attractive. The better I came to know Paula, the more certain I was that here was really a beautiful child. But then, I find this to be true not just with children but with adults also. The more I know about a person and understand his problems, the better I like him.

The day finally arrived when Paula was to come to the Reading Center for her first lesson. And what a day it was—summertime, blazing hot sun, and above all else, five squirming little boys in the class. It took less than five minutes that first day to find who was the toughest child in the bunch. Paula won.

As all teachers know, in every group of children there is a leader. To fail in reaching this child is a certainty of failure with the other children. To succeed with the child opens an avenue toward easy success with all the rest of the children. Had I been wiser, I would never have risked the other five children with such a problem case as Paula.

Consistency has always been the dominant thing in my thinking as the major requirement for a good teacher. But with this consistency, flexibility was, I thought, also necessary. In less than two minutes I knew that my usual methods were not going to work. The seven of us sat down and drew up the rules by which we would abide. It was my desire to use a positive approach and say such things as "everyone will do his best" and the like. Paula put a stop to this. "If we've got to do them, then they've got to say either 'don't' or 'no' and so, the rules of our class came out as these:

1. No loafing
2. No interrupting one and another
3. No leaving the room during the reading lesson

The first two rules were really theirs, the third one was mine. The next step was to make these children understand the rules were not to be broken. After thirty requests for a drink of water during the first lesson, on a blistering hot summer day, I began to wonder if I were not being too rigid. I had never before been so thirsty, but kept thinking that if she would not remind me of it I might make it to the end of the period myself. We survived the first lesson, but there can be little compliment paid to the teaching that went on.

We quickly learned that Paula's definition of loafing and my definition of loafing were quite different. But since I was the teacher, and for no other reason in Paula's understanding, the rules were to be interpreted by me. Her demands for her "rights," in a vote by the other children were quickly squelched by me. I already knew who would win in any such a vote.

The next day Paula delighted her five little boy friends by coming into the classroom through the window. The window, some ten feet above the yard, required a scaling maneuver which only an agile child could have accomplished. Seeing my look of disapproval, amid the joyful glee of the other children, Paula said, "There is no rule against coming in the window." I knew then where the battle line had been drawn. She was willing to abide by my rules, the three which we had established the day before, but no more were to be added. Being unable to foresee anything other than entering through the window, which I supposed I could get used to if I had to, I went along with this unorthodox entree.

From then on, each day Paula had another thing to pull on me which was not governed by the rules. She wore shorts, a hat, chewed gum (which I found particularly objectionable but which she reminded us was not "covered in the rules"), parked her bicycle in the hall out-

side the classroom and brought a cup of water to the door of the classroom to be gulped down the second the class was to begin. But when
Paula discovered that she could do these things providing she still
abided by the three rules the group had set, she settled down into what
resembled an elementary school pupil. She never confessed that these
three rules were the first three that she had ever obeyed. She said
that it was a lot more fun to think of ways to get around the rules than
it was to do what they said.

Beginning with a basic sight word vocabulary, Paula demonstrated
a remarkable ability for learning. She was rather fast at memorization
and when she discovered she was really better at it than the five boys,
she developed a sort of pride at being able to learn faster than they did.

Paula's greatest difficulty was remaining in her seat. Only one
method, not found in the usual educational textbook, worked. In an
affectionate manner, I left my hand on Paula's shoulder at all times.
When the pressure began to be a little stronger coming up, I placed a
little more pressure going down. The balance of the two kept Paula
somewhere near the seat of her chair. When she began giving in to
the pressure and sliding closer to the floor it became necessary to lift
my hand and sometimes bring her with me. Whenever the attention
was too far away from Paula, the pressure on my hand reminded me
that she was still with us.

Working with Paula was a continuous series of trials and errors.
But undoubtedly the greatest mistake was when we came upon the
word *any*. "What does it mean?", asked Paula. Being somewhat
fluent, I talked around what it might mean. I used an example, but I
could never quite tell Paula what "any" did mean. Paula enjoyed the
position in which she had placed me, but finally relieved me by saying,
"Oh well, then draw me a picture of it." Of course, I was unable to do
this. Being in as deep as this, I should have known to quit. And we
had been over the word so many times, I had to say it. "Paula, if it is
the last thing I ever do, I'm going to teach you to read this word." To
this day, some five years later, Paula still says when she comes to the
word *any*, "there's that word that even the man down at the Reading Center couldn't teach me."

Paula actually learned so rapidly that she was able to help some
of the boys in the class. One day, a little boy was having such difficulty
remembering certain words that I asked Paula to take him out of the
room to help him. This was her first experience at being a teacher.
She left with great pride. When the little boy came back, I was somewhat distressed for he seemed to have even more difficulty than before.
I asked Paula how he had done outside of the room and she said that

he had learned the words. I was completely puzzled until I discovered that the little boy was constantly making the same errors as he read the story. The word *boy* was always being read as *Baby* and the word *and* was being read as *in.* After thinking this over, I confronted Paula with it before the class the next day. She readily admitted that she had told the boy the wrong words. When I asked her why she had done this, she explained that he was catching on too quickly and she was afraid that he would get to be better than she was. Paula had been too good a teacher, for the child forgot every word that I told him but seemed to always know the incorrect words that Paula had told him.

Keeping Paula's attention on the lesson was quite difficult. To do this, little tricks were necessary. Since all the children had completed the third grade and had been introduced to cursive writing, they objected to any writing on the board being in mauscript. Being of the old school myself, I had never changed the manner in which I wrote the letter *R.* Paula refused to read any word in which I made this error. She said, "It looks too much like the letter 'n'." She was so indignant about this, that I decided to put it to some use. She was given the assignment of correcting me anytime when I made my *R* incorrectly. No other child was allowed to do this. Whenever her attention began to wane, I would sometimes intentionally write a word using the old-fashioned *R.* Paula soon became so busy watching for the letter *R* that she became somewhat engrossed in the lesson. Almost in spite of herself she began to learn to read.

Paula rejected from the very beginning stories about any little girl. She wanted to read about little boys "Doing somethin." After she had been at the Center for about two years, she asked to be allowed to read a few pages from a novel which I had been reading and she had seen on my desk. It was about a man who had crossed the Atlantic in a boat alone. The first page had many very difficult words but Paula was stumbling along reading silently until she came to one sentence and then she began laughing loudly. I said, "What on earth are you laughing about, Paula? There isn't anything funny in that book." "Oh, yes, there is," she said. "I'm reading about biting gals." As she had been learning her phonic rules, she had only to be reminded about the influence of the final *e* on a word, and its effect on the sound of the preceding vowel. She was then able to read the word as "gale" but, as she said, "It isn't nearly so funny that way."

When Paula was fairly well along in reading ability, she went with me to speak before one of the teachers meetings. As I was wearing a lapel microphone, in order that Paula's and my conversation could be heard by the audience, it was not necessary for either of us to speak loudly. Before we were introduced a man announced from the front of the platform the menu for lunch that day. Paula leaned over toward me and, placing her hand over her mouth, whispered into the mike, "They don't have one thing I like." This was so much the opinion of the entire audience that they were overcome with laughter by the time we were finally introduced. Needless to say, the meeting was highly entertaining. Paula was truly a showwoman and enjoyed the attention which she was able to get.

During the question and answer period, a teacher asked how to keep children from knowing what group they are in. Paula, who was sitting on the stage came forward and said, "Let me answer that." She said, "Well, you have four groups. You have a smart group, an average group, a dumb group, and a very dumb group." To the next question, "And what group are you in, Paula?" She quickly replied, "Are there any more questions?"

After about two and a half years of work with Paula, seeing her twice a week during the year and five days a week for one month each summer, Paula had at last arrived at the point where she was close to the reading level of the other children in the classroom. Feeling very proud when Paula came to the Reading Center for her last lesson, I asked her if she were not very pleased with herself. In a very off-handed manner, she replied, "I could have done it all the time if I had wanted to." My only reply to this was, "I only wish that you had wanted to sooner." She was so right in her answer, but it took so long to build the desire.

Then I did not see Paula for a while, although I did hear favorable reports on her progress from time to time. But her name came up quite forcefully at a poster contest. The Reading Center was having a book fair and each school was invited to submit posters. There, on the largest sheet of paper, was Paula's entry. It was a picture of a bookshelf filled with hundreds of books, painstakingly drawn by hand. While I was not one of the judges, I exerted that influence which teachers use so often on the children and Paula received a prize. Since I was the one who had exerted the influence, I was given the privilege of delivering the prize of a book to her at her school. Arriving at lunch time, I went up to find her. Finally I heard a voice say "Hi" and I knew that she had found me first. When everyone was quiet she stormed over to where I was and said, "Come over here, I want you to meet someone." It was her teacher that she was taking me to and she said, "Miss Brown, I want you to meet my friend, the man who taught me how to read."

Then and there I knew it was all worthwhile and I was ready to go back to work with another Paula.

PRESERVE THEIR LANGUAGE HERITAGE *

Simon J. Chavez

After my first few days in the first grade, I discovered that some of the other first graders already knew English. I wondered why they went to school, since to me the purpose of school was to learn a language different from the one spoken at home.

Changes have taken place since then. Today we find a growing interest in having children at the elementary level learn a second language. Changes have taken place in the youngsters in the small southwestern community where I attended elementary school. It is a rare child who does not speak English before he starts school. Far more significantly, there seems to be a tendency among these children to avoid speaking Spanish, for instance, even though Spanish is used by adults in the home.

PRESERVE OTHER CULTURES

This change displeases some educators and some parents. Why do these children forsake part of their heritage at a time when others have to work hard to try to capture some remnants of this culture?

Several factors are involved in this avoidance. It is quite likely that the children have sensed some of the consequences from the behavior of the adults whom they observe. The teacher who attempts to teach Spanish to these children may well run into considerable resistance. He will be far more effective if he has clear objectives and understands the factors involved.

PROMOTE BETTER UNDERSTANDING

We should first establish a justification for teaching Spanish as a second language. The most valid objective would be that it should serve as an avenue to promote a better understanding of our southern neighbors or of those people in our midst who have inherited the

---

* Reprinted by permission of the Association for Childhood Education International, 3615 Wisconsin Avenue, N. W., Washington 16, D. C. "Preserve Their Language Heritage," by Simon J. Chavez. From *Childhood Education*, December 1956; Vol. 33, No. 4.

Spanish culture. Any progress in this direction is worth considerable time and effort. Approaching the topic realistically, it is doubtful that most children in the elementary school or even in high school will reach a high level of proficiency in the use of Spanish. Any communication between a child from an English-speaking home and one from a Spanish-speaking home will likely continue to be in English.

In a school that includes children of Spanish-speaking origin it might be desirable to begin to teach Spanish to the English-speaking children. The English-speaking children might become more sympathetic toward children who must learn a second language.

ENCOURAGE ACCULTURATION

If there is a noticeable division between children of the two cultures, the school's first responsibility is to eradicate this division so that each child will have the opportunity to "belong to the dominant group" regardless of cultural origin. Providing the opportunity to belong is made more difficult when members of the "in" group observe radical differences in those who are "out." These differences, whether in physical appearance or ways of behaving, are often used by members of a group to prove that "we" are alike and "they" are different.

In a bi-cultural school many children from Spanish-speaking homes will have a primary need to learn the ways of thinking and behaving characteristic of what we might call the dominant group. It is essential that they be accepted by the dominant group and that they be identified as members of the group. There will be some children who will make it their main objective in school life to be accepted and to belong to the larger group. In such a case this could very well explain their desire to avoid the use of Spanish and other behavior patterns that would remind the dominant group of differences. It is to be expected that not until the child feels secure and accepted will he venture to display some of his unusual skills, such as ability in a foreign language.

Until the child feels accepted his efforts to avoid appearing different will likely meet with difficulty. The differences in his use of English will be quickly noted. He may become oversensitive to the way he talks. He may resort to reticence, thus cutting down on his sociability and delaying the process of acculturation.

Noticeable differences in his speech may arise from two main causes. The first is the different sound that the same letters have in the two languages. The other can be ascribed to variations in concepts between the cultures.

DIFFERENCES IN SOUNDS

The first difference, that of sounds, will show itself in several letters. A person whose mother tongue is Spanish will have difficulty in pronouncing many of the English sounds. Among these will be the sound of *h*, which he will tend to make too aspirate. He has to remind himself that in English you don't scrape the sound against your palate—you merely touch it very lightly. Another sound is the *i* in *hit* or *miss*, which has a tendency to come out as *ee* in *meet*. Hence he might say *Mees Jones*. Once aware of this difficulty, he will try to correct and in so doing may overcorrect. He may go to the extreme of sounding the *ee* as *i*.

Another sound that torments many people is the *s* sound, especially when this letter insists on becoming a *z* as in *shoes*. Those who have always spoken Spanish will be unable to make the *sh* sound. The word *show* will carry the *ch* sound as in *church*. The sound of *w* also becomes very aspirate at times. The word *one*, which we pronounce *oo-un*, may be sounded *won* or *gwan*.

The difficulty with sound is further complicated by the many sounds that a letter in English may have. For instance, the letter *o* almost runs the gamut of all vowel sounds in such words as *poor, door, odd, old* and *women*. Individuals or people of a given locality may have difficulty with sounds other than the ones mentioned here.

Unless a person has learned in childhood to make a particular sound it is difficult to learn it later. He is constantly aware that he must either tighten or relax his vocal muscles. The person who has learned only the one language is not even aware of the mechanics in making the desired sounds. They come out automatically.

DIFFERENCES IN CONCEPTS

The second difficulty comes from differences in concepts. Even though there may be no accent or intonation present, the way one expresses himself may cause the hearer to brand him as different. One factor is that in Spanish some words are plural and their English counterpart is singular. In some Spanish localities the word *nose* is plural. A person from such a locality might use a plural pronoun in referring to *nose* and say, "I hit them against the door." The word *skirt* is also plural; you might hear a girl say, "I have to iron them." Why are such words plural? It's hard to say. In English we sometimes refer to *pants* as plural and it is likely that someone might say, "I have to iron them."

The person whose mother tongue is Spanish may inadvertently use direct translations in his English. He may call train cars, *train houses;* peach pits, *peach bones,* etc. He may make other similar mistakes. A woman may say, "I'm going to raise the house," meaning that she is going to straighten things up. She may say that the clock is *walking* instead of running.

DIFFICULTIES ENCOUNTERED

All of these differences and many more exist between the two languages. They all cause untold difficulty to the person who tries to master English as a second language. Such obstacles insist in tying up his tongue, "in tweesting his speech," in branding him as "deeferent." In his daily battling with this other language he may well feel that there is only one conclusion—these differences in speech were designed to torment him.

To school children this struggle is of vital concern. They want to speak well. They want to be accepted like the others. They are aware that they will make mistakes in expression when their guard is down. They will be so thankful when they feel other people are not constantly on the lookout for mistakes.

A second language can become a common denominator—a basis where better understanding of cultural differences prevails among children. Is this not one step closer to achieving better communication?

HELPING THE BILINGUAL CHILD *

J. Post Williams

Among the more common teaching problems met throughout Tulare County is that of how to teach the bilingual children most effectively. These children come from homes of varied language backgrounds and come with control of the English language varying from none to nearly perfect command. Each group of children is unique and the teacher will have to adapt teaching methods to the needs of the particular group. In doing this there are certain common considerations which, taken into account can make teaching more effective.

* Reprinted from *Tulare County Cooperative Language Arts Guide* (Visalia, Calif., Tulare County Schools, 1949), by permission of Tulare County Schools.

Know the home and community in which the child lives.

1. Find out whether the group speaking a language other than English is large or small. In a community where most children share a common foreign language the problem is different from that in a community in which a child is an isolate because of his background. If the child is an isolate the need for acceptance by the group is great.

2. Find out whether the foreign language speaking group represents an accepted or unwelcome minority in the community.

3. Learn the story and meaning of conventions, customs, and traditions held by the group, such as those centering around religious and national holidays, birth, marriage and death.

4. Find out whether there is an English-speaking minority in the community. These children may fail to find acceptance in the group where the majority speak another language.

5. Visit non-English speaking homes even though you do not know the language.

Know the individual child.

1. Find out how much English the child knows. Few are completely unfamiliar with some English. The English they do know should serve as the basis for further development.

2. Know the child's background of experience as thoroughly as possible as a basis for vocabulary building.

With what toys is the child familiar?

What common action words will he identify easily, as: run, jump, etc.

With what objects is he familiar in and around his home?

What are his particular needs and wants?

3. Avoid attributing problem behavior to bilingualism.

Plan instruction which is suited to the developmental needs and interests of these children.

1. Place early emphasis on speech; it comes first in natural development.

.2. Avoid giving new concepts too rapidly.

3. Select materials for older boys and girls which are written at their level of interest as well as their level of reading ability. For example: Primer material may not be geared to the interests of the boy or girl in the middle grades who is an immature reader.

4. Provide many opportunities for children to find real satisfaction as they learn the language.

Read directions for a game; then play it.

Keep records of progress in English usage.

5. Give the child experiences of interest to him: pets, school surroundings, games, home. Build stories around these experiences which they can reread.

Plan a program of instruction in which language is learned through using it in real situations.

1. Keep the bilingual child in the classroom with English speaking children. He learns more readily here than in segregated groups.

2. Talk to the child in English presenting material in such a way that the child will make the correct response.

3. Teach children to play singing games in which action is suited to the word.

4. Provide much opportunity for creative expression.

5. Plan activities in which these children come into daily contact with the accepted customs, traditions, and policies of the democratic way of life such as:

Helping one another.

Working together in the establishment of policies.

Abiding by the decisions of the group.

Respecting property rights of the individual and the group, buying, selling, etc.

Respecting beliefs and practices of individuals and groups.

Provide experiences which have meaning in terms of understandings which children already have.

1. Dramatize action words.

2. Build the playhouse along the lines of the home with which the child is familiar.

3. Plan centers of interest in music, art, science, etc. to which children can make contributions.

4. Encourage children to share their toys, hobbies, etc. using them as a basis for discussion and story-writing.

5. Plan discussions centering around traditions and customs with which children are familiar helping them to learn English terms for familiar experiences.

6. Select reading materials which are related to the life the child knows.

7. Through the social studies help the child to share his culture with others in the group and to see its importance in the cultural development of the United States.

Relate language experiences to the solution of problems the child meets daily in playing, working, buying, and conversing.

1. Dramatize going to the store to purchase needed supplies.

2. Encourage children to help the family secure its groceries.

3. Develop vocabulary around the activities children carry on in school, such as:

Playing games with other children.

Explaining how to travel from home to school and back so they can tell the school bus driver or teacher.

Giving directions for reaching the store, fire-station, clinic, etc.

Entering into conversations with other children where English is spoken.

Helping other children learn new words as they are needed.

4. Plan learning experiences at the level of the child's participation in his home and community activities.

Little children are learning to care for their personal needs, to dress, to care for their clothes, and to keep clean.

Middle grade children are caring for their persons, helping with family chores, running errands.

Older children have definite family responsibilities, help with younger children, sell papers, mow lawns, and work for wages.

Provide meaningful and purposeful drill.

1. Repeat materials and experiences in many situations. Example: Experiences with food are met in buying, preparing, eating, and drawing.

2. Plan the total school program in English at the child's level of comprehension. This will include number, art, music, physical education, home economics, etc.

3. Provide a variety of games and materials for word practice.

"What am I?" games involving description or pantomime.

Word bingo.

Hangman on spelling words.

Matching words to action depicted or played.

Matching words to objects or sounds.

4. Present material in such a way that the child will make the correct response from the first.

5. Avoid fatiguing children with extended drill.

6. Plan a variety of activities utilizing the varied methods by which children learn, such as: visual, auditory, touch, motor, and speaking.

Plan a program of evaluation to check the success of teaching.

1. Keep, or let the child keep, a record of words he uses successfully.

2. Keep anecdotal accounts of situations in which the use of English has been met with a feeling of satisfaction such as:

The first purchase in English.

Giving directions.

Reading a magazine article.

Writing a letter.

3. Delay the use of standardized tests until the child has become proficient in English. Few of these tests have been standardized on non-English speaking children.

IMPROVING THE ENGLISH
OF SPANISH-SPEAKING CHILDREN *

Margaret E. Gott

The very first day of school the child has one word in common in both languages—his name. His experience with language should begin with this one word that he and his teacher have in common. First, the teacher must make sure that the child recognizes his name orally. Some parents use a different name or an abbreviation but give the school the full formal name. This results in some difficulty for the child. Frequently the teacher pronounces the name differently from the way the parents do.

The teacher presents the name cards by attaching one set to the child's table or chair or coat-hook, and teaches the child to find his own place. Then she gathers them in small groups and presents the cards, holding one up, saying the name, and handing it to the child.

GAMES

Testing the mailman. A child who is chosen to be mailman tries to pass out the name cards of his group, giving each one his own card. If a recipient gets the wrong card and does not realize it, the teacher may call for an inspector to check on the mail delivery. This game is good because it involves no competition.

Going to the store. (Tests each participant.) The teacher places all the name cards of the group in the pocket chart. She then calls a child to "go to the store" and get his name. This is especially valuable when

---

* From "Teaching Reading to Spanish-Speaking Children," unpublished thesis. Used by permission of the author.

there are names which begin alike, as it calls for careful discrimination. It can be varied by telling the child to get another child's name.

Storekeeper. (Tests the storekeeper.) The teacher places all the names in the pocket chart. One child is the storekeeper. The others go up one by one, say their names, and the storekeeper tries to give out the correct card. If he misses, the one to whom he gave the wrong card is the new storekeeper. This game provides opportunity to teach new English phrases orally, such as "Good-morning" "What do you want?" "I want" and "Thank you."

Find the stranger. (Tests discrimination of each participant.) The teacher uses a double set of name cards. She arranges each line in the pocket chart so that it contains two identical names and one different one. The children in turn study one line and point out the stranger.

Find the twins. (Test discrimination of each participant.) Using a double set of name cards, the teacher arranges the pocket chart so that each line contains three different names, one of which is repeated. The children in turn study one line and point out the twins.

It is usual for most first grades to have many labels around the room, such as *window, door, books,* etc. If the class will contain many non-English-speaking children it is better not to have these up at the beginning of the term, for the child may associate the label with the Spanish word. The words should be used in every possible class-room situation before being presented in written form. The first word chosen might be *chair;* this is often mispronounced by Mexican-American children but actually contains no phonetic elements foreign to Spanish. When the teacher can say the word *chair* and get a satisfactory response from the child, such as touching the chair or pointing to it, she is ready to present the word. She presents a card to the child with the word *chair* on it. She attaches a duplicate card to the chair. The child then takes the card to the chair to prove that it is identical, saying the words as he does this. This is called matching and will be used in many other lessons.

In presenting the nouns, it is best to present the singular form first, and avoid the plural as much as possible. In Spanish, the final *s* is usually preceded by a vowel, and it is difficult for the child to pronounce the plurals which have a consonant preceding the *s*. There is also another difficulty because the final *s* sometimes has a *z* sound. When the plural form is used in the course of school-room activities, the teacher should try to get the correct pronunciation established as soon as possible.

The following list of words is divided according to the number of pronunciation difficulties. They should be presented slowly and practiced in enjoyable situations. They provide the child with the satisfaction of reading achievement while he is learning the language.

A. *No Pronunciation Difficulties*

ball	game	chair	toy	crayola
clay	house	nail	clock	playhouse

B. *One Pronunciation Difficulty*

table—bl   paper—final r
door—final r   saw—aw
window—short i   box—short o
book—short oo   car—final r
paint—final nt   airplane—no vowel between r-p
pencil—short i   top—short o
rug—short u   crayon—on

C. *Two Pronunciation Difficulties*

hammer—short a, final r
sharpener—sh, final r

D. *Three or More Pronunciation Difficulties*

blackboard—short a, final d, no vowel between syllables
puzzles—short u, z, final s
playthings—th, short i, ng, final s
scissors—short i, z, r, final s
picture—short i, tu, final r, no vowel between c-t
drawing—aw, short i, ng, no consonant sound between syllables

MATCHING GAMES

Testing discrimination of each participant. This should be played with no competition and in the slow group should involve much bodily movement. Each child is handed a card and tries to match it with the label on the object before the teacher rings her bell. When he finds the correct object he stands quietly until his turn to read his word to the group.

Where are you going? (Tests recognition of words by each participant.) In this game the teacher holds up a card and asks a child, "Where are you going?" He tries to remember the word on the card and points to the place where he is going to try to match it up. Then he is given the card and goes to prove the correctness of his recognition, matching the word with the proper label and reading it aloud. If he is in error, he is allowed to go about the room and hunt for the correct label. This game teaches silent reading with comprehension.

Picture-match. The teacher prepares a set of small pictures mounted on cards about 3 × 4 inches and places the pictures in the pocket chart. The children try to place the word cards under the correct pictures. A card incorrectly placed is checked against the labeled object in the room. The children may place one card each in turn, or one child may try to place them all. If this game is used at the stage where the child has been taught only two words, and then each new word added to the set, there will be no confusion.

After the words *door* and *window* have been taught, the teacher may play an oral language game of "Open the Door. Open the Window." This may be done first in the group with the cardboard house and later in the room. The words *open* and *shut* need not be presented in printed form, for they seldom occur below primer or first-reader level. The child hears the word *the* in the complete sentence first. Later the teacher uses it just with the noun. She shows the cardboard house and says, "the door"; the child points to the door. After the child has shown that he is familiar with the article in oral language, the time has come to present it in written form.

For the first presentation the teacher says the words "the door" while showing the phrase on a card, and a child responds by indicating the door. The label on the classroom door has only the noun. Some bright child sees this at once and calls the teacher's attention to it. Her card is different! The teacher then holds up the card with the noun only, saying "door," then holds up the other saying "the door."

Pictures drawn by the children supply a good medium for the first sentences. The child brings his picture to his small group to show. If he knows no English he can quickly learn to hold it up and say, "See." The children will quickly learn to express appreciation for the picture by saying, "Oh, Oh!" These words are easy to say. The teacher should use them many times daily. She should use only the meaning of pleasure and approval at first; later on she can add excitement, dismay, and disapproval.

A number of pictures are now placed in the chalk rail or hung along the blackboard. Then the children learn to indicate their own by saying "my boat" or "my airplane." The teacher can very easily facilitate this by having all the children or all the group draw the same thing. The word *my* is also easily taught, as soon as the children know the word *chair*, by having each child indicate his chair with his name on it and say, "My chair."

On the wall or on a bulletin board the teacher arranges an ever-changing display of children's pictures. As the child displays his drawing he says, "See my ...." The teacher selects, with the children voting, a picture of the day, and puts it up, writing the tag-board label of what the child said, "See my ...." The child goes to the bulletin board, points to the picture and says, "See my ...." The teacher then indicates the label, and moving her whole arm under the line of words in a horizontal position from left to right repeats the phrase. Some pictures are left up for several days and the children play matching games with the duplicate labels. Two or three pictures may be mounted on large sheets of tagboard or paper and hung on the chart-rack with the labels printed below. These are the first experience charts used by the children.

TABLE I. *Words of Basic List That Can Be Formed with Spanish Phonetic Elements*

NOUNS
1. baby
2. ball
3. bear
4. bed
5. boat
6. boy
7. coat
8. chair °
9. cow
10. doll
11. ear
12. egg
13. eye
14. face
15. feet
16. game
17. garden
18. hair
19. home
20. house
21. leg
22. line
23. meat
24. men
25. mail
26. name
27. neck

VERBS
28. ate
29. buy
30. came
31. cry
32. do
33. eat
34. gave
35. get
36. go
37. know
38. like
39. made
40. make
41. may
42. open
43. play
44. said
45. saw
46. see
47. sew
48. take
49. tell
50. walk

GENERAL
51. all
52. blue
53. clean
54. down
55. eight
56. five
57. he
58. hello
59. I
60. me
61. my
62. new
63. nine
64. no
65. out
66. ten
67. to
68. two
69. we
70. who
71. you
72. yellow
73. yes

° Often pronounced *share.*

California Basic Vocabulary

SCHOOL
afternoon
airplane
basket
blackboard
boat
book
boy
children
clay
clock
crayon
doll
door
drum
flag
floor
game
girl
hammer
kite
morning
nail
noon
nurse
paint
paper
pencil

FAMILY, HOME
baby bed
breakfast
broom
brother
cent
chair
cup
dinner
dish
father
fire
fork
home
house
knife
lunch
money
mother
name
plate
sister
spoon
stove
table

CLOTHES
cap
coat
dress
hat
overalls
shirt
shoe
stockings
sweater

PLAYGROUND
ball
bat
circle
line
marbles
slide
swing
top

COMMUNITY
automobile
man
men
people
store
street
train
woman
women
work

FOOD
apple
banana
beans
bread
butter
candy
carrots
egg
lettuce
meat
milk
nut
onions
potatoes
soup

ANIMALS
bear
bird
burro
cat
chicken
cow
dog
goat
hen
horse
kitty
pig
rabbit
rooster

OUTDOORS
flower
garden
grass
ground
leaf
leaves
nest

rain
sky
stick
sun
tree
wind

IDIOMS
at home
at school
at work
good-by
good-morning
I am
I see
may I
lunch time
it is
he is
this is
she is
wake up
I like
I made

BODY
arm
ear
eye
face
feet
fingernails
finger
foot
hand
hair
head
knees
leg
mouth
neck
nose
stomach
teeth
toes

CLEANLINESS
bath
brush
clean
comb
dirty
drink

dry
handkerchief
shower
sick
soap
toilet
towel
wash
water
well
wipe

VERBS
are
ate
bought
bring
brought
buy
came
can
catch
caught
color
come
cry
cut
do
draw
drink
eat
erase
find
gave
get
give
go
have
has
help
is
jump
know
laugh
like
listen
look
made
make
may
open
paste
play

put
ran
run
said
sang
saw
see
sew
shut
sing
sit
sleep
stand
stop
sweep
take
tell
threw
told
walk
want
wash
went

GENERAL
a
after
again
all
an
and
at
away
bad
big
black
blue
brown
clean
cold
dirty
down
eight
excuse me
fast
first
five
for
four
from
good
green
he

hello	no	six	when
her	not	ten	where
him	old	thank you	white
his	on	the	who
hot	one	them	will
I	orange	they	with
in	out	three	yellow
it	please	to	yes
little	pretty	two	you
many	purple	under	your
me	red	up	
my	seven	us	Total: 316
new	she	we	Words: 296
nine	sick	what	Phrases: 20

THE PREADOLESCENT BOYS AND GIRLS
(Grades 5 and 6) °

J. Post Williams

Work with the preadolescent boys and girls is intriguing for they are relatively competent in the basic skills. They read well, see relationships, and do much writing on their own. Their bursting imaginations add to the zest of working with them for they take so much we have to offer, add to, and change it so that the product is ever fresh and interesting. To them we are heroes and sages. They are flattering to be with; they make us feel so knowing and wise.

There are great differences among these children who range in age from 9½ to 13 years. Some are still so childlike and others so grown-up in their general mien. They vary greatly in their physical and social maturity and may undergo growth spurts in which they seem to change overnight. Henry is short and stocky while his friend, Bill, is tall and gangly. They know all the latest slang and use it fluently to gain social acceptance. Mary and Susan are growing rapidly. They have surpassed many of the boys in height. They are able to speak and write more fluently, have better muscular coordination, and show up to better advantage in competitive activities than the boys. Miss Jones, their teacher, is aware of their growth problems and plans activities in which competition between boys and girls is reduced to a minimum.

° Reprinted from *Tulare County Cooperative Language Arts Guide* (Visalia, Calif., Tulare County Schools, 1949), by permission of Tulare County Schools.

These preadolescent boys and girls have become quite self-critical and are often reluctant to perform or display their own work. Depending upon their growth characteristics, it may help if the teacher will read their stories for them anonymously, for it gives them an opportunity to share them without embarrassment.

Many things claim the attention of these boys and girls. They are quite interested in abstract ideas and give consideration to the factors involved in fair play, right and wrong, reality and fiction. They are concerned with boy-girl relationships. They may reject the opposite sex or actually flaunt their boy friends and girl friends. The latter part of this period is dynamic with the boys and girls on the brink of adolescence with all its extremes of alternate discouragement and future dreams.

THESE WAYS OF WORKING HELP THEM GROW

*Plan activities which will help children increase
their. speed in reading.*

1. Encourage interest in voluntary reading for fun. Allow time for much reading of relatively easy, interesting, story material.

Provide material covering a wide range of difficulty and interest.

Plan times when children may discuss and share their free reading experiences.

2. Provide group practice under plans that motivate faster reading.

Use standardized or teacher-made material organized specifically for this purpose, timing child as he works.

Avoid undue stress on thoroughness of mechanics. It is necessary only to get general run of story, or grasp main points. Review mechanics at a later time.

Let children keep individual reading-rate charts so that they may compete against their own rates. When group charts are made they should be made without names, such as a chart to show how many books were read by the group in February, March, and so forth.

3. Provide for individual practice helping each child correct his own difficulties.

Some may need special instruction and practice for the correction of deficiencies in word recognition.

Some may need eye movement training. This may involve providing material with good phrasing and blending, helping them to increase span of recognition, and helping them develop rhythmical eye movements.

Encourage each child to keep a record of his progress so that he may see where he is improving.

PREADOLESCENT BOYS AND

PHYSICALLY, THEY

Are unable to choose sports wisely in terms of their strength and needs.

Are losing grace of childhood as they approach adolescence.

Are healthiest group of elementary school age.

Range from early childhood to preadolescence in levels of maturity.

Are sturdy, though long-legged or chunky.

Are prone to accidents.

Have excellent appetites.

Become skillful with hands.

Attain adult level of hand and eye coordination.

INTELLECTUALLY, THEY

Have many interests including matters world-wide in scope.

Show wide variation in intellectual abilities.

Are very curious.

Seek adventure and excitement.

Have a heightened sense of humor.

Make comparisons and judgments based on objective evidence.

Are oriented in time and space.

Are capable of long-term planning.

Like to startle people.

Grow rapidly in creative expression.

Read extensively.

SO THEY

Sufficient rest and relaxation.

Much outdoor play (survey of home activities may determine kind and amount of school activity needed).

Activities which promote muscular skill, poise, and grace.

Rhythmic activities.

Training in bodily care, health, and sanitation.

Opportunities to practice safety measures.

Construction activities.

Upkeep of materials, equipment, and property used at home and at school.

Knowledge of body and how it functions.

Many methods of sharing ideas, information and skills.

Help in clarifying thinking for writing and speaking through teacher recording of composite thinking.

Help in seeing relationships through graphs, charts, thermometers, and other measuring devices.

Opportunities to hear and tell jokes, funny stories, and strange tales.

Opportunities to initiate and carry out plans for excursions, trips.

Responsibility for planning room organization, projects.

Creative expression through dramatizing, writing, ceramics, and other activities.

GIRLS ARE LIKE THIS

EMOTIONALLY, THEY

May become very aggressive.

May be self-conscious about new activities.

May become highly emotional over matters seeming of little consequence.

May cry easily with beginning adolescence and emotional upsets.

Seek attention from peers and adults.

Rebel if they feel unwanted.

Become modest about sex.

Overt emotion may belie underlying cause: cry when happy, may show antagonism toward person they admire.

SOCIALLY, THEY

Regard the opinion of peers and friends very highly.

Seek group approval; enjoy clubs, gangs, and teams.

Begin to sense social inequalities.

Begin sex antagonism.

Seek adult approval.

Are inclined to hero worship.

Like to help others.

NEED THIS

Permissive understanding from adults who remove every possible tension.

Help in understanding relation between emotions and accidents.

Recognition of their efforts in keeping up their property and their pride in it.

Help in establishing position with members of their own sex.

Emotional counseling of understanding adults.

Privacy to work out emotional problems.

Feeling of competence in their work and a record kept of personal gains rather than too much competition with group.

Acceptance by adults of passive phases of behavior which may be undesirable at the moment.

Opportunities for gatherings.

Freedom to move about in classroom, and help in understanding the rights of others.

Rich personal and social experience as basis for creative expression.

Folk dancing and practice in social graces.

Opportunities to belong to youth organizations.

Skills in social games and etiquette.

Opportunities to write social notes, "thank yous," and invitations.

Conscientious leaders, and opportunities to know leaders of today and yesterday.

Awareness of social mores of their group and community.

THEY NEED TO GROW

PERSONALLY

Caring for personal needs and appearance.
Expressing thoughts and feelings more adequately.
Finding satisfaction in individual as well as group activities.
Understanding of adult problems and reasons for their decisions.
Improving effectiveness of oral and written expression.
Gaining confidence in making decisions and working independently.
Evaluating their own and other's work impartially.
Suspending judgment and foreseeing solutions of problems.
Working independently outside the schoolroom.
Finding creative ways of using their time.

SO THEY NEED THESE

LISTENING

Enjoying stories and poems about animals, adventure, gangs, mystery, western life, hobbies, science, nature study, personal happiness.

Selecting music for special occasions.

Enjoying original work of fellows.

Evaluating radio programs.

Evaluating information from speeches, panels, forums.

Hearing recordings of their own speech patterns.

Selecting and rejecting material pertinent to a particular problem.

SPEAKING

Using courtesies in social situations, e.g., apologies, introductions, departures, compliments.

Telling stories, jokes, poems.

Giving directions, making announcements, and simple explanations.

Conducting class and group activities.

Presenting suggestions for solutions of group and individual problems.

Asking questions to secure pertinent information and to clarify problems.

Sharing items and articles pertinent to given interests.

Serving as a spokesman for the group.

Interviewing people in the community.

IN THESE WAYS

SOCIALLY

Finding satisfactions in group activities.

Considering the welfare of others in the group.

Seeing relationships between individual and group interests.

Using group processes both as leader and follower.

Planning with the group in setting up courtesies in using methods of communication.

Evaluating information sources of social, economic, and political problems.

Appreciating cultural contributions of peoples of other languages, creeds and races.

Contributing pertinent data and observations in conversations.

Entertaining with stories, quotations, jokes, humorous anecdotes, games.

Selecting competent persons to represent the group.

LANGUAGE EXPERIENCES

READING

Reading books in many different interest areas.

Selecting materials for many purposes.

Making books of their own.

Getting acquainted with people and their contributions to literature.

Reading stories, articles, and poems and becoming selective in choice.

Reading about their hobbies.

Reading for specific purposes and selecting and rejecting data pertinent to the problem at hand.

Locating needed information and data from reference materials.

Reading in groups as needed to correct or enlarge use of reading techniques.

Discussing materials read in bringing out finer meanings and expressions.

WRITING

Expressing thoughts and feeling through creative writing in the form of stories, verse, letters, and plays.

Writing announcements, advertisements, notices, editorials, summaries.

Writing adventure stories and tall tales.

Writing business and social letters.

Keeping records of games, activities, skills, tests, needs, accomplishments.

Keeping journals, diaries, logs.

Writing composite letters, stories, and reports.

Sending for free materials, maps, travel literature.

Writing articles for the school or community newspaper.

Collecting interesting poetry, recipes, instructions for making things.

AND THESE SKILLS SHOULD EMERGE

Grouping points of emphasis.

Listening for speech errors in class and playground.

Discriminating rhythms and melodies.

Showing expected courtesies in audience situations.

Following directions and instructions.

Evaluating contributions of group and its members.

Speaking from simple outlines.

Eliminating simple errors in language usage.

Asking pertinent and direct questions.

Using a variety of gestures, intonations, and inflections to color meaning.

Organizing ideas before speaking.

Correcting speech errors and difficulties.

Developing clear and concise expression.

Developing courtesies and techniques for using the telephone.

Developing needed techniques, such as: skimming, main idea, scanning, use of indexes, table of contents, dictionary, library catalogue, encyclopedia.

Interpreting maps, charts, graphs, pictures, diagrams, globes.

Developing mechanics of reading, such as: eye span, eye movement, and accurate return sweep.

Using dictionaries and thesauri to discover finer shades of meaning implied in materials they read.

Increasing speed of reading according to purpose.

Correcting their own writing difficulties.

Taking notes on material read.

Recording selected data for further use in questioning a speaker.

Recording speech errors of pals.

Maintaining and improving previously learned skills in handwriting, spelling, grammar, and punctuation for clear and concise expression.

Using manuscript and cursive writing according to needs.

Developing independence in editing and proofreading.

Filling in forms accurately and neatly such as tests, applications, receipts, money orders, club dues and enrollment blanks.

Evaluating their written work.

Seeking new words to express meaning more clearly on the written page.

Selecting correct forms for written materials.

Plan for the reading of poetry on occasions when it is particularly fitting.

1. Select for reading by teacher or children poems which are tuned to moods or the time of the year, such as: nature poems in the springtime, patriotic poetry on holidays, or adventure poetry when children are planning excursions. Read poetry of different authors to show individuality of style.

2. Limit the amount of poetry read so that it is always an enjoyable experience.

3. Encourage re-reading and memorization when it is really wanted by the child. When adults quote a variety of poems from memory children often wish to learn them too.

*Give children opportunities for participating in and
enjoying choral speaking.*

1. Choral speaking is interpretation of poetry or poetic prose by
many or several voices speaking as one. It is intended for appreciation
and enjoyment and should be developed in an informal manner. In
choosing material for verse speaking choir, less difficult selections
should be chosen first. Ballads with refrains can be used easily. Story
poems should be used first, then lyrics, and lastly dramatic poetry.

2. The group may tap out the rhythm pattern while the teacher or
children read the selection to the class. The group decides on the parts
which suit the high, medium, or low voices.

The parts which are light and airy may be expressed by high voices;
dramatic action may be expressed by low voices; and the less dramatic
parts may be expressed by medium voices. The children will enjoy
taking different parts and experimenting in using the various voice
tones they are able to produce.

Pictures sometimes help children get the mood of a poem and
enable them to put in feeling which is descriptive or emotional.

Plan to produce a school or room newspaper.

The publication of a newspaper may be an on-going activity in
which the paper is published periodically, or it may be that the paper
is published as a culmination activity. In either case, all aspects of
language enter into the planning, working, producing, and evaluating
of the paper.

1. Determine the frequency of publication: annually, monthly,
weekly.

2. Plan the content and organization of the paper. There is much
opportunity here for discussion, evaluating, and recording of suggestions.

The news to be reported: news of the school, local community
news, exchange news from other schools.

Special features, sports page, editorials, features in special columns.

Literary features, original stories and poems, jokes, odd or unusual facts.

Advertisements.

3. Plan the methods by which the paper is to be printed and
published. This will involve such activities as interviewing persons
familiar with duplicating methods to discover which are most satisfactory. Letters will need to be written to find out what supplies are
needed.

Mimeograph liquid process, or gelatin stencil may be used depending upon the facilities available.

Needs may be ascertained by securing from the mimeograph company or duplicating machine company their manual on school papers. Items such as paper, carbon, stencils, letter guides, and colored inks, will be recommended by the commercial companies selling these supplies to the schools. (Check with the county purchasing agent to find out which companies to contact.)

The equipment and supplies suggested will include: table space, one or more typewriters, stapling machine, staples, and accounting books. However, where such equipment is lacking children often find successful substitutes.

4. Select the staff members: editor-in-chief, advertising editor, art editor, sports editor, business manager, reporters. Here is an opportunity for careful evaluation of the type of person needed for each position and for the selection of the one best qualified for each.

5. Plan activities needed to secure necessary information. Some will be individual and some will be group activities. Encourage other rooms to participate.

Visiting a newspaper office.

Examining other school papers and local newspapers.

Interviewing newspaper publishers and reporters for information on publishing the paper.

Contacting business people in the community for advertisements.

Interviewing outstanding persons in the community for the personal column.

Submitting reports and articles for editing before publication.

Plan timing carefully so paper will be issued on time.

6. Publish the paper. Evaluate the success of the activity in terms of the goals which were set up. The teacher and pupils together may be interested in listing the listening, speaking, reading, and writing experiences which have been involved in the activity.

7. Read Edgar Dale's book, "How to Read a Newspaper" and plan how you can make your paper more reliable and effective.

Give children opportunities to write many types of letters helping them to suit each letter to the occasion for which it is designed.

1. Write friendly letters to members of the family, classmates who are ill, to "pen" friends in other parts of the world, and to secret pals.

While content may be more important than form in such a letter, discussion should bring out the characteristics we like to find in a letter we receive. Pool information as to form and style.

Plan ways of making the letter interesting and personal, or writing about the things the other person wants to know.

Share jokes, cartoons, ideas, and experiences with the persons to whom you write.

Write legibly and neatly so the recipient of the letter may follow the train of thought easily.

2. Write needed courtesy notes. These will include invitations, thank-you notes, congratulations, sympathy, and apology. Direct and sincere expression should characterize these notes.

3. Write business letters needed to carry on class and school activities. These may include letters of inquiry, requests for information and materials, invitations to experts to visit school, requests for permission to visit a plant, orders or acknowledgment of services rendered. Check textbooks for mechanics.

Form should be correct.

Expression should be courteous.

The letter should be clear, definite, and concise.

Encourage boys and girls to write original poetry individually or in groups.

Since poetry is a mode of creative expression in which feeling is spontaneous, it should always grow out of real experience. There are many times when group feeling among children is high, and they should be capitalized on. Such times may occur with the first rain of the season, the discovery of a nest of field mice on the school ground, the pet that comes to school, the school picnic or other happenings. Children's spontaneous expression leads naturally into a discussion from which both class and individual poems may emerge with a little help from the teacher.

1. Permit the children to talk freely about the experience, taking turns and sharing their observations and feelings.

2. When the children are ready, let individuals write picture words, phrases, or sentences on the board which describe their feelings and what they have seen.

3. Try out many ways of telling about the experiences.

4. Let the children experience the enjoyment of reading expressions on the board.

5. Encourage those who wish to try to compose poems from suggestions on the board to go ahead.

6. Encourage the children to share their interesting lines or expressions by reading them or writing them on the board.

7. Let the children suggest ways to improve the lines, and from the helps at the board they may compose a class poem. It may be changed many times before they are finally satisfied.

8. Encourage children who compose their own poems to share them with the class.

9. Help the class to respect each student's personality as expressed

in his poetry, encouraging expression of unique thought rather than rhyming jingles.

Help boys and girls correct errors in grammar and usage which they make in their speaking and writing.

1. Encourage them to help themselves by keeping their own personal records of errors made and corrected.

2. Select errors in grammar which are being made by groups of children for correction. Plan drills which are related to the actual language needs of boys and girls in your community.

3. Help children make their own corrections. List the special points at which errors are most apt to be made on the board, and let children check their work to see that it is as nearly right as they can make it.

4. Encourage children to help each other in eliminating spoken errors.

5. Keep graphs showing the number of errors made by the class.

Help children develop skill in using the dictionary.

1. Guide children in examining their individual dictionaries to discover the various types of information they contain.

Explain the location of the table of contents for all books and find it in the dictionary.

Discuss the use of tables of contents and how they help locate units. Try finding the various sections quickly.

Divide the dictionaries into halves and place markers at these pages, then divide them into fourths and place markers. Make a list of the letters on the blackboard that are found in the first part, second part, third part, and fourth part. Discuss ways in which this will make the dictionary easier to use.

Practice letters in alphabetical order, and practice letters that come before or after each letter, but above all practice finding words needed.

Discuss use of guide words and sequence of letters, and how guide words indicate first and last words on the page.

Make up "hunting games" which can be played using the dictionary.

Help children learn the use of guide words.

2. Help children use the dictionary to discover the pronunciation of words with which they are unfamiliar and words which they wish to use correctly in speaking.

Discuss the various types of pronunciation difficulties which our spelling presents and plan how to meet them. Many letters have more than one speech sound. Some speech sounds may be represented by more than one letter or combination of letters.

Discover ways to use pronunciation helps which are provided.

Dictionaries use special pronunciation alphabets. Select and use the preferred pronunciation and spelling.

3. Use the dictionary to discover meaning of new words and new meanings for familiar words. Compare dictionaries as to likenesses and differences.

Stress importance of functional use of dictionary. Select the meaning of the word which best fits in the context you are reading. Read illustrative phrases to discover meaning.

Use the dictionary to find antonyms needed in writing. Sometimes we want to know what the opposite meaning is. Check pictures, captions, drawings, maps, and other pictorial aids which give aid in discovering meaning.

4. Help children to discover the variety of types of information available in the dictionary. Check the table of contents to find what types of information are presented. Compare abridged and unabridged editions for variety of appended material, such as: tables of weights and measures, signs and symbols used in writing, gazetteer, biographical dictionary, common foreign phrases and expressions, and explanatory notes.

Help children develop courtesies needed for social occasions.

1. Discuss courtesies needed for special occasions, such as: excursions, using the telephone, attending parties, riding public conveyances, and entertaining guests at school and home.

2. Dramatize behavior needed on a planned trip, a party, or open house at school.

3. Discuss courtesies practiced or neglected by storybook characters.

4. Discuss and evaluate with children conduct and courtesies, oversights, and particularly appropriate behaviors on a trip, party, or other occasion which they have recently experienced.

Plan ways in which errors made may be avoided in the future.

5. Practice introducing new students and visitors at school.

Encourage boys and girls to plan cooperatively and to take responsibility for attractive room arrangement and displays.

1. Discuss the purpose for displays and centers of interest, and plan how the room can be made a more effective place in which to learn and live.

2. Plan for needed changes in room arrangement and discuss materials needed, sources of supply, and ways of getting them.

3. Encourage boys and girls to share items of current interest, clippings, curios, heirlooms, travel literature, special tools, costumes, pictures, and so on.

4. Let room committees take responsibility for setting up displays and centers of interest.

5. Let boys and girls care for the general appearance of the classroom. This will include keeping the library shelf in order, the window shades straight, waste paper off the floor, and tools and materials in order when not in use.

Help boys and girls correct their own errors in speech and make needed improvements by using recording equipment.

1. Let each child make a recording of his speech while reading and while speaking freely. The teacher may participate in this activity.

2. Replay the recordings letting children analyze the voices and speech habits individually and in groups.

Dramatize the work-day of a telephone lineman.

3. Discuss and make plans for corrections and improvements. Let the class secretary record on a chart the improvements most members of the group need to make. Encourage each child to keep a personal record of the specific errors he wishes to correct.

4. Make recordings again at a later date and note changes in speech habits. Check off improvements the class as a whole has made. Let each child check off his personal list the errors he has eliminated.

Plan to make practice in the use of effective techniques of listening, speaking, reading, and writing an integral part of all school activities.

1. Help boys and girls to present current event topics, items of interest, and sports reports in a way that will hold the interest of their listeners.

2. Develop standards, daily plans, and plans for projects and excursions through group discussion.

3. Plan research techniques, share findings, and evaluate the work of the group cooperatively.

4. Allow time for children to converse and share skits, plays, riddles, poems, and funny stories.

5. Keep well-written minutes for class and club meetings.

6. Listen to radio and recordings for enjoyment, news, and information on specific subjects.

7. Encourage correct spelling and usage in all written work.

8. Provide opportunities for children to read for specific information in the social studies, and to share it by reading aloud to the class, or by oral reports, using maps and graphs to amplify.

9. Give children opportunities to bring outside interests into the classroom. Records of hobbies and collections may be prepared in correct written form to be read by those interested.

10. Encourage children to write accounts of how to do things, such as how to play hopscotch, or keep a box file.

11. Tie home and school together by encouraging children to write stories and poems as well as descriptions, and take them home in attractive form to read to younger children.

Provide many opportunities for boys and girls to read orally.

1. Read parts of a story as a play.

2. Rewrite story into a play and read or reproduce the play orally.

3. Read to the group news articles which relate to activity.

4. Plan reading parties or read to younger children.

5. Read to a group to prove a point.

6. Read to a group to share information on a hobby, crafts, or other interest.

7. Read play parts aloud to discover sounds best fitted to part and action.

8. Read letters or notes received by the class to the group.

9. Read the answer to a particular problem in which the group is interested.

10. Read lists of supplies, bibliography, and places to locate information.

11. Read class minutes and notes.

Plan excursions related to class activities.

In the solution of problems that arise out of the actual needs and interests of children, many sources of information are explored. The planned trip is particularly fruitful in extending experience and language. Suggested trips for grades 5 and 6 are to:

1. Parks.

2. Industries, cotton gins, bakeries, creameries, packing plants, telephone companies.

3. Points of interest.

4. Airports, railroad and bus stations.

5. Public buildings, court house, fire station, police station, city hall, chamber of commerce.

6. Exhibits, Indian early days, fairs, museums, adobe buildings.

7. Public construction work: new schools and homes.

Develop independence in using telephone for social and business calls.

Boys and girls should be familiar with the varied techniques and courtesies involved in the correct use of the telephone.

1. Getting information from the directory.

2. Getting the desired party by dialing or calling the operator.

3. Answering the phone and identifying themselves when making calls.

4. Making calls brief and to the point.

5. Sharing party lines courteously.

6. Receiving and delivering messages accurately and courteously.

Give boys and girls responsibility for securing information and materials needed for their activities.

1. Put markers in books in the classroom and home libraries from which needed information may be secured, such as: farm stories, stories about houses, stories about the post office, and the like.

2. Check encyclopedias to find references dealing with questions and problems.

3. Survey homes for articles needed for construction, displays, diorama, and exhibits.

4. Visit or write to industries, stores, companies, news offices, state or federal resources to secure information or materials. Write to:

a. Lumber office for home booklet.

b. Farm bureau for pamphlets on raising rabbits, chickens, or plants.

c. Travel literature from railroad, steamship, and bus companies.

5. Check with custodian, principal, other teachers, and pupils for materials which they may be able to supply.

6. Search classroom supplementary texts and supplies for needed information and materials.

7. Interview people in the community to find those who may have information.

8. Locate or make pictures, maps, charts, and diagrams for use in solving problems.

Plan to develop meaningful language experiences centered around units pupils are exploring.

The following are based on study of the telephone:

1. Make calls on the telephone.

2. Discuss ways of talking on telephone, purpose and length of calls.

3. Look up names in telephone book for social calls.

4. Look up business houses in the classified index.

5. Discuss the nature of business calls, courtesies and length of time.

6. Discuss kinds of phones, ways of calling through the operator

or dial, numbers, prefixes, rates on phones, one party, two party, business and the like.

7. Plan to improve speech and work on correction using the recorder to discover difficulties.

8. Make telephone calls for school business.

9. Make grocery lists and notes to guide telephone conversations when taking care of needs such as checking the car at garage, calling the chamber of commerce to find out where to dispose of newspapers, and the like.

10. Call fire department, store, doctor, and other places in vicinity when needed.

11. Read poetry, such as Carl Sandburg's "Under a Telephone Pole."

12. Read about the history of the telephone and write letters to the telephone company for films, booklets, and so forth.

13. Get forms for telegrams from telegraph office, and plan how to send a telegram by phone.

14. Plan notes for a long distance phone call so as to limit the length of the conversation.

15. Collect telephone bills, books, directories and so forth.

16. Make telephone or get "Walkie-Talkie" and have telephone conversations across the room, discussing and evaluating.

17. Plan a trip to the telephone office. Write letters requesting permission to visit. Note things to find out. Write to parents to ask permission to go and invite them to go along. Write out plans and note safety precautions. Telephone to telephone office to ask permission to come.

18. Compose the story of the telephone together. Dictating important points for the teacher to record on the board. Copy or rewrite this information carefully, and add anything which is found individually. Each story made may be put into an additional booklet, insuring even the slower children of a story.

19. Read to the group and have stories retold providing oral reports for less fluent readers, and giving listening experience.

20. Find out who workers are in the telephone office and describe their duties.

21. Play telephone, using boys and girls for workers.